Organizational Communication

THIRD EDITION _____

Organizational Communication

R. Wayne Pace
Brigham Young University

Don F. Faules
University of Utah

Prentice Hall, Englewood Cliffs, New Jersey 07632

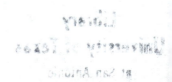

Library of Congress Cataloging–in–Publication Data

Pace, R. Wayne
   Organizational communication / R. Wayne Pace, Don F. Faules.—3rd ed.
    p. cm.
  Includes bibliographical references and index.
  ISBN 0–13–643800–8
   1. Communication in organizations. 2. Organizational behavior. 3. Personnel
management. 4. Interpersonal relations. I. Faules, Don F. II. Title.
HD30.3.P34 1993
658.4′5—dc20

93–31436
CIP

Editorial/production supervision
  and interior design: Shelly Kupperman
Acquisition editor: Steve Dalphin
Editorial assistant: Caffie Risher
Electronic page makeup: Christy Mahon
Production coordinator: Kelly Behr
Copy editor: James Tully
Cover designer: Anne Ricigliano

© 1994, 1989, 1983 by Prentice-Hall, Inc.
A Paramount Communications Company
Englewood Cliffs, New Jersey 07632

Printed in the United States of America
10 9 8 7 6 5 4 3 2 1

ISBN 0-13-643800-8

PRENTICE-HALL INTERNATIONAL (UK) LIMITED, London
PRENTICE-HALL OF AUSTRALIA PTY. LIMITED, Sydney
PRENTICE-HALL CANADA INC., Toronto
PRENTICE-HALL HISPANOAMERICANA, S.A., Mexico
PRENTICE-HALL OF INDIA PRIVATE LIMITED, New Delhi
PRENTICE-HALL OF JAPAN, INC., Tokyo
SIMON & SCHUSTER ASIA PTE. LTD., Singapore
EDITORA PRENTICE-HALL DO BRASIL, LTDA., Rio de Janeiro

Contents

PREFACE   xi

PART I: THE STUDY OF ORGANIZATIONAL COMMUNICATION

1 *ORGANIZATIONAL COMMUNICATION: UNDERLYING CONCEPTS*   1

Alternative Views   2
Impact of World Views on Definitions and Analyses   11
Implications for Organizational Behavior   12
Summary   14
References   14

2 *THE NATURE OF ORGANIZATIONAL COMMUNICATION: WHY PEOPLE STUDY ORGANIZATIONAL COMMUNICATION*   16

Definition of Communication   17
Information as Message–Displays   19

The Fallacy of Meaning Transfer 19
A Communication Unit 21
A Functional Definition of Organizational
  Communication 21
An Interpretive Definition of Organizational Communication 22
A Subjectivist's Reminder 23
Direction of Text 24
Summary 25
References 25

PART TWO: ORGANIZATION THEORIES

3 CLASSICAL STRUCTURAL THEORY 27

Social Organization 27
Formal Organization 29
Characteristics of a Weberian Bureaucracy 29
Positional Communication and Informal Contacts 31
Taylor's Scientific Management 32
Summary 35
A Subjectivist's Reminder 35
References 37

4 TRANSITIONAL THEORIES 38

Behavioral Theories 38
Systems Theories 42
Summary 48
A Subjectivist's Reminder 48
References 51

5 CONTEMPORARY THEORIES: TOWARD SUBJECTIVISM 53

Weick's Theory of Organizing 54
A Cultural Theory of Organization 59
Organizational Culture as Sense Making 64
Summary 71
References 72

PART III: ORGANIZATIONAL COMMUNICATION ISSUES

6 *ORGANIZATIONAL COMMUNICATION AND MOTIVATION:*
X–EFFICIENCY AND COMMUNICATION **75**

A Concept of Motivation   76
Differences between Supervisors and Employees
  on What Motivates Workers   78
Theories of Motivation   79
Deficiency Theories of Motivation   80
Expectations Theory and Motivation   83
Perceptions Theory of Motivation   85
A Subjectivist's Reminder   91
Summary   93
Work Perceptions Profile   94
References   97

7 *ORGANIZATIONAL COMMUNICATION CLIMATE*   **99**

Communication Climate   99
Importance of Climate   100
How Organizational Communication Climate Develops   101
Analyzing Communication Climate   107
Communication Climate Inventory (CCI)   108
Organizational Communication Satisfaction   112
Summary   114
A Subjectivist's Reminder   114
References   115

8 *THE FLOW OF INFORMATION IN ORGANIZATIONS*   **117**

The Nature of Flow   117
Simultaneous Message Dissemination   118
Serial Message Dissemination   119
Patterns of Information Flow   120
The Directions of Information Flow   126
Downward Communication   127
Upward Communication   130
Horizontal Communication   133
Cross-Channel Communication   135
Informal, Personal, or Grapevine
  Communication   136

Relationships 138
Interpersonal Relationships 138
Positional Relationships 139
Serial Relationships 143
Some Current Issues 145
Summary 147
A Subjectivist's Reminder 147
References 151

9 INFORMATION TECHNOLOGY IN ORGANIZATIONS 156

The Problem 156
Forecast 160
Summary 168
References 169

10 POWER AND EMPOWERMENT IN THE ORGANIZATION 171

Power Concepts and Organization 172
Organizational Communication Dynamics 175
Communication and the Empowerment Process 179
Communication and Exercising Power 182
Summary 184
A Subjectivist's Reminder 185
References 185

11 COMMUNICATION, LEADERSHIP AND OPERATING SKILLS 187

The Meaning and Goals of Leadership 187
Assumptions About People That Underlie Styles
   of Leadership 188
Models of Leadership Styles 189
Communicative Behaviors and Leadership Styles 197
Operating Styles 202
Summary 206
A Subjectivist's Reminder 206
References 208

12 TEAMS AND GROUPS 210

Revolution in Progress 210
The Work or the Group 211
Group Formation and Development 212
Group Dynamics 216
Problem-Solving Processes 220
Summary 230
References 231

13 STRESS, CONFLICT, AND ORGANIZATIONAL COMMUNICATION 232

Stress: A Definition 233
Strategies 235
Communicative Strategy One: Strengthen Hope 240
Communicative Strategy Two: Connectedness 242
Communicative Strategy Three: Mindfulness 242
Communicative Strategy Four: Hardiness 244
Communicative Strategy Five: Forgiveness 246
Conflict 249
Conflict and Intergroup Processes 252
Summary 254
A Subjectivist's Reminder 254
References 255

PART IV: CHANGE IN INDIVIDUALS AND ORGANIZATIONAL SYSTEMS

14 INDIVIDUAL ANALYSIS AND CHANGE 259

Definition of Analysis 259
The Process of Analysis 261
Approaches to Documenting Human Resource Concerns 266
Five Approaches to Individual Change 281
Behavioral Theory 284
Achievement Theory 290
Positional Theory 292
Experiential Theory 294
Training Design Model 302
How to Conduct a Training Session 316
Evaluation of Training 317
Summary 318
References 319

15 *SYSTEMS ANALYSIS AND CHANGE* **322**

Interpretive Methods of Analysis 322
Functional Methods of Analysis 329
Strategies and Intervention for Improving Systems
   Effectiveness 344
Conditions, Possibilities, Steps, and Costs 345
Summary 352
References 352

PART V: CAREERS AND ETHICAL ISSUES

16 *WHERE DO YOU USE ORGANIZATIONAL
COMMUNICATION THEORY AND METHODS?* **356**

Where Communication Majors Find Employment! 357
General Management Careers 361
Ethical Issues in Organizations 362
Ethical Guidelines 365
Summary 366
References 366

APPENDIX **367**

Organizational Communication Profile 367

INDEX **373**

Preface

Wayne sits in a seventh-floor office on the campus of Brigham Young University where his view encompasses snow-covered buildings huddled among some trees clinging to the edges of an escarpment known as University Hill, where the campus is located. His view also stretches over twenty-five miles to a lake on one periphery and to some rather majestic mountains on the other.

Don sorts his thoughts in an office on the main floor of one of those classic academic buildings on the lower campus of the University of Utah. His office has high ceilings and a corner window. Outside, trees and shrubbery grow all around. The building looks toward the oval and the wooded area at the entrance to the campus.

Wayne and Don know one another, of course. They have written a book together; in fact, they have written two editions of a book together, although they actually wrote them apart. Well, they were apart but they were together. They would meet at Don's place, then at Wayne's, then some other place. They lived apart but they occasionally came together, mostly to find out what they had been doing while they were apart, apparently working.

They are both evidence of the enduring quality of irascibility, or is it erasability, where one person arrives with a pencil and the other with an eraser. Both of them share the import and impact of maturity. They both labor in organizations and try, as they will, to communicate. They both endure the slings and arrows of outrageous fortune and the comfort and solace of good people of good intentions and good works.

Don and Wayne have been acquainted professionally for almost thirty years, coming from somewhat similar traditions at Ohio State University (Don) and Purdue University (Wayne) during the formative years of the field of organizational communication, but diverging later on. In a sense, they have lived the history and seen the changes and engaged in the dialogue of developing scenarios. Nevertheless, they bring their own unique perspectives to the process of writing a book. Don views things a little more from the vantage point of theory, and Wayne struggles a little more with applications. Don explicates doctrine and Wayne articulates practice. Don reasons around and Wayne runs around reason.

Nevertheless, they have tried to build a text that helps the reader enter the dialogue about understanding organizations and the debate about organization effectiveness. This is a book positioned to express eclectic thoughts and a range of alternative views about organizations, communication, organizational practices, and communication activities. The subject matter builds on paradigms of organization and communication and elucidates analytical methods and strategic practices.

This edition of *Organizational Communication* has been organized to provide more comprehensive packages on certain topics. For example, materials about information and information flow have been centralized and unified into a single chapter, and a new chapter on information technology has been added. Materials about individual analysis and change have been placed together, and the materials about organization systems analysis and change have been combined into a single chapter. The Organizational Communication Profile is presented as an analytical instrument. A new chapter on communication climate has been added with the inclusion of a measuring instrument. In fact, throughout the text, sections on measuring different aspects of organizational communication have been included.

Some new concepts have been added to the book, such as X–efficiency to help explain motivation in a different way, Work Teams to complement new developments in organization theory, Power and Empowerment to enhance and embellish leadership, Stress and Conflict to highlight some of the consequences of dysfunctional organizational life, and Ethics to tug at readers to review some of their individual decisions, and especially some of the potential ways in which organizational systems cultivate dysfunctional decisions and communication.

As authors, we would like to pay tribute to four individuals who have provided insights into the workings of communication and organizational systems: W. Charles Redding, Alfred Korzybski, Elton Mayo, and John Gall.

We quoted Charles in the Preface to the second edition, where he expressed the opinion that the study of organizational communication had exhibited changes in focus, horizons, and models, but that it had not cut itself off from its roots. Charles's telephone book-size treatise, *Communication within the Organization* (1972),* summarized a major perspective or two in the field and generated a lot of talk about organizational communication.

Count Alfred Korzybski wrote a profound tome called *Science and Sanity* (1933)† in which he propounded a wide-ranging thesis that most if not all human and organization problems were caused by the way we talk about things, or, in a broader way, by failures to communicate.

Elton Mayo, widely regarded as the initiator of the human relations movement, explained in one of his books, *The Social Problems of an Industrial Civilization* (1945)‡, that [failure to communicate well] is "the outstanding defect that civilization is facing today."

---

*W. Charles Redding, *Communication within the Organization: An interpretive Review of Theory and Research.* New York: Industrial Communication Council, 1972.

†Alfred Korzybski, *Science and Sanity.* Lakeville, Conn.: International Society for General Semantics, 1933.

‡Elton Mayo, *The Social Problems of an Industrial Civilization.* Cambridge, Mass.: Harvard University Press, 1945.

Finally, John Gall, the author of *Systemantics* (1975),* a pocket-size volume on how systems work and, especially, how they fail—the first book, according to Gall, that attempts to deal with the "cussedness" of systems—offers a series of axiomatic propositions for understanding systems or organizations. One of these is that "complex systems tend to oppose their own proper function." Two corollary propositions are that "people in systems do not do what the system says they are doing" and "the system itself does not do what it says it is doing."

We shall not indict or quibble with any of the above authorities. What they say is probably true. What we say is probable. We think there are opportunities all around and that we should all take advantage of them.

Once again, we wish to acknowledge and thank our colleagues, departments, and universities for their contributions to the completion of this work. Neither the beginning nor the ending of such a task is without disorder, but Linda Veteto and her courageous assistants in the seventh-floor word processing center, Marriott School of Management, Brigham Young University, turned some remarkably sorry-looking pages into a manuscript of elegance. We salute them. Gae Tueller Pace prepared the indexes, and we thank her for that and all the other support she has provided over the years. We wish to thank Steven A. Beebe, Southwest Texas State University and the other reviewers for their helpful suggestions.

Goodnight, Don! Goodnight, Wayne!

R. Wayne Pace
Don F. Faules

*John Gall, *Systemantics: How Systems Work and Especially How They Fail*. New York: Quadrangle/The New York Times, 1975.

1

Organizational Communication

Underlying Concepts

A book about organizational communication must account for at least two basic concepts—organization and communication. The current state of our knowledge about organizational communication has been developing for several decades; both academicians and practitioners from quite different perspectives have analyzed and theorized about organizations and communication. As you shall see, the study of organizational communication is a study of the way people think about things as well as a study of the things themselves.

In our society, we value "good organization." Just about everyone has vowed at some time to "get it together" and "get organized." For example, organization is very prominent in the world of sports. The media seem delighted when they can point to a "no-name team" that defeats its opponents by virtue of "organized team play." Although our culture tends to emphasize individualism, we also revere coordinated activity that produces excellence. In fact, we often hear people say, "We have the team" or "We have the organization to carry that off." Besides being immersed in language that emphasizes "organizing," most of us belong to a variety of organizations. We try to belong to the best organizations, and people expect certain benefits from participating in organized behavior.

Because the concepts of organizing and organization are so pervasive in our everyday lives, it is easy to gloss over their complexity and significance. Making sense of organizational life is more than just arriving at definitions of such terms as *organizing*, *organization*, and *organizational communication*. These concepts can be and are used in very different ways with very different consequences.

We urge readers to maintain their common sense notions of what these terms mean while we explore the forces behind the more specific concepts and definitions. The role that communication plays in the study of organization depends on how "organization" is conceptualized. In this chapter we introduce alternative views of reality, human nature, and organization because these concepts guide our understanding of organizational communication and how it is practiced.

ALTERNATIVE VIEWS

Social Reality

Our major concern in this section is the concept of *social reality* and how we make sense of the social world. We do not intend to solve the puzzle of what reality actually consists of or if things really exist outside of our minds. We feel confident that people experience the existence of physical things, but we are equally confident that people create the experiences they have with people and things.

What is important is that (1) different people behave in different ways toward what they consider to be objects worthy of scrutiny, and (2) those differences are based on how individuals think about those objects. A social object is simply one that has significance to a collectivity or calls for some type of action by people. In that sense, behaviors and things are social constructions, because they depend on people to make them significant.

If one views objects and behaviors as events constructed by people, one can also see human behavior as relying heavily upon social processes to hold the world together. Before we explore this theme in detail, let us provide a contrasting view that may be more familiar.

It is difficult to do justice to all facets of a debate that has spanned many years and disciplines, but the information in Figure 1.1 (Morgan & Smircich, 1980) allows for a general comparison and contrast of views of reality and the accompanying beliefs about human nature. The range of views has been organized on a continuum from highly subjective to highly objective views.

The material contained in Figure 1.1 has numerous implications for the study, practice, and evaluation of organizational communication, but we are using it as a framework for thinking about how theory is related to practice. We want the reader to be aware that there are alternative ways of thinking about communication issues, and different issues are raised by each perspective. This will be discussed in more detail in the section concerning direction of the text. In the meantime, there are basic terms and ideas that require exploration.

In this book the term "objective" refers to the view that objects, behaviors, and events exist in a "real" world. They exist regardless and independent of their perceivers. The term "subjective" suggests that reality itself is a social construction. We caution the reader to remember that we are not using the terms "subjective" and "objective" to represent a value judgment concerning which view is best. The terms refer to alternative views of the world. There is a tendency to assign value to and favor the term "objective" because all of us have been admonished to stand outside our biases and be "objective." Again, this assumes that people can remove themselves from their biases and that "truth" can be found if we can remove human interference when making judgments. Subjectivity suggests that knowledge does not have an objective, unchangeable nature. The study of perception argues for the highly active and selective nature of the process. This in itself throws doubt on whether we can discover the "objective." However, there are those who take the position that individuals do not create the outside world, but interact with it. For example, Brown (1977) maintains that the objects of perception are the results of both theoretical projections and the action of the external world on our senses.

CORE ONTOLOGICAL ASSUMPTIONS	**Reality as a Projection of Human Imagination**	**Reality as a Social Construction**
	The social world and what passes as "reality" is a projection of individual consciousness; it is an act of creative imagination and of dubious intersubjective status. This extreme position, commonly known as solipsism, asserts that there may be nothing outside oneself: one's mind is ones world. Certain transcendental approaches to phenomenology assert a reality in consciousness, the manifestation of a phenomenal world, but not necessarily accessible to understanding in the course of everyday affairs. Reality in this sense is masked by those human processes which judge and interpret the phenomenon in consciousness prior to a full understanding of the structure of meaning it expresses. Thus the nature of the phenomenal world may be accessible to the human being only through consciously phenomenological modes of insight.	The social world is a continuous process, created afresh in each encounter of everyday life as individuals impose themselves on their world to establish a realm of meaningful definition. They do so through the medium of language, labels, actions, and routines, which constitute symbolic modes of being in the world. Social reality is embedded in the nature and use of these modes of symbolic action. The realm of social affairs thus has no concrete status of any kind; it is a symbolic construction. Symbolic modes of being in the world, such as through the use of language, may result in the development of shared, but multiple realities, the status of which is fleeting, confined only to those moments in which they are actively constructed and sustained.
ASSUMPTIONS ABOUT HUMAN NATURE	**Humans as Transcendental Beings**	**Humans Create their Realities**
	Humans are viewed as intentional beings, directing their psychic energy and experience in ways that constitute the world in a meaningful, intentional form. There are realms of being, and realms of reality, constituted through different kinds of founding acts, stemming from a form of transcendental consciousness. Human beings shape the world within the realm of their own immediate experience.	Human beings create their realities in the most fundamental ways, in an attempt to make their world intelligible to themselves and to others. They are not simply actors interpreting their situations in meaningful ways, for there are no situations other than those which individuals bring into being through their own creative activity. Individuals may work together to create a shared reality, but that reality is still a subjective construction capable of disappearing the moment its members cease to sustain it as such. Reality appears as real to individuals because of human acts of conscious or unwitting collusion.
SOME EXAMPLES OF RESEARCH	**Phenomenology**	**Ethnomethodology**

FIGURE 1.1 Assumptions about Ontology and Human Nature

Source: From Gareth Morgan and Linda Smircich, "The Case for Qualitative Research," *Academy of Management Review*, 5 (October 1980), 494–495. Copyright © 1980 by the Academy of Management. Reprinted by permission of the publisher.

$$\longleftarrow \qquad\qquad\qquad\qquad\qquad \longrightarrow$$

Reality as Symbolic Discourse

The social world is a pattern of symbolic relationships and meaning sustained through a process of human action and interaction. Although a certain degree of continuity is preserved through the operation of rule-like activities that define a particular social milieu, the pattern is always open to reaffirmation or change through the interpretations and actions of individual members. The fundamental character of the social world is embedded in the network of subjective meanings that sustain the rule-like actions that lend it enduring form. Reality rests not in the rule or in rule-following, but in the system of meaningful action that renders itself to an external observer as rule-like.

Reality as a Contextual Field of Information

The social world is a field of ever-changing form and activity based on the transmission of information. The form of activity that prevails at any one given time reflects a pattern of "differences" sustained by a particular kind of information exchange. Some forms of activity are more stable than others, reflecting an evolved pattern of learning based on principles of negative feedback. The nature of relationships within the field is probabilistic; a change in the appropriate pattern and balance within any sphere will reverberate throughout the whole, initiating patterns of adjustment and readjustment capable of changing the whole in fundamental ways. Relationships are relative rather than fixed and real.

Humans as Social Actors

Human beings are social actors interpreting their milieu and orienting their actions in ways that are meaningful to them. In this process they utilize language, labels, routines for impression management, and other modes of culturally specific action. In so doing they contribute to the enactment of a reality; human beings live in a world of symbolic significance, interpreting and enacting a meaningful relationship with that world. Humans are actors with the capacity to interpret, modify, and sometimes create the scripts that they play upon life's stage.

Humans as Information Processors

Human beings are engaged in a continual process of interaction and exchange with their context—receiving, interpreting, and acting on the information received, and in so doing creating a new pattern of information that effects changes in the field as a whole. Relationships between individual and context are constantly modified as a result of this exchange; the individual is but an element of a changing whole. The crucial relationship between individual and context is reflected in the pattern of learning and mutual adjustment that has evolved. Where this is well developed, the field of relationships is harmonious; where adjustment is low, the field is unstable and subject to unpredictable and discontinuous patterns of change.

Social Action Theory   **Cybernetics**

FIGURE 1.1 *(continued)*

4

Reality as a Concrete Process

The social world is an evolving process, concrete in nature, but ever-changing in detailed form. Everything interacts with everything else and it is extremely difficult to find determinate causal relationships between constituent processes. At best, the world expresses itself in terms of general and contingent relationships between its more stable and clear-cut elements. The situation is fluid and creates opportunities for those with appropriate ability to mold and exploit relationships in accordance with their interests. The world is in part what one makes of it: a struggle between various influences, each attempting to move toward achievement of desired ends.

Reality as a Concrete Structure

The social world is a hard, concrete, real thing "out there," which affects everyone in one way or another. It can be thought of as a structure composed of a network of determinate relationships between constituent parts. Reality is to be found in the concrete behavior and relationships between these parts. It is an objective phenomenon that lends itself to accurate observation and measurement. Any aspect of the world that does not manifest itself in some form of observable activity or behavior must be regarded as being of questionable status. Reality by definition is that which is external and real. The social world is as concrete and real as the natural world.

Humans as Adaptive Agents

Human beings exist in an interactive relationship with their world. They influence and are influenced by their context or environment. The process of exchange that operates here is essentially a competitive one, the individual seeking to interpret and exploit the environment to satisfy important needs, and hence survive. Relationships between individuals and environment express a pattern of activity necessary for survival and well-being of the individual.

Humans as Responding Mechanisms

Human beings are a product of the external forces in the environment to which they are exposed. Stimuli in their environment condition them to behave and respond to events in predictable and determinate ways. A network of causal relationships links all important aspects of behavior to context. Though human perception may influence this process to some degree, people always respond to situations in a lawful (i.e., rule-governed) manner.

Open Systems Theory

**Behaviorism
Social Learning Theory**

FIGURE 1.1 *(continued)*

The underlying logic of the material in Figure 1.1 poses two general questions that are significant. How "determined" or "voluntary" is human behavior? How does one come to understand and manage the environment? Starting on the "objective" side of the continuum, behavior is highly determined and individuals are truly products of their environment. As one moves toward the other (subjective) end of the continuum, behavior becomes more voluntary and human agency is deemed more of a factor in deciding how the external environment is constructed. One implication is that if individuals are not just responders to environmental cues, it becomes difficult to generalize about them and how they communicate. In addition, if communication action has a voluntary base, as Penman (1992) has suggested, then individuals must be responsible for their actions. This means that there is a moral dimension in the study of communication and that those who subscribe to the more subjective theoretical positions are more likely to see moral issues as central.

The second question provides an important starting point for contrasting views of communication embedded in the positions set forth in Figure 1.1. The extreme "objective" view suggests that people observe their environments, determine the meaning, and use language accordingly. Communication, then, is used as a tool to manage what has been identified. The "subjective" position emphasizes the generation of meaning. It is not just a matter of using language/communication as a tool to describe what is there. Language/communication itself brings about what people are trying to represent. This position concurs with Penman (1992) when she states that "our understanding arises out of our meaning generation process, not out of our physical experiences or observations per se"(p.236). From a subjectivist position the environment is managed by managing meaning. As Weick (1977) suggests, rather than getting control of our environment, a shift of thinking prompts individuals to get in better position to get control of the processes that lead to an enacted environment and the consequent labeling process. If the environment is a creation, then it is prudent to examine the creative process itself rather than place total faith in the notion that there has been a "discovery" of the environment and it just waits to be managed. Communication is not just a tool that represents thought, but it is the thought and it is knowledge. A particular world is generated in communication, and any interpretation of that communication must consider the context in which the communication practices have occurred.

One can understand the wide differences between the positions by analyzing the two extremes. An extreme objectivist looks at the social world in the same way as we think of the physical or natural world, as something concrete and separate from the person who is looking at and touching the world. The extreme subjectivist, on the other hand, maintains that nothing exists outside of the mind of the person doing the perceiving, and that reality is strictly a human process in which we create the physical objects in our minds and respond to them as though they existed as natural events.

We are less concerned with the merits of these two extreme positions and more concerned with *how we might behave if we hold one or the other of the views,* especially in terms of how we might think about an organization. Because significant and specific differences exist between the objective and the subjective approaches, we will contrast them in more detail.

People who approach reality objectively see it as something concrete or physical with a structure that should be and can be discovered. Even if it is not discovered, the structure is still there and is independent of those who are trying to discover it. The world contains a certain order that is, in fact, waiting to be discovered. Most of what we call "science" is based on the objective approach. Scientists, the people who are trying to discover the nature of reality, use telescopes and microscopes to find out what makes things function. The functioning has an order, and a scientist is trying to discover that order—in the planets, in the patterns of animals, in the way in which cells multiply, and in the relationships among atoms and people.

A subjectivist looks at reality as a creative process in which the people create what is "out there." From a subjectivist's view, people *create* an order rather than *discover* the order of things. The world, and all the things in it, is basically unstructured, or at least it operates in ways that do not make sense in and of themselves.

Order is the way in which one thing follows another in a particular sequence of events. In biology, for example, order is the subdivision of classes and subclasses in the classification systems for plants and animals. The question a subjectivist asks is, "Are plants and animals ordered naturally in the same way that biologists order them?" Of course, a subjectivist's answer is that they are not; the biologist creates the order and imposes it on the plants and animals. Once you learn the biological classification system created by biologists, you may *think* the world is ordered in that fashion, but the reality is that scientists created the system and produced the order. The world of plants and animals, according to subjectivists, is not ordered that way.

Organization/Organizing

How one orders people, things, and ideas in an organized fashion is affected by whether one begins from an objectivist's or a subjectivist's point of view. The objective approach suggests that an organization is a physical, concrete thing, that it is a structure with definite boundaries. The term "the organization" implies that something is tangible and actually holds people, relationships, and goals. Some people refer to this approach as the *container* view of organizations. The organization exists like a basket, and all the elements that make up the organization are placed in the container.

A subjective approach looks at an organization as activities that people do. Organization consists of the actions, interactions, and transactions in which people engage. Organization is created and maintained through the continually changing contacts people have with one another and does not exist separately from the people whose behavior constitutes the organization.

From the objective view, organization means structure; from the subjective view, organization means process. The degree of emphasis placed on behavior or on structure depends on which view you hold.

"Organization" is typically thought of as a noun, whereas "organizing" is recognized as a verb (Weick, 1979). Subjectivists regard organization as *organizing behavior*. Objectivists regard organization as structure, something stable. The use of the word "organizing" to refer to an organization may seem awkward regardless of which view you hold.

What do we mean by "organization"? The answer depends on the perspective taken, but, for our purposes, it is important to realize that neither perspective answers the question fully.

The devices used to describe organization provide insight into the challenge of capturing what organization is all about. A primary descriptive device is the *metaphor*. A metaphor compares one thing to another by talking about the first thing as if it were the second thing. For example, to say that "life is a game" is to use a metaphor comparing *life* with *game*. We could say "life is like a game," but the metaphor provides a stronger comparison. Metaphors not only help us see similarities and differences but also convey a feeling that literal descriptions fail to do. When someone says, "Pinning down a bureaucrat is the same as nailing jelly to a wall," a vivid image is conveyed. Metaphors provide the imagery for studying a subject.

The study of something, such as organization, can be based on exploring the features of the metaphors found in the particular subject under inquiry. Morgan and Smircich (1980) maintain that theorists choose metaphors that are based on assumptions about reality and human nature that commit themselves to particular kinds and forms of knowledge. Metaphors have a constraining and enabling influence on the theorists' thought processes.

The use of metaphors to study a subject requires that certain parts of the comparison be ignored while others are emphasized. For example, if you took the metaphor "life is a game" literally, it would be difficult to specify just what the rules are for the game of life. Morgan (1980) argues that a metaphor is based on partial truth, and the metaphor's most creative expression relies on "constructive falsehood," in which certain features are emphasized.

The major implications of this idea, according to Morgan, are that "no one metaphor can capture the total nature of organizational life," and that "different metaphors can constitute and capture the nature of organizational life in different ways, each generating powerful, distinctive, but essentially partial kinds of insight....To acknowledge that organization theory is metaphorical is to acknowledge that it is an essentially subjective enterprise, concerned with the production of one-sided analyses of organizational life" (pp. 611–612).

Metaphors are used widely in the study and practice of organizational communication. For example, managers are fond of using sports metaphors to describe organizational behavior. They refer to "playing team ball," "knowing when to carry the ball and when to pass it," and "going for the home run." However, it is important that metaphors not be confused with what they are intended to describe. Sports metaphors may provide provocative descriptions and some guidelines for expected behavior. But those with organizational experience realize that organizational life is much more complex than most sports. Rules can vary depending on people, status, power, and external forces. In fact, several games with different rules may be operating at the same time, and sometimes unwritten rules dominate the play. Therefore, the differences as well as the similarities in metaphors make for creative and insightful comparisons. Metaphors help explain and illustrate complex concepts, but each metaphor explains in a certain way. We ought to be sensitive to how such devices can both screen out thinking and enrich it.

A way of seeing is also a way of not seeing. For example, a common traditional organizational metaphor, and one that reflects an objective approach, is that of the machine, as in "the organization is a well-oiled machine." Machines are concrete and their various parts can be observed in action. The metaphor simplifies matters by allowing us to see an organization as having interdependent and interchangeable parts that work in harmony. The systematic character of a machine is projected onto the organization. The underlying notion is that we can understand human organization from the same set of principles used to understand machines. However, significant differences must be taken into account when such comparisons are made. Human actors are less predictable, for example, than parts of machines. The differences between human beings suggest that they are not as interchangeable as parts of a machine. Parts of a machine also work in some predetermined fashion. They are programmed to do so. Parts do not care, but people do. Parts shape the machine only in a static sense. People create, maintain, change, and terminate organization through behaviors that are continually changing.

A prominent metaphor that demonstrates the subjective approach to organization is that of culture. The word "culture" is used in a variety of ways when referring to organization (Smircich, 1983, 1985; Pacanowsky & O'Donnell-Trujillo, 1982; Putnam, 1983). When metaphor is used as a way of seeing and knowing the world, culture suggests that organizations exist only through people in interaction. Cultural analysis emphasizes symbolic behavior and the construction of reality through interaction. Although we find it hard to deny the potency of symbolic activity, it does not always represent actions taken. People do not always do what they say! In addition, external forces may be ignored when applying the culture metaphor.

We will elaborate on these and other metaphors in succeeding chapters. At this point, it is important to remember that one's conception of organization depends on one's assumptions about reality. The assumptions depend on whether one holds an objective or a subjective view of the world and people. Both approaches use metaphors that give us insight into some aspects of organization, but each falls short of a complete description of the complexity of organizational life. Because metaphors are incomplete, we need to be sensitive to what is unspoken when a particular metaphor is used. In addition to reflecting a view of reality, metaphors imply certain assumptions about humans. Remember that where and how human beings fit into organization theory depends on which approach you use (see Morgan, 1986, for organizational metaphors).

Human Nature

Ideas about what humans are like and the nature of reality are interconnected (see Figure 1.1). Objective approaches place considerable emphasis on environment as a determining factor in explaining human behavior. People are shaped by their environments, and their success and survival depend on how well they adapt to this concrete reality. A significant part of the adaptive process is defining the environment properly and meeting *its* requirements.

Because the environment and the organization have structure, fitting the two so that maximum adaptation can take place is important. An organization's survival depends on its ability to adapt to and transact with the environment. Human beings are seen as information processors who respond to information found in the environment. The relationship between an individual and the person's context is determined by information exchange.

The subjective approach places humans in a more active and creative role. Humans are not products of an environment, but they create that environment. Their own creations may very well come back upon them ("What goes around comes around," so they say), but that is vastly different from saying that a concrete environment exists independently of people's actions. Human beings live in a symbolic world, and a symbolic environment is subject to change and multiple interpretations. Humans create, sustain, and terminate reality through the use of symbols. Humans do not just respond and adapt to what is out there. They create the environment and participate in the social process of creation. A large part of the human challenge is to recognize and adapt to the social process itself.

Human Action

Human action is also viewed from different perspectives by the objectivist and the subjectivist. From the objectivist's view, action is purposive, intentional, goal-directed, and rational. People think things through; they act with intent, have goals in mind, and weigh the consequences carefully. The essence of this view is well represented in management textbooks. Readers are advised about planning, organizing, and executing their plans (Mintzberg, 1980, p. 9). In addition, action is tightly constrained and controlled by the environment. Actions are environmentally determined, and the actor is constrained to behave in certain ways. For the subjectivist, action emerges from the social process of human interaction. The focus is on emergent behavior that depends on social construction taking place during the process of interaction.

The contrast between these two notions of human action has an impact on the concepts of predictability and control. To believe as an objectivist is to believe that organizations can be managed and controlled by rational decisions that structure activities in accordance with environmental demands and individual capabilities. Plans can be laid out in advance and one should be able to predict outcomes.

Much of the literature on managerial styles of leadership is based on the idea that a manager's behavior produces certain kinds of responses from subordinates. Although this idea will be examined in greater detail later, both experience and the subjective view suggest that prescribed managerial behaviors can result in very different employee responses. It is comforting to think that managers might be able to enter a situation with some universal rules on how to manage. However, even the most routine situations can be problematic and unpredictable. In addition, managers seldom have time to contemplate their decisions with the thoroughness suggested by the objective, rational view.

Both views are "people-oriented," but they view people in different ways. Objectivists suggest that people are predictable, as long as the underlying forces of natural order can be specified. The main objective is to behave rationally and determine how people adapt to situations. Subjectivists emphasize that people create order and situations. Rather than trying to discover a natural order (which, to them, does not exist), it is more useful to become sensitive to how people create order, the meaning it has for them, and the consequences of their creations.

Objective approaches imply that order exists in a real world. That order can be discovered, and the world, as well as human behavior, can be predictable. From this perspective, models for human behavior emphasize order, simplicity, and are based on how organizations *should* operate. The next short step, however, is the idea that once the order is discovered, the organizational participants can be regulated and controlled. Such thinking has stimulated numerous theories of motivation and the search for a way to motivate employees that can be generalized to all settings. From a subjectivist position, understanding motivation demands knowledge about the unique aspects of the participants and the world they have created. This requires knowing what the world and its symbols mean to them.

The phrase *world view* refers to one's assumptions about reality and human nature. In this chapter we will introduce some of the implications different world views have for the analysis and understanding of organizations. It seems clear that human organizations are highly complex, and even though we use metaphors to help us understand them, each metaphor falls short of guiding us toward full comprehension of how organizations work. It is also evident that the metaphor used depends on one's world view. The most provocative question is simply, "What impact do world views have and which one should be followed?"

IMPACT OF WORLD VIEWS ON DEFINITIONS AND ANALYSES

One's world view has an impact on how one defines the concept of organization. An objectivist, as we have pointed out, sees an organization as a concrete structure. An organization is a container that holds people and things; the people in the organization adhere to some common goals. If the organization is healthy, the interdependent parts work in a systematic way to produce desirable outcomes. Knowledge about organizations consists of recognizing what structures or designs produce what outcomes. The objectivist emphasizes structure, planning, control, and goals and places these major factors in a scheme of organizational adaptation. Environment determines the organizing principles. The objectivist seeks the "best form" of the organization, based on environmental conditions. This approach leads to looking for an optimum fit between organ-izational structure and some factor in the environment, such as technology, situational favorability, or uncertainty. Organizations are conceived as large information processors with input, throughput, and output. This structured system of behavior contains positions and roles that can be designed (prestructured) before the roles are filled by actors (Stogdill, 1966).

Objectivists treat the organization primarily as a unit. That is, to study the organization is to study the *entire* organization. The organization is an *entity* that acts or functions in particular ways. Questions may center on how organizations can best adapt to their environment to enhance growth and survival. Some theorists divide the organization into organization, environment, group-to-group, and individual-to-organization areas of study (Lawrence & Lorsch, 1969). However, all of these divisions are considered to be part of an entity called "the organization."

Subjectivists define organization as organizing behavior. Given this definition, knowledge of the organization must be obtained by looking at those specific behaviors and what they mean to the people doing them. Structure is important only to the extent that it is created and re-created by organizational participants. Although knowledge generated by the subjectivist may be used in a variety of ways, its main use is to understand organizational life as it is understood and constituted by organizational participants. A subjectivist seeks not to gain control of the various forces (structure, planning, goals), but to explain them.

When the emphasis is placed on the interaction between the participants, as it is with a subjectivist's view, the concept of organization is not limited to large, complex industries or agencies. A family can be considered an organization just as General Motors can. The unit of analysis is the individual, not the entity called the organization. Organizations do not behave; only people behave (Weick, 1979). The subjectivist is concerned with the actions of the participants and the consequences of their actions and what they mean for the participants.

The objectivist typically views the organization as a large entity with a control structure comprised of procedures and policies. The system is ordered on the basis of logic in order to achieve a goal and contains different degrees of authority at various levels as well as particular kinds of activities performed by individuals (Tosi, 1975). In contrast, a subjectivist advocates a broader notion of organization. For example, the subjectivists Pacanowsky and O'Donnell-Trujillo define an organization as the "interlocked actions of a collectivity" (1982, p. 122). A collectivity may be small or large; the critical aspect of the definition centers on "interlocked actions" and the meaning given to those actions.

Alternative views of reality and human nature have an impact on what is considered important in the study of organizational behavior and communication. The next section discusses some of the general implications for the study of organizational behavior.

IMPLICATIONS FOR ORGANIZATIONAL BEHAVIOR

Structure versus Behavior

Given that objective approaches to reality promote the idea that the world consists of concrete, real things, it comes as no surprise that those approaches emphasize the importance of structure in guiding behavior. Although those who adhere to a structural approach would not maintain that structure alone is enough, they prefer the idea that structure, especially formal structure, represents the organization. McPhee (1985) cites elements of organization that are encompassed under the idea of structure:

> It would include things like official job titles, descriptions, and objectives for employees, along with their conditions of employment or employment contracts; the official differentiation of division, departments, and work units; the book or books of standard operating procedures; the "corporate charter" and other documents establishing the legal basis of the organization, and so on.... I would include in structure the various systems for decision support, management information, work evaluation and compensation, and financial control (p. 149).

Subjectivists recognize structure, but their emphasis is placed on human behavior. Structure does not exist independently of the actions of people. People create structure, sustain it, and terminate it. There are those who maintain that structure is continuously created (see Column 2, Figure 1.1), which makes the concept even of routine activities problematic. A creative process is required for structure to be recognized as routine. Structure is not just there. It is enacted and accomplished through the process of organizing (Garfinkel, 1967; Weick, 1969, 1979).

Objectivists imply that if one understands the structure, one understands the organization. It is but a short step to the metaphor that it is possible to have a well-oiled machine if the right structure can be discovered. Furthermore, from this point of view, it seems reasonable to suggest that management consists of seeing that the right structure is executed in an appropriate fashion. Management is concerned with getting organizational participants to understand and adhere to the structure. Structure can be learned, and one can learn to perform a position and maintain the integrity of a structure.

Subjective views suggest that behavior and specific actions are the dominant forces in the organization. There is no structure until individuals work together to create it. Even then structure is a unique construction that may not last unless it is sustained through further interaction. Through symbolic means, people develop shared but multiple realities. Management, from this perspective, emphasizes the discovery of what those multiple realities are, what is shared, and what impact those discoveries might have on decision making in the organization. Subjective approaches also suggest that managers could benefit from becoming sensitive to the reality-construction processes, because it is those processes that enable people to establish something that is called "routine."

Predictability and Control

Objective approaches imply that humans are products of external forces that condition them to respond in predictable and determinate ways. This view also suggests that there is systematic order to human behavior. The tendency is to want to discover the forces at work so that organizational behavior can be predicted and controlled. Objective study focuses on the discovery of causal relationships (cause and effect). Once causal links are exposed, it is thought that order can be maintained and even altered by manipulating the elements of the organization.

Subjective approaches imply that order is created by the organizational participants. Subjectivists do not deny order but simply argue that there is no order until it is constructed by members of the organization.

Objectivists and subjectivists differ dramatically on how much order and control can be imposed on organizational behavior and the nature of the order and control that the organization has. For example, some maintain that organizational culture can and should be managed, while others contend that culture is an "emergent process" that cannot be controlled (Martin, 1985). While some highlight the control procedures that precede actions, others (Weick, 1977) emphasize the retrospective sense-making processes that follow actions. These ideas will receive more specific treatment in Chapter 5.

Role of Environment

Objective approaches make it clear that environment is the driving force behind organizational behavior. Organizations are conditioned by the environment, and the survival of organizations depends on their ability to interpret the *real* environment and adapt to it. Much emphasis is placed on how well organizational structure and environmental structure fit together. Both structure and environment are considered to be things rather than creations. Theories of environmental determinism have had considerable influence on the study of organizational behavior (Lawrence & Lorsch, 1969; Burns & Stalker, 1961). Again, the organization must attend to the external environment and use its best adaptive strategies to achieve growth and survival.

The subjectivist looks at the importance of environment in a different way. A significant part of organizational behavior is how participants create the environment and how that creation affects their behavior (Weick, 1979). What counts is what is created, not what is "really" there, because what is there (if it is there at all) can only be understood through the symbolic processes and result in a subjective interpretation. Rather than ask questions about what kind of environment exists, the subjectivist asks questions about how participants make sense of whatever is called environment. These ideas will be developed in various portions of the text; a major implication to remember is that if environment is created, then it is possible to think of organizational change as a decision-making process.

Simplicity versus Complexity

Regardless of whether the perspective taken is objective or subjective, numerous metaphors are used to describe the organization. This suggests that organizations seem complex to almost everyone. Nevertheless, objective approaches tend to reduce organizations to interacting parts that respond and adapt to the environment, which implies more stability and routine than may be the case. Subjectivists contend that objectivists gloss over the importance of human creative processes and take them for granted. They argue that the constructive and reconstructive processes of reality are quite complex and changeable. Objectivists, they argue, tend to reduce human behavior to simple, basic terms.

It is appealing to think of humans as information processors, adaptive agents, or responding mechanisms. The terms provide convenient handles, and they seem to fit with our common-sense notions and observations. Nevertheless, subjectivists warn that such conceptions may offer only a grand delusion. When the richness and complexity of human behavior are stripped away, what remains is not human behavior and is not representative of organization. Rather than simplifying, it may be more helpful to analyze all the complexities so that significant human processes can be taken into account.

The objectivist starts with a "real" world that is assumed to be complex and tries to reduce it to parts that are made understandable through the exploration of causal linkages. The subjectivist is interested in the complex notion of "world making" and the impact that process has on organization (Smircich, 1985). For the subjectivist, organizations are made understandable by discovering how organizational life is created by participants.

SUMMARY

We have discussed key ideas that affect the way organizational communication is conceptualized, studied, and practiced. Alternate views of reality and human nature impact on the definition and perceived functions of organizational communication. Such views decide what issues are of concern and how they may be approached for study. In addition, how one views the nature of human action will in large part guide organizational communication practices. Chapter 2 will develop the concept of organizational communication in more detail and present our working definitions for the text.

REFERENCES

BROWN, H., *Perception, Theory and Commitment*. Chicago: University of Chicago Press, 1977.

BURNS, TOM, and G.M. STALKER, *The Management of Innovation*. London: Tavistock, 1961.

GARFINKEL, HAROLD, *Studies in Ethnomethodology*. Englewood Cliffs, N.J.: Prentice-Hall, 1967.

LAWRENCE, PAUL R., and JAY W. LORSCH, *Organization and Environment*. Homewood, Ill.: Richard D. Irwin, 1969.

McPHEE, ROBERT D., "Formal Structures and Organizational Communication," in *Organizational Communication*, Robert D. McPhee and Phillip K. Tompkins, eds. Beverly Hills, Calif.: Sage Publications, Inc., 1985.

MARTIN, JOANNE, "Can Organizational Culture Be Managed?" in *Organizational Culture*, Peter J. Frost et al., eds. Beverly Hills, Calif.: Sage Publications, Inc., 1985.

MINTZBERG, HENRY, *The Nature of Managerial Work*. Englewood Cliffs, N.J.: Prentice-Hall, 1980.

MORGAN, GARETH, "Paradigms, Metaphors, and Puzzle Solving in Organization Theory," *Administrative Science Quarterly*, 25 (December 1980), 605–622.

MORGAN, GARETH, *Images of Organization*. Beverly Hills, Calif.: Sage Publications, Inc., 1986.

MORGAN, GARETH, and LINDA SMIRCICH, "The Case for Qualitative Research," *Academy of Management Review*, 5 (October 1980), 491–500.

PACANOWSKY, MICHAEL E., and NICK O'DONNELL-TRUJILLO, "Communication and Organizational Cultures," *Western Journal of Speech Communication*, 46 (Spring 1982), 115–130.

PENMAN, ROBYN, "Good Theory and Good Practice: An Argument in Progress," *Communication Theory*, 2 (August 1992), 234–250.

PUTNAM, LINDA L., "The Interpretive Perspective: An Alternative to Functionalism," in *Communication and Organizations: An Interpretive Approach*, Linda L. Putnam and Michael E. Pacanowsky, eds. Beverly Hills, Calif.: Sage Publications, Inc., 1983.

SMIRCICH, LINDA, "Concepts of Culture and Organizational Analysis," *Administrative Science Quarterly*, 28 (September 1983), 339–358.

SMIRCICH, LINDA, "Is the Concept of Culture a Paradigm for Understanding Organizations and Ourselves?" in *Organizational Culture*, Peter J. Frost et al., eds. Beverly Hills, Calif.: Sage Publications, Inc., 1985.

STOGDILL, RALPH M., "Dimension of Organization Theory," in *Approaches to Organizational Design*, James D. Thomson, ed. Pittsburgh: University of Pittsburgh Press, 1966.

TOSI, HENRY L., *Theories of Organization*. New York: John Wiley, 1975.

WEICK, KARL, *The Social Psychology of Organizing*. Reading, Mass.: Addison-Wesley, 1969.

WEICK, KARL, "Enactment Processes in Organizations," in *New Directions in Organizational Behavior*, Barry M. Staw and Gerald R. Salancik, eds. Chicago: St. Clair Press, 1977.

WEICK, KARL, *The Social Psychology of Organizing*, 2nd ed. Reading, Mass.: Addison-Wesley, 1979.

2

The Nature
of Organizational
Communication

Why People Study Organizational
Communication

The traditional literature of the field stresses that communication and organizational success are related. To improve organizational communication is to improve the organization. This reasoning suggests the following:

1. There are universal elements that make an organization ideal.
2. These universal elements can be discovered and used to change an organization.
3. These elements and the way they are used "cause" or at least produce outcomes.
4. Organizations that function well have the right mix and use of these elements.
5. These elements are related to desired organizational outcomes.
6. Communication is one of the elements of organization.

This approach implies that ideas exist that can be generalized to produce desirable outcomes. The primary objective in studying communication is to improve the organization. Improving the organization is usually interpreted as "improving things to accomplish the objectives of management." In other words, people study organizational communication to become better managers. Some writers contend that management is communication (D'Aprix, 1982). Thus, most traditional theories and prescriptions about organizations and organizational communication are written from a managerial perspective and lean heavily toward an objectivist's view.

On the other hand, we often hear students say that they are interested in studying organizational communication because of their own difficult experiences in organizations. Much of their discontent seems to stem from their feelings that the organizational system is depersonalized and discourages creativity and productivity. They express their feelings that organizations need to improve the quality of life in the workplace. They seem to be looking at the organization from a worker's perspective and are interested in what the organization does for the people. Their reason for studying organizational communication is to discover ways to improve the quality of work life.

An organization may also be approached as an object of study in its own right. Some people consider the organization to be a fascinating and intriguing subject. Their main goals are to understand the organization by describing its organizational communication, to understand organizational life, and to discover how life is constituted communicatively. The emphasis is on how an organization is constructed and maintained through the communicative process. This approach focuses on what actually goes on in organizations and provides a level of explanation that rarely occurs in other approaches, a decidedly subjectivist view.

Organizations are also studied because people find them oppressive. A radical humanist may be interested in how humans create their own prisons within organizations. The radical structuralist, on the other hand, may be most concerned with organizations as dominating forces (Morgan, 1983). These two lines of thinking produce critics who are interested in how organizational communication is used to control individuals who do not seem to be aware of the domination of the organization. The goal of the critic is to liberate individuals from oppression by providing an analysis and critique of what they see as an oppressive social order. Thus they can provide alternatives for changing the current organization.

Organizational communication is more than something people do. It is a discipline of study that can take a number of legitimate and useful directions. Although we recognize the value of the theorist, the practitioner, and the critic, in an introductory text all needs cannot be given equal time and space.

This text is directed at two types of readers: (1) those who wish to better understand organizational behavior, and (2) those who wish to improve their performance as organizational participants. We see the study of organizational communication as a solid foundation for careers in management, human resource development, corporate communications, and other people-oriented assignments in organizations.

At the same time, we hope you find knowledge about organizations and organizing intriguing. This knowledge is applicable to various types of organizations and its base is grounded in certain basic assumptions. To be knowledgeable in organizational communication is to understand the basis of that knowledge and the questions it raises.

DEFINITION OF COMMUNICATION

Although we have alluded to the concept of communication, we have not yet provided a precise definition of the term *communication*. Dance and Larson (1976) listed 126 different published definitions of communication, but it is neither practical nor feasible to review them here. The question we shall pursue for a moment, however, concerns how we should distinguish communication from other forms of behavior in an organization. The distinctions are both simple and complex. For example, is hammering a nail a form of communication? Is jogging communication? Is filing letters in a cabinet, looking out the window on the twenty-fifth floor of an office building, or writing a memo forms of communication? The answers to these questions depend on the precision with which one thinks about the activities that constitute communication.

The simple answer is that none of the behaviors mentioned are actually communication. The complex answer is that, in a sense, all of them are part of the communication process. If we look at what happens when a person engages in communicating, we find that two general types of actions take place:

1. *Creating messages* or, more precisely, displays and
2. *Interpreting messages* or displays

Figure 2.1 portrays these two processes by dividing the person with a jagged line.

Message-Display

To *display* means that you bring something to the attention of another or others. The *Random House Dictionary of the English Language* (1987) states that "to display is literally to spread something out so that it may be most completely and favorably seen." Thus to display is to put something in plain view and usually in a favorable position for particular observation. Hammering a nail or filing a letter or writing a memo, by themselves, may not constitute forms of communication. However, they would be considered communication behaviors *if* they made something else visible or put something into plain view or brought something to the attention of another person. For a display to be a form of communicative behavior, it must represent or stand for or symbolize something else. When you create a message-display, you engage in one aspect of communication—calling attention to something. For example, when you get dressed in the morning, you create a display of yourself. You put yourself, or at least what you feel you think about yourself, in plain view. We think you are putting yourself in a favorable position for particular observation. Your clothing, jewelry, and facial covering (makeup or beard) represent yourself to others; they are your display.

There is an axiom of communication that says "A person can*not* not communicate" (Smith & Williamson, 1977, p. 61). Technically, that means that a person cannot avoid being a message-display. What you show or put in plain view does represent you. You

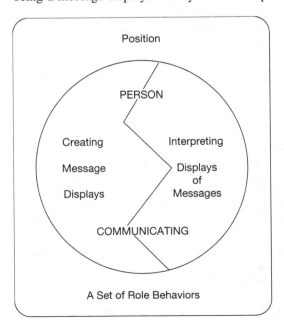

FIGURE 2.1 A Communication Unit

are a walking message-display. The same can be said of your office (Goldhaber, 1979). The office is a message-display. A campus, no matter how it looks, is a message-display for those who visit. Of course, a memo is also a message-display, since the memo represents the ideas being expressed. A speech is a message-display. A drawing, a newspaper, a flower arrangement, and a layout are all message-displays, provided they are designed to stand for something else, such as an idea or image or another object.

Message Interpretation

The second type of behavior that occurs when a person engages in communication is called interpreting message-displays (Redding, 1972). To *interpret* means to set forth, to bring out, or make sense of something. According to the *Random House Dictionary*, to interpret means to construe or understand something in a particular way. Communication can be distinguished from all other human and organizational behaviors because it involves the mental process of making sense out of people, objects, and events, which we call message-displays. The only message that really counts in communicating is the one that results from the interpretative processes (Redding & Sanborn, 1964). You may consciously or intentionally create a display of words, sounds, artifacts, and actions to portray a meaning you have, but the only meaning that has an effect on people is the meaning people assign to the display. What you had in mind makes little difference; how the other person interprets what you did and said is what affects his or her feelings and actions.

INFORMATION AS MESSAGE-DISPLAYS

It is not uncommon for authors to define communication as the *transfer* (Luthans, 1973) or *exchange* (Katz & Kahn, 1966) of information. In this context, for example, *information* refers to the words (in written messages) and the sounds (in spoken messages) in our displays. Luthans (1973), however, included within his definition of information such things as sensory stimuli; languages of all types, including FORTRAN, statistics, and accounting; and nonverbal behavior. Ference (1970) referred to a "five-year forecast of industry sales" as information but defined information as "any input to a person in a communication system" (p. 83). Frequently throughout this book, reference will be made to information, in such contexts as "the flow of information" and "information processing." *Information* is a term used to designate what we have called message-displays and is frequently used to refer to profit-and-loss figures, performance evaluations, personal opinions expressed in letters and memos, technical reports, and operating data.

THE FALLACY OF MEANING TRANSFER

Although we seem to recognize that sending a person a letter, memo, or report, or even talking to him or her face to face, consists only of creating and delivering a display to the other person, we often fail to realize that the delivery of information is different from making sense out of the information. Frequently we behave as though the delivery of information or message-displays is actually the transfer of meaning from one person to another. We think that saying something—such as "Pick up the binder and meet me at the administration building"—should mean exactly the same thing for both people involved. At least when you show up with a ball of string and I was expecting a ring binder, I am surprised that *you* made a mistake. Since I *told* you what to do, you should have done it. I said the words just right, and you should have gotten the meaning. In a statement like that, meaning sounds like something you throw at other people. It's their fault if they fumble it.

The realities of communication suggest that people interpret displays and create meanings. Meanings are *not* contained in the displays or events or words (Lee & Lee, 1957). The fallacy of meaning transfer is expressed in this great principle of communication: "Meanings are in people, not words." Postman and Weingartner (1969) recognized the operation of this fallacy in our schools when they observed that some teachers believe "that they are in the 'information dissemination' business.... The signs that their business is failing are abundant, but they keep at it all the more diligently" (p. 13). The real business of people involved in communicating, including teachers, is helping others create meanings, helping them understand displays. When they assume that meanings are in the displays, they are perpetuating one of the great fallacies of communication.

What is the significance of understanding this meaning-transfer fallacy for a manager, section head, or supervisor? What should an organizational communicator do differently if he or she understands this fallacy? The answer is that the supervisor will *listen to the person, not just to his or her words*. The plaintive appeal to "Listen to what I mean, not what I say" is often heard after something has gone wrong. Remember, there are few, if any, instructions that cannot be misinterpreted by someone. For example, the simple explanation of the flight attendant when handing out chewing gum that "It's for the ears" seemed clear until a passenger complained that gum was all right, but wouldn't something less sticky work better?

The major fallacies of communication are the assumptions that (1) meanings exist in information or message-displays, and (2) meanings can be transferred from one person to another. In reality, information and displays can only be presented or delivered to people; the recipients must make sense out of the displays. Thus, a person can*not* not display. Meanings are in people, not words. Listen to what a person means, not what he or she says.

Messages may be displayed in verbal (involving language) or nonverbal (non-language) forms and by oral, written, or pictorial means. Table 2.1 shows the most common categories of displays.

For a message-display of information to be meaningful, someone must interpret it as standing for something else—that is, the display serves a symbolic function. Any aspect of people and things may be given meaning by someone. Goldhaber (1979) suggests that meaning can be assigned to all of the following: the body and its appearance, especially the mouth and eyes, gestures, touching, posture, and general bodily shape; the volume, tone, rate, pauses, and nonfluencies of vocal expression; the environment, including spaces between people and the territorial cues they offer; time factors such as tardiness and promptness; building and room designs;

TABLE 2.1 Examples of Types of Messages

	VERBAL	NONVERBAL
Oral	Interview	Speaking softly
Written	Report	Diagram or layout
Pictorial	Description of a scene	Sketch of a scene

clothing—dress for success; the display of material things such as artwork; parking spaces; and the number of staff members.

Both verbal and nonverbal message-displays are central to the functioning of an organizational communication system. In fact, the contact that people have with one another and the interpretations they assign to the behavior, objects, and events, both present and absent from the immediate environment, constitute the crux of the organizational communication system.

A COMMUNICATION UNIT

A system has been defined by Pool (1973) as "any continuing entity capable of two or more states" (p. 3). In a communication system the *states* are connections between people. In an organizational communication system the states are connections between *people in positions*. The basic unit of organizational communication is a person in a position. Figure 2.1 symbolizes that important relationship by portraying a person as the circle located inside the square position. As Bakke (1950) and Argyris (1957) explained, the person is socialized by the position, creating a circle that conforms more closely to the shape of the position; at the same time, the position is personalized, producing a figure that conforms more closely to the shape of the person.

A FUNCTIONAL DEFINITION OF ORGANIZATIONAL COMMUNICATION

Organizational communication may be defined as the display and interpretation of messages among communication units that are part of a particular organization. An organization is comprised of communication units in hierarchical relations to each other and functioning in an environment. Figure 2.2 portrays the concept of an organizational communication system. The dotted lines represent the idea that relations are stipulated rather than natural; they also suggest that the structure of an organization is flexible and may change in response to internal, as well as external, environmental forces. Relations among positions, nevertheless, change officially only by declaration of organizational officials.

Organizational communication occurs whenever at least one person who occupies a position in an organization interprets some display. Because our focus is on communication among members of an organization, the analysis of organizational communication involves looking at many transactions occurring simultaneously. The system involves displaying and interpreting messages among dozens or even hundreds of individuals at the same time who have different types of relationships connecting them; whose thinking, decisions, and behaviors are governed by policies, regulations, and "rules"; who have different styles of communicating, managing, and leading; who are motivated by different contingencies; who are at different stages of development in various groups; who perceive different communication climates; who have different levels of satisfaction and information adequacy; who prefer and use different types, forms, and methods of communicating in different networks; who have varying levels of message fidelity; and who require the expenditure of different levels of materials and energy to communicate effectively. The interplay among all of those factors, and possibly many more, is what we call the *organizational communication system*.

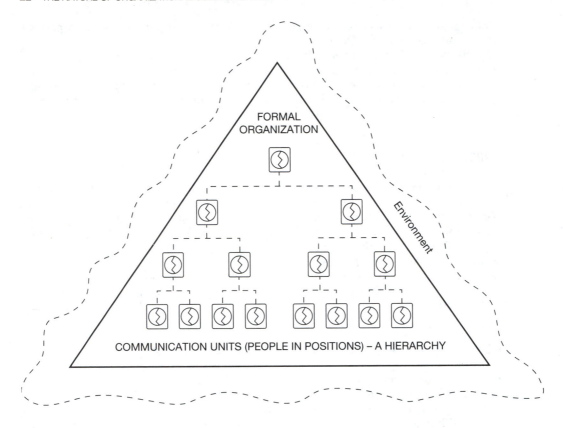

FIGURE 2.2 Organizational Communication System

AN INTERPRETIVE DEFINITION OF ORGANIZATIONAL COMMUNICATION

Traditional (functionalist and objective) definitions of organizational communication tend to emphasize message-handling activities that are contained within an "organizational boundary." To get a view of the primary direction of such definitions return to Chapter 1 and examine "Humans as Information Processors" in Figure 1.1. The focus is on receiving, interpreting and acting on information within a context. The emphasis is on communication as a tool that enables people to adapt to their environment.

Organizational communication from an interpretive (subjective) perspective is the meaning-generation process of interaction that constitutes the organization. The interaction process does not reflect the organization; it is the organization. Organizational communication is the "organizing behavior" that takes place and how those engaged in that process transact and assign meaning to what is taking place. Return to Figure 1.1 and examine the segment titled "Humans Create Their Realities." Notice that reality (organization) is a subjective construction "capable of disappearing the moment its members cease to sustain it as such." To elaborate then, organizational communication is the meaning generation process of interaction that creates, maintains, and changes the organization. In keeping with our earlier discussion, the "objective" view of organization emphasizes "structure" whereas organization from a "subjective" view focuses on "process." Communication is more than a tool, it is a way of thinking.

The concept of "meaning" is both relevant and important to the distinction between functionalist (objective) and interpretive (subjective) perspectives on organizational communication. In the preceding discussion we stressed that an image of communication that places "meaning" in the message will result in behaviors that ignore the "person." It was suggested that the meaning of a message is in the receiver. Another image of communication (subjective) stipulates that the meanings of messages are negotiated *between* participants. Meanings arise and emerge in the interaction that takes place. The relationship (prior or emergent) between participants as well as context will determine what the words mean. The focus of attention is on the verbal and nonverbal transaction that is taking place. Stewart and Thomas (1990) refer to this process as "sculpting mutual meanings." The interpretive (subjective) perspective places emphasis on the role of "persons" and "process" in creating meaning. The "meaning" is not only in the person but in the "transaction" itself.

A SUBJECTIVIST'S REMINDER

The central feature of organizational communication is the message-generating, interpreting, and handling activities of organizational members. What communication does in the organization and what it means depends on one's conception of organization.

If the organization is thought of as a preexisting structure or container, then communication may be conceived of as "a tangible substance that flows upward, downward, and laterally within the container" (Putnam, 1983, p. 39). In that view, communication functions to achieve the goals and objectives of the organizational system. More specific communication functions include work, maintenance, motivation, integration, and innovation messages (Farace, Monge, & Russell, 1977, pp. 56–57). Communication supports the organizational structure and its adaptation to the environment. If the organization is a large information processor, then the purpose of the communication process is to get the right information to the right people at the right times. From this perspective, organizational communication can be seen as "the processes for gathering, processing, storing, and disseminating the communication that enables organizations to function" (Farace, Monge, & Russell, 1977, p. 4).

When the organization is conceived of as people interacting and giving meaning to that interaction, communication becomes an organization-making function rather than just an organization-maintaining one. Communication does not just serve the organization; it *is* the organization. From this perspective, organizational communication "would center on the symbols that make organizational life possible. What are the words, ideas, and constructs that impel, legitimate, coordinate, and realize organized activity in specific settings?" (Smircich, 1985, p. 67). Communication, then, is central to organizational existence and does more than simply carry out organizational plans. In some schemes, communication is theorized to give insight into critical organizational behaviors (i.e., adaptation). For the subjectivist, communication is the critical behavior. To illustrate further, consider the role of communication in decision making. Most people would agree that communication is important to the decision-making process. However, some theorists go further and look at communication as the very fabric of the decision.

The issue of simplicity/complexity discussed in Chapter 1 is relevant here. The notions of organizational structure and functions help us to visualize an organization and the important role of communication. Subjectivists do not deny the usefulness of such concepts; however, they do not take "obvious features" for granted. Understanding is gained through reducing the organization to such simple components, but understanding is also lost by not grasping its complexity. For instance, if we treat structure not as a tool for analysis but as a question of analysis, the complexity of something that was taken for granted becomes evident. What is structure? How is it created, executed, and changed? How is structure enacted or accomplished? These questions generate complexity consistent with subjective approaches.

Can organizational communication exist without people? If messages are treated as physical substances (an extreme objectivist position), communication can exist without people. Objectivists focus on getting information through the system, whereas the role of people is preeminent in a subjectivist's view of organizational communication. Messages are created, interpreted, and re-created in an ongoing process. Organizational communication does not exist until it is created and interpreted by people.

DIRECTION OF TEXT

It is clear that one cannot define and talk about organizational communication without anchoring it in a particular way of thinking. In most cases this will be done implicitly. Even a brief glance at the "objective-subjective" chart (Figure 1.1) suggests the impossibility of covering all facets of this field of study. A case can be made for each of the competing views of "reality" and "human nature." The extreme ends of the continuum may be least defensible, especially when used in a literal sense. So, why have the chart in the first place? Or, as students sometimes ask, "Why look at all those theories?" Theories are linked to action either implicitly or explicitly. The range and nature of action are dependent on the interpretations available. Theories tell us what there is to be thought about and thereby provide alternatives for action.

We would like the reader to become sensitive to what there is to think about and to be better prepared to experiment with some different ways of thinking. We ask that the reader look upon the various frameworks as thought construction tools rather than representations of the "way it really is." It is important to remember that theories may construct the world rather than represent it.

We will not present representative studies and ideas for the entire range of theories on the chart in Figure 1.1. The major portion of this text can be located in the "systems theory," "cybernetics," and the "social action theory" perspectives on the "right" to "middle" side of the chart. Most of the research on and writing about organizational communication represents these views. We not only know these views best, but they have been helpful to us in our own training and consulting activities. That does not suggest that they are the "right" ones or that others do not have merit. Our intention is to recognize other views and at the same time caution ourselves and others to avoid the extremes.

The "subjective" point of view contradicts, elaborates on, and often adds to what the traditional approaches say about organizational communication. Ideas that underlie communication as reality construction (ethnomethodology) and communication as reality enactment (social action theory) stand in sharp contrast to many of the ideas presented in the more "objective" approaches of traditional organizational research. We want to present some of those key "contrasts" for your consideration and use. Throughout the text the more traditional issues are emphasized and then we present comments and questions that are more representative of "subjectivist" thinking. These "reminders" often challenge, criticize, and give an alternative way of thinking about the issues. It must be noted that a strictly "subjectivist" point of view would no doubt generate a different set of issues, but the contrast allows us to see different ways of defining and acting.

The "reminder" and "contrast" sections are to remind us and the reader that (1) there is a tendency not to pay enough attention to the role of humans in creating the conditions that in turn influence their own behaviors, (2) there is a tendency to forget the arbitrary nature of human constructions, and (3) what seems like routine behaviors are reconstituted each time through human interaction. These concepts are critical when considering the issues of communication, control, and power in the organization. Our intent is to provide a "dialectical" approach that promotes the exploration of ideas.

Because objective and subjective perspectives about organizational communication are often on opposite sides of the issues, it is not possible to arrive at a single point of view. One may not be able to meld or bring about a convergence of the two views. We cannot smooth over the differences between objective and subjective approaches to organizational communication, but we can present contrasting points of view so that you can ponder and evaluate them and see where they differ. Our intent is partly to provoke thought about organizational communication. We ask you not to be defensive about either point of view, but to seek to understand what organizational communication is about from both views. You may, as Lauffer (1985) points out, "protect [yourself] from the abuse of others who may be using them [ideas] incorrectly or selectively against your best interests" (p. 20). The theoretical structures presented here will be useful if a sense of perspective is maintained. Most of us go into situations with ideas and then modify them as the situation demands. This text is designed to provide some useful ideas.

SUMMARY

We have discussed the impact that world views have on the study and practice of organizational communication. These views (objective and subjective) influence how one conceptualizes organization, the nature of action, and the function of communication. We have defined organizational communication as the display and interpretation of messages among communication units and we have stressed that organizational communication occurs whenever at least one person who occupies a position interprets some display.

In Part Two, we will examine basic organization theories that have influenced the way organizational communication has been conceived and developed. We are less concerned with the chronology of theories than with the impact of the world views they represent.

REFERENCES

ARGYRIS, CHRIS, *Personality and Organization*. New York: Harper & Row, Pub., 1957.

BAKKE, E. WIGHT, *Bonds of Organization*. New York: Harper & Row, Pub., 1950.

DANCE, FRANK E. X., and CARL E. LARSON, *The Functions of Human Communication: A Theoretical Approach*. New York: Holt, Rinehart & Winston, 1976.

D'APRIX, ROGER, *Communicating for Productivity*. New York: Harper & Row, Pub., 1982.

FARACE, RICHARD V., PETER R. MONGE, and HAMISH M. RUSSELL, *Communicating and Organizing*, Reading, Mass.: Addison-Wesley, 1977.

FERENCE, T. P., "Organizational Communication Systems and the Decision Process," *Management Science*, 17 (1970), 83–96.

GOLDHABER, GERALD M., *Organizational Communication*, 2nd ed. Dubuque, Iowa: Wm. C. Brown, 1979.

KATZ, DANIEL, AND ROBERT L. KAHN, *The Social Psychology of Organizations*. New York: John Wiley, 1966.

LAUFFER, ARMAND, *Careers, Colleagues, and Conflicts*. Beverly Hills, Calif.:Sage Publications, Inc., 1985.

LEE, IRVING J., and LAURA L. LEE, *Handling Barriers in Communication*. New York: Harper & Row, Pub., 1957.

LUTHANS, FRED, *Organizational Behavior*. New York: McGraw-Hill. 1973.

MORGAN, GARETH, *Beyond Method*. Beverly Hills, Calif.: Sage Publications, Inc., 1983.

POOL, ITHIEL DE SOLA , "Communication Systems," in *Handbook of Communication*, Ithiel de Sola Pool and Wilbur Schramm, eds. Skokie, Ill.: Rand McNally, 1973.

POSTMAN, NEIL, and CHARLES WEINGARTNER, *Teaching as a Subversive Activity*. New York: Delacorte Press, 1969.

PUTNAM, LINDA, "The Interpretive Perspective: An Alternative to Functionalism," in *Communication and Organizations: An Interpretive Approach*, Linda L. Putnam and Michael Pacanowsky, eds. Beverly Hills, Calif.: Sage Publications, Inc., 1983.

REDDING, W. CHARLES, *Communication Within the Organization: An Interpretive Review of Theory and Research*. New York: Industrial Communication Council, 1972.

REDDING, W. CHARLES, and GEORGE A. SANBORN, *Business and Industrial Communication: A Source Book*. New York: Harper & Row, Pub., 1964.

SMIRCICH, LINDA, "Is the Concept of Culture a Paradigm for Understanding Organizations and Ourselves?" in *Organizational Culture*, Peter J. Frost et al., eds. Beverly Hills, Calif., Sage Publications, Inc., 1985.

SMITH, DENNIS R., and L. KEITH WILLIAMSON, *Interpersonal Communication: Roles, Rules, Strategies, and Games*. Dubuque, Iowa: Wm. C. Brown, 1977.

STEWART, JOHN, and MILT THOMAS, "Dialogic Listening: Sculpting Mutual Meanings," in *Bridges Not Walls*, 5th ed., John Stewart, ed. New York: McGraw-Hill, 1990.

3

Classical Structural Theory

The next three chapters focus on theories of organization and organizing. Pure objectivist theories are discussed in Chapter 3, some transitional theories are analyzed in Chapter 4, and theories that move toward a subjectivist view are treated in Chapter 5. Each chapter addresses the characteristics and main features of organizations from the perspective of the particular theory. A subjectivist's reminder is appended to the chapters on classical structural theory and transitional behavioral and social systems theories. Contemporary theories are presented from the subjectivist's point of view.

The work of Blau and Scott (1962) serves as the foundation upon which we shall base the classical structural theory of organization. They distinguish between the general structure of social organization and the more specific structure called *formal organization*, about which we shall be concerned.

SOCIAL ORGANIZATION

The term *social organization* refers to the patterns of social interaction (the frequency and duration of contacts between persons; the tendency to initiate contacts; the direction of influence between persons; the degree of cooperation; feelings of attraction, respect, and hostility; and status differences) and the observed regularities in the social behavior of people that are due to their social circumstances rather than to their physiological or psychological characteristics as individuals.

To have pattern or regularity in social interaction implies that there are some linkages between people that transform them from a collection of individuals into a group or from an aggregate of groups into a larger social system. For example, a busload of people going to work at different locations in a city does not really constitute a social organization, but a busload of booster club members on their way to a football game does represent a social organization. The boosters are connected by some shared beliefs that result in a structure that is more than the sum of the individuals composing the group. The patterns of interaction among boosters may result in status differences. For example, highly integrated group members are different from isolates, leaders differ from followers, those who are highly respected are different from those who are not highly regarded. Social status differences develop a hierarchy in the social structure.

Relations also develop between groups, producing a different aspect of social status. The status of the group in the larger social system becomes part of the status of its members. For example, the status of the booster club tends to influence the status of those who belong to it; likewise, membership in an ethnic group, such as Native Americans, also affects one's status.

The networks of contacts and the shared beliefs of a group are usually referred to as its *structure* and its *culture*. Contacts serve to organize human conduct in an organization. As a person conforms to the expectations of group members, that conformity influences relations with others and in turn affects his or her social status; a person's status then begins to affect behavior so that it is consistent with social norms and improves the person's chances of achieving important goals. Socially organized interaction results.

Berlo (1960) suggests that communication is related to social organization in three ways:

First, social systems are produced through communication. Uniformities of behavior and pressures to conform to norms are produced through communication among group members.

Second, once a social system has developed, it determines the communication of its members. Social systems affect how, to, and from whom, and with what effects, communication occurs among members of the system. One's social status in the system, for example, increases the likelihood of talking to people of comparable status and decreases the probability of communicating with people of much higher or much lower status. In addition, the system determines the frequency of messages by restricting the kinds and numbers of people with whom occupants of a particular position can communicate. Finally, the system may affect how members treat their messages. A style develops that is characteristic of members of the social organization. A civic club, a government agency, or a large corporation develops ways of doing things, writing about activities, and talking about their work that are imposed on members of the system. People who communicate with one another over time tend to develop similar behavior patterns. As individuals are immersed in the system, their unique behaviors adapt to the demands of the system, resulting in behavior similar to those of other members of the system.

Third, knowledge about a social system can help us make accurate predictions about people without knowing much more than the roles they occupy in the system. A *role* refers to both a set of behaviors and a given position in a social system. We can, for example, talk about the role of *manager*. A manager is a role in a social system we call a *formal organization*. The term *manager* refers both to a set of behaviors that are performed in the company and to a position in the company. For every role there is a set of behaviors and a position. If we know what behaviors go with a role, we can make predictions about the person who occupies the position. There are, within a range, certain behaviors that go with the role of chief executive officer, supervisor, secretary, union steward, salesperson, clerk, accountant, public relations specialist, or training specialist. When we meet a person who occupies a given role-position, we can predict that he or she will do certain things because of the position. As Berlo summarizes, "Even if we do not know a person as an individual, even if we have had no prior communication with him to determine his attitudes, his knowledges, his communication skills, we still can make fairly accurate predictions from a knowledge of his position in one or more social systems" (p. 150).

FORMAL ORGANIZATION

In contrast to social organization that emerges whenever people associate with one another, there are organizations that are created deliberately for certain purposes. If the accomplishment of a particular objective requires some sort of collective effort, an organization is designed to coordinate the activities of many individuals and to furnish incentives for others to aid them. Businesses, for example, are formed to produce materials that can be sold, unions are organized to increase their bargaining power with employers, government agencies are created to regulate commerce. In these cases the goals to be achieved, the rules to be followed, and the status structure are consciously designed to anticipate and guide interaction and activities of members. The term *formal organization* is used to refer to these kinds of systems.

We shall look at some distinctive characteristics of formal organizations—popularly called *bureaucracies*—in an effort to understand important features of formal systems. The somewhat simplistic analysis that follows is intended to highlight and focus attention on aspects of formal organizations that may have implications for a preliminary understanding of organizational communication. To clarify the characteristics of a formal organization, we shall present ideas derived from the writings of Max Weber (1947), pronounced "Mox Veber," as analyzed and summarized by numerous scholars in the field. The enumeration of characteristics is consistent with those of other analysts, but this list is unique to our view.

To hold an appropriate perspective on Weber's analysis of bureaucratic or formal organizations, we need to realize that he developed his theory of organizations as an *ideal type*. That is, he did not describe organizations as they actually functioned nor did he provide a summary of the usual characteristics of bureaucracies; rather, he identified characteristics that are distinctive of the ideal formal organization. Weber attempted to portray a perfectly bureaucratized organization. He said, in effect, that bureaucracies are those organizations that exhibit the following combination of characteristics. For example, Weber's theory of bureaucracy suggests that efficiency is related to a hierarchical pattern of authority. This may or may not be true. Nevertheless, if a study of a number of organizations were to discover that hierarchical authority was *not* related to efficiency in those organizations, that finding would not be a basis for rejecting Weber's claims; it would only show that the organizations studied were not fully bureaucratized.

CHARACTERISTICS OF A WEBERIAN BUREAUCRACY

Most modern organizations, as well as some ancient ones, are organized consistent with Weber's theory of formal organizations. Although Weber was writing as early as 1910, his theory serves admirably well for comprehending key aspects of organizations from a classical structural point of view and communicative interaction that occurs in that context, even today. Nevertheless, Weber's theory has been criticized and refined, leading to more sophisticated concepts of organizational functioning. Perrow's (1973) description of the rise and fall of bureaucratic theory suggests, however, the continuing interest in Weber's ideas:

At first, with his celebration of the efficiency of bureaucracy, he was received with only reluctant respect, and even with hostility. All writers were against bureaucracy. But it turned out, surprisingly, that managers were not. When asked, they acknowledged that they preferred clear lines of communication, clear specifications of authority and responsibility, and clear knowledge of whom they were responsible to.... Gradually, studies began to show that bureaucratic organizations could change faster than nonbureaucratic ones, and that morale could be higher where there was clear evidence of bureaucracy (p.6).

What are the characteristics of an ideally bureaucratized organization? Analyses of Weber's work suggest the following ten features:

1. An organization consists of stipulated relationships among *positions*. The basic building blocks of any formal organization are positions. Organizational positions are almost always designated by titles, such as supervisor, machinist, lieutenant, sergeant, lecturer, senior analyst, trainer.

2. The broad purpose or plan of the organization is subdivided into tasks; organization tasks are distributed among the various positions as *official duties*. The definitions of duties and responsibilities are inherent in the position. Job descriptions are, of course, one method of meeting this characteristic. A clear division of labor among positions is implied by this feature, which makes possible a high degree of specialization and expertness among employees.

3. *Authority* to perform the duties is vested in the position. That is, the only time that a person is authorized to perform the duties of the position is when he or she legitimately occupies the position. Weber referred to this as *legal* authority. Authority is legitimized by a belief in the supremacy of the law. In such a system obedience is owed to a set of principles, not to a person. This feature includes the requirement to follow directives originating from an office that is superior to one's own, regardless of who occupies the higher office. The government, a factory, the army, a welfare agency, churches, university, and a grocery store are examples of organizations based on legal authority.

4. The lines of authority and the positions are arranged in a *hierarchical order*. The hierarchy takes on the general shape of a pyramid, with each official being responsible to his or her superior for subordinates' decisions, as well as for his or her own. The scope of authority of superiors over subordinates is clearly circumscribed. The concepts of *upward* and *downward* communication express this concept of authority, with information moving down from the position of broadest authority to the position of narrowest authority.

5. A formally established system of general but definite *rules* and *regulations* governs the actions and functions of positions in the organization. Much of the effort of administrators in the organization goes into applying the general regulations to particular cases. The hypothetical case of having the Internal Revenue Service determine your taxes is a good example. If you were to go to an IRS office to argue for a reduced tax load, the decision would most likely be made on the basis of a regulation specifying the rules for making such a decision. The official would then apply the regulation to your case and explain how much tax you owe. Regulations help ensure uniformity of operations and provide for continuity regardless of changes in personnel.

6. *Procedures* in the organization are formal and impersonal—that is, the rules and regulations are applicable to everyone who falls within the category. Officials are expected to assume an impersonal orientation in their contacts with clients and other officials. They are to disregard all personal considerations and to maintain emotional detachment.

Impersonal procedures are designed to prevent the feelings of officials from distorting their rational judgment in carrying out their duties.

7. An attitude of and procedures for enforcing a system of *discipline* is part of the organization. For individuals to work efficiently, they must have the necessary skills and apply them rationally and energetically; however, if members of the organization were to make even rational decisions independently, their work would not be coordinated, making the efficiency of the organization suffer. Individuals who do not accept the authority of those above them, who fail to carry out the duties assigned to their positions, and who apply regulations with capriciousness are not pursuing organizational objectives consistent with the philosophy of efficiency. Thus, the organization needs a program of discipline to help ensure cooperation and efficiency.

8. Members of the organization are to maintain *separate private* and *organizational lives*. Families of organization members, for example, are not to make contact with employees during working hours. Some organizations take great pains to accommodate the personal lives of employees to allow them to devote their complete attention to their jobs. Many corporations buy the homes of employees, care for their families in country club surroundings, and discourage using the telephone for private calls to maintain the separation of private and organizational affairs.

9. Employees are selected for employment in the organization on the basis of *technical qualifications* rather than on political, family, or other connections. Officials are appointed to positions rather than elected by a group of constituents, which makes them dependent on superiors in the organization. The administration of civil service examinations by the U.S. government is one way of trying to select employees on the basis of technical confidence. Recent decisions to require employers to select employees on a basis of bona fide occupational qualifications (BFOQs) are perfectly consistent with this characteristic of Weber's ideal bureaucracy.

10. Although employment in the bureaucracy is based on technical competence, advancements are made according to seniority as well as achievement. After a trial period, officials gain tenure in positions and are protected against arbitrary dismissal. Employment in the organization constitutes a lifelong career, providing *security in the position*.

These characteristics lead toward rational decision making and administrative efficiency. Experts with much experience are best qualified to make technical decisions. Disciplined performance governed by abstract rules, regulations, or policies and coordinated by hierarchical authority fosters a rational and consistent pursuit of organizational goals.

POSITIONAL COMMUNICATION AND INFORMAL CONTACTS

The characteristics of a formal organization lead to a phenomenon that we call *positional communication* (Redfield, 1953). Relationships are established between positions, not people. The entire organization consists of a network of positions. Those who occupy the positions are required to communicate in ways consistent with the positions. Nevertheless, positional communication is upset in practice because not all activities and interactions conform strictly to the positional chart. The relationship between Position A and Position C does not exist separately from the relationship between Andrew and Zébe. The official organization chart can never completely determine the conduct and social relations of organization members. Yet, although it is impossible to completely insulate a position from the occupier's personality, organizational productivity depends most of the time on positional communication. This does not deny or discount the tremendous impact of informal relations on communication. In every formal organization there is likely to develop informal groups. However, since informal relations arise in response to the opportunities created by the environment, the formal organization constitutes the immediate environment of the groups within it and influences greatly the number and functioning of informal relations.

Although Weber's analysis of organization theory appears to describe many current operating organizations, a number of other philosophies and theories have contributed to an understanding of organizational functioning and, especially, organizational communication. Two lines of theory, in addition to communication theory, have provided useful insights: these are management theories and organization theories. Sometimes writers make little distinction between a theory of managing and a theory of organizing because they are often very much alike, but occasionally they differ. We shall briefly report on a classical theory of management that is compatible with Weber's formal theory of organization.

TAYLOR'S SCIENTIFIC MANAGEMENT

Weber's theory of bureaucracy focused primarily on organizing; it is considered to be the most important statement on formal organization, but it may be true that all theories of organization are basically theories of managing. Frederick W. Taylor (1856–1915) lived about the same time as Weber and also wrote about organizations; however, Taylor published *Principles of Scientific Management* whereas Weber's work was translated as *The Theory of Social and Economic Organization*. Both books dealt with issues of business enterprise from similar philosophies. Scott (1961) states that the classical doctrine of organizations and management can be traced directly back to Taylor's interest in functional supervision. Taken together, Weber and Taylor represent theories of organization and management that deal almost exclusively with the anatomy of formal organization and are referred to as classical structural theories. Taylor's approach to management is built around four key elements: division of labor, scalar and functional processes, structure, and span of control. Following Sofer's (1972) analysis closely, we shall briefly review the meaning of these four pillars.

Division of Labor

Division of labor refers to how the tasks, duties, and work of the organization are distributed. In bureaucratic terms the duties of the company are systematically assigned to positions in a descending order of specialization. Taylor suggested that workers should be relieved of the task of planning and of all clerical activities. If practicable, the work of every person in the organization should be confined to the execution of a single function, which is the notion of division of labor. Although not entirely serious, Parkinson (1957) formulated a number of principles that help explain how people in the organization manipulate this element. Parkinson studied the British Navy and concluded that "Work expands to fill the time available for its completion." He called the statement *Parkinson's Law*. His observations led him to realize that in organizations the task to be executed swells in importance and complexity in direct ratio to the amount of time to be spent on the task. Thus, he argued, the amount of work and the number of workers are not related. He illustrates how any small task can expand to fill the time available by describing a person who has all day to prepare a memo. An hour will be spent locating some paper, another in hunting for a pencil, a half an hour in search of the names and addresses, an hour and a quarter composing the memo, twenty minutes deciding whether to distribute it by hand or send it through the mails. The total effort will occupy a busy person for three minutes in total but will leave this person exhausted after a full day of doubt, anxiety, and toil.

Of course, managers, workers, and administrators begin to age and feel reduced energy with such exhausting days. According to Parkinson, the manager has three choices: resign, share the work with a colleague, or ask for assistance in the form of two subordinates. Only the third alternative is ever used. The corollary to Parkinson's Law is that "An official wants to multiply subordinates, not rivals." The inevitable consequence is called the *Rising Pyramid*, the second great pillar of classical management theory.

Scalar and Functional Processes

Scalar and functional processes deal with the vertical and horizontal growth of the organization. The scalar process refers to growth of the chain of command or the vertical dimension of the organization. By acquiring two assistants the manager has increased the size of the organization vertically, creating changes in the delegation of authority and responsibility, unity of direction, and obligations to report.

The division of work into more specialized duties and the restructuring of the more specific parts into compatible units are matters related to *functional processes* and the horizontal expansion of the organization. Both scalar and functional changes lead to the third pillar of classical management theory.

Structure

Structure has to do with logical relationships among functions in the organization. Classical theories concentrate on the two basic structures called *line* and *staff*. The *line structure* involves the authority channels of the organization as they relate to accomplishing the major goals of the organization. For example, in a valve manufacturing company, the line structure follows the order of positions responsible for getting the valves manufactured; the line authority consists of the president, the vice president of manufacturing, the managers, supervisors, and operatives who produce the valves. In the military the line authority involves those who have command functions, such as the company commander, the first sergeant, the squad leaders, and patrol leaders. The *staff structure* represents those positions that provide support for or help the line positions do their work better by offering advice, assistance, or service. Typical staff functions include purchasing and receiving, traffic control, business research, production planning, public relations, and training and development.

Line   The primary value of differentiating between line and staff is in the area of decision making. The term *line* simply means that the final authority rests with positions in that structure. At the university, for example, the line structure for teaching and curricular decisions includes faculty members, department chairpersons, deans, and the academic vice president. The arrangement is hierarchical or pyramidal, since there are more faculty members than there are department chairs, more chairs than deans, and more deans that academic vice presidents. The library of a university is a staff function in support of teaching (and research, of course); however, the library has its own line structure, beginning with the director of the library and moving through functional heads such as circulation, acquisitions, and reference, down to specialty librarians in such areas as the social sciences, education, business, and physical sciences. Secretaries, clerks and researchers represent staff positions.

Staff Staff personnel have traditionally provided advice and service in support of the line. The line has authority to command. The staff advises and persuades on behalf of its recommendations but has no authority to order the line manager to follow the suggestions. When a staff specialist's recommendations are accepted by his or her line superior, they are issued on the line manager's authority, not the staff specialist's. In this way the full authority of the line manager remains intact, and subordinates receive orders only from their line superior, thus maintaining a unity of command.

The role of staff as strictly advisory has changed radically over the years. Staff members are now often assigned limited line or command authority rather than general authority over an organizational unit. For example, the personnel department or the training and development department, even though a staff function, may prescribe the methods for on-the-job training of all new employees, regardless of their line assignment.

Tall and Flat Structures

Organization structures may take many forms, but at the extremes are two main types: the *tall* or *vertical* and the *flat* or *horizontal*. The tallness or flatness of an organization is determined almost solely by the differences in numbers of levels of authority and variations in the span of control at each level. Tall structures have many levels of authority, with managers exercising a narrow span of control. Tall organizations are often characterized by close supervision, team spirit, competition through personal relationships, gradual increases in responsibility, constant insecurity about status, emphasis on the techniques of management, and an abundance of rules and regulations. Flat organizations, on the other hand, seem to be characterized by encouraged individualistic and entrepreneurial activities. Flat structures have only a modest amount of direct supervision and fewer rules and regulations. Personnel assume wider responsibility at lower levels in flat structures, and the manager has less contact with them. The manager has to judge subordinates by less personal, objective standards of performance, and subordinates openly compete with one another in terms of their actual work rather than on the basis of their personal relations with the boss. Flat structures seem to be more appropriate for loosely supervised and technically simple, although individually more challenging, activities such as sales, service, political, and religious organizations. With its greater scope of individual freedom, flat structures more often tend to produce attitudes of enthusiasm and result in higher morale among employees.

Span of Control

Span of control refers to the number of subordinates a superior has under his or her supervision. Although it has frequently been stated that five or six subordinates is about all a manager can supervise, in practice the span of management varies widely. For example, in a retail chain that has only four levels of authority between the company president and first-line store supervisors, a manager may have twenty or thirty supervisors reporting to him or her. In contrast, in a manufacturing operation, with seven levels of authority, a manager may have only five to ten subordinates reporting to her or him. Some companies have as many as twelve levels of authority between the president and the first-line supervisors; in such situations the span of control may run below five.

SUMMARY

This chapter distinguished between two types of organizations: social and formal. Although the regularities in social behavior that produce social organizations make it possible to predict somewhat accurately how people will behave, formal organizations are specifically designed to produce efficiency and predictability in work settings. Ten characteristics of a formal, bureaucratic organization derived from the writings of Max Weber were discussed. Some principles of scientific management consistent with the ideas of Frederick Taylor were also identified. The works of Weber and Taylor represent the classical view of organization and management.

A SUBJECTIVIST'S REMINDER

Weber's ideal model represents the search for order, rationality, and regulation of human behavior. The language of classical structural theory is selective and misleading. Clark (1985) states, "Thoughtful planning, data-based decision making, forceful leadership, responsible action, accountability, responsiveness, efficiency, and cost-effectiveness sound so right and righteous that it is hard to entertain alternative perspectives to the images conveyed by these words" (p.49). The words themselves tend to become guiding principles that are difficult to challenge. It is easy to assume that such principles operate in the organization or *should* be operative. Clark asks, "What, for example, are the antonyms of Weber's characteristics of bureaucratic administration? They are inefficient, unpredictable, irrational, incompetent, ignorant, and prejudicial!" (p. 49). These words and images can prevent us from looking at what actually occurs in the organization. What people do may encompass a wide range of behaviors and may be functional or dysfunctional depending on the situation.

Classical structural theory has a simplicity that is appealing. It suggests that once the right structure is discovered, behavior will be predictable, rational, and efficient. If everyone knows their roles, their responsibilities, and who they are responsible to, organizations can run smoothly. Structure determines behavior and produces predictability.

There are certain "sayings" that apply to these structural notions that are derived from the characteristics of a bureaucracy. Such adages include "The buck stops here" and "Authority should be commensurate with responsibility." But what really happens in an organization? Clark (1985) describes counter-sayings, such as:

> *The buck never stops in an organization.* There is always either someone else to blame or some set of uncontrollable circumstances that no reasonable observer would pin on a single administrator—not even a chief executive officer…. *Authority and responsibility are almost never congruous in an organization.* While some persons are squandering

authority by avoiding responsibility, others are accumulating responsibility in the hope of increasing their authority. Individual authority and responsibility in organizations are variables governed jointly by the day-to-day sense-making activities of organizational participants and designated organizational positions (pp. 49–50).

One might contend that the first saying is what the organization should be like, and it would be if it met Weber's ideal type. However, organizations are created by people through negotiated meaning, and the ideal type is not likely to occur. More important, the term "ideal" is misleading. The idea that "the buck stops here" may not always be functional. It would be a painful world if "face saving" did not exist. Dispersal of blame in an organization is not always dysfunctional. There may be times when it is necessary to protect a person in order to protect a position. If authority and responsibility were always commensurate, it is likely that a great deal of work would never get done. One of the frustrations of coping with bureaucratic systems is presenting a problem to someone only to be told that "I am not responsible for that, it isn't my fault, and don't blame me!" Such people are content to shuffle papers and avoid blame rather than solve a problem.

The idea that relationships are established between positions instead of people places emphasis on structure rather than behavior. Positions become tangible objects that exist prior to and apart from human behavior. This concept ignores the subtleties of organizational behavior. An organizational map of positions might tell us what positions are supposed to exist and what communication should take place between what positions; however, positions do not exist until they have been acted out. In addition, communication establishes relationships, and positions do not communicate—people do. The behavior expected of a position or between positions can only be standardized in a general sense. How that behavior is carried out is unique, negotiated between the people involved. Positions exist only in the abstract until they are performed and validated by the participants. The roles in most organizations follow general guidelines, but a wide latitude of behavior exists in performing those roles. To think only of positions is to think in mechanical terms that mask the creative force of humans.

If the positional emphasis is to make sense, it should certainly do so when one examines sports games. The parameters are set by rules and the method of play is rather straightforward. Let's examine the double play in baseball. This play involves the positions of shortstop, second base, and first base. When an opponent is on first base and a ball is hit to the shortstop, the ball is thrown to second base and relayed to first base in order to put out two players. More is involved here than the positions; the positions only come to life when someone "plays" them. There is a second base in the abstract sense, but there is also Charlie, who plays second base. Yes, the shortstop does throw the ball to second base, but perhaps the real trick is throwing the ball to Charlie—who wants the ball in a certain place so that he can get off his best relay to first. To complicate matters, both the shortstop and second base have to account for an opposing player who is cruising toward Charlie at the speed of a runaway truck. The point is that the positions are not anything until they are played, and anyone who has ever watched a Little League game knows that there is considerable variance in how they are played. Relationships are established between positions only in a general and abstract sense. It is the unique behavior and relationships generated by people that dominate organizational life.

REFERENCES

BERLO, DAVID K., *The Process of Communication*. New York: Holt, Rinehart & Winston, 1960.

BLAU, PETER M., and W. RICHARD SCOTT, *Formal Organizations*. New York: Harper & Row, Pub., 1962.

CLARK, DAVID L., "Emerging Paradigms in Organizational Theory and Research," in *Organizational Theory and Inquiry: The Paradigm Revolution*, Yvonne S. Lincoln, ed. Beverly Hills, Calif." Sage Publications, Inc., 1985.

PARKINSON, C. NORTHCOTE, *Parkinson's Law*. New York: Ballantine, 1957.

PERROW, CHARLES, "The Short and Glorious History of Organizational Theory," *Organizational Dynamics*, 2 (Summer 1973), 2–15.

REDFIELD, CHARLES E., *Communication in Management*. Chicago: University of Chicago Press, 1953.

SCOTT, WILLIAM G., "Organization Theory: An Overview and an Appraisal," *Journal of the Academy of Management,* 4 (April 1961), 7–26.

SOFER, CYRIL, *Organizations in Theory and Practice*. New York: Basic Books, 1972.

TAYLOR, FREDERICK W., *Principles of Scientific Management*, New York: Harper & Row Pub., 1911.

WEBER, MAX, *The Theory of Social and Economic Organization,* trans. A. M. Henderson and Talcott Parsons; Talcott Parsons, ed. Glencoe, Ill.: The Free Press and Falcon's Wing Press, 1947.

4

Transitional Theories

This chapter will explore the transition from classical structural theories of organization and management to the more contemporary behavioral and systems theories. Like eras in the history of people, aspects of earlier traditions form the foundation for future thinking about people and things. The older conceptions continue to exercise important influences on how we conceive of organizations, but refinements in our models begin to bring about curious and often practical changes in our formulations about organizations.

BEHAVIORAL THEORIES

Chester Barnard's Authority-Communication Theory

Perrow (1973) indicates that concerns had been expressed from the beginning about the implications of the classical theory of organization and the scientific doctrine of management. "'Bureaucracy' has always been a dirty word, and the job design efforts of Frederick Taylor were even the subject of a congressional investigation" (p.10). However, it was not until Barnard (1938) published *The Functions of the Executive* that a new line of thought emerged. He proposed that organizations are people systems, not mechanically engineered structures. A good, clear mechanical structure was not enough. Natural groups within the bureaucratic structure affected what happened, upward communication was important, authority came from below rather than from above, and leaders needed to function as a cohesive force.

   Barnard's definition of formal organization—a system of consciously coordinated activities of two or more persons—highlighted the concepts of *system* and *persons*. People, not positions, make up a formal organization. His stress on the cooperative aspects of the organization reflected the importance placed on the human element. Barnard stated that the existence of an organization (as a cooperative system) depended on the ability of human beings to communicate and on their willingness to serve and work toward a common goal. Thus, he concluded that "The first function of the executive is to develop and maintain a system of communication."

Barnard also maintained that authority was a function of willingness to go along. He cited four conditions that must be met before a person will accept a message as authoritative:

1. The person can and does understand the message.
2. The person believes, at the time of the decision, that the message is not inconsistent with the purpose of the organization.
3. The person believes, at the time of the decision to go along, that the message is compatible with his or her personal interest as a whole.
4. The person is able mentally and physically to comply with the message.

This set of premises became known as the *acceptance theory of authority*—that is, authority originating at the top of an organization is, in effect, nominal authority. It becomes real only when it is accepted. However, Barnard recognized that many messages cannot be deliberately analyzed, judged, and accepted or rejected; rather, most types of directives, orders, and persuasive messages fall within a person's *zone of indifference*.

To visualize the idea of a zone of indifference, think of a horizontal line having a scale with zero percent as the center point and 100 at both ends. The wider the person's zone, the farther it extends in both directions toward the ends. A 100 percent willingness to go along shows the zone extending in both directions to the 100 percent marks. A complete rejection of the message (directive, order, request) shows a zone in which the marks are both touching zero.

Many messages in an organization are designed to widen the zone of indifference of employees. The width of a subordinate's zone tends to be different for each order; in one instance the subordinate may be warmly receptive and very willing to accept a request, for another the subordinate may be reluctant although not adamant about rejecting it, whereas in a third the subordinate may completely reject the request.

An instance of total authority communication rejection occurred during the Russo-Japanese War (1904–1905). The Russian ship *Potemkin,* according to the report, was conducting purposeless maneuvers in the Black Sea. The usual grudges held by sailors against officers were multiplied by a policy of harsh discipline. Knowing that the Russo-Japanese War was being badly mismanaged, agitators attempted to incite mutiny but made little progress on the *Potemkin.* However, one day the crew saw some maggoty meat hanging in the galley. In order to assure them that the meat was edible, the ship's doctor had to be called. At dinner the crew was served borscht made with the spoiling meat. As an act of rebellion the crew ate only bread and water, leaving the sickening soup untouched. This enraged the captain, who verbally attacked the crew in an effort to get them to eat. His effort failed, so the next officer in command stepped into the tense situation, called the armed guard, and ordered all sailors willing to eat to step forward. Of all the hundreds of crew members, all but thirty did. The officer ordered the stubborn crew members to be covered with a tarpaulin in preparation for having them shot. As the sailors huddled under the covering, the order to fire was given. The guards hesitated. At that moment other sailors rushed forward urging the guards to turn their rifles on the officers rather than their shipmates. While the senior officer shrieked commands and other officers stood aghast, the guards fired upon them. Most of the officers, including the captain, were shot and thrown overboard. Thus the formal authority was totally ineffective because it was rejected by both the crew and the armed guards (Moorehead, 1958).

Barnard equated authority and effective communication. The rejection of a communication was tantamount to rejection of the communicator's authority. By accepting a message or directive from another, a person grants authority to the formulator of the message and therefore adopts the position of a subordinate. Thus, Tannenbaum (1950) argued, the "sphere of authority possessed by a superior is defined for him by the sphere of acceptance" of his subordinates. The decision *not* to accept the authority and messages of a superior because the advantages may not be sufficient may result in some disadvantages, such as disciplinary action, monetary loss, or social disapproval. In some organizations the fear of such coercive acts may produce a willingness to accept a message even when the disadvantages alone do not.

Beyond a close relationship between authority and communication, Barnard viewed communication techniques (both written and oral) as essential to attaining the organization's goals and as the source of problems in the organization. "Communication techniques," he said, "shape the form and the internal economy of the organization. The absence of a suitable technique of communication would eliminate the possibility of adopting some purpose as a basis of organization" (p. 90). Thus it was largely Barnard who made communication a meaningful part of organization and management theory. He seemed thoroughly convinced that communication was the major shaping force of the organization.

Elton Mayo's Human Relations Theory

A year following Barnard's publication of *Functions,* Roethlisberger and Dickson (1939) issued their massive report on a large-scale investigation of productivity and social relations at the Hawthorne plant of the Western Electric Company. Referred to as *Management and the Worker*, it quickly became known as the *Hawthorne Studies.* The studies were conceived and directed by Elton Mayo with the assistance of Fritz Roethlisberger, both professors at Harvard University. Miller and Form (1951) refer to the Hawthorne Studies as the "first great scientific experiment in industry." A journal reviewer called it "the most outstanding study of industrial relations that has been published anywhere, anytime" (Miller & Form, p. 50). However, Whitehead, the statistician working on the studies, found not a single correlation of enough statistical significance to be recognized by any competent statistician as having any meaning" (Miller & Form, p. 49).

What, then, was discovered that led to such disparate, but at times laudatory, reactions to Mayo's work? The most pertinent results occurred during experiments on illumination. At first the researchers assumed that the brighter the lighting, the higher the worker output. Thus they decided to establish an experimental room with variable light conditions and a control room with constant light conditions. Two groups of workers were chosen to do their work in two different areas. Over a period of time illumination in the experimental room was increased to blinding intensity and them decreased to practically an absence of light. The results went like this: As the amount of illumination increased, so did worker efficiency in the experimental room; however, the efficiency of workers in the control room also increased. As lighting was diminished in the test room, efficiencies of both the test and the control groups increased slowly but steadily. When the illumination reached three-foot candles in the test room, operators protested, saying that they were hardly able to see what they were doing; at that point the production rate decreased. Up to that time the assemblers maintained their efficiency in spite of the handicap.

The results of the illumination experiments intrigued the researchers as well as management. So from 1927 to 1929, a superior team of researchers measured the effects of a wide variety of working conditions on employee production. The results were again consistent with the illumination experiments—regardless of the working conditions, production increased. The researchers came to the conclusion that these unusual and even more amazing results occurred because the six individuals in the experimental room became a team, with group relations being more important and powerful in determining morale and productivity than any of the working conditions—good or bad. The researchers concluded that the operators had no clear idea why they were able to produce more in the test room, but there was the feeling that "better output is in some way related to the distinctly pleasanter, freer, and happier working conditions" (Miller & Form, p. 48).

Two compelling conclusions have evolved out of the Hawthorne Studies, often referred to jointly as the *Hawthorne Effect*: (1) The very act of paying attention to people may change their attitudes and behavior, and (2) high morale and productivity are promoted if employees have opportunities for interaction with each other. Mayo, later in life (1945), wrote what has become a summation of the interests communication specialists bring to the analysis of organizations:

> I believe that social study should begin with careful observation of what may be described as communication: that is, the capacity of an individual to communicate his feelings and ideas to another, the capacity of groups to communicate effectively and intimately with each other. That is, beyond all reasonable doubt, the outstanding defect that civilization is facing today (p. 21).

Taken together, the work of Barnard and Mayo represents a behavioral approach to organizations. Mayo is often attributed with initiating the *human relations movement*. In fact, Perrow (1973), building on the insights of Barnard and Mayo, asserted that the human relations movement came into its own following World War II. Sofer (1973) pointed out that Mayo and his colleagues created a scientific demonstration showing that "a group had a life of its own, complete with customs, norms, and effective social controls on its members" (p. 80). Guilbot (1968) observed that "after the Hawthorne Studies it had to be granted that an informal structure of social relations did exist behind the formal organizational structure and that numerous phenomena could not be explained on any other grounds" (pp. 232–233). One great contribution of the early behavioral theorists was the reorientation of thinking about organizations and management from that of purely structure and task to considerations of people and morale.

One pointed criticism of the human relations movement is its overwhelming preoccupation with people and their relationships and its disregard of the total resources of an organization and its members. A concern about responding to both personal and organizational needs has been a significant consequence of the groundwork laid by early behavioral theorists. An important distinction is made currently between developing good human relations and developing the human resources of an organization. Organizational communication seeks to provide the background for developing the quality of human resources in an organization, rather than just developing the quality of human relations, as important as they may appear.

Bakke and Argyris's Fusion Theory

Sensing the enormity of the problem associated with satisfying both the divergent interests of individuals and the essential demands of the bureaucratic structure, Bakke (1950) proposed a *fusion process*. He reasoned that the organization, to some degree, molds the individual, while at the same time the individual also influences the organization. The result is an organization that is *personalized* by the individual employee and individuals who are *socialized* by the organization. Hence every employee takes on characteristics of the organization, and every position appears to be uniquely like the individuals who occupy them. After fusion (a.f.), every employee looks more like the organization, and every position in the organization is modified to the special interests of the individual.

Argyris (1957), a colleague of Bakke's at Yale University, expanded and refined Bakke's work. He argued that there is a basic incongruity or incompatibility between the needs of mature employees and the requirements of the formal organization. The organization has goals to accomplish that clash with the goals of individual employees. Employees experience frustration as a consequence of the incongruence. Some may leave; some may adapt; and some may stay, lower their work standards, and become apathetic and uninterested. Through this conflict others learn not to expect satisfaction from the job. Many people have learned from personal experience that adjusting to the demands of a formal organization is not easy and should not be expected to occur automatically.

Likert's Linking Pin Theory

Rensis Likert of the University of Michigan is credited with developing what is popularly known as the *linking pin model* of organization structure. The linking pin concept is one of overlapping groups. Each supervisor is a member of two groups: the leader of a lower unit and member of an upper unit. The supervisor functions as a linking pin, tying the work group to another group at the next level. The linking pin structure provides a group-to-group, in contrast to a person-to-person, relationship. Rather than fostering a downward orientation, a linking pin organization encourages an upward orientation. Communication, supervisory influence, and goal attainment are all directed upward in the organization. As Figure 4.1 implies, group processes play an important role in making the linking pin organization function efficiently. All groups must be equally effective, since the organization can be no stronger than its weakest group.

Luthans (1973) argued that the linking pin concept tends to emphasize and facilitate what is supposed to occur in the bureaucratic, classical structure. The superior-subordinate, hierarchical pattern, however, often results in a downward focus, while inhibiting upward and lateral communication. The slowness of group action, which is part of the linking pin organization, must be balanced with the positive advantages of participation—contributions to planning, more open communication, and member commitments—that accrue from the linking pin structure.

SYSTEMS THEORIES

Scott (1961) argues that "the only meaningful way to study organization . . . is as a system" (p. 15). He suggests that the basic parts of an organizational system are the individual and the personality that he or she brings to the system; the formal structure, which we have discussed at length earlier; the informal pattern of interactions; status and role patterns that cre-

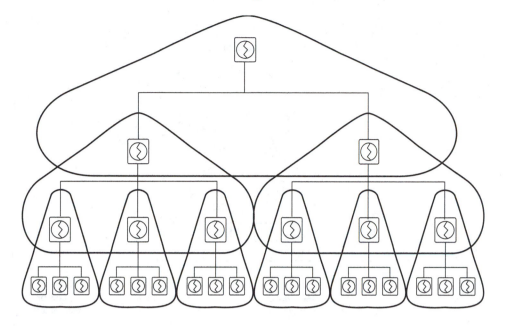

FIGURE 4.1 Linking Pin Model of Organization

ate expectations; and the physical environment of work (Fig. 4.2). These parts are woven into a configuration called an *organizational system*. All of the parts are interrelated and interact with each other. Each part is linked to all of the other parts. Although there are other theories about how the parts are connected, the primary linking process is communication.

The systems concept focuses on the arrangement of parts, relationships between parts, and the dynamics of the relationships that lead to unity or wholeness. The concept of *system* is so encompassing it defies easy definition. A simple definition would screen out the complexity and sophistication of the concept, and yet extensive explanation leads to intricacies that are not readily comprehensible. Although a detailed explanation of the contribution and influence of systems theory to organizational study is beyond the scope of this book, certain items warrant attention. Even at the most general level, systems concepts enable one to conceive of an organization as a whole that is greater than the sum of its parts by virtue of its dynamics. These dynamics take into account structure, relationships, and idiosyncratic behaviors.

General systems theorists (Bertalanffy, 1968; Boulding, 1965; Rapoport, 1968) have identified some principles that apply to all types of systems. That is, machines, organisms, and organizations all have similar processes and can be described with common tenets. We agree with Fisher (1978) that "system theory is a loosely organized and highly abstract set of principles, which serve to direct our thinking but which are subject to numerous interpretations" (p. 196). In the following discussion, we have adapted Fisher's explanation of the tenets of systems theory (pp. 196–204).

Any discussion of systems involves the notion of interdependence. Simply stated, interdependence suggests that a mutual dependence exists among components or units of a system. A change in one component brings about change in every other component. Understanding the concept of interdependence is an integral part of defining systems and systems theory.

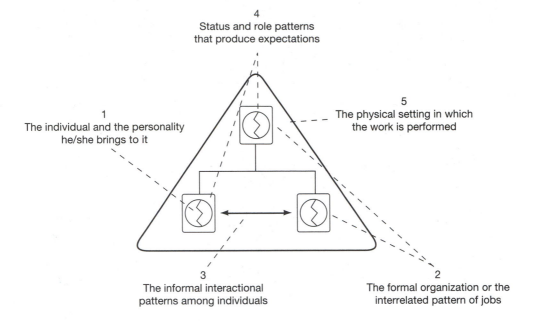

FIGURE 4.2 The Parts of an Organizational System

1. *Nonsummativity.* Nonsummativity suggests that a system is not just a sum of its parts. When the components are related to each other in mutual dependence (interdependent), the system takes on an identity separate from the individual components. For example, what two people might build together through interaction is quite different from what might result by taking each individual's behavior and adding them together. The nonsummativity of components of a system is more important, systemically, than the individual units themselves.

2. *Elements of Structure, Function, and Evolution.* Structure refers to relationships between components of a system. Superior/subordinate relationships, for example, may be distinguished on the basis of status, a structural element. Structure reflects order. A bureaucracy, for example, is a highly structured system that reflects a high degree of order. The actions one performs in conjunction with others are considered to be part of the functional element in a social system. Functions, or actions and behaviors, constitute the primary means by which people are identified in a social system. The person's actions are the events in a social system. The evolution of a system, or the changes and nonchanges in a system over time, affects both the structural and functional elements, and the complexity of a system is related to the extent to which both functional and structural elements vary.

3. *Openness.* Organizations are social systems. Their boundaries are permeable, which allows them to interact with their environments, thereby importing energy and information. Open systems are characterized by *equifinality,* which means that "The same final state may be reached from different conditions and in different ways" (Bertalanffy, 1968, p., 40); it also means that organizations that start with the same initial conditions may reach different end states.

4. *Hierarchy.* A system may be a suprasystem to other systems within it as well as a subsystem to a larger system. The flow of information across the boundaries of a sys-

tem can affect the structural-functional behaviors of the system. Systemic analysis of communication involves subsystems, systems, and suprasystems, and each represents a different level of analysis. Weick (1969, p. 45) suggests that "If there are different levels of analysis (e.g., individual, group, organization, society), the only way we can learn much about any of these levels is if we know how they are tied together, that is, how one level interacts with another level." These tenets will be explored further in the section that examines contemporary theory.

Katz and Kahn's Social Systems Theory

Classical and behavioral theories often refer to communication primarily in terms of forms of communication activity, rather than as a linking process. Communication as a linking process takes on special meaning if we accept Katz and Kahn's (1966) telling point that social structures differ from mechanical and biological structures. Physical and biological entities such as automobiles and animals have anatomical structures that can be identified even when they are not functioning. When a biological organism ceases to function, the physical body can still be examined in a post-mortem analysis.

When a social system ceases to function, it no longer has an identifiable structure. The reason is that social systems are structures of events or happenings rather than physical parts and have no structure apart from their functioning. The communication network of an organization, for example, has little resemblance to the circulatory or nervous system of biological organisms, although we tend to compare the two quite often. Because the analogies seem impelling, we are frequently deterred from grasping the essential differences between social systems and biological systems.

Social systems consist, on the whole, of people. They are imperfect, but the constancy of relationships can be very high. In fact, organizations can have a very high turnover but still exist and function effectively. The *relationships among the people,* not the people themselves, allow an organization to persist far longer than the biological people who fill positions in the organization. Formal organizations have procedures by which the parts (people) can be readily replaced so they can continue to function into an unspecified future. Biological organisms have forces that wear out their parts which often cannot be replaced.

Katz and Kahn explain that most of our interactions with others are communicative acts (verbal and nonverbal, spoken and silent). "Communication—the exchange of information and the transmission of meaning—is the very essence of a social system or an organization" (p.223). They assert that it is possible to subsume under the concept of communication such forms of social interaction as "exertion of influence, cooperation, social contagion or imitation, and leadership" (p.224). As you shall see, we take a perspective consistent with this view and consider communication as the primary linking process in organizations with a number of corollary processes emerging out of the communicating that occurs in organizations. We refer to those special forms of communication as organizational communication skills and activities.

Systems theory recognizes that an organized state requires the introduction of constraints and restrictions to reduce random communication to channels that are appropriate for accomplishment of organizational goals. Organizational development, for example, may require the creation of new communication channels. Katz and Kahn claim that the "very nature of a social system . . . implies a selectivity of channels and communicative acts—a mandate to avoid some and to utilize others" (p.226).

In summary, Scott (1961) points out that "organizations are comprised of parts which communicate with each other, receive messages from the outside world, and store information. Taken together, these communication functions of the parts comprise a configuration representing the total system" (p.18). It might be said that, from a systems point of view, communication is the organization. Hawes (1974), in fact, has expressed this very point: "A social collectivity is patterned communicative behavior; communicative behavior does not occur *within* a network of relationships but is that network" (p. 500). For our purposes in an introductory book on organizational communication, we can assume the existence of organizations and proceed to explain and understand something about their functioning, the manner in which the people interrelate, and some of the impelling issues that affect the way in which the people and the organization develop. We shall treat some of these basic issues in the next part of this book.

Ad-hocracy and the Buck Rogers Theory

Some of our most improbable visions of space exploration have come from the fantasies of the creators of the fictional and famous figure Buck Rogers. Taking the lead from Buck, futuristic authors such as Alvin Toffler (1970) have written about *future shock* and the inevitable consequences of rapid change on all aspects of our lives. Formal organizations have been touched in these analyses. Toffler dedicates an entire chapter to "Organizations: The Coming Ad-hocracy." Bennis (1966) predicts "The Coming Death of Bureaucracy." Luthans (1973) observes that "many practicing managers are becoming disenchanted with traditional ways of organizing" (p. 168). The predictions indicate that we are moving into a postbureaucratic era of organizational theory based on the futuristic concept of rapidly changing organizational structures. Toffler describes it this way: "What we see here is nothing less than the creation of a disposable division—the organizational equivalent of paper dresses or throw-away tissues" (p. 133).

According to Bennis (1966), the social structure of the new bureaucracy will be in a word, *temporary*. The organization will consist largely of *task forces* that are created in response to a particular problem. The manager, in an organization of continuously changing structure, becomes a coordinator, a connector, a linker of various project groups. Skills in human interaction and communication will be of great value, since some of the major tasks will be relaying information and mediating understanding and differences between groups. Bennis argues that people will "have to learn to develop quick and intense relationships on the job, and learn to bear the loss of more enduring work relationships" (p. 35).

Toffler summarizes the characteristics of the new bureaucracy, called an *ad-hocracy,* as fast-moving, rich with information, highly active, constantly changing, filled with transient units and extremely mobile individuals. In the ad-hocracy, it is the work itself, the problem to be solved, the task to be done that attracts the commitment of employees, rather than the organization. Even professional loyalties become short term, because specialists derive their rewards from the intrinsic satisfaction of doing a difficult task well. They are loyal to their standards, not their superiors; to their problems, not their jobs. The ad-hocrats employ their skills and talents in solving problems within the temporary groups and environment of the organization, but only as long as the problems interest them.

Toffler notes that the titles of positions in some ad-hocracies are prefaced by the term *associate*. The term suggests an equality typical of the new organization—that is, *associate* connotes one who works with, rather than is subordinate to, others in the organization. Its use reflects a shift from vertical hierarchies to more lateral communication patterns. In a consulting and training company, we adopted the title *Organizational Associates* to convey the meaning that colleagues are coequals in the attack on organizational problems. The professional staff of associates is highly task oriented, deriving satisfaction from the anticipation of dealing with problems wherever they occur.

Toffler offers some words of caution that may lead us to the next part of this book. He guardedly observes that the "Ad-hocracy increases the adaptability of organizations; but it strains the adaptability of people" (p. 150). Each change of relationship in the organization brings with it some costs in personal adjustment, meaningful relations, and satisfaction. Social tension, psychological strain, and individual coping are all aggravated by the rapid change, temporary work circumstances, and lack of organizational commitment. The constant changes in organizational relationships place a heavy adaptive burden on people. Scrambling, we are propelled by our work into the Buck Rogers organization of the future.

For some the future may be arriving too soon. For most of us the future is now. For example, in 1965 Stewart provided guidelines for "Making Project Management Work." Project organization is the nearest equivalent we currently have to ad-hocracy. Even today the literature on organization theory is replete with descriptions of *matrix* organizational patterns, *intermix* project organization, *aggregate* project organization, *individual and staff* project organization, and *free-form* organization. A common contemporary Buck Rogers theory of organization is the matrix organization. It is a project organization superimposed on the more traditional functional organization. The functional department heads have line authority over projects by collaboration between the appropriate functional and project managers. Many conclude, consistent with Toffler's speculations, that matrix organization has reduced corporate loyalty and identification with the organization. Nevertheless, Luthans (1973) pointed out "that many modern organizations which are facing tremendous structural and technical complexity have no choice but to move to such an arrangement" (p. 177).

Naisbitt and Aburdene (1985) contend that the corporation must be reinvented to meet the demands of the new information society. They point out that companies such as Scandinavian Airlines Systems, W. L. Gore & Associates, Inc., and New Hope Communication have radically restructured their organization charts. These innovative companies represent current efforts to create the corporation of tomorrow.

Gore, Inc., stresses self-management and an open organization. According to Pancanowsky (1987), Gore's structure

> *looks like* a lattice, a regular cross-hatching of lines, representing an unrestricted flow of communication with no overlay of lines of authority. As Bill Gore defines it, a lattice organization means "one-on-one communication" with whomever you need to talk to in order to get a job done, no fixed or assigned authority but leadership that evolves over time and that fluctuates with the specific problems at hand that most need attention, and tasks and functions that are organized through personally made commitments—not through job descriptions and organization charts (p. 4).

Pacanowsky suggests that Gore, Inc., sustains an "empowering culture" by following six rules:

1. Distribute power and opportunity widely.
2. Maintain a full, open, and decentralized communication system.
3. Use integrative problem-solving methods.
4. Practice challenge in an environment of trust.
5. Reward and recognize people to encourage high-performance ethics and self-responsibility.
6. Become wise by living through and learning from organizational ambiguity, inconsistency, contradiction, and paradox.

Matrix, lattice, project, and ad-hocratic organizations are the communication organizations of the present and future. The study of communication is, in such circumstances, the study of organization. Management in matrix and lattice configurations is simply the practice of organizational communication. Present organization practices confirm early theoretical predictions; the first function of an executive is, indeed, to create and maintain a system of communication. The communication system is the organization. Organizational communication is the Buck Rogers theory of organization.

SUMMARY

In this chapter we analyzed behavioral and systems theories of organization. Behavioral theories included Barnard's authority-communication theory, which made the first function of an executive that of developing and maintaining a system of communication; Mayo's human relations theory, which made informal group relations more important and powerful in determining morale and productivity than working conditions; Bakke and Argyris's fusion theory, which proposed an incompatibility between employee needs and organization needs which is minimized by personalizing the organization and socializing the individual and results in the fusion of employee and organization; and Likert's linking pin theory, which conceives of the organization as a number of interconnected groups in which each supervisor is a leader of a lower unit and a member of a higher unit and serves as the linking pin connecting the groups. Katz and Kahn's social systems theory, which focuses on relationships among people and conceives of an organization as parts that communicate with each other, receive messages, and store information, and Toffler's and Bennis's futuristic ad-hocracy, which functions with temporary relationships, disposable divisions, associates, and matrix patterns, were offered as current views of organizations. The lattice scheme of organization has been presented as an example of open communication, shared responsibility, and commitment.

A SUBJECTIVIST'S REMINDER

The behavioral theorists altered classical theories by moving from considerations of pure structure and task to those of people and morale. However, the alterations still only represent variations on underlying themes of objectivist (bureaucratic) views. To elaborate, we will look at the notions of structure, goals, communication, and organization.

Although the work cited in this chapter stresses the importance of informal organization, it does not challenge the legitimacy and predominance of formal organization. A common suggestion is that the informal and formal should be negotiated, or fused together. But it is clear that the resulting structure is still conceived by those in charge. The informal organization is viewed as something that requires attention so that it does not disturb the real work of the organization.

The literature suggests that looking at goals means examining the organization's goals. It is implied that these goals are universal, agreed upon, and understood by everyone. Just as in the classical theories, the behavioral theorists cling to a rational (objectivist) model of organization. Pfeffer (1982) states that "the critical distinguishing feature of organization theories taking the rational perspective is the element of conscious, foresightful action reasonably autonomously constructed to achieve some goal or value" (p. 7). Experience in the organizational setting teaches us that there are multiple goals arising from various factions. These are negotiated with more formally stated goals, and the result may or may not resemble the original concept of a hierarchical organization or structure. The rational (objective) perspective also suggests that organizations and people know what their goals are before they are carried out; therefore, reaching those goals is just a matter of reconciling differences between the individual and the organization. It is more complex than that. Many times organizations do not know what their goals are until they have been achieved. We will develop this idea more fully in the discussion of organizational processes.

The role of communication becomes more visible and central in the behavioral theories, but the function of communication is much the same as in the bureaucratic model. Communication is deemed essential to attaining the organization's goals, and these goals are managerial goals. Communication effectiveness is thought of in managerial terms. Mayo's human relations theory is concerned with the link between communication and productivity. Barnard touts communication technique as a way to exercise authority. In the Likert scheme communication may be directed upward, but its major purpose is to inform the hierarchy so that adjustments can be made. The primary function of communication in these theories is regulation and control.

Although the behavioral models are more people oriented than their predecessors, there is still a clear-cut distinction between something called an organization and the behavior of the people in it. The implied definition still emphasizes organization as a concrete, "real" entity, which can have a formal structure or an informal structure. Which is the "real" organization? The fusion process cited earlier moves back to the formal structure. Behavioral theorists view people and their behavior as an important influence in the organization, but structure is still the dominant force.

Looking at the organization as a social system not only gives a more comprehensive picture but squares with the common-sense notion that an organization is composed of structural and personal dimensions and the interaction of those dimensions. Although this concept moves beyond classical models of organization, it still obscures the human element in organization. The system is often conceived of as having a life of its own, which is generated and guided by underlying principles that are applicable across biological and social structures. This concept promotes a mechanistic view of human behavior and communication. The unique social construction and the interpretation of interaction between individuals is accorded little influence in such schemes.

Silverman (1971, pp. 39–40) states:

> The Systems approach stresses the way in which the action of the parts is structured by the system's need for stability and goal-consensus, and emphasizes the processes of integration and adaptation. The alternative approach argues . . . that organisations are merely the ever-changing product of the self-interested actions of their members . . . . "Society makes Man" (Systems), "Man makes Society" (Action).

Silverman goes on to suggest that the real debate is about the relative merits of analyzing organizations "from the transcendental view of the problems of the system as a whole, with human action being regarded as a reflection of system needs, or from the view of interaction that arises as actors attach meanings to their own actions and to the actions of others" (p. 41). The subjectivist position stresses that individuals and their interactions construct the system, and, although the system may constrain individuals, it does so by meanings that are human products.

When organizations are thought of in terms of interdependent parts that function to sustain the system, there is a tendency to downplay the significance of socially constructed meaning. The system can take on a machine-like image in which the organization is seen as a large information processor whose parts are not only interdependent but interchangeable. Relationships between people are only important in such a formulation because the relationships allow the system to function and sustain itself. One is led to believe that if the people were removed, the organization would still exist by virtue of established relationships, or if people were shifted about, the same relationships would remain. Organization is thought of as very ordered and concrete. Can relationships exist without people? Does "relationship between roles" refer to the prescribed behavior, or the actual behavior and interpretation of that behavior? The subjectivist position maintains that the life given to an organization is just that —given by interacting participants who focus on the meaning of that interaction.

General systems theory emphasizes the similarity of processes that occur with a machine, organism, or organization. If the metaphors of machine and organism are taken too literally, one is likely to forget that organizations have no physical parts and have no structures apart from their functioning. People's actions are significant to what an organization is. The search for similarity of processes can create a false order in which humans are seen as highly predictable and merely reactive.

The open systems approach to organization focuses on the environment in which the system is located. Organizations operate across boundaries and transact with other social systems to ensure their survival. Organizations are systems that are part of other systems, such as institutions and societies. The challenge is to identify those aspects of the environment that the system (organization) must adapt to in order to sustain itself at an optimum level. The factors in the environment are said to provide the basis for organizational structure (Woodward, 1965; Emery & Trist, 1965; Burns & Stalker, 1961; Lawrence & Lorsch, 1967). The approach suggests that organizational adaptation is a rather simple and concrete process. However, Silverman (1971, pp. 36–37) challenges these notions by asking:

> Why, if organisations "must" adapt to their environment, they do so, if at all, at such varying rates? The answer that is normally given is that one of the components of the system ... is the predispositions of the members .... Their predispositions derive from the cultural system of the society and are another input into the organisation which must be taken into account ... It may also be argued, however, that the environment, as perceived by the observer, never exerts this sort of influence on patterns of interaction within organisations. The explanation of why people act as they do may lie not in a combination of "objective" and "subjective" factors, but in a network of meanings which constitute a "world-taken-for-granted."

It may be helpful at this point to review Figure 1.1 in Chapter 1. The systems perspective can be located toward the objective end of the continuum.

Communication from a systems perspective places attention on the acquisition, processing, and dissemination of information. This concept is indeed important, but it is necessary to remember that information and situations are created, and responses are dependent on the meanings held by organizational participants. The following chapter will extend those ideas.

REFERENCES

ARGYRIS, CHRIS, *Personality and Organization*. New York: Harper & Row, Pub., 1957.

BAKKE, E. WIGHT, *Bonds of Organization*. New York: Harper & Row, Pub., 1950.

BARNARD, CHESTER I., *The Functions of the Executive*. Cambridge, Mass.: Harvard University Press, 1938.

BENNIS, WARREN G., "The Coming Death of Bureaucracy," *Think Magazine* (November–December 1966), 30–35.

BERTALANFFY, LUDWIG VON, *General Systems Theory: Foundations, Development, Applications*. New York: George Braziller, 1968.

BOULDING, KENNETH E., "General Systems Theory—The Skeleton of Science," *Management Science*, 2 (1965), 197–208.

BURNS, T., and G. M. STALKER, *The Management of Innovation*. London: Tavistock, 1961.

EMERY, F. E. and E. L. TRIST, "The Causal Texture of Organizational Environments," *Human Relations*, 18 (1965), 21–32.

FISHER, B. AUBREY, *Perspectives on Human Communication*. New York: Macmillan, 1978.

GUILBOT, O. BENOIT, "The Sociology of Work," *International Encyclopedia of the Social Sciences*, Vol. 7, 232–233. New York: Macmillan, 1968.

HAWES, LEONARD C., "Social Collectivities as Communication: Perspective on Organizational Behavior," *Quarterly Journal of Speech*, 60 (December 1974), 500.

KATZ, DANIEL, and ROBERT L. KAHN, *The Social Psychology of Organizations*. New York: John Wiley, 1966.

LAWRENCE, PAUL R., and JAY W. LORSCH, *Organization and Environment*. Cambridge, Mass.: Harvard University Press, 1967.

LIKERT, RENSIS, *New Patterns of Management*. New York: McGraw-Hill, 1961.

LUTHANS, FRED, *Organizational Behavior*. New York: McGraw-Hill, 1973.

MAYO, ELTON, *The Social Problems of an Industrial Civilization*. Cambridge, Mass.: Harvard University Press, 1945.

MILLER, DELBERT C., and WILLIAM H. FORM, *Industrial Sociology*. New York: Harper & Row, Pub., 1951.

MOOREHEAD, ALAN, "The Russian Revolution, Part II: Relentless Rise of the Conspiracy," *Life*, 44 (January 20, 1958), 60–70, 75–82.

NAISBITT, JOHN, and PATRICIA ABURDENE, *Re-inventing the Corporation*. New York: Warner Books, 1985.

PACANOWSKY, MICHAEL, "Communication in the Empowering Organization," Paper presented at the University of Utah Summer Conference on Interpretive Approaches to the Study of Organizational Communication, Alta, Utah, 1987.

PERROW, CHARLES, "The Short and Glorious History of Organizational Theory," *Organizational Dynamics*, 2 (Summer 1973), 2–15.

PFEFFER, JEFFREY, *Organizations and Organization Theory*, Boston: Pitman, 1982.

RAPOPORT, ANATOL, "Foreword" in *Modern Systems Research for the Behavioral Scientist*, Walter Buckley, ed. Chicago: Aldine, 1968.

ROETHLISBERGER, FRITZ J., and WILLIAM J. DICKSON, *Management and the Worker*. Cambridge, Mass.: Harvard University Press, 1939.

SCOTT, WILLIAM G., "Organization Theory: An Overview and Appraisal," *Journal of the Academy of Management* (April 1961), 15, 18.

SILVERMAN, DAVID, *The Theory of Organisations,* New York: Basic Books, 1971.

SOFER, CYRIL, *Organization in Theory and Practice*. New York: Basic Boos, 1973.

STEWART, JOHN M., "Making Project Management Work," *Business Horizons* (Fall 1965), 57–59.

TANNENBAUM, ROBERT, "Managerial Decision Making," *The Journal of Business*, 23 (1950), 22–39.

TOFFLER, ALVIN, *Future Shock,* New York: Random House, 1970.

WEICK, KARL E., *The Social Psychology of Organizing*. Reading, Mass.: Addison-Wesley, 1969.

WOODWARD, JOAN, *Industrial Organization: Theory and Practice*. London: Oxford University Press, 1965.

5

Contemporary Theories
Toward Subjectivism

The behavioral and social systems theories discussed in Chapter 4 were categorized as transitional theories because they represent a more subjective position on the continuum (Figure 1.1). As the interpretations move along that continuum they stress a more central role for the symbolic behavior and creative capacities of humans. We are not suggesting that the more subjective theories are the "right" ones, but that various positions on the continuum are receiving increasing attention today. Some theorists contend that this is not just a slight modification of old theories but a paradigm (world view) revolution (Lincoln, 1985).

Whether we should assimilate and adopt contemporary subjective theories may be arguable, but there is little question that they represent changes in fundamental ways of thinking that challenge the dominant scientific/objective view of the world. In this chapter, we will discuss two theories that contrast with the objective view of organization. They do not, of course, represent all contemporary thinking about organizations, but they are the theories that have had a major impact on the field (Clark, 1985; Geertz, 1973; Schwartz & Ogilvy, 1979). As a preface to a detailed analysis of the two major perspectives, we will briefly summarize dimensions of the corresponding world view so that you might see how it applies to organizational theory. What does the organization look like from this changing perspective?

1. Organizations are viewed as being more complex, and attempts to reduce them to simple elements and processes are questioned. The organization tends to develop a complex culture that has unique characteristics.

2. The idea of an order of natural and social laws is replaced by notions of multiple sets of order and interaction between the orders. Organizations are composed of several sets of order, with dynamics of interaction that are mutual and occurring at the same time.

3. Organization is viewed less in machine terms and more in terms of the holograph metaphor to get at the complex dynamics of the organization. Lincoln (1985) states:

> The power of this metaphor [holograph], is that every piece contains complete information about the whole. This is a particularly powerful concept when considering, for instance, genetic materials, in which a single cell is said to contain information about the entire organism, or in organizations, in which information about some subunit might provide information regarding the whole operation (34–35)].

4. The organization and its future state is seen as less predictable and controllable than suggested by earlier theoretical models.

5. Organizational behavior is better reflected by a complex causal model than one that emphasizes simple cause-and-effect relationships. Notions of mutual causality are more useful in representing the dynamics of growth, change, and evolution.

6. Students of organization are showing increasing willingness to consider various ways of viewing organizational behavior, and the laws-and-instances explanation is giving ground to one that emphasizes cases-and-interpretation. The search for foundational knowledge that can be generalized as truth is giving way to the idea that a particular perspective produces its own branch of knowledge and truth. The search for some grand, comprehensive theory that might deal with the complexity of organization is viewed with increasing skepticism.

In the following sections we will describe two contemporary theories that reflect shifts in thinking that have been taking place in organizational theory.

WEICK'S THEORY OF ORGANIZING

The work of Karl Weick is provocative and influential. Some of the spirit of this work is captured by Lundberg (1982) when he explains:

> To the Alice in each of us, Karl Weick is the white rabbit. The allusion, of course, is to Lewis Carroll's magical tale. Recall the proper English girl, Alice, in her garden, a somewhat formal garden with distinct boundaries. Along comes the white rabbit who catches Alice's attention and prompts her to follow him through the garden boundary, whereupon she fell into a new world. Professor Weick's book does draw our attention and, if we allow ourselves, will enable us to breach conventional conceptual practices and intellectual domains. Like Alice we may explore and achieve new experiences with the paradoxical wonders of what we thought were familiar territories (113–114).

In the following sections we will examine Weick's model by extending the key ideas presented in the previous chapters. The model is heavily invested in systems theory, but that is only one theoretical strand in the overall model. Kreps (1986) explains the model on the basis of "sociocultural evolutionary" theory, information theory, and systems theory. While the model represents a systems theory, the treatment is distinctly different in that human processes receive much more prominence. Our purpose is to illustrate the subjective aspects of the theory and discuss some of the implications for organizational communication.

Conception of Organization

Weick (1979) states that "the word *organization* is a noun, and it is also a myth. If you look for an organization you won't find it. What you will find is that there are events, linked together, that transpire within concrete walls and these sequences, their pathways, and their timing are the forms we erroneously make into substances when we talk about an organization" (p. 88). The focus is clearly on *organizing* rather than *organization*. The process of organizing creates what is called an organization. Emphasis is placed on activity and process. Does an organization have structure? Yes, it does, but "The structure that determines how an organization acts and how it appears is the structure that is established by regular patterns of interlocked behaviors" (Weick, 1979, p. 90). The organization is a system that adapts and sustains itself by reducing the uncertainty that it faces. It is a system of "interlocked behaviors," and that is the key to its functioning. Behaviors are interlocked when the behaviors of one person are contingent on the behaviors of others.

Critical Features of Organizing

Theories discussed in the previous chapters view structure, behavior, and environment as key organizational factors. That is also true of the Weick scheme, but the factors themselves are seen from a different perspective. Structure, in earlier theories, was viewed as hierarchy, policies, and organizational design, whereas Weick sees structure as activity and more specifically, as communication activity. The organizational structure is defined by interlocked behaviors.

The role of people and their behavior is noted in discussions of behavioral and systems theories. However, those approaches look at how people and their behavior serve the organization. In such theories, communication is typically thought to reflect important underlying characteristics of the organization. A distinction is made between behavior and structure. The Weick formulation suggests that structure is identified by its organizing behaviors. Communication does not reflect important processes; it is the important process. Process creates structure. Weick's conception is that a system is clearly human in nature. Humans do not simply serve an organization: they are the organization.

Human beings face a complex and often uncertain environment, which Weick maintains is the reason for organizing. In Chapter 4 we cited a number of theorists who give priority to the role of environment. They have been referred to as *environmental determinists* because they view the environment as determining everything from organizational design to specific organizational behaviors. Again, the notion is that once the environment has been properly identified, a fit can be made between the organization and the environment to ensure continuity and optimum functioning of the organization. A transaction takes place between organization and environment. The term *environment* might refer to market conditions, competition, laws and regulations, and technology.

Weick does not draw a sharp boundary between organization and environment. He takes a more subjective view and argues that people are actively involved in creating the world about them. Organization members do not simply react: they create. They "enact" their environment through interaction and the creation of meaning. The environment in large part is socially constructed, so organizational members are looking at a creation rather than an objective reality. Any event that occurs is a creation—through the interpretation of those who decide what happened and the significance it might have. We will elaborate this idea in the section "Implications for Organizational Communication." The main point for now is that "rather than talking about adapting to an external environment, it may be more correct to argue that organizing consists of adapting to an enacted environment, an environment which is constituted by the actions of interdependent human actors" (Weick, 1969, p. 27).

What is involved in organizing? Weick (1979) defines organizing "as a consensually validated grammar for reducing equivocality by means of sensible interlocked behaviors" (p.3). *Consensual validation* means that organizational reality arises out of experiences that are shared and validated by others. These experiences are shared with others through *symbol systems*. *Grammar* refers to the rules, conventions, and practices of the organization. These conventions help people get things done and provide the basis for interpreting what has been done. *Equivocality* refers to the level of uncertainty or ambiguity that organizational members face. Organizing helps reduce the uncertainty about the information that confronts organizational members when they are trying to make decisions that enable the organization to survive and succeed. The phrase *sensible interlocked behaviors* in Weick's definition represents a key idea embedded in the subjectivist point of view. Interlocked behaviors are communication behaviors in which meaning becomes a socially negotiated process. What is sensible or "real" is dependent upon the consensual validation (agreement and corroboration) between organizational members. Organizational reality is a social construction that takes place through interaction.

Organizations come into being because organizing activity is necessary to combat the ambiguity and uncertainty that humans face. Organizations must manage this equivocality, and they do so by giving meaning to events. Weick is quite specific about the behaviors of organizing. The critical unit of analysis is the *double interact*, in which A communicates to B, B responds to A, and A makes some adjustment or gives some response to B. This kind of specific communication activity forms the basis of organizing. These interlocked communication behaviors enable the organization to process information. Organizations also cope with the equivocality of information by the use of rules. The less equivocal the message input into the system, the more likely it will be that preset rules will be used. The more equivocal the message input into the system, the more likely it will be that communication cycles (double interacts) will be used to deal with the uncertainty. The more uncertainty an organization faces, the greater the requirement for the use of communication cycles.

The Process of Organizing

There are three major phases in the process of organizing. Weick (1979) specifies these phases as "enactment (bracketing some portion of the stream of experience for further attention), selection (imposing some finite set of interpretations on the bracketed portion) and retention (storage of interpreted segments for future application)" (p. 45). Rules and communication cycles are applied in each phase when organizational members process information.

The *enactment phase* simply means that organizational members recreate their environment by assigning and negotiating a particular meaning for an event. In the *selection phase*, rules and communication cycles are used to determine sufficient reduction of equivocality. The *retention phase* allows the organization to store information about the way the organization has responded to various situations. Successful strategies become rules that can be applied in the future. The various phases have an impact on each other. For example, retention knowledge may guide the organization in its enactment and selection processes.

Thus far we have looked at the notions of organization, organizing, and organizing phases developed by Weick. In the following sections we will consider the more general aspects of this work and its implications from a subjectivist stance.

The Nature of Organizations/Humans

It is appropriate to align organizations and humans because the organization is a human system—a system constructed by humans. In the system conceived by Weick, things are in a constant state of change (evolution). Events in human systems are seldom, if ever, of a singular cause-effect nature but are more clearly represented by dynamic interaction and multideterminism. Change rather than stability is the norm and evolutionary change is an inherent function of any organization that tries to maintain itself. The processes of organizing constitute the lifeblood of the organization in this adaptive process. The tenets of systems theory discussed in Chapter 4 are applicable to Weick's theory. The concept of openness is especially relevant. Weick goes beyond the typical systems theorist by suggesting that organizations not only interact with their environments, but they enact them. The creative/adaptive processes in rules and communication cycles exhibit the concept of equifinality. The negotiation of meaning greatly influences the end state of an organization.

We will not detail the relevance of each tenet, but the concept of *interdependence* merits some attention. As you recall, the idea suggests that there is mutual dependence among components or units in an organization. A change in one component brings about change in every other component. This concept further suggests that the systemic character of an organization is a carefully ordered one in which units are tightly bound together. Such systems are said to be *tightly coupled*. Couplings refer to processes that affect the joint behavior of organizational components. Weick (1976) posits the notion of *loosely coupled systems*. An event that takes place in a system might affect other components of that system but not right away. The event could be absorbed by one component and be passed on to others at a later date. An analogy sometimes used to illustrate loose coupling is that of a set of dominoes. If the dominoes are placed standing on end at regular intervals and in a straight line, a push (an event) at the head of the line will bring all of the dominoes down. This version illustrates a tightly coupled system. If the dominoes are spaced at irregular intervals, a push on one will make it fall as well as maybe one or two others. One domino may teeter and fall a bit later than the others—an event analogous to a loosely coupled system. Such systems not only exist, but they are often highly desirable. Loosely coupled systems have both functional and dysfunctional aspects. For example, components of an organization may persist because the organization is less inclined to respond to each change in the environment; but the system may not be selective about what is preserved. When facing a new situation, one component of a system can adapt with relative ease without affecting the rest of the system; of course, this means less uniformity and standardization in the system, which may be a shortcoming. If part of the system fails, that failure may be confined to that part of the system; on the negative side, however, help to that part of the system might be delayed because of its independent nature.

Weick's view of the organization raises questions about the existence and even the desirability of a rational, goal-directed and tightly ordered system. According to earlier theories, in a rational organization a problem could be seen and defined, possible solutions could be carefully generated, and the best solution could be selected. The underlying assumption was that thought precedes action. Weick (1977a) asserts, however, that "organizations talk to themselves in order to clarify their surroundings and learn more about them. . . . Organizations examine retrospectively the very displays that initially they created as pretexts for sense making. Organizations talk in order to discover what they are saying, act in order to discover what they are doing" (p. 282). This idea suggests that action preceding thought may be the rule rather than the exception. This retrospective sense-making process is a departure from classical models. Goals may be formulated and accounted for after action has been taken. For example, Weick (1985) advises administrators to "be willing to leap before you look. If you look before you leap, you may not see anything. Action generates outcomes that ultimately provide the raw material for seeing something" (p. 133). Weick (1985) notes that in contemporary discussions of organization "rationality is viewed (1) as a set of prescriptions that change as the issue changes, (2) as a facade created to attract resources and legitimacy, and (3) as a postaction process used retrospectively to invent reasons for the action" (p. 110).

How much order is there in an organization? The language of organizational theories includes efficiency, predictability, proactive planning, data-based decision making—all terms that imply a high degree of order that is predetermined. Weick (1977b) suggests that "the effective organization is (1) garrulous, (2) clumsy, (3) superstitious, (4) hypocritical, (5) monstrous, (6) octopoid, (7) wandering, and (8) grouchy" (pp. 193–194). This language portrays a very different image of the organization. Weick reminds us that the stream of experience can be chopped up and labeled in arbitrary but reasonable ways. We cannot elaborate on each label here, but let's examine the notion of garrulousness. This term means that organizations talk a great deal and that talk defines and constrains effectiveness. "What organizations say and do provides displays that they can examine reflectively to understand what is occurring" (Weick, 1977a, p. 195). "What is occurring" serves as the data for decision making and is produced by the quality and quantity of talk. Viewed in this way, the garrulous label not only makes sense but also allows us to see different dimensions of the organization. The labels suggest that organizations are human and, as such, their behaviors are subjective in nature. Creations may come about through searching, trail-and-error, and what might be labeled irrational behaviors under other schemes.

Weick (1983, p. 28) presents an analogy that illustrates the value of behaviors that may not fit with traditional theories. Imagine a clear glass jug that contains flies and bees. When the jug is placed in a window and a shaft of sunlight hits it, the flies and bees behave differently. The bees cluster (respond in an orderly way) toward the sunlight even as the heat rises. The flies zing about and bounce off the walls of the jug, but they eventually escape the deadly heat by passing through the jug's mouth. The bees are not so fortunate; they fail to engage in what might be called a variety of searching or random behaviors, which are clearly functional in this case. An organization's capacity for variety, what may be called random behavior, may be very important to survival. This is not to say that order is absent. "Organizations may be anarchies, but they are organized anarchies. Organizations may be loosely coupled, but they are loosely coupled systems. Organizations may resort to garbage can decision making, but garbage cans have borders that impose some structure" (Weick, 1985, p. 109).

Implications for Organizational Communication

To study organization is to study organizing behavior, and the heart of that behavior is communication. Organizations talk in order to know; talk constitutes their intelligence and adaptive capacity. To discover what organizations are thinking, it is critical to examine the interlocked behaviors (double interacts) of the members. What people say and validate with each other produces an environment that organizes their activities—especially their thinking.

Talk is the raw data of sense making and decision making. Individuals actively construct their worlds. The question is not "Have we discovered the correct underlying order?" but "What order have we created and what impact does it have?" Smircich (1983) applies the "enacted environment" concept to management by explaining that "managers must look to their actions and inactions, not to the environment, for explanations of their situation. The environment often serves as a convenient scapegoat for placing blame and denying responsibility" (p. 230).

According to Weick (1977a), people make sense out of experience with the aid of *punctuation* and *connection*. "Punctuation means chopping the stream of experience into sensible, nameable, and named units, and the activity of connection involves imposing relationships, typically causal relationships, among the punctuated elements" (p. 280). Because of the arbitrary nature of this labeling process, it is important to know what the raw data are and how the data are generated. Then it is possible to know how organizations interpret that data and on what basis.

Weick (1985) gives a number of implications for administrative practice. One that is particularly relevant to organizational communication is:

> To manage meaning is to view your organization as a set of procedures for arguing and interpreting. In any organizational assessment ask questions such as these: How do we declare winners of the argument? When do we interpret? What interpretations do we tend to favor (blind spots?)? Whose interpretations seem to stick (p.133)?

He focuses, then, on communication and the role that it plays in structuring a world that prompts one decision over another.

To consider a created world is also to consider the language of that world. The language that sounds so right—"efficient," "cost-effective"—may screen out thinking about how the labels were attached. Perhaps an octopoid organization with gangly tentacles has more to recommend it than a systemic one with an orderly algorithm. In addition, workable disorder casts doubt on the notion of an ideal organization that contains the right mix of the right elements.

Weick's theory of organizing challenges taken-for-granted ways of thinking and allows us to see the significance of a subjective view of the world. We appreciate Weick's (1977a) statement that

> talk about "a reality" is simply one way that people try to make sense out of the stream of experience that flows by them. To say that there is a reality, an environment, and then to search for and discover underlying patterns in those superimposed structures is one way to make sense of that stream. But the tenuousness of this process nevertheless, as well as the actor's central role in its execution, are captured only if we remain attentive to reality as metaphor (p. 278).

This alternative view give us insight into human behavior and communication. In the next part of the chapter we will discuss another prominent subjective world view.

A CULTURAL THEORY OF ORGANIZATION

The "buzz word" for organizational study and consulting in the 1960s and throughout much of the 1970s was *systems*. The rational objective view of the world was, and still is in vogue. However, the term *culture* may certainly be said to have achieved the status of a buzz word in the late 1970s and into the 1980s. Buzz words are "in" words that are usually used in a variety of ways not only because they represent current ideas, but also because they indicate that the user is "with" the state of the art. Such terms are attention grabbing but often misleading. When Hi Fi (high fidelity) sound was new, one restaurant advertised a Hi Fi Sandwich. Explain that one! In the following sections we will discuss why the concept of culture has achieved serious consideration, explore concepts of organizational culture, examine organizational culture issues, and finally point out some implications for organizational communication.

Culture and the Shift toward Subjectivism

In the past twenty years there has been growing concern about the role of human action and symbolic behavior in organizational study. Theorists (Weick, 1969; Silverman, 1970, among a number of others) have raised significant questions about a rational model of organizational behavior. Symbolic behavior is deemed to be significant; yet it is unaccounted for in a rational model that emphasizes structure and environmental adaptation. Because symbolic processes often contradict the premises of objectivity, they cannot be simply tacked on to rational models. Traditional rational models cannot bear the weight of subjective views because they represent a different world view (paradigm). This recognition has enhanced the appeal of subjective approaches.

Although students of organizational behavior tend to expect too much out of theories, it is true that rational theories of human behavior have been a disappointment in terms of predicting behavior. Principles derived from such theories are more articles of faith than a set of reliable prescriptions. Explanations that follow an objective view of the world tend to account for the bare bones of the organization but exclude the soul. People need to get a "feel" for the organization in order to know how to react to any information about it. An organization is not just any object of study: it is a human enterprise. The reaction to past models of organizational behavior, then, has prompted a shift toward subjectivism and the cultural concept.

The market appeal of the term "culture" among academics and practitioners should not be discounted. To explain this statement we must explore some of the language associated with objective and subjective views. Those views that tend toward the objective view of reality and human nature have been labeled as the *functionalist* perspective (Parsons, 1964). Structural, behavioral, and social systems theories represent this perspective. They are concerned with the mechanisms that secure stability of the organization. Organizational analysis focuses on the efficiency of the processes and structures that maintain the system. Some of the metaphors associated with the functionalist perspective include machines, organisms, and systems.

Subjective views of reality and human nature are called the *interpretive* perspective (Morgan, 1980). This perspective maintains that the social world does not exist in a concrete sense, but that it is constructed by the interactions and consensual validation of individuals. Analysis from this perspective centers on how organizational reality is created and the understanding of symbolic discourse that makes up organizational life. Relevant subjective schools of thought for the interpretive perspective include hermeneutics, ethnomethodology, phenomenology, and symbolic interactionism. Some of the metaphors generated by the interpretive perspective include *accomplishment* (Garfinkel, 1967); *enacted sense making* (Weick, 1977a); *language game* (Wittgenstein, 1968); *text* (Ricoeur, 1971); and *culture* (Pondy & Mitroff, 1979; Turner, 1971). Much of the language of subjectivism does not help us have an image of the organization. The metaphors are abstract and removed from experience. But the term "culture" not only captures the imagination but also helps most people make comparisons between the symbolic aspects of a culture and those of a particular organization.

When people talk about an organization as "another world," "a different country," or a "self-contained society," they are on the doorstep of the notion of constructed reality. Of course, a term's appeal can also be its undoing, especially if it is used in so many ways that it becomes meaningless and confusing. Our main point here is that the term "culture" serves as a stimulator of thought and as an anchor, much as the term "system" did for the objective theories.

Finally, we believe that the economic challenges of the 1970s and the 1980s precipitated a close look at the idea of culture. Stiff competition from such rivals as Japan brought about much self-examination. What do they do that the United Stated doesn't do? How do their workers live and what do they believe? How do they achieve their level of quality? The competition might be viewed as culture vs. culture. In 1982, when unemployment was 9.5 percent, the prime rate was over 16 percent, and trade deficits soared, the business world was ready to give serious consideration to ideas that might help them compete in the world market.

At that time several books appeared with popular views of culture. *Corporate Culture* (Deal & Kennedy, 1982) discussed how the stuff of culture—values, symbols, rites, and rituals—might have impact on a company's overall performance. Also in 1982, Peters and Waterman presented *In Search of Excellence*, in which they examined the traits of organizations that had achieved excellence. They identified primary themes that were applicable to the organizations studied. These themes could be construed as cultural in that they represent the values of those organizations.

The culture metaphor is provocative in that it stimulates identification at a number of levels. From a common-sense perspective it fits experience, and at the same time the academic can see the richness of the concept because of the complexity involved. It fires the imagination of both practitioner and theorist. In that sense too much promise may be attached to the metaphor. Smircich and Calas (1987) question whether the notion of culture heralds something different in the study of organization or whether it marks a passing fad and failed project. They maintain that to the extent that the concept of culture represents the more traditional approaches it does not meet its promise as a fresh perspective that challenges what is in place. They argue that the literature should be located in a wider debate that not only questions traditions but also the very logic and politics of labeling something as a tradition.

In terms of the culture concept, the 1970s could be characterized as a time of exuberance and acceptance. The late 1980s and into the 1990s represent the period of critical evaluation and refinement. Recently one of our colleagues said: "If I hear the word culture one more time, I am going to draw my gun!" There are others who are more moderate and optimistic. Sackmann (1991) suggests that the value of the organizational culture concept to researchers and practitioners will be dependent on doing empirical research rather than debating opinions. It is our view that the move toward criticism and refinement enhances the concept of organizational culture rather than signals its demise.

The corporations of the 1990s face global competition and the prospect of change due to the value shifts of members and clients. Naisbitt and Aburdene (1985) assert that "the corporation is an analogue for the rest of society. We are reinventing education, health care, politics, and virtually all our social structures. But the corporation is often the quickest and most responsive to change. . . . Customers, unlike other constituents, vote every day, and that hastens corporate evolution" (p.1). If an organization has a culture and its survival depends on its ability to change, then the question of how to change culture is critical. The notion of cultural change has also given impetus to the study of organizational symbolism and its meaning. Thus far we have used the term "culture" in a variety of ways. In the next section we will explore those usages.

Concepts of Organizational Culture

Sonja Sackmann (1991) traces the term "culture" back to the eighteenth century, and she points out that the notion of culture has been the basic and central concept of anthropology. Although the concept has been a focal point of analysis, there is not consensus among anthropologists on what culture is. According to Sackmann, Kroeber and Kluckhohn list more than 250 different definitions. She derives three broad perspectives of culture that are applied to organizational settings in the managerial literature. Those include (1) a holistic perspective, (2) a variable perspective, and (3) a cognitive perspective. The holistic perspective looks upon culture as patterned ways of thinking, feeling, and reacting. The variable perspective focuses on expressions of culture. The cognitive perspective places the emphasis on ideas, concepts, blueprints, beliefs, values, and norms, the "organized knowledge" that people have in their minds for making sense of reality. Sackmann (1991) follows the tradition of the cognitive perspective in her own conception of culture in organizations. She combines cognitive structuring devices that influence perception, thinking, feeling, and acting with a developmental perspective that looks at the formation and change of cultural cognitions. Cognitions become commonly held in processes of social interaction. In this approach, the essence of culture is the collective construction of social reality.

Smircich and Calas (1987) suggest that culture can be examined as a variable or a root metaphor. When thought of as an external variable, culture is something that is brought into the organization. When framed as an internal variable, emphasis is placed on cultural artifacts (rituals, stories, etc.) that are developed within the organization. Root metaphor analysis looks at organizations as structures of knowledge, shared symbolic patterns, and reflections of unconscious processes.

An examination of only a few conceptual schemes clearly indicates the diversity of views in thinking about and studying organizational culture. In a strict sense any statement about cultural analysis should be accompanied by the unstated assumptions. At the risk of trying to cover too much ground in too little space, we make the following observations.

Generally speaking, when people interact over time, they form a culture. Each culture develops written and unwritten expectations of behavior (rules and norms) that influence the members of that culture. But people are not only influenced by the culture; they create the culture. Each organization has one or more cultures that contain expected behaviors—written or unwritten. Implicit in the concept of culture is an appreciation of the way organizations are molded by unique sets of values, rituals, and personalities. Louis (1985) suggests that a group's culture can be characterized as "a set of understandings or meanings shared by a group of people. The meanings are largely tacit among members, are clearly relevant to the particular group, and are distinctive to the group" (p. 74). Culture, then, involves interaction over time, behavioral expectations, shaping and being shaped, unique characteristics that set one culture apart from another, and a set of meanings/logics that enable group action.

The idea that an organization is "like a culture" captures the interest of both functionalist (objective) and interpretive (subjective) perspectives, but in different ways and for different reasons. Although our task in this chapter is to examine some subjective theories, a brief contrast between perspectives will highlight the subjectivist position. First, there is the matter of *cultural content*. Both perspectives recognize that one culture may be distinguished from another by its values, rites and rituals, practices, vocabulary, metaphors, and stories. The functionalist sees these as elements (variables) that make up an organizational culture. Such elements may be manipulated and controlled so that they affect organizational outcomes. For example, Deal and Kennedy (1982) describe key attributes or organizational culture and then suggest that if these elements are developed, they will lead to business success. Embodied in this approach are the notions of predictability, control, and cause-and-effect linkages, which are found on the objective side of the continuum (Figure 1.1).

The interpretivist focuses on the process of communication and the sense making of organizational members. How do members construct their organizational reality? What do events mean to them? The stories and rituals are displayers and indicators of organizational sense making (Pacanowsky & O'Donnell-Trujillo, 1982, pp. 124–125). It is the sense making itself that is most critical to the interpretivist. While a functionalist might try to determine what stories are in the system and what impact they might have on organizational outcomes, an interpretivist would be more interested in how stories are told, who tells them, and what meaning they hold for organizational members.

How is organizational culture defined? One way is to think of the organization as being made of "things," or cultural artifacts, stories, and rituals. If these artifacts are viewed as concrete entities with "real" existence, the perspective is functionalist, and organizational culture is perceived as artifact. If organizational culture is thought of as sense making, then it is identified through sense-making processes, and symbolic behavior becomes a focal point. It becomes necessary to listen to what people say in order to see how their experience takes on meaning.

The interpretative (subjective) point of view sees organizational culture as processes of sense making that construct organizational reality and thereby give meaning to the membership. The concept of sense making is as important to the interpretive view of culture as enacted sense making is to Weick's (1977a) theory of organizing. The displayers and indicators of organizational culture are not "givens" that just exist. They must be constructed, and the meanings given to them must be generated and regenerated in interaction. The displayers and indicators (stories, rites, rituals) are thought of as action rather than things. Pacanowsky and O'Donnell-Trujillo (1982) maintain that "as members constitute their relevant constructs, practices, rituals, and so forth, these constructs, practices, and rituals are mini-accomplishments embedded in the larger ongoing accomplishment of organizational culture" (p.126). The key term is *accomplishment* in that it indicates action, and ongoing action at that. The displayers and indicators of culture can also be placed under the broad rubric of *organizational symbolism* (Dandridge, Mitroff, & Joyce, 1980). What is significant to the sense-making concept of culture is the meaning of symbolism to organizational members as they shape organizational reality and as they are shaped by their own constructions.

As one proceeds along the subjective-objective continuum, symbolic displayers and indicators are understood in different ways. The complexity of the sense-making process makes it difficult to present a comparison that captures the nuances involved. Perhaps Geertz (1973) says it best when he contends that "man is an animal suspended in webs of significance he himself has spun. . . . Culture [is] those webs, and the analysis of it [is] therefore not an experimental science in search of law but an interpretive one in search of meaning" (p.5). Such an analogy reminds us that much as the spider spins a web, humans spin a reality that has impact on them. Just as in the case of the spider the web that is spun by humans enables their movement and vision; but it also constrains their movement and vision. If webs of significance are thought of as stories, rituals, rites, metaphors, organizational practices, and values, then the prominence of symbolic behavior in culture is clear. There are several drawbacks to these comparisons. From a subjective stance the culture is more than the web; it is also the spinning itself. In addition, humans do not spin alone. Webs of significance must be negotiated between members of the organization. When a spider traverses the web, the process is less complex than when humans share the meaning of webs of significance. Human webs are more fragile and elusive than the tangible web of the spider. They may seem routine, but each new web is negotiated between organizational participants even though members may be unaware of the exchanges that have taken place. The web provides a structure, a context, a network of meaning that has been spun through interaction. It is within this context that people interpret and make sense of events. Organizational culture is identified by discovering the web and its spinning.

Pacanowsky and O'Donnell-Trujillo's (1982) interpretation of Geertz's web analogy recognizes the dual nature of organizational culture. They assert that "if these two components of culture are to be studied—culture as structure and culture as process—then . . . researchers must not be content simply with accounts, but must also be present during occasions of naturally occurring discourse" (p. 123). These features of organizational culture are recognized and explained in a different way by Smircich. She contends that culture is not only something an organization *has* (artifacts, structure), but also something that an organization *is* (process, sense making). The research agenda from this perspective "is to explore the phenomenon of organization as subjective experience and to investigate the patterns that make organized action possible" (Smircich, 1983, p. 348). An interpretive (subjective) approach emphasizes communication patterns within the organization and what those patterns mean to the participant.

Thus far we have discussed how organizational culture might be defined. There are other conceptual issues that should be noted. Louis (1985) presents a conceptual framework organized into natural, purposeful, and reflective levels of analysis. At the natural level, the concerns are origins (Where does culture come from?); outcomes (What does culture lead to?); and manifestations/artifacts (What does culture look like?). The purposeful level of analysis concerns issues of management. What can be done with, to, or about the culture? The reflective level looks at the nature and characteristics of culture. What constitutes the essence of a culture and makes it distinctive? Although any one study may involve several levels of analysis, an interpretive approach would most likely correspond to the reflective level.

In this section we have talked about the nature of culture, the objective and subjective views of culture, and different levels of cultural analysis. These themes raise certain issues that need to be addressed. However, before we embark on that discussion, some focus can be achieved by highlighting a subjective perspective of organizational culture.

ORGANIZATIONAL CULTURE AS SENSE MAKING

Commenting on various usages of and the popularity of the notion of culture, Smircich (1985) contends that "we turned to the idea of culture for a fresh slant on organizational life, for something different. But for the most part, we're not getting it" (p. 59). She stresses that if culture is to be more than just another element (variable) applied to traditional (objective) ways of thinking, it is necessary to concentrate on "meaning" and cultural analysis of organizational life. Cultural analysis of organizational life, from a subjective perspective, focuses on symbols and people in interaction. Organizational life is symbolic construction.

The sense-making (subjective) stance sees culture as a symbolically created context that allows people to make sense of events. They *make* culture and sense through interaction. Organizational life (reality) is put together communicatively. The primary question for the organizational participant is "What do I need to know and say to function in this setting?" The knowing and saying are the sense-making processes that make up the organizational culture. When investigators tap into the "saying" of organizational members, they are examining both sense making and culture.

Organization is symbolic behavior, and its very existence depends upon the shared meanings and interpretations that come about through human interaction. Organization "depends upon the existence of common modes of interpretation and shared understanding of experience which allow day to day activities to become routinized or taken-for-granted. When groups encounter novel situations, new interpretations must be constructed to sustain organized activity" (Smircich, 1981, p. 1). Looking at sense making is looking at the taken-for-granted behavior of the people who have constructed the organization. Symbols and symbolic behavior make organizational life possible. Think of the web analogy cited earlier and how the web both enables and constrains the movement of the spider. Symbolic behavior both enables and constrains the movement and vision of an organization. To understand symbolic behavior is to understand how a particular organization shapes its actions or inactions. More specifically, "what are the words, ideas, and constructs that impel, legitimate, coordinate, and realize organized activity in specific settings? How do they accomplish the task? Whose interests are they serving?" (Smircich, 1985, p. 67). The critical features of culture as sense making focus on shared meaning, symbolic behavior, interaction, and taken-for-granted behavior.

The principles underlying Weick's (1977a) concept of enacted sense making are also applicable here. Humans have a great deal to do with making their world, and the created world comes back to guide their activities. One interpretive critique of management theory points out that "givens" are actually problematic creations. Smircich (1983) looks at the work of Bittner (1965) and Burrell and Morgan (1979) to argue that traditional (functionalism, objective) research has an inherent language problem. While

> such terms as "structure," "resources" and even "organization" are typifications that organizational actors invoke to make sense of their everyday experience . . . social scientists [should] address themselves to the ways organizational members use such terms as "structure," "hierarchy," and "resources," as concepts for constructing an organizational world. In other words these constructs should become the topic of analysis rather than tools for analysis (pp. 223–224).

To get a feel for the "culture-as-sense-making" perspective, substitute displayers and indicators of organizational culture (stories, rites, values) for the preceding organizational terms. The key idea is not that an organization has such displayers, but how organizational members may have created them, how they use them to construct a context that has impact on their interpretation of events, and how they sustain or alter them through communication. The emphasis on a subjectively constructed world is not new (Berger & Luckmann, 1966; Geertz, 1973, 1983; Hallowell, 1955; Schutz, 1967). What is more contemporary is the incorporation and application of the ideas to organizational communication. Because of the variety of meanings attached to culture and because some of those meanings challenge traditional beliefs, certain issues arise.

Organizational Culture Issues

We have explored what organizational culture is and how it might be described. However, it is evident that different definitions of culture lead to different cultural theories. Such definitions are influenced by different objective and subjective views. In addition to what it is and how it should be studied, the concept of organizational culture raises a number of other issues. What is the appropriate level of cultural analysis? What is the purpose of cultural analysis? Can culture be managed? What are the ethical implications of such study? How can such cultural analyses be evaluated? What is the value of cultural analysis?

Level of Analysis   Organizational culture can be studied at different levels, including macroanalytic and microanalytic perspectives. For example, the organization itself can be viewed as being embedded in the larger cultural context of society (Smith & Simmons, 1983); the organization might be seen as participating in a distinctive culture developed within a particular industry (Putnam, 1985); the organization can be studied as a single, unified cultural entity (Meyer, 1982a,b); and a fourth analytic level views organizations as being composed of a number of subcultural groups (Watson, 1983; Riley, 1983; and Schall, 1983). All of these levels represent legitimate areas of study. However, it is important to identify the boundaries of study and the significance of those boundaries. For example, Van Maanen and Barley (1985) state that "unitary organizational cultures evolve when all members of an organization face roughly the same problems, when everyone communicates with almost everyone else, and when each member adopts a common set of understandings for enacting proper and consensually approved behavior" (p. 37). Thus, an organization can be viewed as a homogenous, unitary collective; however, the discovery of cultural action in organizational life is more likely to take place at the group level of analysis. This discovery depends upon finding elements or actions that make one group different from another. Subcultures are more likely to exhibit those actions.

What Is the Purpose of Cultural Analysis?   The answer to this question usually promotes conflict because the traditional literature is so heavily invested in the managerial perspective. This managerial bias assumes that good knowledge is knowledge that helps one manage in the most efficient way. The traditional (functionalist) approach centers on the management of organizations. It emphasizes predictability, control, and an objective world view. Although a number of purposes of cultural analysis could be examined, we will discuss two general ones that contrast the schools of thought. The first looks at cultural analysis as a tool for managing organizational effectiveness. The second considers cultural analysis as a means of understanding. The managerial perspective sees culture as a given—a tool that can be used to analyze a situation in order to improve the situation. It is almost as if an understanding has already been achieved and that the things that make up culture can be used. For example, Deal and Kennedy (1982) explore four key attributes of organizational culture and then emphasize that "strong" organizational cultures lead to bottom-line concerns—profit and continuity. Popular managerial (and simplistic) perspectives treat culture as the magic element (variable) that can be manipulated to lead to high profits and national visibility. When applied as a formula, the notion of culture has not reached expectations (Rhodes, 1986). Even in a more sophisticated treatment (Pfeffer, 1981), the focus is on the management of symbolism for the purpose of meeting the goals of those in charge. If humans are thought of as adaptive agents who respond to forces in their environment, then a manager who controls the symbolic environment would be able to regulate behavior. Of course, the nature of humans and ideas about control are very much at issue. We do not use the term "managerial bias" in a pejorative sense but rather to indicate the purpose and interest of a particular group. When cultural analysis is approached as a means of understanding, the purposes are more inclusive and complex.

Organizational culture does not belong to management; it belongs to all members of the organization. Cultural analysis does not stress what *should* happen from management's perspective but what *does* happen. Organizational culture can exist in any organization and organization can refer to a variety of groups. Size is not the issue; organizing activity is. Culture is not a tool of analysis but an object of analysis. It is not a given that should be taken for granted. It must be discovered through the eyes of the people that create it. Culture is not a concrete thing, but the emergent behaviors that create and sustain the patterns that can be called culture.

Theorists treat the notion of "understanding" in a variety of ways. Pacanowsky and O'Donnell-Trujillo (1982) state: "we are interested in understanding how that organizational life is accomplished communicatively" (p. 122). The purpose of an analysis is to discover how culture is enacted or performed through communication (Pacanowsky & O'Donnell-Trujillo, 1983). If one understands the idea of performance in an organization and what it means, a big step has been taken toward understanding the culture. Smircich (1983), referring to interpretive research and consulting, concludes that "the ultimate purpose is to lead to a more informed, more self-conscious organization (p. 239). Theorists who stress cultural analysis as a means of understanding are careful to avoid the functionalist notions of prediction and control. They focus on taken-for-granted behaviors and concepts because so little is known about how organizations create their realities and the impact of those creations.

Understanding and self-awareness are not sterile concepts. Understanding, or knowledge, has a number of potential and significant uses. It allows an organization to examine its underlying logic so that it might critique and change itself. Just as consciousness-raising groups remind their members of certain inequities, an organization that engages in the reflective process can do the same. A critique of an organization should not be limited to its profit-making ability. The type of knowledge produced by cultural analysis can serve several functions. For the student of organizational behavior, "organizational culture research has theory-generative, theory-contextualizing, and even theory-testing possibilities [for the participant] . . . Each organizational culture study can provide any member (manager, worker, volunteer) with an overall picture of the organization" (Pacanowsky & O'Donnell-Trujillo, 1982, p. 129). This knowledge not only helps people see the underlying logic of what they do; but self-examination and awareness of the sense-making process can also trigger change.

Can Culture Be Managed?   Different schools of thought conflict on this issue.

> Culture pragmatists generally see culture as a key to commitment, productivity, and profitability. They argue that culture can be—indeed, should be and has been—managed. . . . Culture purists . . . find it ridiculous to talk of managing culture. Culture cannot be managed; it emerges. Leaders don't create cultures; members of the culture do. Culture is an expression of people's deepest needs, a means of endowing their experiences with meaning (Martin, 1985, p. 95).

The answer to the question of whether culture can be managed depends on one's definition of culture. The more complex the definition, the more difficult the management issue becomes. It is easier to deal with cultural artifacts than with deeply rooted sense-making processes. When large-scale cultural changes are considered, both objectivists and subjectivists agree that such changes are difficult and quite costly. Even the most popular versions of organizational culture (Deal & Kennedy, 1982) recognize the high costs.

Uttal (1983), writing in *Fortune*, suggests that "for all the hype, corporate culture is real and powerful. It's also hard to change, and you won't find much support for doing so inside or outside your company. If you run up against the culture when trying to redirect strategy, attempt to dodge it. If you must meddle with culture directly, tread carefully and with modest expectations" (p. 72). Although such a statement shows skepticism of cultural change, the key word is *expectations*. Massive cultural overhauls are extremely difficult. That does not mean that managers cannot have impact on significant aspects of a culture. Martin (1985) maintains that when theorists consider the question of managing culture, they prefer to rephrase it to "Are there conditions under which culture can be managed?" She concludes that although different authors hold divergent views about what culture is, these same authors agree about the kinds of conditions that expedite or block the management of culture. The answer to the question of managing culture, then, depends on one's definition of culture, the nature of the process or change, and the conditions underlying the change or management process.

What Are the Ethical Implications? If culture is an "expression of people's deepest needs, a means of endowing their experiences with meaning" as suggested earlier, then once the culture is exposed, whose interest should be served by that knowledge? If cultural analysis gets at the very core of meaning for humans in the workplace, how is that knowledge to be used? Can all voices of the organization be heard? There are many concerns about the interests that dominate workplace decision making (Habermas, 1972, 1975)—certainly more than we can discuss here. We leave that important task to the critic. Nevertheless, it is important to state the issues, even in capsule form. Deetz (1985) asks, "Do we as a society like or want to be what current organizational practices recommend for us? Is there any way we or anyone else can have a say in the matter? In what ways is wider representation possible? To me, these are the critical ethical questions" (p. 266). Deetz suggests that those who do cultural analysis should go beyond the goal of understanding, because "merely understanding the means by which consensual realities are formed and perpetrated says little about whether such a consensus adequately represents different competing interests" (1985, p. 268). Deetz (1992) asserts that corporate organizations provide controlling structures that are embodied in everyday routines and technologies that appear enabling and apolitical. However, they do not rest on open consent, and people are not aware of the control that is being exerted. It is important to examine the conditions of consensus, power distributions, and the interests represented.

How Should Cultural Analysis Be Evaluated? The question of what counts as good cultural analysis may receive a variety of answers. The concept of organizational culture not only has given rise to conflicting definitions but it also has prompted a variety of research methods, goals, and outcomes. The standards for cultural analysis are still being developed. Strine and Pacanowsky (1985) take a cue from Weick (1983) by selecting "good" examples of interpretive research and discussing what makes them good. They do not develop a set of guidelines for evaluating research, but provide a framework within which evaluation can take place. This framework is concerned with the intended audience of the analysis and how an author functions as a source of authority. Cultural analyses may be presented from the authority of an analytic scientist, conceptual theorist, conceptual humanist, or particular humanist. All of the authorized positions require different evaluative guidelines. Each is responsive to a particular audience and nuance of organizational life. This approach illustrates the complex and ongoing nature of creating evaluative criteria for cultural analysis. General guidelines derived from studies of routines and practices in the organizational setting help in assessing cultural studies. The following evaluative questions are derived from statements made by Bantz (1983) concerning criteria for evaluating research that emphasizes the subjective constructions and interpretations of organizational participants.

1. Does the study provide descriptions and interpretations of organizational messages, meanings, and expectations?
2. Are the organization's messages, meanings, and expectations presented as understood by the members of the organization?
3. Is the organization, as presented, recognizable to members of the organization (not identical or accepted, but recognizable)?
4. Do the findings of the study make the organization accessible to nonmembers?
5. Is the final product skillful in its use of argument and language?

Although evaluating cultural analysis is likely to provoke disagreement among theorists, these are some features that appear necessary for "good" studies. Such studies are descriptive—so much so that one can "feel" the organization. Geertz (1973) uses the term "thick description" to refer to the type of narrative that helps one see and feel the subtleties of organizational life. A presentation of this sort works the same way as a good novel or movie. It helps one imagine and get "caught up" in the story. If the purpose is to understand, emphasis is placed on description and interpretation. It is more important to understand what a culture is, and what it makes possible, than to label it good or bad. Judgments will no doubt be made, but studies that concentrate on description and interpretation are more likely to give a complete and full account of organizational life. Good studies reveal how organizational members make sense of and construct their world. They give the reader a sound idea of what it would be like to be a part of such an organization. The reader knows what he or she would have to know to function in the organization and what it would take to fit in or advance in the organization.

Finally, the significance of the use of argument and language cannot be overestimated. Pacanowsky and O'Donnell-Trujillo (1982) contend that "an account of organizational culture begs not for an assessment of its reliability and validity, but for an assessment of its plausibility and its insight" (p. 123). Plausibility and insight are determined by argument and language. The quality of the writing is critical to the evaluation of cultural analysis. Some would go so far as to say that the truth of the interpretive study lies in its writing (Pacanowsky, 1981).

What Is the Value of Cultural Analysis?   What does cultural analysis tell us? There is usually less conflict about such questions when culture is treated as just another element (variable) in the traditional view of organizations. In that case culture is considered to be a potent variable that has impact on organizational performance. But what does a subjective approach tell us? We would contend that an organization that has a better understanding of itself is in a better position to critique and change itself. In a pragmatic sense, to understand the sense-making processes in an organization is also to understand the basis for decision making and managing. Managers have been criticized for not being people oriented and for lacking sensitivity in the management process. To what should they be sensitive? D'Aprix (1982) suggests that a manager must learn the "appropriate touches" with his or her people. An understanding of the sense-making process and how members construct a particular reality gives insight into sensitivity and the appropriate touches.

Because cultural analysis focuses on taken-for-granted behavior and excludes preconceived scientific constructs, it is sometimes accused of not saying much. However, an interesting contradiction arises. This type of research often presents a threat to organizations. Conventional research tends to present findings in a very global, generalized way without specific reference to individuals; cultural analysis can get very specific and tell a great deal about individuals. Specific language is linked to specific individuals and parts of the organization. Conventional research allows the organization to know ahead of time just what will be studied and how. Outcomes may be more a matter of demonstration than discovery. This is not true for cultural analysis, which examines emergent behavior and networks of meaning. Researchers arrive at significant questions; they do not start with them. Just where the inquiry may lead cannot be specified at the outset. Skrtic (1985) states that "Administrators of organizations who would rather not have their problems understood so clearly would do well to choose conventional over qualitative research into their operations" (p. 215). Viewed in this way, cultural analysis may tell too much!

Cultural analysis is useful in that it helps us understand what is going on in particular situations. Smith and Eisenberg (1987) used a root metaphor analysis as a way to gain insight into conflict in an organization. If conflicts can be identified and explicated in this way, it is likely that they can be anticipated and perhaps even managed. Rosen (1991) studied an advertising agency and demonstrated that social drama is the process through which power relations, symbolic action, and their interaction reveal social structure and the mechanisms of control. This type of knowledge is necessary not only to increase awareness but to achieve change. Meyerson (1991) explored hospital social work to develop a theory about how social workers experienced ambiguity. Her findings provide insight into how cultural forces shape what those experiences mean and whether or not they are perceived as legitimate. This adds a significant dimension to traditional views of ambiguity in the organization. Bastien (1992) asserts that organizational culture has been a useful analytic frame for organizational mergers and acquisitions. His study offers insight into the processes of accommodation and change. Many other studies could be cited. The major point is that to "understand" something is to "know" about it. In the case of cultural analysis it may be a different way of knowing, but it provides insight and as such that insight can be used in a variety of ways.

In addition to contributing to pragmatic concerns, cultural analysis adds another dimension to our understanding of organizational life. Understanding can be looked at in a *technical* (cognitive) sense, but there is also a *feeling* (affective) sense that deserves consideration. Smircich (1985) suggests that "organizations are representations of our humanity, like music or art; they can be known through acts of appreciation. . . . Organizations are symbolically constituted worlds, like novels or poems; they can be known through acts of critical reading and interpretation. . . . Organizations are symbolic forms, like religion and folklore; they are displays of the meaning of life" (p. 66). Trujillo (1992) gives some insight into this notion in his study of ballpark culture. He uses the category of "romantic" as a world view to focus on the rich identification and pure joy that many of the participants experience at the ballpark. Our breadth of understanding should have room for more than the technical issues. An understanding that contains feeling not only tells us more about organizational life but it can also tell us something about ourselves. The organization is a fascinating object of study because it is a human object that represents part of all of us. How capable an individual is in "reading" and appreciating an organization demands more than technical knowledge.

Implications for Organizational Communication

The role of communication in organizational culture can be seen differently depending on how culture is conceptualized. If culture is thought of as a collection of symbolic artifacts communicated to organizational members for organizational control, then communication can be conceived of as a vehicle that enables that outcome. If culture is construed as sense making, the process of communication itself becomes the focal point of interest because that is what sense making is. Both stances have value, but we will stress the implications of the subjective view because it adds a different dimension to traditional study.

The study of organizational communication from a cultural perspective involves more than examining only the official exchanges between selected people with status. Everyday talk reveals organizational sense making and networks of shared meanings that may exist. Taken-for-granted behaviors that allow routine and organizing to exist are embedded in communication.

The way messages are interpreted depends on the symbolically created context in which they occur. Predicting the reactions to messages has little chance of accuracy without a knowledge of the organizational context. One cannot be sensitive to a different culture without being sensitive to its language. The same holds true for organizational culture. It is necessary to know and be able to interpret how an organization uses language.

Those who engage in organizational change must inevitably identify and deal with organizational culture. From a sense-making perspective this means knowing how an organization communicates. To know a culture is to understand what it makes possible for its members. Looked at in traditional terms, a particular organization might appear to be irrational and disorganized, but the organization may have created a culture that works for it. Even communication that seems random, contradictory, and obtuse may serve important functions for the members of an organization.

SUMMARY

In this chapter our goal was to illustrate the impact of subjectivism on organizational communication. We selected two prominent contemporary organizational theories that represent subjective thinking, we explained why each theory has achieved recognition, and we described the prominence of communication concepts in each. In addition, we explored the issues raised by the theories. Finally, we discussed the implications each theory has for organizational communication.

In Part Three we will discuss issues in organizational communication arising from a functionalist perspective. If we were to derive the issues from a subjectivist position, they would no doubt be cast in a different way. We believe that the subjectivist view does inform, and for that reason we have added a subjectivist reminder for each issue. Even a note stressing that a point of concern may be a nonissue provides contrast and a note of caution. When ideas stand in opposition, they are more likely to receive greater scrutiny.

REFERENCES

BANTZ, CHARLES R., "Naturalistic Research Traditions," in *Communication and Organizations: An Interpretive Approach*, Linda Putnam and Michael E. Pacanowsky, eds. Beverly Hills, Calif.: Sage Publications, Inc., 1983.

BASTIEN, DAVID T., "Change in Organizational Culture, the Use of Linguistic Methods in a Corporate Acquisition," *Management Communication Quarterly*, 5 (May 1992), 403–442.

BERGER, P. L., and T. LUCKMANN, *The Social Construction of Reality*. Garden City, N.Y.: Doubleday, 1966.

BITTNER, E., "The Concept of Organization," *Social Research*, 32 (1965), 239–255.

BURRELL, G., and Gareth Morgan, *Sociological Paradigms and Organizational Analysis*. London: Heinemann, 1979.

CLARK, DAVID L., "Emerging Paradigms in Organization Theory and Research," in *Organizational Theory and Inquiry: The Paradigm Revolution*, Yvonna S. Lincoln, ed. Beverly Hills, Calif.: Sage Publications, Inc., 1985.

D'APRIX, ROGER, *Communication for Productivity*. New York: Harper & Row, Pub., 1982.

DANDRIDGE, THOMAS, IAN MITROFF, and WILLIAM JOYCE, "Organization Symbolism: A Topic to Expand Organizational Analysis," *Academy of Management Review*, 5 (1980), 77–82.

DEAL, TERRENCE E., and ALLAN A. KENNEDY, *Corporate Culture: The Rites and Rituals of Corporate Life*. Reading, Mass.: Addison-Wesley, 1982.

DEETZ, STANLEY, "Ethical Considerations in Cultural Research in Organizations," in *Organizational Culture*, Peter J. Frost et al., eds. Beverly Hills, Calif.: Sage Publications, Inc., 1985.

DEETZ, STANLEY A., *Democracy in an Age of Corporate Colonization*. Albany: State University of New York Press, 1992.

GARFINKEL, HAROLD, *Studies in Ethnomethodology*. Englewood Cliffs, N.J.: Prentice-Hall, 1967.

GEERTZ, C., *The Interpretation of Cultures*. New York: Basic Books, 1973.

GEERTZ, C., *Local Knowledge: Further Essays in Interpretive Anthropology*. New York: Basic Books, 1983.

HABERMAS, J., *Knowledge and Human Interests*, trans., J. Shapiro. Boston: Beacon Press, 1972.

HABERMAS, J., *Legitimation Crisis*, trans., T. McCarthy. Boston: Beacon Press, 1975.

HALLOWELL, A. I., *Culture and Experience*. Philadelphia: University of Pennsylvania Press, 1955.

KREPS, GARY L., *Organizational Communication: Theory and Practice*. New York: Longman, 1986.

LINCOLN, YVONNA S., *Organizational Theory and Inquiry: The Paradigm Revolution*. Beverly Hills, Calif.: Sage Publications, Inc., 1985.

LOUIS, MERYL REIS, "An Investigator's Guide to Workplace Culture," in *Organizational Culture*, Peter J. Frost et al., eds. Beverly Hills, Calif.: Sage Publications, Inc., 1985.

LUNDBERG, CRAIG, "Open Letter to Karl Weick," *Journal of Applied Behavioral Science*, 18 (1982), 113–117.

MARTIN, JOANNE, "Can Organizational Culture Be Managed?," in *Organizational Culture*, Peter J. Frost et al., eds. Beverly Hills, Calif.: Sage Publications, Inc., 1985.

MEYER, ALAN D., "Adapting to Environmental Jolts," *Administrative Science Quarterly*, 27 (1982a), 515–537.

MEYER, ALAN D., "How Ideologies Supplant Formal Structures and Shape Responses to Environments," *Journal of Management Studies*, 19 (1982b), 45–61.

MEYERSON, DEBRA, "Normal Ambiguity? A Glimpse of an Occupational Culture," in *Reframing Organizational Culture*, Peter J. Frost et al., eds. Newbury Park, Calif.: Sage Publications, Inc., 1991.

MORGAN, GARETH, "Paradigms, Metaphors, and Puzzle Solving in Organization Theory," *Administrative Science Quarterly*, 25 (1980), 605–622.

NAISBITT, JOHN, and PATRICIA ABURDENE, *Re-inventing the Corporation*. New York: Warner Books, 1985.

PACANOWSKY, MICHAEL E., "Writing: Science, Fiction, and the Interpretive Approach." Paper presented at the SCA/ICA Joint-Sponsored Summer Conference on Interpretive Approaches to the Study of Organizational Communication, Alta, Utah, July 26, 1981.

PACANOWSKY, MICHAEL E., and NICK O'DONNELL-TRUJILLO, "Communication and Organizational Cultures," *Western Journal of Speech Communication*, 46 (Spring 1982), 115–130.

PACANOWSKY, MICHAEL E., and NICK O'DONNELL-TRUJILLO, "Organizational Communication as Cultural Performance," *Communication Monographs*, 50 (June 1983), 126–147.

PARSONS, TALCOTT, *Structure and Process in Modern Societies*. Glencoe, Ill.: The Free Press, 1964.

PETERS, T. J., and R. H. WATERMAN, *In Search of Excellence*. New York: Harper & Row, Pub., 1982.

PFEFFER, JEFFREY, "Management as Symbolic Action: The Creation and Maintenance of Organizational Paradigms," in *Research in Organizational Behavior*, Vol. 3, pp. 1–52, Larry L. Cummings and Barry M. Staw, eds. Greenwich, Conn.: JAI Press, 1981.

PONDY, LOUIS R., and IAN I. MITROFF, "Beyond Open System Models of Organization," in *Research in Organizational Behavior*, Vol. 1, pp. 3–39, Larry L. Cummings and Barry M. Staw, eds. Greenwich, Conn.: JAI Press, 1979.

PUTNAM, LINDA L., "Bargaining as Organizational Communication," in *Organizational Communication: Traditional Themes and New Directions*, Robert D. McPhee and Philip K. Tompkins, eds. Beverly Hills, Calif.: Sage Publications, Inc., 1985.

RHODES, LUCIEN, "That's Easy for You to Say," *INC* (June 1986), 63–66.

RICOEUR, PAUL, "The Model of the Text: Meaningful Action Considered as a Text," *Social Research*, 38 (1971), 529–562.

RILEY, PATRICIA, "A Structurationist Account of Political Culture," *Administrative Science Quarterly*, 28 (1983), 414–437.

ROSEN, MICHAEL, "Breakfast at Spiro's: Dramaturgy and Dominance," in *Reframing Organizational Culture*, Peter J. Frost et al., eds. Newbury Park, Calif.: Sage Publications, Inc., 1991.

SACKMANN, SONJA A., *Cultural Knowledge in Organizations*. Newbury Park, Calif.: Sage Publications, Inc., 1991.

SCHALL, MARYAN S., "A Communication Rules Approach to Organizational Culture," *Administrative Science Quarterly*, 28 (1983), 557–581.

SCHUTZ, A., *The Problem of Social Reality*. The Hague: Martinus Nijhoff, 1967.

SCHWARTZ, P., and J. OGILVY, *The Emergent Paradigm: Changing Patterns of Thought and Belief*. Menlo Park, Calif.: SRI International, 1979.

SILVERMAN, DAVID, *The Theory of Organizations*. New York: Basic Books, 1970.

SKRTIC, THOMAS M., "Doing Naturalistic Research into Educational Organizations," in *Organizational Theory and Inquiry: The Paradigm Revolution*, Yvonna S. Lincoln, ed. Beverly Hills, Calif.: Sage Publications, Inc., 1985.

SMIRCICH, LINDA, "Studying Organizations as Cultures." Paper in preparation for *Research Strategies: Links Between Theory and Method*, Gareth Morgan, ed. March 1981.

SMIRCICH, LINDA, "Implications for Management Theory," in *Communication and Organizations: An Interpretive Approach*, Linda L. Putnam and Michael E. Pacanowsky, eds. Beverly Hills, Calif.: Sage Publications, Inc., 1983.

SMIRCICH, LINDA, "Is the Concept of Culture a Paradigm for Understanding Organizations and Ourselves?," in *Organizational Culture*, Peter J. Frost et al., eds. Beverly Hills, Calif.: Sage Publications, Inc., 1985.

SMIRCICH, LINDA, and MARTA B. CALAS, "Organizational Culture: A Critical Assessment," in *Handbook of Organizational Communication*, Fredric M. Jablin et al., eds. Newbury Park, Calif.: Sage Publications, Inc., 1987.

SMITH, KENWYNK, and VALERIE M. SIMMONS, "A Rumpelstiltskin Organization: Metaphors on Metaphors in Field Research," *Administrative Science Quarterly*, 28 (1983), 377–392.

SMITH, RUTH C., and ERIC M. EISENBERG, "Conflict at Disneyland: A Root-Metaphor Analysis," *Communication Monographs*, 34 (December 1987), 367–380.

STRINE, MARY S., and MICHAEL E. PACANOWSKY, "How to Read Interpretive Accounts of Organizational Life: Narrative Bases of Textual Authority," *The Southern Speech Communication Journal*, 50 (Spring 1985), 283–297.

TRUJILLO, NICK, "Interpreting (the Work and Talk of) Baseball: Perspectives on Ballpark Culture," *Western Journal of Communication*, 56 (Fall 1992), 350–371.

TURNER, BARRY A., *Exploring the Industrial Subculture*. London: Macmillan, 1971.

UTTAL, BRO, "The Corporate Culture Vulture," *Fortune* (October 17, 1983), 67–72.

VAN MAANEN, JOHN, and STEPHEN R. BARLEY, "Cultural Organization: Fragments of a Theory," in *Organizational Culture*, Peter J. Frost et al., eds. Beverly Hills, Calif.: Sage Publications, Inc., 1985.

WATSON, TONY J., "Group Ideologies and Organizational Change," *Journal of Management Studies*, 19 (1982), 259–275.

WEICK, KARL E., *The Social Psychology of Organizing*. Reading, Mass.: Addison-Wesley, 1969.

WEICK, KARL E., "Educational Organizations as Loosely Coupled Systems," *Administrative Science Quarterly*, 21 (1976), 1–19.

WEICK, KARL E., "Enactment Processes in Organizations," in *New Directions in Organizational Behavior*, Barry M. Staw and Gerald R. Salancik, eds. Chicago: St. Clair Press, 1977a.

WEICK, KARL E., "Re-Punctuating the Problem," *New Perspectives on Organizational Effectiveness*, Paul S. Goodman and Johannes M. Pennings, eds. San Francisco: Jossey-Bass, 1977b.

WEICK, KARL E., *The Social Psychology of Organizing*, 2nd ed. Reading, Mass.: Addison-Wesley, 1979.

WEICK, KARL E., "Organizational Communication: Toward a Research Agenda," in *Communication and Organizations: An Interpretive Approach*, Linda L. Putnam and Michael E. Pacanowsky, eds. Beverly Hills, Calif.: Sage Publications, Inc., 1983.

WEICK, KARL E., "Sources of Order in Underorganized Systems: Themes in Recent Organizational Theory," in *Organizational Theory and Inquiry: The Paradigm Revolution*, Yvonna S. Lincoln, ed. Beverly Hills, Calif.: Sage Publications, Inc., 1985.

WITTGENSTEIN, LUDWIG, *Philosophical Investigations*, trans. G.E.M. Anscombe. Oxford: Blackwell, 1968.

6

Organizational Communication and Motivation
X-Efficiency and Communication

Of all the issues in the fields of communication, management, and leadership, probably the most popular is that of motivation. When we talk about motivation we are talking about reasons why people devote energy to a task. For example, we hired Sue to serve as a staff assistant to a team of six employees. Her responsibilities included answering the telephone, scheduling appointments, maintaining files, typing correspondence and reports, arranging meetings, keeping the office neat, and handling the budget, including recording receipts and expenditures. When she came to the job, she had to begin filing, typing, recording, and scheduling immediately. The previous staff assistant had taken another job on very short notice and had left the office with numerous stacks of untyped reports, correspondence, and assorted clutter. The telephone rang constantly, and team members asked for schedules and assistance in locating supplies and materials.

At the end of the third day on the job, Sue remained after closing time to assess how she might deal with the demands of everything that needed to be done. She spent an hour sorting through rough drafts of letters and reports, arranging them in a tentative order for typing. She looked through the appointment book and thought about the hours it would take to schedule the interviews and meetings. She stood by the filing cabinets and ran her fingers across the tabs in some drawers, reflecting on how the materials could be sorted and inserted so as to be found at some later time. After two hours of sorting and looking and thinking, she slumped into a chair and stared at the floor.

The next morning she arrived at work before seven and typed several short items before other employees began to stop at her office. Throughout the morning she typed, answered the telephone, and filled requests. During the lunch hour, between bites of a sandwich and sipping a soda, Sue stacked and filed papers. After lunch she completed a report and several pieces of correspondence. By closing time she had made good progress on the pile of typing. For an hour after everyone else had left the building, Sue sorted and filed papers. She arrived at the office at about seven the following morning.

A CONCEPT OF MOTIVATION

Sue was motivated. She was willing to devote large amounts of both physical and mental energy into performing the job. Of course, individuals differ in the amounts of energy, enthusiasm, and persistence they are willing to invest in their work. Nevertheless, the more energy a person puts into a job, the more we say that person is motivated. The question that has puzzled managers for a long time is, "Why do some people work hard whereas others do as little as possible?" The answer lies in the degree to which people are willing to direct their behaviors toward some goal. Sue was willing to do this. She was motivated. Motivation was inside her. No one motivated Sue; she motivated herself.

The field of economics takes as its main concern the efficient use of resources; however, one of its assumptions has been, at least until the development by Leibenstein (1978) of X-efficiency theory, that firms or organizations are internally efficient, which means that they produce maximum output for a particular set of resources (sometimes called *technical efficiency*). This assumption has the corollary assumption that organizations naturally minimize costs.

X-efficiency theory rejects the blatant assumption that organizations function with maximum efficiency and postulates that certain *nonallocative inefficiencies* (versus allocative inefficiencies that derive from the way in which resources are allocated among their competing uses) occur in the organization. Because the nonallocative efficiencies and inefficiencies have been ignored or unidentified in economic theory, they are referred to as *X (or unknown) efficiencies*, and *inefficiencies* (Frantz, 1988, pp. 9–10).

From Frantz's (1988) review of the literature on organization internal efficiency, we discover some of the elements that fall within the scope of X-efficiency:

> Studies of productivity in nine countries, including Burma, Greece, India, Indonesia, Israel, Malaya, Pakistan, Singapore, and Thailand, indicated that "simple alterations in the physical organization of a plant's productive process" lead to relatively large increases in labor productivity and, thus, relatively large decreases in unit costs. The alterations included changes in the layout of the plant, utilization of machines, handling of materials, work flows, waste control, method of payment to employees, worker training, and supervision, none of which are allocative efficiencies.
>
> Studies in thirty-one U.S. and United Kingdom companies showed U.S. labor productivity to be on the average, in 1962, 120 percent higher than that in the United Kingdom, but in cases where the equipment was almost identical there were still major differences in output per worker, suggesting that other factors than resource allocation may have been key in creating efficiencies. Other factors were identified as work flow, factory conditions involving light and heat, hours worked, method of wage payments, work simplification, labor turnover,

and motivation of workers. These other factors, the report indicates, are partly organizational factors and partly factors affecting the willingness and ability of workers to devote effort.

A study of two petroleum refineries in Egypt that were less than a half mile from each other revealed that the productivity of one was double the other for years, but under completely new management the inefficient refinery made spectacular improvements in efficiency with the **same labor force**, clearly suggesting that inefficiencies may be affected by management approaches (Frantz, 1988, pp. 46–53).

The critical difference between X-efficient and X-inefficient organizations lies in the principle of *worker effort discretion*, which says that the performance of employees depend on how well they are motivated, whereas traditional economic theory assumes that work effort is fixed. Worker effort discretion also means that employees make choices that affect the amount of effort they put into their work.

From an economics point of view, four key elements comprise the concept of *effort* at work: (1) the activities (A) that constitute a person's work, (2) the rate (R) at which the activities are performed, (3) the precision (P) or attentiveness with which the person performs the activities that lead to quality, and (4) the time-pattern (T) or rhythm with which the activities are performed (Frantz, 1988, pp. 75–76).

The choices a person exercises regarding the amount of effort to be devoted to or directed at work are affected by individual characteristics and pressures that occur as a member of a group. Effort should, therefore, be viewed as an outcome of individual choices about and responses to both personal—biological and psychological—and environmental or group factors.

Through the employment process, organizations purchase employee *time*, while working efficiently requires *directed effort*, which is *not* purchased, at least not directly. For example, a "contract" to purchase a shirt is different from an employment contract. When you order a shirt, you know pretty much what you will receive as a result of what you pay—you will get a shirt. When an organization purchases "time," however, there is no fixed exchange between the time purchased and the effort expended to produce something. In doing their work, employees have a certain amount of discretion in the amount of effort they expend to get their work done. They can exert a great deal of effort or they can exert minimal effort. This makes an employee's performance pretty much dependent upon what we call *motivation*.

X-inefficiencies result from untapped opportunities due to lack of motivation and behaviors not directed toward cost minimization. X-inefficiencies raise costs and lower productivity. Most of the X-inefficiencies in organizational functioning tie into the way in which individuals communicate with one another in organizations. Frantz (1988) argues that an individual's directed effort is influenced by one's peers and supervisors, as well as by the traditions and history, often called the culture, of the organization (pp. 83–84).

X-efficiencies, we assume, are achieved through vertical relationships that create pressure for more effort, individual satisfactions from avoiding such pressures, and satisfactions from receiving the approval of supervisors; in sum, most organization members may exert more effort to avoid unnecessary hassles and to receive recognition for a job well done. So, without additional costs, we produce more, resulting in efficiencies.

Horizontal relationships create pressure in two ways: (1) through the norm that all group members should carry their share of the load, after which they are free to work as hard as they like, and (2) the norm that individuals may do as little as they want, but they must not work so hard that it makes others look bad (Frantz, 1988, p. 87).

Focus on X-Efficiency Factors

The turnaround of the Ford Motor plant in Louisville, Kentucky, after 1979 is an example of how focusing on X-efficiency factors may make a difference in productivity (Main, 1983). Prior to 1979 the Ford assembly plant was known as a "war zone," characterized as filthy, with openly hostile labor-management relations, autocratic managers, intransigent union leaders, mutual distrust, and little concern for employees. Then, in 1979, the demand for cars made in the Louisville plant declined sharply and the night shift was laid off. Rumors circulated that the plant would be closed.

Both the plant's manager and union head were replaced at the same time. The new leaders recognized that self-destructive behavior was not necessary. It was also announced that the plant had six months to turn things around or it would be shut down.

Small but important employee requests, such as lunch tables, were responded to by management. A quality-of-work-life program was instituted, and serious ongoing discussions with employees resulted in many other small changes. One large change was to replace the tradition of having designers send their plans directly to manufacturing where the product was built. A great deal of needless effort was spent trying to follow plans that seemed unnecessarily difficult. Under the new procedures, the plans were displayed on the plant floor after which comments were invited before the manufacturing phase began.

By early 1980 the plant was turning out high-quality products, and by the end of 1980 the parent company decided to invest $700 million in the production of the Ford Ranger. Quality inspection concerns dropped from 700 per 100 cars to 198, the lowest in Ford's U.S. history. Much of the credit for the Ford turnaround was achieved by focusing on X-efficiency factors, highlighted primarily by changes in communication, motivation, and leadership or management styles.

DIFFERENCES BETWEEN SUPERVISORS AND EMPLOYEES ON WHAT MOTIVATES WORKERS

Although a great deal has been written on the topic of motivation, managers often base their decisions about employee motivation on erroneous information about what actually motivates employees. The sad truth is that supervisors frequently are out of touch with what employees want from their jobs. Kovach (1980) argues that employee attitudes and actual factors that motivate employees change more rapidly than does a supervisor's knowledge about what motivates workers. He claims that most theories of motivation are outdated by the time they are implemented. To support his claim, Kovach replicated the 1946 study completed by the Labor Relations Institute of New York in which first-line supervisors and employees who worked directly for them ranked ten items that provide motivation on the job. The results

TABLE 6.1 What Motivates Employees*

	1946		1979	
	EMPLOYEE	SUPERVISOR	EMPLOYEE	SUPERVISOR
Full appreciation of work done	1	8	2	8
Feeling of being in on things	2	9	3	10
Sympathetic help with personal problems	3	10	9	9
Job security	4	2	4	2
Good wages	5	1	5	1
Interesting work	6	5	1	5
Promotion and growth in the organization	7	3	6	3
Personal loyalty to employees	8	6	8	7
Good working conditions	9	4	7	4
Tactful discipline	10	7	10	6

Source: From Kenneth A. Kovach, "Why Motivational Theories Don't Work," *S.A.M. Advanced Management Journal* (Spring 1980), 54–59. Used by permission of *SAM Advanced Management Journal*.

*Rankings range from 1 to 10: 1, most important; 10, least important.

indicated that a gap existed between what employees wanted from their jobs and what supervisors thought employees wanted. Kovach administered the 1946 questionnaire to a group of over 200 employees and their immediate supervisors to see whether the results were similar. The findings of the 1946 study and Kovach's 1979 study are shown in Table 6.1. An analysis of the results indicates that with the exception of the ranking of "sympathetic help with personal problems," the gap between supervisors and their employees has not narrowed. For example, the items *security* and *wages* were ranked by employees in 1946 as having intermediate importance for them and were ranked by supervisors as having high importance for employees, whereas *appreciation of work* and *feeling in on things* were ranked as having high importance for employees, yet supervisors perceived those items as being of low importance to employees. The same discrepancies were discovered by the 1979 study. Differences in perceptions between supervisors and employees on what motivates employees still appear to exist.

Some of the differences between what employees feel motivates them and what supervisors feel motivates employees may be found in changing attitudes and values. However, most people have choices to make between different ways of satisfying needs and between degrees of effort they will exert toward accomplishing a particular goal. A person's actual motivation (effort directed toward a goal) may be a function of his or her expectations that a certain investment of energy will result in the accomplishment of a particular goal. Vroom's expectancy theory of motivation (1964) helps to explain how what a person values and what a person expects can have an effect on motivation.

THEORIES OF MOTIVATION

The term "motivation" refers to the basic conditions that impel action. The relationship between motivation and action can be diagrammed as shown in Figure 6.1.

CONDITIONS	DECISIONS BASE	RESULTS
Deficiencies	Predispositions	Action
Maslow		
Alderfer		
Herzberg		
Expectations	Goals	Action
Vroom		
Perceptions	Potentials	Action
Pace		

FIGURE 6.1 Factors in Motivation Theories

Figure 6.1 identifies the fundamental conditions underlying decisions to behave in a particular way. One set of theories takes need deficiencies as the impelling condition that leads to certain predispositions to behave, whereas another theory takes expectations in the environment as leading to certain types of goals and subsequent action; a third theory takes perceptions of the workplace as leading to certain types of potentials that impel actions.

Let us look at each of the types of motivation theories.

DEFICIENCY THEORIES OF MOTIVATION

Some of the most common theories of motivation refer to needs as the driving forces of human behavior. We shall review three explanations of how needs function to motivate people:

Hierarchy theory
ERG theory
Motivator-Hygiene theory

A *need* is something that is essential, indispensable, or inevitable to fill a condition. The term *need* is also used to refer to the lack of something. Thus the concept of a need is something that is lacking and must be filled. We are told that all behaviors are responses to satisfy needs. What kinds of needs do we try to satisfy?

Hierarchy Theory

Maslow (1943, 1954) proposed that our needs fall into five categories: physiological; safety or security; belongingness or social; esteem; and self-actualization, as portrayed in Figure 6.2. These needs, according to Maslow, develop in a hierarchical order, with physiological needs being the most prepotent until satisfied. A *prepotent* need has great influence over other needs as long as it is unsatisfied. For example, it is difficult, although not impossible, to give full attention to saving for the future when you feel strong hunger pains. As someone observed, it is tough to be concerned about mosquitoes when you are standing up to your waist in alligators. Thus physiological needs urge to be satisfied before all others. Nevertheless, a lower-order need might not have to be completely satisfied before the next higher one becomes active, as suggested by the overlapping lines of the spiral. You might very easily be concerned about your safety even if you seem fatigued. However, it is quite likely that a major portion of the prepotent need will have to be satisfied before the next order becomes a strong motivator. The concept of prepotency postulates also that a satisfied need is no longer a motivator. Only unsatisfied needs impel people to action and direct their behaviors toward a goal.

The five sets of needs are arranged in a hierarchical order, with *physiological* being the lower order, *safety and security* next, *belonging* in the middle, *esteem* needs higher, and *self-actualization* needs being the highest order. Once bodily needs are satisfied, a person seeks satisfaction for safety and security needs; then when a person feels secure, he or she is motivated by the next level of needs—esteem. When a worker is able to satisfy all of the lower needs, what he or she considers most important or satisfying is to be able to feel that one is doing something of value and is being fulfilled as a person.

FIGURE 6.2 Maslow's Needs Hierarchy

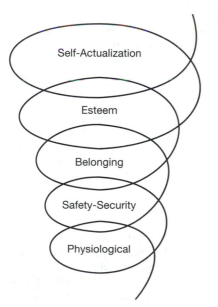

ERG Theory

Alderfer (1972) identified three categories of needs, in comparison to Maslow's five levels of needs. The three types of needs are *existence* (E), *relatedness* (R), and *growth* (G). Existence includes physiological needs such as hunger, thirst, and sex, as well as material needs such as compensation and a desirable work environment. Relatedness needs involve relationships with those who are important to us, such as family members, friends, and work supervisors. Growth needs concern our desires to be productive and creative so as to achieve our potential. These three needs areas are similar to Maslow's and, in fact, span the entire range of needs as suggested by Maslow. In general, the ERG needs concept is a refinement of Maslow's needs system, but they differ in two respects. First, although the order of the needs is similar, the idea of hierarchy is not included. Alderfer argues that if the existence needs are not satisfied, their influence may be strong, but the other need categories may still be important in directing behaviors toward goals. Second, he also claims that even though a need may be satisfied, it may continue as a dominant influence in decisions. You may, for example, have a reasonably good salary and a secure job but continue to seek raises, even though existence needs seem fairly well satisfied. In that case a satisfied need may continue to be a motivator. On the other hand, relatedness and growth needs may increase in intensity as they are satisfied. The more you discover ways to be productive and creative, the more you want to be increasingly productive and creative.

Motivator-Hygiene Theory

Herzberg (1966) attempted to determine what factors influence worker motivation in organizations. He discovered two sets of activities that satisfy a person's needs: (1) those related to job satisfaction and (2) those related to job dissatisfaction. Factors affecting job satisfaction are called *motivators*. These include achievement, recognition, responsibility, advancement or promotion, the work itself, and the potential for personal growth. All of these are related to the job itself. When these factors are responded to positively, employees tend to experience satisfaction and seem motivated. However, if these factors are not present in the work, employees will lack motivation but will not be dissatisfied with their work.

Those factors related to dissatisfaction are called *maintenance* or *hygiene* factors, and include pay, supervision, job security, working conditions, administration, organizational policies, and interpersonal relationships with peers, superiors, and subordinates on the job. These factors are related to the environment or context of the job rather than the job itself. This is why programs to motivate employees using Herzberg's system refer to it as "motivation through the work itself." When these factors are responded to positively, employees do not experience satisfaction or seem motivated; however, if they are not present, employees will be dissatisfied.

Motivators are related to job satisfaction but not to dissatisfaction. Hygiene factors are related to job dissatisfaction but not to satisfaction. Thus to retain or maintain employees, managers should focus on the hygiene factors; however, to get employees to devote more energy to their jobs, managers should focus on the motivators. Managers adjust the job itself to motivate employees and adjust environmental factors to prevent dissatisfaction. For example, a supervisor who does a good job of creating positive relationships with employees will be disappointed if he or she thinks that those employees will be motivated to work harder as a result. Because supervisory relations is a hygiene

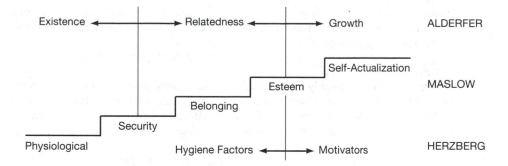

FIGURE 6.3 Three Needs Theories

factor, employees will most likely not be dissatisfied. To motivate employees, the supervisor will need to find ways to give employees greater freedom and more responsibility in doing their work, or at least give them more recognition for work done well. If employees do not get recognition, they will not necessarily be dissatisfied with their jobs, but they will not be motivated to work harder.

Comparison of Maslow's, Alderfer's, and Herzberg's Needs Categories

A great deal of similarity exists among these three ways of talking about motivation. Each system describes self-actualization, growth, and motivators in similar terms. Maintenance or hygiene factors tend to satisfy needs at the physiological and security levels as well as to satisfy the existence needs. Interpersonal relations and supervision might be considered ways to satisfy relatedness, belonging needs, and esteem needs. Figure 6.3 portrays relationships among the three approaches.

EXPECTATIONS THEORY AND MOTIVATION

Expectancy Theory

Vroom (1964) developed a theory of motivation based on the kinds of choices a person makes in seeking to achieve a goal, rather than on internal needs. Expectancy theory has three key assumptions:

   1. Every individual believes that if he or she behaves in a particular way, one will obtain certain things. This is called an *outcome expectancy*. For example, you may believe (or have an expectancy) that if you score at least an 85 on the next test, you will receive a passing grade in the course. Also, you may have the expectancy or belief that if you receive at least a B grade in the class, members of your family will approve of what you are doing. Thus we may define an outcome expectancy as *a person's subjective assessment of the probability that a particular outcome will result from that person's actions.*
   2. Every outcome has a value, worth, or attractiveness for a specific person. This is called a *valence*. For example, you may value a title or the opportunity for advancement, whereas someone else may value a retirement program or nice working conditions.

The valence or value of some aspect of the job usually results from internal needs, but the actual motivation is a more complex process. Thus we may define a valence as *the value a person places on an expected outcome.*

3. Every outcome has associated with it a perception of how hard it will be to achieve the outcome. This is called an *effort expectancy.* For example, you may have the perception that if you study the textbook very hard, you will be able to score an 85 on the next test, but that you will have to devote an exhausting amount of effort to this course in order to score a 90. Thus we may define an effort expectancy as *the probability that a person's effort will lead to accomplishing a particular goal.*

Motivation is explained by combining these three principles. A person will be motivated when he or she believes that (1) a particular behavior will lead to a particular outcome, (2) the outcome has a positive value to him or her, and (3) the outcome can be achieved by the effort one is willing to exert. Hence, a person will choose, when he or she sees alternatives, that level of performance that has the highest motivational force associated with it. When faced with one or more choices about how to behave, you will ask yourself a series of questions such as, "Can I perform at the expected level if I try?" "If I perform at the expected level, what will happen?" "Do I value those things that will happen?" You will then decide to do those things that seem to have the best chance of producing a positive, desired outcome. In other words, you will be motivated. You will be willing to devote the energy to achieve those tasks that you feel will lead to a positive outcome with the amount of effort you are willing to exert. A person's ability to perform a particular task plus the effort that a person is willing to exert to perform the task determines the level of performance. If you do not feel that you have the ability, it may not be worth the effort to try to accomplish the task. Motivation, in expectancy theory, is the decision to expend effort.

Nadler and Lawler's (1976) analysis of expectancy theory suggests some specific ways in which managers and organizations ought to handle their affairs to achieve the maximum motivation from employees:

1. *Determine what kinds of outcomes or rewards have value for employees.* It is easier to find out what people want than it is to change people to want what you have to offer. Thus the skillful manager emphasizes needs analysis rather than changing individual employees.
2. *Define precisely, in observable and measurable behaviors, what is desired from employees.* For example, tell them to "write three term papers" rather than "be a good student."
3. *Make certain that the outcomes are attainable by the employees.* If a person feels that the expected level of performance is higher than he or she can reasonably achieve, the motivation to perform will be low.
4. *Link desired outcomes to desired levels of performance.* For example, if an employee values external rewards, then you should emphasize promotion, financial gain, and recognition. Thus in expectancy theory, environmental factors such as salary may in fact be motivation. If the employee values internal rewards, then increased responsibility, challenge, and achievement should be stressed. We should not forget, however, that people's perceptions, not reality, determine their motivation. Motivation occurs only if an employee sees a relationship between rewards and expectations.
5. *Make sure that rewards are large enough to motivate significant behavior.* Trivial rewards, it is said, result in trivial effort.

6. *High performers should receive more of the desired rewards than do low performers.* Seek an equitable system of rewards, not an equal one. People and organizations usually get what they reward, not what they would like.

PERCEPTIONS THEORY OF MOTIVATION

Most of us have observed employees who reveal vitality in their work. At the same time, we see employees who lack vitality. The primary question is, "What factors contribute to and are associated with negative effects on the vitality of a person?" What fosters animation at work, and what happens to reduce a person's enthusiasm at work and what factors tend to enhance work vitality? Why do some people experience vitality and some people fail in that regard? Both research and the experience of living in organizations indicate that work vitality is revealed by four basic perceptions:

1. How well an employee's expectations are met by the organization.
2. What an employee thinks his or her opportunities are in the organization.
3. How an employee feels about the amount of fulfillment one can derive from working in the organization.
4. What perceptions an employee has of how well he or she is performing in the organization.

The place that these factors hold in a concept of work vitality follows this general line of analysis. The beginning of our careers—our life's work—is comprised, to some extent, of a set of expectations rooted in a series of perceived promises. A promise is some assurance—real or imagined—that someone or something (often the organization) will give us or help us accomplish something in the future. Employment itself is a form of promise. When we get a job, the assumption is tentatively established that the future may turn out the way we imagined it would. Continued employment reinforces the promise. Advancement on the job enables us to confirm that the promises underlying the agreement of employment are being fulfilled. If things go well, we become confident that the promises were sincere. Although some occasional setbacks may occur, on the whole, a career that progresses systematically appears, more often than not, to be based on real and sincere promises.

Expectations

Most of us started working with the anticipation and hope that what we were doing would lead to continued advances in income, position, status, responsibility, or other benefits. Reid and Evans (1983) have observed, for example, that "people begin their careers hopeful that they will be continually promoted" (p. 86). As we live and work in organizations, promises are both kept and unkept, leading to met and unmet expectations, respectively. Expectations represent what people think will happen to them. Promises are the assurances that lead to expectations. When we are assured that something will happen, we are led to expect it to happen. Thus, one major factor that reveals or reflects work vitality is a person's reactions to how well his or her expectations have been met by the organization where the person works.

Individuals who experience a form of mid-life crisis appear to engage in some assessment of how well what they have achieved corresponds with what they expected to achieve. If a difference is seen, they tend to conclude that they have failed to have their expectations met. Hellriegel, Slocum, and Woodman (1986) suggest that "burnout" among professional employees is associated with having "unrealistic expectations concerning their work and their ability to accomplish desired goals, given the nature of the situation in which they find themselves" (p. 531). The lack of vitality in an employee's work life is a failure to match expectations with realities. Niniger (1970) found that the satisfaction levels of employees whose expectations had been met were significantly higher than those whose expectations were not met.

Employees who find that their expectations are based on failed promises tend to become dissatisfied, disillusioned, frustrated, angry, defensive, and insecure. The ultimate consequence for an organization in which expectations are not met is seething unrest, potentially aggressive interaction, and low morale.

Fulfillment

One of the reasons why unmet expectations lead to such negative consequences on employees is the keen sense that failed expectations can be taken as a sign of an unfulfilled life. A fulfilled life is one in which the person feels that he or she has been able to achieve things in personal, unique, and creative ways. Fulfillment at work indicates that employees feel that they have been able to define themselves on their terms and be accepted (see Chapter 11, Power and Empowerment). What they have been able to do shows that the organization's promises and the employee's expectations have been realized and that the person's life is very satisfying. Fulfillment and hopefulness appear to go together. If you feel hopeful, it is because you also feel that promises have been kept, expectations have been realized, and that you will continue to feel satisfied by what is happening to you.

As long ago as 1946, Peter Drucker wrote in the *Concept of the Corporation* that "work appears as something unnatural, a disagreeable, meaningless and stultifying condition of getting the pay check, devoid of dignity as well as of importance. No wonder that this puts a premium on slovenly work, on slowdowns, and on other tricks to get the same pay check with less work. No wonder that results in an unhappy and discontented worker—because a pay check is not enough to base one's self-respect on" (p. 179).

Fromm (1955) explained, however, that dissatisfaction with work could be understood adequately only by differentiating between what people *consciously think* about their satisfaction, and what they *feel unconsciously* about satisfaction with work. He suggested that people may report consciously that they feel satisfied, but their dreams, psychosomatic illnesses, insomnia, and other maladies testify to their underlying unhappiness. "The tendency to repress dissatisfaction and unhappiness," Fromm noted, "is strongly supported by the widespread feeling that not to be satisfied means to be 'a failure,' queer, [or] unsuccessful. . . ." (p. 296).

Discounting the unconscious feelings of lack of fulfillment, and relying only on reports of conscious dissatisfaction, studies of worker satisfaction reported in 1951 indicated that over half of the total population of workers were dissatisfied with their work (Fromm, 1955, p. 296). Satisfaction with work between the 1950s and the 1990s does not appear to have changed considerably. Macleod (1985), for example, reported that many employees "think of the workplace in ways that are remarkably analogous to the way one might describe a *prison*. It is a place that they tolerate only because they feel they are compelled to. They 'escape' at quitting time, on weekends, for vacations—and ultimately, when they retire. Many, including some in highly paid professional and executive positions, would ruefully admit that the term 'wage slave' describes them all too accurately" (p. 215).

Macleod concludes that "prison inmates surely tend to think that their only chance for happiness and satisfaction is 'on the outside.'... [And] many employees (including professionals and executives) seem to look upon their time on the job in much the same way. They watch the clock, they daydream, they expect little satisfaction on the job" (p. 218).

Macleod's final queries seem to capture the essence of the fulfillment issue: "Is it any wonder that full job involvement and satisfaction is the exception instead of the rule? And is it any wonder that productivity, effectiveness, and efficiency are so much less than they could be?" (p. 218). But as she concludes, "surely employers can find ways to make it happen, not only for their own sake but also for the sake of better working effectiveness, productivity, and corporate success" (p. 218).

Writing about Canadian workers, Loo (1985) explained that "managers in the 1980's are faced with increased difficulties in cultivating high levels of job satisfaction among their employees.... Lessened opportunities for promotion and job mobility given the pervasive retrenchment and caution which now characterize much of Canadian business and government...lead to job dissatisfaction and can result in costly effects to the organization as a whole" (p. 22). Failure to find fulfillment at work is a pervasive malady that permeates the workplace and afflicts workers in this country and abroad.

Wenburg and Williamson (1981) articulated worker goals when they said: "to use the quality skills of self-responsibility, commitment, ability to let go of inhibiting mental habits, be willing to take positive risks—simply develop skills for letting ourselves perform life with the *presence of fulfillment*—not just *the absence of illness*" (p. 10). Satisfaction and, even more, fulfillment at work result not only in better work performance and productivity but also in a better quality of life itself. Since we are all "terminally ill" in one sense, we should settle for nothing less than a full and fulfilling work experience so that it can have a constructive effect on the rest of our life.

The search for fulfillment in all aspects of one's existence has been documented by Yankelovich (1982) in his report of cultural changes occurring in the United States since the 1960s. He explains that "the search for self-fulfillment is launching a new cultural revolution. . . . The search for self-fulfillment begins a new story because it introduces important new meanings into our culture, revolving around the struggle to lessen the influence of the instrumental forces in our lives and to heighten the sacred/expressive elements. The freedom that seekers of self-fulfillment pursue . . . is the freedom to choose one's life according to one's own design" (p. 222).

Yankelovich (1982) pinpointed the crux of the new cultural revolution focused on self-fulfillment when he observed that "by the mid-seventies a majority of the American people had reached a conclusion comparable to that reached by intellectual critics of industrial civilization in earlier years, namely, that our civilization is unbalanced, with excessive emphasis on the instrumental, and insufficient concern with the values of community, expressiveness, caring and with the domain of the sacred" (p. 229).

In clarification, Yankelovich provides this supporting analysis: Americans believed that subordinating the self to the institution made sense because it was necessary to give, to work hard, in order to get the benefits of our industrial civilization. "Americans believed that self-denial made sense, sacrifice made sense, obeying the rules made sense, subordinating the self to the institution made sense. But doubts have now set in, and Americans now believe that the old giving/getting compact needlessly restricts the individual while advancing the power of large institutions—government and business particularly—who use the power to enhance their own interests at the expense of the public" (p. 228).

Naisbitt and Aburdene (1985) assert that "corporations that cling to the outdated philosophy and structure of the old industrial era will become extinct in the new information society. Many business people have mourned the death of the work ethic in America. But few of us have applauded the logic of the new value taking its place: 'Work should be fun.' That outrageous assertion is the value that fuels the most productive people and companies in this country. . . . People know that work can be the spiritual and mental high that Peter Senge describes with the word 'alignment.' Or even the physical high that basketball player Bill Russell experienced when he played at peak performance. Or the emotional high someone at People Express feels when he or she still cries after seeing the company's presentation on its goals for the fifth time. People know intuitively that work should be fun. But only a few corporate innovators have created an environment in which fun, profit, and productivity flow" (pp. 5–6).

Naisbitt and Aburdene appear to articulate the features of fulfilling organizations when they explain that a nourishing growth environment "is a workplace where people are talking about their work, exchanging ideas, where top managers and newcomers know one another and often work together, where people are learning at company-sponsored events like lectures and concerts and through travel for specialized training or stimulation. It is a workplace where people are working on what interests them most, although it also means stretching to learn new tasks related to your job or working in new departments to get a feel for the company as a whole. We must re-invent the corporation into a place where people come to grow, instead of expecting people to satisfy the need for growth in their off-hours" (p. 60).

Clurman (1990) describes a small company in Vermont in which an employee can choose everyday "which production task she'll do. Everyday, she runs the risk of getting a free back rub or having a hilarious run-in with the company's Joy Gang. Every day, 7.5 percent of her company's pretax profits go to a worthy social cause—like the environment—that she helps choose. Not to mention such benefits as free health club memberships, profit sharing and college tuition. 'It's what a job should be,' says Carpenter, who persuaded her husband, George, to leave his family's dairy farm and work with her. 'It's not just making money, but doing good things'" (p. 4).

So far we have discussed two key elements that influence the intensity of work vitality in the life of an employee: expectations and fulfillment. Two other elements are equally important in maintaining work vitality: opportunity and performance.

Opportunity

Opportunity may be the most powerful element of the four elements influencing work vitality since it has such potentially devastating consequences when not present. We frequently think of opportunity as something that someone or something gives us. We often remark that we should *take* opportunity when it comes, or the boss is *giving* us an opportunity. Although such assertions may sound true, they fail to reveal the essence of opportunity, which is essential to a clear understanding of the concept.

A dictionary definition indicates that opportunity represents a situation or condition favorable for the attainment of a goal. Thus, if you are employed in an organization and there are few or no conditions that are favorable for you to achieve a goal, we may say that you lack opportunity. If you think that conditions are favorable for you to receive a promotion or a salary increase, you will tend to feel that you have opportunity in the organization. Employees may be considered eligible for advancement and special assignments or opportunities when they meet the conditions for eligibility.

To open up opportunities, we must create a condition that is favorable for doing things that we want to do. For opportunities to exist, employees must have conditions that are favorable to achieving their goals. Abel (1971) found, for example, that to fill a position successfully in the organization that he was studying, it was necessary for prospective applicants to meet certain norms and exhibit particular stylistic tendencies. As employees understood and displayed the styles and met the norms, they were more likely to be promoted to top positions in the organization. These styles included self-confidence, cheerfulness, boldness, and independence.

Employees appear to be able to recognize when they have opportunities in an organization and when they do not. Managers also tend to recognize when an employee meets critical conditions and can report that an employee has opportunity in the organization. The devastating effects of lack of opportunity are no doubt felt by employees and, of course, they are apparent in the lives of individuals; on the other hand, these consequences are often not considered seriously enough as major determinants of employee behavior in the organization.

Without perceived opportunity, employees drift into feelings of despair. All too often, those feelings are considered trivial, but they are serious and undermine work vitality. In our research, one of the most consistent predictors of promotion and salary increases was the evaluation by an employee's manager of the extent of the employee's opportunities in the organization, not how well the employee was actually doing in terms of performance.

To highlight how critical opportunity is to the life of an employee, we shall comment on five categories of behavior (Kanter, 1976; Wheatley, 1981) that are affected by opportunity in organizations—positively if opportunity is present and negatively if opportunity is not present.

Self Esteem   Every employee is susceptible to changes in self esteem through the reflected image that he or she gains from others. Those who receive positive images about their abilities through comments and reward come to value themselves more highly. Those who feel locked into repetitive tasks or who feel invisible to others gradually lose their self-esteem. Experienced and talented employees often voice genuine doubts about their abilities when they face continual rejection. Employees in their mid–forties, for example, who have been passed over for promotion often become highly self-critical and lose confidence in the skills they once proudly displayed. What has changed, usually, is not their skillfulness, but the image they created from messages sent to them by the organization about opportunity.

Aspirations   Opportunity also affects an employee's aspirations or desired achievements. If the organization reinforces and rewards actions that support certain types of goals, employees tend to develop aspirations to reach those goals. Employees who have been stuck in one position for a lengthy period of time tend to curtail any aspirations they might have had initially. In the absence of such aspirations, they fail to see themselves in any other position. If a new position is eventually offered to them, they respond negatively because they have lost the internal vision of themselves that matches the new opportunity. Employees who consistently experience little or no opportunity gradually suppress any larger vision of their potential and represent themselves to others as tentative, self-doubting, and content to stay where they are.

Commitment   Opportunity also affects the extent to which employees remain committed to the organization. Those who experience personal growth and recognition tend to feed their positive feelings back to the organization. They become motivated to do more, to spend extra hours working, to look for additional ways to contribute, and to try innovative ways to improve productivity. Those who receive negative information gradually withdraw from or completely leave the organization. The withdrawal may be subtle in that they continue to do what is asked but at minimally acceptable levels. They may, on the other hand, transfer their energy to another arena, to some other organization or activity, where the response is more positive.

Energy   Employees with blocked opportunity tend to turn to their peers and friends for comfort and recognition. This may have less to do with how well they perform their jobs at work and more to do with how skilled they are in sports, recipes, or gardening. They may devote more energy to contacts and information exchange on tangential activities and less to the work itself. Employees who see high opportunity respond to recognitions of their value by becoming more focused on the task and waste less time in contacts and interactions that are not related to completing their work.

Problem Solving   Employees high in opportunity tend to be proactive in addressing problems in their work and in the organization. If they recognize or identify a potential problem they act on their own initiative to solve it before it becomes a major issue within the organization. For those without opportunity, organizational problems reflect a personal discontent. Instead of acting to resolve problems, they tend to sit passively by and grumble. If someone suggests a solution, they are the first to criticize it. Since their own life in the organization has been primarily negative, they may even derive some satisfaction from seeing the organization in trouble.

Performance

The most commonly evaluated activity in an organization is an employee's performance, which has to do with the way in which he or she does things associated with a job, position, or role in the organization. Two types of behaviors or work tasks appear to encompass the critical elements of job performance: functional tasks and behavioral tasks. Functional tasks relate to how well an employee completes the mechanics of the job, including primarily the completion of technical aspects of the job. Behavioral tasks relate to how well the employee handles interpersonal activities with other members of the organization, including resolving conflict, managing time, empowering others, working with a group, and working independently.

Swanson and Gradous (1986) explain that "within systems, whatever their size, all work is interrelated. The results of one set of work performances are the inputs for other performance efforts." Because of this interrelatedness, what appear to be small performance gains in one aspect of work can result in major gains overall. Thus, the productivity of a system depends upon the accuracy and efficiency of work behaviors.

Gilbert (1978), on the other hand, argues that performance is primarily the product of time and opportunity. "Opportunities without time to pursue them mean nothing. And time, dead on our hands, affording no opportunities, has even less value" (p. 11). "Behavior is a necessary and integral part of performance, but we must not confuse the two. Unfortunately, we often do. To equate behavior and performance is like confusing a sale with the seller" (p. 16). Gilbert argues, further, that one must observe the whole transaction, including both a person's behavior and what was accomplished by it in order to observe performance.

"No sensible person," Gilbert explains, "tries to modify other people's behavior just because it is there, or their performance just because it can be done. When we set about to engineer performance, we should view it in a context of value. We should not train someone to do something differently unless we place a value on the consequence— unless we see that consequence as a valuable accomplishment" (p. 17). He concludes with this aphorism: "Roughly speaking, competent people are those who can create valuable results without using excessively costly behavior" (p. 17).

In the context of work vitality in an organization, Gilbert's view of performance is perfectly consistent with what we consider necessary and important for energizing workers. To perform competently, workers make accomplishments that are valuable to the organization while reducing the cost to achieve the goal. Gilbert explains that great amounts of energy or work, coupled with much knowledge, and applied with lots of enthusiasm, without some comparable accomplishment, represent unworthy performance, and confuses "the plow (behavior) with the crop (accomplishment)" (p. 19).

Finally, Gilbert explains that we have "no need to measure behavior until we have measured accomplishment." By this he means that there can be no real purpose in identifying deficiencies in shooting a rifle until we establish that the person is unable to hit the target, or there is no reason to examine a person's ability to speak French until we determine that the person has a problem communicating to French-speaking people.

Extending this argument to work vitality, we say that the most vital workers in the organization are those who make valuable accomplishments in an efficient manner.

Organizations that fail to recognize and acknowledge the fundamental need for work vitality are the organizations that will fail, that will lack the adaptability to meet the competitiveness of other organizations. Employees who do not want to be vital are holding the organization back. Organizations—their managers and executives—who fail to support the development of vitality in employees are seriously at fault in undermining the competitiveness of the entire organization. The challenge today is to create conditions that contribute to employee vitality.

A SUBJECTIVIST'S REMINDER

Organizational members are best understood by observing their actions and how *they* make sense out of them. People make sense out of what they do before, during, and after their actions. Conscious decision making does not precede all human actions; people act and interact with others to make sense of what they have already done. The literature of symbolic interactionism conceptualizes *motives* as statements that people make about their conduct or the conduct of others (Hewitt, 1976). Viewed in this way, motives do not cause behaviors; they are socially acceptable verbalizations that help people justify their actions. Motives can be determined before, during, or after action.

How are motives selected? A member may select motives because they are acceptable in the organization. In addition, members choose motives on the basis of their understanding or conception of who they are. Foote (1951) suggests that this understanding is decided through interaction and mutual identification. Conceiving of motives as linguistic devices rather than inner drives or psychic forces allows one to see what justifications (accounts, motives) organization members *think* are operative. These justifications require discovery; they provide action linkages; they are contextual; they can be created; and it may be possible to manage them.

Managers should know their people well so that they might "manage meanings." A significant part of knowing people involves an awareness of the accounts given by individuals. Traditional theories of motivation conceptualize people as passive objects who contain forces (motives) that can be energized and directed. "Motivating" someone is just a matter of discovering what those forces are and then communicating in order to link the motives with expected behaviors. However, the level of predictability of behavior based on motive schemes has been disappointing at best. This in itself should indicate the potency of subjective processes. Staw (1977) suggests a move away from traditional concepts of motivation by emphasizing action rather than reaction. He concludes:

> The synthesis of motivation presented here is one in which the individual is an active constructor of his social reality. The individual is viewed not merely as an information processor confronting a number of possible behavioral paths—each with their attendant rewards and costs—but as an actor who can attempt to change the parameters or "givens" of traditional motivation models. The individual can bargain, cajole, and ingratiate in order to change the contingencies between behavior and outcomes. . . . What we are facing, therefore, in describing a theory of individual motivation in organizations, is a highly complex system in which individuals have constructed a social and physical niche for themselves within the larger environment. This niche is built upon relationships developed over time with supervisors, subordinates, and peers in the organization and rests, in part, upon a role negotiation process. . . . This niche is also built upon the individual's idiosyncratic construction of his social reality (p. 89).

Individuals cope with organizational demands and have the capacity to generate their own job satisfaction and motivation. "Vitality" could be considered a managerial concept that serves the interests of management. There is evidence that individuals cope with boredom by constructing their own views of vitality and that the concept might differ in meaning according to context. Pacanowsky and Anderson (1982) point out that police officers make their work more interesting by "spicing up" their role performance. They may do this by hyperbole and use of media nicknames taken from popular television shows. Garson (1977) looks at jobs that represent the extremes in routine work and demonstrates that no matter how mind-numbing the task, such jobs cannot succeed in eliminating the motivation that comes from inside. Workers find ways to make the most routine tasks more interesting and meaningful. Certain types of work may offer more opportunity for self-fulfillment, but "vital" employees can create opportunities for more interesting work.

Determining how individuals have constructed their niche means looking at their unique behaviors and being sensitive to what they are saying. Motives might be provided for people in the sense that individuals can be given *rationalizations* that fulfill their predispositions. But the reasons (accounts, justifications, motives) are not the same for all individuals. Schrank (1978) makes this point when he contends that:

> Engineers, managers, or behavioral scientists, with their compulsive, competitive preoccupation with "making it," tend to see this as a paradigm for all workers. But many workers are not interested in "making it" in a career of power and responsibility, or even in increasing their autonomy and creativity. Some blue-collar workers prefer to make bowling the center of their lives. That may be a greater demonstration of autonomy and creativity than building a better high-speed box (p. 144).

Rather than trying to generalize "psychic unseen forces," it will be more productive for both the researcher and the practitioner to discover *processes* of enactment and adaptation. In addition, it is important to discover what resources might lead to quality of work life and production. What cultural resources are available? Larger cultures may emphasize the very values that can generate "vitality" in the organization. For example, the values of "work ethic," "commitment," and "caring" may be embedded in the political or religious philosophy of the region. When such is the case it is more likely that they will make sense and gain adherence in the organizational setting.

SUMMARY

Motivation, the X-factor in efficiency (the factor that accounts for the willingness of organization members to devote different amounts of energy to their work—the principle of worker effort discretion), may be accounted for in different ways. In this chapter we have briefly outlined the features of five theories of motivation. Three theories—by Maslow, Alderfer, and Herzberg—assume that people are more willing to act when they have deficiencies in their needs. Some argue that a satisfied need is not a motivator.

Maslow's (1943) hierarchy of needs theory postulates five internal needs that are arranged according to an order of prepotency. Thus, physiological needs will be the basis of action until they are satisfied, at which time the safety-security needs serve as the basis of action. When they are satisfied, the belonging and esteem needs impel action, and after they are satisfied, the self-actualizing needs become operable.

Alderfer's (1972) ERG theory of motivation encompasses a range of needs similar to those of Maslow, but it discounts the idea of hierarchy and argues that a satisfied need may continue to motivate action, and some needs, such as growth, tend to become more intense as they are satisfied. In Alderfer's theory, need satisfaction may be the basis of increased motivation.

Herzberg's (1966) satisfier-dissatisfier theory postulates two sets of needs, those concerning job satisfaction and those concerning job dissatisfaction. Satisfiers are the primary motivators, and, in his theory, they are related to the job itself. On the other hand, dissatisfiers have to do essentially with satisfying organization members and keeping them in the organization, and they are related to the environment.

Vroom's (1964) expectancy theory suggests that organization members will be motivated if they believe that their actions will lead to a desired outcome, that the outcome has a positive value for them, and that the effort they are willing to exert will achieve the outcome.

Pace's (1993) perceptions theory explains motivation in terms of the sense that organization members make of their work environment. Four potentialities were identified: how well expectations are met, what kinds of opportunities are provided, what degree of fulfillment occurs, and how well useful organization roles are performed. The decision to devote energy to achieving organization goals is a function of the combination of perceptions of the four potentialities.

All five of these theories contribute to our understanding of why people make the decision to devote energy to accomplishing organization and personal objectives.

Analysis of Motivation

Motivation is often analyzed by informal observation. When asked by *Sales Meetings* magazine to explain what he meant by achievement motivation, David McClelland replied that it was "thinking about doing things better." He said that "we measure this need for achievement by the frequency a person thinks about doing things better" (September 1969, p. 27). Counting the number of times a person thinks about doing something better sounds easier to do than it actually is. McClelland employed a pictorial projective method for measuring achievement and motivation. Individuals are shown eight pictures and asked to answer some questions and create a story from each of the situations viewed. The stories are scored on the extent to which they show a concern for competing to achieve a good performance (Lake, Miles, & Earle, 1973, pp. 191–192).

The *Work Perceptions Profile* (Pace & Mills, 1990) that follows was developed to provide a self-report measure of motivation in the workplace. It is based on the perceptions theory of motivation and elicits reactions to forty-two items organized around the four sets of perceptions that provide the basis for workplace motivation—performance, opportunity, fulfillment, and expectations. An average of responses to all items represents an individual composite score and provides a good indication of a person's level of motivation or vitality in the organization. Average scores may be computed for each of the work perceptions—expectations (Section B; for scoring purposes Section A is dropped), fulfillment (Section C), opportunity (Section D), and performance (Section E).

WORK PERCEPTIONS PROFILE

The *Work Perceptions Profile* describes perceptions that employees have about aspects of their work. Four key variables have been distilled from theory and research on work motivation and represent the focal points of the *Work Perceptions Profile*: expectations met, opportunity, performance, and fulfillment. The *Work Perceptions Profile* approaches these issues from a variety of perspectives and generates new and powerful information upon which work revitalization and organizational renewal plans may be based.

THANK YOU VERY MUCH FOR COMPLETING THIS PROFILE.

DIRECTIONS

1. Using a lead pencil, begin by filling in the circles on the green answer form that represent your Social Security number. Do not put your name anyplace on the answer form.
2. Do not think too long about the questions.
3. Read the directions for each part carefully.
4. Read each question carefully and mark your answer on the answer sheet.
5. Work through each part until you have answered all the questions. Do not leave any blanks.

SECTIONS A & B

Instructions: Mark your answer to each question on the accompanying form using a pencil. The statements are completed by selecting the most appropriate points on the scales. *For example:*

Coming into this organization, I assumed that I would _____ have a personal parking space.

rarely 1 2 3 4 5 almost always

The respondee completed the sentence by selecting choice 2 on the scale because he or she felt that the likelihood of having a personal parking space was quite rare. Mark your choices on the answer form (*not on the questionnaire*) by filling in the appropriate circles. Complete Section A (items 1–6) *first*, and then go to Section B (items 7–12).

SECTION A

Coming into this organization, I assumed that I would _____

1. be treated equitably.
   rarely 1 2 3 4 5 almost always
2. be given promotions at regular intervals.
   rarely 1 2 3 4 5 almost always
3. be given challenging work assignments.
   rarely 1 2 3 4 5 almost always
4. be influential in affecting decisions.
   rarely 1 2 3 4 5 almost always
5. be recognized for my contribution.
   rarely 1 2 3 4 5 almost always
6. be highly respected by my superiors.
   rarely 1 2 3 4 5 almost always

SECTION B

Today in this organization, I am

7. treated equitably.
   rarely 1 2 3 4 5 almost always
8. promoted at regular intervals.
   rarely 1 2 3 4 5 almost always
9. given challenging work assignments.
   rarely 1 2 3 4 5 almost always
10. influential in affecting decisions.
    rarely 1 2 3 4 5 almost always
11. recognized for my contribution.
    rarely 1 2 3 4 5 almost always
12. highly respected by my superiors.
    rarely 1 2 3 4 5 almost always

SECTION C

13. The work which I do _____ be done in unique and clever ways.
    cannot 1 2 3 4 5 can
14. I _____ have the ability to do my work in unique and clever ways.
    do not 1 2 3 4 5 do
15. I _____ trying to do my job in unique, clever, different, and original ways.
    dislike 1 2 3 4 5 like
16. I would _____ to do my work in unique, different, original, and clever ways.
    not like 1 2 3 4 5 very much like
17. This organization _____ my work in unique and clever ways.
    discourages me from doing 1 2 3 4 5 encourages me to do
18. This organization _____ reward employees for doing their work in unique and clever ways.
    does not 1 2 3 4 5 does

19. I am _____ with the support I receive from other employees when I try to do my work in unique and clever ways.

    very displeased 1 2 3 4 5 very pleased

20. I am _____ by the challenges provided by the work I do.

    discouraged 1 2 3 4 5 encouraged

21. I am _____ with the originality and uniqueness with which I do my work.

    very discontented 1 2 3 4 5 very contented

22. I am _____ by the work I do in this organization.

    very unfulfilled 1 2 3 4 5 very fulfilled

SECTION D

23. I believe that I am _____ than well enough known throughout the organization to be appointed to a special task force.

    less 1 2 3 4 5 more

24. I believe that I have _____ than sufficient status in the organization to be consulted about important company problems.

    less 1 2 3 4 5 more

25. I believe that my manager is a _____ advocate in helping me receive regular advancements in this organization.

    very weak 1 2 3 4 5 very strong

26. I believe that _____ positions are available in my functional area to allow me to be promoted within the next few years.

    no 1 2 3 4 5 many

27. I believe that it is _____ that I shall be promoted to the top position (CEO, President, etc.) in this organization.

    unlikely 1 2 3 4 5 likely

28. My manager feels that I have _____ potential to be promoted to the top position in my functional area in this organization.

    little 1 2 3 4 5 great

29. My manager feels that I _____ perform my assigned duties well enough to receive special salary increases periodically.

    never 1 2 3 4 5 always

30. My manager feels that my personality or style of interacting with others may be _____ to me in getting regular advancements in this organization.

    detrimental 1 2 3 4 5 beneficial

31. My manager feels that the quality of my work is _____ than expected to receive an above-average salary increase this year.

    lower 1 2 3 4 5 higher

32. My manager feels that I initiate _____ than enough new ideas to receive special recognition from the organization.

    fewer 1 2 3 4 5 more

SECTION E

33. My manager feels that I _____ motivate other employees to do their very best.

    rarely 1 2 3 4 5 almost always

34. My manager feels that I _____ suggest ways to improve our organizational efficiency.
    rarely 1 2 3 4 5 almost always

35. My manager feels that I _____ work very well on my own.
    rarely 1 2 3 4 5 almost always

36. My manager feels that I _____ do quality work on time.
    rarely 1 2 3 4 5 almost always

37. My manager feels that I _____ offer to help others complete work assignments.
    rarely 1 2 3 4 5 almost always

38. My manager feels that I _____ manage my time effectively.
    rarely 1 2 3 4 5 almost always

39. My manager feels that I _____ make effective contributions when assigned to work in a group.
    rarely 1 2 3 4 5 almost always

40. My manager feels that I _____ resolve conflict I have with other employees on my own.
    rarely 1 2 3 4 5 almost always

41. My manager feels that I _____ use the resources given to me in a prudent manner.
    rarely 1 2 3 4 5 almost always

42. My manager feels that I _____ handle the work skills and technical aspects of my job very well.
    rarely 1 2 3 4 5 almost always

REFERENCES

ABEL, KENNETH ROSS, "Sensitivity to Work Role-Related Expectations and Perceived Promotability." Doctoral dissertation, University of California, Los Angeles, 1971.

ALDERFER, C.P., *Existence, Relatedness, and Growth: Human Needs in Organizational Settings*. New York: Free Press, 1972.

CLURMAN, CAROL, "More Than Just a Paycheck," *USA Weekend* (19–21 January 1990), 4–5.

DRUCKER, PETER F., *Concept of the Corporation*. New York: John Day, 1946.

FOOTE, NELSON N., "Identification as the Basis for a Theory of Motivation," *American Sociological Review* (16 February 1951), 14–21.

FRANTZ, ROGER S., *X-Efficiency: Theory, Evidence and Application*. Boston: Kluwer Academic Publishers, 1988.

FROMM, ERICH, *The Sane Society*. New York: Holt, Rinehart & Winston, 1955.

GARSON, BARBARA, *All the Livelong Day*. New York: Penguin, 1977.

GILBERT, THOMAS F., *Human Competence*. New York: McGraw-Hill, 1978.

HELLRIEGEL, DON, JOHN C. SLOCUM, and RICHARD W. WOODMAN, *Organizational Behavior*, 4th ed. St. Paul, Minn.: West Publishing Co., 1986.

HERZBERG, FREDERICK, *Work and the Nature of Man*. New York: Collins Publishers, 1966.

HEWITT, JOHN P., *Self and Society: A Symbolic Interactionist Social Psychology*. Boston: Allyn & Bacon, 1976.

KANTER, ROSABETH MOSS, "Why Bosses Turn Bitchy," *Psychology Today* (May 1976), 56–59, 88–91.

KOVACH, KENNETH A., "Why Motivational Theories Don't Work," *S.A.M. Advanced Management Journal* (Spring 1980), 54–59.

LAKE, DALE G., MATTHEW B. MILES, and RALPH B. EARLE, JR., eds., *Measuring Human Behavior*. New York: Columbia University Teacher's College Press, 1973.

LEIBENSTEIN, H., *General X-Efficiency Theory and Economic Development*. New York: Oxford University Press, 1978.

LOO, ROBERT, "A Managerial Challenge: Promoting Job Satisfaction," *Canadian Manager* (Summer 1985), 22–23.

MACLEOD, JENNIFER S., "The Work Place as Prison," *Employment Relations Today* (Autumn 1985), 215–218.

MAIN, J., "Anatomy of an Auto Plant Rescue," *Fortune* (4 April 1983), 108.

MASLOW, ABRAHAM H., "A Theory of Human Motivation," *Psychology Review*, 50 (1943), 370–396.

MASLOW, ABRAHAM H., *Motivation and Personality*. New York: Harper & Row, Pub., 1954.

McCLELLAND, DAVID C., "Achievement Motivation," *Sales Meetings* (September 1969).

NADLER, DAVID A., and EDWARD E. LAWLER III, "Motivation: A Diagnostic Approach," *Harvard Business Review* (February 1976), 26–38.

NAISBITT, JOHN, and PATRICIA ABURDENE, *Re-Inventing the Corporation*. New York: Warner Books, 1985.

NINIGER, JAMES ROBERT, "College Graduate Turnover in Industry: A Study of the Role of Expectations in Decisions to Terminate or Continue Participation in One Organization." Doctoral dissertation, University of Michigan, 1970.

PACANOWSKY, MICHAEL E., and JAMES A. ANDERSON, "Cop Talk and Media Use," *Journal of Broadcasting* (Fall 1982), 741-755.

PACE, R. WAYNE, "Managing Worker Vitality: The Opportunity and Challenge of the 90's." Paper presented at the International Management Conference, Cairo, Egypt, January 1993.

PACE, R. WAYNE, and GORDON E. MILLS, *The Work Perceptions Profile*. Provo, Utah: Work Vitality Associates, 1990.

REID, ROBERT D, and MICHAEL R. EVANS, "The Career Plateau: What to Do When a Career Bogs Down," *Cornell Hotel and Restaurant Administration Quarterly* 24 (August 1983), 83–91.

SCHRANK, ROBERT, *Ten Thousand Working Days*. Cambridge, Mass.: MIT Press, 1978.

STAW, BARRY M., "Motivation in Organizations: Toward Synthesis and Redirection," in *New Directions in Organizational Behavior*, Barry M. Staw and Gerald R. Salancik, eds. Chicago: St. Clair Press, 1977.

SWANSON, RICHARD A., and DEANE GRADOUS, *Performance at Work*. New York: John Wiley, 1986.

VROOM, VICTOR H., *Work and Motivation*. New York: John Wiley, 1964.

WENBURG, JOHN R., and JOHN N. WILLIAMSON, "A Business Perspective on Stress Management: The Problem & Current Cures." Paper presented at the Western Speech Communication Association, San Jose, Calif., February 1981.

WHEATLEY, MARGARET, "The Impact of Organizational Structure on Issues of Sex Equity in Educational Policy and Management," in *The Sex Dimension in Educational Policy and Management*, P.A. Schumck and W.W. Charters, Jr., eds. San Francisco, Calif.: Academic Press, 1981.

YANKELOVICH, DANIEL, *New Rules: Searching for Self-Fulfillment in a World Turned Upside Down*. New York: Bantam New Age Books, 1982.

7

Organizational Communication Climate

Have you ever had the experience of working on a job, having your supervisor come by and watch what you're doing for a few moments, and then shrug and say, "Huh"? You ask, "Is there something wrong?" The reply you hear is, "Oh, n-o-o-o-o." Your supervisor walks away. Later you take a break and two other employees working in your area saunter up to the drink dispenser where you are standing. They look at you and then lean against the wall with their backs to you. You decide to go over to the personnel office to check on your overtime. Although you have been in the personnel office many times, the clerk asks your name and the area where you work. The clerk thumbs through the file drawer, looks at you, and shakes his head in a puzzled way. He asks, "What did you say your name is?" You reply "Never mind!" and frown deeply as you slam the door on your way out of the building. Under your breath you mutter, "What is the matter with this place?" You look up at the sky expecting to see dark clouds signaling a thunderstorm. The sun is bright, and the sky is a beautiful blue. You wonder. "It's the climate," you say. "We have a terrible climate in this organization!"

COMMUNICATION CLIMATE

The term "climate" functions as a metaphor. A metaphor is a figure of speech in which one term or phrase with a relatively clear meaning is applied to a different situation in order to suggest a resemblance, such as "this place is a zoo." Although the comparison is figurative, it adds information about the content, structure, and meaning of the new situation. As Sackmann (1989) suggests, "a metaphor can provide vivid images on a cognitive, emotional, and behavioral level, and suggest a certain course of action without determining, however, the actual behavior" (p. 465).

The phrase "organizational communication climate" represents a metaphor of the physical climate. Just as the weather creates a physical climate for a region, the way in which people react to aspects of the organization creates a communication climate. A physical climate consists of the generally prevailing weather conditions of an area. The physical climate is a composite of temperature, air pressure, humidity, precipitation, sunshine, cloudiness, and winds throughout the year that are averaged over a series of years.

The communication climate, on the other hand, is a composite of perceptions—a macro-evaluation—of communicative events, human behaviors, responses of employees to one another, expectations, interpersonal conflicts, and opportunities for growth in the organization. Communication climate is different from organizational climate in that communication climate involves perceptions of messages and message-related events occurring in the organization.

Any particular pattern of weather conditions may give an inaccurate impression of the physical climate of a region; in the same way, one may get an inaccurate impression of the communication climate of an organization based on a short visit or contact with some unusual interpersonal interactions. Sometimes, however, the weather on a particular day does give you a good picture of the general physical climate over a longer period of time, in the same way that perceptions of the organization on a particular day may provide a clear picture of the communication climate of an organization over a longer period of time.

IMPORTANCE OF CLIMATE

Is the physical climate of an area important? Blumenstock (1970) explains that the physical climate "affects our way of life": the clothing we wear, the food we raise, the houses we construct, the transportation we use, the kinds of plants and animals in the area.

Is the communication climate of an organization important? In a similar fashion to the physical climate of an area, the communication climate of an organization affects the way we live: to whom we talk, whom we like, how we feel, how hard we work, how innovative we are, what we want to accomplish, and how we seem to fit into the organization. Redding (1972) states that *"the [communication] 'climate' of the organization is more crucial than are communication skills or techniques (taken by themselves) in creating an effective organization"* (p. 111).

Communication climate is important, also, because it links the organizational context to the concepts, feelings, and expectations of organization members and helps explain the behavior of organization members (Poole, 1985, p. 79). By knowing something about the climate of an organization, we can better understand what impels organization members to behave in particular ways.

It has been pointed out that climate has features that make it appear to overlap with the concept of culture. Poole (1985) explains, however, that "on the whole, climate seems to be a feature of, rather than a substitute for, culture. As a system of generalized beliefs, climate contributes to the coherency of a culture and guides its development" (p. 84). Kopelman, Brief, and Guzzo (1989) tend to concur with this view of the relationship between climate and culture when they state that "organizational culture . . . provides the context in which organizational climate is nested" (p. 8). Thus, an understanding of the communication climate of an organization can tell us much about the culture of the organization.

Some specialists in organizational communication also argue that the concept of "climate" is one of the "richest constructs in organization theory, generally, and organizational communication specifically" (Falcione, Sussman, and Herden, 1987, p. 195). Climate is "rich" because it has received a great deal of attention in theoretical and empirical literature; it is also deceptively simple and complex at the same time, and it has far-reaching explanatory powers.

Poole (1985) indicates that the climate arises from and is sustained by organizational practices (p. 82). Kopelman, Brief, and Guzzo (1989) hypothesize and argue that the climate of the organization, which includes communication climate, is important because it mediates between human resource management practices and productivity. They explain that "when an organization implements a new financial incentive plan or engages in participative decision making, a change in organizational climate may occur. This change in climate may, in turn, affect employee performance and productivity" (p. 12). It would appear that although not all of the consequences of productivity improvement practices reflect changes in climate, many do. Climate in general and communication climate in particular serve as strong mediating factors between elements of the work system and different measures of organizational effectiveness such as productivity, quality, satisfaction, and vitality.

Organizational Communication Climate

The approach taken in this chapter is that communication climate is a macro, abstract, composite image of a global phenomenon called *organizational communication*. We assume that climate develops out of interaction between features of an organization and the individual's perceptions of those features. Climate is viewed as a subjectively experienced quality derived from perceptions of the relatively enduring characteristics of organizations (Falcione et al., 1987, pp. 198, 203).

HOW ORGANIZATIONAL COMMUNICATION CLIMATE DEVELOPS

Organizational communication climate consists of perceptions of organizational elements and the effects they have on communication. The effects are continually defined, confirmed, evolved, and affirmed through interaction with other organization members. The effects provide guidelines for individual decisions and actions and influence messages about the organization.

Figure 7.1 portrays the manner and sequence in which the communication climate of an organization develops, and it identifies the components that contribute to the climate. In this chapter we shall briefly trace the sequence and discuss the components so as to more clearly grasp the manner in which a communication climate functions in organizations.

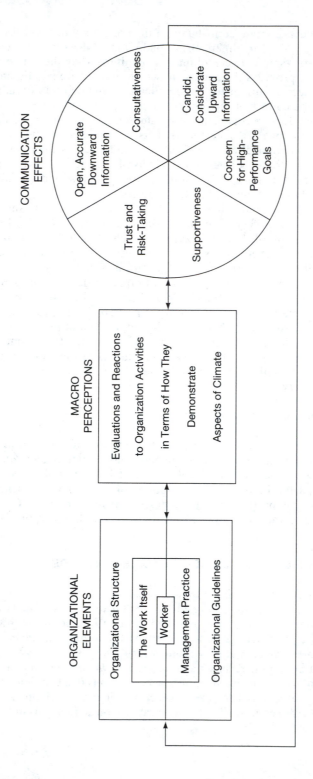

FIGURE 7.1 Interacting Parts of Organizational Communication Climate

Basic Elements of Organization

A communication climate evolves within the context of the organization, theories of which we discussed in earlier chapters. The basic elements that comprise an organization may be summarized, however, under five broad categories: organization members, the work itself, management practices, organization structure, and organization guidelines.

Organization Members   At the heart of the organization are the individuals who perform the work. Individuals who comprise the organization engage in a few primary activities (Bois, 1978, pp. 29–33). They engage in *thinking* activities, which include concepts, using language, solving problems, and generating ideas. They engage in *feeling* activities which encompass emotions, desires, and other nonintellectual aspects of human behavior. They engage in *self-moving* activities, which involve both gross and finite physical actions. Finally, they engage in *electrochemical* activities, which include brain synapses, actions of the heart, and metabolic processes.

These four sets of activities allow individuals to perform skills, to understand symbols, and to care about and experience the world. They combine to allow individuals to perform work within the organization.

The second primary element that constitutes an organization is the work itself.

The Work Itself   The work that people do is comprised of the formal and informal tasks in which they engage so as to produce the products and provide the services of the organization. The primary goal of organization members is to create the output of the organization. The work is characterized by three universal dimensions: content, requirements, and context (Gibson, Ivancevich, and Donnelly, 1991).

Content consists of what organization members do in relation to materials, people, and other tasks in terms of the methods and techniques used, the machines, tools, and equipment employed, and the materials, goods, information, and services created.

Requirements refer to prerequisite knowledge, skills, and attitudes thought to be appropriate for a person to be able to perform the work, including education, experience, licenses, and personal attributes.

Context has to do with the physical demands and conditions of the job location, the kind of accountability and responsibility associated with the work, the amount of supervision required, and the general environment in which the work is performed.

The third basic element of the organization is the management practices.

Management Practices   The primary goal of managerial workers is to get the job done through the efforts of other people. Managers make decisions about how other individuals, usually their subordinates, use resources needed to do their work. Some managers supervise operative workers while others supervise other managers.

The activities of a manager have been described in a variety of ways. First, some consensus has been achieved around the idea that managers engage in approximately five main functions: planning, organizing, staffing, directing, and controlling (MacKenzie, 1969). Second, some sound evidence suggests that managers perform about ten generic roles (Mintzberg, 1973) divided into three basic groups: (1) Interpersonal roles (Figurehead, Leader, Liaison), (2) Informational Roles (Monitor, Disseminator, Spokesperson), and (3) Decision Roles (Entrepreneur, Disturbance Handler, Resource Allocator, and Negotiator).

The fourth basic element that comprises the organization is structure.

Organization Structure Organization structure refers to relationships among the "tasks performed by the members of the organization" (Tosi, Rizzo, and Carroll, 1990, p. 39). Organization structure appears to be defined by three key variables: complexity, formalization, and centralization (Robbins, 1989, p. 398).

Complexity is a function of three factors: (1) *The degree to which differences exist between units (horizontal differentiation) as a result of specializations existing in the organization.* Universities have a large number of specialties and, hence, tend to be horizontally differentiated. (2) *The number of levels of authority between workers and top executives (vertical differentiation).* Whether an organization's structure is taller or flatter depends on the span of control or number of subordinates a manager can supervise effectively. (3) *The degree to which the location of an organization's facilities and personnel are dispersed geographically (spatial differentiation).* An organization with branch offices in twenty different locations tends to be more complex than an organization in which its entire operation is in one location.

Formalization refers to the degree to which jobs and tasks are standardized. If a job is highly formalized, the worker has little discretion over where, when, and how the job is to be done. Formalization occurs when job duties are governed by rules and regulation, whether stated directly or simply understood by workers. Perceptions of workers concerning the extent to which job procedures and activities are specified and enforced provide a fair measure of formalization in an organization. Professionalism also produces standardized or formal behaviors through the socialization of organization members before they even enter the organization through the selection process, by specifying role expectations, by training in job procedures and skills, and through the process of having organization members complete rituals to demonstrate that they have formalized the ideology of the organization.

Centralization refers to the degree to which decision making is concentrated in a single point in the organization. *Decentralization*, in contrast, refers to the extent to which decision-making authority is dispersed throughout the organization. The amount of formal authority given to organization members to make decisions affecting their work activities is a measure of centralization. Policies that limit decision making tend to move organizations toward centralization. Situations in which organization members are prohibited from participating in decisions about their work represents centralization. If some form of discretion is provided at low levels in the organization, but the decisions are closely monitored, the organization is still functioning with high degrees of centralization. The use of self-directed, autonomous teams is an effort to decentralize decision making in organizations.

The fifth basic element of organizations is guidelines.

Organization Guidelines Organization guidelines are the vast array of statements that influence, control, and provide direction for decisions and actions of organization members. Organization guidelines encompass such statements as goals, mission, objectives, strategies, policies, procedures, and rules. These various types of guidelines combine to provide information to organization members about where the organization is going, what they should be doing, how they should think about organization problems and solutions, and what actions they should take to make the organization successful.

Perceptions of Organization Elements

The basic elements of organizations (members, the work itself, managerial practices, structure, and guidelines) are selectively perceived to create evaluations and reactions that indicate what is meant by each of the basic elements and how well they operate for the benefit of organization members. For example, the availability of information is an indication to organization members of how well the basic organization elements function together to provide information for them. Perceptions of information availability cue organization members to aspects of the organization that influence their lives and provide a set of judgments constituting one part of the organizational communication climate.

Perceptions of work conditions, supervision, compensation, advancement, relationships with colleagues, organization rules and regulations, decision-making practices, available resources, and ways of motivating organization members all combine to comprise a body of information that builds what we call the organizational communication climate.

Organization elements do not, directly, create an organization's communication climate. For example, an organization may have many rules and regulations, but their effect on the climate depends on *perceptions* of organization members of (1) the value of rules and regulations; that is, should rules and regulations always be accepted and followed or should some rules and regulations be ignored? and (2) the activities that the rules and regulations affect: regulations about the use of a telephone may be inhibiting whereas a rule about when work starts may be facilitating (see Poole, 1985, pp. 102–104).

Communication Effects

Ultimately, the organizational communication climate is a function of how activities that occur in the organization demonstrate to organization members that the organization trusts them and allows them the freedom to take risks; supports them and gives them responsibility in doing their jobs; openly provides accurate and adequate information about the organization; attentively listens to and gets reliable and candid information from organization members; actively consults organization members so that they see that their involvement is influential in decisions in the organization; and has a concern for high standards and challenging work (Redding, 1972).

Organization members define and confirm the existence of communication effects. Thus, through interactional processes, organization members verify the existence of trust, support, openness, consultativeness, concern, and candidness. Hence, communication effects may vary and change according to the manner in which they are defined and confirmed through interaction among organization members.

Communication effects combine in different ways to evolve a belief and value system that is recognized by organization members as the climate of the organization. Each climate may be characterized by different combinations of communication effects so that they may be called by different names, such as participatory, apathetic, supportive, hostile, invigorating, defensive, positive, or negative.

A particular communication climate provides guidelines for individual decisions and behavior. Decisions by organization members to do their work effectively, to commit themselves to the organization (Guzley, 1992), to behave honestly at work, to pursue opportunities in the organization vigorously, to support colleagues and other members of the organization, to perform tasks creatively, and to offer innovative ideas for the improvement of the organization and its operations are all influenced by the communication climate. A negative climate may decisively undermine the decisions that organization members make about how they will work and contribute to the organization.

Communication climate may be one of the most important influences on productivity in the organization, because climate affects the *effort* of an organization member. Effort refers to both *physical exertion of the body* in the form of lifting, speaking, or walking, and *mental exertion of the mind* in the form of thinking, analyzing, and solving problems (Frantz, 1988, pp. 74–77).

Effort usually consists of four elements: "(1) the activities (A) that constitute the job; (2) the pace (P) at which work is performed; (3) the quality (Q) of output; and (4) the time (T) pattern of work" (Frantz, 1988, p. 75). Organization members choose to vary the amount of effort they devote to activities in the organization, the pace at which work is performed, the attentiveness with which they work—the quality of their outputs, and the amount of time they devote to their work. They make these choices because "directed effort"—the effort to which we are referring—is not directly purchased as part of the contract for labor in organizations, but it represents the outcome of organization members' response to motivations provided by their own psyche and/or by the external environment in which they work (Frantz, 1988, p. 74). From our view, these motivations are derived primarily from one's perceptions of the communication climate of an organization. Thus, communication climate plays a central role in encouraging organization members to devote effort to their work in the organization.

A willingness to exert considerable effort on behalf of the organization is one of three factors of organizational commitment (Mowday, Steers, & Porter, 1979, p. 226). A strong belief in and acceptance of the organization's goals and values, and a strong desire to maintain membership in the organization are the other two factors. In Guzley's research (1992), participation (a dimension of communication climate) emerged as a predictor of commitment for employees with five or more years' tenure in the organization. Guzley reasoned that participation was of greater importance to employees who had established a sense of control over their job situation, which occurred only after they had some degree of tenure in the organization. "Once a sense of control and acceptance has been established, employees' need to feel that their communication has influence may gain importance. In fact, without a sense of such influence employees may become dissatisfied and leave the organization; that is, their organizational commitment is likely to decrease" (p. 397).

Thus, we may conclude that the climate of communication in the organization may have important consequences for employee turnover and tenure within the organization. A positive communication climate tends to encourage and support commitment to the organization.

As an interactive phenomenon, changes in the work system or organization may, conversely, have positive effects on the perception of the communication climate of an organization. For example, the introduction of training programs, self-directed work teams, mentoring programs, special newsmagazines, and organization symbols may influence the perceptions of how the organization is demonstrating trust, supportiveness, or consultativeness. Self-directed work teams appear to have a variety of good effects in organizations, including the enhancement of work effort and productivity, but the most noticeable may be the creation and maintenance of positive perceptions of the organization.

The interactional processes involved in the development of organizational communication climates also contribute to potential effects on restructuring, reorganizing, and revitalizing the basic elements of organizations. Strong, positive communication climates often lead to more supportive managerial practices and organization guidelines. Introduction of mechanisms to enhance climate may in fact do more than just affect climate—they may bring about more fundamental changes in the basic processes that constitute the fabric and substance of what we call an organization.

It is just as likely, for example, for self-directed work teams to engender changes in the way in which work is done in an organization and the way in which organization members are supervised as it is to facilitate a more positive climate. On the other hand, the processes involved predict that mechanisms have a reciprocal influence on perceptions and basic organization elements in which changes in either or both result in making changes in climate, or changes in climate produce changes in the implementation of mechanisms and basic organization elements.

ANALYZING COMMUNICATION CLIMATE

The process of measuring organizational communication climate involves securing perceptions of organization members about the status of communication effects. As a perceptual concept, organizational communication climate is measured by securing perceptual reactions of organization members to macro properties of the organization that are relevant to communication and meaningful to organization members (Dennis, 1974). Although the unit of analysis is individual perceptions, aggregate perceptions provide a useful description of the organization's communication climate when the measures are of macro characteristics. Jackofsky and Slocum (1988) provide support for these premises in their research on the more general concept of organization climate (pp. 320, 331).

Communication Climate Inventory (CCI)

Peterson and Pace (1976) developed a Communication Climate Inventory (CCI) designed to measure the six "communication effects" identified in the model (see Figure 7.1), which were derived from the analysis of "ideal managerial climate" completed by Redding (1972). The CCI has been used by Graff (1976), Bednar (1977), Baugh (1978), and Applbaum and Anatol (1979) in research on climate. Tests of the CCI's internal reliability show coefficients ranging from .80 to .97, which are generally considered very satisfactory. Factor analysis of the CCI reveals the existence of one main factor. Applbaum and Anatol (1979) reported that the CCI "may be a valid index of overall organizational communication climate" (p. 10).

The CCI has been used in consulting activities in organizations as diverse as defense manufacturing, retailing, state government, professional association, community college, federal agency, consulting, warehousing, engineering, computer networking, and banking. Results have been uniformly positive, yielding consistent and positive responses to its face validity. When combined with other types of measures in an *Organizational Communication Profile* (Peterson & Pace, 1985), the CCI provides reliable and supportive evidence of the climate of the organization, especially in the context of triangulation or the use of multiple methods of analysis.

COMMUNICATION CLIMATE INVENTORY (CCI)

R. Wayne Pace and Brent D. Peterson

Please respond to *all questions* as honestly and frankly as you possibly can.

In *no way* will your identity be associated with your responses nor will your responses be used in such a manner as to jeopardize you or your job.

Unless the working of a particular item specifically indicates otherwise, respond in terms of your own impressions of the entire organization in which you work.

Indicate your response to each item by *circling just one of the five numbers* in the right-hand column. PLEASE DO NOT OMIT ANY ITEM! Use the following code to interpret the meaning of the numerical symbols:

5 — Circle this number if, in your honest judgment, the item is a true description of conditions in the organization.

4 — Circle if the item is more true than false as a description of conditions in the organization.

3 — Circle if the item is about half true and half false as a description of conditions in the organization.

2 — Circle if the item is more false than true as a description of conditions in the organization.

1 — Circle if the item is a false description of conditions in the organization.

PLEASE, DO NOT ATTEMPT AN INTENSIVE "WORD ANALYSIS" OF THE QUESTIONS. AND—OF COURSE—YOUR RESPONSES SHOULD REFLECT YOUR OWN JUDGMENTS, NOT THOSE OF OTHER PEOPLE. THERE ARE NO RIGHT OR WRONG ANSWERS.

Answer all questions in terms of your impressions concerning your own organization!

YOU MAY NOW BEGIN.

1. Personnel at all levels in the organization demonstrate a commitment to high-performance goals (high productivity, high quality, low cost).   5 4 3 2 1 (1)

2. Superiors seem to have a great deal of confidence and trust in their subordinates.   5 4 3 2 1 (2)

3. Personnel at all levels in the organization are communicated to and consulted with concerning organizational policy relevant to their positions.   5 4 3 2 1 (3)

4. Subordinates seem to have a great deal of confidence and trust in their superiors.   5 4 3 2 1 (4)

5. Information received from subordinates is perceived by superiors as important enough to be acted upon until demonstrated otherwise.   5 4 3 2 1 (5)

6. All personnel receive information that enhances their abilities to coordinate their work with that of other personnel or departments, and that deals broadly with the company, its organization, leaders, and plans.   5 4 3 2 1 (6)

7. A general atmosphere of candor and frankness seems to pervade relationships between personnel through all levels of the organization.   5 4 3 2 1 (7)

8. There are avenues of communication available for all personnel to consult with management levels above their own in decision-making and goal-setting processes.   5 4 3 2 1 (8)

9. All personnel are able to say "what's on their minds" regardless of whether they are talking to subordinates or superiors.   5 4 3 2 1   (9)

10. Except for necessary security information, all personnel have relatively easy access to information that relates directly to their immediate jobs.   5 4 3 2 1   (10)

11. A high concern for the well-being of all personnel is as important to management as high-performance goals.   5 4 3 2 1   (11)

12. Superiors at all levels in the organization listen continuously and with open minds to suggestions or reports of problems made by personnel at all subordinate levels in the organization.   5 4 3 2 1   (12)

THANK YOU VERY MUCH FOR TAKING THE TIME TO COMPLETE THIS INVENTORY!

Our research indicates that there are at least six major factors that affect an organization's communication climate. A short discussion of each of the six follows:

1. *Trust* — Personnel at all levels should make every effort to develop and maintain relationships where trust, confidence, and credibility are sustained by statement and act.

2. *Participative Decision Making* — Employees at all levels in the organization should be communicated to and consulted with on all issues in all areas of organization policy relevant to their positions. Employees at all levels should be provided with avenues of communication and consultation with management levels above theirs for the purpose of participating in decision-making and goal-setting processes.

3. *Supportiveness* — A general atmosphere of candor and frankness should pervade relationships in the organization, with employees being able to say "what's on their minds" regardless of whether they are talking to peers, subordinates, or superiors.

4. *Openness in Downward Communication* — Except for necessary security information, members of the organization should have relatively easy access to information that relates directly to their immediate jobs, that affects their abilities to coordinate their work with that of other people or departments, and that deals broadly with the company, its organization, leaders, and plans.

5. *Listening in Upward Communication* — Personnel at each level in the organization should listen continuously and with open minds to suggestions or reports of problems made by personnel at each subordinate level in the organization. Information from subordinates should be viewed as important enough to be acted upon until demonstrated otherwise.

6. *Concern for High-Performance Goals* — Personnel at all levels in the organization should demonstrate a commitment to high-performance goals—high productivity, high quality, low cost—as well as a high concern for other members of the organization.

The Communication Climate Inventory attempts to measure attitudes toward each of these factors of climate. The Inventory can also be used to obtain a composite climate score. This is the average of all six factors.

PROCEDURES FOR USING THE INVENTORY:

1. Distribute copies to all personnel in the organization. It is best to distribute copies as close to the same time as possible.

2. Read through the instructions on the cover page as the respondents read silently with you. Ask if there are any questions. Instruct the respondents to turn the page and complete the Inventory.
3. Collect and score all copies in the Inventory.

SCORING AND ANALYSIS

1. Composite Climate Score — To get the Individual Composite Climate Score (ICCS) sum the individual's responses to all twelve items and divide by twelve. This general average gives you a Composite Climate Score (CCS) for each respondent. For the Organization Composite Climate Score (OCCS) sum all the ICC's and divide by the number of total respondents.
2. Trust Climate Score — To get the Trust Climate Score sum number two and number four on each inventory and divide by two. This is an individual score. To get a composite trust score sum all the inventories and divide by the total number of respondents.
3. Participative Decision-Making Score — To get the Participative Decision-Making Score sum number three and number eight on each Inventory and divide by two. This is an individual score. To get a composite participative decision-making score sum all the inventories and divide by the total number of respondents.
4. Supportiveness Climate Score — To get the Supportiveness Climate Score sum number seven and number nine on each Inventory and divide by two. This is an individual score. To get a composite supportiveness score sum all the Inventories and divide by the total number of respondents.
5. Openness in Downward Communication Score — To get the Openness in Downward Communication Score sum number six and number ten on each Inventory and divide by two. This is an individual score. To get a composite openness in downward communication score sum all the Inventories and divide by the total number of respondents.
6. Listening in Upward Communication Score — To get the Listening in Upward Communication score sum number five and number twelve on each Inventory and divide by two. This is an individual score. To get a composite listening in upward communication score sum all the Inventories and divide by the total number of respondents.
7. Concern for High-Performance Goals Score — To get the Concern for High-Performance Goals Score sum number one and number eleven on each Inventory and divide by two. This is an individual score. To get a composite concern for high-performance goals score sum all the Inventories and divide by the total number of respondents.

Some researchers equate measures of quality of organizational relationships with measures of climate (Pincus, 1986, p. 403; Downs, 1988, p. 103). The Organizational Communication Division of the International Communication Association (ICA), as part of a project on the development of an "audit" of organizational communication, created and refined an extensive questionnaire covering many communication variables. One section of the ICA questionnaire asked about communication relationships in the organization. Although not advanced as a measure of communication climate, many of the questions appear to explore issues that we have identified with organizational communication climate. Questions 86 through 127 of an early version of the ICA survey may measure climate; a sample of those questions are part of the public domain and are reproduced below.

Organizational Communication Relationships

Instructions for Questions 86 through 127. A variety of communication relationships exist in organizations like your own. Employees communicate regularly with supervisors, subordinates, peers, and others. Considering your communication relationships with others in your organization, please mark the answer on the answer sheet that best indicates your feelings about the relationship in question.

	To a very little extent	To a little extent	To some extent	To a great extent	To a very great extent
86. Extent to which you trust your boss.	1	2	3	4	5
87. Extent to which you think your boss trusts you.	1	2	3	4	5
88. Extent to which your boss is honest with you.	1	2	3	4	5
89. Extent to which your boss makes you feel confident in doing your job.	1	2	3	4	5
90. Extent to which you trust your subordinates.	1	2	3	4	5
91. Extent to which you trust your co-workers.	1	2	3	4	5
92. Extent to which you trust top management.	1	2	3	4	5
93. Extent to which you feel top management is sincere in their communication with employees.	1	2	3	4	5
94. Extent to which your co-workers get along with each other.	1	2	3	4	5
95. Extent to which your boss is familiar with the type of work you perform.	1	2	3	4	5
96. Extent to which people in your work group respect one another.	1	2	3	4	5
97. Extent to which different work groups share information with one another.	1	2	3	4	5
98. Extent to which your organization encourages differences of opinion.	1	2	3	4	5
99. Extent to which you have a say in decisions that affect you or your job.	1	2	3	4	5
100. Extent to which your boss listens to what you have to say.	1	2	3	4	5
101. Extent to which you feel free to disagree with your boss.	1	2	3	4	5

ORGANIZATIONAL COMMUNICATION SATISFACTION

"Satisfaction with communication" has been, on occasion, confused with "communication climate." The reason is that the climate, some have argued, seems to be a function of how satisfied members are with communication in the organization (Litwin & Stringer, 1968; Pritchard & Karasick, 1973). Satisfaction, however, represents an individual, micro concept whereas climate represents a macro, composite concept.

Satisfaction, in addition, also represents an evaluation of an internal affective state, whereas climate is a description of conditions external to the individual (Schneider, 1975; Dillard, Wigand, & Boster, 1986). Climate consists of a composite image of a global entity or phenomenon, such as communication or organization (see Figure 7.2), and satisfaction represents individual affective reactions to a desired outcome resulting from the communicating that occurs in the organization. Climate is a term that characterizes some properties of an entire organization or one of its complete subunits; satisfaction represents self-evaluation of an internal state.

The similarities and differences in communication climate and satisfaction dimensions are shown in Figure 7.3.

The term *communication satisfaction* has been used to refer to "the overall degree of satisfaction an employee perceives in his total communication environment" (Redding, 1972, p. 429). Although communication satisfaction seems to overlap with communication climate, it tends to enrich the idea of climate by focusing on the individual, personal level.

The most comprehensive analysis of organizational communication satisfaction has been conducted by Downs and Hazen (1977) as part of their effort to develop an instrument to measure communication satisfaction. They identified eight stable dimensions of communication satisfaction: (1) the extent to which communication in the organization motivates and stimulates workers to meet organizational goals and to identify with the organization; (2) the extent to which

FIGURE 7.2 Characteristics of Communication Satisfaction and Climate

	SATISFACTION		CLIMATE	
	Job	Individual Communication	Organization	Organization Communication
Level of Abstraction	Micro (concrete and easy to define)		Macro (abstract, composite)	
Level of Analysis	Individual		Aggregate	
Level of Affect	Evaluate		Descriptive	
Definition	Self-evaluation of an internal affective state. Affective reactions to the amount of desired outcomes that accrue to people as a result of their jobs and their communicating.		Descriptions of phenomena external to the individual. A composite image of a global entity or phenomenon: organization, communication.	

COMMUNICATION SATISFACTION	COMMUNICATION CLIMATE
1. Job-related information	1. Trust
2. Adequacy of information	2. Participative decision making
3. Ability to suggest improvements	3. Supportiveness
4. Efficiency of various communication channels	4. Openness in downward communication
5. Quality of media	5. Listening in upward communication
6. Way in which co-workers communicate	6. Concern for high-performance goals
7. Organization-wide information	
8. Organizational integration	

FIGURE 7.3 Dimensions of Communication Satisfaction and Climate

superiors are open to ideas, the extent to which they listen, and the extent to which they offer guidance for solving job-related problems; (3) the extent to which individuals receive information about the immediate work environment; (4) the extent to which meetings are well organized, written directives are short and clear, and the amount of communication in the organization is about right; (5) the extent to which the grapevine is active and horizontal communication is accurate and free flowing; (6) the extent to which information about the organization as a whole is adequate; (7) the extent to which subordinates are responsive to downward communication and anticipate supervisor's needs; and (8) the extent to which workers feel that they know how they are being judged and how their performance is being appraised.

According to Downs (1988), "the Communication Satisfaction Questionnaire has a noteworthy heritage. Grounded in a firm developmental process, possessing a rich theoretical orientation, and utilized in a variety of organizational settings, it has proved to be a useful, flexible, and efficient means to audit organizational communication" (pp. 130–131).

Overall, satisfaction is concerned with differences between what a person would like in terms of communication in an organization and what a person has in that regard. Satisfaction has little to do with *effectiveness* in displaying messages, but if the communication experience meets a personal goal, it is likely to be regarded as satisfying, although it may not be particularly effective as far as standards of creating, displaying, and interpreting messages are concerned. You may feel a need for certain kinds of information or for having information presented to you in a particular way. When information is communicated in ways consistent with what you feel you would like, then you should experience satisfaction with communication.

Satisfaction is a concept that usually relates to comfort; hence, satisfaction with communication means that you may be comfortable with the messages, media, and relationships in the organization. Comfort has a tendency, on occasion, to lead individuals to prefer current ways of performing, which often fails to lead to increased job performance. Some research on the relationship between organization communication and job performance indicates that satisfaction accounts for only a very small portion of the variance in job performance. That is, satisfaction may not spur individuals to higher levels of performance, although communication satisfaction clearly contributes to job satisfaction (Pincus, 1986, pp. 412–413).

SUMMARY

In this chapter we have defined organizational communication climate, explained its importance in the lives of organization members and in effective organization functioning, explicated the process by which communication climate develops, and presented some alternative ways of measuring organizational communication climate variables or dimensions.

A SUBJECTIVIST'S REMINDER

This chapter has explained that organizational communication climate is created through the interactions of organization members. A subjectivist's view reminds us that the interactions and processes that create, re-create, alter, and sustain climate should be the focus of study rather than each individual's response or a total of all of the responses in an organization. From a subjective perspective, it is the *interaction* that is crucial to climate development.

Climate is *not* an individual property, but it is an attitude that organization members generate, share, and sustain. Imagine a group of workers talking during lunch break. A new worker says, "My supervisor is really on the ball!" Other workers respond, "Must be someone that I don't know. Most of these guys only talk to chew you out." "Yeah, that's my experience." "Me too; in fact, the guys in those positions don't even know what our jobs require." Now suppose that each time the new worker says something positive about a supervisor, fellow workers either say something contradictory or simply don't say anything. It is likely that the new worker will resort to silence until the prevailing view can be sustained in some way. This sort of interaction tells the researcher or manager about climate. It is important to note that what is not said is quite significant in assessing climate. An interpretive emphasis conceives of climate as a collective attitude "continually produced and reproduced by members' interaction" (p. 213). Poole and McPhee (1983) reinforce the interaction idea by pointing out that "it is not enough to characterize this climate as simply a set of expectations and beliefs. We must also discover how these beliefs, attitudes, and values are created and maintained, what the climate means to members, and how it influences organizational life" (pp. 213–214).

What should the observer look for in the interaction? The climate of an organization is revealed through both the content of the messages and the symbolic forms used. Collective attitudes are revealed in vocabulary, metaphors, stories, and accounts. Anyone who has worked in an organization that was on its "last legs" understands the language of pessimism, lost hope, and survival. In such a situation, no one has to distribute a climate inventory to determine climate. Everyday exchanges give insight into how climate is produced and sustained. Schrank (1978) describes informal talk as "schmoozing" and suggests that "though the work itself is important to the workplace community, what is most neglected by those concerned with its problems is the nature of the human relationships. The rituals such as greetings on arrival, coffee breaks, lunchtime, smoke breaks, teasing, in-jokes, and endless talk about almost everything are the important ways in which the community maintains itself" (p. 78).

Climate has some far-reaching implications, and the study of climate involves more than determining whether Company X is a pleasant place to work. Meyer (1981) reports a study that demonstrates how symbolic forms (stories and metaphors) upheld ideologies, substituted for organizational directives, and helped guide reactions during a time of crisis. The employees of one hospital took pride in their self-reliance and efficiency. They characterized themselves as a "lean and hungry organization." Members of another hospital system referred to themselves as a chaotic group, but one that valued innovation, pluralism, and professional autonomy. When the hospitals were faced with a doctors' strike, they responded very differently. Meyer concluded that "Memorial did not foresee the jolt and reverted to its original state when the tremors ceased; Community [Hospital] anticipated the jolt, learned during the adjustment process, and underwent subsequent organizational changes. Although the two hospitals experienced equivalent decline in occupancy, their responses were more consistent with their ideologies than with the objective realities imposed by the strike" (p. 16). When organizational members interact and use symbolic forms, those forms provide rationale for organizational action. They also indicate what is expected from an organizational climate.

REFERENCES

APPLBAUM, RONALD I., and KARL W. E. ANATOL, "An Examination of the Relationships Between Job Satisfaction, Organizational Norms, and Communication Climate Among Employees in an Organization." Paper presented at meetings of the Communication Association of the Pacific, Honolulu, 1979.

BAUGH, STEVEN, "Communication Climate in a School District." Unpublished doctoral dissertation, Brigham Young University, Provo, Utah, 1978.

BEDNAR, DAVID A., "The Measurement of Communication Climate in Organizations: The Reliability of a New Inventory." Unpublished master's thesis, Brigham Young University, Provo, Utah, 1977.

BLUMENSTOCK, DAVID I., "Climate," *The World Book Encyclopedia* (vol. 4), Chicago: Field Enterprises Corp., 1970.

BOIS, SAMUEL, *The Art of Awareness*, Dubuque, Iowa: Wm. C. Brown, 1978.

DENNIS, HARRY S., "The Construction of a Managerial Communication Climate Inventory for Use in Complex Organizations." Paper presented at the annual meeting of the International Communication Association, New Orleans, 1974.

DILLARD, JAMES P., ROLF T. WIGAND, and FRANKLIN J. BOSTER, "Communication Climate and Its Role in Organizations," *Communications*, 12 (1986), 83–101.

DOWNS, CAL W., *Communication Audits*. Glenview, Ill.: Scott, Foresman, 1988.

DOWNS, CAL W., and MICHAEL D. HAZEN, "A Factor Analytic Study of Communication Satisfaction," *The Journal of Business Communication*, 14 (1977), 63–73.

FALCIONE, RAYMOND L., LYLE SUSSMAN, and RICHARD P. HERDEN, "Communication Climate in Organizations," in *Handbook of Organizational Communication: An Interdisciplinary Perspective*, Frederic M. Jablin et al., eds., Newbury Park, Calif.: Sage Publications, Inc., 1987.

FRANTZ, ROGER S., *X-Efficiency: Theory, Evidence and Applications*. Boston: Kluwer Academic Publishers, 1988.

GIBSON, JAMES L., JOHN M. IVANCEVICH and JAMES H. DONNELLY, JR., *Organizations: Behavior, Structure, Processes*. Homewood, Ill: Richard D. Irwin, 1991.

GRAFF, P. W., "Correlational Study Between the Organizational Associates' Climate Inventory and the Job Description Index." Unpublished master's thesis, Brigham Young University, Provo, Utah, 1976.

GUZLEY, RUTH M., "Organizational Climate and Communication Climate," *Management Communication Quarterly* (May 1992), 379–402.

JACKOFSKY, ELLEN F., and JOHN W. SLOCUM, JR., "A Longitudinal Study of Climates," *Journal of Organizational Behavior*, 9 (October 1988), 297–388.

KOPELMAN, RICHARD E., ARTHUR P. BRIEF, and RICHARD A. GUZZO, "The Role of Climate and Culture in Productivity." Working Paper 89-HRMG-03, A.B. Freeman School of Business, Tulane University, New Orleans, 1989.

LITWIN, G., and STRINGER, R., *Motivation and Organization Climate*. Cambridge, Mass.: Graduate School of Business, Harvard University, 1968.

MACKENZIE, R. ALEX, "The Management Process in 3-D," *Harvard Business Review* (November-December 1969), 80–87.

MEYER, ALAN D., "How Beliefs, Stories and Metaphors Uphold Ideologies That Supplant Structures and Guide Reactions." Paper presented at the SCA/ICA Jointly Sponsored Summer Conference on Interpretive Approaches to the Study of Organizational Communication, Alta, Utah, July 16, 1981.

MINTZBERG, HENRY, *The Nature of Managerial Work*. New York: Harper & Row, pub., 1973.

MOWDAY, RICHARD T., RICHARD M. STEERS, and LYMAN W. PORTER, "The Measurement of Organizational Commitment," *Journal of Vocational Behavior*, 14 (1979), 224–247.

PETERSON, BRENT D., and R. WAYNE PACE, "Communication Climate and Organizational Satisfaction." Unpublished manuscript, Brigham Young University, Provo, Utah, 1976.

PETERSON, BRENT D., and R. WAYNE PACE, *Organizational Communication Profile*. Provo, Utah: Organizational Associates, 1985.

PINCUS, J. DAVID, "Communication Satisfaction, Job Satisfaction, and Job Performance," *Human Communication Research*, 12 (Spring 1986), 395–419.

POOLE, MARSHALL SCOTT, "Communication and Organizational Climates: Review, Critique, and a New Perspective," in *Organizational Communication: Traditional Themes and New Directions*, Robert D. McPhee and Phillip K. Tompkins, eds., Beverly Hills, Calif.: Sage Publications, Inc., 1985.

POOLE, MARSHALL SCOTT, and ROBERT D. MCPHEE, "A Structurational Analysis of Organizational Climate," in *Communication and Organization: An Interpretive Approach*, Linda L. Putnam and Michael E. Pacanowsky, eds., Beverly Hills, Calif.: Sage Publications, Inc., 1983.

POOLE, MARSHALL SCOTT, and ROBERT D. MCPHEE, "Bringing Intersubjectivity Back In: A Change of Climate." Unpublished paper presented at the SCA/ICA Conference on Interpretive Approaches to Organizational Communication, Alta, Utah, July 16, 1981.

PRITCHARD, R. D., and B. W. KARASICK, "The Effect of Organizational Climate on Managerial Job Performance and Satisfaction," *Organizational Behavior and Human Performance*, 9 (1973), 126–146.

REDDING, W. CHARLES, *Communication within the Organization: An Interpretive Review of Theory and Research*. New York: Industrial Communication Council, 1972.

ROBBINS, STEPHEN P., *Organizational Behavior* (4th ed.). Englewood Cliffs, N.J.: Prentice-Hall, 1989.

SACKMANN, SONJA, "The Role of Metaphors in Organization Transformation," *Human Relations*, 42 (1989), 463–485.

SCHNEIDER, B., "Organizational Climates: An Essay," *Personnel Psychology*, 28 (1975), 447–479.

SCHRANK, ROBERT, *Ten Thousand Working Days*. Cambridge, Mass.: MIT Press, 1978.

TOSI, HENRY L., JOHN R. RIZZO, and STEPHEN J. CARROLL, *Managing Organizational Behavior* (2nd ed.). New York: Harper & Row, Pub., 1990.

8

The Flow of Information in Organizations

One of the major challenges in organizational communication is how to get information to all parts of an organization and also how to receive information from all parts of an organization. This process is concerned with the flow of information. Why is this an issue? The process is complex, and communication itself cannot be divided from the people who engage in it. What is spelled out structurally may not be what happens at all. Efficiency may be dependent on information flow, but it is not the only consideration. Organizations rely on innovation and must be able to generate information from their members. The flow of information may help determine organizational climate and morale, which in turn impacts on flow of information. New technology raises questions about how information flow may be affected. We will examine these issues in this chapter.

THE NATURE OF FLOW

Technically, information *does not* literally flow. In fact, information itself does not move. What does seem to happen is the display of a message, the interpretation of the display, and the creation of another display. The creation, display, and interpretation of messages are the processes by which information is distributed throughout organizations.

The concept of *process* implies that events and relationships are moving and changing continuously, that events and relationships are dynamic. A *dynamic* relationship or event is one involving energy and action. Thus what we call the flow of information in an organization is actually a dynamic process in which messages are constantly and continuously being created, displayed, and interpreted. The process is ongoing and constantly changing—that is, organizational communication is not something that happens and stops. Communication takes place all the time.

Guetzkow (1965) has appropriately pointed out that the flow of information in an organization may occur in one of three ways: simultaneously, serially, or in some combination of the two. We shall examine the meanings of these ways of disseminating information in organizations.

SIMULTANEOUS MESSAGE DISSEMINATION

A great deal of organizational communication is person to person, or dyadic, involving only a source and an interpreter as the final destination. However, it is also fairly common for a manager to want information to get out to more than one person, such as when changes in a work schedule need to be made or when a group requires briefing on a new procedure. Frequently, messages—called memos or memorandums—are sent to many individuals in an organization. On occasion, such as a university-wide faculty meeting, the top executive or president wishes to send a message to all members of the organization. Many organizations publish a house organ—a magazine or a newsletter that is mailed to all members of the organization. When all members of a particular unit—a department, college, or division—are to receive information at about the same time, we call the process *simultaneous message dissemination* (Figure 8.1).

When the same message needs to arrive at different locations at the same time, plans should be made to use a simultaneous message dissemination strategy or technique. The selection of a dissemination technique on the basis of timing (simultaneous arrival) necessitates thinking about dissemination methods a little differently from how we usually do. For example, one of the main concerns is whether the message can be distributed at the same time. You might think of a written memo as a sure-fire way of sending a message to all members of an organization at the same time. However, the mail service might delay receipt of the memo for some individuals, and others may not pick up their mail for several days. On the other hand, a meeting might be a way of getting information to everyone in the organization at the same time, but, as you can appreciate, the schedule of some individuals may not permit them to attend a meeting, especially if they must travel to attend. The memo is a written medium whereas a meeting is an oral, face-to-face medium. Either or both methods may facilitate the simultaneous dissemination of information to a particular group of organization members; either or both may be ineffective.

With the development of telecommunication media, the task of disseminating information to everyone on a simultaneous basis has been simplified for some organizations. At a given time widely located employees may all tune in to a designated channel on their television monitors and simultaneously see and hear the chief executive officer provide information. Occasionally a large proportion of the population of

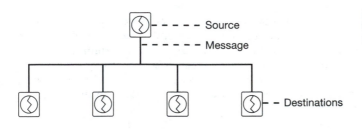

FIGURE 8.1
Simultaneous Message
Dissemination

the United States is able to listen and visually respond to a message from the President by turning on a TV set. Television allows a single speaker to make contact with all members of an organization on an individual basis, without the necessity of them coming together or having a printed document delivered to them. With the development of more sophisticated cable and telephone systems coupled with video images, it may be possible for entire organizations to have visual and vocal contact with one another while remaining at their individual places of work. Simultaneous message dissemination may be more common, more effective, and more efficient than other ways of facilitating the flow of information in an organization.

SERIAL MESSAGE DISSEMINATION

Haney (1962) notes that "serial transmission is clearly an essential, inevitable form of communication in organizations" (p. 150). The serial dissemination of information involves the extension of the dyad so that a message is relayed from Person A to Person B to Person C to Person D to Person E in a series of two-person transactions in which each individual beyond the originator first interprets and then displays a message for the next person in the sequence.

As you can determine by examining Figure 8.2, serial message dissemination represents a pattern of "who talks to whom." It has, as one of its most significant features, a pattern of dissemination. When messages are disseminated in a serial fashion, information spreads on an irregular time schedule, thereby arriving at different destinations at different times. Individuals tend to be aware of information at different times. Because of differences in awareness of information, problems in coordination may develop. Time lags in the dissemination of information may make it difficult to make decisions because people are just not informed. When large numbers of individuals are to be informed, serial processes may require a longer period of time to get the information to them. Of course, as we shall discuss later, the fidelity, or accuracy, of the information may suffer as a result of the frequent interpretations and reproductions involved in the serial dissemination of messages.

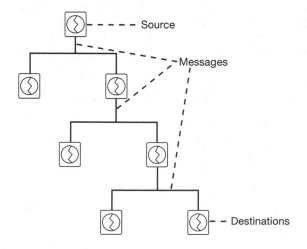

FIGURE 8.2
Serial Message Dissemination

PATTERNS OF INFORMATION FLOW

Although formal organizations rely heavily on general serial processes for gathering and disseminating information, specific patterns of information flow evolve out of regular interpersonal contacts and routine ways of sending and receiving messages. Katz and Kahn (1966) point out that a pattern or organized state of affairs requires that communication among the members of the system be restricted. The very nature of an organization implies limitations on who can talk to whom. Burgess (1969) observed that the peculiar characteristic of communication within organizations is that "message flows become so regularized that we actually may speak of communication networks or structures" (p. 138). He also noted that formal organizations exert control over the communication structure by such means as the designation of authority and work relations, assignment of offices, and special communication functions.

The experimental analysis of communication patterns suggests that certain arrangements of "who talks to whom" have fairly prominent consequences on organizational functioning. We shall compare two contrasting patterns—the wheel and the circle—to illustrate the effects of restricted information flow on organizations (Figure 8.3). The wheel is a pattern in which all information is directed toward the individual occupying the central position. The person in the central position receives contacts and information provided by other organization members and solves problems with the advice and consent of the other members. The circle allows all members to communicate with one another only through some sort of relay system. No one member has direct contact with all other members, nor does any one member have direct access to all the necessary information to solve problems. Several different combinations of contacts are possible: *A* may communicate with *B* and *E* but not *C* and *D*; *B* may communicate with *A* and *C* but not *D* and *E*; *C* may communicate with *B* and *D* but not *A* and *E*; *D* may communicate with *C* and *E* but not *A* and *B*; and *E* may communicate with *D* and *B* but not *B* and *C*. For *D* to communicate with *A*, information must be relayed through *E* or *C* and *B*.

Results of research on the wheel and circle patterns suggest that they produce quite different consequences (Bavelas, 1950; Bavelas & Barrett, 1951; Burgess, 1969; Leavitt, 1951; Shaw, 1958). Table 8.1 summarizes the effects of the wheel and the circle patterns on ten organizational communication variables.

The circle pattern, involving combinations of relay persons, tends to be superior to the wheel pattern, involving highly centralized communication flow, in overall accessibility of members to one another, morale or satisfaction with the process, number of messages sent, and adaptability to changes in tasks; on the other hand, the wheel pattern allows for more control over message flow, experiences rapid leader emergence and a

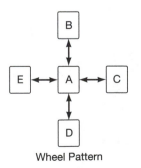

Wheel Pattern

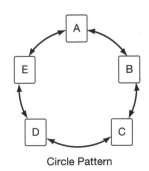

Circle Pattern

FIGURE 8.3
Two Basic Communication Patterns

TABLE 8.1 Effects of Two Patterns on Ten Organizational Communication Processes

ORGANIZATIONAL COMMUNICATION VARIABLE	WHEEL PATTERN	CIRCLE PATTERN
Accessibility of members to one another	Low	High
Control of message flow	High	Low
Morale or satisfaction	Very low	High
Emergence of leader	High	Very low
Accuracy of solutions	Good	Poor
Speed of performance	Fast	Slow
Number of messages sent	Low	High
Emergence of stable organization	Fast	Very slow
Adaptability to job changes	Slow	Fast
Propensity to overload	High	Low

stable organization, demonstrates high accuracy in solving problems, is fast in solving problems, but seems prone to message and work overload.

Burgess (1969) observed that in order to solve problems in experiments, group members had to "learn how to properly and efficiently manipulate the experimental apparatus; and to efficiently transfer messages to the position or positions with which they are linked" (p. 150). This implies that certain complex role behaviors may need to be learned to make the communication patterns function in any optimal way. Some research on communication networks in large organizations suggests that a distribution of network roles is important to the efficient functioning of an organization. We shall summarize some of the concepts on network roles to highlight these developments.

Communication Network Roles

An organization consists of people in positions. As individuals in those positions begin to communicate with one another, regularities in contacts and "who talks to whom" develop. The location of any given individual in the patterns and networks that emerge imposes a role upon that person. Some individuals occupy more central positions, such as Person A in the wheel pattern, that require them to receive and process more information than do other members of the network. Individuals who occupy central positions need to have skills for handling information since they will have to receive, integrate, and see that the appropriate information gets disseminated to the right people in a timely, accurate, and complete manner. Network analysis has revealed the characteristics of a number of communication network roles (Figure 8.4). We shall identify and briefly describe seven roles (Danowski, 1976; Farace, 1980; Farace, Monge, & Russell, 1977; Farace, Taylor, & Stewart, 1978; Richards, 1974; Roberts & O'Reilly, 1978; Rogers & Agarwala-Rogers, 1976).

Clique Member   A *clique* is a group of individuals having at least half of their contacts with each other. Farace and co-workers (1977) indicate that a clique is identified when "more than half of their communication is with each other, when each member is linked to all other members, and when no single link nor member can be eliminated and have the group break apart" (p. 186). You might wonder whether members of a clique are or need to be in close physical proximity to one another, such as occupying adjoining offices or working in the same department. Research on small group ecology (Sommer, 1969) suggests that individuals were more likely to "interact with people whom they could see" (p. 61). The environment also has an impact

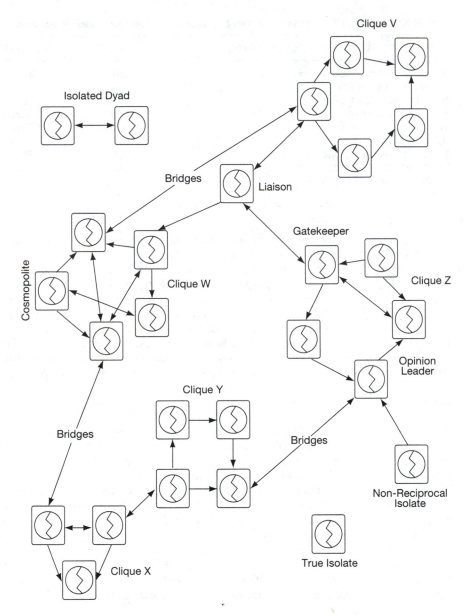

FIGURE 8.4
Hypothetical Network Diagram Showing Communication Network Roles

on the development of contacts. Peter B. Smith (1973) summarized research on constraints of the environment on behavior in organizations and concluded that the environment "may prevent certain patterns of communication. If it permits them, this still does not ensure that those patterns will arise, but the prevented patterns are definitely ruled out" (p. 55). Thus it seems consistent with experience to have Rogers and Agarwala-Rogers (1976) conclude that "most clique members are relatively close to each other in the formal hierarchy of the organization, suggesting the similarity of the formal and informal communication systems" (p. 130).

One requirement of clique membership is that individuals must be able to make contact with one another, even by indirect means. Baird (1977) analyzed the impact of a person's attitudes on the choice of media used in making contacts. He postulated that we might be more attracted to some people than to others and observed that "in communicating with those we like, we usually use the most immediate channel available; face-to-face, even though it may necessitate traveling relatively long distances; telephone calls become too expensive. On the other hand face-to-face contact with those we dislike usually is avoided; we resort to written communication or to sending messages through intermediaries" (p. 260). His concept of *immediate* was derived from Mehrabian (1971) and refers to situations involving "an increase in the sensory stimulation between two persons" (p. 3). Thus face-to-face contact is the most immediate, whereas letters and intermediaries are less immediate.

It is likely that cliques will consist of individuals whose environmental circumstances (offices, work assignments) permit contact, who like one another, and who find contacts of high immediacy satisfying. These three conditions do suggest that cliques may frequently consist of individuals who have both formal, positional reasons for making contacts as well as informal, interpersonal reasons.

Isolate   The first task of network analysis is to identify those who are members of cliques and those who are not. Because clique members are individuals who have more than half of their contacts with other members of the clique, *isolates* are those who have less frequent contact or no contact at all with other group members. The concept of isolate is relative and must be defined for each analysis of communication networks. Networks are usually defined in terms of the content of messages. Thus it is possible for an organization member to be an isolate in a network whose messages concern governmental relations with the organization but to be a central clique member when messages concern the internal administration of a division of the organization. Some organization members are isolates when it comes to the personal lives of other employees but are clearly clique members when messages concern changes in organization policies and procedures.

Goldhaber (1979) has summarized the characteristics of isolates. He suggests that isolates differ from clique members by being

1. Less secure in their self-concepts;
2. Less motivated by achievement;
3. Less willing to interact with others;
4. Younger and less experienced with the system;
5. Less often in positions of power in the organization;
6. More inclined to withhold information than facilitate its flow;
7. Relatively more dissatisfied with the system; and
8. Concerned that the communication system is closed to them.

Bridge   A *bridge* is a member of a clique who has a predominant number of intragroup contacts and who also has contact with a member of another clique. A bridge serves as a direct contact between two groups of employees. Farace and colleagues (1977) estimate that the distortion of messages will increase when contacts between and linkages among cliques are handled primarily by bridges. As one who relays messages and is a central figure in the communication system of a clique, a bridge is susceptible to all of the conditions that produce information forfeiture, message decay, and distortion.

Liaison   The relay relationship discussed earlier in the text is illustrated most clearly by the liaison communication network role. A *liaison* is a person who links or connects two or more cliques but who is *not* a member of any of the groups connected. Liaisons have been the subject of research longer than any other role because they were recognized early as critical to the functioning of an organization or social system (Coleman, 1964; Davis, 1953; Jacobsen & Seashore, 1951; Schwartz, 1977; Schwartz & Jacobsen, 1977; Weiss & Jacobsen, 1955). Liaisons tie units of the organization together and represent people through whom much of the information of the organization is funneled. Ross and Harary (1955) noted that "if a liaison person is a bottleneck, the organization suffers badly, while if he is efficient, he tends to expedite the flow of the entire organization" (p.1).

Most of the evidence suggests that liaisons are important roles for the effective functioning of an organization. They can either facilitate the flow of information or block it. Rogers and Agarwala-Rogers (1976) suggest that "liaison roles may have to be formally created in an organization if they do not exist informally" (p. 138).

The major differences between liaisons and nonliaison members of an organizational communication system have been summarized by Farace and co-workers (1977). Figure 8.5 shows the major differences between liaisons and nonliaisons in terms of their actual communication behaviors, how they perceive themselves, and how others perceive them.

The distinctiveness of the liaison role stems not so much from any special personal characteristic as from the unique relay function they hold in the communication network (Rogers & Agarwala-Rogers, 1976).

Gatekeeper Gatekeeping, report Katz and Lazarsfeld (1955), means "controlling a strategic portion of a channel . . . so as to have the power of decision over whether whatever is flowing through the channel will enter the group or not" (p. 119). In an organizational communication network a *gatekeeper* is a person who is strategically located in the network so as to exercise control over what messages will be disseminated through the system. The gatekeeper is most noticeable in serial communication networks, since information and messages can be controlled at just about every link. Every relay person in a serial chain can be a gatekeeper.

FIGURE 8.5 Characteristics of Liaisons

Objective Characteristics of Liaisons
1. Liaisons have higher agreement (between themselves and others with whom they talk) about the identity of their contacts than do nonliaisons.
2. Liaisons are more likely to serve as first sources of information than are others in the organization.
3. Liaisons have higher formal status in the organization than do nonliaisons.
4. Liaisons have been organizational members for longer periods of time than have nonliaisons.
5. The levels of formal education and the ages of liaisons are similar to those of nonliaisons.

Liaisons Perceive Themselves as
6. having greater numbers of communication contacts in the organization;
7. having greater amounts of information with respect to the content dimensions upon which their role is defined;
8. participating in a communication system that is more "open"—information is seen as more timely, more believable, and more useful;
9. having grater influence in the organization.

Liaisons Are Perceived by Others as
10. having greater numbers of communication contacts in the organization;
11. having a wider range throughout the organizational structure;
12. having more information on the content dimensions on which the network is defined;
13. having more control over the flow of information in the organization;
14. having more influence over the "power structure" of the organization;
15. more competent at their organizational activities.

Source: From Richard V. Farace, Peter R. Monge, and Hamish M. Russell, *Communicating and Organizing* Copyright © 1977 by Richard V. Farace, Peter R. Monge, and Hamish M. Russell. Reprinted by permission of McGraw-Hill, Inc.

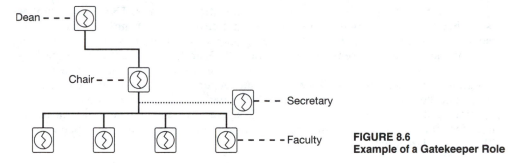

FIGURE 8.6
Example of a Gatekeeper Role

Thus our discussion of the functions of a relay person—linking, storing, stretching, and controlling—represents a description of the activities of a gatekeeper.

In a university, the chair of a department is a fairly clear example of a gatekeeper at work. Faculty are asked to funnel their requests through the chair. The dean, the superior of a chair, in turn funnels information for the faculty back through the chair. The chair controls what information the faculty will receive about the budget, directives and requests from the dean, and information about hiring, firing, and retiring. Figure 8.6 portrays a typical gatekeeper which many of you will recognize. For a faculty member to have access to the chair, he or she must negotiate past the gatekeeper—the department secretary. The secretary provides the chair with information about people who want appointments and with selected information to assist the chair in deciding how the appointment will proceed. One positive consequence of having an efficient secretary-gatekeeper is the reduction in communication load. The secretary-gatekeeper may screen out or handle a great many contacts that may considerably relieve the load on an administrator. A secretary-gatekeeper may also keep a manager from knowing important information and reduce the manager's effectiveness. One interesting research question concerns what guidelines a gatekeeper, such as a secretary, uses in deciding what information should get into the system or to the manager.

Opinion Leader   In contrast to official leaders who exercise authority in organizations by virtue of the positions they hold, there are individuals without a formal position within all social systems who guide opinions and influence people in their decisions. These individuals, called *opinion leaders*, are sought out for their opinions and influence. They are the people who keep up on things and whom others trust to let them know what is really going on. Katz and Lazarsfeld (1955) describe the opinion leader as an "almost invisible, certainly inconspicuous, form of leadership at the person-to-person level of ordinary, intimate, everyday contact" (p. 138).

Formal organizations, as well as communities, have opinion leaders who influence what people believe and do. They serve a key communication function by influencing opinion formation and attitude change. They are asked for their opinions, and members of the organization listen to them (Peterson, 1973).

Cosmopolite   A cosmopolitan person is one who belongs to all the world or one who is free from local, provincial, or national ideas, prejudices, or attachments. A *cosmopolite* is an individual who has contact with the outside world, with individuals beyond the organization. Cosmopolites link organization members with people and events beyond the confines of the organization structure. Organization members who travel a lot, are active in professional associations, and read regional, national, and international publications tend to be more cosmopolitan. They have more frequent contact with sources outside the organization and serve as conduits or channels for new ideas to enter the organization.

Each role plays a special part in communication networks. The clique member is the heart of the system and serves as the final destination for most messages. The isolate challenges the system and creates a degree of uncertainty in the effectiveness of the message dissemination program. The bridge is a central information-processor who provides direct connections between different cliques. The liaison integrates and interconnects cliques. The gatekeeper controls the movement of messages and contacts in order to minimize overload and increase effectiveness. The opinion leader facilitates the formation and changes of attitudes and aids in informal decision making. The cosmopolite connects the organization with people and ideas in the larger environment.

THE DIRECTIONS OF INFORMATION FLOW

In organizational communication we talk about information that proceeds formally from a person of higher authority to one of lower authority—downward communication; information that proceeds from a position of lower authority to one of higher authority—upward communication; information that moves along people and positions of approximately the same level of authority—horizontal communication; or information that moves among people and positions that are neither superior nor subordinate to one another and that are in different functional departments—cross-channel communication. We also refer to information that flows informally along the "grapevine." We shall examine each of these types of directional communication more closely. Figure 8.7 illustrates the four formal directions of information flow in an organization. We shall discuss those first.

FIGURE 8.7 Four Directions of Organizational Communication

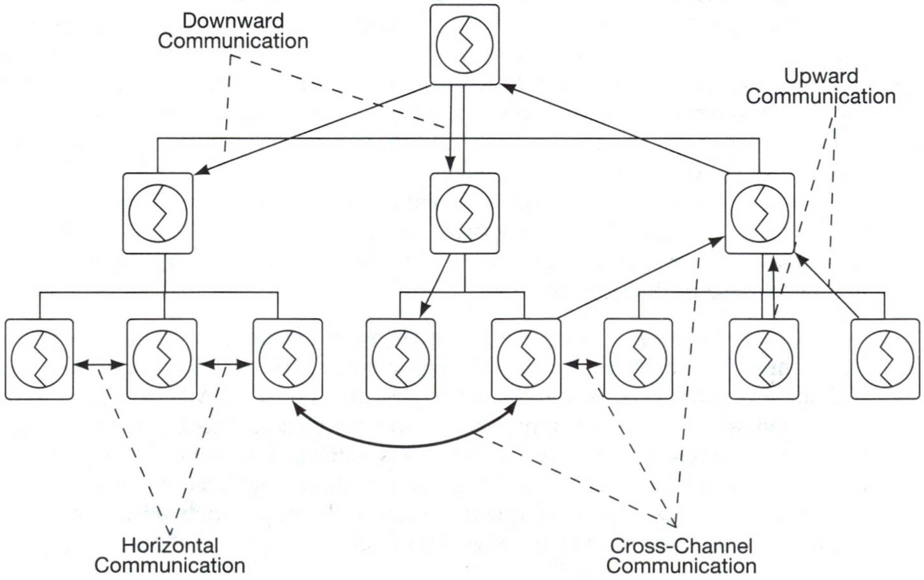

DOWNWARD COMMUNICATION

Downward communication in an organization means that information flows from positions of higher authority to those of lower authority. We usually think of information moving from management to employees; however, in organizations most of the links are in the management group (Davis, 1967). Figure 8.8 shows how the communication structure of a university has six management levels and only one operative level.

You can see how the emphasis in organizational communication can often move toward managerial communication in which the primary concerns are with downward communication, getting information through the management group and *to* the operative group. There are two important concerns: (1) what kinds of information are disseminated from management levels to employees and (2) how the information is provided.

Five types of information are usually communicated from superiors to subordinates (Katz & Kahn, 1966): (1) information about how to do a job, (2) information about the rationale for doing jobs, (3) information about organizational policies and practices, (4) information about an employee's performance, and (5) information to develop a sense of mission.

Employees at all levels in the organization feel a need to be informed. Top management lives in an information world. The quality and quantity of information must be high in order to make meaningful and accurate decisions. Top management must have information from all units in the organization, and it must get information out to all units. The flow of information from top management down to operatives is a continuous and difficult activity. The selection of ways to provide information involves not only the expenditure of direct monetary resources but also psychic and emotional resources.

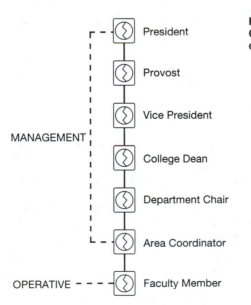

FIGURE 8.8
Organizational Chart Showing Six Levels of Management and One Level of Operative

Selection of Methods and Media

Level (1972) surveyed supervisors and asked them to rate the effectiveness of different combinations of methods for different types of communication situations (Table 8.2). The four methods were (1) written only, (2) oral only, (3) written followed by oral, and (4) oral followed by written. The oral-followed-by-written method was rated *most effective* in six of the ten situations and was never rated as inappropriate for any situation. Situations requiring immediate action but with some follow-up later, those of a general nature with documentation desired, and those involving positive interpersonal relations seemed best handled by the oral-followed-by-written method.

The oral-only method was ranked most effective in situations involving reprimands and settling disputes but least effective in six other situations, although four of the six situations were also ranked most effective for the combination of oral-followed-by-written method. This implies that the oral method is desirable but not by itself.

The written-only method was ranked most effective when information for future action was needed, when the information was general, and when no personal contact was necessary. The written-followed-by-oral method was not ranked most effective or least effective for any situation.

Six criteria are often used for selecting methods of communicating information to employees (Level & Galle, 1988).

1. *Availability*. Those methods that are currently available in the organization will tend to be used. After an inventory of available methods, the organization can decide what methods could be added for a more effective program overall.

2. *Cost*. The method judged to be least costly will tend to be selected for routine and nonurgent information dissemination. When nonroutine and urgent dissemination is necessary or desirable, more costly but faster methods will probably be used.

TABLE 8.2 Most Effective versus Least Effective Methods for Communicating with Employees in Ten Different Situations

SITUATION	MOST EFFECTIVE	LEAST EFFECTIVE
1. Communicating information requiring immediate employee action	Oral followed by written	Written only
2. Communicating information requiring future employee action	Written only	Oral only
3. Communicating information of a general nature	Written only	Oral only
4. Communicating a company directive or order	Oral followed by written	Oral only
5. Communicating information on an important company policy change	Oral followed by written	Oral only
6. Communicating with your immediate supervisor about work progress	Oral followed by written	Oral only
7. Promoting a safety campaign	Oral followed by written	Oral only
8. Commending an employee for noteworthy work	Oral followed by written	Written only
9. Reprimanding an employee for work deficiency	Oral only	Written only
10. Settling a dispute among employees about a work problem	Oral only	Written only

Source: From Dale L. Level, Jr., "Communication Effectiveness: Method and Situation," *The Journal of Business Communication*, 10 (Fall 1972), 19–25. Reprinted by permission of Dale L. Level, Jr., and the American Business Communication Association, publisher of *The Journal of Business Communication*.

3. *Impact*. The method that seems to provide the greatest impact or impression will frequently be chosen over a method that lacks flair or is fairly standard.

4. *Relevance*. The method that seems most relevant to the purpose to be achieved will be chosen more often. A short, informative purpose may be accomplished with a conversation followed by a memo. If the communication of complex details is the purpose, a written technical report may be the method chosen.

5. *Response*. The method selected will be influenced by whether a specific response to the information is desired or necessary. In a training setting it may be desirable to use a method that allows and encourages trainees to react and ask questions. In such a case a face-to-face meeting would probably be the method chosen.

6. *Skills*. The methods that seem to fit the abilities of the sender to actually use *and* the abilities of the receiver to comprehend will tend to be used over those that seem beyond the skills of the communicator or that seem beyond the capabilities of the employee to understand. A glossy brochure will probably not be used if the communicator does not feel capable of producing it; if the employees' level of education is limited, a complex manual of instructions would probably not be a good method to use.

New technologies bring an ever-increasing number of communication options. How should managers choose among the options of electronic mail, teleconferencing, fax, etc.? Trevino, Daft, and Lengel (1990) present a conceptual framework for managerial media choice. Selection of media is dependent on message equivocality. Equivocality refers to multiple and conflicting interpretations. High equivocality results when a situation is ambiguous and sharing meaning is difficult. Daft and Lengel (1984) argue that media have differing capacities for facilitating understanding and that they can be viewed as "rich" or "lean" based on their capacity to resolve ambiguity and facilitate shared meaning. Richness is dependent on the capacity of the media for processing equivocal information.

Trevino, Daft, and Lengel (1990) maintain that the richness of each medium is based on (1) the availability of instant feedback, (2) the capacity to transmit multiple cues—body language, voice tone, etc., (3) the use of natural language to convey subtleties, and (4) a personal focus that allows inclusion of personal feelings and emotions to adapt to the situation of receiver. According to these criteria, face-to-face is considered the richest communication medium, whereas reports are placed in the "lean" category. Individuals are not totally free to make media choices based on message equivocality. Decisions may be based on the resources available and the time pressures involved.

Lengel and Daft (1988) provide some guidelines for the manager:

1. Send equivocal messages through a rich medium (allows for negotiation of meaning).
2. Send equivocal messages through a lean medium (conveying of hard data, official directives, etc.).
3. Be a critical receiver (realize that messages can color understanding because of the medium selected; lean media can filter out information about critical issues).
4. Use the medium for its symbolic messages (be sensitive to the organization's media culture and the meaning that the media itself may convey).
5. Evaluate new technology carefully (capabilities and limitations).

Contractor and Eisenberg (1990) challenge the notion that media characteristics can be matched with task characteristics within organizations. They question whether each medium has an "objective" social presence and each communication task a single goal in actual practice. To suggest that a specific media can be understood in terms of its ability simply to transmit information (1) assumes a passive receiver, (2) ignores the local context in determining the meaning of any given communication, and (3) endorses the idea that clarity and openness should be equated with effectiveness. Effectiveness might be decided by what is political and strategic. In that case ambiguity may serve valuable functions.

Selection of media may be based on considerations of media characteristics, the outcomes sought, cost and time factors, and the cultural context in which the exchange takes place.

UPWARD COMMUNICATION

Upward communication in an organization means that information flows from lower levels (subordinates) to higher levels (supervisors). All employees in an organization, except possibly those at the top level, may communicate upward—that is, any subordinate may have good reason either to request information from or give information to someone with more authority than he or she has. A request or comment directed toward an individual with broader, higher, or more extensive authority is the essence of upward communication.

Values of Upward Communication

Upward communication is important for a number of reasons.

1. The upward flow of information supplies valuable information for decision making by those who direct the organization and supervise the activities of others (Sharma, 1979).
2. Upward communication lets supervisors know when their subordinates are ready for information from them and how well subordinates accept what they have been told (Planty & Machaver, 1952).
3. Upward communication allows—even encourages—gripes and grievances to surface and lets supervisors know what is bothering those who are closer to the actual operations (Conboy, 1976).
4. Upward communication cultivates appreciation and loyalty to the organization by giving employees an opportunity to ask questions and contribute ideas and suggestions about the operation of the organization (Planty & Machaver, 1952).
5. Upward communication permits supervisors to determine whether subordinates got the meaning that was intended from the downward flow of information (Planty & Machaver, 1952).
6. Upward communication helps employees cope with their work problems and strengthen their involvement in their jobs and with the organization (Harriman, 1974).

What Should Be Communicated Up the Line?

Most analyses and research on upward communication suggest that supervisors and managers ought to get information from subordinates that

1. Tells what the subordinates are doing—their work, achievements, progress, and plans for the future.
2. Describes unsolved work problems on which subordinates may need or would like some type of assistance.
3. Offers suggestions or ideas for improvements within their unit or the organization as a whole.
4. Reveals how subordinates think and feel about their jobs, their co-workers, and the organization.

Why Is It Difficult to Get Information Up the Line?

Merrihue (1960) observed that "it would have been wiser to have first bulldozed and paved an uphill street from employees to top management, but that is a much more complex and time-consuming task and most of us are not quite sure that we, as yet, know how to do it" (p. 195). Harriman (1974) reported that "we surveyed hundreds of companies in the United States and Canada. . . . We encountered no experts, studies or programs on upward communications" (pp. 148-149). Both may be right. Upward communication may be too complex and too time-consuming and have too few organization managers who know how to get information up the line.

The difficulty of getting information up the line was alluded to by Davis (1967) when he noted that a manager's

> status and prestige at the plant are different from the workers'. He probably talks differently and dresses differently. He can freely call a worker to his desk or walk to his work station, but the worker is not equally free to call in his manager. The worker usually lacks ability to express himself as clearly as the manager, who is better trained and has more practice in communication skills. Neither can the worker have a specialist prepare his communication, but this service is usually available to the manager. Just as the worker lacks technical assistance, he also usually lacks the use of certain media, such as plant magazines, public-address systems, and meetings. The worker is further impeded because he is talking to a man with whose work and responsibilities he is not familiar (p. 344).

Sharma (1979) lists four reasons why upward communication seems so difficult:

1. *The tendency for employees to conceal their thoughts.* Studies have shown that employees feel that they will get into trouble if they speak up to their supervisors and that the best way to move up in the organization is to agree with their supervisors.
2. *The feeling that supervisors and managers are not interested in employee problems.* Employees report quite frequently that their managers are not concerned about their problems. Managers may not respond to employee problems and may even stifle some upward communication because it might make them look bad to their superiors.
3. *A lack of rewards for employee upward communication.* Frequently, supervisors and managers fail to provide either intangible or tangible rewards for maintaining open upward communication channels.
4. *The feeling that supervisors and managers are inaccessible and unresponsive to what employees say.* Either supervisors are too busy to listen or the subordinates cannot find them. If the supervisor is located, he or she is unresponsive to what the subordinate says.

The combination of these four feelings and beliefs creates a powerful deterrent to the expression of ideas, opinions, and information by subordinates, especially if the process and procedures by which upward communication is to occur are unwieldy and cumbersome.

How Can Information Get Up the Line?

Jackson (1959) noted that the forces that direct communication in an organization are, on the whole, motivational. Employees tend to communicate in order to accomplish some goal, to satisfy some personal need, or to try to improve their immediate circumstances. He suggests that any program of organizational communication must be based on a climate of trust. When trust exists, employees are more likely to communicate ideas and feelings more freely, and supervisors are more likely to interpret what employees mean more accurately.

The importance of creating and maintaining a climate of trust cannot be stated too frequently. Upward communication just will not occur when supervisors feel that they must guard against employees talking to the manager above them. Rogers and Agarwala-Rogers (1976) describe an effort by a large eastern bank to stimulate upward communication with a "sound-off" program. Employees were encouraged to take their complaints and suggestions to the personnel department or to managers above their supervisors if they did not receive satisfaction from their immediate supervisors. It was discovered that supervisors felt that any contact between their subordinates and the supervisors' bosses was threatening and improper. Employees did not think it was improper, but they did feel that it was dangerous. As one employee said, "You bypass the supervisor once and go to Personnel, the first thing they do is get the supervisor on the phone and tell him everything. Next, you're in trouble" (p. 98). Wendlinger (1973) discovered a similar situation in a large West Coast bank. He reported "that there was no way to confidently express an opinion or solve a problem when normal channels had broken down. Some employees feared the possibility of reprisals as a result of bypassing their supervisors with such ideas or proposals, and others were concerned that management—seemingly remote in a rapidly growing organization—was not really interested in their attitudes and opinions" (p. 17).

To facilitate upward communication Wendlinger's organization created an "Open Line" program in which employees were able to submit problems, complaints, or opinions to top management with their identities being kept completely confidential, known only to the Open Line coordinator, with a guaranteed candid written reply from management that was sent to the employee's home. The success of the program was attributed to two factors: The employee's identity was protected, and the answers were honest. The coordinator of Open Line was given one mission: to make the job itself unnecessary, which means arriving at a time when free and open communication precludes the need for Open Line, where mutual trust and understanding make upward communication an easy job.

Principles of Upward Communication

Planty and Machaver (1952) identified seven principles to guide programs of upward communication. The principles seem as applicable today as when they were formulated.

1. *An effective upward communication program must be planned.* Although confidentiality and candor undergird all effective communication programs, supervisors and managers must stimulate, encourage, and find ways to promote upward communication.

2. *An effective upward communication program operates continuously.* Subordinates must initiate information to and request information from higher levels regardless of how things are going. Supervisors and managers must be receptive to information from subordinates and be willing to respond to what they receive when the organization is functioning smoothly as well as when things seem to be going badly.

3. *An effective upward communication program uses the routine channels.* Without denying any employee the opportunity of making contact with and being heard by managers at any level, information should flow upward through the organization following the usual, routine steps. Problems and requests for information should move upward through the organization until they reach the person who can take action; if that person can provide the information or resolve the problem, there should be little need to go beyond that point.

4. *An effective upward communication program stresses sensitivity and receptivity in entertaining ideas from lower levels*. Differences in interpretations and perceptions of events should be expected. A person's position in the organization encourages him or her to see things differently and to assign different meanings to them. Differences in values and priorities lead to differences in inferences and conclusions. Listening in order to understand what a person means is basic to effective upward communication.

5. *An effective upward communication program involves objective listening*. Supervisors and managers must devote the time to listening to subordinates in an objective way. Reactions that distract from the seriousness of information and irritating listening habits show that upward communication is not really desired. Hearing a subordinate out, putting him or her at ease, and reducing tensions reveal a receptive intent and a willingness to hear contrary opinions, implied criticisms, and alternative points of view.

6. *An effective upward communication program involves taking action to respond to problems*. Active listening may get new ideas into the open, but a failure to take action only creates resentment and undermines the good faith in upward communication. When changes in policies or actions should be made, just listening without adjustments denies the idea of effective upward communication. If action cannot be taken, the subordinate should be informed and reasons given for why changes cannot be made.

7. *An effective upward communication program uses a variety of media and methods to promote the flow of information*. The most effective method of upward communication is daily face-to-face contacts and conversations among supervisors and subordinates.

In summary, this section has reviewed the values of upward communication in an organization, discussed what kinds of information should be communicated up the line, analyzed why it is difficult to get information from lower levels to higher levels in an organization, described the climate that seems most conducive to getting information to flow upward, and listed seven principles of an effective program of upward communication. For additional specific analysis of upward influence and message processes, see Schilit & Locke (1982) and Stohl & Redding (1987).

Two directions of information flow have been considered—downward and upward. Together they constitute what is often called *vertical communication*. Information is also shared among organization members who occupy positions of approximately the same level of authority; we refer to it as *horizontal communication*.

HORIZONTAL COMMUNICATION

Horizontal communication consists of sharing information among peers within the same work unit. A work unit is comprised of individuals who are located at the same authority level in the organization and have the same superior. Thus, at a university, a work unit may be a department. A department of communication, a department of organizational behavior, and a department of instructional science all include faculty members who are supervised by a chairperson. Communication among faculty members in one of the departments is what we call horizontal communication. Communication between faculty members in one department and faculty members in another department is what we shall call *cross-channel communication*—that is, information is shared across functional boundaries, or work units, and among people who are neither subordinate nor superior to one another.

Purposes of Horizontal Communication

Research and experience suggest that horizontal communication occurs for at least six reasons:

1. *To coordinate work assignments.* Members of a training and development department have a major training activity to organize and deliver. They need to meet to coordinate who will do what.

2. *To share information on plans and activities.* When ideas from several minds promise to be better than ideas from just one person, horizontal communication becomes critical. In creating the design of a training program or a public relations campaign, members of a department may need to share information on their plans and what they will be doing.

3. *To solve problems.* Recently three student interns were given assignments in the same general location. They met and engaged in horizontal communication in order to reduce the number of unnecessary trips and share rides. They were able to reduce costs and to work together to arrive at their organization assignments with fewer problems.

4. *To secure common understanding.* When changes are proposed in the requirements for an academic major, faculty must work together to produce a common understanding about what changes should be made. Meetings and conversations among faculty members at the same organizational level and within the same department are especially important in achieving understanding.

5. *To conciliate, negotiate, and arbitrate differences.* Individuals frequently develop preferences and priorities that eventually lead to disagreements. When this occurs, horizontal communication among members of the work unit is essential in conciliating differences. In fact, some differences may need to be negotiated or arbitrated. It is only through horizontal communication that priorities can be accommodated and conflicts resolved.

6. *To develop interpersonal support.* Because we spend a great deal of time interacting with others on the job, we all derive some degree of interpersonal support from our colleagues. Much of our horizontal communication is for the purpose of strengthening interpersonal ties and relationships. Co-workers often have lunch together and meet at breaks to strengthen interpersonal relationships. Horizontal communication plays an important part in producing rapport among employees and encouraging a cohesive work unit. Employees at the same level who interact frequently seem to have less trouble understanding one another. Interaction among colleagues provides emotional and psychological support.

Methods of Horizontal Communication

The most common forms of horizontal communication involve some type of interpersonal contact. Even written forms of horizontal communication tend to be more casual. Horizontal communication occurs most often in committee meetings, informal interaction, during breaks, telephone conversations, memos and notes, social activities, and quality circles. A quality circle is a voluntary group of workers who have shared areas of responsibility. It is primarily a normal work group producing a part of a product or service. Members of the circle meet together each week to discuss, analyze, and suggest ideas for improving their work. They are trained in the use of specific problem-solving procedures and specific techniques, such as cause-and-effect diagrams, Pareto diagrams or bar charts with data arranged in order of importance, histograms, checklists, and graphs. Circle leaders are trained in leadership skills, adult learning methods, and motivation and communication techniques. Circle meetings are held on organization time and on organization premises. Quality circles are generally given full responsibility for identifying and solving problems (Yager, 1980).

Barriers to horizontal communication have much in common with those affecting upward and downward communication. Lack of trust among co-workers, intense concerns about upward mobility, and competition for resources can affect the way in which employees at the same level in the organization communicate with one another.

CROSS-CHANNEL COMMUNICATION

In most organizations a need exists for employees to share information across functional boundaries with individuals who occupy positions that are neither subordinate nor superior to their own. For example, departments such as engineering, research, accounting, and personnel gather data, issue reports, prepare plans, coordinate activities, and advise managers about the work of individuals in all parts of an organization. They cross functional lines and communicate with people who supervise and are supervised but who are neither superior nor subordinate to them. They lack line authority to direct those with whom they communicate and must rely primarily on selling their ideas. Nevertheless, they have considerable mobility within the organization; they can visit other areas or leave their offices just to engage in informal conversation (Davis, 1967).

Staff specialists are usually the most active in cross-channel communication because their responsibilities usually influence what occurs in several authority chains of command or positional networks. The training and development unit, for example, may have contacts with production, sales, industrial relations, purchasing, research, and engineering as well as with customers, for customer training. Staff specialists frequently have closer contact with top management, which permits them to short-circuit the authoritative system. Keith Davis (1967) rightly observes that "the results are both good and bad. Communication upward and downward tends to be improved, but lower management often waits in insecurity with the fear that it is being bypassed or criticized without an opportunity to answer" (p. 346).

Because of the potentially large number of cross-channel contacts by staff specialists and others who need to make contacts in other chains of command, it is important to have an organization policy to guide cross-channel communication. Fayol (1916–1940) demonstrated that cross-channel communication was appropriate, and even necessary at times, especially for employees who were lower in a channel. As shown in Figure 8.9, Employee P may save time and conserve resources by communicating directly with Employee Y (through a bridge). Because of the potential for undermining the authority channels and for losing control over the flow of information, two conditions must be met as part of using Fayol's bridge:

1. Each employee who wishes to communicate across channels must secure permission in advance from his or her direct supervisor (in Figure 8.9, Employee P would secure permission from Supervisor H). In some cases the permission may be granted in the form of a general policy statement indicating the circumstances that justify cross-channel communication.
2. Each employee who engages in cross-channel communication must inform his or her supervisor of what happened as a result of the meeting.

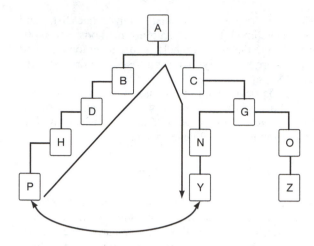

FIGURE 8.9
Fayol's Bridge for Employee P

The importance of cross-channel communication in organization prompted Keith Davis (1967) to suggest that the application of three principles would strengthen the communication role of staff specialists:

1. Staff specialists must be trained in communication skills.
2. Staff specialists need to recognize the importance of their communication role.
3. Management should recognize the role of staff specialist and make greater use of it in organizational communication.

Both horizontal and cross-channel communication involve lateral relationships essential to effective organizational communication. In this section we have focused primarily on *positional communication*, which involves the flow of information between people in positions in an organization. Employees often communicate from their positions. Frequently, however, organization members communicate with others without regard to their positions. This results in one or more *personal communication networks*. Positional communication is usually referred to as *formal communication*; personal communication is usually called *informal communication*. We shall briefly analyze the idea of personal or informal communication in an organization.

INFORMAL, PERSONAL, OR GRAPEVINE COMMUNICATION

When employees communicate with one another without regard to position in the organization, the factors directing the flow of information are more personal. The direction of information flow is less stable. Information flows upward, downward, horizontally, and across channels with little, if any, regard for designated positional relationships. Because this informal, personal information emerges from interaction among people, it appears to flow in unpredictable directions, and its network is referred to as a *grapevine*. The metaphor seems apt; a grapevine seems to grow and send out shoots in all directions, capturing and hiding the fruit under a cover of heavy leaves, almost defying detection.

Information that flows along the grapevine network also appears to be fickle and furtive. In terms of communication, the grapevine has been described as "a person-to-person method of relaying secret reports which cannot be obtained through regular channels" (Stein, 1967, p. 616). Informal communication does tend to consist of "secret" reports about people and events that do not flow through official, formal channels. Information obtained through the grapevine concerns "what someone said or heard" rather than what was announced by authorities. At least the sources seem to be "secret" even if the information itself is not.

Characteristics of the Grapevine

Although research on characteristics of the grapevine is not extensive, enough has been completed over the years to suggest the following factors (W. L. Davis & O'Connor, 1977):

1. The grapevine functions largely through word-of-mouth interaction.
2. The grapevine is generally free of organization and positional restraints.
3. The grapevine moves information rapidly.
4. The grapevine network is described as a *cluster chain* because each relay person tends to tell a cluster of people rather than just one other person.
5. Participants in a grapevine network tend to take one of three roles: liaisons, isolates, or dead-enders (those who usually do not pass on the information).
6. The grapevine tends to be more a product of the situation than of the people in the organization.
7. The sooner a person knows about an event after it happens, the more likely he or she is to tell others.
8. If information being told to a person concerns something in which he or she is interested, that individual is more likely to tell the information to others.
9. The predominant flow of information on the grapevine tends to occur within functional groups rather than between them.
10. Generally from 75 to 90 percent of the details of the message being transmitted by the grapevine are accurate; however, as Keith Davis (1967) notes, "People tend to think the grapevine is less accurate than it really is because its errors are more dramatic and consequently more impressed on memory than its day-to-day routine accuracy. Moreover, the inaccurate parts are often more important" (p. 244).
11. Grapevine information is usually somewhat incomplete, lending itself to misinterpretation even when the details are accurate.
12. The grapevine tends to exert some influence in the organization, whether for good or evil; thus an understanding of the grapevine and how it can contribute positively to the organization is important.

How to Work with the Grapevine

The number and detrimental effects of messages passed along the grapevine can be controlled by keeping the formal channels of communication open, allowing for candid, accurate, and sensitive upward, downward, horizontal, and cross-channel communication. Effective supervisor-subordinate relationships seem crucial to controlling grapevine information. Supervisors and managers should let employees know that they understand and accept information on the grapevine, especially since it reveals something about employee feelings, even if the information is incomplete and not always accurate.

RELATIONSHIPS

One of the most distinctive features of organizational communication is the concept of relationship. Goldhaber (1979) defines an organization as a "network of interdependent relationships" (p. 14). When things are interdependent, this means that they both affect and are affected by each other. The pattern and nature of relationships in an organization may be determined by the positions and prescribed roles for those positions. This gives structure and stability to the organization. However, individuals act outside of role structure, thereby creating communication linkages and structure. This emergent communication structure may not coincide with "positional relationships." Relationships within organizations differ in terms of their "interpersonal" nature.

INTERPERSONAL RELATIONSHIPS

The most intimate relationships we have with other people on a personal, friend-to-friend, peer-to-peer level are usually referred to as *interpersonal*. Our closest friends in an organization, on the job, in church, or at the club tend to care for us more than others. It is with them that we have our most satisfying interpersonal relationships. With them we *resonate*, *vibrate*, and *jibe*, indicating that we care for them. Hoopes (1969) has observed that "the alienated are those people who have been excluded or who have excluded themselves" (p. xii). In authentic interpersonal relationships no one is excluded, nor does anyone want to exclude others.

What are some characteristics of effective interpersonal relationships? One particular analysis (Pace & Boren, 1973) of interpersonal relationships suggests that you will be successful if you do the following:

1. Maintain close personal contact without having feelings of hostility develop.
2. Define and assert your own identity in relation to others without having disagreements erupt.
3. Pass information on to others without having confusion, misunderstanding, distortion, or other unintended changes occur.
4. Engage in open problem solving without provoking defensiveness or breaking off the process.
5. Help others to develop their own effective personal and interpersonal styles.
6. Participate in informal social interaction without engaging in tricks or ploys or devices that put a damper on pleasant communication.

Although you may think of other general goals to be achieved through effective interpersonal relationships, these will suffice to illustrate the direction of our thinking on this issue. Much of the content of later chapters will address the question that usually looms large at this point: How does one achieve those goals? It has been suggested elsewhere (Pace, Boren, & Peterson, 1975) that interpersonal relationships tend to improve when both parties do the following:

1. Communicate feelings directly and in a warm, expressive manner.
2. Communicate what is happening in their private worlds through self-disclosure.
3. Communicate a warm, positive understanding of each other by giving relevant, understanding responses.

4. Communicate a genuineness toward each other by expressing acceptance both verbally and nonverbally.

5. Communicate an ongoing and unconditional positive regard for each other through nonevaluative, friendly responses.

6. Communicate why it may be difficult or even impossible to agree with each other in nonevaluative, accurate, honest, constructive confrontation.

Clearly interpersonal relationships exert a powerful and pervasive influence over organizational affairs. Where the conditions for good interpersonal relationships exist, we also tend to find positive responses to supervisors, responsiveness to personal and organizational needs, sensitivity to employee feelings, and a willingness to share information, all prerequisites for effective upward and downward communication. Sometimes increased productivity is also found. *Quality circles* represent a way of utilizing improved interpersonal relationships to facilitate increased productivity, but their success is contingent upon an organizational climate that may be very difficult to produce generally (see Zemke, 1980). To understand better the important but fragile nature of interpersonal relationships in organizations, we shall look at the second type of relationship: positional.

POSITIONAL RELATIONSHIPS

Positional relationships are defined by the authority structure and functional duties of members of the organization. The rationale for creating an organization based on positional relationships was presented in an earlier chapter on classical theories of organization. Many theories of organization place the concept of positional relationships at their center. Koontz and O'Donnell (1968) highlight these relationships in a chapter titled "Making Organizing Effective." They cite a dozen common mistakes that thwart the effective and efficient performance of individuals in the organization. We shall refer at some length to a few of the mistakes these researchers cite. For example, the first mistake is the failure to plan properly. Part of failing to plan properly is "organizing around people" (p. 407) rather than positions. Organizing around people leads to several problems that positional relationships avoid. In the first place, they suggest, you can never be sure that "all the necessary tasks will be undertaken" (p. 407). In the second place, a danger arises that "different people will desire to do the same things, resulting in conflict or multiple command" (p. 407). In the third place, through retirement, resignation, promotion, or death, "people have a way of coming and going in an enterprise . . . which makes organizing around them risky" (p. 407) and makes their duties hard to recognize and to fill easily. Koontz and O'Donnell cite "failure to clarify relationships" as the second mistake in organizing. They explain that failure to clarify organization relationships accounts for jealousy, friction, insecurity, inefficiencies, and buck-passing more than any other mistake in organizing. Jackson (1959), in discussing the communication problems of organizations, makes a similar observation: "I can think of nothing which would facilitate more the free and accurate flow of communication in an organization than consensus about questions of work, authority, prestige, and status relationships" (p. 20). Those elements are, of course, intimately tied in with positional relationships. For effective and efficient organizational functioning, positional relationships are probably the most critical to specify and clarify.

Superior-Subordinate Relationships

The most common positional relationship, and probably the most crucial to efficient and effective organizational functioning, is that of superior to subordinate. Positions in an organization are arranged in hierarchical order, creating a series of superior-subordinate relationships throughout the organization. In fact, except for the very top and the very bottom of the organization, all positions, and the people in them, have a subordinate relationship to some positions and a superior relationship to other positions. Thus regularities and patterns in superior-subordinate communication have implications for almost the entire organization. Where superior-subordinate relationships can be strengthened, the human resources of the entire organization can be strengthened.

The concept of superior-subordinate relationships rests firmly on differences in authority, which are translated into differences in status, privilege, and control. The superior is perceived, at least, as having higher status, more privileges, and certain areas of control over a subordinate. The subordinate has a lower status, fewer privileges, and is dependent on the superior. Although the subordinate is dependent on the superior and frequently defers to the superior, the superior is also dependent on the subordinate. For example, a supervisor must depend on a subordinate to go along with the directives and suggestions, to complete the work, to accept instructions, to inform the superior of problems, and to relay information to others. The way in which a subordinate responds to a superior, according to research and observation (Sanford, Hunt, & Bracey, 1976), is contingent upon such factors as how much the subordinate trusts the superior, much as we suggested in our discussion of interpersonal relationships, and how badly the subordinate wants to move up in the organization—or upward mobility aspirations. Jackson (1959) suggested, for example, that employees are "always communicating as if they were trying to improve their position" and that they communicate with people "who will help them achieve their aims." That suggests, of course, that the quality of communication between a superior and a subordinate may very well be a function of the interpersonal relationship established between them and how the relationship satisfies the subordinate's needs.

Jablin's (1979) synthesis of superior-subordinate communication identified nine categories of issues: (1) interaction patterns, (2) openness, (3) upward distortion, (4) upward influence, (5) semantic-information distance, (6) effective versus ineffective superiors, (7) personal characteristics of dyads, (8) feedback, and (9) effects of systemic organization variables on the quality of superior-subordinate communication. Figure 8.10 summarizes a few of the major findings on each of the nine issues of superior-subordinate communication.

Research on subordinate-to-superior communication indicates that subordinates tend to tell superiors what they think the superior wants to hear, or what the subordinate wants the superior to hear, and to send superiors information that reflects favorably on the subordinate or, at least, does not reflect badly on the subordinate (Krivonos, 1976; Maier, Hoffman, & Read, 1963: Mellinger, 1956; Pelz, 1952; Read, 1962). These consequences appear to be related to the nature of positional relationships in organizations and especially to the inherent hierarchical, superior-subordinate relationship that comes from the structure of organizations. On the other hand, the hierarchy may be essential and inevitable in handling large numbers of people, in controlling interaction, and, in fact, in getting the work done. In spite of this seeming anomaly, the hierarchy and superiors and subordinates tend to create workable relationships and occasionally to engage in effective communication.

FIGURE 8.10 A Summary of Some Findings on Superior-Subordinate Communication

Interaction Patterns
 1. Between one-third and two-thirds of a supervisor's time is spent communicating with subordinates.
 2. The dominant mode of interaction is face-to-face discussion.
 3. The majority of interactions are about task issues.
 4. Superiors are more likely than subordinates to initiate interaction.
 5. Superiors are less positive toward and less satisfied with interactions with subordinates than with their superiors.
 6. A subordinate's job satisfaction is positively correlated with estimates of communication contact with superiors.
 7. Superiors think they communicate more with subordinates than subordinates think they do.
 8. Subordinates feel they send more messages to their supervisor than their supervisors think they do.
 9. Superiors who lack self-confidence are less willing to hold face-to-face discussions with subordinates.
 10. Role conflict and role ambiguity on the part of superiors are correlated with direct interactions with subordinates.
 11. Subordinates seek informal help in their work setting more from their superiors than from their peers or subordinates.
 12. Superiors are more likely to serve as liaisons about production rather than maintenance or innovation issues.

Openness in Communication
 13. Subordinates are more satisfied with their jobs when openness of communication exists between superiors and subordinates.
 14. Openness of communication appears to be related to organizational performance.
 15. The willingness of superiors and subordinates to talk as well as the actual talk on a topic is a function of perception of the other's willingness to listen.
 16. Superiors and subordinates prefer supervisor responses that are accepting and reciprocating rather than neutral-negative (unfeeling, cold, or nonaccepting).
 17. Subordinates dislike disconfirming responses from a superior and prefer those that provide positive relational feedback.

Upward Distortion of Communication
 18. In superior-subordinate relationships when one person does not trust the other, the nontrusting person will conceal his or her feelings and engage in evasive, compliant, or aggressive communicative behavior and under- or over-estimate agreement on issues.
 19. Subordinates will tend to omit critical comments in their interaction with superiors who have power over them.
 20. Mobility aspirations and low trust tend to have a negative influence on the accuracy of communication between subordinates and superiors; however, even if the subordinate trusts his or her superior, high mobility aspirations reduce the likelihood of communicating potentially threatening information.
 21. Subordinates seem to feel less free to communicate with superiors who have held the subordinate's position.
 22. Subordinates tend to see greater appropriateness, expect fewer harmful consequences, and have a greater willingness to disclose important, yet personally threatening, information to superiors in organic as compared with mechanistic organizational climates.
 23. Subordinate tendencies to disrupt upward communication can be reduced by increasing the superior's consideration or by increasing the accuracy with which the superior transmits downward information.
 24. Intrinsically motivated subordinates tend to distort messages less than do extrinsically motivated subordinates.

Upward Influence of a Subordinate's Superior, or the Pelz Effect
 25. Supervisors who exercise influence upward with their own superiors are more likely to have subordinates with high levels of satisfaction, although extremely high influence may separate subordinates from superiors.

(continued)

26. Subordinates who see their superior as having high upward influence also have a high desire for interaction with, high trust in, and a high estimation of accuracy of information received from the superior.

27. Subordinate confidence and trust in a superior are positively related to the superior's success in interactions with higher levels of management.

Semantic-Information Distance

28. The larger the semantic distance between superior and subordinate, the lower the subordinate's morale.

29. Superiors tend to overestimate the amount of knowledge subordinates possess on given topics.

30. Significant semantic distances exist between union and management personnel and between union leadership and their members.

31. Serious semantic distances are frequent between superiors and subordinates.

Effective versus Ineffective Superiors

32. More effective superiors tend to enjoy talking and speaking up in meetings, are able to explain instructions and policies, and enjoy conversing with subordinates.

33. More effective superiors tend to be empathic listeners, responding understandingly to silly questions; they are approachable and listen to suggestions and complaints.

34. More effective superiors tend to ask or persuade rather than tell or demand.

35. More effective superiors tend to be sensitive to the feelings and ego needs of subordinates.

36. More effective superiors tend to be more open in passing information along by giving advance notice of changes and explaining the reasons for policies and regulations.

37. Supervisory effectiveness tends to be contingent on such factors as task structure, superior-subordinate relations, and superior-position power.

Superior-Subordinate Personal Characteristics

38. Subordinates who have tendencies toward an internal locus of control see their superiors as more considerate than do external-control subordinates and are more satisfied with participative superiors.

39. Superiors who have tendencies toward internal locus of control tend use persuasion to obtain subordinate cooperation, whereas externals tend to use coercive power more.

40. Superiors tend to rate subordinates as competent when they have values similar to those of the superior.

41. Superiors who are apprehensive communicators are not particularly well liked by subordinates.

42. Authoritarian subordinates seem most satisfied when they work for directive superiors.

43. Subordinate satisfaction with his or her immediate superior is related to the subordinate's perception of the superior's credibility.

Feedback from Superiors and Subordinates

44. Subordinate feedback responsiveness is greater when subordinates are told what needs to be done with completed assignments, when the superior makes the assignment to the subordinate, and when the subordinate feels that he or she can secure clarification about assignments from the immediate superior.

45. Positive feedback to a superior tends to make the superior more task-oriented.

46. The performance of superiors tends to improve after feedback from a subordinate.

47. Feedback from a superior that shows a lack of trust results in subordinate dissatisfaction and aggressive feelings.

The Effects of Systemic Organizational Variables on Superior-Subordinate Communication

48. The technology of an organization tends to affect superior-subordinate communication.

49. Upper-level superiors tend to involve their subordinates more in decision making than do lower-level superiors.

50. Organizations with flat structures tend to reward superiors who favor sharing information and objectives with more rapid advancement than do organizations with tall structures.

Source: Extracted from the main points from Fredric M. Jablin, "Superior-Subordinate Communication: The State of the Art," *Psychological Bulletin*, 86 (1979), 1201–1222. Copyright 1979 American Psychological Association. Reprinted by permission of F. M. Jablin.

SERIAL RELATIONSHIPS

As we have seen, people have both interpersonal and positional relationships in organizations. In addition, they have serial relationships. Information is transmitted throughout formal organizations by a process in which the person at the top of the hierarchy sends a message to a second person who, in turn, reproduces the message for a third person. The reproduction of the first person's message becomes the message of the second person, and the reproduction of the reproduction becomes the message of the third person (Haney, 1962). Situations in which information is disseminated by means of this person-to-person format are referred to as *serial*. Three individuals are involved: the person who originates the message, the person who relays the message, and the person who terminates the sequence (Pace, 1976). The key figure in this system is the *relayor* (Pace & Hegstrom, 1977).

Relayor Functions

Alfred G. Smith (1973) points out that some communicators are senders, some are receivers, and some are in-between. The people in the middle are messengers; they are "relayors." The relay person, Smith says, is a "very common figure in communication processes" (p. 313). John Alden, for example, was a relayor for Miles Standish, who wanted to ask Priscilla Mullens to marry him. A librarian, a concert pianist, an actor, a reporter, a professor, a manager, and a supervisor are all relay persons at one time or another. The relayor receives a message and carries it part of the way toward some terminal point in much the same way as a "relay of fresh horses carries the riders along the route, and a relay man carries the baton onward in a track meet" (p. 314). In organizations, messages are carried forward by means of these serial relationships in which a relay passes the work from a superior to a subordinate downward or from a subordinate to a superior upward. The relayors carry the message along and thereby hold the organization together.

A. G. Smith (1973) identified four basic functions served by relay persons: to link, to store, to stretch, and to control. We shall summarize and briefly characterize each of these functions to better understand the serial or relayor relationship in organizations.

Linking

A supervisor tries to link an operative with a manager; the union steward connects union members with management; a line on an organization chart links one organization member to another. Although they may look simple, the links are more complicated than they appear.

Linking processes have at least three troublesome characteristics; they connect those parts of the organizational system, or they can disconnect them. They can send information forward, or they can hold it back. Relayors, as communicators in the middle, can bring the ends together or they can untie the connections. A human relay functions much like a transmission system in a car. The relay connects two independent moving parts. Like a transmission, the relayor adjusts the inertias of one part to those of the other part. Such adjustments avoid lurching, burning rubber, and breaking the system apart. A mediator, for example, adjusts labor and management to one another, using gears and clutches to speed up or slow down, to ease into a situation, or to shift into high gear on the open road. Finally, relayors vary in terms of physical and psychological distance they maintain between those they link. Most professors, for instance, are closer to their books than to their students; some supervisors are closer to the workers than to management. This linking function, Smith argues, creates an ethic in which relayors value adjustment and assimilation of points of view above all else. Because relay persons must work with powerful forces on both sides of them, the task is one of bringing the forces together, of linking them so as to use the power of both. However, the linker cannot be assimilated by either of the sides and still be a person in the middle. The relayor must remain in the middle and not conform wholly to either side.

Storing

Storing is the second function of the relayor. When a section head receives a message from a manager to send on to an operator, he or she must store the message. If the section head forgets the message on the way, that individual would be unable to deliver it and would not be a relayor. Storing accomplishes a number of purposes beyond that of just holding the message. For about the same reason that a farmer stores hay in a barn, the relayor stores messages—to adapt to the needs of sender and receiver, to buffer against fluctuations in what the receiver wants to hear and what the sender wants said. Storing spans the space between the producer of a message and the consumer of a message. Storing implies a conservative ethic, because the relayor who stores preserves the system. As a storer, the relayor values the status quo.

Stretching

The process of adapting the parts of a system to one another involves making some changes. Stretching is a form of change involving the enlargement or amplification of the message. In this sense Paul Revere's ride stretched the light from his lamp from the belfry of a Boston church to Lexington. Reporters stretch the words of a speaker in New York all the way to Los Angeles. This is a matter of distance. Relayors also stretch, up to a point, the meanings associated with a message. They amplify the meaning of a message. Some relayors underinterpret and lose some of the message. The ethic of the relayor is between the under- and the overinterpretation of a message. The relayor analyzes meaning, makes meanings apparent that seem obscure, internalizes meaning, which results in some changes; however, the analysis, the revelations, and the internalizing are all part of preparing the message for relaying.

Controlling

Linking, storing, and stretching are the foundations of the relayor's fourth function—controlling. The first thing that a relayor controls is the means by which links are made. A teacher as a relayor has control over the means by which the lesson will be presented in order to link the student with the source of the lesson. The news reporter controls how the message will be presented in the paper. The travel agent controls information about airline routes. The manager controls how official information will be transmitted to workers. The relayor controls channels and media as well as information itself.

Relayors are the in-between people—midway between senders and receivers. They link the units of a system together by adjusting them to one another. In adjusting and adapting to the units, relayors change messages. Change is often necessary to produce harmony between units in the system, yet change is opposed to the ethic of preserving and conserving the system. Nevertheless, by regulating the transmission, the storage, and the interpretation of message, the relayor has control over the communication system. In the end, the relayor may no longer be the intermediary; the relayor may become master of the system. In the end, you remember, it was John Alden who married Priscilla Mullens.

Likert (1961) recognized the central role of the relayor in organizations when he described the linking-pin structure of organizations. In his model, almost every organization member is a relayor, serving as the link between the upper unit and the lower unit.

SOME CURRENT ISSUES

Impact of Emergent Social Structures

What is the impact of communication networks in the organization? Eisenberg, Monge, and Miller (1983) examined the relationship between involvement in communication networks and organizational commitment. They concluded that for those who are not involved in their job, the communication network involvement has a strong effect on organizational commitment. The workers may be getting what they seek from the organization through the social interaction involved in their jobs.

How do emergent social structures shape organizational processes? Albrecht and Hall (1991a) examined network communication patterns based on innovation in three organization subunits. They found elite groups characterized by dense linkages and high volumes of communication exchange. The innovation networks are dominated by elite groups rather than key individuals. Each network is anchored by a cluster of organizational members. These members receive considerable personal support by "outsiders," which in turn allows them to dominate interaction and manage uncertainty in the organization. Organization members tended to identify "idea persons" on the basis of their communication skills. Albrecht and Hall (1991a) concluded that "the interpersonal behavior of elites, as well as their innovative behavior, thus creates an intriguing stronghold for sustained power and influence in the organization" (p. 557). In additional studies, Albrecht and Hall (1991b) examined the role of personal relationships in organizational innovation. They argue that communication about new ideas in organizations is greatest when there are strong personal ties. Multiplex relationships involving different types of work and social communication offer the best conditions for innovation. Interpersonal communication plays a central role in offering support and "face-saving" considerations. These researchers suggest that power differences, social distance, and a climate that highlights the personal risk of innovation influence the decision to suggest new ideas.

The influence of the organizational climate and structure on the flow of information is of central concern. Nilakanta and Scamell (1990) examined how different information sources (books, people, etc.) influence diffusion of innovation in an organization. One of the implications that they drew from their study is that management must create an environment conducive to the open exchange of information. Courtwright, Fairhurst, and Rogers (1989) examined the communication patterns in organic and mechanistic systems. They concluded that communicative forms are consultative in organic systems (characterized by dispersed control) and command-like in mechanistic systems (characterized by hierarchical control).

Technology

The new technology (electronic mail, voice mail, fax) has raised a number of questions about impact on information flow in the organization. Who will use it? Will it extend and diversify communication networks? What is the relationship among technology, information flow, and networks?

Rice and Aydin (1991) looked at how attitudes developed through social networks might influence individuals' views of new organizational technology. They concluded that social information processing can play no more than a small role in influencing attitudes toward a new information system. They state that "it is possible that the implementation of a new information system itself changes attitudes toward technology and use of that technology, in turn leading to changes in communication patterns, organizational structure, and working location" (p. 240).

According to Rice and Shook (1990) the use of intraorganizational media is one fundamental characteristic of different job categories and organizational levels. Use of media (meetings, memos, etc.) is highly correlated with organizational level. However, upper-level managers do not necessarily use electronic mail less than do lower level workers (clerical). Other issues surrounding the use of technology are explored in Chapter 10.

Communication Processes and Organizational Boundaries

The flow of information has been traditionally studied within a single organization, and network boundaries were not extended beyond organizational membership. Research on interorganizational networks (for example, Eisenberg et al., 1985) extends the traditional notion of boundaries. Cushman and King (1993) argue that the high-technology market has generated a new system of management (high-speed management) that is bringing about a revolution in organizational communication. A competitive and changing global economy demands that organizations use practices that ensure rapid need analysis, and rapid response/adaption. Computers and telecommunications allow for new manufacturing, marketing, and management technologies. A major issue is how to respond to rapid changes in the environment. There must be timely, accurate environmental scanning of information and rapid adjustment and coordination of the system.

What is the impact of the new technologies on flow of information? Russell, Adams, and Boundy (1986) point out that, in the marketing area, Campbell Soup Company can scan the environment to discover the desire for a new soup. They can then model its contents, simulate production, and assess its cost/profit/sales potential. Through the development of an artificial intelligence system the company can control the rate and quality of production. Management can pretest its name, test shelf-placement, and the type and content of its advertising. The company can also run its test market. A management decision that once took years may now only take two or three days.

High-speed management certainly offers significant implications for the role of communication in seeking competitive advantage. In terms of the study of the "flow of information," organizational boundaries must be expanded to include a larger environment. If an organization is conceptualized as networks of interdependent relationships, then information and communication technologies have changed what we typically think of as an organization. If networks tie together various parts of the global economy and if the economy dictates various alliances, just where is the organization located? What information flow is most critical and who should have access to the network?

SUMMARY

The flow of information is a dynamic process in which messages are created, displayed and interpreted. The flow of information impacts on organizational efficiency, climate, adaption, and innovation, and it can be examined from a positional, interpersonal, or serial perspective. Organizational structure can have decided effects on communication patterns and roles. These in turn can facilitate the flow of communication or hinder it. The directional concept of information flow in the organization is concerned with what is communicated to whom and how. The formal directions involve positional communication. However, organization members often communicate with one another without regard to their positions, resulting in a personal communication network, which is often referred to as the *grapevine* and transmits informal or "secret" messages or information that does not flow through formal channels. Because the information on the grapevine is usually quite accurate but often incomplete, it may exert a powerful influence on those who are part of the system. Thus it is important for supervisors and managers to understand and help the grapevine benefit the organization. Each direction of communication flow is related to specific purposes and raises issues of what methods and media are most appropriate for meeting those purposes. Three types of relationships affect the flow of information in organizations: interpersonal, positional, and serial. Interpersonal relationships are based on caring, concern, kindness, and responsiveness. Positional relationships are based on authority, work, prestige, and status. The most common form of positional relationship is that of superior and subordinate. Serial relationships are based on the need for people to serve as relayors of information in organizations. Some contemporary concerns about information flow focus on the impact of emergent social structures, technology, and determining organizational boundaries.

A SUBJECTIVIST'S REMINDER

The flow of information is not an orderly or predictable process, but more than that; what information means depends on context. To find meaning, it is necessary to look at the interrelationships that create the structure and pattern. These interrelationships are complex and illusive (Allen, Gotcher, and Seibert, 1993). Setting aside patterns or networks of communication for examination is a highly arbitrary and artificial undertaking. An interpretative analysis reveals that an organization is made up of interactive influences, mutual constraints, multiple orders, and simultaneous interests. The complexities are obscured if one thinks in terms of a simplistic order and patterns of communication.

Schwartz and Ogilvy (1979) use the metaphor of the holograph and maintain that "everything is interconnected like a vast network of interference patterns" (p. 14). Examining information in one part of an organization can reveal information about the entire organization. The interpretative position emphasizes the meaning attributed to communication exchanges and the meaning derived from the context of these exchanges. If you were to go to several organizations, ask managers how they disseminate information, then ask organizational members how they obtain information, the answers would reveal a discrepancy between the managerial view and actual practice. If you observe information-gathering behaviors, you will see further discrepancies. All of this suggests that the organizational culture provides a context by which information is generated and processed.

Classical studies examining the impact of communication patterns such as the wheel and circle were designed to control and order communication. However, these theoretical patterns do not represent actual communication in organizations. The studies controlled who could speak to them. In more realistic settings, people may have access to others and be able to communicate with them, but that does not mean that they will. Individuals in actual settings may be placed in structured situations, but they alter those structures through emergent negotiated behaviors (Monge and Eisenberg, 1987). The resulting structure or pattern is determined by actual communication.

Network analysis may obscure patterns of interchange and the meanings attached to those exchanges. Richards (1985) describes a study in which medical practitioners were asked from whom they sought advice and information and to whom they gave advice and information. Only one physician in twenty who was listed by a recipient as a source of information said he was a source for the recipient. Richard explains:

> An interpretivist researcher would want to talk with the physicians and uncover how they interpreted both the question about giving or seeking information and the process of giving or seeking information. In this case, the interpretivist would discover that "giving advice or information" is not the inverse of "seeking advice or information." How could this be? It seems that many physicians go to conferences at which other physicians known as experts in their field give presentations. Many of those in the audience feel they are receiving advice or information from the speakers, but the speakers do not count the members of the audience as "coming to them for advice or information." Much advice and information is obtained informally, perhaps over a game of golf. . . . Those who receive information may know they are doing so, while those giving information may feel they are simply having a friendly conversation (pp. 125–126).

This research indicates the complexity of networks. The significance of a network lies in its meaning for the participants.

Information flow may be governed by cultural factors. One of our graduate students traced messages in a retail organization to determine information flow. The managers were interested in getting information through the system in a reasonable amount of time. The student traced several messages in the organization and discovered that they stopped at a certain point. A manager suggested that the messages were not potent enough to travel through the entire organization; thus, he further suggested a message about himself that was sure to raise some eyebrows. This rather "juicy" message was sent through the system. Again, the message stopped at the same point. Through a number of interviews, the investigator discovered that "stories" existed in one organizational unit concerning someone who had been fired for passing along information; those stores tended to regulate the flow of information.

What are the consequences of thinking in terms of directions of flow of information? The most obvious shortcoming is that *meaning*, the very heart of communication, is placed in a secondary role. In other words, this view tends to equate information and communication. As you recall from earlier discussions, communication relies heavily on interpretation. The concepts of direction and flow suggest that communication is a type of substance that moves about in an orderly fashion within well-prescribed boundaries. Putnam (1983) observes: "By treating messages as physical substances, functionalists locate the *essence of communication* in transmission and channel effects" (p. 39). Communication is a process of shared and negotiated meanings; it is not a tangible substance that can be moved along selected channels at will.

Another consequence of emphasizing the direction of flow is that managers start thinking of communication as a highly predictable and mechanical process. We have already provided a caution against this type of thinking in earlier chapters, but once the idea of the direction of flow becomes a focal point, it tends to shape thinking toward an objective and concrete point of view. Reddy (1979) observes that people talk about communication as though it involved an actual pipeline. He suggests that a preponderance (70 percent) of the expressions used in talking or writing about communication emphasize what he has labeled the *conduit metaphor*. This idea suggests that meanings are *in* messages and are transferred by communication. After examining twenty-one management textbooks, issues of *supervisory management*, and the comments of managers, Axley (1983) concluded that conduit metaphorical expressions are predominant.

What is the impact of the conduit metaphor? Of course, words do not *mean*—only people mean—and meanings cannot be transferred like physical objects. Among the communication postulates advanced by Redding (1972) are the notions that (1) anything is a potential message, and (2) the message received is the only one that counts. Communication is not a transferable commodity. When it is conceived as such, the complexity of the process is lost. Axley (1983) contends that "the conduit metaphor ultimately engenders and promotes the viewpoint that *communication is easy* and requires very little effort to be done successfully" (p. 17). Because of the multiple meanings assigned to messages and the negotiation of those messages through interaction, the process of communication requires far more involvement than the term *information flow* suggests. Another consequence of this emphasis is that management information is viewed as *the* information. If organizational reality is to be understood, there must be an effort to examine the information that *drives* the organization. This kind of information may or may not be managerial in nature. What is called informal communication may be just as crucial—and sometimes more so—as formal communication in the achievement of a task.

Rather than accepting the blinders of the terms *direction* and *flow*, it would be more productive to look for *clusters of meaning* and their effect on organizational action. What information is in the system; what information is used or sought; who uses it; and what functions are served by the information? And of course, how is the information interpreted? It must be stressed that just getting information quickly and distributing it "efficiently" does not mean that the consequences will always be beneficial. The information can be interpreted and used in a variety of ways. The scanning of an environment is as much a creative process as a selective one. As Daft and Weick (1984) suggest, interpretation models are linked with organizational differences in environmental scanning, equivocality reduction, strategy, and decision making.

Organizational communication relationships are acted out within a cultural framework that guides the behavior of the participants. An important part of this framework is the power structure. Organizational communication relationships are also power relationships. The different degrees of power held by people in different positions are usually overt and rather obvious. However, the nature of power has prompted theorists to distinguish between *surface* and *deep* structures of power (Clegg, 1979; Conrad, 1983). Conrad (1987) explains that

> deep structures are pre-conscious guidelines and constraints whose appropriateness as ways of interpreting and responding to organizational situations is taken-for-granted by members of an organization. . . . In a sense, deep structures tell employees who they are— what their role in their organization is and where they "fit" in the formal and informal

hierarchies that make up the organization. . . . Employees choose to act in certain ways, not because of overt threats or promises, but because doing so is consistent with their taken-for-granted assumptions about their identities and organizational roles and about what actions constitute natural, appropriate adaptions to the actions of others (p. 14).

Deep structures of power tacitly guide and restrict the actions of organizational members. Conrad (1983) maintains that "deep structures of power are the limits that define and solidify a society or an organization. They *are* the power-related reality of an organization. . . . In normal times deep structures of power are the power relationships in organizations" (p. 187).

An interpretative approach suggests that examining organizational relationships means getting beyond a surface view. The deep structure must be brought to light so that organizations can see how they "organize." It is important to look at not only what is said, but also at what is *not* said. For example, Conrad (1983) points out that there are several *faces* of power. Power can be exerted in overt and covert ways. Conrad contends that "members of organizations may reinforce those norms, values, rules, or practices that ensure that only relatively innocuous issues are ever raised in public" (p. 177). Organization members may also operate under certain parameters that constrain decision making. Organizational relationships involve more than individual feelings and choice.

Consider the following dialogue. We have asked our students to look at the "talk" and describe what is happening.

At the Hospital

JILL: Hello, Dr. Johnson. How is Mrs. Andersen doing?
JOHNSON: She is looking better. I'm going to remove her stitches today.
JILL: (*Enthusiastically*) Great! Do you have everything you need?
JOHNSON: I need a Kelly clamp. Where are they?
JILL: We only have one on the entire floor and we keep it hidden. You'll have to sign in blood for it.
JOHNSON: (*Laughing*) Where do I sign? (*He turns away from Jill to get a patient's chart.*)
JILL: (*Reaches into a drawer and removes a clamp.*) We'll let it go without a signature this time. (*Gives clamp to the doctor who is now facing her.*)
JOHNSON: Thanks. I'll bring it right back.
(*Mrs. South, the nursing supervisor, has come down the hall and overhears the rest of the conversation.*)
JILL: When you're through, put it right back in this drawer. (*She taps on the desk drawer.*)
JOHNSON: The top one?
JILL: Yes. The top one.
(*Dr. Johnson goes into the patient's room, and is out of hearing range.*)
SOUTH: (*With a slight chuckle*) You're treating him like a little boy who has to put his own toys away.
JILL: (*Looks confused*) What?
(*Mrs. South laughs and walks on.*)

Students' reactions vary widely. Some remark that the participants are passing the time of day and the hospital seems like a pleasant place to work. Others suggest that the talk reveals that Jill and Johnson are flirting with each other much as the characters do in hospital soaps on TV. Some criticize Mrs. South and point out that she's a busybody. Some look below the surface and ask why Jill is using this particular approach with the doctor. Of course, we have our favorite answers. There is a power structure in the classroom! We contend that a great deal is going on in this short conversation. Rather than provide those answers, we will suggest some questions that will point you toward the cultural structure that we feel is influencing this exchange. What are the characteristics of the interaction between Jill and Johnson? What is there about the organizational culture that might generate the language used? How aware is Jill of her interpersonal style? Are there factors in this type of organization that promote the strategies used? There are several plausible answers to these questions. The important point is that organizational culture has much to do with how communication relationships are executed and interpreted.

REFERENCES

ALBRECHT, TERRANCE L., and BRADFORD HALL, "Relational and Content Differences Between Elites and Outsiders in Innovation Networks," *Human Communication Research*, 17 (June 1991), 535–561.(a)

ALBRECHT, TERRANCE L., and BRADFORD HALL, "Facilitating Talk About New Ideas: The Role of Personal Relationships in Organizational Innovation," *Communication Monographs*, 58 (September 1991), 273–288.(b)

ALLEN, MYRIA WATKINS, J. MICHAEL GOTCHER, and JOY HART SEIBERT, "A Decade of Organizational Communication Research: Journal Articles 1980–1991," in *Communication Yearbook* 16, Stanley A. Deetz, ed. Newbury Park, Calif.: Sage Publications, Inc., 1993.

AXLEY, STEPHEN R., "Conduit: A Performative Metaphor for Communicating in Organizations." Paper presented at the University of Utah Summer Conference on Interpretative Approaches to the Study of Organizations, Alta, Utah, 1983.

BAIRD, JOHN E., JR., *The Dynamics of Organizational Communication.* New York: Harper & Row, Pub., 1977.

BAVELAS, ALEX, "Communication Patterns in Task-Oriented Groups." *Journal of the Acoustical Society of America*, 22 (1950), 725–730.

BAVELAS, ALEX, and DERMOT BARRETT, "An Experimental Approach to Organizational Communication," *Personnel*, 27 (March 1951), 38–50.

BURGESS, R. L., "Communication Networks and Behavioral Consequences," *Human Relations*, 22 (1969), 137–160.

CLEGG, S., *The Theory of Power and Organization.* London: Routledge & Kegan Paul, 1979.

COLEMAN, J. S., "Relational Analysis: The Study of Social Organizations with Survey Methods," in *Complex Organizations: A Sociological Reader*, A. A. Etzioni, ed. New York: Holt, Rinehart & Winston, 1964.

CONBOY, WILLIAM A., *Working Together . . . Communication in a Healthy Organization.* Columbus, Ohio: Chas. E. Merrill, 1976.

CONRAD, CHARLES, "Organizational Power: Faces and Symbolic Forms" in *Communication and Organizations: An Interpretive Approach*, Linda L. Putnam and Michael E. Pacanowsky, eds. Beverly Hills, Calif.: Sage Publications, Inc., 1983.

CONRAD, CHARLES, "Power, Praxis and Self in Organizational Communication," in *Advances in Organizational Communication Theory and Research.* Beverly Hills, Calif.: Sage Publications, Inc., (in press).

CONTRACTOR, NOSHIR S., and ERIC M. EISENBERG, "Communication Networks and New Media in Organizations," in *Organizations and Communication Technology*, Janet Fulk and Charles Steinfield, eds. Newbury Park, Calif.: Sage Publications, Inc., 1990.

COURTWRIGHT, JOHN A., GAIL T. FAIRHURST, and L. EDNA ROGERS, "Interaction Patterns in Organic and Mechanistic Systems," *Academy of Management Journal*, 32 (1989), 773–802.

CUSHMAN, DONALD P., and SARAH SANDERSON KING, "High-Speed Management: A Revolution in Organizational Communication in the 1990's." in *Communication Yearbook* 16, Stanley A.Deetz, ed. Newbury Park, Calif.: Sage Publications, Inc., 1993.

DAFT, RICHARD L., and ROBERT H. LENGEL, "Information Richness: A New Approach to Managerial Information Processing and Organization Design," in *Research in Organizational Behavior*, L. L. Cummings and B.M. Staw, eds. Greenwich, Conn.: JAI Press, 1984.

DAFT, RICHARD L., and KARL E. WEICK, "Toward a Model of Organizations as Interpretation Systems," *Academy of Management Review*, 9 (1984), 284–295.

DANOWSKI, JAMES A., "Communication Network Analysis and Social Change," in *Communication for Group Transformation in Development*, Goodwin C. Chu, Syed A. Rahim, and D. Lawrence Kincaid, eds. Honolulu: East-West Communication Institute, Communication Monograph, No. 2, September 1976.

DAVIS, KEITH, *Human Relations at Work: The Dynamics of Organizational Behavior*. New York: McGraw-Hill, 1967.

DAVIS, KEITH A., "A Method of Studying Communication Patterns in Organizations," *Personnel Psychology*, 6 (1953), 301–312.

DAVIS, WILLIAM L., and J. REGIS O'CONNOR, "Serial Transmission of Information: A Study of the Grapevine," *Journal of Applied Communication Research*, 5 (1977), 61–72.

EISENBERG, ERIC M., PETER R. MONGE, and KATHERINE I. MILLER, "Involvement in Communication Networks as a Predictor of Organizational Commitment," *Human Communication Research*, 10 (Winter 1983), 179–201.

EISENBERG, ERIC M., R. V. FARACE, P. R. MONGE, E. P. BETTINGHAUS, R. HAWKINS-KURCHNER, K. MILLER, and L. ROTHMAN, "Communication Linkages in Interorganizational Systems," in *Progress in Communication Sciences* (Vol. 6), B. Derrin and M. Voigt, eds. Norwood, N.J.: Ablex, 1985.

FARACE, RICHARD V., "Organizational Communication," in *Human Communication: Principles, Contexts, and Skills*, Cassandra L. Book, ed. New York: St. Martin's Press, 1980.

FARACE, RICHARD V., PETER R. MONGE, and HAMISH M. RUSSELL, *Communicating and Organizing*. Reading, Mass.: Addison-Wesley, 1977.

FARACE, RICHARD V., JAMES A. TAYLOR, and JOHN P. STEWART, "Criteria for Evaluation of Organizational Communication Effectiveness: Review and Synthesis," in *Communication Yearbook* 2, Brent D. Ruben, ed. New Brunswick, N.J.: Transaction Books–International Communication Association, 1978.

FAYOL, HENRI, *General and Industrial Management*, trans. Constance Storrs. New York: Pitman Publishing, 1940. (Original work published 1916)

GOLDHABER, GERALD M., *Organizational Communication* (2nd ed.). Dubuque, Iowa: Wm. C. Brown, 1979.

GUETZKOW, HAROLD, "Communications in Organizations," in *Handbook of Organizations*, James G. March, ed. Skokie, Ill: Rand McNally, 1965.

HANEY, WILLIAM V., "Serial Communication of Information in Organizations," in *Concepts and Issues in Administrative Behavior*, Sidney Malick and Edward H.Van Ness, eds. Englewood Cliffs, N.J.: Prentice Hall, 1962.

HARRIMAN, BRUCE, "Up and Down the Communications Ladder," *Harvard Business Review* (September-October 1974), 143–151.

HOOPES, NED E., ed., *Who Am I?: Essays on the Alienated*. New York: Dell Pub. Co., Inc., 1969.

JABLIN, FREDRIC M., "Superior-Subordinate Communication: The State of the Art," *Psychological Bulletin*, 86 (1979), 1201–1222.

JACKSON, JAY M., "The Organization and Its Communication Problem," *Advanced Management* (February 1959), 17–20.

JACOBSEN, EUGENE, and STANLEY SEASHORE, "Communication Practices in Complex Organizations," *Journal of Social Issues*, 7 (1951), 28–40.

KATZ, DANIEL, and ROBERT KAHN, *The Social Psychology of Organizations*. New York: John Wiley, 1966.

KATZ, ELIHU, and PAUL F. LAZARSFELD, *Personal Influence*. New York: Free Press, 1955.

KOONTZ, HAROLD, and CYRIL O'DONNELL, *Principles of Management* (4th ed.). New York: McGraw-Hill, 1968.

KRIVONOS, PAUL, "Distortion of Subordinate to Superior Communication." Unpublished paper presented at a meeting of the International Communication Association, Portland, Oregon, 1976.

LEAVITT, HAROLD J., "Some Effects of Certain Communication Patterns on Group Performance," *Journal of Abnormal and Social Psychology*, 46 (1951), 38–50.

LENGEL, ROBERT H., and RICHARD L. DAFT, "The Selection of Communication Media as an Executive Skill," *Academy of Management Executive*, 2 (1988), 225–232.

LEVEL, DALE A., JR., "Communication Effectiveness: Method and Situation," *Journal of Business Communication*, 10 (Fall 1972), 19–25.

LEVEL, DALE A., JR., and WILLIAM P. GALLE, JR., *Managerial Communications*. Plano, Texas: Business Publications, Inc., 1988.

LIKERT, RENSIS. *New Patterns of Management*. New York: McGraw-Hill, 1961.

MAIER, NORMAN, L. HOFFMAN, and W. READ, "Superior-Subordinate Communication: The Relative Effectiveness of Managers Who Held Their Subordinates' Positions," *Personnel Psychology*, 16 (1963), 1–11.

MEHRABIAN, ALBERT, *Silent Messages*. Belmont, Calif.: Wadsworth, 1971.

MELLINGER, GLEN D., "Interpersonal Trust as a Factor in Communication," *Journal of Abnormal and Social Psychology*, 52 (1956), 304–309.

MERRIHUE, WILLARD V., *Managing by Communication*. New York: McGraw-Hill, 1960.

MONGE, PETER R., and ERIC M. EISENBERG, "Emergent Communication Networks," in *Handbook of Organizational Communication*, Fredric M. Jablin et al., eds. Newbury Park, Calif.: Sage Publications, Inc., 1987.

NILAKANTA, SREE, and RICHARD W. SCAMELL, "The Effect of Information Sources and Communication Channels on the Diffusion of Innovation in a Data Base Development Environment," *Management Science*, 36 (January 1990), 24–40.

PACE, R. WAYNE, "A Model of Serial Communication." Unpublished paper presented at the fall meeting of the New Mexico Communication Association, Las Cruces, New Mexico, November 1976.

PACE, R. WAYNE, and ROBERT R. BOREN, *The Human Transaction*. Glenview, Ill: Scott, Foresman, 1973.

PACE, R. WAYNE, ROBERT R. BOREN, and BRENT D. PETERSON, *Communication Behavior and Experiments: A Scientific Approach*. Belmont, Calif.: Wadsworth, 1975.

PACE, R. WAYNE, and TIMOTHY G. HEGSTROM, "Seriality in Human Communication Systems." Unpublished paper presented at the annual conference of the International Communication Association, Berlin, 1977, 1–54.

PELZ, DONALD C., "Influence: A Key to Effective Leadership in the First-Line Supervisor," *Personnel*, 29 (1952), 209–217.

PETERSON, BRENT D., "Differences between Managers and Subordinates in Their Perception of Opinion Leaders," *Journal of Business Communication*, 10 (1973), 27–37.

PLANTY, EARL, and WILLIAM MACHAVER, "Upward Communications: A Project in Executive Development," Personnel, 28 (January 1952), 304–318.

PUTNAM, LINDA L., "The Interpretive Perspective: An Alternative to Functionalism," in *Communication and Organizations: An Interpretive Approach*, Linda L. Putnam and Michael Pacanowsky, eds. Beverly Hills, Calif.: Sage Publications, Inc., 1983.

READ, WILLIAM, "Upward Communication in Industrial Hierarchies," *Human Relations*, 15 (1962), 3–15.

REDDING, W. CHARLES, *Communication Within the Organization*, New York: Industrial Communication Council, 1972.

REDDY, M., "The Conduit Metaphor—A Case of Frame Conflict in Our Language About Language," in *Metaphor and Thought*, A. Ortony, ed. Cambridge: Cambridge University Press, 1979.

RICE, RONALD E., and CAROLYN AYDIN, "Attitudes Toward New Organizational Technology: Network Proximity as a Mechanism for Social Information Processing," *Administrative Science Quarterly*, 36 (1991), 219–244.

RICE, RONALD E., and DOUGLAS E. SHOOK, "Relationships of Job Categories and Organizational Levels to Use of Communication Channels, Including Electronic Mail: A Meta-Analysis and Extension," *Journal of Management Studies*, 27 (March 1990), 195–229.

RICHARDS, WILLIAM D., "Data, Models, and Assumptions in Network Analysis," in *Organizational Communication: Traditional Themes and New Directions*, Robert D. McPhee and Phillip K. Tompkins, eds. Beverly Hills, Calif.: Sage Publications, Inc., 1985.

RICHARDS, WILLIAM D., "Network Analysis in Large Complex Systems: Techniques and Methods—Tools." Paper presented at the Annual Meeting of the International Communication Association, New Orleans, 1974.

ROBERTS, KARLENE, and CHARLES A. O'REILLY III, "Organizations as Communication Structures," *Human Communication Research*, 4 (Summer 1978), 283–293.

ROGERS, EVERETT M., and REKHA AGARWALA-ROGERS, *Communication in Organizations*. New York: Free Press, 1976.

ROSS, I. C., and F. HARARY, "Identification of the Liaison Persons of an Organization Using the Structure Matrix," *Management Science*, 1 (April-May 1955), 1–8.

RUSSELL, E., A. ADAMS, and B. BOUNDY, "High-Technology Test Marketing Campbell Soup Company," *Journal of Consumer Marketing*, 3 (1986), 71–80.

SANFORD, AUDREY C., GARY T.HUNT, and HYLER J.BRACEY, *Communication Behavior in Organizations*. Columbus, Ohio: Chas. E. Merrill, 1976.

SCHILIT, W. K., and E. A. LOCKE, "A Study of Upward Influence in Organizations," *Administrative Science Quarterly*, 26 (1982), 304–316.

SCHWARTZ, DONALD F., "Liaison Roles in the Communication of a Formal Organization," in *Communication in Organizations*, Lyman W. Porter and Karlene H. Roberts, eds. Middlesex, England: Penguin Books, 1977.

SCHWARTZ, DONALD F., and EUGENE JACOBSEN, "Organizational Communication Network Analysis—The Liaison Communication Role," *Organizational Behavior and Human Performance*, 18 (1977), 158–174.

SCHWARTZ, P., and J. OGILVY, *The Emergent Paradigm: Changing Patterns of Thought and Belief*. Menlo Park, Calif.: SRI International, 1979.

SHARMA, JITENDRA M., "Organizational Communications: A Linking Process," *The Personnel Administrator*, 24 (July 1979), 35–43.

SHAW, M. E., "Some Effects of Irrelevant Information Upon Problem Solving by Small Groups," *Journal of Social Psychology*, 47 (1958), 33–37.

SMITH, ALFRED G., "The Ethic of the Relay Men," in *Communication: Ethical and Moral Issues*, Lee Thayer, ed. London: Gordon and Breach Science Publishers, 1973.

SMITH, PETER B., *Groups Within Organizations*. London: Harper & Row, Pub., 1973.

SOMMER, ROBERT, *Personal Space*. Englewood Cliffs, N.J.: Prentice-Hall, 1969.

STEIN, JESS, ed., *The Random House Dictionary of the English Language*. New York: Random House, 1967.

STOHL, CYNTHIA, and W. CHARLES REDDING, "Messages and Message Exchange Processes," in *Handbook of Organizational Communication*, Fredric M. Jablin et al., eds. Beverly Hills, Calif.: Sage Publications, Inc., 1987.

TREVINO, LINDA KLEBE, RICHARD L. DAFT, and ROBERT H. LENGEL, "Understanding Managers' Media Choices: A Symbolic Interactionist Perspective," in *Organizations and Communication Technology*, Janet Fulk and Charles Steinfield, eds. Newbury Park, Calif.: Sage Publications, Inc., 1990.

WEISS, R. S., and EUGENE JACOBSEN, "A Method for the Analysis of the Structure of Complex Organizations," *American Sociological Review*, 20 (1955), 661–668.

WENDLINGER, ROBERT M., "Improving Upward Communication," *Journal of Business Communication*, 11 (Summer 1973), 17–23.

YAGER, ED, "Quality Circle: A Tool for the 80's," *Training and Development Journal* (August 1980), 60–62.

ZEMKE, RON, "Honeywell Imports Quality Circles as Long-Term Management Strategy," *Training* (August 1980), 91–95.

9

Information Technology in Organizations

Claire B. Johnson

The C.E.O. of a billion-dollar-a year company called his office while he was on a business trip, but he could not reach his assistant, who was away from his desk. Instead, he reached the company's state-of-the-art voice mail system that had been installed to increase the efficiency of handling telephone calls. A disembodied voice instructed the C.E.O. in all the different ways he could leave messages and assured him that someone would return his call as soon as possible. The decision to install the voice mail system had been made at the vice-presidential level; the decision to uninstall it was made then and there by the C.E.O. He didn't want callers forced to talk to a machine. "That's not the way to treat people," he said (Sproull & Kiesler, 1991, p. 1).

THE PROBLEM

Computer-based communication technologies, such as electronic mail, videoconferencing, voice messaging, facsimile, and computer bulletin boards, are changing the way we work. Computer-mediated communication is playing a central role in the transformation of organizations. This chapter presents a discussion of the implications that new computer communication technology has for organizations and the people who work in them.

Computer-mediated communication facilitates overcoming the obstacles of space and time boundaries; therefore, where an employee is physically located may no longer be relevant. With these new computer-mediated technologies, employees may have potential access to anyone, anywhere in the organization. It no longer matters whether their offices are physically co-located, or if they are separated by geographic distances. Because computer-mediated communication messages can easily cross traditional hierarchical and departmental barriers, organizational boundaries can dissolve. Owing to its inherent relationship with the organization's communication process, computer-mediated communication has the potential to shape organizational norms, behaviors, and options. Thus implications of computer-mediated communication systems should be of vital interest to anyone interested in organizational communication.

How such systems are implemented, managed, and used have the potential to alter, at all organizational levels, the human and communication processes of an organization. For example, compiling a monthly sales report or budget can be done via computer and transmitted to the appropriate individual or group of individuals, bypassing the mail entirely. Not only is the amount of time required to send these materials (via the mail) reduced, but the budget or report arrives ready to print out and be distributed electronically to others who may need access to it. Constraints that are part of the communication process among employees are removed. Contacting a cohort, your manager, or just a friend becomes far easier. "Telephone tag" occurs less often or is no longer relevant. Catching your manager in the office, or out of a meeting, either to seek or provide information, is no longer necessary. Just leave an electronic message at any time of the day or night.

Think about what this means to an organization. The communication process just described eliminates the time lag associated with mailing documents, the need to reconstruct the information on the "correct form," or the need to make multiple copies that then must be distributed to the required personnel. It eliminates leaving multiple messages with the same person, or waiting until they are in the office or available before you ask questions or provide them with information they need. Because the new media can easily cross traditional hierarchical and departmental boundaries, changing these processes with their attendant patterns and intervening effects can fundamentally alter an organization.

Owing primarily to advancements in communication technology, today's organizations differ considerably from earlier ones. In fact, it is argued, here and elsewhere, that computer-based communication is as significant to organizations as was the introduction of the computer. Computer-based communication is often compared to the Industrial Revolution and is referred to as the "technological revolution." Revolution or not, because it is used for communication and communication involves how people interact, computer-based communication is clearly critical to an organization. Communication technology does not exist in a vacuum but becomes embedded in the organization's social processes.

In spite of the technological differences that exist between organizations they can be defined, according to Barnard (1938), as "a system of consciously coordinated activities or forces of two or more persons" (p. 73). Communication is used to "coordinate activities" in an organization. Communication in any form, whether it be the telegraph, telephone, or electronic mail, is clearly central to the process of organizing. Barnard supports this notion when he states:

> In an extensive theory of organization, communication would occupy a central place, because the structure, extensiveness, and the scope of organizations are almost entirely determined by communications techniques (p. 90).

It makes sense then, to say that with transformation of the organization's human and organizational communication processes there is potential for organizations to be transformed. Fulk and Steinfield (1990) posit that, "Effective communication is, in fact, at the very core of goals driving the implementation of information technologies in organizations" (p. 8). New communication technologies can be seen as additional tools that will enhance an organization's ability, and those that work there, to communicate "effectively." This assumption must be carefully scrutinized by organizational communication theorists and practitioners. One question to be considered is: Do communication technologies help an organization communicate more effectively? Another important area to consider is, What will be the short- and long-term implications for the organization and the people who work there?

New communication technologies provide novel challenges and opportunities for those studying or working in an organization. For example, they present a wide array of alternatives as well as a way to augment, complement, or interact with traditional communication media found in organizations, such as the telephone or written documents. Hence, these multiple alternatives create potential for the transformation of communication processes that occur within organizations, whether it be at the individual, group, management, or interorganizational level. Additionally, communication technology is an important issue today both from a pragmatic perspective, such as efficiency and performance, and from a theoretical perspective. For example, Sproull and Kiesler's (1991) two-level perspective, or framework, suggests that new communication technologies have what they refer to as first- and second-level effects. First-level effects refer to the planned technical gains (i.e., increased productivity and efficiency), whereas second-level effects deal with innovation and unanticipated social consequences that are typically long-term changes. Initially, when new communication media were evaluated, organizations and researchers focused on first-level effects. This is no longer the case as it becomes more and more apparent to those studying and working in organizations that long-term, second-level consequences, which become embedded in the organization's communication processes, must be considered as well.

Sproull and Kiesler (1991) argue that second-level effects come about because new communication technology "lead people to pay attention to different things, have contact with different people, and depend on one another differently" (p. 4). By "pay attention to different things," they mean that people spend their time differently, and what they think of as "important" changes. Rather than spend a day preparing hard copy budget reports to be mailed to the main office, they access the information in their computer and transfer it electronically, bypassing a day of report preparation. They have contact with other people because they have new access to other people; there are differences in who they know and how they know people. Change in interdependency means they develop new patterns and abilities in how and what they can do for each other. Kiesler (1986) earlier suggested that we tend to "exaggerate the immediate changes, the significance of transient issues, and we underestimate the social effects" (p. 47). One can clearly see the significance for the organization of both short- and long-term consequences.

Do new communication technologies cause the organization to change? Can one predict and perhaps guarantee an increase in efficiency with the installation of videoconferencing or electronic mail? One of the key theoretical questions for anyone involved with organizational communication is whether new communication technologies "cause" or at least initiate outcomes in an organization. In other words, do they influence the organization toward being more efficient, more productive, more responsive? Do the new communication technologies determine what changes take place as they are assimilated into the organization, or is there more to them than that? Similarly, do they cause the organization's structure to change, say from a typical hierarchy to a matrix organization with multiple communication channels that intersect and overlap? This concept is often referred to theoretically as the "technological imperative" or "technological determinism." It is a somewhat pessimistic view of technology that assumes new communication technologies "determine" what changes take place in organizations, that the people who work there are controlled in a machine-like fashion. Rice (1992) points out that there are many more questions than answers regarding this issue. A transition seems to be taking place that moves away from this deterministic perspective. Rice attributes this to the fact that the theoretical and practical nature of how organizational change comes about is continually evolving.

Organizational change is an enduring subject of study and an area of great complexity. Currently, many organization theorists are moving toward the subjective end of the scale (see Figure 1.1), taking the position that human behavior entails interaction and interpretation. In other words, employees do more than react to their environment; they act upon it. They are not machine-like, but instead co-create their work environment. In fact, Burrell and Morgan (1979) question whether causality can be justified in research on human behavior. The notion of "cause and effect" is not clear-cut when dealing with human communication.

Communication technologies bring together the capabilities of computers and communication media, but they also connect people with other people and with their different activities. Whether and how people communicate is critical to an organization. How individuals perceive and use the new media to accomplish organizational tasks is integral to the effect they ultimately have. This position moves away from a technological determinism perspective toward an "interactionist" frame of reference. The assumption is that communication occurs in a social context. Perceptions, attitudes, and subsequent use of communication technologies are in part co-constructed within that social context. For example, how employees choose to use new communication media to exchange their messages could differ considerably from management's original intent. IBM employees used their company's internal message system to create GRIPENET, to express their complaints about management practices and policies (Kiesler, Siegel, and McGuire, 1984). The first large-scale computer network, ARPANET, installed in the late 1960s as a way to provide extended computer power from other locations to universities and research institutions (a first-level goal), rapidly became an electronic mail community (a second-level effect). Initially, electronic mail was a minor feature of the network, but its popularity grew as researchers, project heads, and other collaborators "discovered it" (Rice & Case, 1983; Sproull & Kiesler, 1991).

Both of these examples highlight the fact that, for the people who work in organizations, and their use of new communication media, a potential exists for unanticipated and often unplanned organizational change. This is because there are long-term social issues to consider, beyond the first-level pragmatic perspective, that are directly related to the communication process and practices in an organization. Organizations are more than assemblages of things; they are social entities, and "media use occurs in a web of social relationships…social context effects must be considered" (Fulk et al., 1987, p. 546).

The fundamental point is that communication processes and communication technologies are not objective, independent entities but, as Rice (1992) points out, need to be viewed as subjective and socially constructed. People are constructing their understanding of how communication should be used in their particular day-to-day work practices as they interact and work together. For example, the installation of electronic mail does not guarantee it will be used or used in the expected way. Employees may decide among themselves that it is impersonal or too time-consuming to learn and opt to continue with their current way of doing things. In addition, it is clear that social acceptance by employees of the new medium is necessary. Organizational members may also select media due to, among other things, ease of use, accessibility, and personal perception (Culnan & Markus, 1987). Rice (1992) states that new communication media are "products of, become embedded in, and re-institutionalize, ongoing social processes" (p. 6). Organization members may perceive the new media as too formal, impersonal, and difficult to use. They could also perceive a particular technology as a way to save time, increase their efficiency, or provide an opportunity for new contacts and information.

There are many new communication technologies, such as electronic mail, videoconferencing, voice messaging, video text, fiber optics, laserdisks, facsimile, computer bulletin boards, computer conferencing, group decision support systems, and interactive TV talk shows. The sheer vastness of new technologies far exceeds a single chapter. Therefore, this chapter will limit its focus primarily to a current communication technology that is "new" in the sense that it is one of the latest technologies enjoying widespread acceptance in organizations, and will be "new" for many organizations in the future: electronic mail. It provides a current and useful framework with which to understand the use, social implications, and adoption of new communication technologies in organizations.

FORECAST

The focus of this chapter is on the organization as a socially constructed entity. Technical details regarding the use of new communication technology will not be covered here. Instead, the new opportunities and new problems that surround organizational communication processes will be explored. We will look first at organizational structure, next consider a concept termed "media richness," and finally move to a discussion of the potential for increased efficiency and productivity. It would be wise to consider, as organizations continue to adopt new computer-based communication technology, just what the implications for employees, and the organization, might be.

Structural Issues and Range of Communication

This textbook presents a discussion of both "formal" and "social" organizations. Both of these notions deal with how an organization is structured, either formally, as in Weber's (1947) ideal type, or socially through negotiated meanings. In a similar vein, McPhee (1985) tells us that the structure of an organization can be viewed in various ways, as an empirical object, a negotiated set of relationships, a system, or a carrier of social processes. In other words, an organization can be viewed as a formally created entity or as socially constructed patterns of behavior.

Organizational structure is a key area of concern for people who work in organizations. Why? Because the direction of information flow relates directly to how the work should be done, and who has access to, and control over information. The structure of an organization can be either "tall" as in a pyramid or "flat" as in a matrix design with its multiple and overlapping channels of communication. Depending on the organization's structure, the flow of information will be different. Does communication move horizontally, crossing functional boundaries, or primarily downward as in most bureaucratic organizations? However, communication is more than the flow of information; it involves meaning. For example, what does it mean to receive an instruction from the boss compared to receiving it from a fellow employee? Consequently, the implications of communication technologies, as they relate to the structure of an organization, are an important focus of study because new communication technologies create the possibility that the direction or flow of communication can change.

A central feature of electronic or computer mail is its ability to overcome space and time constraints. It provides the opportunity to change the range of and direction of one's communication. For example, month-end reports, accounting details, and marketing updates can be sent in seconds to office locations geographically distant. This eliminates waiting for what some employees call "snail mail," which seems to be getting slower all the time. Further, groups of people can coordinate their work and activities over any distance. With electronic mail connections, the direction and patterns of communication are limitless. Space, time, and geographic location are no longer factors in the communication process. Electronic mail provides an alternative to the traditional forms of communication; one has access to a broader range of employees, and messages can now be sent to the other side of the globe in minutes. They can also be directed to multiple destinations and employees. There is the potential, when employees use electronic mail, for their communication network, size, density, and range to be altered. However, Rice (1992) cautions that, while electronic mail provides the ability to cross organizational and geographic boundaries, task and resource interdependency may be intervening factors. They could easily constrain, change, and/or reduce the motivation to change (p. 20). For example, if two employees' work is interdependent, they may choose not to use electronic mail to make "new" contacts since they are already heavily invested in the current "work relationship."

Malone and Rockart (1991) suggest that a new form of organization termed "ad-hocracy" is becoming more viable since "new media such as electronic mail, computer conferencing and electronic bulletin boards can make the coordination easier" (p. 133). An ad-hocracy contrasts with a conventional hierarchical structure since it has abundant lateral communication and flexible shifting teams or work groups. Malone and Rockart note, however, that there are potential difficulties owing to an increase in overall information. For example, centralization of the additional information that has been created (on a main computer) could provide management with greater control and power. The opposite fear is one of organizational chaos that may come with decentralization as employees assume more authority and begin to serve their own organizational interests.

Kiesler (1986) supports Malone and Rockart's argument when she discusses the effects of computer-mediated communication and the way it can change work habits and communication practices, stating that it allows employees to cross "hierarchical and department barriers, standard operating procedures and organizational norms" (p. 47). New communication technologies have the potential to reshape the organization's communication processes and structure (Depaoli, Fantoli, and Miani, 1988; Kanter, 1983; Morgan, 1988; Peters & Waterman, 1982; Sproull & Kiesler, 1991). Therefore, by changing the direction in which information flows, relationships can change. Typically, managers have access to their employees, but with electronic mail employees may have new access to management.

Culnan and Markus (1987), for example, reported consistent findings in the increase of upward and downward hierarchical communication. In other words, there was more "talk" moving up as well as down in the organization. An increase in upward communication may help management identify issues and problems earlier. Culnan and Markus take the position that the introduction of new communication technologies in organizations has the potential to alter communication activities, thus altering and influencing "key aspects of organizational structure and process" (p. 421). Kiesler and colleagues (1984) also report the potential for increased lateral relationships and a change in "the flow of information in organizations, altering status relations and organizational hierarchy" (p. 1124). For instance, employees might "discover" others in the legal department who have overlapping goals with them, and use them as a resource.

Sproull and Kiesler (1991) report that as the form of work changes (i.e., it is no longer constrained by a nonelectronic world) organizations become more flexible and, therefore, less hierarchical. They cite examples of "broadcast" messages that begin with the question "Does anybody know. . . ?" This kind of message can seek information from an entire organization or network as was the case at Tandem Computers, Inc. Typically, Tandem reports that about eight employees respond daily to these kinds of inquiries. Additionally, those employees receiving responses can redistribute the information to others, thus increasing the information pool and range of messages even further. Ideas and information are shared across the organization in an expanding network that is much different from traditional nonelectronic behavior. Another example is Digital Equipment Corporation's sales organization. Electronic mail allows sales reps to increase their range of communication and decrease turnaround time. It provides them with the capability to broadcast messages to other sales representatives around the world, asking for help with a specific sales proposal. They routinely use the system to gather information about sales prospects that may have DEC equipment in other locations (Sproull & Kiesler, 1991). Further, employees who are geographically dispersed or those who do shift work can now be included in organizational information sharing and decision making.

Contrary to these findings, C. B. Johnson (1992) found that electronic mail did not significantly alter the range and direction of communication in a local utility company. Why not? This could be attributed to the task and resource interdependency requirements already mentioned, or it could be strict administrative sanctions against personal use of electronic mail. In other words, we cannot assume that the implementation of electronic mail will change an organization's structure. There are other factors to consider such as culture, norms, and who needs to work with whom. This highlights the importance of social construction of media use and moves away from technological determinism. Others have also found little or no evidence of change in formal structures as a result of the introduction of electronic mail (Eveland & Bikson, 1987; McKenney, Doherty, & Sviokla, 1986; Robey, 1981; Sherblom, 1988).

Electronic mail can be used to overcome traditional boundaries and constraints, yet it can also serve to reinforce existing norms and reflect an organization's traditional hierarchy, if dictated by organizational policy. For example, if there are sanctions against upward communication or contacting other departments without first "checking with the boss," electronic mail will do little more than reinforce these norms. In one organization, Johnson (1992) found strict sanctions against the use of the traditional mail system for personal purposes. When electronic mail was installed, employees felt this sanction extended to it, and therefore did not see it as a medium for new or social use. Obviously, organizational structure may or may not change with the introduction of electronic mail or any other new communication technology. Change is less likely in organizations with a long history of prohibited use and no new and explicit policy to encourage use of the new system in a way that would change structure (Rice, 1992). Also, an organization's culture may constrain the ability of an organization to change its communication range, pattern, and direction. For instance, if it is made entirely clear to employees that electronic mail is to be used only as a replacement for some other form of communication, and *not* as an additional channel, the culture may not "allow" employees to contact others beyond their normal work activities.

Media Richness

Media richness or social presence has been defined as the potential information-carrying capacity or feedback responses of a medium; these include nonverbal communication, social cues, equivocal information, physical proximity, and status (Daft & Lengel, 1984; Short, Williams, & Christie, 1976). The capacities are arrayed along a continuum with face-to-face considered the richest medium owing to its rapid response and multiple cues, followed next by the telephone, then written personal, written formal, and finally numeric formal representing the leanest medium. Communication technologies reduce the amount of "social presence" or "media richness" one has in face-to-face communication.

Steinfield and Fulk (1986) argued that electronic mail should be included on the richness continuum between telephone and written documents. It does provide rapid feedback but lacks other interpersonal nonverbal cues such as voice inflection and affect display. It is not clear yet just where electronic mail should be positioned on the rich to lean continuum, or if it should be. Part of the difficulty may be that we are trying to compare electronic mail with existing forms of media or see it as a replacement for other media. Instead, we should look at it, and perhaps most of the new communication media, on the technology's own terms and as "new" media that may not fit within our current understanding or perspectives about media.

Often people who work in organizations are concerned that a lack of "richness" in communicating with fellow employees may be detrimental to the organization. Face-to-face communication has a long history as a standard by which other media are evaluated. Hence, they believe that replacing face-to-face conversations with electronic mail messages, or videoconferencing, may contribute to feelings of alienation, dissatisfaction, marginalization, or a feeling that "this place has really gotten impersonal."

Media richness theory, or rational choice, proposes that people consciously select communication media based on the inherent "richness" of the medium, and how well the degree of "richness" matches the communication event. In other words, the choice would be considered "rational" based on the context of communication. For example, in highly equivocal situations, such as an employee counseling session, one might select a rich form of communication that provides multiple feedback cues. The theory argues that communication is facilitated by selecting "rich" communication media in a highly equivocal context. Conversely, communication is effective when one selects "lean" media in unambiguous situations. As equivocality increases, the need for feedback increases. Fairly straightforward situations with low equivocality, like a change in the company car rental plan, may be handled with a lean medium such as a written memo. Media-richness theory makes the point, for instance, that choice of medium is not necessarily an intentional or conscious decision. Whether a communication medium, like the telephone, is perceived as "rich" or "lean" is inherent in the medium. From this perspective, face-to-face communication is always considered "rich."

In fact, Trevino, Lengel, and Daft (1987) argue that effective managers, those who advance and are successful in an organization, are better at matching the "correct" medium with the situation. In other words, such a manager seems to know when it is appropriate to select either "rich" or "lean" media and match them correctly to the situation. The idea is to correctly match the degree of richness of the medium with the requirements of the communication task at hand, resulting in "effective" communication.

Fulk and co-workers (1987, 1990) and Ryu and Fulk (1991), drawing upon the social influence model of communication, take the position that perception of new media, and therefore media-use behavior, varies among individuals and across groups. This model assumes that if a group socially constructs that electronic mail use is acceptable in ambiguous situations, then selection and use of it will be appropriate and effective in that situation. In this view, media-use behavior is socially influenced. Use behavior is not constrained solely by the objective features of a medium; constraint is not inherent in a medium; rather, constraint is socially constructed. The form of media in and of themselves will not determine how they should be used; people do.

Unlike Daft and Lengel's (1984) information-richness theory, which posits that media-use outcomes are the result of objectively rational choices based on the medium's capacity to provide feedback, Fulk and others (1987, 1990) argue that media use is socially constructed. Therefore, selection of media may be different across groups and from person to person. For example, a particular work group or department could adopt a "media style," while other departments have different norms of media use. They build their argument on the notion that media-use behavior is "at its core, subjectively rational. Behavior need not meet efficiency criteria in order to be considered rational within the particular context" (Fulk and others, 1990, p. 125). For example, textual communication does not have to be considered "lean." There are numerous examples of heavy electronic mail use by upper level managers. According to Mintzberg (1973), managers, owing to the ambiguous nature of their work, spend a great deal of time in "rich" face-to-face communication. This supports Daft and Lengel's (1984) proposition.

However, a multiorganizational study by Rice, Hart, Torobin, and Shook (1989) found that electronic mail, a less rich medium, was used more heavily by managers than clerical or technical workers. Heavy use of electronic mail by management is contrary to implications of media-richness theory, but indicates that these managers, within their social context, spend time using electronic mail instead of face-to-face communication. This provides support for the notion that "rational use" is interrelated with social context. What this means is if a group socially constructs that electronic mail use is acceptable in ambiguous situations, then selection and use of it will be appropriate in that situation. In this view, media-use behavior is socially influenced. Fulk and co-workers (1990) provide further evidence for social influence effects. They cite recent findings that indicate that electronic mail is being used for highly interpersonal interactions such as negotiation and conflict resolution. Also, Rice and Love (1987) found that electronic mail (E-mail) seems to support more socio-emotional content, which is required for media richness.

Which model supports the use of electronic mail for negotiation purposes? The media-richness model assumes that, owing to its inherent richness of face-to-face communication, it would be the objectively rational choice for negotiation. The social influence model subsumes the media-richness model, pointing out that social influence must also be considered as a factor in media selection. The research of Trevino and colleagues (1987) informs us that message ambiguity, symbolic cues, and situational constraints are all factors in media choice. However, their argument that face-to-face communication is "rich" and preferred by managers in ambiguous situations only lends credence to the notion that in the past we have used face-to-face communication as a criterion by which we judge all other communication media. By that, we mean it is seen as the preferred form of communication and the standard by which all other communication media are judged. In light of new communication technology, this assumption may no longer hold.

Based on the above discussion it can be seen that there may be organizations where other forms of communication media, particularly electronic mail, are as acceptable as face-to-face communication. In fact, Shook and Rice's study (1990) found that in two of the sites E-mail usage was higher for managers. They found, instead, that the distinction between managers and clerical workers lay in the amount of time spent in meetings, not the amount of time spent using electronic mail.

Efficiency and Productivity

A frequent and popular justification for the installation of new communication technology is the assumption that, as a result of anticipated increases in efficiency and productivity, an organization can be more efficient. Organizations consider increases in efficiency and productivity as improvements in how the organization functions. For example, organizations seem willing to spend billions of dollars on the "automated office" in a desperate move to increase white-collar productivity (Immel, 1986). The reasoning is that improvement in how an organization functions should improve the "bottom line." Furthermore, Buchanan's (1986) research identified seven different types of new technology introduced in six companies with increased productivity as one of the stated strategic objectives. In addition, the COMSERVE hotline (November 1991), an electronic mail forum, broadcast a request for any information that would provide cost justification for the installation of E-mail at a major university. Their goal, as stated, was to reduce their telephone and fax transmission costs. This was based on the assumption that electronic mail would substitute for, replace, or decrease the use of other media.

Caution

With this in mind, this section begins with a word of caution to anyone who anticipates that new communication technology will result in increased efficiency and productivity. A way to think about this might be, "Don't kill the messenger." In this case the "messenger" is new communication technology. Expecting it to deliver an improvement (good news), might lead to blaming it if there is no significant improvement (bad news).

Simply said, an organization's efficiency goal may be typically, either increased output for the same amount of input, or decreased input for the same amount of output, or both. Organizational efficiency criteria are derived from a sought-after "preferred state" wherein its targets are met in a clear and objective way (Harrison, 1987). In a nutshell, it is often seen as a way to save money. There is an underlying assumption by far too many organizations that they will benefit economically as the organization "automates" and becomes more "productive and efficient." However, the possibility exists that a decrease in efficiency may occur with no appreciable change at all. A new communication medium like electronic mail can result, for example, in "information overload," including an increase in "junk" mail, which creates more to do (one has to at least look at it, if not deal with it) with no associated organizational benefit (Harrison, 1987, p. 33).

It has always been difficult to measure an increase in efficiency for a knowledge worker. Increases in material output—for example, in manufacturing—can be quantified. It can also be determined whether production rates and quality of a product have improved. But how does management determine when a knowledge worker is "more efficient or productive"? For instance, the number of research projects produced in one year does not provide information about quality, just quantity. Are employees or organizational members more efficient just because they have produced more work? Producing more work does not equal an increase in quality or efficiency. In other words, there are types of organizational tasks and work that cannot be measured or quantified. Quality of work life is one example. Instead, when evaluating electronic mail, management should consider the overall success of a department or organization. With that word of warning we can now turn to a discussion of electronic mail as an example of how a new technology may enhance productivity and efficiency.

It is costly for organizations to process and transmit information. Because E-mail is fast, asynchronous, and expands communication beyond one-to-one contacts to include mass or "broadcast" messages, cost savings and efficiency gains are possible as a first level effect (Sproull & Kiesler, 1991, p. 21). Electronic mail can in fact provide a viable substitute for other media. Businesses do enjoy the cost savings that can derive from increased speed in communication, bypassing the regular mail, and the ability to reduce telephone costs. Rice and Case's (1983) study of a project, Terminals for Managers (TFM), at a large university included questions about the perceived effects of the new communication medium on the manager's work and other media. Managers reported perceived benefits owing to TFM in the quality and quantity of their work (p. 141). This obviously relates to productivity and efficiency issues.

Another striking example is the use of computer based information by Manufacturer's Hanover Trust. "Manufacturer's Hanover Trust estimated that employees saved an average of 36 minutes a day by using computer-based communication. This translates into an annual net opportunity value of about $7 million" (Sproull & Kiesler, 1991, p. 23). Further, Digital Equipment Corporation estimated a $28 million cost savings to its managers using electronic mail (Crawford, 1982).

Hiltz identifies cost displacement as one justification for the E-mail system used by Owens Corning:

> Experienced users typically replaced four to six communications a day, which, with a future projected population in the company of 1500 users, would show replacement savings of $600,000 a year (1984, p. 166).

However, as mentioned earlier, Hiltz (1984) points out that an add-on effect might occur (i.e., electronic mail is added on to other communication rather than replacing it), or there may very well be an expansion effect (i.e., the additional communication created by electronic mail stimulates more communication via other media). For instance, Hiltz reports that early users experience an add-on effect for telephone use and mail and that over time when the system use increased (or with those who were heavy users) there was likely to be an expanded use of all communication media. Electronic mail follows this pattern in a similar way. Interestingly, Hiltz reports that an increase as well as a decrease in mail among medium to heavy users occurs more frequently. Hiltz (1983) speculates that,

> A probable explanation is that on-line communication substitutes for some mail or telephone but stimulates other contacts that might not otherwise take place. For instance, users may apprise one another of available preprints or other documents, which are then sent by mail. If a subject of mutual interest is likely to take a great deal of discussion, participants who find themselves on-line at the same time frequently decide to talk it over on the telephone to resolve an issue or to get another set of cues about each other's feelings (p. 169).

Thus, an increase in overall volume of communication occurs. This relates directly to the issue of an organization's structure discussed earlier. As size of networks increase, (i.e., number of connections) and range of communication expands, there is potential for the organization's structure to be broadened. It can be seen from this discussion of first-level effects that efficiency, productivity, and the structure of the organization are interrelated.

It is often management's intent to increase productivity and efficiency by installing electronic mail, but it does not always do so. One of the problems organizations face is that a narrow focus on production capability only (i.e., output) limits the organization's ability to implement new technology successfully. Johnson and Rice (1987) conducted a study of organizational innovation in almost 200 organizations, noting that some entities were more successful in adapting to change than others. They argued that the emphasis should be on second-level effects: An organization's ability to adapt to change and to innovate, rather than the traditional bureaucratic notion of production capability and efficiency, should be the primary goal when a new communication technology is adopted. "Managers of information workers should pay increasing attention to adaptation rather than solely to narrow definitions of production" (Johnson and Rice, 1987, p. 2). Further, they cite one large-scale study in which "only 10 percent of the 110 organizations had successful implementations of office automation" (p. 2).

Another way to look at the outcome of rapid and easy electronic mail communication is to consider other effects beyond efficiency. Kiesler and colleagues (1984) report that a company president, sending computer mail from Pittsburgh at dinner time, expects his subordinates in Singapore to respond with their quarterly projections by breakfast. The explicit expectation of a rapid response, which entails more than the capability of electronic mail, could be one more outcome of instantaneous communication availability. New norms are created.

It would seem, then, that beyond the obvious first-level effects that management is striving for, there are long-term second-level effects that must be considered in any organization's implementation of new communication technologies. Second-level effects also include changes in the social interaction that takes place among co-workers. Johnson and Rice (1987) cite the classic diffusion study by Coleman and others (1966) in which information about new drugs was received through varying forms of media by doctors but that a colleague's opinion was most important in the decision process. This lends support to the importance of the social influence model. It is important to remember that first-level efficiency goals may not always be achieved.

In a review of information overload literature, Hiltz and Turoff (1985) point out that, although a balance must be struck between open and structured electronic communication systems to control volume, there is a definite potential benefit to the organization in adopting electronic systems. They cite reports by users that the most valuable feature of a system is the flexibility it allows them, thereby enabling them to contact and converse with "new" people on line. The result was an increase in new ideas, a second-level innovation (pp. 683–684).

Trevino and colleagues (1987) studied managerial media choice. In one instance they gave anecdotal evidence about the importance of the choice of medium:

> Harold Geneen discovered that how he communicated with European subsidiaries of ITT made a big difference in his subsequent actions. He discovered that his response to a question or request from Europe was different if received by teletype in New York versus talking to the sender face-to-face in Europe (p. 554).

The impact of electronic media on communication clearly moves beyond efficiency. The point is that while first-level effects of increased productivity and efficiency are important to an organization, so are the second-level effects that deal with long-term organizational issues such as innovation.

In fact, Kiesler (1986) points out that the social effects of computer networks may be far more important than efficiency gains. For example, Kiesler refers us to the long-term social effects of prior technical innovations such as the elevator and the telephone and suggests that researchers learn from these histories. Kiesler argues that,

> first, the social effects of new technologies are hard to foresee, Hence we tend to exaggerate the technical changes and the significance of transient issues, and we underestimate the social effects. Second, the long run social effects of a new technology are not the intended ones, but have more to do with the technology's indirect demands on our time and attention, and with the way it changes our work habits and our interpersonal relations (p. 47).

The social effects of a new communication medium, such as electronic mail, in an organization create new issues about work habits and interpersonal communication structures, quality, and quantity. Social interaction occurs in a dynamic web of co-constructed meanings.

There are as many stories about failures as there are about successes in organizations when new communication media such as electronic mail are introduced (Johnson & Rice, 1987). These same authors point out that, to a great extent, success depends on many factors. One must consider how employees' interactions, perceptions, and attitudes about the new medium, *in addition to what the medium itself can do*, affect its use. For example, employees may perceive electronic mail as an "un-secure" means of communication and decide among themselves not to use it in certain situations or for sensitive topics. In a research institution, employees could be concerned about "losing secrets" to competitors via electronic mail. Or they may decide among themselves, as they socially construct their understanding of this new medium, that it will make work seem impersonal. These are a few of the many examples of obstacles that can be created by employees as organizations look to new technology for increased productivity and efficiency. What's the point here?

The point is that an understanding of any new communication technology and particularly new medium such as electronic mail should include the employees' use and perception of it. There is no other way to understand or make sense of its deployment in the organization. Admittedly, there is a rational use for electronic mail or any new communication technology as additional tools for the organization, but employees create and come to understand the organization and the tools in it as they interact and work together.

SUMMARY

The issues that the organization's participants must consider in connection with a new communication technology center around their use of the new medium as well as its technical capabilities. Along with changes in the patterns of communication there is potential for the organization's structure to change. Concepts of what constitutes "media richness" may no longer apply as new media and communication technology enter organizations. Efficiency and productivity cannot be assumed based on the technical merits of the medium. It is clear that communication media are embedded in organizational communication processes and practices, including the human communication practices that constitute the organization.

Finally, anyone interested in additional areas and issues surrounding new communication media and organizations should look at computer-supported group decision technologies, information processing and its relationship to organizational design, new opportunities for interorganizational communication, and communication network analysis.

REFERENCES

BARNARD, C. I., *The Functions of the Executive* (30th anniv. ed.). Cambridge, Mass: Harvard University Press, 1938.

BUCHANAN, D.A., "Using the New Technology," in *Information Technology Revolution.* Tom Forester, ed. Cambridge, Mass.: MIT Press, 1986.

BURRELL, G., and G. MORGAN, *Sociological Paradigms and Organizational Analysis.* London: Heinemann, 1979.

CRAWFORD, A.B., "Corporate Electronic Mail—A Communication Intensive Application of Information Technology," *MIS Quarterly*, 6 (1982), 1–14.

CULNAN, M.J., and M.L. MARKUS, "Information Technologies," in *Handbook of Organizational Communication*, F. Jablin, L. Putnam, K. Roberts, and L. Porter, eds. Newbury Park, Calif.: Sage Publications, Inc., 1987.

DAFT, R.L., and R. LENGEL, "Information Richness: A New Approach to Managerial Behavior and Organization Design," in *Research in Organizational Behavior* (Vol. 6), B. Staw and L.L. Cummings, eds. Greenwich, Conn.: JAI Press, 1984.

DEPAOLI, P., A. FANTOLI A., and G. MIANI, *Participation in Technological Change: The Role of the Parties Concerned in the Introduction of New Technology.* Dublin: Loughlinstown House, Shankill Co., 1988.

EVELAND, J.D., and T. BIKSON, "Evolving Electronic Communication Networks: An Empirical Assessment," *Office: Technology and People*, 3 (1987), 103–128.

FULK, J., and C.W. STEINFIELD, "Editorial introduction," in *Organizations and Communication Technology.* Newbury Park, Calif.: Sage Publications, Inc., 1990.

FULK, J., C.W. STEINFIELD, J. SCHMITZ, and J.G. POWER, "A Social Information Processing Model of Media Use in Organizations," in *Communication Research*, P.R. Monge, ed. Beverly Hills, Calif.: Sage Publications, Inc., 1987.

FULK, J., C.W. STEINFIELD, J. SCHMITZ, and J.G. POWER, "A Social Influence Model of Technology Use," in *Organizations and Communication Technology*, J. Fulk and C. W. Steinfield, eds. Newbury Park, Calif.: Sage Publications, Inc., 1990.

HARRISON, M.I., *Diagnosing Organizations: Methods, Models and Processes.* Newbury Park, Calif.: Sage Publications, Inc., 1987.

HILTZ, S.R., *Online Communities: A Case Study of the Office of the Future.* Norwood, N.J.: Ablex, 1984.

HILTZ, S.R., and M. TUROFF, "Structuring Computer Mediated Communication Systems to Avoid Information Overload," *Communication of the ACM*, 28 (1985), 680–689.

IMMEL, R.A., "Automated Office: Myth Versus Reality," in *Information Technology Revolution*, Tom Forester, ed. Cambridge, Mass.: MIT Press, 1986.

JOHNSON, B.M., and R.E. RICE, *Managing Organizational Innovation: The Evolution From Word Processing to Office Information Systems.* New York: Columbia University Press, 1987.

JOHNSON, C.B., "New Communication Media and the Potential for Change in the Organization." Unpublished manuscript, 1992.

KANTER, R.M, *The Change Masters*. New York: Simon & Schuster, 1983.

KIESLER, S., "The Hidden Messages in Computer Networks," *HBR* (January–February 1986), 46–53.

KIESLER, S., J. SIEGEL, and T.W. MCGUIRE, "Social Psychological Aspects of Computer-Mediated Communication," *American Psychologist*, 39 (1984), 1123–1134.

McKENNEY, J., V. DOHERTY, and J. SVIOKLA, "The Impact of Electronic Networks on Management Communication: An Information Processing Study." Unpublished manuscript. Boston: Harvard Graduate School of Business, 1986.

McPHEE, R.D., "Formal Structure and Organizational Communication," in *Organizational Communication: Traditional Themes and New Directions*, R.D. McPhee and P.K. Tompkins, eds. Beverly Hills, Calif.: Sage Publications, Inc., 1985.

MALONE, T.W., and J.F. ROCKART, "Computers, Networks and the Corporation," *Scientific American* (September 1991), 128–136.

MINTZBERG, H., *The Nature of Managerial Work*. New York: Harper & Row, Pub., 1973.

MORGAN, G., *Riding the Waves of Changes: Developing Managerial Competence for a Changing World*. San Francisco: Jossey-Bass, 1988.

PETERS, T.J., and R.H. WATERMAN, *In Search of Excellence*. New York: Harper & Row, Pub., 1982.

RICE, R.E., "Contexts of Research on Organizational Computer-Mediated Communication: A Recursive Review," in *Contexts of Computer Mediated Communication*. Ed. M. Lea, United Kingdom: Harvester-Wheatsheaf, 1992.

RICE, R.E., and D. CASE, "Electronic Message Systems in the University: A Description of Use and Utility," *Journal of Communication*, Winter (1983), 131–150.

RICE, R.E., P. HART, J. TOROBIN, and D. SHOOK, "Task Analyzability, Media Use and Performance: A Multi-Site Test of Information Richness Theory." Unpublished manuscript presented to International Communication Association, San Francisco, 1989.

RICE, R. E., and G. LOVE, "Electronic Emotion: Socioemotional Content in a Computer-Mediated Communication Network," in *Communication Research*, 14 (1987), 85–108.

ROBEY, D., "Computer Information Systems and Organization Structure," in *Communications of the ACM*, 24 (1981), 679–687.

RYU, D., and J. FULK, "Group Cohesiveness and Perceptions of Media Richness in the Work Place." Unpublished manuscript. Forty-first annual conference of International Communication Association, Chicago, IL, May 1991.

SHERBLOOM, J., "Direction, Function and Signature in Electronic Mail," *The Journal of Business Communication*, 25 (1988), 39–54.

SHOOK, M., and R.E. RICE, "Relationships of Job Categories and Organizational Levels to the Use of Communication Channels Including Electronic Mail, a Meta-Analysis and Extension," *Journal of Management Studies*, 27 (1990), 194–229.

SHORT, J., E. WILLIAMS, and B. CHRISTIE, *The Social Psychology of Telecommunications*. New York: John Wiley, 1976.

SPROULL, L., and S. KIESLER, *Connections: New Ways of Working in the Networked Organization*. Cambridge, Mass.: MIT Press, 1991.

STEINFIELD, C.W., and J. FULK, "Task Demands and Managers' Use of Communication Media: An Informational Processing View." Unpublished manuscript. Academy of Management, Organizational Communication Division, Chicago, Illinois, 1986.

TREVINO, L.K., R.H. LENGEL, and R.L. DAFT, "Media Symbolism, Media Richness, and Media Choice in Organizations," in *Communication Research*, P.R. Monge, ed. Beverly Hills, Calif.: Sage Publications, Inc., 1987.

WEBER, M., *The Theory of Social and Economic Organization*. New York: Free Press, 1947.

10

Power and Empowerment in the Organization

Organizations by their very nature seek to achieve some level of order so that they may sustain themselves and achieve their goals. This means that the organization must be able to get participants to behave in ways that are beneficial to the organization. This may involve a negotiated order, but it is an ordering of people that involves exercising power. Individuals who join organizations or who are born into them seek certain advantages. Their attempts to do this are exercises in power.

Clegg (1989) tells us that "organization is basically about control…in extending power through delegation one must be able to bind delegates to the power that authorizes" (p.272). In most cases individuals within organizations also want a sense of control. It is not only a matter of where one "fits" but where one is "going." People desire some "voice" in the outcome of their organizational lives. There is a "tension" between organizational demands and individual freedom. What power is used and how it is used is important to the issue of whose interests are being served and for what purpose. Individual capacity to exert power and have some sense of control over self is not a peripheral issue. The organization is not just a place where services are rendered and profits made. Organizations represent a significant part of an individual's life and identity. The term "empowerment" refers to the process by which individuals exert power on an organization.

This chapter discusses power concepts and attendant issues. Our major concern is with communication-based issues. These are significant enough to warrant major attention. There have been long standing theoretical issues in the study of power, and much has been written that exposes the complexity of those issues. We will discuss some of the major areas of concern, but the focus will be on those questions that most directly affect the way one communicates as an organizational participant. This means becoming more aware of what constitutes power, how it is executed, and how the distribution of power influences organizational life and outcomes.

POWER CONCEPTS AND ORGANIZATION

What Is Power?

Traditional definitions of power have focused on individual capacity to determine or restrict outcomes. This seems straightforward enough, but the concept of power raises multiple issues. Dahl (1957) suggests that "A has power over B to the extent he can get B to do something B would not otherwise do" (pp. 202–203). This definition not only narrows the concept of power but requires that one identify special types of behaviors. Riker (1964) maintains that the differences in the notions of power are really based on different ideas of causality. In his words, "Power is the ability to exercise influence while cause is the actual exercise of it" (p. 347). Is power an ability to do something or the actual act of doing it?

Russell (1986) defines power as the production of intended effects. Does power only take place when it is intended? Clegg (1989) points out that the foundational tradition of power suggests several major questions. "Is power distributed 'plurally' or held by an 'elite'? Is power intentional or not intentional? Is power confined to decision making or is it evident in non-decision making? Is not making a decision an action or a non-action? Is power a capacity for action or the exercise of action?" (p. 37).

Mintzberg (1983) not only remarks about the quagmire of issues surrounding the concept of power but also asserts that in terms of the organization the interest should be focused on who gets power, when they get it, how they get it and why, rather than on what it is. Perhaps part of the frustration of studying power results from trying to devise an all-encompassing definition that contains and resolves divergent issues.

Our approach will be to explore several facets of power and elaborate on the complexity of the concept. We do not advocate or seek the one true concept of power. What is important is how the various notions of power relate to organizational communication. Although definitions of power do not embrace and resolve all the complexities of the concept, taken by themselves they have merit. Boulding (1989) advances the notion that power is simply, in the broad sense, to what extent and how we get what we want. If this is applied to the organizational setting, it is a matter of determining the circumstances of how the organization gets what it wants and how individual contributors get what they want. We consider power as the capacity of individuals and collectivities to influence, regulate, and control outcomes.

Where Does Power Reside?

Traditional notions about power have focused on the individual and the exercise of power. Power is something that is held by people. It is held by virtue of certain sources of power. French and Raven (1959) suggest that A may have power over B on the basis of five types of power. These bases of power are differentiated by the meaning A's acts have to B and by the relationship they imply. (1) *Reward Power:* Can A determine perceived rewards for B? (2) *Coercive Power:* Can A mete out what is considered punishment for B? (3) *Legitimate Power:* Does B believe that A has a right to exert influence and that B should accept it? The source of legitimate power may be acceptance of a social structure or cultural values. (4) *Referent Power:* Does B identify with A? Does B aspire to be like A or have a desire for a feeling of oneness with A? (5) *Expert Power:* Does B believe that A possesses special knowledge or skills that are beneficial or necessary for the well-being of B?

Contemporary views recognize that power does not reside in people alone but in the social structure in which they act (Lukes, 1977; Giddens 1979, 1984). This suggests that the structure, or the "rules of the game" as socially constructed, decides what can be talked about and in what ways. The structure itself may decide what issues can be considered in the decision-making process. Anyone who has entered a new organization and has sat in a meeting knows that people are not speaking in a vacuum. There is more operating than the overt statements. What can be talked about? What is considered outrageous or disloyal? Will an opinion be shared by anyone? A social structure is present. The concept of power then must take into consideration what is said and what is not said by virtue of the social structure in which power is exercised. This has been referred to as the "two faces of power" (Bachrach and Baratz, 1962).

Organizations represent certain values and practices that are embedded in their structure. This "structure" is acted out and reinforced by organizational behaviors that are constrained by the "structure" itself. Power resides in the structure because it is a controlling force on those who would exercise power. Schattschneider (1960) asserts that organization itself is the "mobilization of bias." In other words, some issues become part of the political scene and some are organized out.

Individuals may have the capacity to influence others by virtue of a particular resource or position, but power involves more than a commodity or property that can be employed in any situation or social structure. Power resides in the relationships between people and within the social system itself. Contemporary views treat the concept of power as a multidimensional concept (Clegg, 1989; Gaventa, 1980; Lukes, 1974, 1986). For example, when talking about the power of A over B, Gaventa suggests that the first dimension of power may involve A's control of superior bargaining resources. The second dimension is concerned with A constructing barriers to participation of B. These barriers may be signified by the decisions that are *not* made and those issues that are excluded from discussion or negotiation. A third and more subtle dimension focuses on how A influences and shapes the thinking of B through the production of myths, information control, and ideology.

Although discussion of these dimensions appears to focus on the individual, it must be kept in mind that individuals are acting out of a structure. There may or may not be an awareness of the power structure that exists. This raises the question: Whose interests are being served within a particular social system, and is there an awareness of whose interests are being served? The central concern is whether the social system allows for rational choice. The system itself may have produced people who do not understand what their best interests are and consequently they act against their own self-interests (Lukes, 1974; Habermas, 1972). Although such a view has merit, we are primarily interested in what it says about the concept of power. The exercise of power is embedded in a context, which is especially true of the organizational context.

Organization/Power Interface

We use the term *interface* to indicate the close interaction between the concepts of organization and power. The amount of order and how that order is achieved in any social system may be open to a variety of interpretations, but eventually decisions must be made if the system is to sustain itself. Even chaos must be managed. Some voices (individuals, groups, ideologies, philosophies, cultural norms) will be heard more, sustained more, and permitted more than others. From a common-sense view it is a question of what is organized "in" and what is organized "out."

Clegg (1989) asserts that

> any generally applicable theory of power must also be a theory of organization. Much of the theory of power in organizations has been oriented towards the explanation of how organizational obedience is produced. In the penultimate chapter this orientation is built on to develop a framework in which both "obedience" and "resistance" can be located.... Agency is something which is achieved by virtue of organization, whether of a human being's dispositional capacities or of a collective nature, in the sense usually reserved for the referent of "organizations" (p. 17).

Power is not reduced to human agents or structure alone. Clegg maintains that an understanding of either "organization" or "power" involves a reciprocal conceptualization of both terms. A theory of power must look at the context in which it is arranged and determine what "practices" are privileged and sustained. His approach is to regard power "as a process which may pass through distinct circuits of power and resistance" (p. 18).

The notions of "obedience" and "resistance" are important to the growth and survival of organizations. The healthy social system contains both. A certain level of order is necessary while at the same time individuals must be able to challenge the thinking of the organization. This allows for innovation and change. The contradiction between obedience and resistance represents a fundamental challenge to organizational leadership. Parents usually want their children to become independent, but when that process occurs they find it difficult to give up controls that are assumed to represent the best solutions. Challenging the status quo in an organization becomes even more difficult because individuals do not always have immediate access to power centers.

A central concept in organizations (especially large organizations) is that of hierarchy. The various levels of an organization represent positional power. As Boulding (1989) points out, decisions are made by individuals, but in most cases they are made on behalf of a larger entity. As people rise in hierarchies, what they are deciding and on whose behalf becomes more complex. This suggests that the organizational structure itself both enables and constrains the exercise of power. Positions may allow people to exercise certain powers, but at the same time decisions are not "individual" because of the requirements of the position (see Chapter 3).

As important as organizational structure is, it cannot sustain itself without individuals who legitimate it through behavior, especially communication behavior. Positions and roles do take on a power of their own by what they represent. For example, when it is suggested that one should "respect the position if nothing else," it is clear that the position represents certain values and the holder is in a position to exercise power. People want to respond because of a basic belief that anyone who holds the position should embody the values of that position. It is easier to be "presidential" if you are the president. At the same time, the position or role cannot be influential unless it has been legitimized by those who respond to it. Each time there is a riot in a major city, it is abundantly clear that police have little impact unless there is a legitimizing response by those involved. What the police represent symbolically is more potent than what they can do physically to maintain order.

As organizations become large and complex, it becomes difficult to monitor behaviors and assure that organizational concerns are receiving maximum attention and support. Some types of power may be more effective than others in sustaining the organization. Boulding (1989) explores three types of power—destructive, productive, and integrative. Destructive power is threat power and the capacity to destroy. Productive power is economic in nature and involves the power to produce and exchange. To be able to make something is having productive power. Integrative power involves inspiring loyalty, bringing people together, and being able to move people toward a common vision. Boulding's major thesis is that integrative power is the most dominant and significant form of power. In terms of the organization this certainly appears to be true. Such power places the focus on legitimacy. A hierarchical organization has to rely on information and support throughout its structure. The degree to which this occurs depends on how legitimate organizational requests are perceived to be. Organizations by their very nature develop structure and roles that are created, maintained, and transformed through the communication process. In addition, the language of structure and roles represents an organizational reality that achieves a legitimacy through its use.

To organize is to create power relationships in which the nature of these relationships is communication dependent. If we were forced to choose any one factor that distinguishes organizational communication from other types, we would select the concept of power. It could be said that power relationships exist in any exchange, but in the organization they become more pronounced, focused, and omnipresent. It could be argued that the difference is one of degree and not of kind. Either way, the difference is no small matter. Certainly part of the interest in organizations arises from the apparent political structure that each represents. Participants in an organization do not act with free and independent agency. Wittingly or unwittingly they act out of the pressures of a complex context. The middle manager, department head, or director feels the push and pull of a variety of interests.

ORGANIZATIONAL COMMUNICATION DYNAMICS

The more traditional notions of communication focus on the concepts of "transmission" and "tool." In the case of "transmission," Carey (1975) reminds us that the definitions of communication have emphasized notions of sending, transmitting, and giving information to others for the purpose of control. He then develops a "ritual" view of communication that links the term to sharing, participation, and association. The emphasis of the ritual view is on the representation of shared beliefs and the construction of a meaningful cultural world. For Carey the organization would not only exist *by* communication, but *in* communication. Similar ideas are expressed by Pearce (1989), who points out that communication has been thought of as an instrument whereby people accomplish certain purposes, such as instructing, persuading, or achieving power. In this case communication is a "vehicle" of thought, a tool used to get something done. He presents a contrasting view that sees communication as the process by which thought is constituted. Reality itself is located within the language. This assertion would suggest that an organization not only exists *by* communication but *in* communication. Both of these contrasting ideas are important to an understanding of organizational communication and power.

Communication as a Mechanism of Power

Communication can be considered as a tool for implementing the traditional notions of power. For example, let us return to some of the bases of power cited earlier. *Reward power* and *coercive power* produce effects only insofar as recipients perceive that there are indeed rewards and punishments that can be carried out by another. Success in using such power is communication dependent. A threat is not effective if it is not perceived as such. *Legitimate power* usually comes from a "position" as a perceived "right" that one person's role allows the prescription of behavior for others. The effectiveness of legitimate power depends very much on how individuals communicate their positions and rights. For example, the status of the company president may be significantly affected by how presidential he or she appears to others. Much the same can be said for *referent power*. People identify with and follow another primarily through what has been communicated. The impact of communication on *expert power* is well documented. In many cases expertness is determined by how well people communicate that expertness, as both politicians and salespersons would attest. Communication is the mechanism by which influence (power) is executed. In the organizational context, communication is used to establish norms, goals, and organized behavior. It can be looked upon as a vehicle of power. A person has power, exerts it through communication, and thereby creates organized action.

Communication as Power

An individual's perception and interpretation of the environment is communication dependent. In the "objective" sense what individuals know of the "real" world comes to them through a filter of social reality. This filter consists of a shared symbolic world of beliefs, experiences, and meanings generated and maintained through communication. Therefore anyone who can withhold, provide, or alter information has potential power. A more "subjective" view suggests that communication does more than reflect the world; it is the world! To have control of communication is to decide what the world is and how people should behave. Those who can decide what something means have power. Bosmajian (1983) develops this theme in his exploration of language. People have power when they can define themselves in their terms and others accept and support that definition. One can identify groups without power by examining how they are defined and where this places them in the social order.

The options that individuals have for belief and action depend heavily on shared and validated communication. The organization is held together by a symbol system whose very texture is symbol born and symbol sustained. Just as fish sustain themselves by swimming in water, humans swim in a sea of symbols. They are not always aware of their heavy reliance on those symbols and the control exerted by them. Berger and Luckmann (1966) assert that the social structure moves from *here is what we do*, to *this is the way it is*. In our view organizations are constructed through communication, and those who can decide the labels and sustain those labels can exert power because the labels themselves direct action. A world is constructed that is shared and confirmed by others. People "construct" in contexts composed of rules, players, objects, others, and situations. All of us "construct" from the information that is in communication.

Put simply, communication is power because of its capacity to determine outcomes—knowledge, beliefs, and actions. People act on the basis of available information and the alternatives and choices such information provides. Organizations may have both explicit and implicit prohibitions against certain ideas. Individuals may be unable to see alternative views, and the capacity to generate alternative views may be severely restricted. Power is exercised through the alternatives presented and the way in which they are presented. For example, an organization may permit its participants to take part in decision making but also state the criteria that any decision must meet. Tompkins and Cheney (1985) explore the unobtrusive use of power by pointing out that control can be exerted when individuals buy into unstated premises of policy or belief systems. Such premises operate at a low level of awareness and are seldom challenged.

The subtlety and impact of communication as power can best be seen by examining the works of Foucault (1972, 1977, 1980), who maintains that knowledge is made up of a shared body of discourse and given discursive practices. Because the discourse has followed particular rules and has passed certain expectations, it is understood to be true. For example, if a CEO of an organization makes a pronouncement, it is attended to not only because it comes from the CEO, but because it is seen as grounded in special knowledge that a CEO has. The discourse itself provides a framework with which to view the world, and the power is anchored in the discourse. Knowledge is generated by discursive practice and this knowledge specifies the form the discourse assumes. Certain rules and procedures govern a discursive formation. These rules may be carried out on an unconscious level so that individuals may not be able to specify the rules of discourse that determine the possibilities for the content and form of communication.

What type of rules that regulate behavior exist in organizations? Foucault (1980) suggests that rules decide *what* can be talked about. Certain topics of conversation or suggestions may not be recognized as legitimate objects of discourse. Certain groups may be recognized as having the authority to name and define. Rules decide who is allowed to speak and write with authority and what kinds of discourse are appropriate. Rules also specify what behaviors and places are used when performing the discourse. They also indicate the form that various concepts and theories must take to be accepted as knowledge. In organizations those who submit reports soon learn what constitutes a "good argument." Rules may allow only certain individuals to be a participant in the formulation of concepts and theories. The organizational roles that individuals assume in speaking and writing are created and constrained by the rules of the discursive formation. Power is anchored in organizational discourse and its practice. Power and knowledge (discursive formation) are bound together. Each organization has a type of discourse that it accepts and "makes function as true." To Foucault (1980) power is a set of relations established and implemented through discourse. Power is omnipresent and produced in all relationships; the form of power depends on the type of relationship.

Power relationships exist at the individual/individual; individual/group; group/group; and individual/organization levels in the organizational setting. Of course, one cannot exclude the organization/organization and organization/environment levels of analysis. Although the discourse may contain common components across these levels, each relationship also contains its special discourse. For example, speaking with an "organizational voice" is quite different from speaking as an independent individual. When managers speak with subordinates they may use the "language" of the organization and may even drop the names of their superiors. Power is being exercised through the discourse itself.

Some Implications

We have argued that communication is a mechanism of power, and that communication itself is power. Individuals may use communication to exert power and achieve certain ends, but there is also power in the linguistic structure that people act out of in which language becomes the very fabric of organizational life. Language initiates, maintains, and transforms the organization. Individuals carve up experience in certain ways so as to make sense by labeling what they have done. The resultant structure takes on a life of its own that constrains the behavior of the original creators. Berger and Luckmann (1966) stress that there is a tendency to forget that social reality is indeed a social construction rather than some preexisting object to which people must adhere.

A number of theorists have explored the relationship between power (human agency) and structure (Giddens, 1976,1979,1984; Lukes, 1974). The issue revolves around just how "free" human behavior is versus how much human behavior is "determined" by the very structure in which humans live. Some of the research approaches listed in Figure 1.1 (i.e., phenomenology, ethnomethodology) stress human agency whereas others (open systems theory, behaviorism) emphasize the structural constraints on social action. Our main concern is not with resolving the issue of the relationship between human agency and structure. We wish to explore what that relationship means to organizational communication. Again, the focus on human agency emphasizes sense-making that creates organizational reality, whereas structure (determinism) looks at the reproduction of reality through structural forms, which themselves shape human agency. By engaging in organizational practices, individuals are reproducing a structure that in turn sets up the conditions which constrain what is done in the future. Power is exercised when individuals are in a position to draw upon rules and resources to produce and reproduce structure. Giddens (1981) asserts that all interaction involves the use of power in that it is concerned with the production and reproduction of structure.

Power within organizations can be viewed as the capacity of individuals to make a difference in the production and reproduction of structure (rules, policies, practices, and values). This may take the form of getting others to adhere to structure, resist structure, or engage in structural change. An inherent part of structure is language and its discursive practices that include speech, writing, and argumentation. Those who have access to organizational discursive practices, who know the approved language, and who are recognized by virtue of position or special resource have "voice" in the organization. They have the capacity to be heard and influence outcomes.

We suggested at the outset that organization is about control, which means inherent power relations. To sustain themselves, organizations must be able to achieve a certain level of adherence from their members. But a sustaining, healthy organization is about more than control. It requires innovation, adaptation, and the maximum contribution from its members. Organizations must also be able to obtain "resistance" from its members. The issue involves how an organization maintains stability and at the same time ensures individual creativity that allows for change and adaptation. Organizations must be able to "see" alternatives. Thus far we have emphasized organizational needs. While it is true that a healthy organization provides returns (economic rewards, skill development) for its members, there are individual needs that relate to privacy and a sense of control over self and situations. For example, supervisors may listen in on employees' phone calls to monitor behavior. Individuals may be unaware of the organization's attempt to influence them and in what ways. Individuals may not have access to information that may affect their future. Control and surveillance techniques may destroy the quality of work life.

It is our contention that organizations that are able to generate the strongest commitment and contributions from their members are those whose members feel that they can make a difference in the pursuit of worthwhile goals. The major question is: What kind of power and what kind of communication facilitates this outcome? Boulding's (1989) notion of integrative power focuses on binding people together and developing legitimacy. It is power that generates loyalty. The values of the organization are perceived as legitimate. This in turn inspires individuals to give their best effort.

Power sharing is inherent to democracy. There is a fundamental belief that individuals have the right to influence policies and procedures that impact on their lives. The notion of democracy raises a number of issues. Who is in the best position to decide what is best for the collective? Who defines and labels the world? Are all people capable of knowing what is best for them? Are there some people who just cannot be trusted to make responsible decisions? Democracy can be torturous in terms of the time spent in "searching behaviors" and disappointing when results seem less than perfect. Anyone who has watched a political convention can also attest to some of the general silliness that accompanies the democratic process. What is sometimes called the democratic process is clearly undercut by dominant self-interest groups. Thus, there is both reverence and suspicion of the democratic process. With all of its potential faults, most of us probably prefer to work in organizations that try to practice some form of democratic procedure. It is important to note that when we use the terms "power sharing" and "empowerment" we are aiming at a democratic ideal. There has been increasing recognition of the value of people and the importance of the quality of worklife in organizations. This does not mean that all organizations give more than lip service to such concepts. Managers may recognize that people are the most important asset of an organization but still choose to coerce and manipulate that resource. In economic downturns, integrative power may give way to threat and economic blackmail. We cannot deny that there is much distrust in the workplace, and not without good reason in a number of cases. Nevertheless, it is our contention that forward-looking organizations will consider the nature and distribution of power.

COMMUNICATION AND THE EMPOWERMENT PROCESS

Organizational theorists and practitioners have always had a primary interest in determining the conditions under which individuals give maximum effort. Various management practices have been aimed at getting organizational participants to use their creative talents to better the collective. Such approaches have included "participatory management," "human relations," "human resources," "quality circles," and "total quality management." One of the underlying notions is that individuals perform better when their value is recognized and when they have input into the decision-making process. Contemporary views have not thrown out the premise of human worth and the desire to develop self, but have brought the issue of power into focus.

Nature of Empowerment

The concept of empowerment has several dimensions. Conger and Kanungo (1988) point out that empowerment can be considered in a relational or motivational sense. The relational aspects emphasize sharing power between managers and subordinates. There is an attempt to de-emphasize hierarchy and stress shared problem solving. One such example is that of the Gortex Company where attempts are made to distribute power more evenly (Pacanowsky, 1988).

When the referent to empowerment is motivation, it is said that "power...refers to an intrinsic need for self-determination or a belief in personal self-efficacy...; any managerial strategy or technique that strengthens this self-determination need or self-efficacy belief of employees will make them feel more powerful" (Conger and Kanungo, 1988, p. 473). To empower, then, is to believe in self-determination for everyone, which includes the need and right for others to feel a sense of effectiveness and accomplishment. Bandura (1977) suggests that how strongly people feel about their own effectiveness determines whether they will even cope with certain situations. Efficacy expectations help decide how much effort people will put forth and how long they will persist in adverse conditions. The manager who helps people experience a sense of personal mastery in their actions is empowering others. If individuals are given responsibility and expected to participate in decisions concerning work practices, they have the opportunity to test their personal effectiveness. Mistakes may be made, but as they are overcome, feelings of self-efficacy will be strengthened. Of course, success generates feelings of self-worth which are empowering.

Thus far we have emphasized the linkage between "performance" and empowerment. Participating in decision making and mastering tasks both constitute performance. There is another dimension to empowerment that is no less important. In fact, it may be the most critical because it is more subtle and constitutes the "taken for granted power" that occurs at such a low level of awareness that it is seldom seen or questioned. We are talking about the communication practices themselves. Some of these practices include language usage, the act of communication, communication content, and implicit and explicit roles. It is obvious that those who control the communication mechanisms (computers and copy machines) and forms (meetings and memos) usually have "voices" that are grounded in power positions. Each organization has its preferred and endorsed language that makes up its reality. Who can initiate communication is an indicator of power. What can and cannot be talked about and what issues are deemed significant are all part of the power structure. The hierarchical and specialized task roles of an organization indicate who has voice and when they can speak.

Much of the emphasis in the "empowerment literature" is placed on individual actions and how the individual feels about power or the lack of it. Empowerment also involves structures that constrain people. Just as society at large has dominant values, rites of passage, and ways of behaving, the organization has its structure that validates acceptable behavior. All of us are born into ways of seeing and believing through the most elaborate structure of all—our language. To have access to the "right language" is to have power. To be defined in acceptable ways by the language of the collectivity is to have power.

Communication practices are certainly relevant to relational and motivational views of empowerment. Perhaps even more significant, they represent structures that create and maintain power.

Communication Practices and Empowerment

Some have stressed (Foucault, 1980) that what is perceived as knowledge is constituted by a shared body of discourse and given discursive practices. To be empowered in an organization is to know the acceptable arguments and the acceptable ways of using them. Communication practices themselves may exclude some from "organizational knowledge" or may also disempower them. Bosmajian (1983) stresses that language that appears to protect may indeed exclude. For example, terms such as "lady" may place women on a pedestal, but it is also a way of controlling them by implying that certain groups need protection and men are just the ones to do it! The terms "girl" and "baby" applied to women are cast in the same mold. As noted earlier, rules may decide what can and cannot be talked about, but there are also rules that decide communication practices other than content. There is also the matter of rituals that accompany the discourse. These may include dress, setting, timing, and method of discourse.

For Habermas (1972) the "ideal speech situation" exists when individuals are unconstrained in their ability to take part in the discourse that may affect their lives. Habermas elaborates a model of the conditions that allow individuals to see alternatives and make rational choices. There is an emphasis on communication competence, shared community of language, and dialogue. Such a community is built on trust because power tends to distort communication.

Weick's (1977) concept of "punctuation" is also relevant to communication practices and empowerment. To "punctuate" is to chop up the stream of experience in certain ways and then assign labels to make sense. The labels then become part of the discourse and a particular way of thinking. Because the assigning of labels is rather arbitrary in that different labels can be reasonable, there is power in who can define things and which definitions stick (see Hall's (1980) notion of "definition of the situation"). These definitions become part of the discourse so that each time the discourse is used, the definitions become more "real." Again, individuals are empowered when they recognize that much of their world is created and they have opportunities to influence that creation. In that sense the terms "education" and "consciousness raising" are descriptive of the empowerment process.

Communication Conditions and Empowerment

A significant part of empowerment is the identification of those conditions that generate feelings of powerlessness. People in organizations feel powerless when they do not have access to information affecting their work and well-being. A common finding of organizational studies is that people usually express a need for more information. This indicates the importance of information as a source of power. My department head makes the budget available to faculty. I do not pore over the budget, but the notion that I am allowed access to this information means that I have opportunity to speak about it and thereby potentially influence outcomes.

The bureaucratic structure poses conditions that can lead to feelings of powerlessness and distorted communication. Macher (1988) cites political maneuvering, resistance to change, and lack of support as common conditions of the bureaucracy. Block (1987) asserts that the bureaucratic context and management styles of the bureaucracy actually encourage powerlessness. He insists that the essence of the "mind-set" in such an organization is not to take responsibility for what is happening so that the bureaucracy characterizes someone else, not ourselves.

As a former worker in several government agencies in Washington, D.C., one of the authors of this book can identify with those feelings. Much of his work involved the routing of messages. When he had doubts, he simply sent the message through the hierarchy of offices. He felt that someone would know what to do with the report, memo, etc. If the paper came back, he would re-route it again, because after all, it wasn't his responsibility! He was depending on others to know, rather than using individual initiative to find out.

The concept of empowerment does not suggest a system where everyone does what comes to mind. Enabling others to use their abilities is empowerment. The communication climate must be safe, open, and coherent. Role ambiguity, excessive role expectations, and conflict are contextual factors that also create powerlessness (Conger and Kanungo, 1988; Byham, 1989). The condition that allows people to know what their role is and the importance of the role to the overall enterprise—and that allows for mutual influence of outcomes—is an empowering environment. Considerable emphasis has been placed on removing the barriers to empowerment that are created by the hierarchical structure of organizations. Organizational features and contextual conditions are important considerations in the empowerment process, but they are only part of the empowerment concept.

COMMUNICATION AND EXERCISING POWER

Power should not be thought of in only a prohibitive, negative sense or as something that inherently corrupts people who hold it. The facilitative nature of power has long been recognized (Parsons, 1967). Power is positive in that it can achieve goals and get things done. Foucault (1977, 1980), who does not separate power and knowledge, asserts that the exercise of power creates new knowledge and bodies of information. Power is both a creative force and a restrictive one. In *Men and Women of the Corporation*, Kanter (1977) considers power not as hierarchical domination but as the ability to get things done. When power is viewed as an enabling process that leads to the ability to accomplish, the significance of the empowerment concept is quite clear.

We are not taking a Pollyanna position that suggests that power sharing is an easy process that is always equitable, productive, and risk free. Nor are we suggesting that organizations are morally obligated to use a particular type of power or to empower their members. In terms of power, many organizations still operate structurally, behaviorly, and communicatively in ways that suggest domination and distortion as opposed to equity and openness. When organizations want their members to do their bidding, there is talk about loyalty, debt to the collectivity, the significance of the work being done, and the setting aside of selfish motives. However, when members of an organization want more than a place to work and are desirous of self-development, the organization may point out that they cannot be social centers or places of welfare that are permanently obligated to their members. Contradictions of expectations are part of the reality of the workplace.

At the interpersonal level, other seemingly contradictory behaviors mitigate against the empowerment principle. American culture has placed emphasis on individual achievement and achieving a power position. There can be a concern that sharing power with others detracts from one's own power. In addition, sharing power with others usually means that one has the confidence to do so, but it is also necessary to achieve power so that one has confidence.

Organizations that wish to survive, grow, and compete at a high level will consider "integrative power" and "empowerment" as integral parts of managerial practice. To believe in such concepts there must also be a fundamental belief that the organization that exercises power based on legitimacy will garner maximum support and creative effort from its members. What is the ultimate state of legitimacy? When does the participant believe that the collective has the right to demand obedience? When the interests and needs of both are seen as similar and when they serve both. *When the communication binds all together by a language that not only affirms this, but celebrates it*, then authentic empowerment occurs.

Both past and contemporary theorists have advocated moving away from an authoritarian and controlling environment to one that emphasizes learning and self-efficacy. Senge (1990) maintains that organizations that will be able to excel and compete in the future will be those that can tap into people's commitment and capacity to learn. Weick (1977) has cautioned that there may be too much organization rather than too little, and Block (1987) insists that traditional controlling techniques have created dysfunctional dependency. Block asks that management give up the dogma of planning, organizing, and controlling and concentrate on enabling conditions. What type of communication promotes the enabling process?

Communication in an organization should reflect the judicious use of power. Boulding (1989) contends that maintaining power may depend on knowing when to use it. Power that is exercised wisely may not be exercised at all. For example, if a manager delegates authority to a subordinate to carry out a task, communication should support the notion of some independent judgment by the subordinate. The manager who hovers over the subordinate or sends a constant barrage of memos that detail exactly what should be done is not delegating and is certainly not empowering the subordinate. This form of over-management is demoralizing and antithetical to the enabling process. It hardly promotes the concept of self-efficacy.

Communication to control can lead to gamesmanship and political maneuvering that closes out voices that may provide valuable input for decision making. Manipulation and managing information for one's own advantage may offer only short-term advantage, if that. Block (1987) states that this type of behavior is due to a "bureaucratic cycle" that leads to myopic self-interests, manipulative tactics, and, ultimately, to a dependency in which people do not claim responsibility. Communication that defines what the alternatives are in a given decision-making setting exercises power. Individuals who are involved in such an arrangement may feel that there is democracy at work. However, the power lies with those who can define the alternatives using their language or who can establish the criteria by which a judgment will be made. Schattschneider (1960) asserts that the definition of the alternatives is the supreme instrument of power. It seems to us that an integral part of that process is the labeling that is placed on the alternatives and how those alternatives are communicated to others. The use of communication then is the exercise of power. What may be a very efficient process is also one that excludes multiple voices. The stated or unstated "rules" may allow only certain individuals to be involved in the development and application of criteria of judgment. It is their communication that counts.

Communication that places individuals in a lesser position is an exercise in power. It connotes a relationship that may not always be conscious to the person who is unknowingly asserting dominance. Many of the gender issues (sexist language, sexual language) are power issues. It is not uncommon for those in power positions to be surprised by the feelings and reactions of the less powerful to communication that dominates or excludes them. What may be seen as innocent by some is viewed as oppressive by others. For example, as of this writing there is a controversy in some colleges over the term "freshman." The argument is that the word is gender exclusive and simply doesn't include everyone. The suggestion is that the term "first-year" student is more appropriate. Those who have opposed the change say that the change is unnecessary and a little ludicrous because "freshman" is a term that lost its gender some time ago. In terms of communication, what is important is the "message created." Language is not simply a matter of political correctness. If the support of everyone is important, it is dysfunctional to alienate those who feel a lack of power. In addition, the question of equity transcends the idea of political correctness.

What type of communication enables and has the potential to achieve the best efforts from all organizational members? How does one get at power sharing in a communicative sense? Senge (1990) makes the point that most people in an organization have been taught to establish territory through advocacy and then hold that ground. This exercise in power has the effect of restricting alternative views and stifling inquiry for ourselves and others. Advocacy by itself is likely to promote more advocacy. If the organization is to learn and adapt to change, its managers must acquire reflection and inquiry skills as well as advocacy skills. This means that the skills of inquiry must be embedded in the communication itself. Views are stated to reveal the underlying thinking so that everyone is invited to inquire into that thinking. Inquiry and advocacy are combined into expanded alternatives. Encouraging multiple voices may lead to an openness to data that may change the advocate's mind as well as others. This is a step in establishing "open critique." If the matter of giving voice to organizational members is to be more than a technique, it must rest on core values of the organization. Diversity must be seen as an opportunity rather than a problem. Managers, who think in terms of expanding the power of the organization by providing the conditions that will empower all, will feel most comfortable with "open" communication. The core value of open communication rests on the belief that all participants have something to offer. It is a pragmatic matter that suggests that the best way to move others to action is to enable them to move themselves.

In those organizations that wish to make the best use of human resources, there will always be a tension between obedience and resistance. There will be a certain level of order, but there must also be a resistance that stimulates innovation and change. This resistance manifests itself in communication that ensures open critique and self-examination. Whether there is a hierarchical structure or some other arrangement, the conditions for mutual influence must exist if the concept of empowerment is to have any substantial meaning. A significant part of these conditions includes communication that clearly indicates that the organizational member and their work are taken seriously, that there is a shared responsibility in mistakes as well as achievements, and that the development of all individuals is a part of organizational life.

SUMMARY

Power is the capacity to influence, regulate, or control and is an inherent part of the organizational process. Power not only resides in people and resources but also in the social structure itself. Power is a relational concept that is multidimensional and involves both inaction and action. Organizational structure enables and constrains the use of power. This structure is legitimized through communication behavior. Organizational structure is created, maintained, and transformed through the communication process. Communication serves not only as a mechanism of power but also *is* power in that rules, practices, and ways of seeing are embedded in the discourse itself. All interaction involves the use of power because it deals with the production and reproduction of structure. The discursive practices of talk, writing, and argumentation are an inherent part of structure. Organizations that look to innovation, change, and maximum contribution from their members will engage in communication that empowers all participants. Power is a positive force when it is shared, developed in others, and used judiciously. This is best achieved by communication that permits multiple voices, promotes self-efficacy, stimulates inquiry as well as advocacy, and ensures conditions for mutual influence.

A SUBJECTIVIST'S REMINDER

We have discussed "subjective" views in our examination of power. However, there is a tendency to forget that "power" is a process that relies heavily on the relationships created and sustained by all participants. Deetz (1992) explores the social processes by which experience, knowledge, and identity are formed and sustained as political formations. He contends that control and influence are dispersed into norms and standard practices. In this way all participants (superordinates and subordinates) in an organization are subject to a "discipline." This discipline is produced together in the day-to-day routines. It may even be built into the organization by training programs or various technologies.

Examination of everyday interaction may reveal power relations that are otherwise invisible. Power relations not made explicit are those that are the most potent. This is true in the sense that they are viewed as "that is the way it is" if they are seen at all. They do not require costly monitoring or enforcement procedures. When power is hidden in discourse that sustains organizational practice, it receives very little resistance. If organizations wish to achieve "open critique," the discourse itself must receive scrutiny. Such investigation reveals anonymous rules and structural principles that constitute power.

It must be stressed that power relations may involve more than one discourse. Scott (1990) asserts that every subordinate group creates a "hidden transcript" that represents a critique of power of the dominant. He also points out that the powerful develop a hidden transcript that represents practices that are not openly discussed. This struggle is referred to as the *infrapolitics* that provide the underpinnings of visible political action.

REFERENCES

BACHRACH, P., and M.S. BARATZ, "Two Faces of Power," *American Political Science Review*, 56 (1962), 947–952.

BANDURA, A., "Self-efficacy: Toward a Unifying Theory of Behavioral Change," *Psychological Review*, 84 (1977), 191–215.

BERGER, P.L., and T. LUCKMANN, *The Social Construction of Reality*. Garden City, N.Y.: Doubleday, 1966.

BLOCK, P., *The Empowered Manager: Positive Political Skills at Work*. San Francisco: Jossey-Bass, 1987.

BOSMAJIAN, H.A., *The Language of Oppression*. New York: University Press of America, 1983.

BOULDING, K., *Three Faces of Power*. Newbury Park, Calif.: Sage Publications, Inc., 1989.

BYHAM, W.C., *Zapp! The Lightning of Empowerment*. New York: Harmony Books, 1989.

CAREY, J.W., "A Cultural Approach to Communication," *Communication*, 2 (1975), 1–21.

CLEGG, STEWART R., *Frameworks of Power*. Newbury Park, Calif.: Sage Publications, Inc., 1989.

CONGER, J.A., and R.N. KANUNGO, "The Empowerment Process: Integrating Theory and Practice," *Academy of Management Review*, 12 (1988), 471–482.

DAHL, R.A., "The Concept of Power," *Behavioral Science*, 2 (1957), 201–205.

DEETZ, STANLEY A., *Democracy in an Age of Corporate Colonization*. Albany: State University of New York Press, 1992.

FOUCAULT, M., *The Archaeology of Knowledge*. London: Tavistock, 1972.

FOUCAULT, M., *Discipline and Punish: The Birth of the Prison*. Harmondsworthy: Penguin, 1977.

FOUCAULT, M., *Power/Knowledge: Selected Interviews and Other Writings 1972–1977*, C. Gordon, ed. Brighton: Harvester Press, 1980.

FRENCH, J. JR., and B. RAVEN, "The Bases of Social Power," in *Studies in Social Power*, D. Cartwright, ed. Ann Arbor: Institute for Social Research, University of Michigan, 1959.

GAVENTA, J.P., *Power and Powerlessness: Quiescence and Rebellion in an Appalachian Valley*. Urbana: University of Illinois Press, 1980.

GIDDENS, A., *New Rules of Sociological Method*. London: Hutchinson, 1976.

GIDDENS, A., *Central Problems in Social Theory*. London: Macmillan, 1979.

GIDDENS, A., *A Contemporary Critique of Historical Materialism*. London: Macmillan, 1981.

GIDDENS, A., *The Constitution of Society*. Cambridge: Polity Press, 1984.

HABERMAS, J., *Knowledge and Human Interests*, trans., J. Shapiro. Boston: Beacon Press, 1972.

HALL, P.M., "Structuring Symbolic Interaction: Communication and Power," in *Communication Yearbook* 4, Dan Nimmo, ed. New Brunswick, N.J.: Transaction Books, 1980.

KANTER, R.M., *Men and Women of the Corporation*. New York: Basic Books, 1977.

LUKES, S., *Power: A Radical View*. London: Macmillian, 1974.

LUKES, S., *Essays in Social Theory*. London: Macmillian, 1977.

LUKES, S., ed., *Power*. Oxford: Blackwell, 1986.

MACHER, K., "Empowerment and the Bureaucracy," *Training and Development Journal*, 42 (1988), 41–45.

MINTZBERG, H., *Power in and Around Organizations*. Englewood Cliffs, N.J.: Prentice-Hall, 1983.

PACANOWSKY, M., "Communication in the Empowering Organization," in *Communication Yearbook* 2, J. Anderson, ed. Newbury Park, Calif.: Sage Publications, Inc., 1988.

PARSONS, T., *Sociological Theory and Modern Society*. New York: Free Press, 1967.

PEARCE, W.B., *Communication and the Human Condition*. Carbondale: Southern Illinois University Press, 1989.

RIKER, WILLIAM H., "Some Ambiguities in the Notion of Power," *American Political Science Review*, 58 (1964), 341–349.

RUSSELL, B., "The Forms of Power," in *Power*, S. Lukes, ed. Oxford: Blackwell, 1986.

SCHATTSCHNEIDER, E.E., *The Semi-Sovereign People: A Realist's View of Democracy in America*. New York: Holt, Rinehart and Winston, 1960.

SCOTT, JAMES C., *Domination and the Arts of Resistance*. New Haven: Yale University Press, 1990.

SENGE, P.M., *The Fifth Discipline*. New York: Doubleday, 1990.

TOMPKINS, P.K., and G. CHENEY, "Communication and Unobtrusive Control in Contemporary Organizations," in *Organizational Communication: Traditional Themes and New Directions*, R.D. McPhee and P.K. Tompkins, eds. Beverly Hills, Calif.: Sage Publications, Inc., 1985.

WEICK, K., "Re-punctuating the Problem," in *New Perspectives on Organizational Effectiveness*, P. Goodman and J. Pennings, eds. San Francisco: Jossey-Bass, 1977.

11

Communication, Leadership, and Operating Styles

Leadership and motivation are some of the most widely discussed issues in most organizations. We analyzed the concept of motivation in an earlier chapter and concluded that motivation has to do with why people do what they do. Low productivity, absenteeism, low morale, dissatisfaction, and turnover are symptoms of lack of motivation. When organization members fail to work in ways that achieve desired results, they are considered to lack motivation.

THE MEANING AND GOALS OF LEADERSHIP

The goal of leadership, on the other hand, is to help others to regain, maintain, and enhance their motivation. That is, a leader is one who helps others to achieve desired outcomes or results. Leaders behave in ways that facilitate productivity, high morale, energetic responses, quality workmanship, commitment, efficiency, few defects, satisfaction, attendance, and continuation in the organization.

Leadership is expressed by means of a person's *operating style*—or consistent way of working with others. It is through what a person says (language) and what a person does (actions) that others are helped to achieve desired outcomes. The way a person talks to others and the way a person behaves in the presence of others constitute an operating style.

The concept of style implies that we are dealing with combinations of language and actions that appear to represent a fairly consistent pattern. What might be some patterns of language and actions that one might use to help others achieve a desired outcome? Without considering any particular point of view, some different approaches might involve (1) controlling or directing others, (2) challenging or provoking others, (3) explaining to or instructing others, (4) encouraging or supporting others, (5) entreating or persuading others, (6) involving or empowering others, and (7) rewarding or reinforcing others.

Each one of these approaches to helping others achieve desired outcomes is implemented through specific ways of talking and acting toward others. Controlling, for example, is achieved through language and actions that restrict or limit what another person can do. A controlling style implies a tone of voice, a way of reacting, the use of particular words and phrases, and certain gestures and actions that are complementary, interrelated, and patterned. To recognize a controlling style, all of the elements of style—tone of voice, actions, words, and phrases—must combine into a consistent and coherent perception that we call controlling.

Initial Summary

In this chapter we shall look at some theoretical models used to identify different leadership styles. We shall also examine various leadership styles and their associated communicative behaviors. Finally, we shall explore some general principles that shed light on what many feel may be the most effective styles of leadership for this day and age.

ASSUMPTIONS ABOUT PEOPLE THAT UNDERLIE STYLES OF LEADERSHIP

A person's leadership style is grounded in some assumptions about people and what motivates them. McGregor (1967) identified two bipolar sets of assumptions or beliefs that leaders have a tendency to hold about others. He called them *Theory X* and *Theory Y*. Most leaders probably do not embrace either of McGregor's theories in any pure sense, but the characterizations help us to visualize the mental set of an ideal type so that we can get a clearer image of the thinking of a person who leans strongly in one direction or another.

Theory X

Theory X assumptions appear to be derived from a view of people as machines who require a great deal of external control. Theory X assumptions may be summarized as follows:

1. Most people think work is distasteful and try to avoid it.
2. Most people prefer to be directed and must often be forced to do their work.
3. Most people are not ambitious, do not want to go ahead, and do not want responsibility.
4. Most people are motivated primarily by their desire for basic necessities and security-safety needs.
5. Most people must be closely controlled and are incapable of solving problems in the organization.

It is probably fair to say that leaders who hold Theory X assumptions about people think of employees as tools of production, motivated by fear of punishment or by a desire for money and security. Managers who view workers in this way probably tend to watch them closely, make and enforce strict rules, and use the threat of punishment as a means of motivating them.

Theory Y

Theory Y assumptions tend to be derived from a view of people as biological organisms who grow, develop, and exercise control over themselves. Theory Y assumptions may be summarized as follows:

1. Most people think that work is as natural as play. If work is unpleasant, it is probably because of the way it is done in the organization.
2. Most people feel that self-control is indispensable in getting work done properly.
3. Most people are motivated primarily by their desire for social acceptance, recognition, and a sense of achievement, as well as their need for money to provide basic necessities and security.
4. Most people will accept and even seek responsibility if given proper supervision, management, and leadership.
5. Most people have the ability to solve problems creatively in the organization.

Leaders who base their styles on Theory Y see others as having a variety of needs. They believe their job is to organize and manage work so that both the organization and the employees can satisfy their needs. Theory Y managers assume that personal and organizational goals may be compatible. There is some evidence, however, to suggest that both cannot be achieved within the organizational context. Some personal and some organizational goals may be quite contradictory. Nevertheless, the manager who accepts Theory Y assumptions works with employees to set goals for the organization, encourages them to share in the decision-making process, and seeks to set high standards.

MODELS OF LEADERSHIP STYLES

The most common systems used in describing consistencies in ways of working with others are derived from the work of the Ohio State Leadership Studies and the research of Stoghill and Coons (1957).

Ohio State Leadership Studies

Bass (1960) explains that the factor "initiating structure" accounted for a third of the total variation in leadership studies, and "consideration" and "initiating structure" accounted for 83 percent of the variance (p. 102), thus establishing these two variables as the most critical in leadership styles.

A leader who earns a high score on consideration emphasizes promise, reward, and support as motivational techniques and acts in a warm and supportive manner, showing concern and respect for subordinates. A leader who scores low exhibits threatening, deflating, inconsiderate behavior, and defines and structures his or her own role and those of subordinates toward goal attainment.

From among a multitude of models, theories, and analyses, we have chosen to examine the following six popular systems for classifying and describing leadership styles:

1. Leadership Grid Theory (Blake & Mouton)
2. 3-D Theory (Reddin)
3. Situational Leadership Theory (Hersey & Blanchard)

4. Four-Systems Theory (Likert)
5. Continuum Theory (Tannenbaum & Schmidt)
6. Contingency Theory (Fiedler)

Each of these ways of looking at leadership and managerial styles is associated with the researcher, writer, or theorist who popularized the point of view.

Leadership Grid

One of the most widely discussed theories of leadership styles is that advanced by Blake and Mouton (1964), originally called the *managerial grid* but now called the leadership grid (1991). The grid is derived from the basic concerns of managers: concern for production or that which the organization is designed to accomplish, and concern for the individuals and elements of the organization that affect people. The grid portrays the ways in which a leader's concern for production and people intertwine to produce styles of managing and leading. Figure 11.1 diagrams how these concerns are related to one another. The five extreme styles suggested by the Grid model are presented in summary form.

1,1 Impoverished style. This style is characterized by very low concern for both production and people. The impoverished leader tends to accept the decisions of others; to go along with opinions, attitudes, and ideas of others; and to avoid taking sides. When conflict arises the impoverished leader remains neutral and stays out of it. By remaining neutral the impoverished leader rarely gets stirred up. The impoverished leader just puts out enough effort to get by.

5,5 Middle-of-the-road style. This style is characterized by moderate concern for both production and people. The middle-road leader searches for workable, although usually not perfect, solutions to problems. When ideas, opinions, and attitudes different from those of the middle-road leader develop, the middle-road leader initiates a compromise position. When conflict arises the middle-road leader tries to be fair but firm and to evolve an equitable solution. Under pressure the middle-road leader may be unsure about which way to turn to avoid tension. The middle-road leader seeks to maintain a good steady pace.

9,9 Team style. This style is characterized by high concern for both production and people. The team leader places high value on arriving at sound, creative decisions that result in understanding and agreement of organization members. The team leader listens for and seeks out ideas, opinions, and attitudes that are different from his or her own. The team leader has clear convictions about what needs to be done but responds to sound ideas from others by changing his or her own mind. When conflict arises the team leader tries to identify reasons for the differences and to resolve the underlying causes. When aroused, the team leader maintains self-control, although some impatience may be visible. The team leader has a sense of humor even under pressure and exerts vigorous effort and enlists others to join in. The team leader is able to show a need for mutual trust and respect among team members as well as respect for the job.

1,9 Country club style. This style is characterized by low concern for production but high concern for people. The country club leader places a high value on maintaining good relationships with others. The country club leader prefers to accept opinions, attitudes, and ideas of others rather than to push his or her own. The country club leader avoids creating conflict, but when it does appear, tries to soothe feelings and to keep people working together. The country club leader reacts to events in a consistently warm and friendly way so as to reduce tensions that disturbances create. Rather than lead, a country club leader extends help.

9,1 Authority-compliance style. This style is characterized by a high concern for accomplishing tasks but a low concern for people. The leader places a high value on making deci-

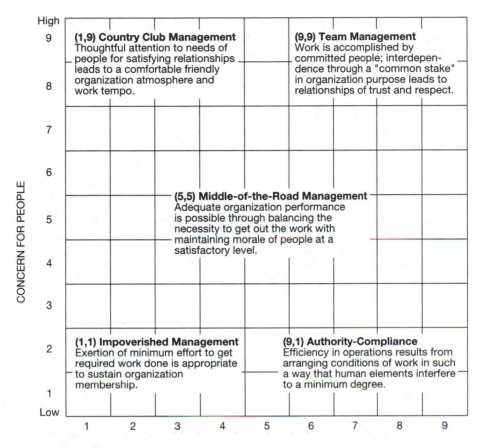

FIGURE 11.1 The Leadership Grid® Figure

Source: The Leadership Grid Figure for *Leadership Dilemmas—Grid Solutions*, by Robert R. Blake and Anne Adams McCanse. (Formerly the Managerial Grid figure by Robert R. Blake and Jane S. Mouton) Houston: Gulf Publishing Company, Page 29. Copyright 1991 by Scientific Methods, Inc. Reproduced by Permission of the owners.

sions that hold. The task leader is a person whose main concern is with efficiency of operations and getting the job done. The 9,1 style leader tends to stand up for his or her ideas, opinions, and attitudes even though they may sometimes result in stepping on the toes of others. When conflict arises the task leader tries to cut it off or to win his or her position by defending, resisting, or coming back with counterarguments. When things are not going just right, these kind of leaders drive themselves and others.

According to Blake and Mouton, the "9,9 team style" is the most desirable. A team style of leadership is based on an effective integration of both production and people concerns. In general, the 9,9 leadership style assumes that people produce best when they have the opportunity to do meaningful work. Behind the 9,9 style is a commitment to involve organization members in decision making so as to use their abilities to achieve the highest possible results.

3-D Theory

Reddin (1967) builds upon the task-person grid of Blake and Mouton by adding a third dimension, *effectiveness*. The three dimensions are defined as follows:

Task Orientation—the extent to which a manager directs subordinates' efforts toward attaining a goal.

Relationship Orientation—the extent to which a manager has personal job relationships with subordinates characterized by mutual trust, respect for their ideas, and consideration of their feelings.

Effectiveness—the extent to which a manager achieves the production requirements for his or her person.

The 3-D grid results in eight managerial or leadership styles. Figure 11.2 shows the three aspects of the model and the resulting styles. Four others are less effective, and four others are considered more effective. This implies that a low relationship orientation and a low production orientation, considered by Blake and Mouton (1,1 grid style) to be generally undesirable, may be effective when the person is viewed as being primarily conscientious about the following rules and procedures in order to get the job done. A brief description of each of the eight styles follows:

MORE EFFECTIVE

Executive
High task, high relationships; seen as a good motivator who sets high standards, who treats everyone somewhat differently, and who prefers to allow team management.

Benevolent Autocrat
High task, low relationships; seen as knowing what he or she wants and knowing how to get it without creating resentment.

Developer
Low task, high relationships; seen as having implicit trust in people and as being primarily concerned with developing harmonious relationships.

Bureaucrat
Low task, low relationships; seen as primarily interested in rules and procedures for their own sake and as wanting to maintain and control the situation by their use; often seen as conscientious.

LESS EFFECTIVE

Compromiser
High task, high relationships where only one or neither is appropriate; seen as a poor decision maker and one who allows pressure to influence him or her too much; seen as minimizing pressures and problems rather than maximizing long-term production.

Autocrat
High task, low relationships where such behavior is inappropriate; seen as having no confidence in others, as being interested only in the immediate job.

Missionary
Low task, high relationships where such behavior is inappropriate; seen as being primarily interested in individuals.

Deserter
Low task, low relationships where such behavior is inappropriate; seen as uninvolved and passive.

Reddin (1967) explains that the four *more effective* styles may be equally effective, depending on the situation in which they are used. On the other hand, some managerial jobs require all four styles to be used at one time or another, whereas other jobs tend to demand only one or two styles consistently.

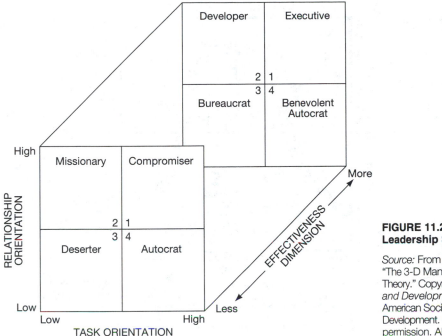

FIGURE 11.2 3-D Model of Leadership Styles

Source: From William J. Reddin, "The 3-D Management Style Theory." Copyright 1967, *Training and Development Journal,* American Society for Training and Development. Reprinted with permission. All rights reserved.

Situational Leadership

Hersey and Blanchard (1974, 1977) developed the concept of situational leadership from studies of leadership completed at Ohio State University (Stogdill & Coons, 1957). The studies showed, much as in Blake and Mouton's theory, two dimensions of leadership style: consideration and initiating structure, resulting in a grid similar to that of Blake and Mouton. In addition, Hersey and Blanchard identified a third variable—maturity—that functions in a way similar to Reddin's effectiveness dimension. Hence, Hersey and Blanchard's model of situational leadership has an appearance like Reddin's model. In fact, their interpretation of "effective" leadership is also quite similar: "The difference between the effective and ineffective styles is often not the actual behavior of leader, but the appropriateness of this behavior to the situation in which it is used" (Hersey & Blanchard,1974, p. 6). The factor that determines effectiveness is described by Hersey (1985) as the follower's readiness. *Readiness* is defined by a person's willingness and ability to take responsibility. In other words, if the followers of a leader have high willingness and ability to take responsibility, and are experienced with the task at hand—a particular leadership style will be more effective than if the followers are less ready.

As the level of readiness of one's followers increases, the leader reduces the amount of supportive or relationship behavior accordingly. Figure 11.3 shows the patterns of leadership styles as they follow a bell-shaped curve going through the four leadership quadrants. For purposes of making quick diagnostic judgments, four styles of situational leadership are identified:

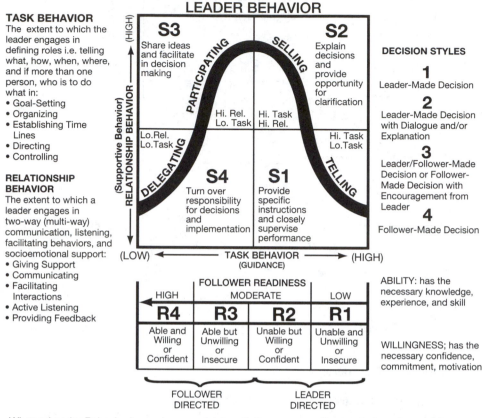

FIGURE 11.3 Expanded Situational Leadership Model

Source: Paul Hersey, *Situational Selling.* Escondido, Calif.: Center for Leadership Studies, 1985, p. 32.

Style 1—Telling. High task, low relationship. This style is characterized by one-way communication in which the leader defines the roles of followers and tells them what, how, when, and where to do various tasks.

Style 2—Selling. High task, high relationship. This style is characterized by some effort at two-way communication, although most of the direction is provided by the leader. The leader also provides socioemotional support to get the followers to accept some responsibility for the decisions to be made.

Style 3—Participating. High relationship, low task. This style is characterized by having the leader and followers share in decision making through authentic two-way communication. The leader engages in much facilitating behavior since the followers have the ability and knowledge to do the task.

Style 4—Delegating. Low relationship, low task. This style is characterized by the leader letting the followers take responsibility for their own decisions. The leader delegates decisions to the followers since they are high in readiness, being both willing and able to take responsibility for directing their own behavior.

In contrast to both Blake and Mouton's and Reddin's theories, Hersey and Blanchard seem to regard low-task, low-relationship orientations as highly desirable when the followers are high in readiness. They argue that with people of high task-relevant readiness, Style 4 has the highest probability of success.

Four-Systems Theory

One of the most frequently discussed theories of managerial and leadership styles is that of Likert (1967). He devised four managerial styles or systems based on an analysis of eight managerial variables: (1) leadership, (2) motivation, (3) communication, (4) interaction, (5) decision making, (6) goal setting, (7) control, and (8) performance. Likert refers to the styles as:

1. Exploitive-Authoritative
2. Benevolent-Authoritative
3. Consultative
4. Participative

We shall briefly characterize each of the four systems.

System 1—Exploitive-Authoritative. This style is based on the assumptions of McGregor's Theory X in which the manager-leader provides strong guidance and control on the premise that employees are motivated best by fear, threats, and punishments. Superior-subordinate interaction is minimal, with all decisions coming from the top and with downward communication consisting primarily of directives and orders.

System 2—Benevolent-Authoritative. This style is basically authoritarian but encourages upward communication to voice the opinions and complaints of subordinates; however, interaction between levels in the organization is through the formal channels. Communication is rarely frank and candid.

System 3—Consultative. This style involves fairly frequent interaction at moderately personal levels between superiors and subordinates in the organization. Information flows both upward and downward but with slightly more emphasis on ideas that originate from the top. The manager has substantial, but not complete, trust and confidence in employees.

System 4—Participative. This style is highly supportive, with goals for the organization being set through true employee participation. Information flows in all directions, and control is exercised at all levels. People communicate freely, openly, and candidly with little fear of punishment. The participative style is similar to Blake and Mouton's 9,9 team style. Generally the informal and formal communication systems are identical, ensuring authentic integration of personal and organizational goals.

The central issue in Likert's systems theory is decision making. System 4 (participative), with the highest level of employee participation, results in the highest level of productivity also. Likert's research indicated that most organizations prefer System 4 but, regretfully, actually use System 1.

Continuum Theory

Tannenbaum and Schmidt (1957) make control over decision making the key concept in their continuum of leadership behavior. They describe seven behavior points on a continuum from boss-centered leadership to subordinate-centered leadership. The seven points characterize leader-managers ranging from those who maintain a high degree of control to those who release control to subordinates. The continuum may be described as follows:

1. The manager makes the decision and announces it.
2. The manager makes the decision and sells it.
3. The manager presents the decision and invites questions.
4. The manager presents a tentative decision that is subject to change.
5. The manager presents a problem, gets suggestions, then makes the decision.
6. The manager defines limits and asks the subordinate to make the decision.
7. The manager permits subordinates to make decisions.

Although the possible range of leadership styles may exist along a continuum as suggested, Tannenbaum and Schmidt characterize the successful leader as neither strongly control-oriented nor highly permissive. Rather, the most effective leader is one who adopts a style consistent with the demands of the situation. If direction seems appropriate, the leader gives direction; if participation in decisions is required, the leader releases control and allows the group to function in making decisions. The question generally left unanswered concerns what kinds of demands within a leadership situation call for each of the different styles. Some ideas for how to decide when to use a particular leadership style are suggested by *contingency theory*.

Contingency Theory

Many of the theories examined here implicitly, if not explicitly, acknowledge that effective leadership may be a function of or contingent upon the situation in which leadership is being exercised. Fiedler (1967) was instrumental in developing a theory of leadership styles based on the concept of contingencies. According to contingency theory the leader's effectiveness depends on the relationships within his or her style, as well as certain features of the situation. A leader's style is described in terms of variables already familiar to us: task and relationship. Hence, leaders are considered to be task-motivated or relationship-motivated.

The characteristics of a given leadership situation that seem most important are (1) leader-member relations, (2) task structure, and (3) leader's position power. Good *leader-member relations* exist when members like, trust, and respect the leader; this is regarded as the single most important condition for effective leadership. *Task structure* refers to the degree to which the way a job is to be done is explained in step-by-step detail; the more structured the task, the more influence the leader has over the group. *Position power* is defined in terms of the degree to which a leader can punish, reward, promote, discipline, or reprimand members; leaders have more position power when they can reward and punish.

Leader effectiveness is determined by the match between the style of leadership (task or relationship) and the favorableness of the situation. The most favorable situation exists when leader-member relations are good, the task is highly structured, and the leader has strong position power. The least favorable situation exists when leader-member relations are poor, the task is unstructured, and leader position power is weak. Of course, any situation may have varying levels of favorableness, which would include aspects of both better and poorer characteristics.

Table 11.1 portrays various combinations of style, characteristics, and favorableness. Eight basic contingencies result from the combinations. Research on the contingency model has shown that (1) task-motivated leaders are more effective in highly favorable *and* highly unfavorable situations and (2) relationship-motivated leaders are more effective in moderately favorable situations. Thus, task-motivated leaders tend to be more effective in situations in which they have either very much or very little influence. Relationship-motivated leaders tend to be more effective in situations in which they have moderate levels of influence.

Why certain leadership styles seem to be more effective in different situations is explained by looking at the requirements of favorable and unfavorable situations. In favorable situations you, as a leader, are well liked, have a clear task, and have high position power; under those conditions you obviously have everything going for you and should be able to exert influence over the group. The group should be willing to go along with your efforts to direct them; the strongest style for this situation is the task-motivated one. On the other hand, if you are disliked, have a vague assignment, and have little position power, then you are unlikely to have much influence over the group. In that case you should focus on the task and direct the group, relying on whatever influence you might have through the authority derived from the position. In either case—highly favorable and highly unfavorable—the task-motivated leader has the greatest likelihood of success.

Relationship-motivated leaders tend to perform most effectively in moderately favorable situations. When the situation is favorable, members do not require strong control. Tasks can be accomplished by subordinates with little task direction, but they need encouragement, support, and interpersonal trust, all of which are provided by the relationship-motivated leader.

COMMUNICATIVE BEHAVIORS AND LEADERSHIP STYLES

Up to now we have used several models of leadership to identify the primary focus of leadership attempts. That is, in one theory the focus is concern about the people who are supposed to accomplish certain results or about production or results to be accomplished; in another theory, the focus is on relationships and tasks; other theories fix on relationships, tasks, and either effectiveness or maturity; still another theory looks at control and freedom in decision making. Although the focus of each theory contains useful information for individuals interested in evolving an approach to helping others achieve goals, it is actually the style that results from taking a particular focus that is of greatest interest to us. That is primarily because the style is what indicates the behaviors (talking, acting) to be used in helping in a particular way.

Type Approaches to Leadership Style

As far as we know, Hippocrates may have been the first person to speculate about factors that create and characterize an individual's behavioral style. Hippocrates suggest-

TABLE 11.1 Leadership Effectiveness (Based on a Leader Style, Situational Favorableness, and Contingencies)

MOST EFFECTIVE LEADER	TASK-MOTIVATED			RELATIONSHIP-MOTIVATED			TASK-MOTIVATED	
Situational Favorableness	Highly Favorable			Moderately Favorable			Unfavorable	
Leader-member relations	Good	Good	Good	Good	Poor	Poor	Poor	Poor
Task structure	Highly structured	Structured	Unstructured	Unstructured	Structured	Structured	Unstructured	Highly structured
Leader position power	Strong	Weak	Strong	Weak	Strong	Weak	Strong	Weak
Contingency	1	2	3	4	5	6	7	8

ed that bodily structure and physiology determine one's personality or habitual way of behaving. He described four personality types that were supposed to be the result of the predominant influence of one of the four "humors" of the body.

James Deese explains, however, that "there was, of course, no evidence for such a notion, and about the only remaining vestige of Hippocrates' types are the adjectives still in use to describe traits: phlegmatic, choleric, sanguine, and melancholic" (1967, p. 429). Littauer (1983), nevertheless, developed an extensive analysis of behavioral styles using the four temperaments as the foundation.

Jung

Carl Jung (1923) also developed a system of character types based on two *attitudes* and four *functions*. The two attitudes are *introversion* and *extroversion*. "Everyone now agrees, however, that the dichotomy [introversion vs. extroversion] does not serve as a useful typology" (Deese, 1967, p. 429).

The four functions are *thinking, feeling, sensing,* and *intuiting*. The thinking function is concerned with ideas. Through thinking, people try to comprehend the nature of the world and themselves. Feeling is the valuing function. Feelings give value to things and are responsible for the experiences of pleasure and pain, anger, fear, sorrow, joy, love, etc. Sensing is the perceptual or reality function and reveals concrete facts and information about the world. Intuiting refers to gaining knowledge and getting at the essential nature of the world by means of mystical experiences and from unconscious sources (Dushkin, 1970, p. 470).

Deese suggests that since "our mental processes work by reducing the complexities of the world to simple schemes, type descriptions of personality will be with us in popular thought for a long time" (1967, p. 430).

The most common number of categories of personality/style types is four, possibly due to the strong influence of Jung's work and the resulting four basic functions. Subsequently, the concepts associated with the four basic styles are, also, suspiciously consistent, although the specific terms differ somewhat. A comparison of a few of the major instruments used to identify operating styles may reveal similarities and differences.

Myers-Briggs

One of the most widely used and replicated instruments is the Myers-Briggs Type Indicator (Briggs & Briggs Myers, 1976) based on Jung's four basic functions and is often called a "personality type theory." Myers and Briggs explain that Jung's theory posits that much apparently random behavior is actually quite orderly and consistent, due to certain basic similarities and differences in the way people perceive the world and make judgments about it.

Perceiving involves the ways in which we become aware of things, people, and happenings. Judgments involve all the ways we have of coming to conclusions about what has been perceived. There are two contrasting ways of perceiving—sensing and intuiting—and two contrasting ways of arriving at judgments—thinking and feeling. If people differ systematically in how they perceive, and in how they reach conclusions, it is reasonable to believe that they will differ in the kinds of operating style they show.

Other Instruments Based on Types

Drake Beam Morin, Inc., consultants in the management of human resources (277 Park Avenue, New York, NY 10172), developed an I-Speak Test based on Jung's four personality types that is used to create a profile of a person's communication style. The four styles in the I-Speak survey are Intuitor, Thinker, Senser, and Feeler.

Paul Mok and Associates (14455 Webbs Chapel Road, Dallas, TX 75234), now Mok-Bledsoe International, help clients identify their four styles using a Communicating Styles Survey (CST) that reveals an Intuitor, a Senser, a Thinker, and a Feeler style (Lynch, 1976, 1977; Mok & Lynch, 1978).

Kolb (1976a & 1976b) based his study of "learning styles" on Jung's concept of personality types. Four learner activities were identified: thinking, feeling, watching, and doing. Combinations of each of these activities resulted in four learning styles: Converger, Diverger, Assimilator, and Accommodator. Convergers are relatively unemotional and prefer to deal with things rather than people. Divergers tend to be emotional and imaginative and are interested in people. Assimilators excel in inductive reasoning and assimilating disparate observations into an integrated explanation, and they are less interested in people and more concerned with abstract concepts. Accommodators' greatest strengths lie in doing things, in carrying out plans and involving themselves in new experiences. They tend to solve problems in an intuitive trial-and-error manner.

Harrison and Bramson (1982) began with work on "inquiry modes" and identified five styles derived from the approaches to thinking of "certain seminal thinkers and philosophers" associated with major historical eras. The Idealist is associated with philosophy, government, and politics; the Analyst reflects the foundations of Western intellectual methods; the Realist represents thought and activity associated with scientific methods; the Pragmatist is associated with nontraditional, progressive thinking and action; and the Synthesist is grounded in the dialectical method and represents an integrative style.

Consistent with qualifications provided by most of the theorists, Harrison and Bramson (1982) explain that "each person is truly unique and never completely predictable. Our Style of Thinking characterizations only describe prototypes (or "ideal types"). No one is a total Analyst or a total Synthesist. Yet, Analyst thinking is a human characteristic and knowing how much one has of it makes it possible to predict a good deal about how he or she is going to think about things" (pp. 186–187).

Traits Approaches to Styles

The approaches of four individuals or teams who have conducted research using adjectives to describe operating styles are discussed below. Although they use slightly different styles, terminology, and different adjectival measures from those of Myers-Briggs, four basic types are, nevertheless, apparent in their conceptualizations.

NREL Using a different database and methods, but starting from a similar theoretical framework (people vs. task orientation and extrovert vs. introvert orientation), the Northwest Regional Educational Laboratory (710 S.W. Second Avenue, Portland, OR 97204) created the *Leadership Styles: A Behavioral Matrix* (Sayers, 1978) that elicits data on four different styles: Promoting, Controlling, Analyzing, and Supporting.

MALONE   The Malone Training & Development Company (Akron, OH) developed the *Behavior Style Survey* (Oravecz, 1981) that provides information about four basic styles: Director, Persuader, Analyzer, and Supporter.

TRACOM   The TRACOM Corporation (200 Fillmore Street, Denver, CO 80206) markets the *Social Style Profile* (Reid & Merrill, 1987) that reveals four styles: Analytical, Driving, Amiable, and Expressive that seem somewhat equivalent to Thinking (analytical), Feeling (expressive), Intuition (amiable), and Sensing (driving).

PERFORMAX   Performax Systems International (12755 State Highway 55, Minneapolis, MN 55441) markets the *Personal Profile System*, a styles instrument based on the research of John G. Geier (1967) and the general theory of William Moulton Marston, author of *Emotions of Normal People* (1979). Marston identified four primary emotions around which behaviors tend to cluster: dominance, influence, submission, and compliance. Geier verified a quartet of styles to which he gave the title DISC (dominance, influence, steadiness, and compliance).

Although not directly derived from the same research, there are obvious equivalents to the styles identified by Geier (1977), Sayers (1978), Oravecz (1981), and Reid and Merrill (1987) because they come from a similar "traits" approach to styles. Dominance seems much like Director, Controller, and Driving; Influence shares features with Promoter, Persuader, and Expressive; Compliance has many of the characteristics of Supporter, Amiable, and Supporter; and Steadiness appears to be something like Analyzer, Analytical, and Analyzer.

Transactional Analysis

Styles can also be viewed from the perspective of Eric Berne (1964) and what is currently called Transactional Analysis. Berne derived his theories from psychoanalytical theory and postulated three ego states: Adult, Parent, and Children as part of each person's behavioral repertory.

James R. Noland (1978) developed and distributes an instrument called Personalysis, in which responses are interpreted in terms of each of Berne's primary ego states and four attributes that characterize each ego state. The Adult ego state, for example, represents a person's preferred style of managing self and others and is organized around implementing, organizing, structuring, and planning activities. The Parent ego state represents one's preferred style of being managed and includes four preferred styles: authoritative, bureaucratic, democratic, and self-directed. The Child ego state represents a person's motivational needs and includes power, control, flexibility, and freedom.

Wofford, Gerloff, and Cummins (1977) infer six basic communication styles from Transactional Analysis theory, loosely derived from each of the primary ego states. The Controlling Style, the Equalitarian Style, the Structuring Style, the Dynamic Style, the Relinquishing Style, and the Withdrawing Style are distributed among the three ego states: Parent uses controlling and structuring styles; Adult uses equalitarian and dynamic styles; Child uses relinquishing and withdrawing styles.

Hill Interaction Matrix

The Hill Interaction Matrix (HIM) was developed to articulate recurring patterns that characterize a wide variety of behavioral phenomena and verbal content of group interaction. The categories "make stylistic distinctions between groups" (Hill, 1973). Whether the categories involved in the HIM are valid "must remain with the reader who can validate it against his [or her] experience with groups to determine whether these categories are useful in the understanding and management of groups" (Hill, 1973, p. 160). Four style categories were produced by the results: Confrontive, Speculative, Assertive, and Conventional.

Miller, Nunnally, and Wackman (1975), however, extrapolated four variables that they felt accounted for the styles—emphasizes feelings, emphasizes thinking, emphasizes personal issues, and emphasizes relationship issues. They created four styles of their own, described as follows:

Style I: Friendly, sociable, playful; keeps the world going.
Style II: Directing, persuading, blaming, demanding; usually used when you want to be persuasive or to control what is happening.
Style III: Tentative, expanding, elaborating, exploring, searching; a speculative style whose intention is almost to stop the world, reflect on it, and explore it.
Style IV: Aware, active, accepting, disclosing, caring, and cooperative; pursues the process of dealing with issues openly and directly; a committed style.

Miller and co-workers (1975), conclude that "if your intention is to socialize and participate in some activities together, Style IV is too heavy. Style I would be better here. If your intention is to direct and persuade, then Style IV doesn't fit. Try Style II. If your intention is to explore tentatively and get a general overview of an issue, then Style IV is too focused. Style III is better for that" (pp. 209–211). Style IV expresses a deeper commitment to deal with the issue. Style IV is best when you and your partner have an issue and want to work on it.

There may be a multitude of additional ways of looking at and analyzing individual operating styles. Some, for example, look at Assertive, Nonassertive, and Aggressive styles of interacting (Bolton, 1979; Alberti & Emmons, 1982). The above summary of the major approaches to creating, measuring, and classifying styles represents the vast range of current ways of looking at operating styles and reveals considerable similarity in theoretical perspective and methods used in describing operating styles.

OPERATING STYLES

In summary, certain decisions that people make are predictable from what is popularly called their style; being able to predict a person's decisions allows us to understand how they may respond to a variety of directions, opportunities, challenges, and changing conditions. Thus, many researchers have been attempting to discover and describe people's styles. If we can recognize a person's style, we may be able to explain *why* that person reacted the way he or she did to the direction, challenge, opportunity, or change. It may be, also, that certain styles or patterns of behavior are more conducive to accomplishing certain types of organizational and personal goals.

An operating style is a person's consistent pattern of behavior as perceived by others when a person is attempting to assist others to achieve goals. To many, someone's operating style is the single most important factor in working successfully with employees. The theory and research cited above suggest that two sets of behavioral inclinations comprise most styles: (1) an initiating versus a sustaining inclination and (2) a relational versus a notional inclination. These inclinations combine to make a four-cell matrix and identify four stylistic tendencies or inclinations (Figure 11.4).

Initiating tendencies are revealed when a person takes the first step to begin something, and shows energy and direction in bringing about the action. A person with initiating tendencies is usually active, looking to get things done, and pushing things forward.

Sustaining tendencies are revealed when a person lends support, endures without failing or yielding, and helps others to continue their actions. A person with sustaining tendencies is usually committed to minimizing conflict and promoting the happiness of everyone. They are often thorough and able to bear up under pressure.

Relational concerns focus on the emotional connections between human beings. A person reveals relational concerns by placing value on people and caring for them. A person with relational concerns is people-oriented and nonaggressive.

Notional concerns focus on ideas, objects, and abstract conceptions. A person who reveals notional concerns places value on things and data, often appears aloof and cool, and may prefer to work alone.

Combinations of initiating tendencies and relational concerns produce a *Dealer* style, whereas combinations of sustaining tendencies and notional concerns produce a *Holder* style. On the other hand, combinations of initiating tendencies and notional concerns result in a *Mover* style. Finally, combinations of sustaining tendencies and relational concerns result in a *Giver* style.

Dealers are very diplomatic, socially outgoing, imaginative, and friendly. Dealers get things going, but may settle for less than the best in order to get on to something else. They have creative ideas but may be less likely to follow through to get a task done. Dealers tend to value information that gives them power to manage the situation so they can realize their goals in a socially acceptable way.

BEHAVIORAL OR STYLISTIC INCLINATIONS

```
                    Initiating Tendencies
                              |
                              |
             Dealer    |    Mover
                              |
Relational   _____|_____   Notional
Concerns                  |            Concerns
             Giver     |    Holder
                              |
                              |
                    Sustaining Tendencies
```

FIGURE 11.4 Operating Styles

Holders are problem solvers and like to get all the data before making decisions. Some say they are thorough but others say they are slow. These people like to work alone; they esteem conceptual skills, and, interpersonally, may seem aloof and cool. They value information that allows them to make substantive decisions on the basis of fact and evidence.

Movers are results-oriented individuals who love to run things their own way. They manage time and are efficient, but they are often viewed as unfeeling and threatening in their relationships with others. Movers make sure the job is done and are often impatient with people or policies that stand in their way.

Givers value interpersonal relations. These people try to minimize conflict and promote the happiness of others. They are seen by many as accommodating and friendly, while some view them as wishy-washy. They like to please others and rely on others to give directions about how to get their work done.

How to Describe Operating Styles

Studies on the use of symbols indicate that language functions not simply as a device for reporting experiences, but as a way of defining experience itself. Meanings are imposed on experience. Existence is based on assumptions that predispose people to see the world in a way that is consistent with the manner in which they talk about it. "Saying is seeing" rather than "seeing is believing" may be the more accurate way of expressing the relation between language and what we see as the world in which we live.

A language device used widely for expressing the meaning of experience is called a *metaphor*. A metaphor makes sense of a situation by comparing it with something else, by talking about the first situation as though it were the second situation. For example, we might refer to a colleague as a "tiger" or say that Elbert is a tiger. We are using a metaphor comparing Elbert to a tiger.

Metaphors influence the way we think, and they help us think by succinctly chunking together certain characteristics and transferring them from one thing to another without enumerating the characteristics, thus providing a compact and coherent whole. Metaphors tend to be highly memorable because they often are novel and vivid as well as succinct.

Metaphors structure complex situations by highlighting certain elements and obscuring others. Metaphors transport conceptions of the familiar to the less familiar and articulate topics for which we may not otherwise have language to express them.

Saying that Elbert is a tiger fits the description of a metaphor. It is succinct, novel, and vivid, and chunks the characteristics of a "tiger" into a compact and coherent whole, highlighting certain traits as the term is applied to Elbert. It would be possible to describe Elbert in great detail, enumerating features that characterize his ferocious attack on problems, but the idea of Elbert as a tiger captures the essence more quickly and also captures some inexplicable attributes.

In this same fashion, it is possible to encourage individuals to characterize themselves through the use of metaphors. While we can succinctly describe Elbert as a tiger, it is equally feasible for Elbert to select the metaphor of tiger to describe himself. When given a list of metaphors from which to choose, we have found that individual employees can select the most appropriate metaphors for characterizing their styles of interacting with others. In fact, they find it involving, intriguing, and fascinating to frame their typical way of interacting in the form of metaphors.

Instructions: Choose one term from each set of four that most clearly represents the way in which you work with other people. Select one term in each group that characterizes the way in which you work with others.

A. Bear
B. Fox
C. Tortoise
D. Bluebird

Key: A = mover, B = dealer, C = holder, D = giver

FIGURE 11.5 Excerpt from Operating Styles Inventory

Operating style (Pace, Mills, & Stephan, 1989) is assessed using fifteen sets of metaphors that allow the person to characterize ways of interacting with others holistically. The Operating Styles Inventory (Figure 11.5) reveals a person's tendencies toward initiating versus sustaining and a person's concerns for relationships versus notions.

The Operating Styles instrument elicits a score that indicates the preferred and typical operating style of respondents. Operating Style is a holistic measure of a person's tendencies to behave in more or less habitual ways. Although the results from the Operating Styles instrument are similar to a number of other instruments available for use in styles assessment, this one is unique in that it uses metaphors to describe styles. The instrument is both easy and interesting to complete and appears to derive patterns that have face validity. If the styles described by this instrument are consistent with longer and more cumbersome surveys, then this may be a superior approach to deriving styles because of its simplicity and interest value.

Most Effective Leadership Style

The logic of a one-best leadership style versus a conditional-best leadership style is grounded in assumptions about the nature of influence. From a one-best style perspective, it is argued that the orientation and skills of the influencer make the difference. If you are going to help another person to achieve some desirable outcomes—exercise leadership—you will be most effective if you use the style that has the highest probability of being responded to in a positive way.

Stephan and Pace (1991), for example, have advised executives who want to exhibit more effective leadership to "treat others as friends." They suggest that "friends are generous and hospitable, devoted and genial, happy to be in the presence of each other. They are willing to place the needs of the other ahead of their own. They are willing to accept the burdens of others.... Being a friend is the simpler, easier, more effective way to achieve leadership. Being a friend opens the door to exciting, moving, powerful leadership, without the use of complex strategies for winning and influencing people" (p. 7). Being a friend is a one-best leadership style.

Manz and Sims (1991) argue for a form of "SuperLeader" whose goal becomes "largely that of helping followers to develop the necessary skills for work" or what they call self-leadership. SuperLeadership consists of an "array of behavioral and cognitive strategies." Nevertheless, the concept of SuperLeadership appears to imply a one-best leadership style, "to lead followers to discover the potentialities that lie within themselves" (pp. 22–23). They contend that "the best results derive from a total integrated system that is deliberately intended to encourage, support, and reinforce self-leadership *throughout* the system" (p. 29).

A conditional-best leadership style is one in which the leader uses different combinations of communicative behaviors that respond to the circumstances in which the leader is attempting to help another to achieve desired outcomes. No single style or approach to leadership guarantees just the right type of help for everyone to achieve desirable goals. Different styles result in different goal attainments, depending on the conditions under which the styles are being used. Completing a highly structured task, for example, may require a different leadership style than accomplishing an ambiguous, unstructured task. A situation in which the people whom you are attempting to help are uncooperative or even hostile may require a slightly different leadership style and approach from one in which those being helped are friendly, cooperative, and supportive.

SUMMARY

What we may have learned from this chapter is that there are various models for explaining what one needs to focus on in order to help people achieve desirable results—the essence of leadership. Some theorists suggest that leaders must be concerned about both achieving production goals and responding to the individual needs of people. Other theorists explain that leaders must be concerned with achieving tasks and maintaining relationships, but they must also be concerned with or take into account the maturity of those being led and the effectiveness of the techniques being used. Still other theorists feel that leaders should be more concerned about control over decisions and whether control should be shared or held by the leader, and under what conditions. Finally, a small but growing number of theorists assert that the best form of leadership is that which teaches others to lead themselves.

Leadership style has to do, primarily, with the communicative behaviors used to help others to achieve desired outcomes. For ease of analysis, communicative behaviors are usually grouped into categories. The most common groupings are those identified by Carl Jung and identified as *thinking, feeling, sensing,* and *intuiting* behaviors. In fact, Mok and associates have used a "communicating styles survey" to reveal the intuitor, sensor, thinker, and feeler communication styles. Other practitioners have employed designations such as director, promoter, supporter, and analyzer to characterize the communicative behaviors of different types of leaders. Finally, Pace, Mills, and Stephan use a metaphors test to distinguish among four operating styles that are typical of people who work in organizations.

A SUBJECTIVIST'S REMINDER

Leadership has meaning only as constructed and defined by organizational members. The same management styles in different contexts are likely to be perceived in different ways. But what about all the literature on management and communication that gives advice about the leadership styles that should be used? As Calder (1977) contends:

> Leadership cannot be taught as a skill. Skills may certainly help a person to per-
> form more effectively, but leadership depends on how this performance and its
> effects are perceived by others. To teach leadership is to sensitize people to the
> perceptions of others—that is, to sensitize them to the everyday, common-sense
> thinking of a group of people. The transfer of leadership from one group of actors
> to another thus becomes highly problematic. The would-be-leader must respond
> to attributions based on the meaning of leadership for each group with which he
> interacts (p. 202).

Managers can become sensitive and responsive to organizational demands by
understanding the interactions of members. Each organizational culture makes different demands in terms of what a manager can do and what the response of the
manager ought to be in a particular context.

A provocative study is provided by Pettegrew (1982). After a review of leadership literature, he concludes:

> Conceptualizations of management style hold in common the notion that organi-
> zational leadership exerts a strong stylistic pressure on other members of the
> organization. Depending upon certain needs and assets of its members, particular
> styles will have predictable outcomes for their attitudes and behaviors, the pro-
> ductivity of the organization as a whole, and the kind of communication which
> takes place laterally, vertically, and horizontally (p. 181).

The traditional functionalist literature, then, suggests that managerial and leadership styles are strong determinants of the behavior of subordinates, and that different styles produce different outcomes.

Pettegrew examines the effects of leadership styles in his study of academic
medical centers. In essence, the findings indicate that in the particular organization
studied, employees perceived leadership as being the same in spite of the divergent
leadership styles employed by managers. This conclusion gives rise to a different
kind of framework for understanding the effects of leadership behavior on the
organization. Pettegrew states:

> This alternative is termed "The S.O.B. Theory of Management." Its basic tenet
> holds that in nonprofit health and human service organizations . . . it doesn't matter
> what kind of management style one uses (from delegative to directive). The force
> of being a decision-maker within this particular organizational context makes one
> an S.O.B. to the majority of interest groups in such organizations (pp. 178–180).

This statement generalizes more than interpretive researchers may like, but the
important point is that the context, or culture, is a dominant factor in determining
what behaviors mean. Pettegrew maintains that "there are frequently both situational and contextual factors which render received theories important. The schol-
ar must be willing to abandon the received view and search for other, perhaps
more rhetorical, interpretive frameworks for understanding the organization and
the communication which takes place therein" (p. 191).

We would suggest that managers could benefit from an understanding of the
ways organizational members interpret different management styles. Although the
S.O.B. label seems harsh, it may not only be realistic but quite functional. Some
cultures (organizations) may operate better with S.O.B.'s.

REFERENCES

ALBERTI, ROBERT E., and MICHAEL L. EMMONS, *Your Perfect Right: A Guide to Assertive Living*. San Luis Obispo, Calif.: Impact Publishers, 1982.

BASS, BERNARD M., *Leadership, Psychology and Organizational Behavior*. New York: Harper & Row, Pub., 1960.

BERNE, ERIC, *Games People Play*. New York: Grove Press, 1964.

BLAKE, ROBERT R., and ANNE ADAMS MCCAUSE, *Leadership Dilemmas—Grid Solutions*. Houston: Gulf Publishing Co., 1991.

BLAKE, ROBERT R., and JANE S. MOUTON, *The Managerial Grid*. Houston: Gulf Publishing Co., 1964.

BOLTON, ROBERT, *People Skills: How to Assert Yourself, Listen to Others, and Resolve Conflicts*. Englewood Cliffs, N.J.: Prentice-Hall, 1979.

BRIGGS, KATHARINE C., and ISABEL BRIGGS MYERS, *Myers-Briggs Type Indicator*. Palo Alto, Calif.: Consulting Psychologists Press, 1976.

CALDER, BOBBY J., "An Attribution Theory of Leadership," in *New Directions in Organizational Behavior*, Barry M. Staw and Gerald R. Salancik, eds. Chicago: St. Clair Press, 1977.

DEESE, JAMES, *General Psychology*. Boston: Allyn & Bacon, 1967.

DUSHKIN, DAVID A., *Psychology Today: An Introduction*. Del Mar, Calif.: CRM Books, 1970.

FIEDLER, FRED E., *A Theory of Leadership Effectiveness*. New York: McGraw-Hill, 1967.

GEIER, JOHN G., *Personal Profile System*. Minneapolis: Performax Systems International, 1977.

GEIER, JOHN G., "A Trait Approach to the Study of Leadership in Small Groups," *Journal of Communication* (December 1967), 316–323.

HARRISON, ALLEN F., and ROBERT M. BRAMSON, *The Art of Thinking*. New York: Berkley Publishing Group, 1982.

HERSEY, PAUL, and KENNETH H. BLANCHARD, "So You Want to Know Your Leadership Style?" *Training and Development Journal*, 28 (February 1974), 22–37.

HERSEY, PAUL, and KENNETH H. BLANCHARD, *Management of Organizational Behavior: Utilizing Human Resources* (3rd ed.). Englewood Cliffs, N.J.: Prentice-Hall, 1977.

HERSEY, PAUL, *Situational Selling*. Escondido, Calif.: Center for Leadership Studies, 1985.

HILL, WM. FAWCETT, "Hill Interaction Matrix (HIM): Conceptual Framework for Understanding Groups," in *The 1973 Annual Handbook for Group Facilitators*. San Diego: University Associates, 1973.

JUNG, CARL J., *Psychological Types*. New York: Harcourt, Brace, Inc., 1923.

KOLB, DAVID A., *Learning Style Inventory*. Boston: McBer and Company, 1976(a).

KOLB, DAVID A., "On Management and the Learning Process," *California Management Review* (Spring 1976)(b).

LIKERT, RENSIS, *The Human Organization*. New York: McGraw-Hill, 1967.

LITTAUER, FLORENCE, *Personality Plus*. Old Tappan, N.J.: Fleming H. Revell Co., 1983.

LYNCH, DUDLEY, "Intuitors, Sensors, Thinkers, Feelers," *Texas Parade Magazine* (April 1976): 26–29.

LYNCH, DUDLEY, "In Sync With the Other Guy," *TWA Ambassador Magazine* (March 1977), 28–31.

MANZ, CHARLES C., and HENRY P. SIMS, JR., "SuperLeadership: Beyond the Myth of Heroic Leadership," *Organizational Dynamics* (Spring 1991), 18–35.

MARSTON, WILLIAM MOULTON, *Emotions of Normal People*. Minneapolis: Persona Press, 1979.

MCGREGOR, DOUGLAS, *The Human Side of Enterprise*. New York: McGraw-Hill, 1967.

MILLER, SHEROD, ELAM W. NUNNALLY, and DANIEL B. WACKMAN, *Alive and Aware*. Minneapolis: Interpersonal Communication Programs, Inc., 1975.

MOK, PAUL, and DUDLEY LYNCH, "Easy New Way to Get Your Way," *Reader's Digest* (March 1978), 105–109.

NOLAND, JAMES R., *Personalysis*. Houston: Management Technologies, 1978.

ORAVECZ, M.T., *Behavior Style Survey*. Akron, Ohio: Malone Training & Development Co., 1981.

PACE, R. WAYNE, GORDON E. MILLS, and ERIC STEPHAN "Operating Styles." Unpublished manuscript, Brigham Young University, Provo, Utah, 1989.

PETTEGREW, LOYD S., "Organizational Communication and the S.O.B. Theory of Management," *Western Journal of Speech Communication*, 46 (Spring 1982), 178–191.

REDDIN, WILLIAM J., "The 3-D Management Style Theory," *Training and Development Journal*, 21 (April 1967), 8–17.

REID, ROGER, and DAVID W. MERRILL, *Social Style Profile*. The TRACOM Corporation, 1987.

SAYERS, SUSAN, "Leadership Styles: A Behavioral Matrix." Portland, Ore.: Northwest Regional Educational Laboratory, 1978.

STEPHAN, ERIC, and R. WAYNE PACE, "Five Keys to Effective Leadership," *Executive Excellence* (January 1991), 7–8.

STOGDILL, RALPH M., and ALVIN E. COONS (eds.), *Leader Behavior: Its Description and Measurement*. Research Monograph No. 88. Columbus: Bureau of Business Research, Ohio State University, 1957.

TANNENBAUM, ROBERT, and WARREN H. SCHMIDT, "How to Choose a Leadership Pattern," *Harvard Business Review* 36 (March-April, 1957), 95–101. Reprinted in May-June 1973.

WOFFORD, JERRY C., EDWIN A. GERLOFF, and ROBERT C. CUMMINS, *Organizational Communication: The Keystone to Managerial Effectiveness*. New York: McGraw-Hill, 1977.

12

Teams and Groups

REVOLUTION IN PROGRESS

A revolution is in process in the United States and other countries; it is a work revolution in which insignificant and often invisible people (Scott & Hart, 1989, pp. 65–76) are being given significance and visibility. This revolution is being accomplished in two ways: (1) through changes in the values and assumptions of the managers, executives, and technological professionals who are the significant people in organizations, and (2) through changes in the way in which the work itself is being done.

Changes in Values and Assumptions

The primary change in values and assumptions is from assuming that managers are important in getting employees to do their work to assuming that employees will actually make the decision on their own to work more effectively (Coonradt, 1984, pp. 1–11). Work is being viewed more as a collaborative, holistic experience than as a private or sequential experience (LeBaron, 1988, p. ix). The most effective organization members tend to work with others, to contribute their own character to an organizational character (Wilkins, 1989, p. 3), and to build on the skills, motivation, and vision of other organization members. Both the assumption and the value that organization members should be empowered in their work have contributed to the work revolution.

The team concept is spreading rapidly among industries such as auto manufacturing, aerospace, electrical equipment, electronics, food processing, paper, steel, coal, and financial services (Hoerr, 1989). However, adopting work teams is no small matter. It means wiping out tiers of managers and tearing down bureaucratic barriers between departments. Nevertheless, companies appear to be willing to undertake such radical

changes to gain workers' commitment and the productivity gains that someti
30 percent in some industries.

Changes in the Work Itself

Specialists in the design of work observe that "lots of jobs are not so well designed. They demotivate people rather than turn them on. They undermine rather than encourage productivity and work quality. They aren't any fun" (Hackman & Oldham, 1980, p. ix). The work revolution has jolted organization leaders and managers to reconsider how work in their organization is being done. The goal is to make work more motivating, more encouraging, and more fun. New assumptions about how the work itself should be done appears to be creating a revolution in the way in which organizations themselves are put together. Changes in the work itself have, in many organizations, reduced the need for middle managers and supervisors, or at least it has changed the definition of what supervisors, foremen, and managers are supposed to do in the organization.

The Ultimate Change

The consequence of these two fundamental changes on the life of organization members finds its ultimate expression in a reconceptualization of the meaning of "groups at work." It has been traditional to approach group processes in an organization from the perspective of social psychology, with a focus on relationships and social processes (Smith, 1973, pp. 1–13; Bormann & Bormann, 1980, pp. 1–4). What has been called "work groups" is really a group having a meeting, not a work group. The fundamental change in our thinking about groups turns on the way we understand what controls the creation and structure of work groups—the work or the group.

THE WORK OR THE GROUP

Work Team (WT)

Ketchum and Trist (1992) reason that "while individual character traits are not to be ignored, there is a strong relationship between behavior on the job and the way work is organized. We create the workplace, and the workplace creates us" (p. 7). Why is it that we use teams as the mechanism for creating "good work"? Ketchum and Trist explain that "generally, overcoming the limitation of scope and variety means putting workers into teams. Teams, as units, can be given a very broad scope of responsibility and thus greatly expand the scope and variety of each person. For this reason the team becomes the basic building block of the new organization" (p. 143).

Groups that are created as a result of the work itself are called "work teams." A work team is a group of workers responsible for creating a product or handling a process in an organization. The WT plans the work, completes it, and oversees many of the regular supervisory tasks such as scheduling, setting goals, providing performance feedback, and even hiring new team members and firing those who do not contribute adequately to the work of the team. The team is accountable for production, quality, costs, statistical controls, and coordination with other teams and departments. The WT is governed by the work itself. Members are a team because the work dictates that they work together. The WT is charged with responsibility to manage itself, increase the skills of team members, and improve the process, the product, and/or the service the team provides. When a WT functions fairly independently, it may be referred to as an "autonomous" or "self-managed" team.

Self-managing work teams usually consist of five to fifteen members who produce an entire product. Members learn all tasks and rotate from job to job. Teams take over managerial duties, including scheduling vacations and ordering materials. Many managers resist self-managed WTs because it entails sharing power with employees. Owners and managers who fear hostile takeovers think twice about investing in work teams since they require continual training to help workers improve their technical and social/managerial skills.

Project Groups (PG)

The "project group" is created primarily for purposes of planning and coordination. Project group members are usually assigned to the group and are selected because they have information or talents that will aid the planning and coordination processes. They usually talk about work problems, but the team itself is not responsible for doing the work. Project group members engage in problem solving and make recommendations, but most of the time they return to their work units to actually engage in their work. The term "meeting" is often used to refer to those occasions when the PG comes together to discuss problems, share information, and plan and coordinate activities.

Common Factors

Whether a team or a group, organization members who work and plan together have in common the need to manage the processes and dynamics of interaction among their members. Both types of groups—project or work teams—must deal with several process issues. They include (1) how the PG or WT comes together and develops into a cohesive body, (2) how the group or team dynamics are managed, and (3) how the group or team solves problems and makes decisions.

GROUP FORMATION AND DEVELOPMENT

Because much of the work of professionals in organizational communication involves building productive groups and teams, it is desirable to understand how groups are formed and how they develop.

Group Formation

There appear to be at least three ways to create groups or teams: through need satisfaction, through assignment to projects, and through restructuring the work people do on a daily basis.

Forming Groups through Need Satisfaction The formation of a group or team through need satisfaction is based on the assumption that people want to have associations with other people. Schutz (1958) described three needs that constitute his theory of interpersonal relations, called FIRO (fundamental interpersonal relations orientation): (1) the need for inclusion, (2) the need for control, and (3) the need for affection.

Inclusion is the need to interact with other people. Some people like a lot of contact and others prefer to work alone and maintain their privacy. Each person, to some degree, tries to interact with others while at the same time tries to maintain a certain amount of solitude. We like to have other people initiate contact with us, but we also want to be left alone.

Control is the need to have power and influence. We all vary in terms of the degree to which we want to be controlled by others versus the degree to which we wish to control them. You may know someone who wants to be controlled completely by a friend or spouse. On the other hand, you may know, or be, a person who has strong feelings about being independent and in control of your own decisions.

Affection is the need to have warm, close, personal relationships with others. Some individuals feel a strong need to maintain close contacts with others, but others prefer somewhat impersonal and distant relationships. Each of us has our preferences. Some individuals may want others to show warmth and affection toward them but find it difficult to express affection to others.

Each interpersonal need has two parts to it: the *expressed behaviors*, or the behaviors a person initiates toward other people; and the *wanted behaviors*, or the behaviors a person prefers to have others express toward him or her. Your fundamental interpersonal relations orientation (FIRO) is your usual approach to interpersonal relations in terms of the three needs (inclusion, control, and affection) and the degree to which you want and express behaviors relevant to each need. Schutz (1958) developed a questionnaire called FIRO-B (for "behavior") that allows individuals to locate themselves in a matrix on the basis of scores in each need area. Table 12.1 shows the matrix. *FIRO-B* is available from Consulting Psychologists Press, Palo Alto, Ca.

Groups or teams formed exclusively on the basis of interpersonal needs are usually voluntary and allow members to choose whether to join and to determine what they will do as members of the group or team. Nevertheless, if given an opportunity, most of us will attempt to affiliate with groups that provide satisfaction for at least some of our interpersonal needs. In fact, since most of us must function in one or more groups, we often try to affiliate with groups that appear to have the potential for comfortable inclusion, control, and affection need satisfaction. Rather than be coerced into a group or team that may not have the highest potentials for satisfaction, we often volunteer to affiliate with a group or work in a team that may provide at least some minimal satisfaction.

Forming Groups through Assignment to Projects Evidence supports the idea that groups are created through voluntary association in response to the impelling pressure of interpersonal needs. Nevertheless, we also have evidence that group or team membership is often brought about by assignment. That is, in organizations in particular, individuals are more often elected, selected, appointed, and assigned to committees, projects, and

TABLE 12.1 Matrix of Scores on the FIRO-B Inventory

	INCLUSION *I*	*CONTROL* *C*	*AFFECTION* *A*
Express (E)			
Want (W)			

Source: From William Schutz, *FIRO: A Three-Dimensional Theory of Interpersonal Behavior*, New York, Holt, Rinehart & Winston, 1958.

teams with little choice on their part. A considerable amount of group and team activity occurs as a consequence of assignment to a task force, a committee, or a project team. However, the very act of being assigned to a team or group allows for the development of group ties that strengthen and satisfy our interpersonal needs.

Assignment to a committee in the organization provides for opportunities to participate in group problem solving, information sharing, and informal interaction. People who are in close proximity to one another tend to interact more, and interaction tends to help develop feelings of attraction. Assignment to a committee gives one a chance to experience emotional reactions that aid in unifying a group. People are usually attracted to others who share common emotional experiences. The accomplishment of a task often leads to positive emotional experiences and strengthens group cohesiveness.

Forming Groups through Work Restructuring The argument for restructuring work around teams is complex, but Ketchum and Trist (1992) make this concise observation:

> Bad work must go and with it the inordinate reliance on extrinsic motivation, especially coercive supervision. Good work requires increasing the scope and variety of each person's work far beyond that normal to the old way. Generally, overcoming the limitation of scope and variety means putting workers into teams. Teams, as units, can be given a very broad scope of responsibility and thus greatly expand the scope and variety for each person. For this reason the team becomes the basic building block of the new organization (pp. 142–143).

This means that the work of organizations can be accomplished most effectively if it is restructured around the concept of teams. The work is done by teams because the work is organized for team work. Taylor and Felten (1993) list six conditions that need to exist for work to be done by a team:

1. Several workers must be jointly responsible for their own performance.
2. The tasks of the workers must be interdependent.
3. The interdependence of tasks must be a function of the whole work process, flow, or end product.
4. The work must require workers with different skills.
5. To be performed effectively, the skills of the workers must be integrated.
6. Workers share a conscious and common goal or purpose.

These six conditions focus on arranging the work so that the tasks performed are interdependent and are all essential to the completion of an end product, and the skills of those doing the work must be different and integrated so as to effectively complete the end product (Taylor & Felten, 1993, pp. 174–175). If the work itself is organized according to these six guidelines, then those who do the work will automatically be working in teams.

Group or Team Development

The mere fact that a group or team has been created voluntarily, by assignment, or by restructuring the work itself is no guarantee that individual members will function effectively as a group or team. The group or team must develop into a positive, functioning unit. This is achieved by moving through a number of developmental stages just as individuals grow and mature.

TABLE 12.2 Stages in Group Development

	STAGE	INTERPERSONAL RELATIONS ISSUES	TASK FUNCTION ISSUES
1.	Forming	Dependence/Independence	Orientation
2.	Storming	Interpersonal Conflict	Organization/Structure
3.	Norming	Cohesion	Information Sharing
4.	Performing	Interdependence	Problem Solving

For a group or team to progress from one stage to another, it must arrive at a general understanding of both interpersonal relationships and task aspects of group processes. If agreement has not been reached at any one stage prior to proceeding to another, a regression often occurs later. What is particularly important to remember is that groups and teams need to go through each of the stages. If they do not, they are frequently stymied at the point where they should be accomplishing their objectives.

Several systems for describing development stages have been identified over the years (Bales & Strodtbeck, 1951; Bennis & Shepard, 1956; Fisher, 1970), but we shall use Tuckman's (1965) general approach. It reflects the major stages identified in the research and represents a systematic way of thinking about stages in group and team development. The four stages with the interpersonal and task issues associated with each stage in the model are summarized in Table 12.2. We shall briefly describe the major dimensions of each of the stages in the process.

Stage 1: Forming At this early stage, it is not surprising to find team members concerned about being included, liked, and accepted into the group. The task function is to ensure that team members are oriented to the work to be done—why they are on the team, what they are supposed to do, and how they are going to get it done. Team members may be instructed on these points, or they may evolve the goals and orientation through interaction. On the interpersonal relations side, team members must resolve a number of dependence issues, such as the extent to which a designated leader will provide direction, the ground rules on which the group will operate, and the agenda that will be followed. At this stage, team members are getting oriented to one another and to the work to be accomplished.

Stage 2: Storming As teams members get oriented and begin to feel comfortable with one another, the next step is to determine who is in control and what kind of influence that person will have on the team. Different feelings about authority, rules, and leadership surface in the form of interpersonal conflict. The team fails to work in a unified direction, cliques may develop, and conflict intensifies. This is a critical stage in development for groups and teams and some may even fall apart. Unresolved conflict tends to deter the group from becoming a smoothly functioning team. In task functions, the team is seeking answers to questions about who is going to be responsible for what tasks, what the work rules are going to be, and what rewards will ensue. The creation of assignments and rules to govern work and interaction imposes organization and structure on the group. It is important for the team to evolve an orderly process for making decisions that allows team members to exercise independent judgments.

Stage 3: Norming As the differences are resolved and the team acquires structure, individuals begin to experience a sense of cohesion and a feeling of catharsis at having resolved conflicts and survived. Team members begin to engage in constructive cooperation, and conflict is viewed as necessary in order to explore all sides of an issue. Members begin to share ideas and feelings, provide feedback to one another, explore actions related to completing the task, and share information—the primary task function. Group members begin to feel good about what is going on. There is an emerging openness with regard to the task, and some playfulness even occurs. Groups that get stuck at this stage experience high levels of pleasantness about interacting with other members and evolve into what has been called a happy circle, or a group with high morale and intense levels of interaction. Unfortunately the feelings of cohesiveness often stall the group and keep it from moving to the next stage.

Stage 4: Performing As the team continues to work and develop processes and methods to accomplish their tasks, members work singly, in subgroups, and as a total unit. They begin functioning as a group of mature and interdependent individuals. They both cooperate and compete; there is support for experimenting with alternative ways of making decisions and solving problems. In interpersonal relations, team members feel highly interdependent, but neither dependent nor counterdependent. Harmony for its own sake is replaced by individual freedom and a strong emphasis on productivity.

In real-life working groups, of course, the interpersonal relations issues and the task issues are dealt with jointly and simultaneously. Although we separated them at times for convenience, organizational groups cope with interpersonal problems and task problems as though they are pretty much the same. The ability to recognize some differences, however, may allow members to catch thorny issues that may be stalling the team.

All too often the major concern of the team is to solve a specific task problem, without considering how group processes might be improved so as to solve problems more effectively in the long run. More attention should usually be paid to how the team itself functions, to what behaviors help the team accomplish its work. Groups, especially work groups, seldom examine how they operate. Except for the expletives uttered when something goes wrong, team members usually focus almost exclusively on difficulties with the task. It may be that the group has interpersonal problems that interfere with the way in which it functions. If a little time were devoted to discovering why the team functions so badly, it might be making a solid investment with great dividends in the future.

GROUP DYNAMICS

A group usually serves three functions for its members: (1) It satisfies interpersonal needs, (2) it provides support for individual self-concepts, and (3) it protects individuals from their own mistakes (Hampton, Summer, & Webber, 1973). Besides helping individual members in those areas, the group takes on an identity, or self-concept, of its own. The group acquires some goals of its own. Occasionally individual goals conflict with group goals; sometimes group goals differ from those of the larger organization, but sometimes the goals are all very similar. The way in which the group or team progresses through the four stages from getting organized to being productive is related to how the group copes with three important aspects of group life: (1) the roles or activities performed by group members, (2) the norms and differences in status that develop as members interact, and (3) the conflict that evolves from pressures to behave competitively rather than cooperatively (Huse & Bowditch, 1973). The interaction among individual needs, group goals, and the roles, norms, and conflict of group functioning is what we call the *dynamics* of the group. Let us now look at the three aspects of group life and how they contribute or detract from the way in which groups and teams accomplish their goals.

Roles of Team Members

The two broadest objectives of team interaction and group dynamics are:

1. To keep the group or team together and functioning smoothly (to maintain a highly cohesive group), and
2. To keep the group or team working on the task at hand (to maintain a task-orientation through a systematic approach to solving problems).

Because individual group members possess different skills, tastes, and abilities, various members usually discover rather quickly that they can perform different behaviors effectively and that all or many of these behaviors can contribute to group cohesiveness and productivity. As work on the task progresses, group members may discover that still other skills are required to move the interaction forward. One or possibly several members may have such skills. If so, certain members of the group will then have to accept the required specialized roles and thus become differentiated from one another. In a limited sense, task specialization occurs in most groups and teams, although not in the same sense that "job descriptions" are specified by business organizations. In groups and teams, only for such task specialists as secretary or recorder are fairly precise behaviors specified.

Benne and Sheats (1948) identified and classified the functional roles enacted by group and team members into three broad categories:

1. Those that facilitate group effect in problem solving (task roles).
2. Those that maintain, strengthen, regulate, and perpetuate the group or team itself (maintenance roles).
3. Those that hinder group progress and effort by focusing on the satisfaction of individual needs that are irrelevant or antithetical to task accomplishment and group maintenance (hindering roles).

Task Roles Behaviors such as offering ideas, suggesting methods and plans, asking for information and opinions, prodding people along, and handling procedural activities, such as distributing papers and recording ideas, all contribute to the smooth functioning of a group or team. These types of behaviors help to get the job done.

Maintenance Roles Behaviors such as providing praise, expressing warmth and support, mediating differences, listening to others, accepting group decisions, introducing some humor to relax the group, and bringing in group members who might not otherwise speak also contribute to the smooth functioning of a team. These types of behaviors keep the team together.

Hindering Roles Behaviors such as opposing or resisting anyone in the group who represents authority, attacking the status of others, opposing group ideas stubbornly and for personal reasons, asserting superiority to control and interrupt others, using flattery to patronize group members, clowning and engaging in horseplay and ridicule, and staying off the subject under discussion to avoid making a commitment represent ways to thwart the progress of the team. These types of behaviors prevent the group from getting the job done and discourage members from staying together.

Group Norms and Status

As a group progresses through the stages in group development, it begins to acquire a life of its own, a history and culture, that is revealed through the expression of similar feelings, beliefs, and values among team members. A commonality of feelings and beliefs is often referred to as a *norm*, or standard of appropriate and acceptable behavior. The tendency to associate with people who share common feelings, beliefs, and values; to listen to and accept their ideas; and to defend their points of view also strengthens team and group solidarity and exerts pressure on members not to deviate from team decisions.

If you are assigned to or find yourself functioning in a team whose values are different from your own, you will probably find yourself in a position in which you must decide whether (1) to accept the new values, (2) to try to bring about a change in the values of the team, or (3) to leave the team. Employment may bring you into a team in which the values of the overall organization are different from yours. You will have to decide how to cope with the norms of acceptable behavior in that organization and team.

Although norms in a group are strong influences toward conformity or similarity in behavior, they also reveal differences among members. Once you have established yourself in a group or team and demonstrate that you are able to respond according to group norms, a conflicting need often emerges: the need for status or prestige. Even within small work teams, some subtle differences in status are usually apparent. The norms that indicate how we should behave in the team often define your status—the respect or disrespect, familiarity or unfamiliarity, reserve or frankness we are to show in your presence indicates how you are different from the rest of the group (Hampton, Summer, & Webber, 1973). If you fail to treat people with the appropriate degree of respect or disrespect, you may be subject to punishment for violating group norms.

The factors that accord individuals status in any particular group vary from group to group. A person's family background, name, or relatives may provide status in some organizations. In some jobs, education, seniority, age, sex, or ethnic background may contribute to higher status. Such personal characteristics as physical size, dress and general appearance, sociability, friendliness, self-confidence, and status in another group (such as an athletic club) may all influence perceptions of status. On the job, a person's title, job description, compensation, privileges, freedom from direct supervision, office location, furnishings, and potential for upward mobility may be considered when others assign status. Regardless of what elements determine status in your group or team, you can be pretty certain that the best positions will be occupied by high-status individuals.

Competition and Conflict within the Team

Individual roles and group norms and status affect the way in which team members communicate with each another. In addition, most team members have occasion to cooperate and to compete with each other. A situation in which rewards are limited so that one group member gets rewards and other members lose them is usually called one of *competition*. If group members believe that no one will be rewarded unless they all contribute to the task, the situation is usually called one of *cooperation*.

In some work teams, an external authority determines how the rewards are to be distributed among team members. The boss creates or works within a system in which pay, recognition, promotions, and other rewards are given according to conditions established by the organization. Thus, whether team members are to function in a competitive or a cooperative atmosphere is decided by the organization.

On the other hand, a single team member may create a competitive atmosphere even if the organization is attempting to have groups work cooperatively. By monopolizing the time, using more space than others, consuming a large number of supplies, or traveling more than other team members, one individual may be viewed as taking something that is scarce and of value to all team members. If the resource is considered limited, the one member may make competition an inevitable consequence of being a team member just by getting more than his or her share.

Most groups, of course, have some cooperative activities and some competitive ones. To accomplish a task, they may be required to cooperate. Nevertheless, individual team members may still compete for personal rewards such as admiration, approval, affections, and power. Few rewards, whether personal or material, are distributed equally. Differences in roles and status lead to perceptions that rewards are distributed competitively.

In self-directed or self-managed work teams, however, cooperation is far more important than in traditional organizations. Teams require players who are empowered and feel that they are authorized to guide and coordinate their own work. The need for communication accelerates so that more face-to-face contacts occur so that everyone is involved and communicated with. To manage their own lives, team members must be heard and feel committed to the team. There is little doubt that the one area in which the skills of organizational communication specialists can be brought to bear with maximum benefit to organizations is in the implementation and development of self-managed work teams.

Self-directed or self-managed teams are so different from what we are accustomed to in traditional organizations that those involved will need training in this new way of working. The training issues range throughout the topics covered in this chapter as well as others and include problem solving, communication skills, team meetings, managing conflict, team development, and information flow and availability. The major barrier to the adoption of self-directed work teams and practices is insufficient training in the critical areas of self-management.

Effects of Competition on Team Functioning

When team members view their roles as highly competitive, they tend to listen less to what other members say, to understand less well what was actually said, become less interested in high achievement, help one another less, have more difficulty coordinating their team's efforts, are more likely to duplicate efforts of others so as to do the work themselves, tend to be less efficient, and tend to do lower quality work. In addition, they may not like what they have accomplished, and may not like the group with whom they worked or each other as individuals.

Effects of Cooperation on Team Functioning

When team members view their roles as highly cooperative, they tend to show more coordination of their efforts. There is greater diversity of contributions per group member, with more subdivision of activities. Group members tend to be more attentive, have higher mutual comprehension of information, and make more common appraisals of information. Cooperative teams tend to exhibit a clearer orientation and orderliness with more pressures toward achievement. Communication seems more friendly, and the group and its products are evaluated more favorably.

Not all jobs demand the same degree of competition and cooperation. Some kinds of work require creative performances that may receive strong stimulation from competition; other work requires the careful and complete cooperation of every team member to be successful. The ideal balance between competition and cooperation is a continuing issue and relates directly to the type of work that is being done. Regardless, competition and cooperation have different effects on team work. Competition is more likely to lead to conflicts within the group.

PROBLEM-SOLVING PROCESSES

In most organizations we can observe people working in groups and teams to solve problems. The quality of any decision is a function of the process used in arriving at the decision. That is why so much time and effort is put into designing systems and procedures for doing things. Law enforcement agencies have been obligated over the years to adopt procedures for ensuring that the rights of criminal defendants are protected. How defendants are handled, what is said to them, and when they are to be advised have been determined because the sequence has been found to influence the way in which decisions are made and how civil rights are protected. Problem solving is based on a similar philosophy. The process that a group follows in solving problems affects the quality of the solutions. There are some generally accepted stages through which any problem-solving group should proceed to cover adequately the major issues involved in finding solutions to problems. We list four of these basic steps below.

1. Recognize and clearly describe the existence of a problem.
2. Generate ways to respond to the problem.
3. Select the most useful or effective solution/ideas.
4. Make a decision about which ideas to implement and proceed to take specific steps necessary to resolve the problem.

These are ordinarily viewed as the broad stages in problem solving; however, certain intermediate steps must be taken if there is to be productive interaction and if an ultimate solution is to be reached. Although some of these intermediate phases may seem obvious, they are often omitted, which negates or nullifies the team's effort to achieve a good and workable solution.

Recognize and Describe the Problem

One of the first concerns in effective team problem solving is to get agreement from team members that they have a mutual problem or set of problems that need considering. Such an agreement should not be assumed or taken for granted. To explore the nature of probable or potential problems requires an openness and a willingness to investigate and accept different ways of perceiving and behaving. All of us tend to resist change; and since solving a problem strongly implies the possibility of making changes, many of us carry around a kind of built-in resistance—a resistance that can mount at the moment we discover that a task group is to be assembled. In a sense, we interpret the event as a personal criticism of the status quo—the way in which we have been handling things; we are offended at the mere thought that something might be wrong. We stress this point because the very act of assuming the existence of a problem can set up a serious, initial barrier to continued communication on the issue.

Mutual recognition of the existence of a problem, while essential, is not enough. Group members must make a commitment, explicitly or implicitly, of their willingness to discuss the possible problem. If this kind of group commitment is not achieved very early in the process, numerous irrelevant, nontask interactions and messages are almost sure to intervene. This, of course, can waste much valuable time and create additional barriers.

The necessary willingness to talk about the difficulty can be facilitated if all group members feel impelled to interact because of a similar intensity of desire to engage in an analysis of the problem. If the group as a whole lacks sufficient concern to take such a problem-solving posture, or if even individual team members seem uninterested and uninvolved, attempts to pursue the task seriously very probably will create disruptive or at least nonproductive relationships rather than a positive, congenial, and enthusiastic focus on the task at hand. Underlying all of these initial phases of the process is the necessity for establishing an atmosphere in which team members will want to begin to talk about the conditions that seem to be provoking their interest or disturbing it. Out of such talk, the real nature of the problem should begin to emerge.

Usually, in the beginning, the nature of the problem tends to be only partially understood or is only dimly defined. In fact, group members may not even be sure that they have a problem. Therefore, to determine whether you, in fact, have a problem that needs solving, merely ask yourself such questions as:

"What would I like to have that I do not now possess?"

"What would I like to accomplish that I am being prevented from accomplishing?"

"What feeling or feelings would I like to have that I do not now have?"

Implicit in these questions are at least three major dimensions of a problem: (1) The ways things are now, (2) the way we think they ought to be, and (3) a desire to reduce the discrepancy between (1) and (2). In other words, problems arise from looking at what we have, wanting something else, and being unable to get it. Therefore, when we want something and cannot seem to obtain or achieve it, we have a problem. Viewed from this perspective, one of the easiest and quickest ways to solve problems is to stop wanting things. Quite likely you are acquainted with some people who take that approach in coping with their difficulties; they simply stop wanting and passively accept the world as it develops. For most of us, however, the mainspring of human action surges from our desire to improve what we have and what we do. We want to articulate, dissect, discuss, and—if possible—find workable solutions to our dilemmas.

One useful way in which we can try to identify and analyze a problem is to diagram it into the three essential parts so as to visualize the components. At this stage of the problem-solving process, we recommend that you "translate" whatever looks like any problem-producing incident, condition, or situation into the dimensions portrayed in Figure 12.1.

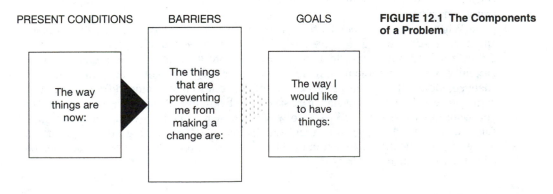

PRESENT CONDITIONS   BARRIERS   GOALS

FIGURE 12.1 The Components of a Problem

The way things are now:

The things that are preventing me from making a change are:

The way I would like to have things:

Obstacles may occur, of course, in any one or more of these area-dimensions. Part of the subprocess of analyzing a problem is to locate it as specifically as possible within the scheme of things. Sometimes it is necessary to pinpoint the source of the "problem within the problem," so to speak. This involves discerning the point-of-obstruction or bottleneck that is interfering with an otherwise desirable and possible solution to the difficulty. Usually this requires looking at the situation in the light of the problem-solving process as a whole and then pointing to the place in the process where the obstacle or obstruction can probably be found.

In team work, the most likely and common trouble spots occur in (a) the procedures used, (b) team member behaviors, (c) team member feelings, (d) team member possessions, and (e) team member's involvement in events. For example, procedures cause problems when they are too long and drawn out—when we sense that better procedures might solve the problems in a shorter time. Procedures are viewed also as problems when they are too complicated, or too inefficient, or too disorganized, or are not dependable, or when they make us uncomfortable.

Team member behaviors create problems when they appear to be irresponsible, discourteous, condescending, or too impersonal. All of us, no doubt, have observed how people allow their feelings to obstruct productive work; they are "hypersensitive" or they believe that others are "treading on their toes." Possessions pose a problem when ownership seems to be threatened by the approach or the line of development being taken by the team, when there is a suspicion or fear that one or more of the possible solutions will affect vested interests in or change the ownership of the possessions. Finally, events—real, described, or imagined—may, in themselves, have uncertain outcomes; and fear of the unknown can be considerable, especially as a deterrent to any decision or proposed action. Locating and handling these problems calls for a continuing sensitivity to and an awareness of human needs and a skill in reducing defensiveness both in ourselves and in others.

At the identification stage of problem solving, we endeavor to come to some agreement among team members on what ought to be changed. If, for instance, we agree that a given procedure ought to be better organized, we have identified a problem. Of course, we ought to be able to explain why or in what way the procedure should be improved, because problem analysis involves getting the group to agree on the reasons why the proposed change is desirable. We must not lose sight of the fact that, very often, making a change is based on knowing what to change. If we can agree on what needs to be changed and why it ought to be changed—be it procedure, feelings, possessions, or events—we have actually analyzed the problem. However, before we can proceed to a consideration of the ways to solve the problem there is one other highly important step that we must take.

When we reach the point where, as team members, we have identified the problem and have made at least a tentative analysis of it, we must state the problem in the most discussable and potentially solvable terms. The problem question is a clear, concise, carefully worded statement—usually in interrogative form—of exactly what is to be changed. Quite often, phrasing this question turns out to be the most difficult part of the entire process. If you cannot state here—near the beginning of the process—exactly what you want to change, you will have no way of knowing whether—at the end—you have succeeded in developing a sound and satisfactory way of bringing about that change. Some of the difficulties inherent in the phrasing of the problem question are demonstrated in the following examples:

Example One

Suppose you have a mouse in your home. What is your problem? Some say that it is to find a mousetrap. Is that really the problem? Consider for a moment what it is that you want to change. Do you want to change from not possessing a mousetrap to possessing one? We doubt it! What you probably want is to get rid of the mouse. The problem question could be phrased: How can we rid our home of the mouse? Or: In what ways might we catch the mouse in our home? The important feature to note here is that in both problem statements the question raises an issue directly related to the kind of change you would like to make.

Example Two

Suppose you have an employee who does not seem to be working as hard as you, the team members, would like. What is your problem? You might say that it is to decide whether to dismiss or not dismiss this employee. But is the state of the employee's employment/nonemployment what you really want to change? You will need to make that decision before you can determine whether you do, in fact, have a problem. If you decide to dismiss the employee, you have no problem. Just do it. If you decide to retain the employee's services, you also have no problem. Just do it. You have a problem only when you want to change the employee. Assuming for the moment that you wish to retain the employee, how—in what specific way or ways—do you want the employee to change? Presumably, you want the person to work harder. Your problem could be stated: How can we get this employee to work harder? Or: In what particular ways might we influence this employee to perform more effectively on the job? You might need to ask yourself: "What specific behaviors do we want this employee to change?" The more precisely you can identify the particular behavior or behaviors that need changing, the higher will be the probability of developing a satisfactory way of bringing about the change. For any given employee, incident, or event, you may have to ask yourself several questions of this kind.

In group and team work in which several individuals must formulate the problem question and eventually agree on a solution, the difficulties demonstrated in Examples 1 and 2 will enlarge considerably and grow proportionately more complex. Getting the entire team to participate in and agree upon the phrasing of the problem question is clearly a major task involving all of the organizational communication skills you can muster. The willingness of the team to incorporate the point of view of each of its members will almost inevitably be revealed by a readiness to incorporate modifications, concessions, and compromises in the tentative and final phrasing of the problem question.

Always attempt to get complete agreement on the phrasing of the problem questions, even if you must return again and again to the phrasing as the team evolves and develops. The problem question and way in which it is worded is the solid launching base from which the remainder of the work proceeds; it is the compass that guides the direction of the team; it is the meter by which, from time to time, you measure team progress; and, finally, it is the navigational device pointing the way to the destination at which you hope to arrive.

Generate Ideas

Once you have recognized and stated the problem accurately, the next major step in team problem solving is to find ways of accomplishing what you want to do. We refer to this phase of the process as *idea-generation*. To illuminate this stage of the process more clearly, we offer this example.

In the forests of this country, a great deal of timber is cut for commercial use in the building industry, for making paper, and for other important purposes. As timber is cut, the limbs are trimmed and left lying in the area; only the larger logs are hauled away. The limbs, small logs, and broken pieces of tress that are left behind are referred to as "slash." Slash accumulates, tends to be unsightly, and is often difficult for animals, as well as hunters and other who use the forest, to get through. Suppose, for purposes of this example, that we are confronted with the problem question: What can be done with slash after an area has been logged?

What we want, first of all, are a lot of ideas. We are not very much concerned with whether the ideas are feasible or acceptable, but only whether the ideas suggest ways of doing things with slash. Matters of feasibility and acceptability will be deferred until a later time. Parnes (1966) refers to the procedure of generating ideas first and evaluating them later as the Principle of Deferred Judgment (p. 35). Applying this principle, you attempt to list as many different ways of disposing of slash as you can. Your emphasis should be on ways. As Osborn (1963) observed, "The more ideas you think up, the more likely you are to arrive at the potentially best leads to solutions" (p. 124). So, suspending judgment and listing as many ways (both good and bad) as you can possibly think of, generate a long list of potential, alternative ways to dispose of slash. Some of the methods in use at this time are listed below. See how many new ideas you can add to this list:

1. Do nothing; let slash decompose naturally.
2. Burn the area with a controlled fire.
3. Pile slash with a bulldozer and burn in large stacks.
4. Cut slash into small pieces, pile them by hand, and burn.
5. Cut slash into small pieces and disperse them somewhat evenly over the logged area.
6. Cut slash into small pieces and feed them into a wood chipper for hauling to a pulp mill.
7. Chop slash into uneven pieces and let them lie.

Once you have a large number of ideas, the next phase involves grouping the ideas for an analysis of their feasibility and usefulness in accomplishing the desired change. Grouping consists primarily of placing together those ideas that use similar approaches. For example, we might group the methods listed above for handling slash under such categories as:

Burning

Burn the area with a controlled fire. (2)
Pile slash with a bulldozer and burn in large stacks. (3)
Cut slash into small pieces, pile them by hand, and burn. (4)

Leaving

Do nothing; let slash decompose naturally. (1)
Cut slash into small pieces and disperse them somewhat evenly over the logged area. (5)
Chop slash into uneven pieces and let them lie. (7)

Removing

Cut slash into small pieces and feed them into a wood chipper for hauling to a pulp mill. (6)

In problem solving, such grouping can trigger new ideas, reveal complementary ideas, identify duplicate suggestions, and—possibly—suggest groupings in which additional ideas might be desirable or necessary.

During the idea-generating stage of team problem solving, no concern should be given to eliminating duplicate, irrelevant, or inadequate ideas. Just list them all. When you have written down all of the ideas that the team can think of, begin to rearrange them into groups. As the ideas are grouped, pay particular attention to ways of modifying them to make them more usable or more striking. Once the ideas are grouped, move to the next step: selection of useful ideas.

Selecting the Most Useful Ideas

The selection of useful ideas is the first phase in the actual decision-making process. With a large accumulation of useful ideas in mind, we can begin to discriminate among those ideas for purposes of determining which ones can be utilized in making the proposed change or changes. At this point in the process, the communicative activity should center around examining the consequences of the various alternatives that are being proposed. The purpose is to select those ideas that provide the maximum benefit and the minimum detriment. Benefit and detriment are, of course, often personal, individualized conceptions and involve values and feelings. For instance, certain solutions may seem the "soundest" to some of the team members; other members might feel that the solutions are not the most "beneficial" because they violate personal values.

This balancing of values, of weighing one idea against another, is unquestionably the most difficult phase for teams and is the one most likely to arouse defensive responses. Disagreements flourish when people attempt to decide which consequences are essential, which ones are not essential, which ones are entirely unacceptable, and which ones can at least be tolerated. Despite the obvious complexities of the task and its inherent pitfalls, however, the most likely and potentially useful ideas must be identified and cataloged for tentative implementation. This can be accomplished if everyone involved will reveal his or her preferences and explain the reasons for preferring those particular ideas. In this phase, methods of conflict resolution may prove especially valuable in resolving differences and selecting the most beneficial ideas.

Make a Decision

The culmination of the selection process arrives when the actual decision is made to adopt a particular solution for the problem. Although in any given case there may be several ways of reaching a decision, it is of utmost importance that team members agree on the method to be used. Again, this need for maximal agreement can prove to be a difficult communicative task in a small group like a team. The team's goal in this regard must be to reach a level of acceptance where each individual abides by a decision arrived at in a particular way. To achieve such an objective is often time-consuming and likely to engender a considerable amount of conflict. Nevertheless, the decision-making process cannot be completed unless a systematic way of resolving differences or overcoming indifferences can be accepted by all. Paradoxical though it may seem, even a refusal or failure to make a choice involves the making of a decision. The following is a brief, descriptive summary of some of the most commonly used strategies for making choices in the culminating phase of problem solving:

1. *Bypassing.* An idea is offered, but before it can be discussed or brought before the group for formal action, another idea is presented. The first idea is simply bypassed and allowed to fail through inaction.
2. *Power.* The most important, prestigious, authoritative, or otherwise powerful person in the group actively supports the idea and acts on the assumption that all others agree. Holding the power, the holder is able unilaterally to make the choice.
3. *Vocal Coalition.* A vocal minority of the group creates the impression that widespread support exists for an idea. Because the other members of the group fail to offer their objections, the seeming strength of the vocal coalition makes the choice.
4. *Majority Vote.* Through the procedures of a poll (show of hands, voice vote, or secret ballot), the idea supported by more than one half of the group is accepted.
5. *Plurality.* On occasion, although a choice must be made, a majority cannot be developed in favor of a particular idea. Plurality allows for the idea having the largest number of supporters to be accepted as the group decision. Political elections, for example, are often determined by plurality rather than majority vote.
6. *Consensus.* When communication among members of the group has been genuinely open and receptive, and when each person has been able to express his or her opinion and tender objections, agreements can be reached at the point when members are willing to subscribe to the idea even if they have some reservations about it. Consensus represents support for a majority opinion given willingly and as a consequence of the members' understanding of that opinion and the fact that they have influenced its shape during interaction.
7. *Unanimity.* Unanimity occurs when all members of the group actually agree on the selection of an idea or a solution. Usually, important group decisions are reached by consensus; but there are times when complete agreement by all members should be sought.

Decisions, we must remember, do not represent the end of the problem-solving process. The group—having decided upon a solution to a problem facing it—must proceed to take whatever steps it can to set in motion the machinery necessary to achieve the end result. To be effective and bring about the desired change, ideas must always be translated into workable plans and implemented on the job, in the reality of the pertinent situation.

Often the actual task of putting the chosen solution into practice is assigned to a group of technical specialists. In some organizations, decisions are made at the management level, and plans are then implemented at the operational level. When a decision made at one level must be carried out at another level, continuing communication ought to be maintained between both levels. Indeed, those responsible for implementing the solution might well be brought into the problem solving process at the earliest possible moment because this will help ensure adequate understanding, intelligent involvement, and meaningful participation in determining the change or change for which members will be held accountable.

Team Building

A team is a complete work group or work unit in which its members have at least one common goal and the accomplishment of that goal requires cooperative behavior on the part of all members (Burke, 1982, p. 268). Team building is an intervention conducted in a work unit to improve its operations (Dyer, 1977, p. 41). Four purposes of team building have been identified by Beckhard (1972):

1. To set team goals and priorities;
2. To allocate work among team members;
3. To improve the way in which the team works; and
4. To improve team procedures and processes.

We shall discuss each of these purposes and some of the methods employed to achieve them.

Setting Goals and Priorities The first step in team building is to assist the members in clarifying the primary goal of the team and to establish subgoals to be accomplished in some order of priority. Goal setting should be accomplished first because interpersonal difficulties may be a result of failure of the team to recognize and agree upon what is to be achieved. In addition, problems with the way (procedures and processes) in which the team works may also be associated with lack of clarity about team goals and priorities. Starting a team building effort by first focusing on interpersonal problems or roles and responsibilities or procedures and processes may be a misuse of time and effort.

Procedures for goal setting and establishing priorities with a team have been described by Dyer (1977) and Burke (1982), among others. Helping a team set goals may be achieved in the following way:

> Have each member of the team privately write down the central or core purpose or goal of the team; that is, members should state what each person thinks is the reason why the team was created. Out of the central purpose of the team should come the subgoals and purposes and the priorities of the team. Team members should reveal their statements by means of posting them on newsprint or sharing them orally. Then, team members should discuss the statements and create a single goal statement that represents the most accurate reflection of the central purpose of the team. This final statement should be printed on newsprint and displayed prominently in the work area. In fact, each team member should have a personal copy of the statement. During subsequent team discussions, this central purpose statement should serve as the standard against which other plans and actions are evaluated in terms of whether or not they will help accomplish the central purpose.

During this first step, team members should also evolve a clear statement of some subpurposes or goals to be accomplished by the team. The subpurposes should contribute to achieving the central purpose. The same procedure as used for stating the central purpose could be used again. Individually, team members write down what each one feels are the three or four primary subpurposes or goals that come out of the central purpose. They each post their lists, and together they select, state, and list the subgoals in an order of importance or priority to be implemented.

After the central goal, purpose, or mission of the team has been identified, recorded, and agreed upon, and the subgoals, purposes, or objectives have been identified, recorded, and agreed upon, the team is ready to move to the second phase in team development.

Formulating Operating Guidelines and Allocating Work The development of operating guidelines means determining how the team will work during its period of existence. During this period of time, team members should discuss and decide how the team will make decisions. For example, members could use a majority vote (more than half), consensus (agreement by the entire team), or by a plurality (the largest number of votes).

To allocate work means making decisions about what roles and responsibilities each member of the team will perform. Decisions about roles and responsibilities in a group may be made by having team members share their views about roles and responsibilities with one another, after which they can negotiate the best fit for purposes of the team. During the negotiation phase, team members may be asked to indicate for other team members what they should do more of or do better, do less of or stop doing, or continuing doing in order to fulfill their roles and responsibilities more effectively.

The team also needs to decide how it will make certain that everyone gets a chance to talk about the issues and raise concerns that seem of importance to each team member. Such discussions may involve differences of opinion, so it is important to have ways of resolving differences. A third party could be appointed to meet and help participants talk through the differences, or the third party could in fact be empowered to recommend compromises.

Finally, teams need to have procedures for making certain that they will complete their work. That is, team members must be committed to devoting the time and energy necessary to fulfill assignments. It may be helpful to have summaries of activities to be completed, reports of work accomplished, and procedures for making contact with team members while they are working independently. If the assignments do get finished, alternative ways must be available for transferring tasks and for producing results.

Improving the Way in Which the Team Works At the heart of team functioning are relationships among team members. Difficulties in interpersonal relations and communication are revealed by symptoms that surface during group dynamics (Varney, 1989, pp. 100–102). For example, team members may complain about and find fault with one another or express suspicion and distrust of select members of the team. In some instances, some team members may verbally blow up and yell at one another or exhibit other signs of distress. On occasion, team members may seek endless details having to do with both major and minor actions of the team, resulting in excessive time in reaching decisions. Frequently, the team shifts position or changes its decisions after they have been made.

The goals of a facilitator or person working to improve team functioning by focusing on relationships and communication should be to keep the discussion and interaction focused on the task or topic and moving toward a decision or action. The facilitator should intervene in the discussion to help team members maintain respect, trust, and support, to help them to express their ideas, opinions and feelings openly, and to help team members manage differences so as to arrive at an integrated decision. The facilitator should tactfully prevent any single team member from dominating the discussion or from being ignored by the team, and to assist the team in using the variety of skills of team members. Finally, the facilitator should seek to bring some resolution to discussions so that decisions may be made, and within particular time restraints. If the team is unable to bring a discussion to a close within the time limits, team members should decide whether to continue the discussion at the expense of other items of business or to delay discussion to another time.

Moosbruker (1988) has identified specific interpersonal behaviors associated with each stage in team development. At the forming or orientation stage, for example, team members may direct their comments exclusively to the leader. They may continually seek clarification and direction, with most issues being discussed quite superficially. The status of team members may be based on their roles outside the team.

At the storming or conflict stage, team members attempt to gain influence through subgroups and coalitions. The leader is challenged and tested both overtly and covertly, and team members judge and evaluate one another, resulting in ideas being rejected and the task not being achieved.

At the norming or cohesiveness stage, team members may disagree with the leader and withhold support from one another, but the group laughs, has some fun, and makes jokes at the leader's expense; overall, however, they have a sense of cohesiveness and respond to groups norms. Members tend not to challenge one another as much as they should.

Finally, at the performing or problem-solving stage, team members take the initiative and accept one another because their roles are clear and each person is able to make a distinctive contribution. Discussion is open, members challenge one another and seek feedback from one another, as well as from the leader in order to improve their performance. Team members engage in authentic problem solving.

Team building requires helping the team move through the four stages in development. Focusing on the relevant interpersonal behaviors may be a critical form of intervention.

Improving Team Procedures and Processes The final purpose to be achieved in team building is the improvement of processes and procedures that facilitate team work. Two categories of activities are relevant in team building at this point. One is the creation and use of an agenda and the other is facilitating human processes. Schein (1969) has identified six crucial human processes relevant to effective organization functioning: communication, functional roles, problem solving, norms, authority, and cooperation. These same processes find their most common expression in team work. Process consultation, an intervention discussed in Chapter 16, focuses on methods for improving these processes, so we shall defer specific discussion of process issues to Chapter 16.

Because of the central nature of agendas to effective team functioning, we shall devote the remainder of this section to a discussion of agendas. The use of an agenda is usually discussed in the context of team structuring (Pace, Peterson, & Burnett, 1979). Structuring a team consists of three somewhat distinct steps that involve planning for team discussion, acquainting team members with procedures, and orienting the team to the topic, objectives, and tasks.

A team should create and use an agenda for each meeting. An agenda is a systematic presentation of the topics to be discussed at a meeting of the team. An agenda is constructed by creating a tally sheet of important topics to be discussed by the team. Then, using the tally sheet, one or two team members select the items to be discussed. The agenda should include some standard items such as the call to order, roll call, reading and approval of minutes of previous meetings, and the introduction of guests.

The formal part of the agenda consists of the topics to be discussed and the order in which they are to be discussed. Time should be allocated for each item of business. The role of a facilitator often includes helping the team deal with agenda items in the time allocated. The agenda often identifies the name of the person who originated or raised the item or the person who is most knowledgeable about it. Team meetings and the agenda include a short time period for reviewing the agenda itself.

Part of the team-building process involves helping the team learn how to create an agenda and use one. A sample agenda for the first meeting of a team might look like the following:

PROJECT TEAM _____ **DATE** _____

1. Call to order [tap a bell or the table, say, "Please come to order"], and call the roll [to make certain everyone is present] (2 mins).
2. Review the agenda and/or approve the minutes of previous meeting [delete items, add pressing items, check to see whether estimated times are appropriate, and comment on action to be taken, such as announcing decision, discussion, vote] (5 mins).
3. Brief introductions of team members (10 mins).
4. Review primary purpose of team (15 mins).
5. Help team members get acquainted with each other by conducting an ice breaker/introductions exercise (20 mins).
6. Explain any special roles, such as facilitator, quality advisor, and process evaluator (15 mins).
7. Discuss ground rules, norms, and housekeeping (10 mins).
8. Introduce concepts basic to proceeding to next meeting (10 mins).
9. Give assignments for the next meeting; set day and time (10 mins).

Sample Agenda for a Regular Meeting of a Team

PROJECT TEAM _____ **DATE** _____

1. Call to order
2. Review agenda
3. Status reports on assignments and responsibilities
4. Other presentations and discussion of items
5. Review status of project
6. Give assignments for follow-up activities
7. Review events, special meetings, etc., for future
8. Review items on action list
9. Review items on future action list
10. List agenda items for next regular meeting
11. Refreshments or special activity
12. Adjourn

SUMMARY

In this chapter we have described teams, groups, and communication. We touched upon differences between ways in which teams are formed, the stages through which they develop in order to move from infancy to maturity, the dynamics that affect how teams function, and the processes by which teams and groups solve problems.

The move toward the implementation of self-managed work teams in business and industry both in this country and globally poses a challenge and an opportunity for specialists prepared in organizational communication. At the center of group and team processes is the factor of communication. Critical to the effective functioning of self-managed teams are communicative processes and practices.

REFERENCES

BALES, ROBERT F., and F.L. STRODTBECK, "Phases in Group Problem Solving," *Journal of Abnormal and Social Psychology*, 46 (1951), 485-495.

BECKHARD, RICHARD, "Optimizing Team-Building Efforts," *Journal of Contemporary Business* (Summer 1972), 23–37.

BENNE, KENNETH, and P. SHEATS, "Functional Roles of Group Members," *Journal of Social Issues*, 4 (1948), 41–49.

BENNIS, WARREN G., and H.A. SHEPARD, "A Theory of Group Development," *Human Relations*, 9 (1956), 415–437.

BORMANN, ERNEST G., and NANCY C. BORMANN, *Effective Small Group Communication*. Minneapolis: Burgess, 1980.

BURKE, W. WARNER, *Organizational Development: Principles and Practices*. Boston: Little, Brown, 1982.

COONRADT, CHARLES A., *The Game of Work*. Salt Lake City: Shadow Mountain, 1984.

DYER, WILLIAM G., *Team Building: Issues and Alternatives*. Reading, Mass.: Addison-Wesley, 1977.

FISHER, B. AUBREY, "Decision Emergence: Phases in Group Decision-Making," *Speech Monographs*, 37 (1970), 53–66.

HACKMAN, J. RICHARD ,and GREG R. OLDHAM, *Work Redesign*. Reading, Mass.: Addison-Wesley, 1980.

HAMPTON, DAVID R., CHARLES E. SUMMER, and ROSS E. WEBBER, *Organizational Behavior and the Practice of Management* (rev. ed.). Glenview, Ill.: Scott, Foresman, 1973.

HOERR, JOHN, "The Payoff From Teamwork," *Business Week* (July 10, 1989), 56–62.

HUSE, EDGAR F., and JAMES L. BOWDITCH, *Behavior in Organizations: A Systems Approach to Managing*. Reading, Mass.: Addison-Wesley, 1973.

KETCHUM, LYMAN D., and ERIC TRIST, *All Teams Are Not Created Equal*. Newbury Park, Calif.: Sage Publications, Inc., 1992.

LEBARON, MEL, *Workable Workplace*. Brea, Calif.: Et Cetera, Et Cetera Graphics, 1988.

MOOSBRUKER, JANE, "Developing a Productivity Team: Making Groups at Work," in *Team Building: Blueprints for Productivity and Satisfaction*, W. Brendan Reddy and Kaleel Jamison, eds. Alexandria, Va.: NTL Institute for Applied Behavioral Science, 1988.

OSBORN, ALEX F., *Applied Imagination*, (3rd rev. ed.). New York: Charles Scribners's Sons, 1963.

PACE, R. WAYNE, BRENT D. PETERSON, and M. DALLAS BURNETT, *Techniques for Effective Communication*. Reading, Mass.: Addison-Wesley, 1979.

PARNES, SIDNEY J., *Instructor's Manual for Institutes and Courses in Creative Problem-Solving*. Buffalo, N.Y.: Creative Education Foundation, 1966.

SCHEIN, EDGAR H., *Process Consultation: Its Role in Organization Development*. Reading, Mass.: Addison-Wesley, 1969.

SCHUTZ, WILLIAM, *FIRO: A Three-Dimensional Theory of Interpersonal Behavior*. New York: Holt, Rinehart & Winston, 1958.

SCOTT, WILLIAM G., and DAVID K. HART, *Organizational Values in America*. New Brunswick, N.J.: Transaction Books, 1989.

SMITH, PETER B., *Groups Within Organizations*. New York: Harper & Row, Pub., 1973.

TAYLOR, JAMES C., and DAVID F. FELTEN, *Performance by Design*. Englewood Cliffs, N.J.: Prentice-Hall, 1993.

TUCKMAN, B.W., "Developmental Sequence in Small Groups," *Psychological Bulletin*, 63 (1965), 384–399.

VARNEY, GLENN H., *Building Productive Teams*. San Francisco: Jossey-Bass, 1989.

WILKINS, ALAN L., *Developing Corporate Character*. San Francisco: Josey-Bass, 1989.

13

Stress, Conflict, and Organizational Communication

One of the most serious problems facing organization members today is that of *Stress!* Ray (1991) has pointed out that the literature on job-related stress consistently demonstrates that stress has destructive, harmful, and detrimental effects on both the physical and psychological well-being of workers. Heaney and van Ryn (1990) explain that occupational stress has been linked to both short-term effects such as job anxiety, job tension, and job satisfaction, and longer-term outcomes such as depression, ulcers, cardiovascular disease, and mortality (p. 413). Wallis (1983), in a special cover story in *Time* on stress, reported that stress is estimated to cost business and industry between $50 billion and $75 billion a year (p. 48). This is obviously a heavy burden on both personal and organizational well-being.

Communication scholars have recently taken an interest in studying stress and its relationship to communication (Albrecht, Irey, & Mundy, 1982; Ray, 1983a, 1983b; Albrecht & Adelman, 1984; Albrecht & Adelman, 1987; Miller, Zook, & Ellis, 1989; Miller et al., 1990; Ray, 1991). However, communication behaviors and reactions have long been considered both antecedents and consequences of stressful circumstances. In other words, the way in which people communicate may generate stress in both themselves and in others, and stress may affect the way in which people communicate.

Because communication both precipitates stress and is a response to stress, strategies for alleviating stress can be introduced at a great variety of points. As Heaney and Ryn (1990) explain, "The target for change may be individual attitudes or behavior, group norms or behavior, or organizational policies and priorities" (p.415). Thus, the literature on ways to manage stress is varied and wide-ranging (Selye, 1976; Chase, 1972; Adams, 1979; Greenwood & Greenwood, 1979; Warshaw, 1979; Yates, 1979; Ivancevich & Matteson, 1980; Cooper & Marshall, 1980; Lenhart, 1981; Charlesworth & Nathan, 1985; Barnett, Biener, & Baruch, 1987).

We are interested in communication as a tool in managing stress. We are not suggesting that all problems of stress are really communication problems. Although the act of communication is certainly relevant to stress, it is not necessarily the heart of such problems. At the same time, communication practices are not peripheral in the release of stress. The application of communication to the analysis of stress, nevertheless, should not be extended beyond its logical limits. For example, individuals do have much more control over their feelings and how they see the world than they might realize. We do have a choice about what is going to make us angry and, certainly, we can decide what is worth getting mad about. At the same time, the control of one's feelings may depend on the situation. External forces cannot always be defined away, and communication activities such as the labeling process may be only part of the problem.

STRESS: A DEFINITION

The communicative features of stress are highlighted most clearly by examining a contemporary definition of stress. For purposes of our analysis, we define stress as

> the physical, mental, or emotional pain that results from an interpretation of an event as a threat to an individual's personal agenda.

This definition can be translated into a model of stress development and release that is based on the premise that the *interpretation* of an event is what leads either to positive or painful consequences.

Figure 13.1 portrays the sequence of actions that lead to a stress reaction. The model is based on the philosophy expressed by the wise Greek thinker Epictetus when he said that "men [people] are disturbed not by things, but the view which they take of them," another pointed reference to the critical connection between assigning meaning and stress.

An *event* is any real of imagined happening in one's life. In this model, the concept of event refers to almost anything that happens to a person. Some events that appear to elicit negative interpretations that translate into painful reactions include the death of a close relative or spouse, divorce, personal injury or illness, being fired from work, marital arguments, foreclosure of a mortgage or loan, trouble with boss, arrest for minor violation of the law, and any number of changes in residence, work hours, sleeping habits, work responsibilities, living conditions, and number of family gatherings. Each event, especially those that encourage negative responses, tend to pose some form of threat to an individual's *personal agenda.*

A personal agenda consists of the activities or the actions a person engages in to achieve the important goals in life. Csikszentmihalyi (1990) explains that "each of us has

FIGURE 13.1 Sequence Leading to a Stress Reaction

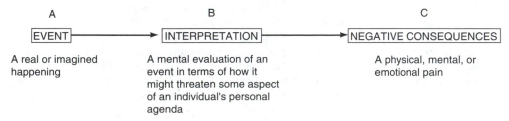

a picture, however vague, of what we would like to accomplish before we die." How close we come to achieving these goals becomes the measure of the quality of our lives. If the goals remain beyond our reach, we grow resentful, but if at least some of the goals are achieved, we experience a sense of happiness and satisfaction (p. 9). For most of us, the events that we think generate negative reactions are those that threaten how well or how soon we are able to reach some of our goals.

You can understand why, for example, the loss of a job can be such a powerful stress producer. If you lose your source of income, you may think that many of your goals or agenda items are threatened. A change in your financial status could be very stressful if it appears to threaten the achievement of one or more of your goals. To determine whether any particular event has the potential for producing a stressful reaction, simply trace what you think might be the consequence of the event on some goal or agenda item. If the consequence appears to threaten the accomplishment of the goal or agenda item, the event is likely to be stressful.

According to Rosch (1984), "the response to stress in humans is highly personalized and varies with each one of us or even in the same individual at different times. It is equally clear that what is distressful for one individual may be pleasurable for another or evoke no response at all. It is not the nature of the external stimulus but rather our perception of it and what techniques have been developed for coping or adapting that appear to be most important" (p. 16). Whether an event precipitates a stressful response depends on how the event is interpreted.

To *interpret* an event means that you make some sense of it and are able to explain what the event means to you; or, in other words, you are able to explain to yourself, at least, what kind of potential effect the event may have on some aspect of your personal agenda or goals. If your interpretation suggests that the event will be a threat to a goal or agenda item, then it will potentially lead to the negative, painful reaction that we call stress.

A *negative consequence* consists of a physical or emotional pain. At least five categories of negative consequences have been identified: physical, emotional, mental, relational, and spiritual. Negative *physical* consequences include the full range of bodily changes and diseases such as insomnia, headaches, eczema and psoriasis, neck and shoulder aches, muscular twitches and nervous tics, gastritis, stomach and duodenal ulcers, irritable colon, menstrual disorders and impotence, asthmatic conditions, cardiovascular disease and hypertension, mouth ulcers and excessive dryness, and instances of excessive hair loss and some forms of baldness (Palmer, 1950; Syme, Hyman, & Enterline, 1964; Blair, 1989; Springer, 1990).

Negative *emotional* consequences include not only personality changes, irritability, anxiety, and depression (Seligman, 1975), but also nightmares, crying spells, worrying, frustration, bad tempers, and a belief that no one cares (Pace, 1992). Closely related to emotional problems are negative *mental* consequences such as forgetfulness, poor concentration, negative attitudes, confusion, lethargy, boredom, negative self-talk, and a general dulling of the senses (Lazarus, 1981).

Negative *relational* consequences include such conditions as feelings of isolation, intolerance, resentment, loneliness, clamming up, nagging, distrust, lack of intimacy, and lashing out at others (Kobasa, 1979; Sweetland, 1979). Finally, negative *spiritual* consequences are experienced as a loss of meaning, emptiness, martyrdom, doubt, loss of direction, cynicism, apathy, and being an unforgiving person (Frankl, 1959; Green, 1964; Kushner, 1981). Any event interpreted to be a possible threat to a person's goal or a personal agenda item may produce one or more negative consequences of a physical, emotional, mental, relational, or spiritual type.

The notion that perceived negative consequences associated with some event could produce actual physical illness is not new. Plato observed that "all the diseases of the body proceed from the mind or soul." Rosch (1984) explained that John Hunter, the person "who raised surgery from a mechanical trade to an experimental science, suffered from angina and being a keen observer complained, 'My life is in the hands of any rascal who chooses to annoy and tease me.' His remarks turned out to be somewhat prophetic since, in fact, an argument did precipitate his death from a heart attack" (p. 13).

The research of Thomas at Johns Hopkins and that of Vaillant at Harvard provide evidence that "emotional well-being and the ability to cope with stress are highly predictive of good health" (Rosch, 1984, p. 16). The bottom line in dealing with stress is that the release of stress makes one feel better and it helps people live longer.

STRATEGIES

From the model of stress, we are able to identify three types of strategies for releasing stress by (1) minimizing the effects of the physical consequences through temporary relief, (2) strengthening the person's ability to cope with physical consequences on a long-term basis, and (3) interpreting events in our lives so as to remove the negative mental, emotional, relational, and spiritual consequences for lifelong peaceful living.

Temporary Relief

Three general strategies are available to most people to provide temporary relief from stress. Let us look at each of them in more detail.

Escape   One of the most common remedies for dealing with stress is to get away from or *escape* from the event that appears to be producing stress. To escape means to flee from, to avoid, or to get out of the way of; it carries the strong implication of separating oneself from the event or the consequences. To stay away from events, one needs to have a lot of control over one's life. One needs to avoid seeing people who trigger negative reactions and to avoid places and activities that stimulate negative responses. On the other hand, if one cannot avoid those stressful situations, a person will probably have to deal with the consequences. That may mean, taking a pain reliever, like an aspirin, to escape from the headache (Jacobsen, 1938; Wallace, 1970) induced by stress.

Instant Calming   Another way to find temporary relief from stress is to engage in a procedure called the *instant calming sequence*. Often, in our lives, we find some negative consequences creeping through our bodies as a result of perceptions of a threat to a personal goal. When these negative effects begin to bother us, we can attack them through an instant calming process. On a personal level, when you experience a sense of tension and stress, immediately begin to breathe deeply; don't hold your breath or strain, but continue breathing normally. Then smile broadly, stand up straight, and relax all of your muscles. Let the tension go and say to yourself, "What is happening to me is real, but I am taking the best possible action I can right now!" The important act is to experience a wave of relaxation and a concentration of effort, rather than tension and constriction of effort. Seek for an instant calming sensation (Benson, 1974, 1975).

Exercise for Pleasure   Another way to escape from stress and the situations that engender it is to engage in some form of physical exercise. This exercise is not necessarily to get in shape; it is designed to help us forget about the negative effects of living and working. When we are deeply involved in physical activity, we tend to forget about many of our worries and the things that precipitate stressful reactions. Some people get out and jog; others play a sport; still others do side-straddle jumps or push-ups. Taking a hike or strolling through the woods can also provide the physical activity necessary to temporarily relieve the pressure of stressful situations (Springer, 1990).

Long-Term Physical Health

Health Check   To monitor the level of your physical health, it is important to have a regular *targeted physical checkup*. That does not mean that you need a complete physical every year, but you do need to target certain aspects of your health and have those checked annually. Up to about age forty, you need to have your blood pressure and weight checked regularly, and if you are female, you need to have breast and pelvic exams, including a Pap smear to check for cancer. When a person turns forty, a complete physical exam should be done annually. This exam should include testing of blood pressure and also for glaucoma. Cholesterol levels should be checked. Women are advised to have a mammogram, and men a rectal exam to detect possible prostate cancer.

The best time to schedule an annual physical exam is during your birth week. That way you will be less likely to forget it. Regular physical examinations will tell you the state of your health and provide early warning signs of possible dangers. Along with regular checkups, you need to establish good nutritional habits (Allsen, Harrison, & Vance, 1984).

Good Nutrition   Proper nutrition contributes to our ability to cope with stress. As a general rule, people who eat properly feel better about themselves and experience higher self-esteem. When your self-esteem is positive, other aspects of your life seem less stressful.

Good nutrition can be described by six principles:

1. Reduce your intake of refined carbohydrates, especially white sugar. Eat fewer foods containing sugar, such as candy, soft drinks, ice cream, cakes, and cookies. Risks to your health increase with the frequency with which you eat sugar and sweets, as well as with the amount you eat. How *often* you eat sugar is as important as how *much* sugar you eat.

2. Decrease your fat consumption, including cholesterol. Eat lean meat, fish, poultry, dried beans, and peas as a source of protein, but limit eggs, liver, butter, cream, shortenings, palm and coconut oil, and avocado in your diet. Broil, bake, or boil rather than fry foods. Read the labels on packaged foods to determine the amount and type of fat in them.

3. Increase your intake of complex carbohydrates, such as whole grains, raw fruits, vegetables, beans, and potatoes. Most diets are relatively low in fiber, and complex carbohydrates contain more fiber. High-fiber foods also tend to reduce the symptoms of chronic constipation and other gastrointestinal disorders.

4. Avoid too much sodium, including table salt. Most Americans desire more salt than they actually need. Use less table salt by learning to enjoy the flavor of unsalted foods. Add little or no salt to food at the table. Finally, limit your intake of salty foods, such as potato chips, pretzels, salted nuts and popcorn, cheese, pickled foods, and cured meats.

5. Drink six to eight glasses of water each day. This will help you control the amount of food you eat and rinse out your system more frequently. If you are uncertain whether you are hungry, just drink a glass of water. As a rule, you should drink a couple of glasses of water with each meal.

6. Finally, eat only when you are actually hungry. It is best to eat regularly and not to skip meals. Hunger appears to occur about every four to six hours, so you should not eat more frequently than that. Breakfast is an important meal, because missing breakfast sets you up for bigger lunches and more night eating.

Exercise for Endurance   Exercise is a wonderful alternative to stress. By exercising, you can increase your body's tolerance for or resistance against stressful events. The advantages associated with regular exercise include a greater sense of concentration, reduced risk of heart attack, more energy and vitality, a firmer looking appearance, sounder sleeping, better control of body weight, more positive moods, and reduced anxiety and hostility. Through exercise, the heart becomes more powerful and efficient and acquires a greater pumping capacity.

Exercise tends to result in three positive and basic consequences: stamina or endurance, suppleness or flexibility, and strength or power. Endurance is the ability to perform moderately strenuous, large-muscle exercises for relatively long periods of time. Walking, cycling, swimming, and jogging develop endurance or stamina. Suppleness or flexibility involves the range of motion that a joint or a body part can engage in. Touching your toes is an example of flexibility. Stretching activities enhance suppleness. Strength includes muscular power or the force that a muscle can exert against some form of resistance. Push-ups, weightlifting, and long-distance running develop strength.

The training-effect principle indicates that if you perform the same exercise every day, you will not increase your strength or endurance. Increases come about only by doing a little more each day.

The most important exercises are those that use your entire body and involve continuous movement for long periods of time. Walking, jogging, swimming, jumping rope, bicycle riding, aerobic dancing, hiking, and cross-country skiing are types of exercises that improve cardiorespiratory endurance. They require the body to use oxygen to produce energy.

The most accurate way to tell whether your exercise is effective and of proper intensity is to check your pulse rate while exercising. When you begin exercising, your heart rate should increase until it levels off. Do not be over-strenuous when you begin exercising. If you are breathing too hard to carry on a conversation, you are probably exercising too hard. Your heart rate will increase in direct proportion to the intensity of the exercise. To achieve benefits from exercise, the heart should work at 70 to 85 percent of a person's maximum heart rate.

Do the right kinds of exercise, those that improve cardiorespiratory endurance. Engage in a routine that involves moderate intensity, but establish and maintain your proper heart rate. If you are over thirty-five years of age, it is advisable to have a physical examination and a treadmill stress test before beginning an exercise program.

If you feel physically well—that is strong, flexible, and able to endure—you will be better able to focus on developing the skills to maintain a long-term program of mental, emotional, relational, and spiritual endurance that will allow you to take full advantage of your communicative abilities in releasing stress and enjoying life.

Long-Term Mental, Emotional, Relational, and Spiritual Strength

The management of stress through communication results in long-term mental, emotional, relational, and spiritual strength (Ellerbroek, 1978). In this section, we shall provide a model and procedures for using the power of communication to release stress and sustain a life of harmony and tranquility.

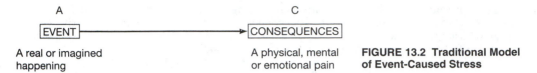

FIGURE 13.2 Traditional Model of Event-Caused Stress

A   C
EVENT ————————————→ CONSEQUENCES

A real or imagined happening   A physical, mental or emotional pain

A communicative approach to stress rejects the traditional model of event-caused stress that is portrayed in Figure 13.2.

This model is based on the assumption that events cause consequences directly. That is, something happens and you feel stress. For example, a change in a zoning ordinance could put a factory near your house. You have an assignment due Monday, and Friday you have to go out of town to help a member of your family. The event occurs and you feel pain.

The model of stress shown in Figure 13.3 identifies the key communicative aspects of stress, indicating that it is the *interpretation* of an event that leads to either positive or negative (stress) consequences in a person's life. This could be called a meaning-centered model of stress creation that makes use of the idea of "punctuation" (see Chapter 5 and section titled "Implications for Organizational Communication"), which involves dividing the stream of experience into nameable units so they can be connected by us in sensible ways.

Try this experiment. Read the three incidents below and then select one of the words in the list at the end that best describes how you would feel as an observer of the event. Write the word on the line at the end of each incident.

Incident 1

You are heading home after a hard day's work. You are passed on the freeway by a couple driving a car similar to yours. They are obviously close to each other; in fact, you wonder if the driver can safely drive the car while the passenger tousles the driver's hair and nibbles the driver's ear lobes.

     Feeling _____

Incident 2

At lunchtime you decide to walk a few blocks for a quick sandwich. As you are crossing the street at a busy intersection, a car races through the intersection, apparently trying to beat the red light. The car comes so close that you literally jump out of the way to avoid being hit.

     Feeling _____

Incident 3

While riding the subway, you see a man with three small boys ranging in ages from about two to six. The boys run noisily up and down the aisles, yelling and screaming. The father sits totally oblivious of the behavior of the youngsters.

     Feeling _____

Words to Describe How You Feel

alarm	anger	concern	curiosity	disapproval
disinterest	envy	excitement	fear	gratitude
happiness	humiliation	interest	irritation	joy
kindness	love	resentment	sadness	worry

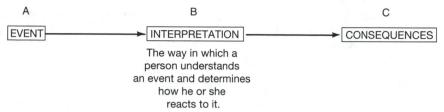

FIGURE 13.3 Stress Model

Now, read the incident again as described below, and using the list of words, as before, select one that describes how you feel.

Incident 1: New View

You are heading home after a hard day's work. You are passed on the freeway by a couple driving a car similar to yours. They are obviously close to each other; in fact, you wonder if the driver can safely drive the car while the passenger tousles the driver's hair and nibbles the driver's ear lobes. As the car passes, you notice that the passenger is your spouse and they are driving your car.

Feeling _____

Incident 2: New View

At lunchtime you decide to walk a few blocks for a quick sandwich. As you are crossing the street at a busy intersection, a car races through the intersection, apparently trying to beat the red light. The car comes so close to you that you literally jump out of the way to avoid being hit. As you watch the car speed away, you realize the driver is your 80-year-old mother who recently had an eye operation.

Feeling _____

Incident 3: New View

While riding the subway, you see a man with three small boys ranging in ages from about two to six. The boys run noisily up and down the aisles, yelling and screaming. The father sits totally oblivious of the behavior of the youngsters. Another passenger leans over to you and explains that the father and children are on their way home from the hospital where his wife died after weeks of suffering from cancer.

Feeling _____

Compare the feelings you selected for the first reading of the incidents with the feelings you selected for the second reading. Reflect on whether the saying of Epictetus—that people are disturbed not by things, but by the view they take of them—rings true. Were you disturbed by the incidents themselves or by the view you had of them? If you think you were concerned by the incidents themselves, then why did you change your feelings the second time around? The incidents were the same, only your view of them changed the second time (Holmes & Houston, 1974).

During the discussions that follow, we shall focus on the way in which we view incidents or events that *produce pain* in our lives, because that is what we call stress. Communication involves the interpretation of events; thus, the long-term release of stress must come from understanding how we can interpret events so as to minimize pain and maximize peace and comfort. We have identified five communicative or interpretative strategies that contribute to long-term stress release and reduction. Implementing these strategies will help you feel better and live a more comfortable, longer life.

COMMUNICATIVE STRATEGY ONE: STRENGTHEN HOPE

The most fundamental, basic, raw ingredient of peace, achievement, and success is a feeling we call *hope*. Having hope is believing and acting as though what you want is actually achievable. Hope is seeing, perceiving, and interpreting the conditions of life in such a way as to believe that what you would like to have is actually possible to hold, possess, or achieve (Bandura, 1977; Bandura, 1985; de Vries, Dijkstra, & Kuhlman, 1988). Conversely, hopelessness is believing and acting as though what you want is not possible to get. Hopelessness underlies all failure, disappointment, discouragement, and loss. From hopelessness comes dejection, depression, dread, and inaction. When you want to have something happen—to achieve a personal agenda item—but you don't think that it will happen, then you have the makings of hopelessness (Seligman, 1975; Pace, 1992).

Naturally, your entire life is not hopeless; on the contrary, you may be very hopeful about most aspects of your life, but there is one small part that is just not going very well. You wish it were—you want it to be—but it isn't. You feel, in fact, that there is nothing you can do to make a difference. You say, "I want things to be different, but I just cannot figure out what to do; it is hopeless." You begin to feel *stress*! What we must realize is that when we want something, and want it badly, but we can see no way in which we are going to get it, we will experience stress. If you desperately want your local sports team to win a game but you can see that it is not going to happen, you want it to happen anyway, then you are going to have stress. Consider the following:

Salmarene was a lovely woman who had a fine marriage. She had five children and wanted very badly to continue enjoying the good life to which she had become accustomed. She and her husband operated a small contracting business and were active in church, social, and community affairs. Although her husband traveled on a regional basis to make business contacts, the family vacationed together and were recognized in the community as a happy and positive influence. She and her husband worked together, owned a large house in an established part of town, and traveled in a large motor home.

Salmarene realized that her husband was traveling on business quite often to a city located more than 300 miles away. She asked him one day what was it that required him to spend so much time there. He said he was trying to collect some money owed for sales he had made. Then, casually, he mentioned that he was going to his high school class reunion, which was being held the following week in a neighboring town. He asked whether she would like to go along. Salmarene thought that would be nice and said she'd like to go.

Salmarene accompanied her husband to the reunion and met many of his former classmates. One of them was a beautiful, stately woman who was not married at the time, but who was employed in the city that Salmarene's husband visited frequently. A few weeks after the reunion, Salmarene's husband invited his wife to make the trip with him to the city. Arrangements were made for the older children to look after the younger ones while they were gone. They drove in their new Lincoln and talked about their life together. During the trip, Salmarene learned that, during his visits to the city, her husband had been seeing the woman who was at the class reunion .

As they approached the outskirts of the city, her husband explained that he was going to stay at a local hotel and that Salmarene was to take the car and continue on to the next town and stay over the weekend with some friends. He told her to pick him up

Sunday night. Salmarene dropped her husband off at the hotel and drove to the next town to stay with her friends. On Sunday evening she returned, picked up her husband at the hotel, and both returned home.

A few weeks later they made the same trek, Salmarene dropping him at the hotel and then proceeding to stay with friends in another town and returning home Sunday. This same routine continued over a period of several months. On one occasion, Salmarene delayed her departure just long enough to see the former classmate greet her husband warmly as he got into her car and the two drove away together. On the return trip, Salmarene asked her husband what had happened. He explained that it saved money for him to stay at the woman's apartment.

During the next trip to the city, Salmarene's husband told his wife that he no longer loved her and wanted a divorce. Nevertheless, Salmarene continued to drive the 600 miles round trip, drop him at the hotel, and attempt to reason with her husband to give their marriage another chance. At the same time she began to have feelings of failure, disappointment, discouragement, and loss. She could see that the relationship was hopelessly ended, resulting in additional feelings of dejection, depression, and dread. Her husband finally announced that he was filing for divorce, but Salmarene continued to insist, especially to herself, that they would get back together, although the feelings of rejection and failure continued to plague her. As the divorce proceeded, Salmarene realized there was no way the marriage could be saved, but she continued to want the marriage to succeed. The more she wanted things to work out, the more intense her dread and tension and sense of failure became. The stress proved almost unbearable. Salmarene entered therapy and counseling, continuing for almost five years, still insisting that she wanted to be reunited with her former husband. She spent most of her time crying.

This incident is based on an actual case and illustrates the principle that stress occurs in our lives when the achievement of a personal agenda item that we want badly to attain seems hopeless (Pelletier, 1977). Making things possible is the real force in bringing about hope in one's life and in overcoming stress. Research on "self-efficacy" (de Vries, et al., 1988) tends to support this general view of hope. What must we do to make the accomplishing of something seem possible? The things we want to have happen seem possible when we meet four basic requirements.

1. We must be clear in our minds about what we really want. Thus, we must distinguish between an actual, legitimate, authentic agenda item and a feigned one. Authentic agenda items are those that we seriously want to achieve, whereas feigned items are those for which we have little commitment.

2. We must feel that we have enough energy to get what we want. That means we need to distinguish between literally not having the energy to achieve something versus thinking or imagining that we do not have the energy.

3. We must feel that we have the talents, skills, and abilities to get what we want. This means we must often distinguish between not having or lacking skills versus merely not wanting to develop the skills we have so that they can be used to achieve what we want (Bandura, 1977).

4. We must feel that we will be able to get what we want if we exert the energy and apply our abilities to the task. Thus, we must distinguish between not wanting to exert the energy versus not being able to apply ourselves to achieving our goals.

In sum, to have hope you must be certain that you want to achieve a particular goal. You must have the energy and the talents to achieve the agenda item. Then, you must estimate the likelihood of achieving the agenda item using the available energy and talents, and conclude that it is possible to achieve the goal. At that point you will have the distinct feeling of having hope.

COMMUNICATIVE STRATEGY TWO: CONNECTEDNESS

Stress develops, flourishes, and grows when we have the feeling of being shut out, isolated, and separated from others (Bruhn & Wolf, 1979). We can live in an apartment in New York City or in the sprawling suburbs of Los Angeles and still feel alone. In a society that is so severance-prone, with frequent transfers and moves and almost epidemic divorce rates, there is a multitude of people who feel disconnected, separate, and alone.

Connectedness is the nurturing influence and social support of family, friends, neighbors, community organizations, national identification, and world ties. Experts have discovered that social support is one of our greatest resources for releasing stress. Close family and social ties created by effective interpersonal communication have a major impact on our positive interpretations of events.

House (1981) reports, however, that work-related stress is moderated most effectively by having supportive supervisors and co-workers, even more than having a supportive spouse and friends outside of work. Ray (1991) also comments that "fostering support groups may not be the answer [to reducing stress] and may actually be a stressor," but people who have intensive interpersonal contacts in their work may find that "fewer ties may be more desirable" and find "forced interaction stressful" (p. 99). This is not to say that nonwork contacts and support are not important, but that for work-related stress, work-related support connections might be more helpful.

An increasing body of research indicates that "social support" in the form of positive interpersonal relationships in the workplace is a strong influence in stress reduction (Albrecht et al., 1982). This may be because organization members understand the subtle stresses in a particular workplace and provide ways for reducing stress within the same interpretative context. Nevertheless, social support in the workplace may be risky because it requires colleagues to trust each other in situations where they may be most vulnerable. This necessitates the ability to predict accurately the extent to which the other will respond with supportive communication (Albrecht & Adelman, 1984).

Organizations, ideally, ought to be structured to encourage social support to occur naturally. If that is not the case, each organization member should pay special attention to the quality of communication and social support he or she gets and gives. Some organization members may struggle to acquire the interpersonal communication skills necessary for quality relationships and support to develop. Moreover, some organization members may decide that the organization has such a negative climate and such inadequate communicative support that they choose to leave it. Nevertheless, the effort expended to develop skills, build a supportive climate, and make supportive connections may be well worth it.

COMMUNICATIVE STRATEGY THREE: MINDFULNESS

One of the most impressive communicative strategies for dealing with stress is that of mindfulness (Borysenko, 1987; Salomon & Globerson, 1987; Langer, 1989). Mindfulness is the art of taking life as it comes and enjoying it moment by moment. Mindfulness encourages us to live as though each moment were important, which means that each and every moment should be noticed, watched, accepted, and valued. By absorbing each moment to the fullest, we become mindful. Mindfulness means being willing to see things as they actually exist without any effort to deny, change, or distort them. It means simply acknowledging what is going on and taking it as it is. Mindfulness is articulated through five basic principles.

Principle 1: Nonstriving

Nonstriving means to let things occur rather than to force them to happen. Much, if not most, of the stress we create comes from our need to achieve, whereas we can actually accomplish more by allowing things to happen naturally. One reason for this is that we distract ourselves by focusing our energies so ferociously and narrowly. We tend to obscure the innate abilities and mental powers we have so that we don't recognize them. Viktor Frankl (1959) explained this when he cautioned that we shouldn't aim at success. "The more you aim at it and make it a target, the more you are going to miss it. For success, like happiness, cannot be pursued; it must ensue . . . as the unintended side-effect of one's personal dedication to a course greater than oneself" (p. 5).

Principle 2: Nonjudging

We have learned that most of us use enormous amounts of energy judging the events in our lives. We try to decide whether the events are good or bad, helpful or hindering, or acceptable or unacceptable. Simply put, nonjudging means to witness the events of life and notice what is actually happening—accept events for what they are.

Principle 3: Open Perspective

An open perspective means to see life from a fresh point of view, to see events with new-ness. This principle is reflected in the interpretation of events exercise presented at the beginning of this section. Let us look at another incident to refocus our minds on this issue.

Incident 4

You are on a committee for a club to interview and select a citizen of the year. During the interviews of candidates, you are informed that a real hero has been nominated and will arrive shortly for an interview. The candidate saved a drowning child last summer and donated the reward money to create a CPR training program for youth leaders. He is kind and courteous.

Feeling _____ (Turn to page 238 to review possible words to describe your feelings.)

Incident 4: New View

You are on a committee for a club to interview and select a citizen of the year. During the interviews of candidates, you are informed that a real hero has been nominated and will arrive shortly for an interview. The candidate saved a drowning child last summer and donated the reward money to create a CPR training program for youth leaders. He is kind and courteous, but you learn that he was accused of sexually molesting a child, although evidence at the trial was insufficient to convict him.

Feeling _____ (What word best describes your feeling now?)

Well, now, what do think about that? How do you feel now? Can you recognize what this principle means? Can you look at the incident with an open perspective? Does life seem to play tricks on people? What is the meaning of this principle in terms of Incident 4?

Principle 4: Self-Trust

As used here, trust refers to the willingness to believe in and rely on our own experience as much as on someone else's. The principle of self-trust says that each of us needs to develop the confidence to depend on our own observations, on our own abilities to discover the meaning of things in the midst of chaos. Mindfulness is based on trusting yourself to notice great treasures all around you (Langer & Rodin, 1976). Self-trust implies having confidence in your own goodness and to find the goodness in others and in the universe.

Principle 5: Patience

By patience we mean "wise waiting." This involves enduring pains without complaint, exercising forbearance when you are under provocation, and being undisturbed by obstacles, delays, and failures. Epictetus noted in his *Discourses* (Chapter 15) that

> No great thing is created suddenly any more than a bunch of grapes or a fig. If you tell me that you desire a fig, I answer you that there must be time. Let it first blossom, then bear fruit, then ripen.

Thus it is with progress in all facets of life that we must allow time for things to happen. Have you run a marathon? If so, you can testify to the truth of what we are about to say. We want you to imagine that you are a couch potato. You are a little overweight; you *never* exercise—never, never. If the temptation to exercise even a little bit starts to overcome you, you quickly lie down until it passes. You get out of breath just climbing a flight of stairs, and two flights send you to a chair for a five-minute rest before it is safe to walk and breathe at the same time.

Now, imagine that, for whatever reason, you decide to run a marathon. How long do you think it will take you to prepare to run 26 miles 385 yards without stopping? How long do you estimate it will take you to run even one mile without a break? Patience is associated with what athletes call the "training effect." The training effect is what happens to you after you run around the track for thirty days in a row, one right after the other. You discover that you are able to gradually increase your distance. You get better at running. Running becomes easier. You cannot run every day without getting stronger.

The point is that mindlessness begins to abate and mindfulness begins to grow as you engage in the processes of re-interpreting, re-understanding, and re-creating the events around you. With greater ability to engage in mindfulness, you will become stronger and experience less stress.

COMMUNICATIVE STRATEGY FOUR: HARDINESS

The work of Maddi and Kobasa (1984) has revealed that stress may be ameliorated through the buffering effects of a quality of personality called "hardiness." Hardiness consists of a set of beliefs about oneself, events in the world, and the interaction between the two that derive from three factors: a sense of commitment, a sense of control, and a sense of challenge.

Commitment

If you have a feeling of self-confidence that you can find something interesting or important about what you are doing, you have commitment. Goethe, the German philosopher, observed that "until one is committed, there is hesitance, the chance to draw back, always ineffectiveness . . . The moment one definitely commits oneself, then providence moves you." This is sense of commitment. Failing commitment, alienation and chronic boredom set in, which lead to meaninglessness and uninvolvement.

Control

If you believe that you can influence things going on around you and you also have a willingness to act on that belief, then you have control. Hobbs (1987) articulated this principle when he wrote: "Self-reliance is at the core of time management because it yields confidence in one's judgment to exercise the most appropriate control over selected anticipated events" (p. 9). Hardiness articulates a similar philosophy by suggesting that without control, one feels powerless or the victim of circumstances.

Challenge

If you think of your life as lived best in pursuit of development in which disruptions and failures appear to be experiences from which you can learn and grow, then you have a sense of challenge. Gardner (1963) noted that "there is no learning without some difficulty and fumbling. If you want to keep on learning, you must keep on risking failure—all your life" (p. 15). Without challenge, you may think life is best when it is characterized by ease, comfort, and security. In such a case, every change is viewed as a threat to some goal you have in mind, which, as we explained earlier, results in feelings of stress.

Dealing with stress through hardiness means developing commitment, exercising control, and finding challenge in living to such an extent that you evolve a resilient personality (Kobasa, 1982). In that way, you are able to cope with stressful circumstances by transforming them into less stressful events. Some evidence indicates that hardiness leads a person to seek and be open to social support and more supportive interpersonal communication (Kobasa et al., 1985).

Authentic commitment involves engaging in those activities that you feel are interesting and important to you. Through true commitment, you leave the rat race and join the human race because you are doing things that you want to do. The key to exercising control is to influence things that can be influenced and to adapt to things that cannot be influenced. Recognizing the difference is critical in developing control. Finally, challenge means finding the opportunity in every difficulty rather than the difficulty in every opportunity. Transforming difficulties into opportunities necessitates locating a positive outcome in a pattern of negative outcomes. This requires looking past the immediate negative consequences and imagining what good might come from the event itself. In a sense, to feel challenge, one must ignore the negative effects and visualize positive ones.

The development of hardiness relies almost entirely on the re-interpretation of stressful circumstances so that a person substitutes a sense of commitment, control, and challenge for feelings of alienation, powerlessness, and threat.

COMMUNICATIVE STRATEGY FIVE: FORGIVENESS

Fundamental insights into the healing effects of communicating forgiveness are expressed by philosophers throughout the centuries. Henry Wadsworth Longfellow wrote in *Driftwood* (1857), for example, that "if we could read the secret history of our enemies, we should find in each man's life sorrow and suffering enough to disarm all hostility." In a more contemporary vein, Harold S. Kushner (1981) explained that "the facts of life and death are neutral. We, by our responses, give suffering either a positive or a negative meaning. Illnesses, accidents, human tragedies kill people. But they do not necessarily kill life or faith. . . . If suffering and death in someone close to us bring us to explore the limits of our capacity for strength and love and cheerfulness, if it leads us to discover sources of consolation we never knew before, then we make the person into a witness for the affirmation of life rather than its rejection" (p. 138).

These words impress upon us how we can act positively in the face of affronts, scorn, derision, insults, and all form of negative communication in our lives (Buscaglia, 1972). We can respond with forgiveness rather than hostility, since we all share the bonds of human tragedy, although at first glance we may not detect the common suffering. That may be why mindfulness is such a critical variable in sensitizing us to the frailties of human relationships (Langer, Blank, & Chanowitz, 1978). We need that focus and concentration on events and circumstances. At the same time, it is we who give meaning to those affronts, that hostility, that insult. We can find a capacity for love and cheerfulness. We can, in the language of this strategy, find and express forgiveness. By doing so, we strengthen ourselves, we find peace, calm, and even pleasure and joy in life (Ten Boom & Sherrill, 1971).

Forgiveness is necessary to the reduction and release of stress in our lives because it involves giving up resentment. A resentment is any *negative feeling*, however slight, toward a person, object, or event, although most resentments appear to involve what people say and do toward us. We tend to have the most intense resentments toward those who appear consciously or deliberately to threaten us. That is, resentments develop when we interpret other people to say and do things intentionally so as to threaten some aspect of our personal agenda, thus meeting the fundamental condition for stress to occur.

The interesting thing is that even if someone else has tried deliberately and maliciously to hurt us, it is our own negative feelings, not their attempt to hurt us, that produce stress in our lives. The act of forgiving is to cease to feel resentment against an offender—to give up resentment of, or revenge for, an insult. If you want to get even with that other person, you will suffer the consequences in your own life and experience stress, which may result in mental anguish, emotional trauma, and physical deterioration. Resentment takes its toll on how we communicate and how we live our lives.

When we choose to resent what someone else has said or done, we are choosing to live with the emotional pain that we call stress. Forgiveness means that we relinquish our resentments so that we can be free to choose peace. Stress is released when we elect to interpret another person's words and actions as not threatening to us and we cease resenting what others say and do.

Joan (not her real name) was driving along a street in an East Coast city. In front of her was a family in an old, battered car. A young boy leaned out of the rear window and, for no apparent reason, made a vulgar gesture toward her. Joan later reported handling the situation like this: "It was easy to see that his behavior had nothing to do with me, but must have been caused by pain created by societal or family concerns. Instead

FIGURE 13.4 The Forgiveness Strategy

of adding to his pain, I mustered up all the love I could and beamed it out to him in a big smile. He suddenly began to smile in return, and we waved at one another until his car was out of sight."

Forgiveness is not a self-righteous or Pollyanna-like turning of the other cheek by which we condone undesirable behavior. Rather, it is based on an understanding of the deep pain from which the hurtful actions inflicted upon us arose. By understanding the pain of others, we sense the suffering of others, leading us to compassionate communication that turns aside our own resentment. In that communicative spirit of forgiveness, we move out of the role of victim and see beyond the negative actions to the person who is speaking and acting.

Figure 13.4, The Forgiveness Strategy, shows the communicative stress-release model in the center of the diagram, beginning on the left with an *Event* and moving to the right with the *Interpretation* and ending with the *Consequence*. When you interpret the event as a threat—first step above the line toward Resentment—you move toward stress. However, when you choose to interpret the event without judging (nonjudging) and focus on what is happening behind the words and actions, you move toward Acceptance and Peace.

You might think of Figure 13.4 as an upper and lower arc in a chain of dominoes—an Arc of Dominoes. When you interpret an event as a threat to you and items in your agenda of life, you tip over the first domino, leading all the way to some form of stress. That same event, interpreted nonjudgmentally as not a threat, triggers a sequence of events leading to peace.

Here is a story that illustrates the concept of forgiveness as applied in the resolution of conflict flooding from authentic human pain and suffering (Dass & Gorman, 1988, pp. 167–171):

The train clanked and rattled through the suburbs of Tokyo on a drowsy spring afternoon. Our car was comparatively empty—a few housewives with their kids in tow, some old folks going shopping. I gazed absently at the drab houses and dusty hedgerows.

At one station the doors opened, and suddenly the afternoon quiet was shattered by a man bellowing violent, incomprehensible curses. The man staggered into our car. He wore laborer's clothing, and he was big, drunk, and dirty. Screaming, he swung at a woman holding a baby. The blow sent her spinning into the laps of an elderly couple. It was a miracle that the baby was unharmed.

Terrified, the couple jumped up and scrambled toward the other end of the car. The laborer aimed a kick at the retreating back of the old woman but missed as she scuttled to safety. This so enraged the drunk that he grabbed the metal pole in the center of the car and tried to wrench it out of its stanchion. I could see that one of his hands was cut and bleeding. The train lurched ahead, the passengers frozen with fear. I stood up.

I was young then, some twenty years ago, and in pretty good shape. I'd been putting in a solid eight hours of aikido training [Japanese art of self-defense] nearly every day for the past three years. I liked to throw and grapple. I thought I was tough. The trouble was, my martial skill was untested in actual combat. As students of aikido, we were not allowed to fight.

"Aikido," my instructor had said again and again, "is the art of reconciliation. Whoever has the mind to fight has broken his connection with the universe. If you try to dominate people, you are already defeated. We study how to resolve conflict, not how to start it."

I listened to his words. I tried hard. I even went so far as to cross the street to avoid the *chimpira,* the pinball punks who lounged around the train stations. My forbearance exalted me. I felt both tough and holy. In my heart, however, I wanted an absolutely legitimate opportunity whereby I might save the innocent by destroying the guilty.

"This is it!" I said to myself as I got to my feet. "People are in danger. If I don't do something fast, somebody will probably get hurt!"

Seeing me stand up, the drunk recognized a chance to focus his rage. "Aha!" he roared. "A foreigner! You need a lesson in Japanese manners!"

I held on lightly to the commuter strap overhead and gave him a slow look of disgust and dismissal. I planned to take this turkey apart, but he had to make the first move. I wanted him mad, so I pursed my lips and blew him an insolent kiss.

"All right!" he hollered. "You're gonna get a lesson." He gathered himself for a rush at me.

A fraction of a second before he could move, someone shouted, "Hey!" It was ear-splitting. I remember the strangely joyous, lilting quality of it—as though you and a friend had been searching diligently for something and he had suddenly stumbled upon it. "Hey!" the voice repeated.

I wheeled to my left; the drunk spun to his right. We both stared down at a little old Japanese man. He must have been well into his seventies, this tiny gentleman, sitting there immaculate in his kimono. He took no notice of me, but beamed delightedly at the laborer, as though he had a most important, most welcome secret to share.

"C'mere," the old man said in an easy vernacular, beckoning to the drunk. "C'mere and talk with me." He waved his hand lightly.

The big man followed, as if on a string. He planted his feet belligerently in front of the old gentlemen and roared above the clacking wheels of the train: "Why the hell should I talk to you?" The drunk now had his back to me. If his elbow moved so much as a millimeter, I'd drop him in his socks.

The old man continued to beam at the laborer. "What 'cha been drinkin'?" he asked, his eyes sparkling with interest.

"I been drinkin' sake," the laborer bellowed back, "and it's none of your business!" Flecks of spittle splattered the old man.

"Oh, that's wonderful," the old man said, "absolutely wonderful! You see, I love sake too. Every night, me and my wife (she's seventy-six, you know), we warm up a little bottle of sake and take it out into the garden, and we sit on an old wooden bench. We watch the sun go down, and we look to see how our persimmon tree is doing. My great-grandfather planted that tree, and we worry about whether it will recover from those ice storms we had last winter. Our tree has done better than I expected, though, especially when you consider the poor quality of the soil. It is gratifying to watch when we take our sake and go out to enjoy the evening—even when it rains!" He looked up at the laborer, eyes twinkling.

As he struggled to follow the old man's conversation, the drunk's face began to soften. His fists slowly unclenched. "Yeah," he said. "I love persimmons, too. . . ." His voice trailed off.

"Yes," said the old man, smiling, "and I'm sure you have a wonderful wife."

"No," replied the laborer. "My wife died." Very gently, swaying with the motion of the train, the big man began to sob. "I don't got no wife, I don't got no home, I don't got no job. I'm so ashamed of myself." Tears rolled down his cheeks; a spasm of despair rippled through his body.

Now it was my turn. Standing there in my well-scrubbed, youthful innocence and my make-this-world-safe-for-democracy righteousness, I suddenly felt dirtier than he was.

Suddenly the train arrived at my station. As the doors opened, I heard the old man cluck sympathetically. "My, my. That is a difficult predicament, indeed. Sit down here and tell me about it," he motioned to the drunk.

I turned my head for one last look. The laborer was sprawled on the seat, his head in the old man's lap. The old gentleman was softly stroking the filthy, matted hair. As the train pulled away, I sat down on a bench. What I had wanted to do with muscle had been accomplished with kind words. I had just seen aikido tried in combat, and the essence of it was love. I would have to practice the art with an entirely different spirit. It would be a long time before I could speak about the resolution of conflict.*

CONFLICT

As the above incident so vividly illustrates, stress and conflict are intimately connected. Perceived negative consequences issuing from interpersonal contact incite feelings of stress; conversely, feelings of stress may serve as the basis of potential conflict.

Conflict has been defined as an "expressed struggle between at least two interdependent parties, who perceive incompatible goals, scarce rewards, and interference from the other party in achieving their goals" (Frost & Wilmot, 1978, p. 9). In this view the "struggle" represents differences between the parties that are expressed, recognized, and experienced. For conflict to occur, the difference must be communicated. Conflicts may be expressed in different ways, from very subtle nonverbal movements to all-out physical brawling; from subtle sarcasm to overt verbal attack.

The concept of struggle is related to efforts designed to achieve goals, to secure resources, and to obtain rewards that are also being sought after by the other party. The implication is that people want to do different things and they also desire the same

*From *How Can I Help?* by Rom Doss and Paul Gorman. Copyright © 1985 by Rom Doss and Paul Gorman. Reprinted by permission of Alfred A. Knopf.

things. These are the concepts of incompatible goals and scarce rewards. Early signs of conflict may be identified by an increase in the rate of disagreements among group members. Previously neutral comments take on an unfriendly tone. As the tension mounts, more explicit signs of disagreement surface. The conflict is expressed through sighs, uneasy twitches in facial muscles, faltering silences, lapses in attention, slouching, doodling, turning away, and curt verbal utterances.

If members of a group have common goals, the likelihood of conflict developing is lowered. Goals involve a wide variety of desires that people would like to achieve, some of which are real and tangible and others of which are imagined and intangible. The goal of a company to reduce costs may in fact be quite incompatible with the goal of an employee to increase his or her income. However, some superordinate goals may encompass both of the incompatible goals to allow conflict to be managed to the advantage of both the company and the employee.

Rewards are of different kinds. Most of us are familiar with salaries, bonuses, promotions, corner offices, and vacations, but more personal reactions such as respect, time together, warmth, pride, listening, and love are also rewards. Frost and Wilmot (1978) argue that in interpersonal conflict, "regardless of the content issue involved, the parties usually perceive a shortage of power and/or self-esteem reward" (p. 12). Thus conflicts may often be averted by showing that those rewards are less scarce than supposed.

Personal Conflict Styles

There seems to be general agreement that people have preferred ways of handling conflict, or at least habitual ways of dealing with conflict (Filley, 1975; Frost & Wilmot, 1978). A habitual way of behaving is one that is somewhat fixed and resistant to change because it is comfortable and natural. When two people come together expecting to claim their share of scarce resources, they somewhat habitually think about themselves and the other person. Thus conflict styles appear to be some combination

FIGURE 13.5 Personal Conflict Styles

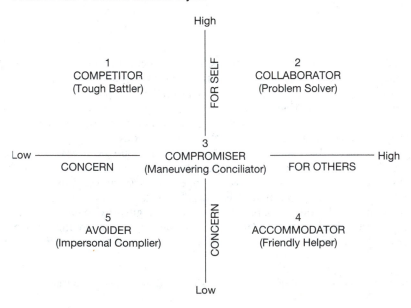

of the amount of concern you have about accomplishing your own goals and the amount of concern you have about the other person accomplishing his or her goals. These concerns can be portrayed by two axes running from low concern to high concern. The resulting cells with mixtures of concern for accomplishing particular goals represent styles that people have for dealing with conflict. Figure 13.5 identifies five personal conflict styles that we shall briefly characterize. The terms used to label the styles are derived from the writings of Hall (1969), Blake and Mouton (1980), and Kilmann and Thomas (1975).

1. *Competitor or tough battler.* The person who employs this style pursues his or her own concerns somewhat ruthlessly and generally at the expense of other members of the group. The tough battler views losing as an indication of weakness, reduced status, and a crumbling self-image. Winning is the only worthwhile goal and results in accomplishment and exhilaration.

2. *Collaborator or problem solver.* The person who employs this style seeks to create a situation in which the goals of all parties involved can be accomplished. The problem solver works at finding mutually acceptable solutions. Winning and losing are not part of his or her way of looking at conflict.

3. *Compromiser or maneuvering conciliator.* The person who employs this style assumes that everyone involved in a disagreement stands to lose, and he or she works to help find a workable position. A pattern of "giving in" often develops.

4. *Accommodator or friendly helper.* The person who employs this style is somewhat nonassertive and quite cooperative, neglecting his or her own concerns in favor of those of others. The friendly helper feels that harmony should prevail and that anger and confrontation are bad. When a decision is reached, the accommodator may go along and wish later that he or she had expressed some reservations.

5. *Avoider or impersonal complier.* The person who employs this style tends to view conflict as unproductive and somewhat punishing. Thus the avoider gets away from an uncomfortable situation by refusing to be concerned. The result is usually an impersonal reaction to the decision and little commitment to future actions.

Unfortunately, when conflict occurs we have tendencies to do and say things that perpetuate the conflict rather than reduce or eliminate it. Although frequently very difficult to do, there are usually a few actions that can be taken to start the de-escalation of conflict. Disagreements seldom resolve themselves. In small groups, conflict is usually handled best through the process of *integration*—the combination of each person's ideas into a group idea (Barnlund & Haimam, 1960).

Integration

The goal of integrative decision making is to achieve consensus. The philosophical basis underlying consensus is that differences in thinking, feeling, and behaving are best resolved by incorporating the points of view of all parties into the decision or plan. Cooperative effort is achieved by finding, isolating, and clarifying areas of agreement and disagreement, thus systematically narrowing the area of difference and enlarging the area of acceptability (Pace, Peterson, & Burnett, 1979). Two areas of difference need to be managed: differences in understanding and differences in feelings.

Differences in understanding can be managed in three ways:

1. *By discovering what the other person or party means.* Often a simple statement of what a person means prevents disagreements from escalating.

2. *By checking the validity of evidence and reasoning.* Disagreements and conflicts often develop because it is possible for two people to reason from the same data and arrive at totally different conclusions. You might want to locate the source of evidence in order to determine how accurate it is.

3. *By identifying a more basic value or goal, sometimes called a* superordinate *goal.* When a disagreement is based on differences in preferences or values, understanding may be increased by identifying a more basic value that is acceptable to all parties.

Differences based on feelings may be managed in five ways:

1. *By increasing the self-esteem of those with whom you have the disagreement.* A basic source of emotional resistance is loss of face. No one wants to appear foolish, illogical, or misdirected. Reduce disagreements based on feelings by providing ego support and ways of strengthening self-esteem.

2. *By creating an atmosphere of inquiry.* Get group members to probe into the issue by asking open-ended questions. Resistance often occurs because all alternatives have not been explored.

3. *By involving each group member in the discussion.* Emotional barriers and negative feelings flare up when we feel uninvited or discouraged from making contributions. Avoid squelching anyone, regardless of what the person may have said.

4. *By using summaries to show the group where it has been and where it is going.* Summaries can help objectify comments and reduce excessive generalizing and over-statement. Group members are allowed to respond to a more objective summary rather than the original emotional comments.

5. *By providing for the release of feelings.* Participants should have the opportunity to make highly emotional statements without argument or refutation. Many disagreements can be resolved simply by letting the other person dissipate the underlying feelings (Pace, Peterson, & Burnett, 1979).

The use of integrative decision making to reduce disagreements capitalizes on a merger of information, logic, and feelings to achieve the best collective judgment of the entire group. Conflict is used creatively and constructively.

CONFLICT AND INTERGROUP PROCESSES

One of the most important aspects of organizational life concerns relations among groups within the organization (Schein, 1969). The symptoms of bad relations are often somewhat easy to recognize. A breakdown in the flow of work or lack of coordination between groups usually stands out. Poor communication or a failure to exchange information adequately may be a symptom that accompanies lack of coordination. Delays and mistakes often lead to tensions and negative feelings. If groups must rely on one another to get their work done, the symptoms are often more dramatic. Conflict between groups is expressed in much the same way that interpersonal conflict is. "Criticisms, bickering, snide remarks, and intentional ignoring of others are clear indicators of difficult relations, just as the opposites indicate satisfying ones" (Coffey et al., 1975).

Intergroup Conflict

When several groups feel frustrated because they are being kept from accomplishing their goals, intergroup conflict occurs. Some groups look for the source of frustration inside their group—their own skills, methods, equipment, and procedures. Other groups look for the source of their frustrations outside their group. When they think they have found the source of their frustrations in some other group, a downward spiral of conflict develops. Seven stages seem to characterize the cycle:

1. Beginnings of doubt and distrust appear, and the climate between the groups deteriorates.
2. Perceptions of the outside group become distorted or stereotyped and polarized, with verbal comments dividing the "good" groups from the "bad" ones.
3. Cohesiveness and related feelings such as friendliness, attractiveness, closeness, and importance within each group increase.
4. Adherence to group norms and conformity also increase in each group.
5. Groups ready themselves for more authoritarian leadership and direction.
6. Hostile behaviors, reduced communicative contacts, and other signs of negative intergroup relations become apparent.
7. Complete separation is mutually desired, and any form of positive collaborative effort ceases (Coffey et al., 1975).

What happens to the competing groups when a decision is made and one is the winner and the other is the loser? Schein (1969) indicates that the winning group retains its cohesiveness and may even increase in that area. It also experiences a letdown and becomes complacent and casual. Along with the loss of its fighting spirit, the winning group experiences higher intragroup cooperation and concern for its members with an accompanying decrease in concern for task accomplishment. The winning group tends to feel that its positive image and the negative stereotype of the other group have been confirmed.

Conversely, the losing group looks for an explanation for its loss in some external source such as the decision makers or dumb luck. When the group accepts its loss, it begins to splinter, internal fights break out, and unresolved internal conflicts surface. The losing group becomes more tense, gets ready to work harder, and appears desperate to find something to blame for the loss. The losing group places a high concern on recouping its losses by working harder, with less concern for member needs. The losing group tends to learn something about itself because its positive image was upset by the loss, forcing a re-evaluation of the group's perceptions. Once the loss has been accepted realistically, the losing group tends to become more cohesive and more effective.

Reducing Intergroup Conflict

Huse and Bowditch (1973) suggest five ways for minimizing conflict within the existing organizational framework:

1. Make certain that information for solving problems is discovered and held in common by the groups involved. Representatives of different groups might meet regularly to study problem areas and to develop joint recommendations.
2. Rotate people among different groups. This suggestion implies the Buck Roger's era of organization theory with temporary work groups and project management. Some groups are too specialized to use this method of reducing conflict, but some work areas are well suited for rotating members.
3. Bring groups into close contact with one another. Bring opposing groups together to clear the air and allow them to share perceptions.

4. Locate a common enemy. A competing company, the government, or some other group may allow the groups in conflict to join forces and cooperate to repel the invader. This may bring the groups into closer contact and dissipate conflict.
5. Identify or develop a common set of goals. This is the idea of locating a superordinate objective that both groups have in common.

SUMMARY

In this chapter we discussed a model of stress development that includes an event, an interpretation of the event, and consequences that follow from the interpretations. Specific suggestions were discussed for providing temporary relief from stress, for strengthening ourselves for long-term resistance to the effects of stress, and for developing strategies for acquiring and developing long-term mental, emotional, relational, and spiritual health. Five personal conflict styles were discussed: the competitor, the collaborator, the accommodator, the compromiser, and the avoider. Ways of resolving conflict through the process of integration were also analyzed. Finally, intergroup conflict was examined. A seven-stage cycle of frustration leading to intergroup conflict was explained. Finally, the effects on groups of winning and losing in competition and five ways of reducing intergroup conflict were offered.

A SUBJECTIVIST'S REMINDER

Any number of factors can create groups that have subcultural possibilities within an organization. Specialization places the people who do the same kind of work together. Professionalization puts people together who share occupational identities. Automation groups individuals together who work with specific machines. Each group develops its own language, practices, and ideas about organizational goals. Subcultures are also created by acquisitions, mergers, and technological innovation. As interactional opportunities are altered, contrasting interpretative systems are constructed (Van Maanen & Barley, 1985).

Management of groups involves more than the consideration of individual personalities. Groups that have evolved into subcultures share organizational views that are constructed and reinforced by symbolic behavior. Van Maanen and Barley (1985) point out that although members of subcultures may be aware of each other as persons, they may not recognize subcultural differences unless some unexpected event occurs. Although culture can be portrayed as a force for organizational solidarity, cultures are just as likely to provoke disintegration of organizational unity. Van Maanen and Barley contend that, "whereas proponents of organizational culture sometimes argue that modern corporations suffer from a lack of culture, we submit that organizations often get more culture than they bargained for. . . . The study of cultural organization is therefore closely bound to the study of organizational conflict" (p. 48). Group processes, then, become a significant issue in the study and practice of organizational communication.

Groups that have continuity develop cultures and thereby share similar feelings, beliefs, and values. It is rather obvious that when groups compete for resources or a greater voice in organizational operations, differing perspectives produce conflict. It is less apparent that conflict itself is an organizational practice. Organizations differ on how they "do" conflict. Conflict may be carried out in active or passive ways. Denying conflict or pretending that it does not exist is a way of "doing" conflict. The purpose here is not to discuss the merits of various conflict behaviors. Different modes of conflict may be functional for different subcultures. After conflict behaviors have been negotiated and become routine in groups, they operate at a low level of the members' awareness. When groups confront each other, they must not only deal with the matter of conflicting goals and attitudes, but also with the conflict that results from the differing practices of conflict.

Both authors of this text have been involved in the mergers of university departments, and both can attest to what cultural clashes are all about. Mergers of academic departments produce the anxiety that comes from perceived loss of turf and the uncertainty of change. The conflict style of the groups comes into play. These conflict behaviors are easier to analyze in retrospect but are difficult to see objectively during the actual interactions. The following personal account of the author's experience during a department merger illustrates the impact of different conflict styles on an organizational activity.

> It was clear that the university administration wanted the merger of two departments. The college dean decided to bring the two departments together to start preliminary talks. The first step was the creation of a committee made up of representatives from each department. The committee was asked to discover areas where resources might be shared between the two departments. All of the committee members knew that the committee was the first step toward a merger and all were wary. All had investments in programs of study and research. The two groups sat on opposite sides of the table. One group engaged in behaviors that were interpreted as hostile by the other group. The other's behaviors were thought to be devious because they were not openly combative. It was as though two families had been thrown together. One family had been accustomed to shouting and taking extreme positions during negotiation while the other group had worked out a system of more moderate exchange. One group felt bullied while the other felt it was being "sweet-talked" into a loss of identity. In one meeting I became so angry that I had to leave the room. I returned after cooling down. I had felt insulted by what I considered an inflammatory speech. The person who made the speech felt insulted because I wasn't willing to "face the issues."
>
> In retrospect, all of this seems strange. The merger was accomplished some time ago and a culture has been created that has incorporated all behaviors. Those behaviors have had a moderating influence on one another. The greatest change has come about through the understanding and acceptance of the way conflict is "done." Conflict is healthy for the organization; it keeps significant issues in full view.

REFERENCES

General

ADAMS, JOHN D., "Guidelines for Stress Management and Life Style Changes," *The Personnel Administrator*, 24 (June 1979), 35–38, 44.

BARNETT, ROSALIND C., LOIS BIENER, and GRACE K. BARUCH (eds.), *Gender and Stress*. New York: Free Press, 1987.

BARNLUND, DEAN C. and FRANKLYN S. HAIMAN, *The Dynamics of Discussion*. Boston: Houghton Mifflin, 1960.

BLAKE, ROBERT R. and JANE SRYGLEY MOUTON, *Grid Approaches to Managing Stress*. Springfield, Ill.: Charles C. Thomas Publisher, 1980.

CHARLESWORTH, EDWARD A., and RONALD G. NATHAN, *Stress Management*. New York: Ballantine, 1985.

CHASE, DENNIS J., "Sources of Mental Stress and How to Avoid Them," *Supervisory Management,* 17 (November 1972), 33–36.

COFFEY, ROBERT E., ANTHONY G. ATHOS, and PETER A. REYNOLDS, *Behavior in Organizations: A Multidimensional View,* 2nd ed. Englewood Cliffs, N.J.: Prentice Hall, 1975.

COOPER, CARY LYNN, and JUDI MARSHALL, *White Collar and Professional Stress.* New York: John Wiley, 1980.

FILLEY, ALAN C., *Interpersonal Conflict Resolution.* Glenview, Ill.: Scott, Foresman, 1975.

FROST, JOYCE HOCKER, and WILLIAM W. WILMOT, *Interpersonal Conflict.* Dubuque, Iowa.: Wm. C. Brown, 1978.

GREENWOOD, JAMES W. III, and JAMES W. GREENWOOD, JR., *Managing Executive Stress: A Systems Approach.* New York: John Wiley, 1979.

HALL, JAY, *Conflict Management Survey.* Austin, Texas: Teleometrics, Inc., 1969.

HEANEY, CATHERINE, and MICHELLE VAN RYN, "Broadening the Scope of Worksite Stress Programs: A Guiding Framework," *American Journal of Health Promotion,* 4 (July/August 1990), 413–420.

HUSE, EDGAR F., and JAMES L. BOWDITCH, *Behavior in Organizations: A Systems Approach to Managing.* Reading, Mass.: Addison-Wesley, 1973.

IVANCEVICH, JOHN M., and MICHAEL T. MATTESON, *Stress and Work: A Managerial Perspective.* Glenview, Ill.: Scott, Foresman, 1980.

KILMANN, RALPH, and KENNETH THOMAS, "Interpersonal Conflict—Handling Behavior as Reflections of Jungian Personality Dimensions," *Psychological Reports,* 37 (1975), 971–980.

LENHART, LEVI, *Preventing Work Stress.* Reading, Mass..: Addison-Wesley, 1981.

PACE, R. WAYNE, BRENT D. PATERSON, and M. DALLAS BURNETT, *Techniques for Effective Communication.* Reading, Mass.: Addison-Wesley, 1979.

ROSCH, PAUL J., "Stress and Illness: Fact or Fantasy?" *PA Practice: The Practical Clinical Journal for Physician Assistants,* 3 (1984), 13–16.

SCHEIN, EDGAR H., *Process Consultation: Its Role in Organization Development.* Reading, Mass.: Addison-Wesley, 1969.

SELYE, HANS, *The Stress of Life.* New York: McGraw-Hill, 1976.

SWEETLAND, JOHN, *Occupational Stress and Productivity.* New York: Work in America Institute, 1979.

VAN MAANEN, JOHN, and STEPHEN R. BARLEY, "Cultural Organization: Fragments of a Theory," in *Organizational Culture,* Peter J. Frost et al., eds. Beverly Hills, Calif.: Sage Publications, Inc., 1985.

WALLIS, C., "Stress: Can We Cope?" *Time* (June 6, 1983), 48–54.

WARSHAW, LEON J., *Managing Stress.* Reading, Mass.: Addison-Wesley, 1979.

YATES, JERI E., *Managing Stress.* New York: AMACOM, 1979.

Mindfulness

BORYSENKO, JOAN, *Minding the Body, Mending the Mind.* New York: Bantam, 1987.

CSIKSZENTMIHALYI, MIHALY, *Flow: The Psychology of Optimal Experience.* New York: Harper & Row, Pub., 1990.

ELLERBROEK, W.C., "Language, Thought, and Disease," *The Co-Evolution Quarterly,* 17 (Spring 1978), 30–38.

HOLMES, D., and B.K. HOUSTON, "Effectiveness of Situation Redefinition and Affective Isolation in Coping with Stress," *Journal of Personality and Social Psychology,* 29 (1974), 212–218.

LANGER, ELLEN J., *Mindfulness.* Reading, Mass.: Addison-Wesley, 1989.

LANGER, ELLEN J., A. BLANK, and B. CHANOWITZ, "The Mindlessness of Ostensibly Thoughtful Action: The Role of Placebic Information in Interpersonal Interaction," *Journal of Personality and Social Psychology,* 36 (1978), 635–642.

LANGER, ELLEN J., and J. RODIN, "The Effects of Enhanced Personal Responsibility for the Aged: A Field Experiment in an Institutional Setting," *Journal of Personality and Social Psychology,* 34 (1976), 191–198.

SALOMON, G., and T. GLOBERSON, "Skill May Not Be Enough: The Role of Mindfulness in Learning and Transfer," *International Journal of Educational Research,* 11, (1987), 623–627.

Forgiveness

BUSCAGLIA, LEO, *Love: A Warm and Wonderful Book About the Largest Experience in Life.* New York: Ballantine, 1972.

DASS, RAM, and PAUL GORMAN, *How Can I Serve?* New York: Knopf, 1988.

FRANKL, VIKTOR E., *Man's Search for Meaning.* New York: Pocket Books, 1959.

GREEN, HANNAH, *I Never Promised You a Rose Garden.* New York: Holt, Rinehart, & Winston, 1964.

KUSHNER, HAROLD S., *When Bad Things Happen to Good People.* New York: Avon Books, 1981.

TEN BOOM, CORRIE, with JOHN and ELIZABETH SHERRILL, *The Hiding Place: The Triumphant True Story of Corrie Ten Boom.* New York: Bantam, 1971.

Hope

BANDURA, ALBERT, "Self-Efficacy: Toward a Unifying Theory of Behavior Change, *Psychological Review,* 84 (1977), 191–215.

BANDURA, ALBERT, *Social Foundations of Thought and Action: A Social Cognitive Theory.* Englewood Cliffs, N.J.: Prentice Hall, 1985.

DE VRIES, HEIN, MARGO DIJKSTRA, and PIET KUHLMAN, "Self-Efficacy: The Third Factor Besides Attitude and Subjective Norm as a Predictor of Behavioural Intentions," *Health Education Research,* 3 (1988), 273–282.

GARDNER, JOHN W., *Self-Renewal.* New York: Harper & Row, Pub., 1963.

LAZARUS, R.S., *The Stress and Coping Paradigm.* New York: Spectrum Publ., 1981.

PACE, R. WAYNE, "When Bad Things Happen to Good Semanticists: New Thoughts on All-Inclusive Generalization," *ETC.: A Review of General Semantics,* 49 (Spring 1992), 20–33.

PELLETIER, KENNETH. *Mind as Healer, Mind as Slayer.* New York: Dell Pub. Co., Inc., 1977.

SELIGMAN, MARTIN E.P., *Helplessness: On Depression, Development and Death.* New York: W.H. Freeman & Company Publishers, 1975.

Connectedness

ALBRECHT, T. L., K.V. IREY, and A.K. MUNDY, "Integration in a Communication Network as a Mediator of Stress," *Social Work,* 27 (1982), 229–234.

ALBRECHT, T. L., and M.B. ADELMAN, "Social Support and Life Stress: New Directions for Communication Research," *Human Communication Research,* 11 (1984), 3–32.

ALBRECHT, T. L., and M. B. ADELMAN, *Communicating Social Support.* Newbury Park, Calif.: Sage Publications, Inc., 1987.

BRUHN, JOHN G., and STEWART WOLF, *The Roseto Story: An Anatomy of Health.* Norman: University of Oklahoma Press, 1979.

HOUSE, J.S., *Work Stress and Social Support.* Reading, Mass.: Addison-Wesley, 1981.

MILLER, K.I., B.H. ELLIS, E.G. ZOOK, and J.S. LYLES, "An Integrated Model of Communication, Stress, and Burnout in the Workplace," *Communication Research,* 17 (June 1990), 300–326.

MILLER, K.I., E.G. ZOOK, and B.H. ELLIS, "Occupational Differences in the Influence of Communication on Stress and Burnout in the Workplace," *Management Communication Quarterly,* 3 (1989), 166–190.

RAY, EILEEN BERLIN, "Identifying Job Stress in a Human Service Organization," *Journal of Applied Communication Research,* 11 (1983), 109–119. (a)

RAY, EILEEN BERLIN, "Job Burnout from a Communication Perspective," in R.N. Bostrom, ed., *Communication Yearbook 7.* Beverly Hills, Calif.: Sage Publications, Inc., 1983. (b)

RAY, EILEEN BERLIN, "The Relationship Among Communication Network Roles, Job Stress, and Burnout in Educational Organizations," *Communication Quarterly,* 39 (Winter 1991), 91–102.

Relaxation

Benson, Herbert, "Your Innate Asset for Combatting Stress," *Harvard Business Review,* 52 (1974), 49–60.

Benson, Herbert, *The Relaxation Response.* New York: Morrow, 1975.

Jacobsen, E., *Progressive Relaxation.* Chicago: University of Chicago Press, 1938.

Palmer, R.S., "Psyche and Blood Pressure: One Hundred Mental Stress Tests and Fifty Personality Surveys in Patients with Essential Hypertension," *Journal of the American Medical Association,* 144 (1950), 295–298.

Syme, S.L., M.M. Hyman, and P.E. Enterline, "Some Social and Cultural Factors Associated with the Occurrence of Coronary Heart Disease," *Journal of Chronic Diseases,* 17 (1964), 277–289.

Wallace, R.K., "Physiological Effects of Transcendental Meditation," *Science,* 167 (1970), 1751–1754.

Hardiness

HOBBS, CHARLES R., *Time Power.* New York: Harper & Row, Pub., 1987.

KOBASA, S.C., "Stressful Life Events, Personality, and Health: An Inquiry into Hardiness," *Journal of Personality and Social Psychology,* 37 (1979), 1–11.

KOBASA, S.C., "The Hardy Personality: Toward a Social Psychology of Stress and Health," in *Social Psychology of Health and Illness,* J. Suls and G. Sanders, eds., Hillsdale, N.J.: Erlbaum, 1982.

KOBASA, S.C., S. R. MADDI, M.C. PUCCETTI, and M.A. ZOLA, "Effectiveness of Hardiness, Exercise, and Social Support as Resources Against Illness," *Journal of Psychosomatic Research,* 29 (1985), 525–533.

MADDI, S.R., and S.C. KOBASA, *The Hardy Executive: Health Under Stress.* Homewood, Ill: Dorsey Professional Series, 1984.

Physical Fitness

ALLSEN, PHILIP, JOYCE M. HARRISON, and BARBARA VANCE, *Fitness for Life.* Dubuque, Iowa: Wm. C. Brown, 1984.

BLAIR, STEVEN, *et al.,* "Physical Fitness and All-Cause Mortality: A Prospective Study of Healthy Men and Women," *Journal of the American Medical Association,* 262 (1989), 2395–2401.

SPRINGER, ILENE, "A New Miracle Cure: It's Called Exercise—You Ought to Try It," *AARP Bulletin,* 31 (December 1990), 2, 10.

14

Individual Analysis and Change

It has been long claimed that effective analysis is critical to the selection and implementation of appropriate interventions for enhancing the effectiveness of individuals and organizations (see Mills, Pace, & Peterson, 1988; French & Bell, 1990). Unfortunately, more effort is often spent on refining organizational interventions and individual change packages than is spent on the development of analytic models and methods that could be useful in diagnosing problems involving people and organizations before change is attempted (see Lawrence & Lorsch, 1969).

The field of organizational communication has haltingly evolved some methods of analysis (see Downs, 1988), but the existence of a model of the process of analysis is so rare that it is almost an admission that less thought has been given to the full process than ought to have been. The most comprehensive model of the analytical process that is available for use in organizational communication is that devised by Mills and co-workers (1988, p. 9) and elaborated in the previous edition of this book.

DEFINITION OF ANALYSIS

Analysis is the activity of examining the constituent elements of a process or phenomenon so as to identify and recognize which conditions are contributing to the functioning of the unit and which conditions are creating problems in the unit being analyzed. Organizational communication (OC) analysts are interested in communication phenomena as both the antecedent and the consequent of organi-

FIGURE 14.1 Organizational Communication as a Mediating Factor between Human Resource and Organizational Functioning and Organizational Outcomes

zational functioning. That is, OC analysts might focus on communication activities directly to determine whether they are part of the conditions that are creating problems in organizational functioning. On the other hand, OC analysts may choose to focus on aspects of organizational functioning to determine whether these are creating problems in communication. An analysis of organizational communication may shed light on key processes that are detrimental to effective organizational functioning; conversely, an analysis of select organizational processes and activities might reveal critical influences that could be detrimental to effective communication.

Most of the time, OC analysts are interested in communication activities as mediators of organizational functioning. Figure 14.1 shows the primary focus of OC analysis.

Using the model shown in Figure 14.1, an organizational communication analyst might also examine organizational outcomes for signs of weak organizational functioning and attendant dysfunctions in communication. The comprehensive, holistic approach to analysis implied in Figure 14.1 would require an understanding of analytical methods that go beyond those designated to understand organizational communication, including general business practices, accounting and finance, organizational strategies, marketing, and personnel, as well as organizational processes such as goal setting, decision making, conflict resolution, and group functioning. It is not unusual, however, for OC analysts to be skilled in and knowledgeable about organizational processes and to draw upon the skills of business management specialists to provide analytical prowess in dealing with general business practices.

As we have conceived of organizational communication in this book, it is the central, key, critical, and necessary process and activity constituting organizations and organizational life; hence, a broad-stroke approach to analysis seems appropriate. We shall, therefore, review methods of analysis that elicit an understanding of communication as central to the effective functioning of organization members and of organizational life.

The remainder of this chapter will look at the model and process of analysis, along with three categories of individual analysis—task, performance, and needs methods, and the processes and methods of individual change. Five theories of change and relevant methods and procedures for designing and conducting training sessions will be described.

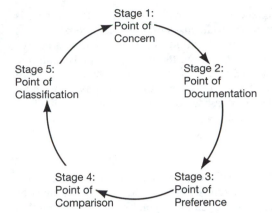

FIGURE 14.2 Model of Analysis

THE PROCESS OF ANALYSIS

Before dealing with specific issues of analysis, we shall discuss a general model of the process of analysis that involves a five-stage process (see also Figure 14.2):

1. Point of concern
2. Point of documentation
3. Point of preference
4. Point of comparison
5. Point of classification

Stage 1: Point of Concern

Most organizational performance has some history. A drop in productivity is a move from one level of production to a lower one. The need to make an analysis is usually provoked by a change that hurts. A *hurt* is some consequence indicating that a single person or the entire organization is beginning to suffer; it is one of those points of concern that impel us to take some type of analytical action.

Points of concern are usually of two types: (1) symptoms of a more basic problem, or (2) consequences of the basic problem. The difference between a *symptom* and a *consequence* lies primarily in the relationship between the problem and the manifestation of the problem. A symptom is a sign that the problem exists, but it is not the result of the problem. For example, absenteeism could be a symptom of some other condition, such as an undesirable organization climate. Lower sales figures are not usually considered to be the consequence of problems in the sales department, but they are symptoms of a problem. A consequence, on the other hand, is the result of some undesirable condition in the organization. A consequence results from the problem, whereas a symptom merely signals that the problem is present. For example, complaints and grumbling are usually symptoms of a problem such as poor working conditions or undesirable supervision; ineffective supervision, however, is more likely to be the consequence of inadequate selection and training programs.

In either case, symptoms and consequences both provoke a sense that something is wrong; what has been done in the past is now producing symptoms and consequences that appear different and undesirable. If the organization is producing only positive results, it is unlikely that it will move to the next stage in the process of analysis. Some point of concern usually triggers interest in analysis. Most of the time, the point of concern is subtle; things just feel a bit different from how they felt in the past. The more someone in the organization hurts from the consequence or symptom, the more likely it is that someone will suggest moving to the next stage.

Stage 2: Point of Documentation

Once a concern has been recognized, the next stage is to provide some documentation for the hurt or concern. The example of a medical diagnosis reveals the process that most of us go through when moving from Stage 1 to Stage 2. Suppose you hurt your foot and it is quite painful. Most likely you will go home and lie down to see if the pain goes away. Isn't that also the way most organizations function? Even with a hurt and some pain, we usually choose to see whether it will just go away.

Now, suppose it doesn't go away. Your choices may be to endure the pain or to go to a doctor to determine what the problem is. You decide to go to a doctor. You limp over to the office and sit for a while in the waiting room, holding your hurting foot. When your time comes, you hobble into the examining room.

The doctor enters and asks you, "What seems to be wrong?" You explain the problem. You remove your slipper and sock for the doctor to examine your foot. The doctor squeezes your foot and wiggles it a bit and you flinch with pain. The doctor says, "Hmm" and explains that it seems like you've hurt your foot. You think, "Of course, that's why I'm here."

Before we go further with this case, think some more. What do you want the doctor to do? One thing could be to make your foot better. But in most cases, the body has to make itself better. Another thing could be to determine for you what might be some of the causes of the pain in your foot. You choose the latter.

The doctor then volunteers that you could check into the hospital (at a daily cost of $900), have an X-ray ($250), and rest, but it seems likely that you just have a sprain, that the X-ray would not show much, and you can rest at home. Which plan do you choose? If you were the manager of a department and the pain was a little absenteeism, the manager might elect to endure the pain. The doctor presented you with a plan for documenting the concern. In your case, let us assume that you select the hospital and X-ray route.

Although the doctor indicates that the analysis suggests a simple sprain, you want to have further documentation; thus, you opt for the X-ray and some wiggling of your foot in the hospital. You are paying for some documentation just as an organization would pay for some evidence to support the feeling of organizational hurt.

The real objective of the second stage in analysis is to discover *why* the individual or organization is hurting. The point of concern indicates that something is apparently wrong, and the task at the second stage is to provide information that reveals what the cause could be.

A *cause* is the source of the hurt or concern; it is the reason why you—or the organization—are hurting. In the case of your foot, the cause could be either a sprained ligament or a broken bone. The documentation procedures should provide information that reveals the cause. Likewise, an analysis of organizational processes should provide information that reveals the cause of undesirable consequences and symptoms in the organization.

A case for "cause analysis" is effectively presented by Plunkett and Hale (1982), who suggest that locating the cause of some consequence is a function of "isolating some unique differences" between or among two or more people, machines, work groups, or organizations. They cite the case of four machines in which one is malfunctioning. The malfunction is likely to be something unique to that one machine.

One of the key objectives of the documentation phase of analysis is to discover what is different or unique about the people or organization being analyzed in comparison to some other set of data, principles, or circumstances. The methods, instruments, and procedures of documentation involve measuring and recording characteristics of the people or the organization being analyzed in an effort to provide a basis for comparison.

In human resource analysis, we have found that it is possible to document differences from three points of view: (1) from the view of the task to be performed, (2) from the view of the person performing the task, and (3) from the view of the supervisor (or other third party) of the person performing the task. These types of documentation are referred to, respectively, as *task analysis, needs analysis,* and *performance analysis.* The methods, instruments, and procedures involved in task, needs, and performance analyses will be presented later in this chapter.

Stage 3: Point of Preference

The third stage in analysis, as suggested earlier, involves the development of a set of data, principles, or circumstances that could serve as guidelines or preferences against which to compare the documentations secured in Stage 2. The purpose of the guidelines is to help identify the differences between a situation in which there are no problems and the situation being analyzed.

The set of data, principles, or circumstances should help direct the analyst's thinking about what kind of performance, behavior, attitude, skill, or practice would be preferred in the situation being analyzed. These preferences are usually found in five different places: job and position descriptions; performance standards statements; organization policies; excellent practices and performances in other organizations; and organization, communication, and other theories.

Job and position descriptions indicate what employees are supposed to do in the organization. They define the authority, responsibility, and accountability of each person and position within the organization, and they describe the requirements for occupying a position and for coordinating the activities of the position.

Performance standards statements indicate the level of proficiency at which employees should work. They reflect the expectations of the organization about how seriously each employee is to take his or her duties.

Organization policies are more general statements that reveal how employees should think about the decisions they make while carrying out the functions of their positions. Policies state what ought to be done in order to have an efficiently run organization. Behaviors that are inconsistent with policies, performance standards, and job descriptions should be suspect, if not taken as clear symptoms that the organization has problems.

Excellent practices in other companies often serve as standards against which to compare practices of the organization being analyzed. If you compare your performance against someone who is doing something similar without problems, you may find some key differences that are the source or cause of your problems.

Theories more often than not describe ideal situations. If your personal and organizational practices differ significantly from what theories suggest, you may find that the differences provide some excellent clues about the source or cause of your difficulties.

Analysis requires a clear set of guidelines or preferred models to determine where potential causes of problems lie. The next stage in the process of analysis involves the actual comparison and the decision about whether and where a problem exists.

Stage 4: Point of Comparison

Patton and Giffin (1973) state that "in its simplest terms, the process of analysis consists of determining the difference between what you have and what you would like to have" (p. 141). The point of comparison is an attempt to determine whether the documented concerns represent activities in the organization that deviate from the preferences and guidelines. The point of comparison attempts to answer two key questions: (1) Are there differences between what is happening and what ought to be happening? and (2) Are there differences important enough to do something about? If the documentation and the guidelines and preferences are clear, the differences may be easy to recognize as definitely detrimental to the organization. In other instances, the differences may be more subtle and difficult to relate to objective data.

Comparisons and problem definitions can be approached from two different perspectives: (1) from a *reactive* stance, after the act has occurred, or (2) from a *proactive* stance, or before the act has occurred. A reactive approach looks at how the organization is currently functioning and defines a problem as anything that deviates from the usual way of doing things. If things seem to be going smoothly, no problem exists; as soon as the organization shows signs of functioning differently from what has been the case, that is a clue that a problem may be developing.

A proactive approach defines a problem in the same way as a reactive approach—as the difference between what is happening and what ought to be happening—but recognizes a problem before some deviation in current functioning occurs. A proactive person may think that what is happening now may not be adequate, even though it meets minimal requirements. To discover "what ought to be happening" involves an effort to project into the future and picture something better than what now exists. Analysis, from a proactive perspective, is an effort to visualize better ways of doing things. A problem is the difference between the better way and the way it is presently being done.

Figure 14.3 pictures the idea of a problem from the reactive and the proactive points of view. The baseline (what is happening now) is the point from which we view deviations in both cases. The proactive perspective projects a line into the future and suggests that we have a problem if we are not already accomplishing what is possible. The reactive perspective takes the baseline as satisfactory or even desirable and looks for deviations that dip below the baseline.

Creative analysis attempts to locate problems that involve projections of the future and determine how the resolution of those problems could lead employees and the company to do better. Nevertheless, reactive problem analysis often provides information of great value to the development of human resources and the organization. Both approaches to analysis can have benefits.

A human resource problem (proactive or reactive) involves a person who is not performing as well as someone feels the person should be. That is, the person may lack information necessary to do the job well, or exhibit counterproductive attitudes, or lack the skills to do a job as well as it should be done. Through the process of analysis, diffi-

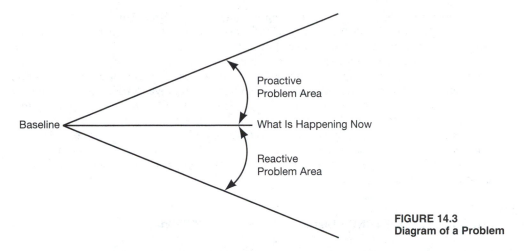

Baseline

Proactive
Problem Area

What Is Happening Now

Reactive
Problem Area

FIGURE 14.3
Diagram of a Problem

culties can be recognized and classified so as to make them amenable to improvement. Human resource analysis can provide important information about knowledge, attitude, and skill deficiencies that affect both the organization and the individuals.

Many efforts in analysis are stymied at this point. Managers might recognize and accept the documentation of concerns and the preferences and guidelines, but they may disagree about the extent to which the differences actually represent important deviations from the guidelines. If key people fail to recognize or accept the fact that the differences cause problems for the organization, little support will be given to proposals to remove the deficiencies. Thus, the point of comparison may need to be developed very carefully, with the best data available and the clearest possible demonstration that the differences are the causes for the negative consequences in the organization.

Stage 5: Point of Classification

The fifth and final stage in the analytical process is to determine what kinds of problems exist in the organization. The basic types of problems tend to correlate with the types of documentation used. Three types of problems can exist:

1. Those having to do with deficiencies in employee knowledge, attitudes, and skills.
2. Those having to do with deficiencies in the ways in which supervisors and managers plan, organize, staff, direct, and control the physical and human resources in the organization.
3. Those having to do with deficiencies in the conceptualization and design of the mission, positions, duties, responsibilities, and authority of the organization.

Deficiencies in knowledge, attitude, and skill that interfere with the competent performance of an employee's job are called *training problems*. Deficiencies in knowledge, attitude, and skill that keep an employee from moving into higher-level jobs, positions, and careers are called *development problems*. These two deficiencies can be removed through human resource training and development strategies.

Deficiencies in the way in which supervisors and managers carry out their duties and responsibilities are called *performance problems*. Performance problems can be resolved through changes in management practices.

Deficiencies in the way in which an organization is conceived and designed are called *organization problems*. Deficiencies in organizational design can be alleviated through organization development procedures.

Stage 5 is devoted primarily to classifying clearly the types of deficiencies existing in the organization. This stage is particularly critical because so many of the resources of an organization can be frittered away by attempting to remove deficiencies in knowledge, attitude, and skill by using organization development procedures; by attempting to remove deficiencies in supervisory and employee performance by using training and development procedures; or by attempting to remove deficiencies in organization design by using procedures to change management practices. The careful classification of problems confronting the organization can lead to more appropriate and powerful methods and strategies for solving problems.

APPROACHES TO DOCUMENTING HUMAN RESOURCE CONCERNS

We now turn our attention to the ways in which human resource concerns can be documented. Several general approaches can be used. Deficiencies in individual employee task performance can be documented through task analysis, performance analysis, and needs analysis.

Task Analysis

Task analysis is a method for determining the specific performance requirements of a job to identify what an employee must know and do to complete the job. "Task analysis is a method for specifying in precise detail and in measurable terms the human performance required to achieve specific management objectives, the tools and conditions needed to perform the job, and the skills and knowledge required of the employee" (Michalak & Yager, 1979, p. 43). A task analysis encompasses ten steps.

1. *Make a list of all major tasks and subtasks necessary to perform the job.* The idea is to identify what is to be done and what the steps are to get the job done. The tasks are usually listed in chronological order or in the time sequence in which they are performed. Jobs that require quite a bit of physical activity usually have the steps in the job listed chronologically. For example, a good practice exercise involves listing the steps required to change a flat tire. Assume that you are driving down the freeway and suddenly have a flat tire. List the tasks you need to do in order to stop the car, change the tire, and get back on the road. List them in the order that they should be done.

Jobs that involve less systematic tasks may be analyzed more efficiently by completing a highly detailed job description. Some jobs have tasks to do but not in any particular order. For example, an executive secretary may answer the telephone, make appointments, schedule travel arrangements, brief the boss, supervise typists and clerks, and maintain surveillance over certain budget items. A task analysis of the executive secretary's job might be accomplished by preparing a list of the different types of tasks that are done from time to time, although not necessarily in any particular order. Of course, each of the tasks, such as answering the telephone, could be analyzed by listing the steps chronologically.

2. *Record when and how often each task is to be done.* The frequency with which tasks are completed should be noted. If a task is done each Tuesday, it may be treated

differently from one that is done only every six months. The kinds of problems that may develop and the discrepancies that surface might imply quite different approaches for making changes, designing training sessions, and reinforcing learning.

3. *State the levels of acceptable performance associated with each major task.* Whenever possible, a specific quantifiable measure of acceptable performance should be noted. The best standards refer to such measures as time, distance, and number of errors. For example, scores of 90 percent; within 3 seconds; with a tolerance of .005 of an inch; a maximum of three typing errors, etc. Some jobs are less amenable to objective measures and require a consensus of judgments. "With the concurrence of three of the five team members" might be an acceptable level of performance. "Written in a manner consistent with the guidelines provided by the manual" might also be an acceptable standard of performance.

4. *Note the perceived importance of each task in accomplishing the overall objective of the job.* In performing the job of a student, there may be a difference in the importance assigned to attending class every period and completing the final exam. Missing the final may have considerably greater consequences on a positive evaluation of the student's performance than missing a day of class discussion. The importance of the task may reveal quite a bit about the types of problems that might develop if the task is not done well.

5. *List the skills and knowledge required to do the job.* At this stage in the task analysis we are interested in what the employee needs to know and what skills the employee needs to have to complete each task. To construct a sidewalk, knowing what cement to use and how to mix it might be helpful.

6. *Note the type of learning activity involved.* Some tasks require the employee to tell the difference between two or more items; others require remembering names for tools; a third may require determining whether something is correct; a fourth might necessitate executing some physical movements, whereas a fifth could require special uses of speech.

7. *Record the conditions under which the task is to be performed.* Some tasks must be performed under a great deal of pressure with people watching, whereas others are done in relative solitude where corrections can be made in private. Some tasks are performed with other people whereas others are done alone.

8. *Make an estimate of how difficult it seems to learn to perform the task.* On a scale from 1 to 10, some tasks are 1 and others are 9 in terms of figuring out how to do them. More time and effort may have to be expended in alleviating problems with difficult-to-learn tasks.

9. *Itemize the equipment, tools, and materials needed to do the task.* Difficulties in the performance of some tasks may be related to the number and quality of tools and other equipment to be used. Complicated pieces of equipment may create more problems than they solve.

10. *Note where the skills seem to be acquired best.* Some skills, such as operating a computer terminal on a sales floor, may be introduced in a simulated situation, but the actual learning and skill acquisition may take place more effectively on the sales floor.

Task analysis is frequently the basis for identifying and solving problems in industrial settings. The development of an industrial or technical training program, for example, is usually grounded in a task analysis of each task and piece of equipment. A training manual, leader's guide, and tests are all part of a technical training package. They nearly always evolve from a sound task analysis (Dowling & Drolet, 1979).

Once the task analysis has been completed, it must be validated or compared to the way in which the task is performed in the actual work location. Observation and on-site interviews with those who do the work are essential.

Performance Analysis

The way in which the task is done is clearly an important component in documenting a concern about what is happening in the organization. The ability of employees to do tasks and the motivation with which they do the tasks are important considerations in achieving high productivity. Documentation that employees are unable to do particular tasks or are unable to do them with peak efficiency would clearly reveal evidence that something is wrong in the organization.

How well employees are doing their jobs is frequently determined by a performance appraisal. Appraisals are performed not only to help maintain control over the organization's resources but also to measure the efficiency with which the human resources are being utilized and to identify places where improvement needs to take place (Cummings & Schwab, 1973). Appraisals can be an important factor in increasing both employee performance and satisfaction. Areas of deficiency in employee abilities can be identified and relationships between performance and on-the-job goals and rewards can be clarified, thus leading to increased motivation. With the ability to perform tasks efficiently and with high-intensity motivation, employees have the potential for increased productivity.

Cummings and Schwab (1973) describe four major appraisal methods: (1) comparative procedures, (2) absolute standards, (3) management by objectives, and (4) direct indexes. *Comparative procedures* focus on employee-to-employee evaluations; *absolute standards* focus on employee-to-common-standards assessments; *management by objectives* focuses on employee-to-specific-objective appraisals; and *direct indexes* focus on objective measures of behavior.

Comparative Procedures   These procedures usually involve comparing one employee with another on one or more global or general criteria that attempt to assess the employee's overall effectiveness in the organization. The question to be answered is something like, "Which one of the employees is the most successful, competent, effective, and valuable?" Two general types of comparative procedures are used: ranking and forced distribution.

RANKING   Three types of ranking procedures are the most common: straight ranking, alternative ranking, and paired comparison.

Straight Ranking   This procedure involves arranging the employees being appraised in the order of excellence on the criterion being used, assigning the very best performer a ranking of 1, the next best a ranking of 2, and so on through all employees being evaluated.

Alternative Ranking   This procedure is a little more complex and begins with an alphabetical list of employees being appraised. The evaluator is asked to identify the very best employee and the very weakest employee from the list. The best employee is ranked number 1, and the weakest employee is ranked last. Their names are removed from the list, and the best employee and the weakest employee are again identified from among the remaining employees on the list. Each time the best and weakest employees are removed from the list and added to the separate rankings. In this way the evaluation alternates between selecting the best and the poorest employee from an ever-reducing list.

TABLE 14.1 Paired Comparison Matrix for Five Employees

	SARA	DON	JIM	JO	MEL	TIMES CHOSEN	RANK
Sara		Sara	Jim	Jo	Mel	1	4
Don	Sara		Jim	Jo	Mel	0	5
Jim	Jim	Jim		Jo	Mel	2	3
Jo	Jo	Jo	Jo		Mel	3	2
Mel	Mel	Mel	Mel	Mel		4	1

Paired Comparison   This procedure has each evaluator compare each employee being appraised with every other employee, one at a time. A matrix listing every employee along both the X and Y axes, as illustrated in Table 14.1, is used. The evaluator simply picks the one employee from the pair who ranks highest. The employee's final evaluation and ranking are determined by how many times he or she is chosen.

FORCED DISTRIBUTION   This system requires the evaluator to assign a percentage of the employees being appraised to each of several categories based on several performance factors. Typically, a forced distribution assigns 10 percent of the employees to a superior category, 20 percent to an excellent category, 40 percent to an average category, 20 percent to a below-average category, and 10 percent to a poorest category. Table 14.2 illustrates the forced distribution system of appraising employees. The forced distribution system minimizes leniency in ratings, but the employees as a group may not fit the distribution all that well in terms of actual performance.

Absolute Standards   Systems that evaluate employees using absolute standards compare individuals with an authoritative model or measure rather than with other employees. A *standard* is a statement that describes what is expected in terms of behavior, value, suitability, and other characteristics. There are two basic ways of applying absolute standards: qualitative and quantitative.

QUALITATIVE METHODS   We shall comment on three qualitative methods, all of which ask the evaluator to determine whether a particular standard applies to a specific employee. In general, the appraiser makes an either-or judgment—the employee does what is asked or the employee does not do what is asked.

The Critical-Incident Method   The steps involved in using critical incidents begin with the collection of examples of when any employee is considered very effective or very ineffective—the middle group is usually not included—from supervisors and others who are familiar with employees who do a particular job. The examples, illustrations, or incidents are analyzed for similarities and grouped under a number of general categories. In the International Communication Association (ICA) Organizational Communication Audit Project, researchers collected hundreds of critical incidents reflecting highly effective and highly ineffective communication in organizations. Eight general categories of

TABLE 14.2 Forced Distribution System for Appraising Employees

EMPLOYEES BEING EVALUATED	POOREST	BELOW AVERAGE	AVERAGE	ABOVE AVERAGE	SUPERIOR
20	2	4	8	4	2
9	1	2	3	2	1

issues emerged from the analysis of incidents: (1) clarity of role, (2) adequacy of information, (3) syntactic disparity, (4) adequacy of feedback, (5) channel usage, (6) participation in decision making, (7) perception of interpersonal relationships, and (8) personal communication competencies.

After the categories are identified and defined, each evaluator is given a list to use in recording positive and negative incidents involving the employee being appraised. The incidents secured are used as the basis for determining whether the employee does what is expected of effective employees.

Weighted Checklists Checklists are developed by collecting a comprehensive list of statements about employee performance when they are doing the job to be rated. Each statement is evaluated by a group of supervisors or individuals familiar with the job in terms of how favorable or unfavorable the statement is for successful performance on the job. On a 7-point scale, unfavorable values have low scores, and favorable values have high scores. Statements on which the judges cannot agree are eliminated from the list. The items retained are weighted by the average score obtained from the group of evaluators.

Each evaluator is given a copy of the checklist, without the weightings, and indicates whether the employee performs the behavior mentioned in each item in the checklist. The final evaluation is determined by summing the scores of the items that have been checked.

The Forced-Choice Method This method involves gathering statements about the performance of a job from individuals familiar with the job. Judges evaluate very effective and very ineffective employees using information in the statements. Items that distinguish between the best and the worst employees are given weights. Judges also classify each statement according to whether it is favorable or unfavorable to job effectiveness. Items are then clustered so that several are capable of discriminating between effective and ineffective employees and at the same time determining favorability or unfavorability.

A forced-choice instrument, for example, might have four items. The evaluator would choose between A and B and between C and D. Items A and B would both be favorable to the job, but only B would discriminate between effective and ineffective employees. Items C and D would both be unfavorable to the job, but only C would discriminate between effective and ineffective employees. The person doing the appraisal would have the items without knowing which ones were favorable or unfavorable or which ones distinguish between effective and ineffective employees. The evaluator would check those items among the four that were most descriptive and least descriptive of the employee. The employee's score consists of the sum of the indexes for the items checked. High scores represent more desirable performance; low scores indicate less desirable performance.

QUANTITATIVE METHODS Two general types of quantitative methods are used: conventional rating scales and behaviorally anchored rating scales. Unfortunately, conventional rating scales permit a *halo effect* to occur, which may consistently bias evaluations for or against an employee. They also tend to focus on personality characteristics rather than on performance. Nevertheless, conventional rating scales are widely used. Behaviorally anchored rating scales are designed to reduce bias and error while providing useful information for employees during a development program.

Conventional Rating Scales This method generally consists of a series of statements about employee characteristics. A scale is established for each characteristic, usually ranging from unsatisfactory to outstanding on a 5-point scale. The evaluator places a check along the scale to represent his or her evaluation of the employee. From five to twenty-five

RATING SCALE

PERFORMANCE CATEGORIES	Unsatisfactory	Satisfactory			
		Meets minimum	Average	Above average	Outstanding
1. Accuracy, thoroughness, and completeness of work					
2. Presentability of work					
3. Care and maintenance of property and space					
4. Judgment					
5. Communication (oral and written expression)					
6. Leadership					
7. Public relations					
8. Safety of self and others					
9. Productiveness					

FIGURE 14.4 Conventional Rating Scale Form

characteristics may be evaluated. Figure 14.4 illustrates a typical conventional rating form for appraising employee performance.

Behaviorally Anchored Rating Scales   These scales are developed by using critical-incident procedures. Supervisors and others familiar with those being evaluated describe incidents in which the employees have been highly effective or highly ineffective. The incidents are grouped under a small number of categories based on similarities in behaviors. Judges, supervisors, and others then rate each incident on the basis of how well it represents extremely good performance or extremely poor performance. The incidents are ordered according to the average value assigned by the judges, and the incidents are placed along a scale from extremely poor performance to extremely good performance. The evaluator is given the scale with the critical incidents describing specific behaviors at each point on the scale. The employee is evaluated on each general category; the sum of the assigned scores across all categories is the employee's rating. A specific development program can be devised on the basis of weaknesses as revealed by the ratings.

Management by Objectives   In addition to the use of comparative procedures and absolute standards, a third type of appraisal method is that of management by objectives. MBO, as it is called, is based on the assumption that goals can be accomplished better if a person knows what is to be achieved, and progress toward a goal should be measured in terms of the goal to be accomplished. These seem like simple-minded premises, but they call our attention to the fact that clearly understood goals are easier to accomplish than unclear ones.

Another assumption of MBO is that both the subordinate and the supervisor are to be involved in defining and clarifying the goals to be accomplished. Moreover, a well-stated goal is one that is as quantitative as possible, with specific figures and dates. The process of involvement continues through the period of MBO, with the employee doing what is necessary to accomplish the goals. Finally, the supervisor and the employee periodically compare the employee's performance against the goals that were set. During the meeting the level of goal accomplishment is discussed, and the reasons why shortcomings occurred and how performance can be improved are reviewed. MBO is clearly a human resource development procedure that can be used to upgrade below-standard performance, to maintain acceptable levels of performance, and to strengthen high levels of performance that may lead to advancement, unique contributions to personal growth, and organization accomplishment.

The four basic phases in MBO can be summarized as follows (Cummings & Schwab, 1973):

1. Planning the objectives.
   a. The manager and employee meet and discuss the goals to be accomplished during the next review period—4, 6, or 12 months.
   b. The goals, stated in written form, identify (i) the specific tasks to be accomplished and (ii) the measures of satisfactory performance.
   c. During the meeting the manager and the employee discuss and resolve any differences between their perceptions of the size of the goals to be accomplished and where accomplishment of the goals will lead.
   d. The meeting to establish objectives should also include the identification of specific operational and measurable targets against which a performance program can be compared.
2. Working toward accomplishment of objectives.
   a. The employee implements a plan leading to the accomplishment of the objectives.
   b. The observable checkpoints are used to measure progress.
3. The manager and the employee meet later at some specific time to review jointly what has happened during the performance period. This usually begins with a self-appraisal by the employee, which is submitted to the manager in writing. The self-appraisal is reviewed jointly by the manager and the employee. An analysis of why some goals were not met and others were and the success experienced is made.
4. New objectives are set and continuing objectives reinforced.

Both the strength and weakness of the MBO system lies in its ability to provide unique objectives and standards for each employee. Individual differences and personal contributions can be considered. Regretfully, the identification and allocation of rewards on an equitable basis is much more difficult to achieve. Because the employee plays a fairly direct role in identifying, setting, and evaluating goal accomplishment, employee performances may vary considerably, or the entire system may be subverted to the interests of employees.

Direct Indexes of Performance Cummings and Schwab (1973) refer to two direct indicators of performance: (1) units of output and (2) turnover and absenteeism. Number of items made, number of items sold, number of students taught, number of majors in a program, number of clients interviewed, and number of cartons shipped are all units of production. The frequency of absences and tardiness and the number of permanent terminations and resignations are special measures of employee productivity, especially the performance of supervisors. Complaints, grievances, and reprimands may also be indicators of supervisory performance.

Thus far we have discussed methods associated with two forms of documenting individual employee task performance: task analysis and employee performance appraisal. Straight ranking, alternative ranking, paired comparison, forced distribution, critical incident, weighted checklists, forced choice, conventional rating scales, behaviorally anchored rating scales, and management by objective have been discussed as measures of individual employee task performance. We shall continue our discussion of methods for documenting the concern by examining needs analysis procedures.

Needs Analysis

A needs analysis looks at those things that are keeping employees from making their strongest contribution to the organization. Procedures for conducting a needs analysis consist mainly of talking to employees about their work and having employees respond to feelings about their work in writing. Two other basic approaches also provide information about what is keeping employees from making the best of their resources: files analysis and clinical observation. We shall discuss the methods of conducting a needs analysis by looking at files analysis, clinical observation, interviewing, and the use of questionnaires.

Files Analysis   Files analysis consists of a study of (1) organization policies, plans, organization charts, and position descriptions; (2) employee grievance, turnover, absenteeism, and accident reports; (3) records of meetings and program evaluation studies; (4) past performance appraisals and attitude surveys; and (5) audits and budget reports. The files and documents are examined for indications of deficiencies and circumstances that appear to interfere with optimal performance of employees.

Clinical Observation   *Clinical observation* refers to making a set of observations that are extremely objective and realistic, in contrast to highly subjective observations in artificial settings. Objectivity is achieved by observing behaviors that can be counted and verified. Realism is achieved by observing employees working at their jobs. The purpose of clinical observation is to identify and record the frequency with which critical behaviors occur. Clinical observation represents a system for discriminating between very high and very low performing individuals or groups. Clinical observations are most useful when differences between employees concern frequency or quantity of performance rather than quality of performance.

Clinical observations help to verify critical incidents and represent an application of Vilfredo Pareto's principle of the unequal distribution of wealth. Pareto discovered that about 80 percent of the wealth of Italy was controlled by 20 percent of the population. This principle has been demonstrated in other ways, such as 20 percent of a company's sales force makes 80 percent of it sales; that 20 percent of the sales generates 80 percent of the profits; and 20 percent of a person's effort results in 80 percent of his or her productivity. Clinical observations seek to identify those behaviors in the 20 percent category that differentiate between high and low producers and result in 80 percent of the organization's effectiveness.

Three general steps are involved in making clinical observations: (1) Determine the behaviors to be observed. Tentative decisions about specific behaviors to be observed could be derived from interviews and, possibly, experience. Eventually a clearly stated description of some clusters of behaviors to be observed should be used. Four types of behaviors might be observed in public-contact situations: rude behaviors that are curt, short, and argumentative; indifferent behaviors, such as speaking to a customer only when addressed, making few eye contacts, speaking in an impersonal tone; pleasant behaviors, such as smiling and greeting the customer warmly, making definite eye contact, and ending the contact with a personal comment; and value-added behaviors, such as smiling at, greeting, and chatting with customers during the transaction, offering information, and making statements that are adapted to the customer, with a personal salutation at the end. (2) Observe some highly effective employees and some highly ineffective ones and write the observations on separate record forms. (3) Make observations of each group of employees for a specified period of time, such as thirty minutes at a time in the morning and in the afternoon for five days.

Portray the data in a Pareto-type diagram. (See Figure 14.5.) The procedures for creating a Pareto diagram include summarizing the data from the record form to show the number of times (frequency) each employee being observed engaged in the types of behaviors described. Arrange the data in order from the largest to the smallest numbers and total them. Compute the percentage of behaviors exhibited by each person observed. Plot the percentages on a graph. Construct a bar graph putting the longest bar (highest frequency) on the far left. The vertical scale (up the left-hand side) shows the percentage, usually in multiples of 10 percent, and the horizontal scale (along the bottom) shows the types of behaviors. Separate charts should be constructed for both high and low performers. The arrangement of the bar graphs from highest frequencies on the left to lowest frequencies on the right provides a quick visual picture of where the problems are occurring. By developing a behavioral frequency Pareto-type diagram before and after training and development, the effectiveness of certain strategies can be determined.

Interviewing Interviewing or talking to people about their work is one of the most commonly used methods for conducting a needs analysis. Interviews are also a basic method for gathering information for task analyses, performance appraisals, and organizational communication systems analyses. Interviews in needs analysis are often referred to as *gap interviews* and are designed to gather information about opinions and attitudes, values, thoughts and ideas, and expectations. Interviewing allows employees to talk about their perceptions of a problem or need and their proposed solutions.

Interviews are frequently used at different stages of documenting a concern, but they are especially helpful early in a needs analysis to get an idea of the general feelings of select organization members. An early interview is usually called *exploratory* since it seeks to get a sense of what is happening in order to select other procedures and develop instruments.

Interviews can be conducted with one person or with a group, often employing brainstorming or nominal group processes, and can be either face to face or over the telephone. Interviews can be formal or casual, structured or unstructured, lengthy or brief.

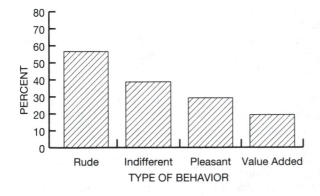

FIGURE 14.5 Pareto Diagram of Behaviors of Ineffective Public-Contact Employees

Interviews are probably most effective in revealing employee feelings, causes of problems, and expectations and anticipated difficulties. Because they are usually personal and involve predominantly oral communication, interviews help establish and strengthen relationships between parties involved in the needs analysis.

Interviews have their disadvantages also. They may be somewhat costly when one interviewer works with one employee. They may seem quite slow when only four or five individuals are interviewed in a day. Employee responses are almost entirely qualitative, making them difficult to analyze and interpret. The quality of an interview may depend heavily upon the interpersonal skills of the interviewer, particularly in face-to-face interviews. Employees can feel very uneasy and self-conscious with an unskilled interviewer. If employees doubt that their comments will be held in confidence, they may be reluctant to answer questions openly, fully, and candidly. Interviewers must be sensitive to nonverbal behaviors that tell when employees want to say more, when they desire to talk in greater confidence, or to discuss something controversial.

INDIVIDUAL INTERVIEWS   One-on-one interviews are conducted near the employee's place of work and cover certain basic questions while allowing the employee to comment on what topics he or she prefers. Procedures for conducting a needs analysis interview are similar to those used in other types of analyses and involve arranging for a private location in which to conduct the interview, such as an office or secluded work area.

Put the interviewee at ease and assure the individual that what is being discussed will be handled so as to maintain confidences and the anonymity of information and the interviewee. Ask each question in the order presented on the interview schedule. Record the interviewee's answers to the questions as accurately as possible. The responsibility of the interviewer is to secure and record precise and accurate answers to each question asked. You may find, however, that interviewees provide information relevant to some other question; record answers as unobtrusively as possible, but under the question for which they are the answers, then guide the interview back to the original question and continue with the sequence. When you arrive at the later question and discover that you have already recorded answers, simply pose the question to verify that the responses are accurate and to allow the interviewee to elaborate on answers. Record replies to each question on a separate sheet of paper. This will facilitate the analysis later.

The interview schedule for a supervisory needs analysis might include the following questions (Kirkpatrick, 1971):

1. What problems exist in your department?
2. What problems do you expect will develop in the future?
3. What ought to be included in a training program to resolve the problems?
4. What information would help you to do your job better?
5. When would be a good time to hold a training session?
6. What is the best time for you to attend a training session?

The interview should be opened with some comments to establish rapport and goodwill with the interviewee, then reveal the purpose of the interview. Give some assurances that the confidences will be maintained and that no names or personal identification will be associated with any response. Mention that only general needs and group concerns will be included in any reports. Request permission to take notes. Make a transition to the first question.

ANALYSIS OF INTERVIEW RESPONSES   Interview responses are analyzed in an eight-step procedure:

1. Assign a code number to each interview schedule; put the code on all pages.
2. Place the answers to Question One from all schedules together.
3. Sort the answers to Question One according to some prearranged category system—position, years in service, level of authority, etc.
4. Bring all answers to a single question together on one or more pages—cut, paste, and photocopy or type the answers.
5. Identify themes occurring in respondents' answers to each question.
6. State each theme and excerpt some typical responses from the lists—appropriately disguised to protect the anonymity of interviewees—to illustrate how you arrived at the theme.
7. After all responses to all questions of all interviewees have been reviewed for themes, look for similarities and differences among the themes and compare and contrast individual and group responses of different categories of employees.
8. Write an analysis of the interview response to indicate what the needs are.

GROUP INTERVIEWS   Group interviews are often held to elicit the ideas and needs of a work group or team. In addition to following the procedures for personal interviews, including having a set of clear questions in the form of an interview schedule that is adapted to the group, several techniques are used to obtain maximum benefit from group interaction and to reduce the pressures toward conformity implicit in face-to-face interaction. These techniques are discussed below (Pace, Peterson, & Burnett, 1979).

Brainstorming   This is a group session in which members think up ideas without being critical or giving judgmental reactions. A question such as "What do we need to do our jobs better?" could be used in brainstorming. A brainstorming session is most effective when some simple guidelines and rules are adhered to; the leader should call the meeting to order and review the following:

1. No questions should be asked during the brainstorming period; all questions should be answered before the start of the session.
2. To maintain order, the leader recognizes each person, as quickly as possible, who has an idea; if you are not called upon immediately, jot down your idea for use later.
3. Avoid elaborating on, defending, or editorializing on any suggestion; merely state the idea without personal reservations, as quickly and concisely as possible.
4. Suggest even the obvious, since some apparent need may trigger some ideas in others; don't be guilty of self-criticism.
5. Don't be afraid to restate an idea in a different way.
6. Strive for a workable solution but allow the ridiculous to occur.
7. Follow all brainstorming rules faithfully. Four rules must not be violated; the leader should ring a bell or slam a gong if even one rule is violated:
   a. Criticism is not allowed.
   b. Freewheeling is encouraged.
   c. Quantity is wanted.
   d. Combination and improvement are sought.

The person doing the needs analysis is usually the leader. After the session is over, the ideas and needs are processed and grouped in much the same way that ideas from an interview are handled.

POOR INTERPERSONAL RELATIONSHIPS

Producing Factors	Deterring Factors
Managers treat employees like machines rather than as employees	Similar backgrounds in the professional area
Excessive authoritarian management styles	Genuine interest in having a successful work unit
Excessive yelling and screaming at employees	Company policy on conflict

FIGURE 14.6 Sample Force-Field Analysis
Source: From Donald F. Michalak and Edwin G. Yager, *Making the Training Process Work,* New York: Harper & Row, Pub., 1979.

Force-Field Analysis   This is the special application of group interviews and brain-storming (Michalak & Yager, 1979). Its basic objective is to provide a way of systematically identifying factors that produce and deter action in the organization. The idea of a force-field is one of balance. In an organization, the current way of doing things is a result of counter-balancing factors, some producing and some deterring. As shown in Figure 14.6, the technique is relatively simple and involves a flip chart with newsprint, a felt pen, and a brain-storming group. The leader/interviewer draws a force-field diagram on the flip chart, with the issue stated at the top of the page. A vertical line running down the page represents the way things are being done now. The arrows represent the producing and deterring factors.

As group members call out forces that produce or deter the current status, the leader/interviewer should record each item as close to verbatim as possible to avoid inter-rupting the group with questions of interpretation and meaning. Along with each force, the leader/interviewer draws a horizontal line toward the vertical line to represent the strength of the producing or deterring force. Each line will be a different length depending upon the strength of the force. The current circumstances are a balance between the forces. To make a change, a force-field analysis suggests, remove or strengthen the forces that produce or deter the kind of action that you want.

Nominal Group Process   This is a structured group meeting in which participants alternate ideas silently, listing ideas in serial order orally for posting on a flip chart, offering pro and con and clarifying comments, and voting on ideas.

Nominal group process (NGP) balances the influence of high-status, highly expres-sive, strong personalities, allowing equality of participation and consideration of ideas. NGP facilitates more open discussion and the contribution of unusual and controversial ideas while applying simple mathematics to reduce errors when individual judgments are com-bined into group decisions.

Nominal group process involves a number of stages plus some preparation. Since NGP relies heavily on the posting of ideas in front of the group, it is essential to have a flip chart and newsprint to be mounted on an easel or attached to the wall. A roll of masking tape, 3-by-5-inch cards, felt pen, and paper and pencil for each participant are important also. The NGP develops as follows:

1. Welcome the participants and explain the process. Place the question before the group: "What kinds of problems are you experiencing in your work?"
2. Each member writes ideas in response to the question, working silently and independently.
3. The leader-recorder asks for one idea from each group member, going around the table one at a time; the recorder writes the ideas on the flip chart without comment about the ideas until all are posted.

FIGURE 14.7 Sample Consensus Ranking Form for Needs Analysis

INDIVIDUAL TRAINING NEEDS RANKING FORM

Instructions: Below are listed 15 training needs identified by typical employees. Your task is to rank-order them in terms of their importance to your personal needs. Place a 1 in front of the type of training that you feel to be your greatest need, and so on, to 15, your lowest training need.

_____	Coping with stress	_____	Interviewing
_____	Fulfilling management functions	_____	Training new employees
_____	Maintaining interpersonal communication	_____	Problem solving and decision making
_____	Writing memos and reports	_____	Developing self
_____	Inducting new employees	_____	Supervising ethnic minorities
_____	Appraising employee performance	_____	Motivating employees
_____	Listening	_____	Handling complaints and grievances
_____	Planning		

4. Each idea in the list is taken in the order listed, and comments of clarification are made about each one; the purpose of this period is to clarify, not to argue, the merits of any idea.

5. From the list of ideas on the flip chart, the group selects a specific number that seem to be the most important—from five to ten items. Each group member writes the priority items on separate 3-by-5-inch cards and rank-orders the items from 1 to 10. The cards are collected, shuffled, and recorded on newsprint in front of the group. The sum of the rankings across all group members is the final order of items. Group members can discuss the final rankings and rate the importance to them of each need. The results represent the needs analysis.

Consensus Ranking   This is a two-stage group activity in which employees (1) individually rank a list of potential needs and (2) as a group arrive at consensus on a ranking of the same items. A sample ranking form is illustrated in Figure 14.7. Instructions for the group consensus step should look something like those in Figure 14.8.

Card Sort   Another approach to interviewing employees about needs is to use a card-sort activity (Bellman, 1975). Use of the card-sort technique involves (1) preparing the cards and (2) conducting the survey interview. Pick a target population, such as supervisors, and develop a long list of responsibilities. Translate the responsibilities into questions. Group the questions into common areas, such as motivation, delegation, training, planning, time use, teamwork, or communication. Transfer the questions to cards. Put only one question on a card. Number each card on the reverse side so that each group of ques-

FIGURE 14.8 Sample Instructions for Group Consensus Exercise

GROUP RANKING FOR TRAINING NEEDS

Instructions: This phase of the needs analysis is designed to discover the most important *group* needs. Your group is to reach consensus on rankings for the 15 employee needs. This means that the final rankings for each of the needs must be agreed upon by each group member before it becomes part of the group decision. Consensus may be difficult to achieve; therefore, not every item will meet with everyone's complete approval. Try, as a group, to make each ranking one with which all group members can at least partially agree. Here are some guidelines in reaching consensus:

1. Avoid arguing for your own individual judgments; approach the task on the basis of logic.
2. Avoid changing your mind only in order to reach agreement and avoid conflict; support only needs with which you are able to agree somewhat, at least.
3. View differences of opinion as helpful rather than as a hindrance to reaching agreement.

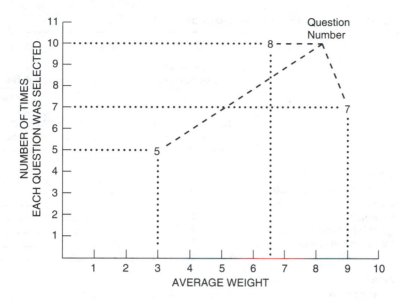

FIGURE 14.9 Sample Matrix for Displaying Card-Sort Data

tions is represented by a sequence of numbers, such as 1,2, 3, 4. With the questions on cards, a supervisor can quickly compare one question with another and physically separate the cards into stacks and sequences. You are now prepared to conduct the survey interview.

Begin the interview by explaining the purpose of the interview, how the employee can help, and the card deck. Give the cards to the employee while asking, "If you could have the answers to ten of these questions, which ten would be most helpful to you in doing your job?" Ask the employee to select the ten most important questions and to place them in order from most important to least important. Explain that after the cards have been selected and ordered, you will return and discuss them. Leave the room until the employee has finished, about ten to fifteen minutes.

When you return, have the employee read the number of each question (on the reverse side) while you record the rank order of the ten questions for later analysis. Assign the most important question 10 points, the second most important 9 points, down to the least important question, which is given 1 point. Review the sheet on which you recorded the rankings and the weightings, answering questions for the employee. Ask the employee to respond to the question "What is happening in your job that caused you to select this question?" Ask the question in a variety of ways for each of the ten questions selected. Elicit specific job performance comments. Record the employee's comments on index cards, putting one to a card for easier sorting later. Code the index cards and the cards with questions in the same way so they can be sorted according to location, work group, position, and demographic characteristics such as experience or age, depending on what might be important.

At the end of the interview, review the cards with the employee to make certain they are accurate. Assure the employee that the comments are for your use only and no identities will be revealed. Conclude by explaining when the analysis is to be finished, how the employees will learn about the results, and how the data will be used to determine needs.

Analyze the card sorts by portraying the results in a matrix like that illustrated in Figure 14.9, with the horizontal axis reading from 1 to 10 and the vertical axis running from 1 to the number of times any question was selected most frequently. Using the matrix, the more important questions are located in the upper-right-hand quadrant.

FIGURE 14.10 Sample Needs Analysis Questionnaire

SURVEY OF TRAINING AND DEVELOPMENT NEEDS

	This Ability Is Important to My Job					I Could Do My Job Better If	
	Not Important		Very Important			I Had More Training	Some Conditions Were Changed in the Organization
	(circle a number)						
Planning Abilities							
1. Set objectives or develop projects	1	2	3	4	5	_____	_____
2. Develop plans	1	2	3	4	5	_____	_____
3. Set priorities for work	1	2	3	4	5	_____	_____
4. Use program budgeting procedures	1	2	3	4	5	_____	_____
5. Use special budgeting systems	1	2	3	4	5	_____	_____
6. Use time effectively	1	2	3	4	5	_____	_____
Managing Abilities							
7. Assign work to people	1	2	3	4	5	_____	_____
8. Delegate	1	2	3	4	5	_____	_____
9. Motivate people	1	2	3	4	5	_____	_____
10. Understand people of different ages, races, backgrounds	1	2	3	4	5	_____	_____
Problem-Solving Abilities							
11. Recognize and analyze the problems	1	2	3	4	5	_____	_____
12. Identify solutions to problems	1	2	3	4	5	_____	_____
13. Decide which solution is best	1	2	3	4	5	_____	_____
14. Make decisions in emergencies	1	2	3	4	5	_____	_____
Communication							
15. Inform supervisor	1	2	3	4	5	_____	_____
16. Inform subordinates	1	2	3	4	5	_____	_____
17. Answer questions about programs	1	2	3	4	5	_____	_____
18. Answer questions about merit, production, EEO, and classification	1	2	3	4	5	_____	_____
19. Conduct formal briefings	1	2	3	4	5	_____	_____
20. Lead meetings	1	2	3	4	5	_____	_____
21. Listen and accept views of others	1	2	3	4	5	_____	_____
22. Provide negative information	1	2	3	4	5	_____	_____
23. Complete reports and forms	1	2	3	4	5	_____	_____
24. Write formal letters	1	2	3	4	5	_____	_____

TELEPHONE INTERVIEW   A final interviewing procedure is to use telephone surveys. Interviewing over the telephone is a common market-research technique (Downs, Smeyak, & Martin, 1980). Calls are usually made to a random sample of individuals using an interview guide or schedule. The schedule must be developed carefully. Downs and colleagues suggest that the schedule should be as simple as possible in order to reduce fatigue, that respondents should not be asked questions they cannot answer, that the questions should be restricted to essential information, and that the small sample size consistent with the objectives of the study should be used.

The telephone interviewer should ask questions exactly as they are worded so as to have comparable information from all respondents. Interviewers should probe answers when necessary to avoid incomplete or unclear responses. The interviewer should not be drawn into giving answers. Finally, some answer should be recorded for every question. Avoid leaving blank spaces, either by probing or writing in "don't know." Telephone interviewing requires a great deal of skill and patience, but few survey techniques are as quick and economical.

Questionnaires   Questionnaires and other written instruments and procedures are probably the most widely used methods for conducting a needs analysis. Questionnaires can provide fairly precise information from large and small groups of employees. A variety of questions can be used and combined with other written instruments, such as rating scales, rankings, and free-response questions. Questionnaires can be administered individually or in groups or can be mailed to employees. They are relatively inexpensive to use and can reach a large group of people in a fairly short time. Responses to a questionnaire are about as easy to summarize, analyze, and report as any needs analysis procedure. Questionnaires can be simple or complex. The major problem associated with questionnaires is that they often require a great deal of time and expertise to develop effective instruments.

An effective questionnaire for use in needs analysis should be as simple as possible to achieve the purpose of the survey (Zemke & Walonick, 1980). Questionnaires of two or three pages may appear unnecessarily complex and may intimidate employees. Longer questionnaires can be used, of course, but they require special expertise to construct. Wilson (1980) argues that needs analysis can profitably use "demonstrably valid surveys" developed by professionals. Although well-constructed questionnaires are important in securing accurate information, some simple instruments can be very effective.

Figure 14.10 illustrates a needs analysis questionnaire that covers four general areas and includes twenty-four items about specific abilities. The items are fairly specific and the response categories ask for indications of importance to the job as well as the need for training or organizational changes.

From an analysis of the differences between what is required and what the employee possesses in areas of importance, some critical needs can be identified.

FIVE APPROACHES TO INDIVIDUAL CHANGE

Rational Theory

An approach to change based on rational theory begins with the assumption that *what we believe determines how we behave*. Beliefs are those statements we make to ourselves and others that represent what we accept as true. Rational theory suggests that what we accept as true determines the strategies we select and use to perform tasks and to deal with others. For example, if you believe, as a supervisor, that you can influence an employee to work harder if you are direct, you will tend to speak more directly to employees and act in more direct ways toward them. As a supervisor, you will communicate more directly if you believe that directness is more effective.

From the perspective of rational theory, a program to change the behavior of an employee should focus on changing beliefs. The change in beliefs would then affect how the employee behaves. The old adage "a person convinced against his will is of the same opinion still" reflects the philosophy of rational theory. Without a change in beliefs, a person will continue to follow old patterns of behavior or revert back to them at the earliest opportunity.

In discussing the training of professional workers, Combs, Avila, and Purkey (1971) argue that they should be provided with "opportunities for discovering personal meanings" (p.9), which are the guides for day-to-day behaviors they will use in carrying out their professional duties. *Personal meanings* are the images one holds about people, events, and objects. Personal meanings are expressed in the ways we talk about things.

Craighead, Kazdin, and Mahoney (1976) note that "individuals respond to language in the form of instructions, commands, and rules that govern behavior. However, there are more subtle means, such as in self-verbalizations, through which language influences behavior" (p.145). A rational approach to change builds on the powerful impact that beliefs, personal meanings, language, and self-verbalizations have on behavior.

The foundational premise of rational-emotive training (RET), one rational approach, is expressed by Ellis and Harper (1975) as follows:

> Unlike lower animals, people tell themselves various sane and crazy things. Their beliefs, attitudes, opinions, and philosophies largely . . . take the form of internalized sentences of self-talk. Consequently, one of the most powerful and elegant modalities they can use to change themselves . . . consists of their clearly seeing, understanding, disputing, altering, and acting against their internal verbalizations" (p. x).

Rational theory assumes that problems result from irrational thinking and verbalizing; thus, the emphasis is on the cultivation of rationality. In this context, rational thinking means that our beliefs and verbalizations accurately represent reality and that our actions are consistent with our beliefs and verbalizations. Irrationality, in contrast, occurs when our beliefs and verbalizations do not match reality and our actions are inconsistent with our beliefs.

Rational theory argues that individual change is facilitated by presenting problems in which one's perceptions, beliefs, and personal meanings of reality are tested for accuracy by comparing them with external sources. Rationality is cultivated by confronting so-called irrational concerns and by implementing specific ways of thinking and talking about them.

Rational-emotive training has been called a form of *semantic therapy*. Ellis and Harper (1975) acknowledge that they may have developed a way of applying the teachings of general semantics, which Bois (1978) says "deals with the meaning we find or put in whatever we do and whatever happens to us" (pp. 43–44). Rational theory deals directly with the verbal communicative aspects of behavior and is belief-oriented. Even our desires and emotions have deep biological and social foundations that are directly related to our thinking processes and are, consequently, also largely under our control when approached as personal meanings and beliefs.

The work of Martha Spice (1982) on *thought selection* is typical of those attempting to apply rational theory. She observes that "thought selection, self-suggestion, belief development, affirmation, self-talk, internal dialogue, and possibility thinking are all phrases alluding to the notion that what we say to ourselves about ourselves at a conscious or subconscious level affects our results." The formula, she says, is simple: "knowledge + congruent beliefs = action . . . knowledge + negating beliefs = 'good intentions' (and often guilt)" (p. 58).

Chamberlain's book (1978) on self-defeating behaviors (SDB's) illustrates how to develop a program for change based on rational theory. He identifies seven steps through which a person moves to alter behavior.

1. *Identify a behavior (a way of responding, reacting, or acting) that is keeping you from accomplishing some goals.* If you are not able to recognize a behavior that is a hindrance to a more complete and satisfying life, look at the following list and select one or more behaviors that seem to fit you:

Feelings of inferiority
Attitude of superiority
Lack of motivation
Procrastination
Compulsive lying
Uncontrollable temper
Excessive worry
Feelings of loneliness
Inability to say "no"
Wasting time
Forgetfulness
Fear of commitment
Extreme nervousness
Feeling inadequate

Choose only one behavior to focus on at a time. Choose a behavior that you would like to change and that causes problems not only for you but also for others. Write down the behavior you would like to change. Finally, describe *how you do the behavior you want to change.* For example, if you wrote "withdrawing under pressure" as the behavior, you should describe what you do to withdraw under pressure, how you withdraw, etc.

2. *Accept responsibility for the behavior.* Part of the process of eliminating behaviors that hinder you is to accept responsibility for them. We often disown our behavior by *labeling ourselves,* which shifts responsibility for the behavior to our heredity. Labels indicate that we *are* something. To be something indicates that we have an inherited condition. Identify a label that represents the behavior to be changed. It should be a negative label, such as "I am a withdrawer."

Change the label to give a more positive connotation by changing the label from a state of existence to some action. Thus, in the withdrawing example, the label might read, "I do withdrawing" rather than "I am a withdrawer." In some cases it is necessary to change the negative label to the exact opposite, such as "I stay involved," in order to give the positive connotation.

Another way to shift responsibility is to blame other people for the behaviors that hinder us. "My mother made me do it," "I can't control my feelings," and "My family hurt me" are statements that shift responsibility. Your task is to write about the behavior so as to accept responsibility for it. Thus, rewrite how you do the behaviors by inserting terms of personal responsibility such as "I choose to withdraw."

3. *Identify the short- and long-range costs paid for the hindering behavior.* Some costs we pay for behaviors include the following: not being fully happy, feeling depressed, poor relationships, lack of energy, shame, and loss of control. Make a list of all the costs you pay for the hindering behavior. Continue listing until the cost is too high to accept. Now, list ways that you minimize the costs. For example, "I joke about the costs," "I conclude that I was destined to be that way," "I ignore that I am being hurt," "I feel that the bad behavior can't be helped," or "I keep busy and occupied so as to avoid the cost."

4. *Recognize that you can make inner choices.* All of our outer choices are based on some inner, deeply felt values and priorities. To gain control over our behavior, we need to control the inner choices that lead to behaviors. The inner choices or beliefs are with you all the time. It may appear to you that behaviors are activated automatically, but the inner choices are often made in a split second and you may find it difficult to catch yourself making the choices or to recognize the choices you actually make. You need to realize that you do make inner choices based on values or beliefs in order to activate external behaviors. You decide to carry out the inner choices in a series of outer movements and behaviors. Work through these seven phases:

a. List some inner choices that help you maintain the behavior you want to eliminate.
b. Catch yourself making an inner choice and become aware of the behavior that follows from it.
c. Practice making other choices.
d. Monitor yourself and catch yourself making choices, then consciously make alternative self-enhancing choices.
e. Get ahead of your own game; lessen the time between making a choice and your recognition of having made the choice.
f. If you suffer a relapse, learn from it.
g. Experience alternative choices in advance by closing your eyes and visualizing or imagining yourself responding in your best, controlled self.

5. *Recognize the techniques that are used to activate hindering behaviors.* Techniques such as getting discouraged, comparing yourself to others, and behaving in an impatient manner are used to activate hindering behaviors.

6. *Face the fears you may have of being without the hindering behavior.* Fears are a form of belief. "I will fail" represents a fear that encourages hindering behaviors. Recognize that you will have fears if you change your behavior. For example, you may fear that you will find out that "I am a person I don't like," or "I am dumb and incompetent after all." These are statements that most of us fear, even though they may be untrue.

7. *Face your fears by testing them against reality.* Let go of the hindering behavior and see what happens.

BEHAVIORAL THEORY

Behavioral theory is firmly rooted in the assumption that changes in the way people behave can be produced more efficiently by focusing on observable behaviors than by focusing on beliefs and ways of thinking, as rational theory suggests. In fact, both attitudes and internal thought processes are understood by observing and measuring overt behavior. This is not to say that behaviors are unaffected by internal processes and thinking; it simply means that *observable behaviors* are the focus of attention. The behavioral philosophy also assumes that changes in behaviors typically produce corresponding changes in thoughts and attitudes. Bartlett (1967) argued that "it is easier to change behavior than attitudes! Why launch a direct onslaught upon the latter when they will follow if the former is changed?" (p. 39).

The basic premise underlying the behavioral approach to training and development is that behavior occurs as a consequence of reinforcement. Williams and Long (1975) apply the principles of behaviorism in a program for developing self-management and argue that "effective self-management primarily involves the rearrangement of behavioral consequences so that desired behavior is *immediately* reinforced" (p. 22).

Three Behavioral Strategies

Three general strategies represent the applications of behaviorism in training and development: (1) structuring contingencies, (2) simulations, and (3) modeling.

Structuring Contingencies   *Contingencies* are consequences that positively reinforce desirable behaviors or punish undesirable behaviors. Contingencies may be a natural part of the work environment, such as assignments to work shifts, use of old versus new equipment, reporting procedures, arrangements of offices, and communication contacts and channels. They may all involve positive or negative consequences that serve as contingencies. Organization development strategies frequently involve structural changes in the organization that serve to reduce negative consequences and increase positive consequences. Changes in behavior are often a direct result of structural changes in both task and nontask situations in organizations. Because most training and human resource development departments do not have the power to create structural changes in the organization, training and development programs tend to focus on making behavioral changes in organizational members.

Communication behaviors are frequently the focus of training and development programs, especially when a behavioral approach is used. This is understandable if we accept Schein's (1969) observation that "one of the most important processes in organizations, and one of the easiest to observe, is how the members communicate with each other, particularly in face-to-face situations" (p. 15). Communicative behaviors can be changed by the external management of reinforcement contingencies, by self-directed efforts in which individuals regulate their own behavior by arranging appropriate contingencies for themselves, or by both methods.

Williams and Long (1975) describe an approach to self-management of a person's life that is based on behavioral principles. They suggest that "effective self-management primarily involves the rearrangement of behavioral consequences so that desired behavior is *immediately* reinforced" (p. 22). The principle of immediate reinforcement of desired behaviors is fundamental to a behavioral approach. Frequently the unwanted behaviors are rewarded naturally; thus the program of self-management requires the individual to administer his or her own punishment for unwanted behaviors and to reward the desired behaviors more vigorously.

Five steps epitomize the implementation of a behavioral training program involving the structuring of contingencies.

1. *Select a goal*. Identify a single goal so that you work on one change at a time. There are four considerations involved in selecting an appropriate goal:

   a. *Select a goal that is important to you*. If you experience some form of pain, such as embarrassment or anxiety, any positive improvement will be noticeable and reinforcing. You should be somewhat cautious in trying to change well-entrenched behaviors at the beginning. It may be better to take a goal that seems important but that involves behaviors that might be changed more easily.

   b. *Define the goal in measurable behavioral terms*. In this context *behavioral* means some type of overt action that can be seen and recognized by others. Nodding, smiling, speaking up, stepping back, and holding hands are overt behaviors. Feeling better, being more confident, and doing what's right must be translated into some type of behavior before we understand what is actually happening. For example, being more confident is expressed in some overt behavior. What do you do? How about looking right into the eyes of a person who disagrees with you? At least you can tell when you are being more confident with that kind of goal. By identifying the overt behaviors clearly, you can carefully select contingencies that help strengthen new and desirable ones. By changing overt behaviors, the behavioral approach contends, you change the internal feelings associated with them.

c. *Set a goal that is readily attainable.* One mistake often made in behavioral modification programs is to set goals too high. It is important to set goals that are only a little bit higher than your present level of behaving. When you can regularly perform a new behavior, then raise your standards and set a higher goal. Behaviorally, we change in small increments.

d. *State the goal positively.* The end result of the behavior-change program is to develop the presence of positive behaviors. You might eliminate a great many negative behaviors and still not produce much improvement in what you do. It is also easier and more motivating to recognize and experience the presence of positive behaviors than to notice the absence of negative ones.

2. *Record the quantity and the context of behaviors.* This step allows you to recognize the extent to which offending behaviors occur and the circumstances in which they take place. You might discover that you say, "Oh yea!" more frequently when someone disagrees with you in a group than at any other time. Keeping a record of the behavior to be changed will sensitize you to the progress you are making. Three major types of records of behavior can be used in behavior modification.

a. *Frequency counting.* This involves tabulating the number of times a particular behavior occurs. To be counted, a behavior must be defined in terms of discrete cases. The behavior must occur over a short period of time and have an identifiable beginning and ending.

b. *Duration of behavior.* Staring, crying, dozing, and other types of behaviors do not occur in discrete instances all of the time and are best recorded in terms of the amount of time devoted to the behavior. The simplest approach to recording the duration of behavior is to indicate when it starts (with a stopwatch or by recording the time) and when it stops.

c. *Results of behavior.* Rather than recording the behavior directly, occasionally you can monitor the behaviors by keeping track of what happens as a result of the behavior. By recording the amount of waste in a manufacturing plant, it is often possible to tell a great deal about the behaviors occurring in the plant. Weighing yourself can give you information about your eating habits. Nevertheless, to make changes, you will need to identify the specific behaviors that lead to waste or to being overweight.

The very act of making a recording may lead to changes in behavior. When a person is able to see an objective report of a behavior, he or she may be motivated to change. Identifying the behavior and maintaining a record of how frequently it occurs might be all that some people need to do to implement a behavior modification program. Some, on the other hand, may need to proceed to the next step.

3. *Change the situation in which the behavior occurs.* Some behaviors are triggered by the situation in which they occur. One way to modify behavior is to change the situation that encourages it. This can be done in two different ways:

a. *Avoid the situation.* Although staying away from someone because he or she tends to provoke an angry response in you will not eliminate your undesirable behavior entirely, it will do much to limit the situations in which it does occur. Ultimately you will need to deal with the behavior directly; nevertheless, at the beginning, avoidance may help you get control of and start to modify the behavior.

b. *Alter the situation.* If you tend to get sleepy sitting in a lounge chair, modify the behavior by sitting in a chair that seems less conducive to sleeping. On the other hand, if you tend to eat snacks at your desk, you might put the snacks in a sealed container and place the container in a file drawer so that you have to think about what you are doing before engaging in the behavior. You might even put a mirror on the desk so that you have to watch yourself eating.

By altering the situation, you are providing yourself with supportive settings in which to control behavior. These are ways of applying contingencies to modify behavior. The direct application of contingencies, however, is important in a behavioral approach to change.

4. *Arrange reinforcing or punishing consequences.* A behavioral approach assumes that a person's behaviors are controlled by the consequences resulting from them. If you unnecessarily argue with other people, but in the end you receive a lot of praise and encouraging comments, you will tend to be reinforced in your arguing. A difficulty in arranging consequences is that most of us have not thought about how things affect us. We are not sure how a particular event will affect our behavior. Thus we nearly always need to broaden the list of consequences that might be used as reinforcers or punishers.

a. *Require yourself to exhibit the preferred behavior before participating in the reinforcing activity.* This means that you earn certain privileges by behaving in certain ways. If speaking in a negative manner to others is the behavior you wish to change, a highly satisfying or reinforcing privilege should be made contingent to or conditional upon speaking in a positive way to others. The reinforcers will be most effective if they are applied immediately after the desired behaviors are exhibited and if the new behaviors are not too hard to perform. Because it is not entirely feasible to give direct rewards immediately, a system of credits can be used. When you earn five or ten credits, they apply toward the direct reward, such as going to a movie or having some quiet time.

b. *Use punishers as well as reinforcers.* Although the idea may not seem very appealing, the idea of flipping yourself with a rubber band or administering pain in some other way when you fail to carry out the new behavior is clearly a procedure consistent with a behavioral approach to changing behavior. Pain can also be administered though social disapproval. You can arrange a punishing contingency by telling those with whom you work about what you are trying to accomplish and asking them to administer the contingency or to simply remind you to administer the punishment.

5. *Focus on and verbalize the contingencies.* The strongest program for managing behavior change through contingencies keeps a person aware of and focusing on the consequences of his or her behavior. One of the main problems in behavior change is impulsive responses. We often react before we have had a chance to think about the consequences. Behavior modification seeks to heighten a person's awareness so he or she thinks about the consequences of one's behavior before acting. One way to do this is to talk about the consequences to yourself prior to acting. The verbalizations must be said aloud, at least in the beginning. It appears that the sound, as well as the statements, heighten awareness more than just the thought or silent verbalization of behavior.

Craighead and colleagues (1976) describe procedures for modifying marital problems by using contingencies. Couples are taught how to "pinpoint" the behaviors they wish to change, how to discriminate between positive and negative responses, how to improve their listening skills, how to share communication equally, how to reduce aversive behaviors, how to solve problems as a unit, and how to contract for the application of contingencies—consequences that positively reinforce compliance with agreed-upon changes and punish failures to comply. The entire process represents a training program based on a behavioral approach.

Simulations   A second strategy for applying the principles and philosophy of behaviorism to training and development is called *simulation,* which refers to some type of vicarious experience. The behaviors in which a person participates have the characteristics of or are similar to those that occur on the job. The term *simulator* is frequently used to refer to machines that have the appearance of the real thing but that are mounted in a laboratory rather than in the field. In a simulation the trainee gets to engage in the behavior that is desired back on the job without taking all of the risks associated with authentic work conditions.

Odiorne (1970) has referred to the use of simulations in training as *action training* and explains that "the specific forms of action training break down into different kinds of simulations. The common element is that all of them simulate the situation in which the trainee must operate in the real world and require him to behave in a way that he might behave back in that environment if he were to apply the new behavioral skills desired" (p. 264). In simulation the important requirement is to have a plausible resemblance to the main task.

Using task analysis the specific behaviors to be acquired are identified and defined. Behavior is changed by having the trainee engage in the desired behaviors in a progression of small steps. At each step in the training the trainee obtains information on how well he or she is performing the behaviors.

Bartlett (1967) has suggested that simulation is "one unconventional method for changing behavior, strong enough to pierce the 'attitudinal' sound barriers" (p. 40). Consistent with the behavioral theory on which it is based, he notes that "this involves, under the guise of skill training, having subjects (Ss) practice doing differently (in a laboratory situation). As they are given rewards for doing differently, their attitudes will (absent pressure) tend to soften." Bartlett proposes that a training program to upgrade communication should be the primary vehicle to use when attempting to improve interpersonal competence on the job.

Communication training is a more or less neutral subject that focuses on processes and behaviors rather than on company policies and procedures. Skill training in communication provides employees with practice in listening and telling and lends itself naturally to broadening their perspectives with regard to perceptions of human behavior. Interpersonal competencies develop by doing things differently, by behaving as a communicatively competent person. To bring about changes in a person's communication skills and to enhance the transference of the new patterns of behavior from classroom simulations to the real world of the job, Bartlett urges that the training should be conducted in a company conference room that is used exclusively for the program.

There are two basic strategies for conducting simulations: role playing and games. We shall look at each of these briefly to illustrate how a behavioral philosophy can be implemented through simulations.

ROLE PLAYING   As a simulation method, role playing involves acting out a situation that parallels real-life experiences (Pace, Peterson, & Burnett, 1979). Role playing can be carried out in two different ways: structured and spontaneous (Wohlking & Weiner, 1981). Wohlking and Weiner compared structured and spontaneous role playing on four stages involved in the use of role playing: (1) objectives, (2) warm-up, (3) enactment, and (4) post-role-playing techniques. We shall briefly review their analysis to highlight the training applications of role playing.

Structured role playing is accomplished by having a series of written role descriptions with guidelines for the facilitator that structures the situation and sets the scene.

Spontaneous role playing evolves somewhat naturally from the discussion of a problem, during which a potential solution is identified and tested through role playing.

Objectives Structured role playing is designed to develop skills in areas such as problem solving, interpersonal communication, and interviewing; it is used to teach procedures and instruct in how to do tasks and to modify attitudes involved in superior-subordinate relationships. Spontaneous role playing, on the other hand, is designed to provide insight into a person's own behavior and the behavior of others, to modify attitudes and perceptions, and to develop ways of diagnosing problem situations.

Warm-up Regardless of how the role playing is conducted, time should be spent preparing participants to engage in the role-playing activity. They should be ready to participate by understanding the relevance of the problem and by wanting to be involved physically in role playing. The warm-up for structured role playing can be accomplished by presenting a lecture on a principle related to some aspect of effective organizational communication, for example, or by showing a film on the topic, which includes principles that can be translated into skills in role playing. In addition, the written case itself can be analyzed, or a general discussion conducted on a problem area, which can lead to the question, "How would you handle such a situation?" The warm-up period for spontaneous role playing often consists of identifying problems that the group would like to explore.

Enactment In structured role playing, separate roles are distributed to the participants prior to conducting the activity. The written statements give role descriptions and identify role behaviors and points of difference. The trainer avoids intervening during the enactment, allowing the entire scene to proceed uninterrupted until the situation reaches a climax. In contrast, during the enactment of a spontaneous role play, the trainer intervenes frequently in an effort to highlight feelings and focus on individual responses.

Post–Role-Playing Techniques All role playing should be followed by a period of discussion in which the insights developed during the enactment are articulated by participants and observers. A discussion led by the trainer should focus on how the methods used in the role playing facilitated or hindered communication between the roles, not on the individuals taking the parts. Observers could be asked to report what they noticed, which may lead to a discussion about the problems of translating principles into actual communication skills. In spontaneous role playing the trainer asks each player to react to the feelings, emotions, and tensions that developed during the enactment. The group is then asked for its reactions to the role play.

Role playing is an effective way of helping people understand the behavior of others. Much can also be learned from another type of simulation—games.

Games A game is "any simulated contest (play) among adversaries (players) operating under constraints (rules) for an objective (winning)" (Alice Gordon, 1972, p.8). In human resource development, serious games are used. They tend to simulate real-life problems and include a complex combination of cooperation, competition, winning, and losing. Some players or even teams of players may be more successful than others, and in some cases, if the problem is solved, all players may win. In some instances winning is not the most crucial part of the game; how the participants use their resources to attain the maximum benefit can be more important than accomplishing the objective.

In training and development, games tend to follow two basic approaches: board games and role-playing games (A. Gordon, 1972). Board games are designed to be played on a gameboard on which the action occurs. Role-play games usually have written materials that include a scene and profiles of the players. In most cases all the players receive the same background information, but each one receives a unique role description that describes his or her specific role and relationship to other players and the player's objectives. The information is provided to give players some basis for responding during the action. Rules are the only other information required. In role playing the rules are generally quite broad and define activities and decisions in which the player may be involved. Olivas and Newstrom (1981) concluded that "games can change attitudes, develop interpersonal skills, and achieve ready acceptance by the trainees. Most critical, simulations generally incorporate active participation and practice opportunities, thereby increasing the probability of learning and ease the transfer to the work environment" (p. 66).

Behavior Modeling   The third and final strategy for implementing a behavioral approach to human resource development is called *behavior modeling*. Zenger (1980) refers to behavior modeling as "the most exciting new technology in training" (p. 45). Research suggests that nearly all learning that results from direct experience can be acquired vicariously through observation of another person's behavior and the results that accrue to the person being observed (Bandura, 1969). Bandura suggests that a person can "acquire intricate response patterns merely by observing the performances of appropriate models" (p. 118).

Behavior modeling is based, according to Zenger (1980), on the idea that people learn by "(a) seeing a good example, (b) being provided a cognitive framework to understand the important elements of the skill to be learned, then (c) practicing or rehearsing the skill, and finally (d) receiving positive feedback when one succeeds in doing it properly" (p. 45). Behavior modeling assumes that (1) specific skills are learned by practice and that (2) such activities as managing, leading, and problem solving involve a series of concrete behaviors that can be modeled, observed, practiced, reinforced, and integrated into the total behavioral repertoire of a manager.

Behavior modeling is implemented best through the preparation of a series of videotapes that participants can view, identify with the situation, rehearse the modeled behavior under the coaching of a trainer, and transfer the skills back to their jobs (Rosenbaum, 1979). In a typical videotape modeling how a supervisor should handle a corrective interview, the model supervisor is to do the following:

1. Define the problem in terms of lack of improvement since the previous discussion.
2. Ask for, and actively listen to, the employee's reason for the continued behavior.
3. If disciplinary action is called for, indicate what action you must take and why.
4. Agree on specific actions to be taken to solve the problem.
5. Assure the employee of your interest in helping him/her to succeed and express your continued confidence in the employee.
6. Set a follow-up date.
7. Positively reinforce any behavior change in the desired direction (Rosenbaum, 1979, p. 42).

ACHIEVEMENT THEORY

Many popular behavior-change programs are based in what some authors call *motivational* or *success theory* (Gorman, 1979, pp. 61–85). Our preference is to refer to this large body of literature as *achievement theory,* because much of the basic philosophy is derived from research and practice on personal achievement and persuasion processes.

Some superficial similarities may appear between rational theory and achievement theory, but they should not be confused, because significant differences exist between the two perspectives on change.

Achievement theory is based on the assumption that changes in behavior occur because an individual wants to be successful. Individuals who have a strong predisposition toward doing things better have the highest probability of making changes and achieving something. Another major assumption is that if a person spends most of his or her time thinking about doing things better, that individual will exhibit drive, energy, and a desire to become successful and, most likely, will achieve greater objectives.

According to McClelland and others (1953), a pioneer in achievement research, individuals with a high need for achievement can be differentiated from others by four characteristics:

1. *They like work that involves moderate challenges.* If the work is too easy they get little satisfaction; if it is too hard, they tend to falter.
2. *They like to have concrete feedback on whether they have succeeded or not.* If they cannot tell when they are achieving, they tend to dislike the task.
3. *They like to be personally responsible for working on the task.* If they need to work on a committee or take a big chance, they feel they are not in charge. They prefer to do it themselves because they can feel satisfied with the outcome.
4. *They are restless, tend to be innovative, and travel a lot.* When something gets routine, the probability of success goes up and they are sure they can do it. They start searching for more challenging tasks, leaving the old ones and finding new ones.

Achievement theory of change can be expressed by five principles that lead people to change their behavior in the direction of achievement.

1. *Change is a result of achieving psychological success.* Hill (1967), for example, argues that the act of psychologically foreseeing success as a reality is the beginning of success itself. Bandura and Cervone (1983) conclude from their empirical research on goal accomplishment that "by representing foreseeable outcomes symbolically, future consequences can be converted into current motivators and regulators of behavior" (p. 1017).

Achievement theory initiates the change process by inducing or at least facilitating psychological success. Techniques of visualization are often employed. Teaching the martial artist to visualize his or her hand on the other side of the broken board, rather than visualizing his or her hand breaking the board, is an example of psychological achievement.

2. *Inadequate performance or achievement is a result of low aspirations.* This principle is essentially the contrary of Principle 1 because it argues that individuals who assume that they cannot achieve are adopting a self-defeating, pessimistic attitude and will be unable to exceed the lower expectations. The factor affecting achievement and behavioral change is not skill and capability but low aspirations. Maltz (1960) has suggested that "within you right now is the power to do things you never dreamed possible."

Deese (1967) concludes from his analysis that "clearly, our expectancies do determine our behavior, and they do so by not only telling us what we think is going to happen but by telling us how much we are going to like or dislike what is going to happen" (p. 128). A person with a history of not succeeding may be excessively cautious and set his or her level of aspiration much too low. Research has shown that the things we think about and *how* we think about them have an enormous influence upon both our levels of aspiration and the direction our energy takes us.

3. *Change occurs when our attention is persistently focused on a goal.* James Winans (1917), a pioneer in the field of persuasion, observed that "what holds attention governs action." Writing down and reviewing goals, for example, directs both our conscious and unconscious attention toward them. The persistent focusing of attention on what you want or need to accomplish, in and of itself, leads the mind and body to pursue that goal. If you give full, fair, and undivided attention to a goal, you are much more likely to achieve it.

The use of the technique of stating "positive affirmations" is one way to focus persistently on a goal. To have a person stand and say confidently, "I can say 'No'! I can say 'No'! I can say 'No,'" focuses the person's attention on that goal and blocks out distracting interferences.

4. *Achievement is enhanced through group support.* Research on crowd behavior, conformity, and contagion attest to the motivating force of group support (Davis, 1969; Gordon, 1971; King, 1975; McGuire, 1969). The old adage that "It is easier to do anything if someone else is doing it with you" implies that achievement will tend to increase when group support is given. The effect may be explained in various ways, but Birch and Veroff (1966) see an *affiliation incentive* as the prime stimulator. They suggest that a person feels reassured that he or she is accepted and subsequently devotes more energy to accomplishing the goal.

The *standing ovation* is a technique used in achievement training that provides spontaneous support from the group for the accomplishment of one of its members. As the target person watches and hears his or her group stand and applaud, the feeling that achieving is important intensifies.

5. *With the realization that one is achieving, efforts intensify and more energy is devoted to accomplishing the goal.* As people complete a task successfully, they tend to view themselves as more capable. This phenomenon is observed each year on Easter when children search for candy and eggs hidden the night before. If a youngster cannot find a piece of candy or an Easter egg before someone else finds one several times in a row, discouragement sets in; but the child who locates a treat right away immediately gets a surge of confidence and intensifies the search to find more. The adage "success breeds success" illustrates this principle.

Failure to succeed does not necessarily deter a person, however, especially if he or she feels that success is possible. For example. Bandura and Cervone (1983) concluded, following one of their studies, that "the higher the self-dissatisfaction with a substandard performance and the stronger the perceived self-efficacy for goal attainment, the greater the subsequent intensification of efforts" (p. 1017). Stated in simpler terms, their conclusion suggests that people tend to work harder if they are dissatisfied with their performance and believe attaining the goal is important.

POSITIONAL THEORY

Positional theory is based on the premise that a person's behavior is largely determined by the role he or she occupies, although each person may have separate sets of expectations for different positions. A role is a repertoire of behaviors characteristic of a person in a position; it is a set of expectations, standards, norms, or concepts about how to behave in a social position.

Positional theory derives its concepts from role theory (Biddle & Thomas, 1966), and role analysts study *patterned forms* of real-life behavior using concepts of role theory. Individual patterns of behavior, aggregates of individuals, and institutional behavior are examined with an emphasis on how one's past and present environment influence behaviors and produce predictable patterns.

The fundamental premise of positional theory is that the behavior of individuals is influenced and shaped by the demands, expectations, and rules of others, as well as by the individual's understanding of what behavior he or she should exhibit in situations. Although this view does not deny the facts of individual differences, it does focus attention on the conditions under which expectations, norms, rules, and sanctions are influential.

The corollary assumption is, of course, that changes in role expectations bring about changes in role behaviors. This assumption means that people learn and develop new behaviors by changing their attitudes toward their own roles and the roles that surround them. For an individual to exhibit behaviors appropriate to a particular role, the person must understand the demands on the position and have the ability to respond with relevant behaviors.

Positional theory has been implemented with the technique called *role negotiation* described by Roger Harrison (1972). Role negotiation involves "changing by means of negotiation with other interested parties the *role* which an individual or group performs in the organisation" (p. 85). Role, in this context, means the work requirements; what duties a person performs; what decisions the person makes; to whom the role occupant reports and about what and how often; and who can give him or her orders and under what circumstances. It also includes the informal understandings and agreements with others that determine how the person or group fits in with others.

For the technique to work, one basic assumption must be met: Participants "must be open about what changes in behaviour, authority, responsibility, etc., they wish to obtain from others in the situation" (Harrison, 1972, p. 86). Harrison notes that if those involved in role negotiation take the risk and specify concrete changes they would like to see on the part of others involved in the negotiation, then important changes in behavior and work effectiveness can be achieved.

Stubbs, Hill, and Carlton (1978) reported on the use of role negotiation in a behavior-change program instituted at Diamond Shamrock, a multinational chemical and petroleum company. Richard Hill (1983) has developed a training program based on positional theory and role negotiation that is patterned after Harrison's work. He notes that "the change process is essentially a give-and-take situation in which two or more members each agree to change behavior in exchange for some desired change on the part of the other. The emphasis is on behavior rather than upon feelings, thus making the process safer for the team members" (p. 7). Hill reports that there are seven basic steps in the process, all of which must be completed for the program to be effective. They all depend on clearly identifying the work group or team that will serve as the focus of change.

1. *Identification process.* For each member of the team, list three sets of activities: (a) things that each team member should do more or do better, (b) things that each team member should do less, and (c) things that each team member does that facilitate the effectiveness of the others and should not be changed.
2. *Clarification process.* Post the lists and review each item for each team member to make certain that all members of the team *understand* every item. This process does not mean that anyone either accepts or agrees to make any changes. The entire focus should be on understanding what the statements mean.

3. *Setting priorities*. Using only the *Do More and Do Less* lists, sort out the issues in terms of their importance. If a particular request holds some personal interest for an individual, that individual should initial the item so that the target individual can engage in negotiation with those who initialed the particular item.

4. *Negotiating process*. The negotiation process takes place in two formats: one-on-one and group. Every attempt should be made by all team members to deal with all items and to meet with others to help them complete their negotiations.

Each person meets with every other person and negotiates changes in behaviors on a "something for something" basis. That is, each pair or group agrees to do something if the other party agrees to do something. Each member must stick with the procedure until all needs are met.

5. *Contracting*. When the negotiations between team members near resolution, a contract should be drafted to reduce agreements to a few written words. Contracts should specify the following:

With whom the agreement is made

What you agree to do

In exchange for doing what

Date on which agreement is to be reviewed and evaluated

Signatures of both parties to the agreement

6. *Group meeting*. Team members meet as a group, briefly summarize their agreements with others, and acquaint the team with the significant contract issues. This step should be done in a round-robin fashion, with each member in turn describing the agreements and the exchanges.

7. *Contract review*. After approximately three months, a contract review should be held on each agreement. The review should indicate information on four results:

Agreements that were achieved

Agreements that were overachieved

Agreements that were underachieved

Special circumstances that negated agreements

The review process should be very open, to the extent of posting a grid on newsprint on the wall so that all agreements may be viewed by all team members.

As Hill points out, role negotiation may expose which organization members have real power and influence and may threaten those who bluff and those who operate behind the scenes. Nevertheless, much is to be gained through open, honest communication and negotiation, possibly even more than through coercion, private competition, withholding of information, and other strategies.

EXPERIENTIAL THEORY

An experiential approach to behavior change is based on the premise that people are more likely to believe their own experiences than those of others. People change their behaviors, according to this view, by examining their current beliefs in light of their reactions to situations in which they feel some significant emotional arousal. By reflecting on what happened to them, individuals develop a personal explanation for their reactions and make a conscious effort to try alternative ways of behaving in another setting.

There seems to be fairly widespread agreement that learning that results from direct experience is significantly different from learning that results from more cognitive methods (Springer, 1981). Part of the reason for the stronger impact of experiential learning is the combination of physical activity and thinking activity that occurs when a person experiences something. In some ways, change through experiential learning is a natural extension of the rational approach to change, because experiential learning allows individuals to test reality in safe situations. Each experience is a form of reality testing in which a person senses how he or she reacts to a concrete activity.

Behavior change as a result of experiential learning may occur both inside and outside the training area. People have experiences, create meaning from them, and try new ways of behaving, regardless of where they are. Unfortunately, there is often little analysis of the experience outside the training room, and the discussion that does occur may be unguided or misdirected. Experiences in the training area should be structured so that trainees learn how to learn from their own experiences.

The major advantages of using an experiential learning approach can be summarized in five key points (Hall, Bowen, Lewicki, & Hall, 1975):

1. Experiential learning is more active than other approaches.
2. Experiential learning is problem centered but also incorporates theory for a solid base.
3. Experiential learning involves two-way communication to a greater extent than do other forms of learning.
4. Experiential learning shares control over and responsibility for the learning process with participants.
5. Experiential learning integrates thoughts, feelings, and actions into a more holistic approach to behavior change.

Experiential Learning Model

Contemporary concepts of experiential learning have evolved from the work of Kolb in the development of a *learning styles inventory* (Kolb, Rubin, & McIntyre, 1974). He describes a four-stage cycle through which a person proceeds to learn from experience:

1. An immediate, concrete experience is the basis for
2. observation and reflection; the observations are assimilated into an explanation consisting of
3. abstract concepts and generalizations, which serve as guidelines for testing
4. new behaviors in different situations.

In this view a person learns by participating in a concrete experience, reflecting on the experience, formulating generalizations from the reflections, and trying new behaviors that test the generalizations.

Michalak and Yager (1979) designed a six-stage experiential learning model that expands Kolb's sequence and creates a systematic design process. Their six stages include (1) experience, (2) content input, (3) analysis, (4) generalizations, (5) practice, and (6) transfer. In this model, each training sequence begins with an experience, followed by the presentation of content information and an analysis of the experience in terms of the information and principles. Trainees then formulate generalizations that can be tested in the practice stage. The final step is devoted to preparing trainees to use their new knowledge and skills back on the job.

Although all aspects of designing and conducting training for purposes of changing behavior—such as writing objectives and evaluating the process—are not represented in

FIGURE 14.11 Experiential Training Model

the preceding models, they suggest four types of activities that go into an experiential training sequence (see Figure 14.11).

1. The *experience,* which involves supervising an exercise that allows a trainee to encounter some aspect of reality to the extent that it evokes an emotional response in the trainee.
2. Explanatory *information,* which consists of presenting theory that explains what happened to the trainee or why the exercise was able to evoke the response.
3. An *analysis,* which involves assisting participants to make sense out of the experience by using the theory to explain what happened, to formulate principles for use later, and to identify and recognize specific skills involved in the reality.
4. A *practice* session, which consists of preparing and leading trainees through the recognition and rehearsal of the skills to provide for transfer of the skills to the workplace.

Experiential Training Methods

The steps in producing behavior change through an experiential approach can be described according to each of the four activities involved in the training model.

Supervising Experiences An experience is an encounter with some aspect of reality that evokes an emotional response. Examples of experiences that may evoke emotional responses include taking a field trip to a new and exotic site, participating in a "trust walk" in which a person is blindfolded and led through a maze of unpredictable events, or hiking in the mountains. All of those activities meet the conditions of an experience.

To bring about behavior change, experiential learning should involve a degree of structuring; a point of view imposed on the process allows participants to generalize and recognize patterns and skills. The term *structured experience* has been coined to refer to this special type of experience.

Middleman and Goldberg (1972) describe a structured experience as a closed system, deliberately constructed and set in motion by the facilitator. The experience might consist of simple or complex activities in which participants actually do something. It might take the form of role playing or making an object. It could involve completing a questionnaire or inventory. Some structured experiences have participants solve puzzles, analyze problems, create designs, or engage in activities like brainstorming and simulations.

Pace (1977) identified thirty-six different exercises for teaching concepts in organizational communication, all of which have been used in training sessions over the years.

One of the most common sources of structured experiences is the Pfeiffer and Jones handbooks for human relations training and for group facilitators. The *Reference Guide* (1985) classifies the contents of twenty-four books of exercises. The structured experiences are classified according to six categories: (1) personal, including self-disclosure, feelings, values, life and career planning; (2) communication, including oral and nonverbal awareness, trust, listening, interviewing, and assertion; (3) group characteristics, including process, power, styles, motivation, leadership, and stereotyping; (4) task behavior, including problem solving, generating alternatives, feedback, competition, collaboration, conflict, and consensus; (5) organizations, including diagnosis, team building, decision making, and consultation skills; and (6) facilitating learning, including getting acquainted, forming subgroups, expectations, blocks to learning, building trust, openness, energizers, evaluating group process, facilitator skills, and closure.

Casse (1981) has prepared a unique manual for international/intercultural trainers that includes seventeen workshops with exercises and materials to prepare individuals for crossing cultures. The entire book illustrates the use of structured experiences in experiential learning.

Each structured experience should include a statement of the goals of the exercise, the materials necessary, the physical setting and group size for which it is best suited, step-by-step procedures and the estimated amounted of time required to complete the exercise, and copies of worksheets, questionnaires, scales, or tests used in the exercise (Grove, 1976).

To set the stage for analysis of the experience and to get the most out of the process, participants should be encouraged to

1. Get involved in the exercise and participate with enthusiasm in the activities.
2. Think consciously about the relevance of the exercise to the theory and information presented for use in the analysis phase.
3. Contemplate and make notes on what kinds of generalizations might be developed from the exercise and what specific skills might be identified that could be practiced.

The following exercise illustrates how a structured experience is designed and supervised:

The Fractured Puzzle Exercise

Goal   To demonstrate that the critical act of communication is assigning meaning or significance to people, objects, and events.

Group size   Minimum of five individuals, with one to serve as communicator and the others to serve as communicatees.

Time required   About forty-five minutes.

Materials and equipment needed

1. A master five-piece puzzle
2. Copies of puzzle for audience members
3. A 2-by-3-inch cardboard screen
4. Small table on which to put puzzle and screen
5. Chair for communicator
6. Student desks or tables and chairs for communicatees

Physical setting   Communicator is seated at table, behind screen, with completed puzzle in front of him or her; communicatees are seated at student desks or tables with scrambled pieces of puzzle in front of them.

Procedure or process   The following ten steps should be completed.

1. The facilitator explains to the group that he or she would like to conduct an exercise that demonstrates a major characteristic of communication.
2. The facilitator explains that to perform the demonstration it will be necessary to select a person whom others consider to be a reasonably effective communicator.
3. The volunteer or person selected takes a seat at the front of the room at the table so that the small cardboard screen is between the volunteer and the group. The communicator and the group should be able to hear each other, but they should not be able to see one another.
4. The facilitator distributes pieces of the puzzle to communicatees, either singly or as a group, depending upon the number of puzzles available. If in groups, one person is assigned to work with the pieces of the puzzle while the others observe quietly. The five pieces of the puzzle should be gently tossed onto the table in front of the individual with instructions to remove the rubber band holding them together and to wait for instructions.
5. The volunteer communicator is given the five pieces of the master set, identical in size and shape, but having a different color combination. The communicator's set should be assembled behind the screen out of view of the group, in front of the communicator by the trainer.
6. The facilitator explains the nature of the problem to the communicator and communictees. Communicatees are to play the role of machine operators who have been given the parts of a new machine, but with no instructions on how to assemble the machine. The communicator is to play the role of a manager who must explain to the operators how to do the assembly. The manager has an assembled machine in front of him (or her), made of pieces that are the same size and shape as those that the operators have.
7. The facilitator explains that the manager may say anything he or she wishes to the operators, but the operators may *not* talk back, ask questions, or make any audible sounds during the explanation.
8. As the manager gives instructions, the facilitator monitors the operators for violations of the no-talking rules and for examples of misinterpretations of what the manager says on the part of operators as they attempt to assemble machines.
9. The manager completes the instructions on how to assemble the machine, which may take fifteen minutes or less. As soon as the manager has completed giving instructions, the facilitator asks everyone to "freeze" (not to move puzzle pieces any further) while the manager walks around and observes the results of his or her instructions. The facilitator asks the manager to look for information (called *feedback*) about the results of the instructions given and anything that might be useful in modifying them.
10. The facilitator interviews the manager for a few minutes about what he or she observed, attempting to draw out and highlight some of the sources of misinterpretation that occurred, such as assuming that all of the pieces were the same color, using unfamiliar or complex terminology, giving instructions too rapidly, or neglecting to explain the ultimate objective of the instructions—to assemble a figure that looks like the shape of his or her puzzle (a block T or F or H). Whenever possible, the reactions and behavior of the operators should be related to the main idea that assigning meaning is the key feature of communication.

This ends the exercise on structured experience. The next step in the experiential process would be the presentation of explanatory information or theory, which helps participants to understand *why* problems in communication occur.

Presenting Information   Forceful delivery is developed by the adoption and practice of behaviors that highlight the five characteristics of effective presenters. Presenters must discover the range of expression within each of the key characteristics of their style of delivery and then engage in consistent practice with some exaggeration. A range of expression can be developed by pressing the characteristic to its limit. As muscles are strengthened through exercise, so good delivery is developed through concentration and expanding the range of expressiveness associated with each characteristic. The test of forceful delivery is in whether an audience sees you as dynamic and energetic, not in how you think you look. Thus, practice so that you will be viewed as:

1. *One who appears as confident and in control of the situation.* This implies that you should keep a bold front, even in the face of inconsequential errors, some self-consciousness, and an occasional shortcoming. Remember that fear and trembling is much more apparent to you than it is to members of the audience.

2. *One who communicates a sense of urgency.* Your manner must indicate that what you have to say is important to you and for members of the audience. It is the quiet intensity that communicates urgency and a genuine enthusiasm for the ideas being presented. To find the most acceptable level of urgency, exaggerate beyond what you think seems to express the appropriate degree of enthusiasm. You still may find that you have not adequately externalized the importance and urgency of your message.

3. *One who communicates a full understanding of what is being said.* The way in which you utter words and phrases should indicate to the audience that you comprehend the full meaning and import of the message. The meanings need to be communicated with vocal sounds and physical movements that are consistent with the meanings. Where events are gigantic, the voice must sound enormous and the movements should indicate size comparable to the event. If the concept is solemn or sacred, let your voice and movements portray that.

4. *One who communicates with a keen sense of directness.* This is accomplished by forgetting yourself and concentrating on getting your ideas across to the audience. Talk to all members of the audience in turn; be friendly and look friendly; speak directly to members of the audience. Look your audience right in the eye and speak as though you wanted to influence them.

5. *One who uses animated and expressive vocal and physical behavior.* Avoid monotony by infusing variety into your vocal pattern. Give emphasis to important ideas but avoid painful or unpleasant extremes in force, loudness, and explosiveness. Generate variety by drawing out the meaning of passages. Be physically active by gesturing and punctuating points with your entire body. Dramatize your meanings with bodily action to give nonverbal support to your words. Be alert, however, to the need to make your gestures and actions natural and spontaneous.

Facilitating Analysis   This phase in the experiential learning process is designed to assist the participants in discovering the meaning to them of the exercise and in formulating some generalizations and principles that can serve as guidelines for behaving differently in the future. Participants must be encouraged to develop generalizations from the activities in which they partake. Talking about experiences, films, diagrams, role playing, and reading immediately after participants are exposed to them is often more important than the experiences themselves. When experiences are related to information presented as part of the content input, we refer to the discussions as *information processing*.

Analysis and information processing are facilitated by creating an atmosphere of inquiry among participants. Inquiry is accomplished by stimulating participants to probe into the meaning of the exercise and to explore alternative interpretations of what happened. As a facilitator, pose questions, then wait and listen; when during long silences almost everyone is thinking, it is important for you to allow sufficient time for participants to think through what they wish to say. Work to get participants to offer suggestions and analyses of the experience. Assist them in phrasing their ideas clearly, concisely, completely. Strive to have everyone contribute to the analysis and avoid allowing one member to monopolize the interaction. Keep the comments moving among all participants by frequently asking for more ideas. When discussion is slow, gently play devil's advocate by introducing ideas that provide other ways of thinking about a situation. Throughout the analysis period, maintain and enhance the self-esteem of the participants by acknowledging any reactions, praising ideas, pointing out positive behaviors and their effects on others, and recording participants' ideas on a flip chart.

Analysis can be facilitated by letting participants engage in small-group discussions and by making reports.

DISCUSSION FORMATS   Analysis can be facilitated by using one or more of these formal group formats:

1. Buzz groups—Divide participants into groups of three and let them discuss the experience.
2. Phillips 66—Groups of six participants who discuss for six minutes.
3. Ring response—Start the discussion with a buzz group, then enlarge the discussion as others get involved.
4. Fishbowl—This consists of arranging the participants in a double circle—half inside and half outside; the inner group analyzes the experience while the outer group listens; the groups then change places.

REPORTING FORMATS   Analysis frequently continues as participants prepare for and listen to reports presented in front of the groups; on other occasions private reports in the form of notes or journal entries are effective ways to facilitate the analysis of experiences. Four reporting formats are:

1. Individual summaries of reactions given to small groups.
2. Team representative reports.
3. Consultative or listening group reports.
4. Private journal reports or diary entries.

Following small-group analysis and reports, the trainer should assemble the entire group and facilitate a large-group analysis designed to formulate workable generalizations. Specific suggestions should be stated and printed on newsprint for group members to study, analyze, and modify. The next step in the training process is to have participants engage in the practice of specific skills that might be used to do their jobs.

Directing Practice   The basic idea of practice is to apply the skills learned to the job. Although the practice session occurs in the training setting, the principles for effective practice are essentially the same as on-the-job instruction. Figure 14.12 summarizes the four standard steps in directing the practice of on-the-job skills.

PREPARE THE TRAINEE FOR PRACTICE   Let the trainee know that the skill can be learned with some reasonable effort and that you are interested in helping him or her learn a skill that will make work more efficient. Create motivation to learn the skill by relating the skill to the trainee's ability to do his or her work more easily and more effectively and to make a better living.

FIGURE 14.12 Four Steps in Directing the Practice of a Skill

STEPS	HOW TO DO IT
1. Prepare the trainee for practice.	A. Put the trainee at ease. B. Mention the name of the skill. C. Comment on the purpose of the skill. D. Relate the skill to the trainee's past experience.
2. Set the pattern or sequence of the skill in the trainee's mind.	A. Explain any materials needed to perform the skill. B. Demonstrate the skill, explaining each step slowly and clearly. C. Review the name, purpose and steps in performing the skill.
3. Help the trainee perform the skill and begin to form a habit.	A. Listen and watch as the trainee performs the skill. B. Question the trainee on weak and key points. C. Have the trainee repeat the performance until the manual skills *and* the habits of thought have been acquired.
4. Check how well the trainee has acquired the skill.	A. Have the trainee perform the skill alone. B. Compare the performance against the standards of excellence. C. Review both areas of excellence and weakness for additional repetition.

SET THE PATTERN OR SEQUENCE   The steps to complete simple skills should be presented in some sequence. Explain and demonstrate the pattern or sequence for doing the skill one step at a time. Focus on the main steps and key points. Avoid giving too much information at one time. Use simple, direct language. Demonstrate how the skill is to be performed. Highlight those behaviors that are essential to executing the skill well. Set a high standard. As a trainee watches, you will be serving as a behavior model. The performance you give not only demonstrates how to do the skill but also represents how to do it well.

When the skills are more complex, mental traces or patterns must be established prior to learning meaningful motor skills. That is, mental rehearsal must precede the motor development of skills. With communication skills, especially, some well-established ways of behaving have already been formed. Learning, in those cases, is as much an *unlearning* process as it is a direct learning one. For individuals to display key actions and overcome "old" behaviors effectively, it is essential that the rehearsal of physical motor skills be preceded by visualization and mental rehearsal.

BEGIN TO FORM A HABIT   Habits are formed by doing, so the trainee should actually perform the skill. In addition, through guided practice the trainee builds self-confidence and strengthens his or her willingness to try other skills. Start with simple behaviors and gradually work toward the more difficult ones. As the trainee practices, have him or her tell you how and why the skill is done that particular way. Correct errors and omissions as the trainee makes them. Rather than criticize the trainee, show the person how the skill could be executed better; a correction becomes instruction and is usually accepted more eagerly. The best way to make corrections is to have the trainee make the adjustments. Thus a good procedure is to compliment the trainee on the practice effort and then ask whether the trainee can think of anything that could be done to make the performance better. If the trainee is unable to identify what needs to be corrected, then make the instructional suggestion. Avoid correcting too frequently. Exercise restraint in correcting during practice.

CHECK ON HOW WELL THE SKILL HAS BEEN LEARNED   Allow the trainee to perform the skill without your help. Encourage the trainee to ask questions about performing the skill. No matter how simple the question appears, respond with instructions that are serious and respectful. Check the trainee's performance as he or she does it alone, but gradually taper off as the person's ability to perform the skill increases. Finally, if the trainee is doing well, say so.

TRAINING DESIGN MODEL

Carnarius (1981) has provided a model for design that fits the realities of management training; thus, we shall structure this chapter around his design model, with some minor modifications to adapt it to our overall philosophy. As Figure 14.13 indicates, the model consists of seven steps: (1) Identify and outline content, (2) List possible activities, (3) Write objectives, (4) Consider methods and match with objectives, (5) Sequence the session, (6) Check agenda, and (7) Prepare materials.

Step 1: Identify and Outline Content

The content of any given training session is usually identified jointly by the training staff and the line managers based on practical experience and the theory that evolves out of an analysis.

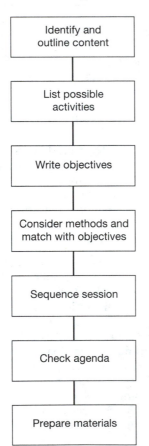

FIGURE 14.13 Training Design Model

Source: From Stan Carnarius, "A New Approach to Designing Training Programs." Copyright 1981, *Training and Development Journal,* American Society for Training and Development. Reprinted with permission. All rights reserved.

SUPERVISION

The supervisor's role and functions
  The basic functions of the supervisor
  The essentials of planning
  The requirements of good plans

Assigning work
  The role of organizational level in affecting work assignments
  The reasons why supervisors fail to assign work effectively
  Guidelines for making effective work assignments

Decision making
  Learning to make a decision
  Decision making and other supervisory functions
  Implementing the decision

Motivating employees
  The basics of motivation
  The overestimated role of money
  Current theories of motivation

Realities that shape managerial style
  The traditional leadership role
  Newer approaches to leadership
  The essence of effective leadership

Supervising for results
  Setting job objectives for employees
  Creating performance standards
  Scheduling
  Getting commitment

Managing supervisory time
  The pressures of time
  Guidelines for effective use of time
  Basic questions concerning time utilization

Training employees
  Instillation of good work habits
  Principles of effective training
  Follow-up with the learner

Communication: A Management Tool
  What makes effective communication
  What leads to good communication
  How to improve listening skills
  What body language can reveal

FIGURE 14.14 Topics Used in Supervisory Training

We usually begin with the content in training design because this information often represents prerequisite concepts that the trainee needs to know to accomplish the objectives and perform the job up to standard. To outline the content, describe in a general way what trainees ought to know to perform the skills or do the work to be addressed in the training session; next make an outline of what information ought to go into the session. The result should be a two- or three-level outline of the topics as illustrated in Figure 14.14 for a seminar on supervision.

A typical outline on how to manage meetings more effectively is shown in Figure 14.15, and a training session designed to strengthen skills in managing employees who do not perform up to par might contain the content outlined in Figure 14.16.

CONDUCTING MEETINGS

Why meetings are important
    The role of effective meetings in increasing productivity
    The incredible costs of meetings

What goes wrong at meetings
    Confusion between process and content
    Hidden agendas, repetition, wheel-spinning

When to hold a meeting and when not to
    Hierarchical vs. horizontal meetings

How managers can increase group participation
    How to increase participation without losing control
    How to become a more effective participant

How to handle key meeting behaviors
    Facilitative methods and behaviors
    Things you can do to avoid problems
    Use of win/win decision methods

How to arrange meetings
    How to manage them
    How to build effective agendas
    How to set up a meeting room
    How to ensure meeting follow-up

How to analyze your problem-solving style
    What is a model of human problem solving
    How to be a better problem solver

How to solve meeting problems
    How to reach consensus
    How to deal with difficult people
    How to remove organizational blocks
    How to get more people solving more problems
    How to use problem-solving training
    How to set up an internal problem-solving center

FIGURE 14.15 Topics for Training in Conducting Meetings

Step 2: List Possible Activities

In the process of designing a training sequence, the identification and selection of possible activities—which include experiences, instruments, simulations, role plays, questionnaires and inventories, and puzzles—and all of the material and instructions necessary to direct the activity, occur early, usually before the clear statement of objectives.

On the other hand, after the objectives have been stated and refined, focus on the activities and make final decisions about which ones will actually be used during the session. Most people who design training programs have large files of activities and boxes of materials that they consult at this stage in the design process.

One of the most extensive and useful collections of activities is that of University Associates, a publishing company in San Diego, California. Since about 1972 they have published annual collections of structured experiences (including instruments, lecturettes, instructions, and other aids) for use in leadership and management training and development as well as personal growth.

In 1985 University Associates published a *Reference Guide to Handbooks and Annuals* (ten volumes including entries for the years 1972-1985) that classifies, describes, and indexes over 400 activities (Pfeiffer & Jones, 1985). The materials themselves are published in a single 81/2-by-11-inch format and distributed in a box for immediate and convenient use. Materials are divided into six categories:

UNSATISFACTORY EMPLOYEE

How to recognize unsatisfactory performance
    The marginal employee
    The unsatisfactory employee
    Definitions of poor employees

Causes of problem performance
    Managerial causes
    Organizational causes
    Individual problems
    Outside influences
    Abrasive employees

Laziness
    Reasons for apparent laziness
    Lack of motivation
    Unsatisfactory employee syndrome

Deciding who to salvage
    Moral and ethical considerations
    A matrix for making decisions

Managing the unsatisfactory employee
    Preventative approach
      Selection and screening
      Early detection of potential problems
    Therapeutic approach
      Coaching, counseling, training
      Getting commitment to improve
    Punitive approach
      Discipline
      Demotions, transfers, retirement

Problems with marginal employees
    Performance inadequacies
    Personal problems

How to handle people problems
    Age
    Sex
    Children

How to sever if you don't salvage
    How to handle fear of firing
    How to terminate

FIGURE 14.16 Topics for Training in How to Manage the Unsatisfactory Employee

1. Personal activities that focus on the expansion of personal insight, awareness, and development of interpersonal skills.
2. Communication activities that emphasize verbal and nonverbal skills in interpersonal and intragroup relationships.
3. Activities of group characteristics that examine how individuals affect group functioning.
4. Group task-behavior activities that focus on how groups organize and function to accomplish objectives.
5. Organizational activities that help individuals and groups function within an organizational context.
6. Facilitating learning activities that create a climate of responsiveness and encourage skill development.

Ninety paper-and-pencil instruments are included and classified as personal, interpersonal, management/leadership, organization, and group behavior.

Although the activities published by University Associates constitute a valuable collection, activities are also published by many other groups. Consult your library and training and development professionals in your community for additional sources.

Pfeiffer and Jones (1985) explain that "each activity within the training experiences should build from the previous sequence of activities and toward the next one" (p. 20). In addition, the activities should incorporate relevant content, especially in leadership and management development. The concerns and problems that participants face in their own work should be reflected in the activities.

Pfeiffer and Jones also argue that an "organic sequence of activities" exists in leadership development. They offer the following sequence as an "organic, logical, and effective flow of activities that need to take place in leadership development workshops" (p. 28).

1. *Getting acquainted.* These activities help create a climate in which participants have easy access to one another.
2. *Closing expectation gaps.* These activities help make the goals and objectives of the workshop explicit and correlate them with the goals and objectives of participants.
3. *Roles and shared leadership.* These activities introduce the concept of roles and functions of different group members and the notion of individuals as leaders in relation to others.
4. *Learning about feedback.* These activities provide instruction in the feedback process so that effective sharing can occur throughout the workshop.
5. *Developing an awareness of process.* These activities explore the dynamic processes emerging in the workshop and provide skills for occasionally stopping the interaction to examine the process that is occurring.
6. *Competition.* These activities examine the functional and dysfunctional effects of interpersonal competition.
7. *Collaboration.* These activities demonstrate that collaboration is possible within a culture that rewards the competitive spirit.
8. *Consensus.* These activities illustrate the concept of synergy and involve a number of people in arriving at collective judgments that are superior to individual judgments.
9. *Planning back-home application.* These activities help participants make definite plans for using particular behaviors in the work environment.

Although the identification of activities may start even before the precise statement of objectives, it may be very helpful to keep in mind this general sequence for the development of leadership as you tentatively select activities.

Step 3: Write Objectives

Two somewhat different philosophies govern the statement of objectives in training and development. The first philosophy argues that individual development is achieved most effectively when the skills and behaviors to be acquired are specified in advance. The statement of objectives to be reached describes what the person is to be like after the training and development experience. A well-stated objective successfully communicates to the trainees or participants what you want them to do; a poorly stated objective allows for more interpretations and fails to indicate directly the trainer's or developer's intentions (Mager, 1962). Barton (1973) argues, however, that stating objectives in advance is useful only when trainees are to acquire a "predetermined behavioral outcome" (p. vii).

Three conditions need to be met:

1. Trainee and trainer efforts need to be focused to develop specific behaviors in a minimum amount of time.
2. The results of training should be evaluated.
3. The behaviors to be mastered need to be precisely defined.

Thus if it is not desirable to concentrate on the development of specific, well-defined behaviors that can be clearly assessed, then the statement of performance objectives in advance may not be particularly useful. Those who advocate a performance or behavior objective approach to development also argue that it is possible, more often than not, to specify the kind of behavior that should be demonstrated by the trainee at the end of the training period. If the objectives cannot be stated, they contend, it is impossible to determine whether the program is meeting the objectives.

The second philosophy relating to the statement of objectives suggests that specific behaviors are not particularly important, that specific competencies or behaviors often do not tell the difference between effective and ineffective employees, especially in complex and not well defined situations. When the task consists of problems for which there may be many appropriate solutions, training in specific competencies may be more limiting than helpful. Barton (1973) explains that when the major concern is the process of having a new experience, or where trainees are attempting to discover the value or meaning of something, or where the situation consists of problems with few common characteristics, the statement of predetermined behavior objectives is less useful than is the design of trainee-centered activities. Combs (1965) has argued effectively that, in education, the effective teachers use "themselves as instruments" (p. 9) to accomplish their goals. Some tasks are immensely personal and cannot be translated into behavior competencies.

Dyer (1978) suggests that managers need to develop abilities to "move into any situation and then learn how to observe, gather feedback, and learn what is happening" (p. 55). He contends that "complex organizational training exercises are needed to give managers experience in the total cycle from the gathering of data to implementation of action and evaluation of the consequences of the action" (pp. 55–56). Although some specific behaviors may apply in many situations, the implication is that many problems call for different actions from different managers and that the ability to recognize those differences may be more important than any specific behaviors; hence, training with behavior objectives may be counterproductive.

As you may recognize, these two philosophies tend to express the theories of change represented by the rational and the behavioral strategies discussed earlier. The former stresses discovering the meaning to the individual of experiences, and the latter stresses the acquisition of specific behaviors that are measurable and identifiable in advance. The effort to meld the rational and behavioral philosophies into a single, unified approach that integrates belief and action was referred to earlier as an experiential approach. Regardless of whether the activity is individual training and development—which emphasizes both technical and interpersonal skills acquisition—or organization development—which emphasizes intergroup and system analysis and change—the ultimate concern is with what the trainee can do at the end of the training period. This suggests that the objectives of a training and development program ought to be stated in terms of performances. At the same time the development process should be structured so as to allow individuals to examine their beliefs and assumptions and develop personal meanings and explanations to undergird the specific behaviors and competencies.

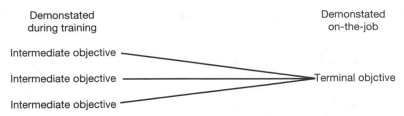

FIGURE 14.17 Types of Performance Objectives and Where They Are Demonstrated

In general, objectives are used to identify the performances expected of participants during and after a training session. *Intermediate objectives* indicate the specific performances that are expected of trainees when they successfully complete a particular segment of a training session. *Terminal objectives* refer to the performance that is expected of trainees when they complete the entire session and prepare to return to their jobs. If trainees successfully complete each section of a training course, they should be able to demonstrate a group of behaviors (one or more for each segment of the course). If the trainees are able to demonstrate all of the specific behaviors at the end of the complete course, general skills can be used and maintained in the organizational setting to which they return. Figure 14.17 shows the relationship of intermediate objectives to terminal objectives. The design of any training and development program begins with the statement of terminal objectives. Each terminal objective can be classified according to the content or deficiency that it is designed to alleviate.

In most cases three factors account for training deficiencies: (1) lack of information, (2) lack of psychomotor skills, or (3) lack of appropriate attitudes (which include beliefs, feelings, values, and preferences). Figure 14.18 shows how these three factors interrelate to affect performance. For an employee to perform at a minimally acceptable level, he or she must *understand* (have accurate and acceptable personal interpretations of the information), *appreciate* (have a favorable set of beliefs, feelings, values, and preferences), and have the *ability* (skill to physically and mentally execute the behaviors) to do the job.

FIGURE 14.18 Three Factors that Account for Adequate Performance

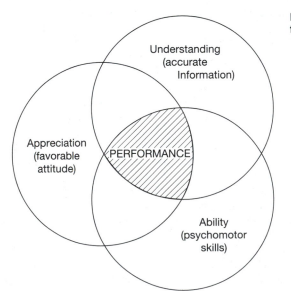

Deficiencies in any or all of the three areas may lead to inadequate job performance. The statement of terminal objectives for any training program should be based upon the analysis completed and the concerns documented. If attitudinal concerns were identified, the training program should include terminal objectives designed to increase favorable attitudes; if informational concerns were identified, terminal objectives designed to increase understanding should be included; if inabilities to perform relevant psychomotor skills were identified, terminal objectives designed to improve those skills should be included.

Training objectives of any type require that individuals alter their behavior. Training deficiencies cannot be alleviated by changing the system or by managing people more carefully. Hence, objectives to be accomplished during the training session are usually stated in specific behavior terms. Intermediate objectives should be related directly to one of the terminal objectives and refer to trainee behaviors. The statement of the intermediate objectives will tell both the trainer and the trainee exactly what the trainee should be able to do at the end of a given segment of the training session. Because intermediate objectives influence the selection of training methods most directly, we shall discuss how to state those kinds of objectives next.

An *intermediate objective* can be defined as the statement of a specific performance or set of behaviors that will be expected of the trainee upon completion of a specified training segment. Acceptable statements of intermediate objectives must meet the following criteria:

1. *They must make direct reference to some observable behavior.* The verb in the statement must refer to some action, or product of some action, that can be observed by a person. Verbs that refer to observable behavior include the following:

define	diagram	rate
list	compare	choose
underline	categorize	revise
describe	distinguish	install
explain	compose	rearrange
identify	assemble	write
use	create	imitate
demonstrate	set up	role-play
sketch	design	report
solve	fix	replace

2. *They must omit any reference to instructions, directions, and training activities.* The mastery of objectives by the trainees can be determined at any time, regardless of whether they are engaging in the training program. Learning activities should help trainees master the objectives, but engaging in the learning activities is not part of the measurement process. Such phrases as "after participating in . . . ," "following an analysis of . . . ," and "observe a dyad interacting . . ." are either training activities, directions, or instructions and are inappropriate for performance objectives.

3. *They must include reliable and easily understood qualitative and quantitative ways of measuring the performance.* Performance objectives should indicate quantitative and qualitative standards for determining whether trainees have achieved the objectives. A *quantitative* standard is expressed in terms of how many, how frequently, or with what percentage something occurs. A *qualitative* standard is expressed in terms of how well something is done or qualities of excellence.

4. *They must refer to the important conditions under which the performance is to occur.* Some examples of relevant and important conditions are "with the aid of an organization chart," "in a ten-minute interview," "on a timed-test," "working in a group of five individuals," "when verbally presented by the trainer," and "by interacting for five minutes with another person." The main physical and psychological circumstances and pressures associated with the task to be accomplished should be indicated.

5. *They must specify the tools and supplies or reference materials available to the trainee; if no references are mentioned, the trainee is to perform the task from memory.* Statements such as "by looking at a picture," "given the use of a list," "by using only newsprint on a flip chart and a felt pen," and "with the aid of one person and a standard set of Tinkertoys" refer to supplies, references, and assistance available for demonstrating the skills.

Some sample statements of objectives for training in communication skills are listed below. Each statement includes the phrase "At the end of the training period, trainees will be able to . . . ," which is a reminder that the objective describes what the trainee is to do, *not* what the trainer does. Thus, at the end of the training period:

1. When given a written communication incident, trainees will be able to underline examples of five elements of communication.
2. Using an official organization chart of the unit in which they work and working in teams of five or six individuals, each team will be able to trace and explain how three different types of messages are disseminated into the organization along upward, downward, and horizontal channels.
3. Trainees will be able to identify in writing at least one different scene from the film *The Eye of the Beholder,* which illustrates each of the following principles:
   a. Desires, goals, and purposes influence how and to what a person responds in any given situation.
   b. People describe what they believe an event, person, or object to be rather than what it really is.
4. Trainees will be able to recognize self-disclosure statements that occur during five minutes of interaction with an individual who has been instructed to communicate explicitly one bit of information from each of five different headings on a list of self-disclosure items. After five minutes participants will prepare a written list of the five bits of information and compare them with those intended to be communicated by the other person. Four of the five items should appear on the presenter's list.
5. Trainees will be able to interact with a presenter who is role playing an emotionally agitated employee for five minutes during which they use each of the following techniques at least three times: reflection, paraphrase, open question, extending support. An observer should be able to identify each of the techniques by writing brief quotations of representative statements and/or describing behaviors exhibited by them in using each technique. During a ten-minute discussion period the presenter, the subject, and the observer should agree on the accuracy of the observer's identification on three out of four techniques.
6. Trainees will be able to demonstrate procedures for handling a complaint interview consistent with principles presented during the training session by interacting for ten minutes with a complainant in a role-playing interview. An observer should report that the procedures used are consistent with those described during the training session.

Objectives should be stated that indicate both terminal and intermediate performances desired of trainees. Clearly stated objectives should provide trainees with precise

descriptions of the intentions of trainers. Well-stated objectives also provide specifications for the preparation of evaluation procedures and instruments. In fact, if objectives
are carefully stated, actual evaluation procedures are suggested. Of course, objectives aid
in focusing training methods in order to accomplish the goals established for the training
session, to reduce irrelevancies, and to eliminate inadequacies.

Step 4: Consider Methods and Match with Objectives

Once the precise terminal and intermediate objectives are stated, you need to return to
the possible activities and match them with the objectives. The match, of course, should
be made on the basis of how well the activity achieves the objective. Your first task is
simply to come up with as many relevant activities as you can. With a large number of
activities for each objective, you can select those that are most appropriate. With few
activities, you are limited in the choices you can make.

As Carnarius (1981) suggests, you are something like a chef, "with things cooking
at various stages in your kitchen. What you need to do is serve it up in the right fashion
so it will not only be nourishing, but pleasing as an experience" (p. 43). Matching objectives and considering methods are refined in the next stage, because sequencing requires
putting things in the order that will achieve the greatest impact.

Step 5: Sequence the Session

A *training sequence* consists of those activities associated with the accomplishment of an
intermediate objective. Training sequences combine to constitute a *training session,*
which may run from one hour to two weeks in length. Training sessions combine to constitute a *training program,* which is made up of all of the training sessions available to a
particular group of employees. A supervisory training program, for example, consists of
all of the training sessions that a supervisor might take.

The arrangement of a training sequence is governed largely by the basic approach
chosen: rational, behavioral, achievement, positional, and experiential. However, the
design of a training sequence within any basic approach may be strengthened by adher-
ing to four principles of *activity alternation* (Lynton & Pareek, 1967):

Principle 1: Alternate stimulation with reflection

Training sequences are something like great dramas; they provide tension but allow for
relaxation. Continuous activity should not be regarded as the primary method. Trainees
need time to reflect on the activity and to make sense out of what is happening.

Principle 2: Alternate personal involvement with safe distance

Training sequences need to be balanced between intense personal experiences and
opportunities to offer detached, analytical, and conceptual comments. Continuous intensity may produce stress rather than learning, so alternate intensity with detachment.

Principle 3: Alternate talking about something with practicing it

Training sequences need to provide practice opportunities until improvement in the
skill tapers off. Time then needs to be devoted to thinking and talking about those
things that still present problems in order to prepare for the next practice session.

8:00–8:10	Clearing the Agenda Activity	Experience
8:10–8:20	Ice-Breaker Activity	
8:20–8:30	Lecturette	Information
8:30–8:45	Large-Group Discussion	Analysis
8:45–9:00	Self-Analysis Instrument	Experience
9:00–9:05	Lecturette/Summary	Information
9:05–9:15	Small-Group Discussion	Analysis
9:15–9:30	Break/Informal Conversation	
9:30–10:00	Assertiveness Exercise	Experience
10:00–10:15	Lecturette	Information
10:15–10:45	Small-Group Discussion to Identify Relevant Skills	Analysis
10:45–11:00	Break/Informal Conversation	
11:00–12:00	Role-Play Skills	Practice

FIGURE 14.19
Sample Training Sequence Illustrating the Application of Elements in the Experiential Training Approach

Principle 4: Alternate individual tasks with group processes

Training sequences ought to have a balance of individual events and group events, in which the group activities provide stimulation and the individual activities allow participants to push themselves along as individuals.

An Experiential Training Sequence The experiential approach contains the elements of training that quite naturally provide for the alternation of stimulation and reflection, personal involvement and detachment, talking and practicing, and individual and group tasks. The model includes four distinct types of activities—experience, information, analysis, and practice—as shown in Figure 14.19. The order of activities in the training sequence should follow the order in the model.

The process of ordering activities can be illustrated by arranging a half-day sequence. Figure 14.19 shows how the experiential activities combine to make a training sequence. The training sequence develops in approximately the same order as the elements in the experiential model, moving from experience to information to analysis; the sequence then returns to experience and moves to information and to analysis twice more before the culminating practice session. The number of preliminary rounds (from experience to information to analysis) that needs to be completed before a practice segment is introduced depends upon the complexity of the skills being developed and the amount of prerequisite information and analysis desirable for successful performance of the skills. The final stage in the design of a training session is the selection and refinement of exercises, instruments, discussion questions, and lecturettes so they fit the time periods and are consistent with the principles of alternation.

The completed design of a training session might consist of a large number of sequences, each involving several rounds of experience, information, analysis, and practice, plus detailed instructions for supervising experiences, presenting information, facilitating analysis, and directing practice. In addition, a comprehensive daily training guide is usually prepared for use by the session leader in conducting the training. The entire package often extends to a hundred pages or more; this is because it contains copies of all materials to be used with exercises, including detailed instructions for conducting them, outlines of lecturettes, a list of equipment and material needs, evaluation forms, and the training-room floor plan with indications for placement of equipment, tables, and chairs.

Step 6: Check the Agenda

A training session consists of a set of objectives, some division of labor between staff and participants, a temporal sequence of time periods, and some identifiable training

Daily Schedule

8:00 A.M.–9:15 A.M.	Activities (75 min.)
9:15 A.M.–9:30 A.M.	Break
9:30 A.M.–10:45 A.M.	Activities (75 min.)
10:45 A.M.–11:00 A.M.	Break
11:00 A.M.–12:00 P.M.	Activities (60 min.)
12: 00 P.M.–1:00 P.M.	Lunch
1:00 P.M.–2:15 P.M.	Activities (75 min.)
2:15 P.M.–2:30 P.M.	Break
2:30 P.M.–3:45 P.M.	Activities (75 min.)
3:45 P.M.–4:00 P.M.	Break
4:00 P.M.–5:00 P.M.	Activities (60 min.)

FIGURE 14.20 Sample Daily Schedule for Training Program

activities (Havelock & Havelock, 1973). The combination of objectives, activities, labor, and time periods is called an *agenda*.

Time Blocks   The amount of time to be devoted to any given training session is usually decided by a combination of organizational factors such as staff budgets available, number of employees who should be trained, physical facilities, costs, and workload. When those issues are settled, the length of the training session is usually determined by the specifications of different training methods. Frequently, however, three days are assigned to a particular training program. The task of the training staff is to design a program that will fit the amount of time available. Thus, you start with a one-, three-, or five-days and select the objectives, methods, and activities that can be handled during that period. Although some training programs run for as long as eighty hours, most training occurs in sessions of eight to forty hours.

Daily Schedule   When working with adult employees, the day often begins at 8:00 a.m. and ends at 5:00 p.m., although it can vary from 7:30 to 9:00 a.m. for starting times and from 3:30 to 6:00 p.m. for quitting times. Most training programs should provide for segments long enough to conduct exercises and analyze them but short enough to keep participants from getting tired. In general, the schedule for any given day should appear somewhat like that portrayed in Figure 14.20, ranging from 60- to 75-minute blocks. As illustrated in the sample daily schedule, planning for detailed training events occurs within 75- and 60-minute blocks. Each period is usually planned so that it is self-contained and that exercises, simulations, lecturettes, analysis, and practices will fit within the allotted time.

Each 75- and 60-minute block usually has one or more intermediate objectives associated with it. Each day or half-day culminates in the accomplishment of a terminal objective.

To check the agenda, it is a good idea to lay out the entire training session according to small time periods showing the discrete activities associated with each of the goals to be accomplished. Objectives to be achieved by the trainees will be associated with each time block and portrayed at the beginning of the 60- or 75-minute time block. The agenda is often checked best by looking at what the *trainer* is to do within each of the 60- or 75-minute time spans to accomplish the objective for that time period.

To illustrate this process, we have created a series of time periods for a training session on customer service with descriptions of the trainer goals and the instructions for what should be done during each time period to accomplish the goals. Even though some time periods may consist of only a few minutes, it is a good idea to put all of the information for each time period on a separate page; hence, as often as possible, each page in the trainer's manual is somewhat self-contained.

Sample Agenda

TIME BLOCK: 9:00–10:15 A.M.

Intermediate Objectives
At the end of the time block, each participant will (1) appreciate the importance of great customer service (affective objective) and (2) be able to explain the elements that constitute the *fast-action model* of customer service (cognitive objective). (These are abbreviated forms of the actual statement of intermediate objectives used to prepare the workshop.)

TIME PERIOD 1: 9:00-9:05 A.M.

Goals
To welcome participants, review housekeeping details, and create some structure.

Instructions

1. Get the attention of participants.
2. Greet them warmly.
3. Explain smoking policy.
4. Point out restrooms and other facilities.
5. Review agenda and breaks.

TIME PERIOD 2: 9:05–9:15 A.M.

Goals
To introduce the trainer, explain why the workshop is being presented, demonstrate that customer service is important to the company, describe how the session was designed, and present the objectives of the workshop.

Instructions

1. State your name and position and give information (such as education and experience) that enhances your credibility as a trainer.
2. Explain that customer service is widely misunderstood because customers demand greater service and expect a different type of service than in the past.
3. Explain that this workshop is being presented to provide a new philosophy and tools that will build on a legacy of customer service.
4. Explain that great customer service has benefits that will make the employees big winners for themselves and for the company.
5. Show poster-size quotations from company officials illustrating their commitment to customer service.
6. Explain that the workshop consists of doing, reading, listening, discussing, and trying out and experiencing new ideas and values.
7. Present the objectives of the workshop in terms of what participants will get out of it:
   a. They will have a clearer idea of what modern customer service means.
   b. They will discover that great customer service is based on "fast action" and self-actualization values.
   c. They will see how visions lead to victories for themselves and for the company.
   d. They will learn how to make customer service a positive difference in their own lives.

Time Period 3: 9:15–9:30 a.m.

Goals
To show the relationship between values and actions.

Instructions

1. Explain that you would like each participant to stand at his or her seat and explain something each participant did recently that represented good customer service and then explain *why* he or she did it.
2. Give an example of what might be said, such as "I suggested that a customer going on a trip take traveler's checks rather than cash." The reason: "I thought it would be dangerous to take cash."
3. As workshop leader, condense the "why" statement into the form of a value; in the above explanation, the value might be "concern for others" or "helpfulness."
4. After all the participants have shared their experiences and explained why and have listed their values on a flip chart, point out that the values were the keys to what they did and how they acted.

Time Period 4: 9:30–10:15 a.m.

Goals
To show and describe the *fast-action model* of customer service.

Instructions

1. Explain that customer service involves three general levels of employee activity: nonresponsive, reactive, and fast-action.
2. Divide participants into small groups of five individuals each. Ask each group to prepare three role-playing skits to illustrate the three types of employee reactions to customers.
3. Ask each group to assign members of their group to enact the three examples, then contrast the responses of the three customers, and relate them to what the employees said and did.
4. Explain the theory of fast-action customer service to the entire group.
5. Lead a discussion about how the role-playing skits illustrated the theory.
6. Divide into small groups again and have members make a list of behaviors that seemed to make the greatest difference in customer satisfaction, both positive and negative.
7. Call up the groups and have each one select a specific behavior that makes a positive difference in customer satisfaction and prepare to practice the behavior. Break for restroom and refreshments.

With this outline, it is possible to check the agenda for consistency, flow, the relevance of the activities to the objectives, and the quality of the entire sequence.

Step 7: Prepare Materials

As soon as the agenda has been checked and the workshop schedule is ready, you now begin the task of preparing materials. You will need to develop the trainer's guide; lecturettes and other ways of presenting information; instruments and other items for supervising exercises; questions for discussion and ways of facilitating the analysis; handouts that go with lectures, discussions, exercises, and practice periods; and audiovisual materials.

The final task is to make copies of both the trainer's manual and the participants' workbooks for use in the training session. At that point, you will want to review all of the other details associated with conducting a training session, including how to evaluate the effectiveness of the training.

HOW TO CONDUCT A TRAINING SESSION

To conduct a training session involves considerably more than standing in front of a group. Although the design of the session and the preparation of a leader's guide should provide most of the basic information and directions for supervising, presenting, facilitating, and directing activities, other details must also be taken care of. The list that follows is a summary of most of the major issues that need attention (Davis & McCallon, 1974).

1. Dates (month, week, days) for the session must be established and scheduled.
2. Facilities (meeting rooms) must be secured and scheduled.
3. Equipment (projectors, screens, flip charts) must be located and scheduled or rented.
4. Materials (prereadings, handouts, instructions, instruments, puzzles, and other items involved in the activities) must be prepared, reproduced, sorted, stacked, and ordered for use.
5. Aids (pencils, felt pens, paper and notebooks, newsprint, overhead projections, pictures, and other aids) must be purchased, located, and boxed.
6. Participants (trainees) must be identified, recruited, and prepared to attend.
7. Promotion (advertising, notices, clearances) must be prepared and distributed with adequate information to make it simple for people to attend.
8. Accommodations and travel (sleeping quarters, ground and air transportation) often need to be arranged.
9. Food and refreshments (special luncheons, banquets, regular meals, refreshments for breaks) must be arranged, menus studied, and guarantees made.
10. Meeting room setup (arrangements of tables, chairs, screens, microphones, and easels) must be negotiated or handled by the training staff.
11. Staff and consultants (those who will conduct and assist with the session and invited guests, including organization officials who may wish to extend greetings and openings, as well as award certificates of completion at the end) must be determined, con-tacted, and contracted with or invited.
12. Budget sheets (itemized list of funds available and disbursed and projected costs) must be prepared to account for and explain expenditures. Items for which there is usually a chargeable cost include materials, staff, consultants, aids, facilities, accommodations, travel, meals, refreshments, promotion, and participant salaries.

After taking care of the many issues that must be considered in preparing for a training session, the actual training activity may seem like a very small part of the entire process.

Getting a Training Session Started

When all of the participants are assembled, materials are in place, and the physical surroundings have been checked for comfort and workability, you are ready to open the training session. Sometimes a formal welcome or greeting is in order, but in any case you will need to create a warm and cordial atmosphere. Frequently participants need to get acquainted with and accustomed to each other. Ice-breaker and get-acquainted exercises are very helpful at the beginning. The ground rules for participating in the session should be reviewed and participant expectations acknowledged. A review of the schedule and the topics and skills to be developed often help establish anticipations and increase motivation. Check the seating arrangements, ventilation, temperature, acoustics, and lighting as you proceed so that adjustments can be made before starting the first training segment. When the schedule is right, move into the first exercise. Materials should be nearby and a system set up to distribute them quickly to participants. Follow the plan, supervising experiences, presenting information, facilitating discussions, and directing practice sessions. At the end of each day have a dramatic motivational closing to leave trainees on an exciting high.

EVALUATION OF TRAINING

Few people working in human resource development deny the claim that the evaluation of training is not only the most important aspect of the entire process but also the most difficult. Smith (1980) argues convincingly that failures to evaluate the training process may be explained by three reasons: (1) *No one sees a need for evaluation.* The sessions and the support activities seem to be going along fairly well, so the actual need to evaluate does not seem particularly important. (2) *Evaluators do not know how to evaluate.* The major deficiencies lie in not knowing how to state evaluation objectives in precise and measurable terms or how to analyze the data once the data have been gathered. Many trainers just do not know how to summarize data so that the information collected can be interpreted and understood. (3) *The complexity of the trainer's job leads to other tasks having higher priority.* Training courses are often without adequate instructional guides, and frequent changes occur in course content. In addition, there may be a long time lag between the training activity and the trainee's opportunity to apply the skills to improve job performance. Finally, the trainers and trainees may feel that they, rather than the training, are the subjects of evaluation, and they may not cooperate with evaluators.

Four problems result from these causes:

1. No evaluation data are collected.
2. Evaluation data are unreliable and misleading.
3. Evaluation data fail to be presented in a timely fashion, often too late to be used effectively.
4. Evaluation data are incomplete, frequently lacking information about potential causes.

Planning an Evaluation

As with other aspects of training, to be effective, evaluation must be planned. The first step in the process is to identify what should be known about training. The second step is to decide what should be measured. The third step is to identify ways of obtaining the data.

Answers to five questions seem critical in evaluating a training program:

1. Are the trainees satisfied?
2. Did the trainees experience information gain?
3. Did the trainees acquire the skills being developed?
4. Do the trainees use the skills on the job?
5. Does using the skills have a positive effect on the organization?

TABLE 14.3 Summary of Evaluation Issues

WHAT SHOULD BE INVESTIGATED	WHAT SHOULD BE MEASURED		WHAT SHOULD BE EXAMINED
	DURING THE SESSION	AFTER THE SESSION	
Trainee satisfaction	Perceptions after training segments	Perceptions on the job	Oral and written comments and reactions to questionnaires
Trainee information gain	Knowledge of concepts	Explanations of concepts to others	Scores on objective tests, performance during exercises, observations of work
Trainee skills acquisition	Skills exhibited in practices	Skills used on the job	Performance review reports, observations of work, employee-reported problems
Effect of skills on the organization	Perceptions of others of value of changes to the organization	Actual value of changes to organization	Perceptions of supervisors, cost-effectiveness figures, problems reported by supervisors

Finding answers to those questions constitutes the evaluation process. Table 14.3 summarizes what should be measured to answer each question and what kinds of data might produce relevant answers.

To evaluate the satisfaction with the training experience, some measurement of trainee perceptions both during the training session and after the session when trainees return to the job is important. Satisfaction with program content, instructor styles, learning experiences, facilities, and related accommodations may all affect quality of the training session. Information gain is usually measured directly by administering some type of test, either objective or subjective; however, much can be learned about what a person knows by listening to the person explain ideas to others.

Evaluation of how well a trainee has developed the psychomotor skills needed to perform behaviors more effectively is a difficult task. Measures of performance are frequently based on observation and are quite subjective at times. How well a person performs a particular skill in practice sessions during training is often difficult to determine, and whether the skills are actually transferred and used on the job is generally not easy to determine either. Performance review reports, observations of work, and employee-reported problems may all give some indication of how well the trainee has acquired and uses the skills presented during the training session.

Whether the behaviors developed in the training session will have a positive effect on the functioning of the organization is something that can only be predicted, especially when evaluated during the training session. Instructions to select the two or three most important job-related objectives and to evaluate how well they have been accomplished during the training may give an indication of the value of the objectives to the organization. As supervisors observe the work of employees, they may recognize problems or may notice trainees using behaviors that are of value to the company. Naturally, production figures and other objective indicators of performance that can be related to employee behaviors are usually excellent indicators of the effect of training on the organization.

SUMMARY

The design, conduct, and evaluation of strategies of training and development were reviewed. Two philosophies of specifying objectives were summarized: (1) performance objectives can be stated and are essential for determining the effectiveness of training programs; (2) specific behaviors and competencies often do not tell the difference between effective and noneffective employees, and trainee-centered activities develop more flexible employees. It was suggested that an experiential approach to training combines the major benefits of both philosophies. Terminal objectives describe what trainees should be able to do back on the job, whereas intermediate objectives indicate what trainees should be able to do following specific training sequences. Appreciation and understanding of and the ability to perform behaviors were identified as factors that account for a person's performance. Objectives designed to produce favorable attitudes, provide accurate information, and develop psychomotor skills should be included in training programs.

The characteristics of acceptable performance objectives were discussed. They include reference to observable behaviors, omission of references to directions and training activities, reliable and easily understood qualitative and quantitative ways of measuring the performance, inclusion of important conditions under which the performance is to occur, and inclusion of the tools, supplies, and references available to the trainee. Sample statements of performance objectives were given.

The content of a training program is usually determined by what the trainees need to know and is portrayed in a two-level outline of topics. Examples of program content were presented.

A training program was described as consisting of a set of objectives, a division of labor, blocks of time, and identifiable training activities. The sequence of training events was described in terms of a weekly and a daily time schedule. It was explained that training sessions are developed around 60- and 75-minute self-contained time blocks.

A training sequence was defined as those activities associated with the accomplishment of an intermediate objective. The principles for alternating training activities were discussed. The experiential training sequence was analyzed as an approach that naturally provides for the alternation of the key principles. A daily schedule for implementing the elements in experiential training was described. Twelve major issues in preparation for conducting a training session were listed. How to get a session started was discussed.

The reasons why evaluation of training fails to be done and the problems resulting therefrom were explained. Questions critical to evaluating a training program were analyzed. Finally, trainee satisfaction, trainee information gain, trainee skills acquisition, and the effect on organization function of using the skills were identified as the key variables to be evaluated.

REFERENCES

BANDURA, ALBERT, *Principles of Behavior Modification.* New York: Holt, Rinehart, & Winston, 1969.

BANDURA, ALBERT, and D. CERVONE, "Self-Evaluative and Self-Efficacy Mechanisms Governing the Motivational Effects of Goal Systems," *Journal of Personality and Social Psychology* 45 (1983), 1017–1028.

BARTLETT, ALTON C., "Changing Behavior Through Simulation: An Alternative Design to T-Group Training," *Training and Development Journal,* 21 (August 1967), 38–52.

BARTON, GRANT E., *Performance Objectives.* Provo, Utah: Brigham Young University Press, 1973.

BELLMAN, GEOFFREY, "Surveying Your Supervisory Training Needs," *Training and Development Journal* (February 1975), 25–33.

BIDDLE, BRUCE J., and EDWIN J. THOMAS, eds., *Role Theory: Concepts and Research.* New York: John Wiley, 1966.

BIRCH, D., and J. VEROFF, *Motivation: A Study of Action.* Belmont, Calif.: Wadsworth, 1966.

BOIS, J. SAMUEL, *The Art of Awareness* (3rd ed.). Dubuque, Iowa: Wm. C. Brown, 1978.

CARNARIUS, STAN, "A New Approach to Designing Training Programs," *Training and Development Journal,* 35 (February 1981), 40–44.

CASSE, PIERRE, *Training for the Cross-Cultural Mind* (2nd ed.). Washington, D.C.: The Society for Education, Training and Research, 1981.

CHAMBERLAIN, JONATHAN M., *Eliminate Your SDBs*. Provo, Utah: Brigham Young University Press, 1978.

COMBS, ARTHUR W., *The Professional Education of Teachers*. Boston: Allyn & Bacon, 1965.

COMBS, ARTHUR W., DONALD L. AVILA, and WILLIAM W. PURKEY, *Helping Relationships: Basic Concepts for the Helping Professions*. Boston: Allyn & Bacon, 1971.

CRAIGHEAD, W. EDWARD, ALAN E. KAZDIN, and MICHAEL J. MAHONEY, *Behavior Modification: Principles, Issues, and Applications*. Boston: Houghton Mifflin, 1976.

CUMMINGS, L.L., and DONALD P. SCHWAB, *Performance in Organizations: Determinants and Appraisal*. Glenview, Ill.: Scott, Foresman, 1973.

DAVIS, JAMES H., *Group Performance*. Reading, Mass.: Addison-Wesley, 1969.

DAVIS, LARRY NOLAN, and EARL McCALLON, *Planning, Conducting, and Evaluating Workshops*. Austin, Texas: Learning Concepts, 1974.

DEESE, JAMES, *General Psychology*. Boston: Allyn & Bacon, 1967.

DOWLING, JOHN R., and ROBERT P. DROLET, *Developing and Administering an Industrial Training Program,* Boston: CBI Publishing Company, 1979.

DOWNS, CAL W., *Communication Audits*. Glenview, Ill.: Scott, Foresman, 1988.

DOWNS, CAL W., G. PAUL SMEYAK, and ERNEST MARTIN, *Professional Interviewing*. New York: Harper & Row, Pub., 1980.

DYER, WILLIAM G., "What Makes Sense in Management Training?" *Management Review,* 67 (June 1978), 50–56.

ELLIS, ALBERT, and ROBERT A. HARPER, *A New Guide to Rational Living*. North Hollywood, Calif.: Wilshire Book Company, 1975.

FRENCH, WENDELL L., and CECIL H. BELL, JR., *Organization Development* (4th ed.). Englewood Cliffs, N.J.: Prentice Hall, 1990.

GORDON, ALICE KAPLAN, *Games for Growth*. Chicago: Science Research Associates, 1972.

GORDON, GEORGE N., *Persuasion: The Theory and Practice of Manipulative Communication*. New York: Hastings House, 1971.

GORMAN, WALTER, *Selling: Personality, Persuasion, Strategy*. New York: Random House, 1979.

GROVE, THEODORE G, *Experiences in Interpersonal Communication*. Englewood Cliffs, N.J.: Prentice Hall, 1976.

HALL, DOUGLAS T., DONALD D. BOWEN, ROY J. LEWICKI, and FRANCINE S. HALL, *Experiences in Management and Organizational Behavior*. Chicago: St. Clair Press, 1975.

HARRISON, ROGER, "Role Negotiation: A Tough-Minded Approach to Team Development," in *Group Training Techniques,* M.L. and P.J. Berger, eds. New York: John Wiley, 1972.

HAVELOCK, RONALD G., and MARY C. HAVELOCK, *Training for Change Agents*. Ann Arbor: University of Michigan Press, 1973.

HILL, NAPOLEAN, *Think and Grow Rich*. New York: Hawthorn Books, 1967.

HILL, RICHARD L., *Role Negotiation: Participant Workbook*. Plymouth, Mich.: Human Synergistics, 1983.

KING, STEPHEN W., *Communication and Social Influence*. Reading, Mass.: Addison-Wesley, 1975.

KIRKPATRICK, DONALD L., *A Practical Guide for Supervisory Training and Development*. Reading, Mass.: Addison-Wesley, 1971.

KOLB, DAVID A., IRWIN M. RUBIN, and JAMES M. McINTYRE. *Organizational Psychology: A Book of Readings* (2nd ed.). Englewood Cliffs, N.J.: Prentice Hall, 1974.

LAWRENCE, PAUL R., and JAY W. LORSCH, *Developing Organizations: Diagnosis and Action*. Reading, Mass.: Addison-Wesley, 1969.

LYNTON, ROLF P., and UDAI PAREEK, *Training for Development*. Homewood Ill.: Richard D. Irwin, 1967.

MAGER, ROBERT F., *Preparing Instructional Objectives*. Belmont, Calif.: Fearon, 1962.

MALTZ, MAXWELL, *Psycho-Cybernetics*. Englewood Cliffs, N.J.: Prentice Hall, 1960.

MCCLELLAND, DAVID C., J.W. ATKINSON, R.A. CLARK, and E.L. LOWELL, *The Achievement Motive*. New York: Appleton-Century-Crofts, 1953.

MCGUIRE, WILLIAM J., "The Nature of Attitudes and Attitude Change," in *The Handbook of Social Psychology* (2nd ed.), Gardner Lindzey and Elliott Aronson, eds. Reading, Mass.: Addison-Wesley, 1969.

MICHALAK, DONALD F., and EDWIN G. YAGER, *Making the Training Process Work*. New York: Harper & Row, Pub., 1979.

MIDDLEMAN, RUTH R., and GALE GOLDBERG, "The Concept of Structure in Experiential Learning," *The 1972 Annual Handbook for Group Facilitators*. San Diego, Calif.: University Associates, 1972.

MILLS, GORDON E., R. WAYNE PACE, and BRENT D. PETERSON, *Analysis in Human Resource Training and Organization Development*. Reading, Mass.: Addison-Wesley, 1988.

ODIORNE, GEORGE S., *Training by Objectives*. New York: Macmillan, 1970.

OLIVAS, LOUIS, and JOHN W. NEWSTROM, "Learning Through the Use of Simulation Games," *Training and Development Journal* (September 1981), 63–66.

PACE, R. WAYNE, "An Experiential Approach to Teaching Organizational Communication," *The Journal of Business Communication,* 14 (Summer 1977), 37–47.

PACE, R. WAYNE, BRENT D. PETERSON, and M. DALLAS BURNETT, *Techniques for Effective Communication*. Reading, Mass.: Addison-Wesley, 1979.

PATTON, BOBBY R., and KIM GIFFIN, *Problem-Solving Group Interaction*. New York: Harper & Row, Pub., 1973.

PFEIFFER, J. WILLIAM, and JOHN E. JONES, "Design Considerations in Laboratory Education," *Reference Guide to Handbooks and Annuals*. San Diego: University Associates, 1985.

PLUNKETT, LORNE C., and GUY A. HALE, *The Proactive Manager*. New York: John Wiley, 1982.

ROSENBAUM, BERNARD L., "Common Misconceptions About Behavior Modeling and Supervisory Skill Training (SST), *Training and Development Journal* (August 1979), 40–44.

SCHEIN, EDGAR H., *Process Consultation: Its Role in Organization Development*. Reading, Mass.: Addison-Wesley, 1969.

SMITH, MARTIN E., "Evaluating Training Operations and Programs," *Training and Development Journal* (October 1980), 70–78.

SPICE, MARTHA B., "The Thought Selection Process: A Tool Worth Exploring," *Training and Development Journal* (May 1982), 54–59.

SPRINGER, JUDY, "Brain/Mind and Human Resource Development," *Training and Development Journal* (August 1981), 42-49.

STUBBS, IRVING, RICHARD L. HILL, and G.G. CARLTON, "Training and Development of Internal Consultants at Diamond Shamrock." *The Personnel Administrator* (July 1978), 17–20, 42.

WILLIAMS, ROBERT L., and JAMES D. LONG, *Toward a Self-Managed Life Style*. Boston: Houghton Mifflin, 1975.

WILSON, CLARK, "Identifying Needs With Costs in Mind," *Training and Development Journal,* 34 (July 1980), 58–62.

WINANS, JAMES A., *Public Speaking*. New York: The Century Co., 1917.

WOHLKING, WALLACE, and HANNAH WEINER, "Structured and Spontaneous Role-Playing," *Training and Development Journal* (June 1981), 111–121.

ZEMKE, RON, and DAVE WALONICK, "The Non-Statistician's Approach to Conducting and Analyzing Surveys," *Training/HRD* (September 1980), 89–99.

ZENGER, JACK, "The Painful Turnabout in Training," *Training and Development Journal* (December 1980), 36–49.

15

Systems Analysis and Change

In the preceding chapter we discussed individual or "micro" approaches to analysis and change. In this chapter we shall focus on a systems or "macro" approach to organizational communication. In the first part of the chapter we shall introduce analytical methods that are part of the two major theoretical traditions—interpretive and functional. We shall look at interpretive methods of analyzing organizational communication. We shall then explore the concept of functional analysis and introduce an instrument for completing a functional analysis of organizational communication that encompasses the major dimensions of communication in organizations.

In the second part of the chapter we shall examine strategies or methods for making changes in organizational communication itself or in elements of the organization or work system that affect organizational communication.

INTERPRETIVE METHODS OF ANALYSIS

This section will explore basic interpretive methods, such as participant observation, account analysis, story analysis, metaphor analysis, and in-depth interviews. The definitions and methods of interpretive research vary considerably. Strine and Pacanowsky (1985) remark, "Some pieces of interpretive research strongly resemble traditional 'org. comm.' studies complete with numbers. But others look like critical analyses of plays, filled with indented dialogue. Still others resemble new Journalism or fiction" (p. 284). It is obvious that each interpretive method requires a different level of sophistication. Although this section may not prepare you to write a novel or engage in rhetorical criticism, it should provide the basic concepts that will enable you to do some useful analysis. We will discuss some of the basic insights and procedures that must be mastered before one can move to an intermediate level of sophistication. The analytic concepts we discuss are selected for illustrative purposes and should not be thought of as *the* concepts to use.

General Considerations

Traditional studies rely mainly on instruments such as inventories, attitude questionnaires, and structured interviews. The interpretive method of analysis relies more heavily on the researcher as the instrument; hence, it is up to interpretive researchers to present a strong case for their findings. The investigator cannot rely on such statements as "My findings are valid because my questionnaire is valid and reliable." An interpretive study must persuade readers that they are gaining knowledge through the discoveries made by a careful and insightful researcher. The critical question is, "Can the researcher 'discover' and 'interpret' significant organizational behaviors?"

What does the researcher look for? The search is for symbolic behavior that has organizational significance. What do the symbols allow organization members to see and do? How might they enable or constrain organizational activity? To repeat Smircich (1985), "What are the words, ideas, and constructs that impel, legitimate, coordinate, and realize organized activity in specific settings? How do they accomplish the task? Whose interests are they serving?" (p.67). We suggested earlier that a culture can be "imaged" by considering its indicators and displayers. These indicators and displayers appear in a variety of cultural schemes. Lundberg (1985) discusses four levels of organizational culture: artifacts, perspectives, values, and assumptions. *Artifacts* can be verbal, behavioral, or physical. A verbal artifact could be a story, for instance. Behavioral artifacts include rituals and ceremonies. The visual images (pictures, plaques, prints, clippings, and cartoons) and actual objects, such as golf clubs, sculptures, or vases exhibited by members of an organization, are examples of physical artifacts. *Perspectives* refer to the shared rules and norms of an organization. *Values* represent those ideas that organizational members use for judging situations, acts, and goals. They are the standards and ideals of the organization. *Assumptions* are the tacit beliefs that organizational members hold. They are often implicit and so taken for granted that members do not consciously think about them. In that way, assumptions are the underpinning of the first three levels. Deal and Kennedy (1982) posit four key attributes of organizational cultures: values, heroes, rites and rituals, and cultural-communication networks.

Although Lundberg's and Deal and Kennedy's categories are helpful, it is important at this point to issue a caution. In our view the best cultural analyses focus on *discovering* the symbolic behavior that *drives* organized activity. The idea is not to select the best system of cultural categories and then apply them. Finding indicators and displayers of organizational culture and cataloging them does not tell much about the significance of such factors. Barley (1983) cautions the researcher to avoid focusing only on the symbolic phenomena that lie on the surface of everyday life. Rather than belaboring the obvious, the investigator should reveal the core of the interpretive system. Each list of cultural components should be regarded as some potential categories that may emerge as important anchors of meaning. In one organization a particular component of culture may guide behavior whereas in another it has little significance. Because culture is constructed by its members, it is unique; the researcher must discover the uniqueness. The researcher observes and records specific behaviors, develops themes out of those behaviors, and then assigns the theme to a category. A new category may have to be developed.

Interpretive research requires that the investigator be able to *see* taken-for-granted behavior and its significance. Taken-for-granted behavior is embedded in everyday talk and routines. Sometimes when organizational members have agreed to be observed, they say, "Well, you can observe us, but you will be disappointed because nothing ever happens here." However, to an outsider who is trying to understand an organization, a great deal is going on and much of it is unclear. If you have seen the television show *The Waltons* then the following example will make sense. In one episode, a family member, upon discovering that John Boy plans to become a writer and that he plans to write about the family, says, "I don't see how he can write about the family; we never do anything!" All of us are so accustomed to certain behaviors that we do not see them or understand how they have structured our world. When the behaviors are made visible and interpreted, one might be fascinated, amused, and even prepared for change. Comedians (Bill Cosby and George Carlin, for example) have a special talent for taking the everyday language and routines that people take for granted and making them not only quite visible but also problematic. It is the capacity to make people conscious of their unconscious behaviors that must be developed by the interpretive researcher.

Gathering data presents another challenge. Pacanowsky and O'Donnell-Trujillo (1982) stress that interpretive researchers must become very "familiar" with the organizational behavior that is being studied, but at the same time they must remain in a position to experience the behavior as "unfamiliar" so that it can be questioned and understood. As the researcher becomes more familiar with organizational routines, it becomes more difficult to see or question them. Students who are assigned a cultural analysis project often ask if they can do an interpretive study of an organization that employs them. The good news is that they are familiar with the organization, but it is also bad news that they are familiar with the organization. When individuals examine their own workplace cultures, particular care must be taken to make organizational behaviors "strange." We will elaborate on this notion in the discussion of procedures.

What may appear to be mundane language or interaction can embody significant organizational processes and beliefs. For example, Roy (1960) describes and analyzes the interaction that takes place within a group of factory machine operators. His account of the "first awareness" of what was happening around him is important to the interpretive researcher. He states, "What I heard at first, before I started to listen, was a stream of disconnected bits of communication which did not make sense. . . . What I saw at first, before I began to observe, was occasional flurries of horseplay so simple and unvarying in pattern and so childish in quality that they made no strong bid for attention" (p. 161). As he developed familiarity with the communication system, the interaction started to reveal structure. He discovered that there were "times" and themes that emerged out of the communication. The breaks during the day were labeled: There was coffee-time, peach-time, banana-time, fish-time, coke-time, and lunch-time. The themes were those of verbal interplay and included such items as "kidding themes." His interpretation contends that the times and themes were used as a source of job satisfaction and as a way of coping with monotony. There are certainly more implications, but the important point for the researcher is that what appears to be mundane has meaning, pattern, and significance.

If a researcher intends to make some sense of an organizational culture, it is difficult, if not impossible, to specify what is being looked for except in a general way. There is a search for the *sense patterns* of the organizational membership that drive, legitimate, coordinate, and make possible their activity. Although there is value in understanding the available methods of analysis and the cultural components to which the methods are applied (Bantz, 1981, 1983, 1987), these represent *potential* methods and components. The researcher must discover the sense of making that is taking place and then describe its significance.

Procedures

What Culture Is Examined? We suggested earlier that an organization is likely to have several subcultures. In view of this a researcher will have to set some boundaries at the outset, even if they are arbitrary ones. The size of the organization may dictate those boundaries. Cultural analysis requires time, and in this regard it is not an inexpensive process. The boundaries selected at the outset may be altered as the study progresses. Even small organizations may contain several subcultures that become apparent in the course of study. There is also the alternative of studying what happens at the interstices between subcultures. Frost and colleagues (1991) called this the differentiation perspective.

What Is the Focus of Study? Our discussion of culture indicated that studies of workplace culture can focus on different issues, such as the origins, manifestations, outcomes, and management of cultures. Our focus has been on obtaining an "understanding" of organizational culture. This approach has the advantage of presenting a more comprehensive picture of the organization and focuses on significance that is generated by members of the organization. The language of the other foci of study treats culture as given— an end product that is made up of certain elements that have an impact on other elements. In that sense it represents functional research more closely than interpretive research.

What Constitutes Data? *Talk* is the primary data of cultural analysis. It is in the talk that cultures are brought to life and acted out or, as Pacanowsky and O'Donnell-Trujillo (1983) would suggest, organizational reality is brought into being. In traditional studies data usually consist of numbers, whereas the data in interpretive studies are organizational *messages*. These messages may be selected from communicative interactions, organizational documents, organizational outputs, and physical artifacts. Language is the dominant subject in analyzing interaction, but nonverbal aspects should not be discounted. Ideally, interactions should be videotaped so that nonverbal cues can be included in the analysis. However, even a description of the nonverbal behavior can help the reader understand the interaction. The analysis of documents can give insight into the official version of an organization, and the congruence or divergence between document statements and actual behavior may add an interesting dimension to cultural analysis. Bantz (1983) suggests that organizational messages that are actual products of the organization as well as those that serve an image-building function for the organization can be analyzed by (1) examining how they are discussed and reconstructed by organizational members, and (2) studying the way in which the output (report) is used by the members to construct meanings and expectations of the organization. Physical artifacts of the organization also send messages about the culture of that organization. Furniture, art, space, and design are artifacts that convey meaning and feeling in an organization. They are a type of data.

How Are the Data Gathered? The two major means of gathering data are participant observation and interviewing. *Participant observation* means that the researcher observes, then interviews organizational members about the observations and what they might mean. The observer gets involved with the meanings of organization members who are observed. *Interviews* are used to clarify observations. Pacanowsky and O'Donnell-Trujillo (1982) point out that "what is required then are details—detailed observations of organizational members 'in action' and detailed interviews (formal or informal) of organizational members accounting for their actions" (p. 127). Detailed data are necessary for a rich description and plausible presentation of an organizational culture. Enough time must be spent to become very familiar with the organization. Depending on the situation, the researcher takes notes, makes tape recordings, takes pictures, and collects documents. Field notes are extremely important for illustrating communicative exchanges. Writing down or recording exactly what was said is a real challenge. If the researcher is going to capture the nuances of organizational communication, however, precise and accurate records are important.

How Are Data Generated? The discovery of sense-making processes necessitates techniques that illuminate taken-for-granted behavior. In this regard, data are generated or "brought to light." People engage in everyday routines without thinking about them, and they hold tacit knowledge or understanding that they never verbalize. How are taken-for-granted behavior and tacit knowledge revealed so that the investigator can see how people are making sense of their behaviors? Pacanowsky and O'Donnell-Trujillo (1982) suggest that researchers should constantly ask organizational members "Why?" when referring to particular behaviors for statements. This sort of digging can produce accounts that reveal sense making. It must be remembered that "why" questions are used to determine *how* organizational members are making sense. Nevertheless, *why* people are *really* doing or saying something is *not* the issue. Louis (1985) suggests that the researcher can get at tacit knowledge by looking for (or provoking) conditions under which such knowledge becomes accessible. Conditions that allow for getting at tacit knowledge include disruptions or crises, because what is normal is disturbed and brought to light. Individuals who experience *contrast* (multiple roles) can often provide descriptions or tacit knowledge held by various groups. The investigator might probe (or provoke) by asking a group to produce an image of itself or discuss what epitomized that group. Another technique is to focus on a *critical incident*, and then ask the group to reflect on its meaning.

How Are Data Interpreted? The researcher must have sufficient data, be able to see what organizational members are experiencing, discover patterns of sense making, and, finally, interpret the significance of the sense making. In the final analysis the researcher is responsible for the interpretation. However, the thorough researcher will seek out supplemental inputs and perspectives. This step enables greater scrutiny of data and permits an investigator to state the type of bias that may be in a final report. Louis (1981, 1985) discusses levels of interpretation in a research process. She suggests that they include (1) the member's interpretations, (2) negotiated interpretations between member and researcher, (3) the researcher's interpretations, (4) negotiated interpretations between two researchers, (5) validation of a researcher's interpretations between two researchers, (6) validation of a researcher's interpretations by an organizational member, and (7) critical interpretations of the researcher. The appropriateness of these levels depends on the particular study and researcher. What is important is the notion of various perspectives so that different nuances of the organizational culture do not elude the investigator.

Up to this point we have stressed the basic considerations and procedures for analyzing organizational culture from an *emergent* perspective. That is, the researcher determines what is important to the culture in terms of what drives it; labels may be attached to or created for particular constructs.

Bryman (1991) explores the classic work of Whyte as a model for research into organizational culture. He suggests that Whyte viewed culture as something in flux and as emergent and that organizational culture research should be no exception. Getting at the "interpretive core" means identifying patterns of behavior and showing how these mesh with and underpin culture. Trujillo (1992) asserts that communication scholars may have unique access to multiple interpretations because they are enacted and revealed in communication actions and interactions. Wuthnow and co-workers (1984) suggest that cultural analysis should focus on visible behaviors such as verbal utterances and gestures. The performance aspects of communication are emphasized and communication and culture are closely linked.

Although we favor the emergent approach, there are other ways to conduct interpretive analyses. One such approach, a *preconceptualized* one (Bantz, 1987), lays out what is important in advance on the assumption that the items examined will give significant insights into organizational culture. Bantz states that

> the Organizational Communication Culture (OCC) approach entails a methodology that (1) gathers messages; (2) analyzes the messages for four major elements—vocabulary, themes, architecture, and temporality; (3) analyzes the symbolic forms in the messages—metaphors, fantasy themes, and stories; (4) infers patterns of organizational meanings from the elements, symbolic forms, and the messages themselves; (5) infers patterns of expectations from the elements, symbolic forms, meanings, and the messages themselves; and (6) weaves these patterns of meanings and expectations into a tapestry of the Organizational Communication Culture (p. 6).

Researchers who adopt a preconceptualized approach tend to analyze messages in terms of symbolic forms. Three such symbolic forms that have been found useful in organizational study include *account analysis, story analysis,* and *metaphor analysis*. These forms tell about organizational cultures, although it must be stressed that they do not tell all.

Account analysis involves asking people to provide explanations for their behavior. *Accounts* are the kinds of statements people use whenever their actions are challenged (Scott & Lyman, 1968). In other words, people usually give accounts when they are asked to justify their actions; givers of accounts provide explanations that they perceive as socially acceptable. For example, if you were asked why your term paper was late, you would no doubt try to present verbal justifications that you thought were socially (culturally) acceptable. This account would tell how you make sense of the culture and what you think is important. Getting at *legitimate* behavior in the organization tells us a great deal about organizational constraints. When an individual accounts for a particular behavior, more is involved than giving reasons. The verbalization is an act that has a number of implications. Account analysis has been used to illustrate (1) organizational identification (Cheney, 1983), (2) the link between organizational decision making and identification (Tompkins & Cheney, 1983), (3) the reconstruction of an event's context (Buttny, 1985), (4) account acceptability in the organizational setting (Buckholdt & Gubrium, 1983), and (5) identification of organizational culture (Faules & Drecksel, 1991). Accounts can be obtained by observing naturally occurring interaction, by interviewing, and by administering a questionnaire. Account analysis can help the *change agent* discover what justifications members *think* are operative in the organization. Knowledge of accounts may also help managers realize that different cultural contexts require different managerial strategies.

Story analysis examines organizational narrations or stories. The *story* is a form of organizational symbolism that "members use to reveal or make comprehendible the unconscious feelings, images, and values that are inherent in that organization" (Dandridge, Mitroff & Joyce, 1980, p. 77). Stories are used to give meaning to critical events. There are different types of stories and story analyses, including *myths* (Sykes, 1970), *legends* (Brunvard, 1980), *sagas* (Bormann, 1972, 1983), and *master symbols* (Smith, n.d.). Stories are used for sense making. Members use stories to determine what organizational events and activities mean. You have probably been involved in an organization where stories have been used to socialize new members (Brown, 1985), convey policy, make a particular point, epitomize what the organization is "all about," or illustrate what really counts "around here."

Stories are potent anchors of meaning. Martin (1982) suggests that the story is an effective tool for communicating a policy in that it is more memorable and believable than other symbolic forms. Wilkins (1978) found that the number and types of stories told may be related to the level of employee commitment. The content of stories, who tells them, and how they are told can give insight into significant organizational behaviors.

Myrsiades (1987) maintains that organizational stories can provide the context of meaning in the culture. In that way they do more than transmit information or guide behavior. They are symbolic realities and extended real-life metaphors. She suggests that the study of organizational stories is useful for understanding the systems of events that make up a culture.

How does the researcher obtain stories? Mitroff and Kilmann (1975) suggest that "stories are like dreams. Most of us have to be trained not only to recognize them, but also to appreciate their significance. For this reason, it is almost impossible to get at the stories that govern organizations directly. Like dreams they have to be gotten at indirectly" (pp. 19–20). Of course, it would be ideal to observe stories as they are told in everyday interaction. However, this method may require an excessive amount of time. Observation may provide data, but the researcher must rely primarily on the interview. Faules (1982) used story analysis to examine performance appraisal.

> The interview strategy was to (1) get respondents to talk about what organizational members talk about in reference to performance appraisal, (2) get respondents to focus on stories about performance appraisal, and (3) get respondents to develop those stories with as much detail as possible. A typical sequence of questions would include: What do people talk about when they are discussing performance appraisal? What are the major concerns? What are the favorable and unfavorable factors in the appraisal system? Can you give me an incident that would illustrate that factor? Describe the incident in as much detail as you can. How often are such incidents discussed? Are there other incidents that you have seen or heard about? Describe those for me (pp. 153–154).

Stories should be looked upon as creations. In the creating and re-creating process, organizational members reveal the sense making of that organization. Members can be asked to create stories that embody the practices, aspirations, and climate of an organization. Stories can be analyzed by looking for dominant themes and patterns of thought.

As for *metaphor analysis*, we have already discussed the *metaphor* as a potent device in the construction of reality. The metaphor is certainly a way of thinking that is used so often that it operates at a low level of awareness. What is important is how metaphors shape thinking. As the reader has already discovered, metaphors employed to describe an organization can limit and direct what is possible to think about in regard to the organization. For example, if organizations are thought of as "garbage cans" or places where problems, people, situations of choice, and solutions are dumped (Cohen, March & Olsen, 1972) rather than as "machines," a variety of behaviors can be considered. In addition, it must be remembered that from a subjective position, "rather than a person perceiving a world and then giving it an interpretation or meaning, perception is of an already meaningful (interpreted) world" (Koch & Deetz, 1981, p. 2). Metaphors, then, make up the organizational world and operate as an inherent part of the thinking and behavior of members.

Metaphors are gathered by observing and recording members' talk. In addition to naturally occurring exchanges, the researcher can interview, set up group sessions, or ask members to write on topics that might generate metaphors. Burrell, Buzzanell, and McMillan (1992) use metaphoric analysis derived from questionnaires and seminar content to see how people approach and manage conflict. Organizational documents may also provide useful data. To analyze metaphors, the researcher should look for patterns and dominant themes.

We have isolated some of the more recognized sense-making displayers, but the language and arguments used in an organization can tell us much about the culture. Riley, Hollihan, and Freadhoff (1991) analyzed the language games and argumentative structures that emerged during an organizational transformation. In their view, to understand the language game is also a key to understanding power in an organization.

Some Final Comments

In an earlier discussion of cultural analysis we pointed out that this type of study may tell *too much*. It is highly descriptive, and individuals may be identified by the specific language they use. This raises the issue of how cultural analysis should be conducted and presented. Even when presented in nonevaluative terms, such research can be threatening. Should an organization's culture be put on public display? This question raises more arguments than we can possibly deal with here. However, we would like to specify some of the conditions that lead to responsible research. The confidentiality of participants should be protected. Participants should be informed that they have the right to refuse observation or questioning. Final reports should be available to participants. The participant-observer process depends on trust, and the researcher should think very carefully about the impact of what is finally written. If someone is gracious enough to allow the researcher to enter a private world, the researcher has a responsibility to avoid destroying that world for the sake of a "good story."

Cultural analysis reports should take advantage of the nature of this type of research. Write for effect! If the interpretive analysis includes the dimension of "feeling," then the writer should not be tied to the format of a technical report. Much of the style of the report depends on the audience and its expectations. However, such reports ought to contain *thick description*. This means dialogue and description that provokes imagery. The *display* might take the form of dialogue, debate, a diary, novel, or short story. There are different ways of knowing, and these ways can be portrayed in a variety of formats.

FUNCTIONAL METHODS OF ANALYSIS

Throughout this book we have discussed various aspects of organizational communication and presented illustrative functional methods for analyzing select components. Thus, in this section we shall discuss the general concept of organizational analysis and limit our discussion of functional methods of analyzing communication primarily to the Organizational Communication Profile (OCP).

Harrison (1987) uses what we call a functional approach to organizational diagnosis and explains that "it involves the use of behavioral science knowledge to assess an organization's current state and to help discover routes to its improvement" (p. vii). Underlying nearly every approach to organization change is the process of organizational diagnosis. Harvey and Brown (1992) explain that "organization diagnosis is aimed at providing a rigorous analysis of data on the structure, administration, interaction, procedures, interfaces, and other essential elements of the client system" (p. 160).

Schein (1969) explains that "most organizations could probably be more effective than they are if they could identify what processes (work flow, interpersonal relations, communications, intergroup relations, etc.) need improvement." He says that no manager should "leap into an action program, particularly if it involves any kind of changes in organizational structure, until the organization itself has done a thorough diagnosis and assessment of the strengths and weaknesses of the present structure" (p. 6).

Harvey and Brown (1992) further explain that organizational diagnosis examines various subelements of the organization such as the divisions, departments, and products, and the organizational processes such as "communication networks, group problem solving, decision making, leadership and authority styles, goal setting and planning methods, and the management of conflict and competition" (pp. 160–161).

Schein (1969) identified six critical human processes in organizations that may be amenable to diagnosis and, subsequently, to change: (1) communication, (2) member roles and functions in groups, (3) group problem solving and decision making, (4) group norms and group growth, (5) leadership and authority, and (6) intergroup cooperation and competition (p. 13).

The fundamental purpose of diagnosis, according to experts in the field, is to look for *causality*—that is, for situations in which one factor such as rewards produces a change in another factor such as commitment to the organization. The analyst attempts to identify factors that are causing problems so that they can be resolved (Harvey & Brown, 1992, p. 161; Harrison, 1987, p. 3).

In the field of organizational communication, as one of the organizational sciences, similar reasoning is used to argue for the use of a "communication audit" in organizations to obtain information about how well the organization is doing in the area of communication. Downs (1988) explains that "more than anything else, the audit is a diagnostic technique. It answers the questions 'What characterizes this organization?' 'What does it do well?' and 'What needs improving?'" (p. 3).

From this very functional perspective, it is necessary to view organizational communication as either a cause of effective or ineffective organization functioning or as a symptom that the organization is functioning effectively or ineffectively, or as both a cause and a symptom. For example, Harrison (1987) says that clients are often able to recognize symptoms or effects of ineffective functioning, such as low morale, poor work quality, and conflicts and tensions that polarize people and groups, misunderstandings and communication failures (p. 2). They may not, however, be able to identify the causes or explain *why* the symptoms arose.

Schein (1969), on the other hand, talks about communication and the subtle communication processes that lead to or cause effective work relations and high productivity. Downs (1988) says that communication audits can "yield information that explains or predicts critical organizational events such as dissatisfaction, lapses in productivity, union activity, turnover, and lack of teamwork" (p. 7). Both Schein and Downs tend to talk about organizational communication as the cause of effective and ineffective organizational functioning.

In reality, the organizational communication variables discussed earlier (message distortion, communication climate, information flow, communication technology, power messages, team and interpersonal processes, leadership, and conflict) may be both the cause of differences in organizational functioning and the effect. Communication may be at the root of an organizational dysfunction or it may be only a symptom of a more basic cause. Thus, the analyst of organizational communication must be constantly alert to the changing role of communication as both a symptom and a cause of effective and ineffective organizational functioning.

Let us speculate about this issue for a few moments and assume that something about communication is the *cause* of organizational dysfunctioning. What, then, would be the symptoms or effects? One might answer such a question in this way: If employees get distorted information (cause), they will be less efficient in their work (effect). What are some clues that employees are not doing their work as efficiently as they could? They may miss deadlines or do things at the wrong times.

Another answer might be this: If the communication climate is undesirable (cause), employees will be fearful and defensive in their relations with other organization members (effect). What are some clues that employees feel fearful and defensive? They may limit their contacts with other organization members to only formal requirements or they may be quick to defend mistakes rather than to accept mistakes and to learn from them.

If you think that the way people talk and react represents some effects of organizational dysfunctioning, what might be the causes? If communicative responses seem reserved and tentative, they may be a symptom of resistance to change. If communication is terse and emotional, it may be a symptom of lack of empowerment. Thus, we can see that communication can be both the cause and the symptom of organizational dysfunctioning.

Instruments for analyzing various aspects of organizational communication have been included in earlier chapters. Figure 15.1 summarizes six key communication variables and lists procedures and instruments that are appropriate diagnostic tools.

Procedures for conducting an organizational communication analysis have been described by a number of different analysts (Goldhaber & Krivonos, 1977; Goldhaber & Rogers, 1979; Downs, 1988; and Mills, Pace & Peterson, 1988). However, Pace and Peterson have outlined fourteen specific steps for completing an analysis of organization communication. Figure 15.2 summarizes these steps, which range from visiting the organization to determining, whether an analysis could be done in a way that is helpful to the organization, to

---

FIGURE 15.1 Designing a Functional Organizational Systems Analysis

Step 1: Portray and describe the authority structure, duties, and responsibilities of *communication units—people in positions.*
  a. Locate or create an organization chart, position descriptions, and operating procedures with accompanying manuals, directives, and instructions.
  b. Complete an equipment and documents inventory.
  c. Complete a linear responsibility chart for the unit under analysis.

Step 2: Describe the flow of information and the technology to facilitate it.
  a. Make a diagram of the location of the communication equipment and technology.
  b. Create a flow chart of paper production.
  c. Complete a log of mail procedures and processing.
  d. Complete a personal contact record form for selected personnel.
  e. Conduct a network analysis.

Step 3: Measure message fidelity and distortion in information flow.
  a. Conduct a modified ECCO analysis focusing on the fidelity of messages using tests, unit analysis, or theme analysis.
  b. Look at communication load scores and locate sources of overload and underload in the system.

Step 4: Measure information adequacy as related to downward communication.
  a. Identify areas of key information and prepare and information adequacy test and administer to employees.
  b. Prepare and administer a Bateman-type information adequacy inventory.

Step 5: Measure communication satisfaction.
  a. Administer Downs and Hazen's Communication Satisfaction Questionnaire.
  b. Interview employees about their satisfaction with communication.

Step 6: Measure communication climate.
  a. Administer the Peterson-Pace Communication Climate Inventory.
  b. Administer Siegel and Turney's Survey of Organizational Climate.
  c. Complete a communication rules analysis.
  d. Gather and analyze critical communication incidents.
  e. Interview employees about the communication climate in the organization.

FIGURE 15.2 Pace-Peterson Organizational Communication Analytical Process

Step 1: *Feasibility Visit:* Analysts make organization on-site feasibility visit to determine whether doing the analysis is possible.

Step 2: *Initial Meeting:* Analysts meet with all unit personnel to preview philosophy, assumptions, expectations, and procedures associated with the analysis.

Step 3: *Administer Profile:* Administer the *Organizational Communication Profile* (Peterson-Pace) instrument to all personnel in the unit being studied to secure data on key features and variables.

Step 4: *In-depth Data on Variables:* Exploration of key features and variables of OCP using interviews, observations, and other procedures and instruments.

Step 5: *Complementary Units Data:* Gather data from complementary units, the public or community, and related groups concerning perceptions of organizational effectiveness and communication practices of organization members. Structured interviews and simple measuring instruments are used where appropriate.

Step 6: *Comparison of Data:* Compare organization profile data (step 3), in-depth data (step 4), and complementary units data (step 5) to locate points of similarity and difference.

Step 7: *Data Sharing Meeting:* Meeting with all unit personnel and select invited guests to review preliminary data on item-by-item basis to identify, examine, elaborate, and delete problem areas.

Step 8: *Interim Report:* Analysts write preliminary report and distribute it to all unit personnel and, if desired, to invited participants.

Step 9: *Form Task Groups:* Create and organize task groups consisting of unit personnel and, if desired, invited participants, for purpose of evaluating preliminary report.

Step 10: *Task Group Evaluations:* Task groups meet and review preliminary report in terms of personal meaning for them. Groups identify and enumerate problems and provide tentative alternative ways for taking corrective action. Task groups prepare their own reports.

Step 11: *General Meeting:* All task groups meet together to share their reports with one another. Select task members, usually elected by groups, assigned to merge group reports and prepare a single, unified document.

Step 12: *Analysts' Final Report:* Using their own preliminary report, the final report of task groups, and other data, analysts prepare final report and list of specific recommendations.

Step 13: *Final Report Meeting:* All unit personnel, invited guests, and analysts meet for purposes of having unit administrators and managers respond to report of task groups and analysts, and to discuss how to proceed after report.

Step 14: *Turnover Meeting:* Analysts meet with administrative staff to review procedures for organization members to assume full responsibility for continuing analysis and implementation of recommendations on long-range basis.

administering the instruments, gathering complementary data through interviews, to analyzing the data, conducting data-sharing meetings, and preparing the final report.

The procedures listed in Figure 15.2 include the use of a comprehensive instrument called the Organizational Communication Profile (see Appendix). The OCP is a written questionnaire that is relatively easy to administer and interpret and provides information about the functioning of the organization's overall communication system.

The OCP secures information on eight communication variables. Figure 15.3 portrays the variables and their relationships to one another. Definitions of the eight variables diagnosed by the OCP and how to score each part of the profile are presented in the next section.

The OCP provides a way for organization members to report how satisfied they are with the organization, what kind of communication climate exists in the organization, how information is shared in the organization, and features of the culture of the organization.

Definitions

The variables measured by the OCP are defined as follows:

1. *Organizational Satisfaction:* Perceptions of the extent to which organization members are satisfied with their work, supervision, pay and benefits, promotions, and co-workers.

   Scoring instructions: To arrive at individual scores, sum the items indicated and divide by four. To calculate a score for the entire organization, sum all of the individual

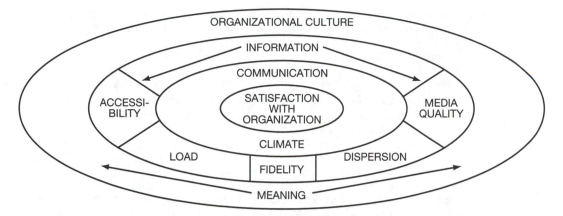

FIGURE 15.3 Model of OCP Variables

scores and divide by the total number of respondents. (See the Appendix, where the OCP is reproduced in its entirety.)

Work Satisfaction Score: Sum items 19, 20, 25, and 32.

Supervision Satisfaction Score: Sum items 1, 9, 14, and 22.

Pay and Benefits Satisfaction Score: Sum items 3, 7, 16, and 17.

Promotions Satisfaction Score: Sum items 8, 13, 23, and 26.

Co-workers Satisfaction Score: Sum items 5, 11, 28, and 30.

2. *Communication Climate:* Perceptions of the extent to which organization members feel that the organization trusts, supports, is open to, attends to, and actively consults them, and has a concern for high performance standards.

   Scoring instructions: To arrive at individual scores, sum the items indicated and divide by two. To calculate a score for the entire organization, sum all of the individual scores and divide by the total number of respondents.

   Trust Score: Sum items 4 and 10.

   Participative Decision Making Score: Sum items 6 and 21.

   Supportiveness Score: Sum items 18 and 24.

   Openness in Downward Communication Score: Sum items 15 and 27.

   Listening in Upward Communication Score: Sum items 12 and 31.

   Concern for High Performance Goals Score: Sum items 2 and 29.

3. *Media Quality:* Perceptions of organization members of the extent to which publications, written directives, reports, and other media are viewed as appealing, appropriate, efficient, and reliable.

   Scoring instructions: To arrive at individual scores, sum the items indicated and divide by three. To calculate a score for the entire organization, sum all of the individual scores and divide by the total number of respondents.

   Media Quality Score: Sum items 33, 34, and 35.

4. *Information Accessibility:* Perceptions of organization members of the extent to which information is available to them from a variety of sources in the organization.

   Scoring instructions: To arrive at individual scores, sum the items indicated and divide by eight. To calculate a score for the entire organization, sum all of the individual scores and divide by the total number of respondents.

   Information Accessibility Score: Sum items 36, 37, 38, 39, 40, 41, 42, and 43.

5. *Information Dispersion:* Perceptions of organization members of the extent to which a message is dispersed throughout the organization, or who knows something about a specific message.

   Scoring instructions: There are no individual scores for this variable. To calculate the score for the entire organization, look at item 52 in the OCP, determine who knew about the information and who did not, and calculate the percentage for each group.

   Information Dispersion Score: The percentage of respondents who marked item 52.

6. *Information Load:* Perceptions of organization members of the extent to which they feel they receive more or less information than they can cope with or need to function effectively.

   Scoring instructions: To arrive at individual scores, sum the items indicated and divide by eight. Then subtract this score from the Information Accessibility score. This will give an Information Load score for the individual. A minus (-) score indicates under-load and a plus (+) score indicates overload. To calculate a score for the entire organization, sum all of the individual scores and divide by the total number of respondents.

   Information Load Score: Sum items 44, 45, 46, 47, 48, 49, 50, and 51, and divide by eight. Subtract this score from the Information Accessibility score.

7. *Message Fidelity:* Perceptions of organization members of how many bits of information they know about a particular message in contrast to the actual number of bits of information in the message.

   Scoring instructions: The number circled for item 53 is the individual score for this variable. To calculate the score for the entire organization, sum all scores on item 53 and divide by the total number of respondents.

   Message Fidelity Score: Record the number circled for item 53. This number represents the percentage of the bits of information that respondents knew.

8. *Organization Culture:* The perceptions of organization members of the key values and shared concepts that constitute the image they have of the organization.

   Scoring instructions: Use the list of words collected during the timed test at the beginning of the OCP. Assign a number to each word according to the following weightings for the first ten words: 6, 5, 4, 3, 3, 3, 2, 2, 1, 1. Assign a 1 to all other words. The words and scores are then grouped into categories on the basis of similarity of meaning or referent.

   Organization Culture Score: See Figure 15.4 for the calculation of a sample, hypothetical organization culture score.

How to Interpret Data from the OCP

Data from the OCP is descriptive; that is, the data reveal areas and issues that may bear looking into, but the data do not indicate whether an authentic problem exists or what to do about a problem if it does exist. Because the data are descriptive, it is essential to make some sense out of the data and point toward the issues that may be of greatest concern.

To illustrate how the OCP is used, we shall discuss some data derived from a recent administration of the instrument and review some possible interpretations of what the data may mean. Nevertheless, the decision as to whether an actual problem exists still resides with organization members.

From a statistical point of view, any difference between scores of a + 20 or − .20 is considered significant. For example, the difference between a composite climate score of 3.39 (hourly employees) and 2.94 (salaried employees) is .45 and represents a statistically significant difference in perceived climate between the two groups of employees. On the surface, the difference may not seem very great, but the difference in actual organization climates experienced by the two groups is likely to be quite different.

The data from the OCP will be reviewed in the order in which the definitions were presented.

FIGURE 15.4 Calculation of Organization Culture Score

In the box below, write the name of your organization. As you are timed for one minute, write all the words that come to your mind when you think of your organization. *Use only one word for each line.*

Pipsqueak Market

WEIGHT	WORDS LISTED
6	1. Encouraging
5	2. Quality
4	3. Clean
3	4. Understanding
3	5. Good
3	6. Safe
3	7. Communicating
2	8. Service
1	9. Neat
1	10. Listening
1	11. Best
1	12. Secure
1	13. Helping
1	14. Growth
1	15. Caring

Thank you! You have completed this portion of this instrument. *Do not turn the page until given further instructions.*

The following word categories were selected from this sample data sheet.

RELATIONSHIPS		WORTH		ENVIRONMENT	
6	encouraging	5	quality	4	clean
3	understanding	3	good	3	safe
3	communicating	2	service	2	neat
1	listening	1	best	1	secure
1	helping	1	growth		
1	caring				

To calculate the percentage of importance of each category, use the weights as follows:

Relationships:	sum the weights of each word	15
Worth:	sum the weights of each word	12
Environment:	sum the weights of each word	10
	Total the sums of all weights	37

Use the total to calculate the percentage of weights in each category.

Relationships:	15/37 = 41%
Worth:	12/37 = 32%
Environment:	10/37 = 27%

Organizational Satisfaction

The concept that appears at the core of one's workday is satisfaction with the organization; without an acceptable level of organizational satisfaction, employees tend to leave or at least to withdraw from the organization. The level of organizational satisfaction that characterizes employees in effective organizations is about 4.00. Higher levels of satisfaction encourage employees to prefer satisfaction to performance. In fact, some theorists indicate that motivation is negatively related to satisfaction; that is, motivation occurs when an employee is dissatisfied. Our data indicate that low levels of satisfaction (scores below 2.8) may be disruptive to the organization. Thus, scores that move toward 3.0 are generally considered less desirable.

The satisfaction scores summarized in Table 15.1 indicate that the composite score across all employees responding is 3.31. It falls toward the lower range of acceptable scores and is significantly below the preferred score of 4.0 and well below the composite score of 4.08 of a comparable type of organization. Composite scores of groups of employees indicate that there is a comparable level of satisfaction (3.25 to 3.36) among the groups.

In contrast, scores for satisfaction with "supervision" (3.69 for salaried employees to 4.28 for hourly employees) and "co-workers" (3.73 for in-town employees to 4.56 for out-of-town employees) are closer to the preferred levels. Clearly, scores on "pay and benefits" (2.47 for hourly employees to 3.08 for salaried employees) are quite low, as are scores on "promotion" (2.39 to 2.69 for salaried and hourly employees, respectively). Composite scores of 2.58 (promotion) and 2.76 (pay and benefits) for all employees indicate quite low levels of satisfaction. Nevertheless, scores on pay and benefits and promotion are customarily lower than other satisfaction scores. In a comparable organization, the pay and benefits satisfaction score was 3.75 and promotions 3.67.

Some of the responses to item 60 in the OCP, "how you really feel about your organization," tend to support these empirical data:

"while the equipment to put out more work has increased, the benefits for workers have not increased at all"

"working conditions are good here, but improvements are needed in employee benefits and salaries"

"it is frustrating to not be compensated adequately"

"it is difficult to not be able to pay bills after putting in 60–70 hrs/wk"

In addition, another open response tends to support the composite scores on work satisfaction (3.25 for all employees; 3.13 to 3.56 for in-town and out-of-town employees, respectively):

"it has a long way to go in being a great place to work"

TABLE 15.1 Organizational Satisfaction Scores

	ALL EMPLOYEES	HOURLY EMPLOYEES	SALARIED EMPLOYEES	IN TOWN	OUT OF TOWN
Composite score	3.31	3.33	3.25	3.27	3.36
Work	3.25	3.14	3.31	3.13	3.56
Supervision	4.00	4.28	3.69	4.02	3.88
Pay and benefits	2.76	2.47	3.08	2.89	2.38
Promotion	2.58	2.69	2.39	2.57	2.44
Co-workers	3.93	4.06	3.78	3.73	4.56

Communication Climate

The communication concept that most closely parallels the idea of motivation in organizations is that of "climate." High levels of trust, support, openness, attentive listening, participative decision making, and concern for high standards create the basis for a motivated work force. We would expect to find employees who have low communication climate scores to be disenchanted, lethargic, unmotivated, and discouraged. Our data tend to support this general line of analysis. The preferred communication climate scores are slightly lower than those for satisfaction scores, but climate scores should be about 3.80. It appears that organizational life tends to affect perceptions of climate more negatively than do perceptions of satisfaction. Thus, we often find higher levels of satisfaction and lower levels of motivation. Low climate scores tend to be at 2.80 and below.

Communication climate scores for the demonstration organization are summarized in Table 15.2. The composite score for all employees responding is 3.21, which falls toward the lower range of preferred climate scores. The composite communication climate score for a comparable organization is 3.83. Nevertheless, the overall composite score of 3.21 is above the 2.80 level considered undesirable.

The composite scores of groups of employees indicate that salaried employees scored the lowest (2.94) whereas hourly employees scored the highest (3.39). A difference on "trust" scores appears to exist between groups of employees, with those out of town scoring highest (4.25) and salaried employees scoring lowest (3.11). This range no doubt points to a problem, just in terms of the difference in scores. High-trust employees tend to respond differently to information from the organization and, potentially, to other employees. Employees out of town also have the lowest scores (2.63) on supportiveness, but salaried employees and those out of town have the lowest scores on participative decision making (2.89 and 2.88, respectively). However, hourly employees feel that the organization has less concern for high performance goals (2.89).

Some of the responses to item 60 on the OCP, "how you really feel about your organization," tend to support the pattern of these scores:

"I don't always feel my efforts and abilities are recognized"

"my future is not guaranteed"

"we are not being creative and forward-thinking enough"

"there is an air of everything being second-rate"

"the organization seems timid, reluctant, slow to make the working place one that will attract and retain qualified, enthusiastic employees"

TABLE 15.2 Communication Climate Scores

	ALL EMPLOYEES	HOURLY EMPLOYEES	SALARIED EMPLOYEES	IN TOWN	OUT OF TOWN
Composite score	3.21	3.39	2.94	3.14	3.25
Trust	3.42	3.67	3.11	3.14	4.25
Participative decision making	3.21	3.44	2.89	3.25	2.88
Support	3.03	3.11	2.94	3.14	2.63
Open down	3.18	3.44	2.78	3.07	3.25
Listen up	3.32	3.78	2.72	3.25	3.25
High goals	3.08	2.89	3.17	2.96	3.25

TABLE 15.3 Media Quality Scores

	ALL EMPLOYEES	HOURLY EMPLOYEES	SALARIED EMPLOYEES	IN TOWN	OUT OF TOWN
Composite score	3.21	3.22	3.11	3.26	2.83

Salaried employees reported that they do not feel a climate of openness in downward communication and attentive listening in upward communication exists in the organization. Salaried employees appear to score considerably lower than other employees on openness and upward communication. This seems like a management contradiction, since salaried employees are usually more closely associated with decision-making and information systems.

Media Quality

As a rule, media quality relates to the pride employees have in the company. If the publications, reports, and other media of the company are appealing, appropriate, and reliable, employees tend to express pride in the quality of outputs of the company. Nevertheless, the cost of maintaining a steady output of high quality media products may be excessive, leading most employees to feel that some of the publications, reports, and memos do not meet their expectations. Thus, we anticipate preferred scores to be high, but in fact they are often low. This means that acceptable media quality scores begin at about 3.50. Low media quality scores range below 2.50.

Table 15.3 indicates that all of the media quality perceptions are below expected levels of excellence. However, none of the scores falls below the low quality score (2.83 is the lowest score). Nevertheless, the media products distributed by the organization ought to be reviewed for ways to increase their quality.

Information Accessibility

One of the open-ended responses to item 60, "how you really feel about your organization," provides the focus for this interpretation: "The communication line needs *vast* improvement." Information accessibility has to do with perceptions of organization members concerning the extent to which information is available from a variety of sources in the organization.

The information accessibility score is derived by getting the average of eight items that ask about the amount of information received from various sources. Because of the difficulty in keeping employees informed about issues on which they would like to have information, scores usually run lower than scores discussed above. Preferred scores are 3.50 or higher. Undesirable scores are 2.80 and lower (see Table 15.4).

Scores on information accessibility support the widespread assumption that employees feel that they are not always well informed. None of the composite scores across groups and for all employees reach the preferred level. In fact, the highest score (salaried employees: 3.23) is statistically well below the preferred level. Hourly employees and those outside of

TABLE 15.4 Information Accessibility Scores

	ALL EMPLOYEES	HOURLY EMPLOYEES	SALARIED EMPLOYEES	IN TOWN	OUT OF TOWN
Composite score	3.12	2.90	3.23	3.10	2.94

TABLE 15.5 Information Dispersion Scores

	ALL EMPLOYEES	HOURLY EMPLOYEES	SALARIED EMPLOYEES	IN TOWN	OUT OF TOWN
Percentage who knew about the message	89.4	77.8	100.00	92.8	75.0

town report receiving the least amount of information. This is an issue that needs to be studied in more depth, and one that definitely warrants serious consideration.

Information Dispersion

Information dispersion has to do with the extent to which organization members report knowing about a specific message. Organization members are presented with a brief mention of a message; in this analysis, the message concerned "new membership renewal procedures." Employees were asked to indicate whether they knew something about this message prior to completing the OCP.

Table 15.5 indicates that almost 90 percent of all employees reported knowing something about the message. This may appear to fly in the face of data about information accessibility and information load scores. However, knowing about one particular message may not represent the full range of information that employees would like to have. After-the-fact information about decisions or announcements of new policies and practices may actually highlight the problem. Employees may feel that they want more information before decisions are made, and that information prior to decisions is what is not accessible.

Information Load

The information-load score is calculated by subtracting the information accessibility score from an information-wanted score. Information load indicates the perceptions of organization members with regard to the extent to which they feel they receive more or less information than they can cope with or need to function effectively. Employees vary in terms of the amount of information they want to have. Thus, different groups of employees may score quite differently.

Plus scores indicate that employees are receiving more information than they want to have; *minus* scores indicate that employees feel that they should have more information. Generally, employees report that they would like more information than they are getting. Both employees and organizations prefer information-load scores that are near .00, since that indicates a balance between information wanted and information received.

Results from the OCP on information load are reported in Table 15.6. All figures are minus, indicating an underload of information. Using the general statistical pattern, any difference of .20 from zero is significant. Even for some allowances for unusual circumstances, the scores clearly show a need for more information, especially for employees out of town and for salaried employees.

TABLE 15.6 Information Load Scores

	ALL EMPLOYEES	HOURLY EMPLOYEES	SALARIED EMPLOYEES	IN TOWN	OUT OF TOWN
Composite score	−.65	−.58	−.73	−.53	−1.09

TABLE 15.7 Message Fidelity Scores

	ALL EMPLOYEES	HOURLY EMPLOYEES	SALARIED EMPLOYEES	IN TOWN	OUT OF TOWN
No. of items recognized	5–6	5–6	5–6	7–8	0–2

Message Fidelity

Fidelity in communication concerns the accuracy of messages. The OCP measures message fidelity by having organization members study the points included in an actual message distributed to them earlier and then indicate the number of items they knew prior to completing the OCP. We generally expect individuals, even when confronted with the details of a message that is routinely distributed to employees, to recognize a larger number of items than to recall and report the details of a message. Hence, we normally expect employees to report recognizing seven or more items from the message. Employees who recognize four or fewer items have low fidelity in receiving information.

Table 15.7 indicates that employees out of town appear to have the lowest fidelity (0–2 items recognized) or accuracy (completeness) in the receipt of information from the organization. Employees in town report knowing the largest number of items within the range of high fidelity. These results seem consistent with generally accepted assumptions; that is, employees who are farther away from the source of messages are likely to have lowest levels of fidelity, and employees closest to the source tend to recognize the largest number of items or have the highest levels of fidelity.

These data suggest that the organization should consider ways of enhancing communication channels and information-distribution systems.

Sources of Information

Employees reported the source from which they received the message used to measure fidelity. No particular source is expected to be used, but the organization should check the actual source of the message against the source reported by employees. If employees are getting messages from sources not anticipated by the initiator of messages, some questions may be raised concerning the information network.

Table 15.8 indicates that employees predominantly identified a meeting as the source of the message included in this analysis; however, employees out of town exclusively identified the telephone as the source. Many employees identified various sources for the message. Some employees may have heard about the message from various sources, which may account for the variety of sources mentioned.

TABLE 15.8 Frequency of Sources of Messages

SUBJECTS	HOURLY EMPLOYEES	SALARIED EMPLOYEES	IN TOWN	OUT OF TOWN
Memo	3	2	5	0
Supervisor	5	2	7	
Telephone	1	3	1	3
Meeting*	6	7	13	0

*18 Subjects; totals may exceed numbers of respondees owing to multiple sources indicated.

Organization Culture

The *Organizational Communication Profile* derives information about the culture of an organization through an "associative group analysis" (AGA) method. The AGA attempts to discover the shared constructs comprising an organization's culture by means of word associations. The words generated by organization members reveal the subjective meanings they have for the focus concept. When the words are grouped and classified, the categories represent the shared constructs of organization members, which we refer to as the "culture" of the organization.

What does the cultural analysis of the OCP reveal about the organization? First, a word of caution: Because of a relatively small number of subjects involved in the analysis (responses from eighteen individuals), we must consider the description somewhat tentative; nevertheless, if the words were generated as authentic open responses to the organization, then we may clearly anticipate that the categories tend to represent the general culture of the organization. Second, the creation of categories follows from the thought processes and intuitive assumptions of the professionals engaged in the analysis. Thus, this analysis may be considered tentative, depending on the perceived accuracy of categories. The categories portrayed in Figure 15.5 represent a conscientious effort to represent the results as accurately as possible.

This analysis resulted in eight categories describing organization culture: (1) positive climate, (2) negative effects, (3) excellence qualities, (4) growth potential, (5) organizational elements, (6) educational activities, (7) small and immature organization, and (8) active/upbeat.

Positive Climate

As portrayed in Figure 15.5, the most dominant construct is that the organization operates in a positive climate (18.6 percent of the total words generated fell into this category). The construct of "positive climate" is defined by the terms listed (e.g., *well-intentioned, friendly, casual, good-spirited, concern, caring*). Employees appear to feel that they are working in an organization where there is unity, sharing, and a relaxed atmosphere. This is no doubt a strong cultural influence on employee perceptions.

FIGURE 15.5 Concepts in the Culture of the Organization

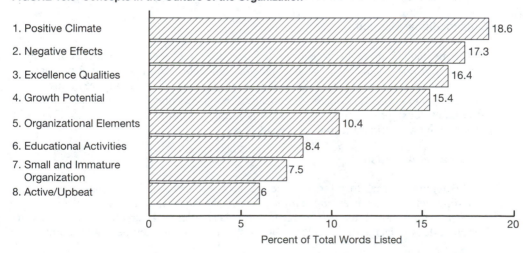

Negative Effects

The second most dominant construct (17.3 percent), on the other hand, appears to reflect areas of concern to employees; we have called it "negative effects." This construct is defined in terms of words such as *confusing, frustrating, disorganized, incoherent, combative,* and *dysfunctional.* Clearly, the size of this category argues that a negative dimension appears to be permeating the culture of the organization and should be examined. Employees appear to feel that they are working in an organization that is chaotic, stressful, messy, and misguided, at least at critical times.

Excellence Qualities

In contrast, employees also tend to regard the culture as one that promotes "excellence"; 16.4 percent of the terms referred to qualities of excellence in organizations, such as *service, professional, skilled, dependable,* and *respected.* This category represents a dimension of culture that should probably be cultivated and reinforced. Adopting a philosophy and practices that reinforce total quality performance could be accomplished in a culture in which excellence is regarded as highly as it is in this organization.

Growth Potential

A big plus in the culture of the organization is this dimension of its culture—growth potential. Although fourth in strength, growth potential appears to be one of the four strongest features of the organization's culture (15.4 percent of the terms). Growth potential is revealed by such terms as *growing, developing, opportunity, progressive, potential,* and *changing* (see Figure 15.5, category 4). This suggests that employees expect the organization to continue to grow and to provide them opportunities to participate in the growth. It would seem important that everything possible needs to be done to help employees meet those expectations.

The remaining four categories seem to exercise less influence (6 to 10 percent of the terms in each category) on the overall culture of the organization than do the prior four categories; nevertheless, they reveal some specific constructs that probably influence some decisions in the organization or, at least, indicate some characteristics of the organization.

Organizational Elements

The terms that comprise this category (10.4 percent) tend to refer to elements or benefits derived from the organization, such as *members, benefits,* and *insurance.* This category seems to reflect a concern with the organization itself and how employees conceive of the main goals and features of the organization. It appears that the culture has a small but prominent "customer" focus, although this emphasis could be strengthened so as to become a more dominant feature of the culture.

Educational Activities

This category appears to refer to some primary services provided by the association, including activities such as *conventions, meetings, exhibits, education,* and *knowledge and learning.* Although the percentage of terms is smaller (8.4 percent) than earlier categories, it does reflect a strong cultural bias toward service to members, and it appears to reinforce a common goal of organizations that serve their own membership. It would probably be a mistake to discontinue these activities since they comprise a significant feature of the culture of this organization.

Small and Immature Organization

This category may be a reflection of an earlier category (negative effects), but it appears to focus on an important (7.5 percent of the words) although somewhat narrower characteristic of the organization; the words combine to create a picture of a young, small, fledgling, but naive and inexperienced organization. The implications of this element of the culture are not entirely clear, but the category does suggest some tolerance of the negative effects that may be attributed to the youth and size of the organization.

Active/Upbeat

The final category comprises the smallest weighted percentage of words (6.0 percent), but reveals another important element of the culture: an active/upbeat place to work. The terms used to reveal this feature were *unique, cool place, fun, interesting, enthusiasm,* and *busy*. Taken in the context of a caring, positive, and relaxed climate, this element of the culture may need to be reviewed to determine whether it conflicts with other elements; if it does not, then some steps should be taken to strengthen the active/upbeat aspect of the culture. Most employees are motivated by a "fun" culture, provided it does not detract from the main goals of the organization.

Conclusions and Recommendations

1. Employees appear to be most dissatisfied with pay, benefits, and promotions. However, they feel satisfied with co-workers and supervisors.
2. Employees in different locations and with different classifications appear to view the climate of the organization differently. Hourly employees and employees in town report low concern for high performance goals, but salaried employees and employees outside of town report low participative decision making.
3. Employees appear to feel that the media distributed by the organization could be of higher quality.
4. Although most employees feel that information could be more accessible, hourly employees and those out of town show the greatest concerns.
5. Despite a concern about accessibility of information, when employees do get messages, most employees appear to process them fairly completely, but employees out of town report knowing the least and having the lowest fidelity (completeness) scores. Employees out of town also have the highest *under*load of information scores, although all employees report wanting more information than they get.
6. Data from the cultural part of the OCP indicate that the culture of the organization consists of eight elements, most of which combine to reveal an organization with a positive climate, dedicated to excellence, with growth potential, and active/upbeat practices; on the other hand, employees recognize a dimension of the culture that is confusing, incoherent, and dysfunctional, and may be attributed to the size and lack of maturity of the organization. Employees appear to consider the organization to be customer focused and to provide primarily educational activities. Although these categories are based on responses from a somewhat small number of employees, they do reflect actual responses of the employees and should be taken seriously.

We have attempted to illustrate how the Organizational Communication Profile (OCP) can be used to gather data for an analysis of organizational communication. The actual OCP instrument is included in the Appendix at the end of this text.

STRATEGIES AND INTERVENTIONS FOR IMPROVING SYSTEMS EFFECTIVENESS

Changing individuals who work in organizations by means of processes that enhance their knowledge base, modify their attitudes, and strengthen their skills is an important way to improve both individual and organizational or system effectiveness. However, organization effectiveness can also be increased by making changes in aspects of organizational communication and work systems.

Systems effectiveness can be improved through processes that involve affecting macro, global, or organizationwide phenomena. Communication climate is an example of a macro, global concept that is often the focus of organization change efforts. In fact, the communication variables of information patterns and flow, leadership practices and styles, decision making and problem solving, conflict resolution, superior-subordinate relations, and communication technology, as well as work flow, rewards, strategic planning, and financial management, are all variables and issues that comprise macro, organizationwide processes.

Macro organization change efforts involve strategies and interventions designed to affect communication processes directly, and the strategies and interventions to bring about macroorganization change efforts are based on and are implemented through communication activities and practices. The heart of both organizational processes and organization change interventions is communication. Organizational communication is both the method of change and the object of change. Making an organization more effective involves changing communication processes and practices, but changing an organization involves using communication processes and practices.

Models and Methods of Systems Change

Change in organization systems can occur in one or more of three subsystems: the social, the technical, and the administrative (Kur, 1981), and among different levels: the individual, the structural, and the cultural (Goodstein & Burke, 1991). It is on these subsystems and levels of phenomena that the organization change agent must focus in order to bring about change in the overall system.

Systems change programs are usually coordinated by a change agent (Pace, Smith & Mills, 1991, pp. 129–136), but practical considerations dictate that organization members work collaboratively or together as a team with the change agent. A basic assumption underlying most systems change interventions is that organization members must take control of the problems and "own" the solutions, or at least feel that the procedures to be used are ones that they have selected. The change agent is involved in the process not to provide answers to problems, but to show organization members alternative ways to work on the problems.

Even though systems change efforts are directed toward subsystems and process levels, of which communication is the most prominent, organization systems, and especially bureaucratic or formal organizations, run so counter to the assumptions on which change efforts are based that it may not be possible to make any far-reaching

| Present Conditions Creating Problems | Possibility of Improving Conditions | Practical Steps for Making Changes |

COSTS OF MAKING CHANGES

FIGURE 15.6 Elements of the Change Process

changes in organization systems. For example, Schein and Greiner (1977) argued that interventions work best in an "organic" or open systems rather than in a functional system, which are characterized by open communication, interdependence among groups, considerable trust, joint problem solving, and risk taking. Bureaucracies tend, on the other hand, *not* to be very open, making change interventions somewhat difficult to use. In addition, bureaucracies are *not* particularly amenable to change in order to become open systems. Thus, to bring about more open communication, more trust, more risk taking, and more joint problem solving, which are some of the primary goals of organization change interventions, one needs to have an organization that already embodies those goals.

This dilemma—or better, this paradox—may be resolved by using interventions that improve or refine the operations of bureaucratic organizations, rather than attempt to bring about significant overall systems change. Working within the confines of the social, technical, and administrative subsystems, change interventions should look to reduce interdepartmental conflicts, increase coordination, improve communication across functions, reduce frustration and boredom, accentuate innovation, and enhance vitality.

Burke (1980) has also conceded that what is practiced as organization change does not usually make systemwide changes anyway, but results in a form of "tinkering" with the system. In fact, most interventions fail to bring about any fundamental change in the way in which things are done in organizations. They are, nevertheless, clearly helping organization members to adapt to and cope more effectively with environmental and internal work conditions. In fact, change interventions fine-tune and stabilize organizations so that they can become more effective.

Let us now look at the elements involved in the change process, the concept of interventions, and some procedures that are often used to increase the effectiveness of subsystems and organization processes.

Organization Change Elements

Models of change have some similarities (Schein, 1964; Beckhard & Harris, 1987; Goodstein & Burke, 1991) that suggest a three-stage process running from unfreezing to moving to refreezing, or beginning with the present state, moving to a transitional state, and arriving at a future state. An in-depth look at what happens during each of these stages suggests four elements involved in organization systems change (Figure 15.6).

CONDITIONS, POSSIBILITIES, STEPS, AND COSTS

To bring about change in an organization, interventions must take into account the *present conditions that are creating problems, the extent to which it may be possible to improve the conditions, practical steps that allow the changes to be made,* and *costs involved in making changes.*

The Process of Change

The first step in the process of creating change in organization systems involves identifying the present conditions in the organization—among the processes, functions, relationships, and structures—that are creating problems; a problem exists when something within the organization is keeping it from achieving a goal. The second step involves analyzing the factors that are creating the problems to determine to what extent it seems possible to change or alter the present conditions so as to alleviate the problems. The third step involves identifying and establishing a series of practical steps through which organization members may proceed to make the changes to alter the present conditions to alleviate the problems. The fourth step is to account for the costs involved in making changes.

The practical steps in the change process are what we usually call *interventions*. To be effective, each intervention must involve a series of action steps that have an effect on some process, relationship, function, or structure. What are some specific organizational processes that might be influenced in such a way as to result in more effective organizational functioning?

Processes, by definition, consist of actions that occur in a special order; thus, interventions appear, themselves, to be processes. Nevertheless, the three basic categories of processes—social, technical, and administrative—each include several sets of subprocesses. Let us explore the processes associated with each of the basic categories.

Social Processes   Social processes are those involving the way in which organization members relate and interact with one another. Social processes include such actions as one person interacting with another; interaction between groups; procedures used to distribute information, to make decisions, to plan actions, and to set goals, guidelines, and policies that provide direction to organization members; the norms, values, and ground rules that help members maintain relationships with one another; the attitudes of people toward their work, the organization, and authority systems; and the way in which effort is devoted to work. It is *communication* that comprises the heart of the social processes of an organization.

Technical Processes   Technical processes are those involving the creation of the output of the organization, including such subprocesses as the work itself, the work flow, the methods of work, the type of production—assembly line, process, batch, or unit—the physical work setting, the complexity of the work process, acquisition and distribution of raw materials, and the time demands and constraints involved in creating outputs. *Communication* affects the technical processes by making the work easier or difficult.

Administrative Processes   Administrative processes are those involving the support dimensions of the technical and social processes, including personnel systems, union and labor relations, wages, salaries, and benefits, budgeting and financial systems, reporting and data processing, legal activities, and purchasing and accounting. *Communication* allows the administrative processes to function to provide useful assistance to the other processes.

Present Conditions that Create Problems in Organizations

The concept of conditions creating problems is critical in understanding organization system interventions. The intervention into social, technical, or administrative processes depends on how well the *analytical* activities discussed in the preceding section have revealed problems in the organization. As we have explained in other places, problems are perceived differences between what we have and what we would like to have. Thus, at this point, we shall assume that the need to intervene in a process is a function of someone having recognized a problem.

Beckhard (1969) has identified ten organizational conditions that call for some type of intervention. The need to change the climate of the organization is one of the conditions. As you may recall, a negative communication climate was characterized by a lack of trust and lack of risk taking; a lack of supportiveness and responsibility; a lack of open and accurate downward communication; a lack of attentive and considerate responses to the upward flow of information; a lack of consultativeness and influence in decision making; and a lack of concern for high performance goals and challenging work. If key organization members recognize, verify, and certify that the negative communication climate was such that it created a problem in the organization, we assume that one or more interventions should be implemented to bring the climate closer to that which the key organization members would prefer, thereby closing the gap between what existed and what the organization would like to exist. That is the general line of reasoning that justifies the introduction of interventions to improve organization effectiveness.

Problems in the technical system are illustrated by differences between optimal levels of technical functioning and that which is observed. Pasmore and others (1979) have pointed out that tasks within a job should have an optimum variety. A task should have enough variety to allow an operator to take a rest from high levels of attention or effort or to stretch after a period of routine activity. By reports from organization members and through direct observation, it may be possible to recognize, verify, and certify that tasks involved in some jobs fail to have the optimal level of variety and to justify an intervention to change the variety level.

Administrative processes also function at less than desirable levels. In fact, lack of adequate rewards, inadequate information about personnel matters, and performance review processes that fail to recognize the difference between moderate and exceptional contributions of employees may be recognized, verified, and certified as the source of problems in an organization, thus leading to interventions to correct or improve administrative processes.

Data from the analytical procedures discussed above should provide verifications of the existence of problems in various processes of the organization. Beckhard (1969, pp. 16–19) lists these organization activities as conditions that call for interventions: a need to change; managerial strategy; cultural norms; structure and roles; motivation of the work force; coping with mergers; organization climate; communication system; and a need to adapt to a new environment and better planning.

Other phenomena that could be changed are the state of morale, the way work is done, reporting procedures, location of decision making, effectiveness of top teams, ways of setting goals, and relationships between levels in the organization.

It is generally accepted that organization members work hard when they

1. have a sense of ownership and are responsible for whole tasks or processes;
2. have multiple skills and can perform a variety of tasks at high levels of proficiency;
3. have a feeling of autonomy and independence in what to do, how to do it, when to do it, and where to do it;
4. work cooperatively and have strong supportive relationships in the workplace;
5. are well enough informed to recognize problems in their work and in the organization, and have the knowledge to relate their work to the larger organization;

6. are involved in making decisions and influencing what happens in the organization and to them as part of the workforce; and

7. are recognized and rewarded for their contributions to the organization and for the value that they add to goods and services.

Thus, any time that the analytical processes reveal violations of any of these general principles, the organization should consider the use of appropriate interventions to make changes in organizational processes at the social, technical, or administrative levels.

Definition of Intervention

Organization systems interventions are activities that intervene in the workday activities of organization members in such a way that they positively affect organizational processes such as communication, problem solving, planning, decision making, leadership, and organization culture, as well as structural changes that affect work flow, technology, and authority relationships. Interventions are usually directed toward or involve specific sets of organization members, such as a work group, two or more work-related groups, a distinct unit within the organization, or all the members of the organization.

We are concerned, in this chapter, with interventions that affect systems and processes of a complete unit such as an intact work group, a unit or division, or an entire organization. Three types of interventions represent the core of systems and process interventions: Survey Feedback, Process Consultation, and Sociotechnical Systems Design.

These interventions are intended to achieve several general goals: to enhance employee involvement and empowerment in the organization; to increase the effectiveness of team functioning; to heighten intergroup relations; to improve organization goal setting; and to increase the motivation, commitment, and dedication of organization members. Central to all of these goals is the improvement of the communication system and communication processes.

Survey Feedback

One of the most widely used interventions in unitwide change is that of *survey feedback*. This method was developed by the Survey Research Center at the Institute for Social Research, University of Michigan, during the early 1960s (Taylor & Bowers, 1967). It consists of collecting data about the organization, unit, or group by means of a standard questionnaire, then reporting the results back to individuals and groups at all levels in the organization. Both the individuals and groups analyze the data, interpret what it means for them, and take steps to correct the problems identified.

The survey questionnaire secures responses of organization members to macro-level or organizationwide issues, such as communication. The Organizational Communication Profile (OCP) described earlier (see the Appendix) represents a survey feedback instrument, and the processes described for using it also represent a form of intervention. Other questionnaires get responses about leadership, decision making, superior-subordinate relations, job satisfaction, and organization vitality. The *Survey of Organizations* (Taylor & Bowers, 1967) included the primary variables of leadership, organizational climate, and satisfaction.

Several advantages accrue to using a standard questionnaire based on relevant research in providing data for development purposes. First, individually tailored questionnaires lack norms, standards, or reference points for estimating the significance of organizational problems, allowing important circumstances to be overlooked. Second, individually tailored questionnaires are time-consuming to construct, and the data from them are difficult to interpret. Third, individually tailored questionnaires may contain large numbers of items that may not be relevant to the process of change.

In survey feedback, data should be collected from all members of the organization being studied, and the results should be reported back to everyone from whom data were collected. All organization members should be involved in analyzing the data as reported back so as to help identify problem areas. A process for obtaining concurrence on an organizationwide strategy for change and for the use of additional interventions must be devised. Finally, at least teams of organization members should be involved in planning action to change the organization (see Figure 15.2, steps 7 through 11 for an illustration of the feedback process).

As a rule, feedback meetings appear on the surface to be similar to team-building sessions, but they are much less likely to deal with interpersonal and human processes. Thus, survey feedback and process consultation often go hand-in-hand as ways to focus on both task and process factors in organization change.

Process Consultation

When an organization feels that the source of reduced effectiveness lies in its human and communicative processes, then an appropriate intervention is *process consultation*. Schein (1969) defined process consultation as "a set of activities on the part of the consultant which help the client [organization or unit] to perceive, understand, and act upon process events which occur in the client's environment." Human processes most critical for effective organizational operations are communication, interaction of functional roles, problem solving, influence of group norms, authority relationships, and activities associated with bringing about cooperation. These processes operate at the individual, interpersonal, and intergroup levels in organizations.

Process consultation consists of a set of activities designed to help organization members learn to solve their own problems. Organization members become aware of human processes in the organization, how they occur, what effects they have, and how to use their own problem-solving abilities and resources to modify processes to make the organization more effective.

Process consultation involves helping organization members understand the human processes in which they are involved, to diagnose the source of difficulties, and to make adjustments in those processes so as to allow the organization to increase in effectiveness. Process consultation may be carried out by organization members themselves, but most of the time attempts to change organizational processes must be guided by deliberate actions on the part of a consultant/facilitator. Process *interventions* are concerned with *how* organization members are going about accomplishing their goals. Process *interventions* do not involve the facilitator in the technical tasks of organization members.

The facilitator's focus should be on the human processes as they occur in the organization or unit. Schein (1969) identified four types of *interventions:* (1) those dealing with agenda setting, (2) those involving feedback of observations or other data, (3) coaching or counseling of individuals or groups, and (4) structural suggestions.

Agenda-setting interventions direct attention to the way in which the team or unit establishes and works through its items of business. The facilitator often suggests ways in which organization members can determine what to put on an agenda, how much time to allocate to each item, and how to prioritize the items. This is a central issue in team development, demonstrating how organization interventions may be used for various purposes. One key issue in agenda setting involves getting organization members to devote time to discussing human, interpersonal processes. The group could spend fifteen or twenty minutes at the end of a meeting talking about how they interacted and what interfered with getting their work done.

Giving feedback about behaviors observed during group meetings is another form of process intervention. Comments may be offered during meetings and as they occur or to individuals after the meeting is over. It is crucial that organization members be willing and ready to receive the feedback. As members become accustomed to talking about process issues, they tend to be more open and take more responsibility for initiating discussions.

Coaching or *counseling* has become a popular and widely used intervention because it has the ability to center right on key interpersonal issues. Suggestions for ways to exhibit more appropriate behavior and to interact with other group members can be very powerful if the person is interested and willing to devote the time and effort to understand the effect of changes and to engage in the behaviors suggested.

Suggestions for structural changes are considered to be lowest in priority for process consultation. Even though changes in the way in which work is organized might be paramount in improving organization effectiveness, process consultation focuses on human processes and allows organization members to propose their own suggestions. However, task and technical changes are high priority in sociotechnical systems change. Thus, we shall look at these interventions next.

Sociotechnical Systems Change

An intervention process that combines elements of many of the processes already discussed is called *sociotechnical systems* (STS) change, or the integrated design of both social and technical work systems to improve organization effectiveness. Sociotechnical systems change is the mechanism that leads from simple organization development to advanced organization renewal and revitalization. This intervention assumes that the organization is an open sociotechnical system involving the coordination of human processes and technical activities (Taylor & Felten, 1993).

The organization can be conceived as an open system of five dimensions in interaction with the organization's environment (Kast & Rosenzweig, 1979, p. 19; Pace, 1991). The five primary components are represented by subsystems designated as (1) the *worker* or psychological subsystem, (2) the *work itself* or technical subsystem, (3) the *organizational structure* or structural subsystem, (4) the *organizational guidelines* or the goals subsystem, and (5) the *management practices* or the managerial subsystem, all of which are encompassed by the *environment,* which consists of *society* and its national social institutions, and the culture, ideology, technology, and communication that define the way of life of groups.

Sociotechnical systems change represents a holistic approach to organization change in which a change in one subsystem affects the functioning of other subsystems. The initial focus of change may begin with any subsystem, but it is more traditional to begin the change effort by examining the work itself or the technical subsystem. Once the STS analyst has a clear picture of the technical system, its operations and interdependencies, the tasks can be arranged so they can be performed by individuals and groups in the most satisfying ways. A number of principles govern the allocation process (Pasmore and colleagues, 1979):

1. Tasks within a job must have optimum variety. That is, too much variety may be inefficient and too little may encourage boredom.

2. Each job should constitute a single overall task. That is, a job should have some meaningful pattern among its tasks so that some interdependence among them can be perceived.

3. Each job should have an optimum length in its work cycle. That is, a short cycle means too much starting and stopping and too long a cycle frustrates the development of a work rhythm.

4. Each job should have a range of standards of quantity and quality and a way to get feedback about results. That is, minimum standards may be expected, but workers need to have some freedom in setting higher standards and adequate feedback to see whether the work is proceeding according to form.

5. Each job should include some of the preparatory and/or auxiliary tasks that exist at the "boundary" of the worker's job. That is, the worker should have some control over what precedes and follows from the assigned job.

6. Each job should include tasks that represent some level of skill, knowledge, and effort worthy of respect in the community. That is, every job should enhance the reputation of the worker in the eyes of others.

7. Each job should add some value to the product or service. That is, the tasks involved in the job should make some definite, noticeable, and positive change in the output.

8. Where there is a perceived interdependence of jobs, based on technical or psychological considerations, the jobs should be located in close proximity and allow for job rotation and the formation of work groups. That is, where possible, natural, autonomous work groups should be installed.

9. Where there is a high degree of stress in jobs, provide for "interlocking" tasks, job rotation, and physical proximity to reduce strain and enhance communication.

10. Where a number of jobs are linked together, make certain that various jobs meet the requirements established for individual jobs regarding meaningful patterns, optimum length of cycles, and control over quality standards and auxiliary tasks.

Although these guidelines may be quite useful in the design of specific jobs and even clusters of interlocking jobs, the specific use of STS interventions depends on the problems identified.

According to Taylor (1975), STS change begins by conducting an informal seminar with a design team, which consists of three to five persons from the organization who are line and staff from supervisory and nonsupervisory ranks. The seminar consists of about ten hours of class time and an equal amount of outside reading time on the topics of organizational behavior, technical systems, general systems, society, and culture.

The second step involves making an analysis of the technical system, as described above, which involves a multiple-stage process itself:

1. *Scanning:* This is defined as getting an overview of the system to be redesigned, its boundaries, inputs, products, staff, and their relationships to the environment and any immediate problem of productivity, quality, or vitality. The scanning procedures are critical since that is where the system boundaries are initially defined.

2. *Technical Analysis:* The technology involved in the creation of the product is defined in terms of its inputs and outputs rather than by its processes or techniques. The technical system is analyzed separately from the jobs and the work of people and the management and control systems. All of the mutually exclusive "unit operations" are identified. In a laundry, for example, ironing and folding clothing is a point at which some identifiable change occurs in the output, but inspecting for spots does not change the final product and would not be identified as one of the unit operations.

In addition to the unit operations, the design team identifies "key variances," or places where the input or materials of production are affected by the technical system that result in high quality and quantity, and low cost. Variances are not errors, but situations where deviations may occur in the quality, for example, of a product through the usual production processes. Having inadequate raw materials to complete a product or sending materials to the wrong location *might be* variances, even though they might occur as a result of some human decision; however, the volume of mail received or the number of requests for a product *would be* variances, since they are more likely to vary in the regular process of business and affect the ability of the organization to deliver timely services and products.

Finally, the design team identifies where the key variances can be controlled by purely technical solutions; however, a great principle of variance control is that variances should be controlled closest to the point of variance. The team should note where the variance occurs, how it is observed, how it should be controlled, and who or what controls the variance.

3. *Social Systems Analysis:* The social system consists of work-related interactions among organization members, including both vertical and horizontal relationships that are both internal to the work group and that cross its boundaries. Social systems analysis looks at who talks to whom, about what, and how effective they are. Social systems analysis usually focuses on some key or focal roles, but especially the roles of individuals who are responsible for the timely and accurate delivery of services and products. In organizational communication, the techniques of network analysis are relevant here.

This brief description does not fully convey the detail and complexity involved in STS change, but it does suggest how some of the techniques of analysis discussed earlier may be integrated into and applied to systems design. For example, STS design utilizes aspects of network analysis and role negotiation, as well as other organizational communication methods. For a comprehensive analysis of sociotechnical systems design, consult the work by James C. Taylor and David F. Felten, *Performance by Design*: Sociotechnical Systems in North America. Englewood Cliffs, N.J.: Prentice Hall, Inc, 1993.

SUMMARY

This chapter examined the models and methods of communication systems analysis and change. Two general approaches to analysis were discussed: interpretive and functional. A functional organizational communication analysis was illustrated by the Organizational Communication Profile, a comprehensive survey method.

Strategies and interventions for improving systems effectiveness were discussed. A general model of change was explained and three basic interventions were reviewed: Survey Feedback, Process Consultation, and Sociotechnical Systems Change.

REFERENCES

BANTZ, CHARLES R., "Interpreting Organizational Cultures: A Proposed Procedure, Criteria for Evaluation, and Consideration of Research Methods." Paper presented at the SCA/ICA Summer Conference on Interpretive Approaches to the Study of Organizational Communication, Alta, Utah, 1981.

BANTZ, CHARLES R., "Naturalistic Research Traditions," in *Communication and Organizations: An Interpretive Approach,* Linda L. Putnam and Michael E. Pacanowsky, eds. Beverly Hills, Calif.: Sage Publications, Inc., 1983.

BANTZ, CHARLES R., "Understanding Organizations: Analyzing Organizational Communication Cultures." Paper presented at the University of Utah Summer Conference on Interpretive Approaches to the Study of Organizational Communication, Alta, Utah, 1987.

BARLEY, STEPHEN R., "Semiotics and the Study of Occupational and Organizational Culture," *Administrative Science Quarterly,* 28 (September 1983), 393–413.

BECKHARD, RICHARD, *Organization Development: Strategies and Models.* Reading, Mass.: Addison-Wesley, 1969.

BECKHARD, RICHARD, and REUBEN T. HARRIS, *Organization Transitions: Managing Complex Change* (2nd ed.). Reading, Mass.: Addison-Wesley, 1987.

BORMANN, ERNEST G., "Fantasy and Rhetorical Vision: The Rhetorical Criticism of Social Reality," *Quarterly Journal of Speech,* 58 (1972), 396–407.

BORMANN, ERNEST G., "Symbolic Convergence: Organizational Communication and Culture," in *Communication and Organizations: An Interpretive Approach,* Linda L. Putnam and Michael E. Pacanowsky, eds. Beverly Hills, Calif.: Sage Publications, Inc., 1983

BROWN, MARY HELEN, "That Reminds Me of a Story: Speech Action in Organizational Socialization," *Western Journal of Speech Communication,* 49 (Winter 1985), 27–42.

BRUNVARD, JAN H., "Urban Legends: Folklore for Today," *Psychology Today,* 14 (June 1980), 50–62.

BRYMAN, ALAN, "Street Corner Society as a Model for Research into Organizational Culture," in *Reframing Organizational Cultures,* Peter J. Frost et al., eds. Newbury Park, Calif.: Sage Publications, Inc., 1991.

BUCKHOLDT, D. R., and J. F. GUBRIUM, "Practicing Accountability in Human Service Institutions," *Urban Life,* 12 (1983) 249–268.

BURKE, W. WARNER, "Organizational Development and Bureaucracy in the 1980s," *The Journal of Applied Behavioral Science,* 16 (1980), 423–427.

BURRELL, NANCY A., PATRICE M. BUZZANELL, and JILL J. MCMILLAN, "Feminine Tensions in Conflict Situations as Revealed by Metaphoric Analyses," *Management Communication Quarterly,* 6 (November 1992), 115–149.

BUTTNY, RICHARD, "Accounts as a Reconstruction of an Event's Context," *Communication Monographs,* 52 (March 1985), 57–75.

CHENEY, GEORGE, "On the Various and Changing Meanings of Organizational Membership: A Field Study of Organizational Identification," *Communication Monographs,* 50 (December 1983), 342–362.

COHEN, M. D., J. G. MARCH, and J. P. OLSEN, "A Garbage Can Model of Organizational Choice," *Administrative Science Quarterly,* 17 (1972), 1–25.

DANDRIDGE, THOMAS, IAN MITROFF, and WILLIAM JOYCE, "Organizational Symbolism: A Topic to Expand Organizational Analysis," *Academy of Management Review,* 5 (1980), 77–82.

DEAL, TERRENCE E., and ALLAN A. KENNEDY, *Corporate Cultures: The Rites and Rituals of Corporate Life.* Reading, Mass.: Addison-Wesley, 1982.

DOWNS, CAL W., *Communication Audits.* Glenview, Ill: Scott, Foresman, 1988.

FAULES, DON, "The Use of Multi-Methods in the Organizational Setting," *Western Journal of Speech Communication,* 46 (Spring 1982), 150–161.

FAULES, DON F., and G. LLOYD DRECKSEL, "Organizational Cultures Reflected in a Comparison of Work Justifications Across Work Groups," *Communication Reports,* 4 (Summer 1991), 90–102.

FROST, PETER J., LARRY F. MOORE, MERYL REIS LOUIS, CRAIG C. LUNDBERG, and JOANNE MARTIN, eds., *Reframing Organizational Cultures*. Newbury Park, Calif.: Sage Publications, Inc., 1991.

GOLDHABER, GERALD, and PAUL KRIVONOS, "The ICA Communication Audit: Process, Status, and Critique," *Journal of Business Communication*, 15 (1977), 41–56.

GOLDHABER, GERALD, and DON ROGERS, *Auditing Organizational Communication Systems*. Dubuque, Iowa: Kendall/Hunt, 1979.

GOODSTEIN, LEONARD D., and W. WARNER BURKE, "Creating Successful Organization Change," *Organizational Dynamics* (Spring 1991), 5–17.

HARRISON, MICHAEL I., *Diagnosing Organizations: Methods, Models, and Processes*. Newbury Park, Calif.: Sage Publications, Inc., 1987.

HARVEY, DONALD F., and DONALD R. BROWN, *An Experiential Approach to Organization Development*. Englewood Cliffs, N.J.: Prentice Hall, 1992.

KAST, FREMONT E., and JAMES E. ROSENZWEIG, *Organization and Management*. New York: McGraw-Hill, 1979.

KOCH, SUSAN, and STANLEY DEETZ, "Metaphor Analysis of Social Reality in Organizations." Paper presented at the SCA/ICA Summer Conference on Interpretive Approaches to the Study of Organizational Communication, Alta, Utah, 1981.

KUR, C. EDWARD, "OD: Perspectives, Processes and Prospects," *Training and Development Journal* (April 1981), 28–34.

LOUIS, MERYL REIS, "A Cultural Perspective on Organizations: The Need for and Consequences of Viewing Organizations as Culture-Bearing Milieux," *Human Systems Management*, 2 (1981), 246–258.

LOUIS, MERYL REIS, "An Investigator's Guide to Workplace Culture," in *Organizational Culture*, Peter J. Frost et al., eds. Beverly Hills, Calif.: Sage Publications, Inc., 1985.

LUNDBERG, CRAIG C., "On the Feasibility of Cultural Intervention in Organizations," in *Organizational Culture*, Peter J. Frost et al., eds. Beverly Hills, Calif.: Sage Publications, Inc., 1985.

MARTIN, JOANNE, "Stories and Scripts in Organizational Settings" in *Cognitive Social Psychology*, A. Hastorf and I. Isen, eds. New York: Elsevier North-Holland, 1982.

MILLS, GORDON E., R. WAYNE PACE, and BRENT D. PETERSON, *Analysis in Human Resource Training and Organization Development*. Reading, Mass.: Addison-Wesley, 1988.

MITROFF, IVAN I., and RALPH H. KILMANN, "Stories Managers Tell: A New Tool for Organizational Problem Solving," *Management Review*, 64 (1975), 19–20.

MYRSIADES, LINDA S., "Corporate Stories as Cultural Communication in the Organizational Setting," *Management Communication Quarterly*, 1 (August 1987), 84–120.

PACANOWSKY, MICHAEL E., and NICK O'DONNELL-TRUJILLO, "Communication and Organizational Cultures," *Western Journal of Speech Communication*, 46 (Spring 1982), 115–130.

PACANOWSKY, MICHAEL E., and NICK O'DONNELL-TRUJILLO, "Organizational Communication as Cultural Performance," *Communication Monographs*, 50 (June 1983), 126–147.

PACE, R. WAYNE, "A Work Systems Model." Unpublished manuscript, Marriott School of Management, Brigham Young University, Provo, Utah, 1991.

PACE, R. WAYNE, PHILIP C. SMITH, and GORDON E. MILLS, *Human Resource Development: The Field*. Englewood Cliffs, N.J.: Prentice Hall, 1991.

PASMORE, WILLIAM A., KAREN GAERTNER, JEFFREY HALDEMAN, CAROL FRANCIS, and ABRAHAM SHANI, "Sociotechnical Systems: An Integrated Literature Review and Analytical Model." Unpublished manuscript, Department of Organizational Behavior, Case Western Reserve University, November 1979.

RILEY, PATRICIA, THOMAS A. HOLLIHAN, and KEITH FREADHOFF, "Scientific Argument in Organizations: Power and Advocacy in a Late Modern Environment," in *Proceedings of the Second International Conference on Argumentation,* Frans H. van Eemeren, Rob Grootendorst, J. Anthony Blair, and Charles A. Willard, eds. Amsterdam: International Centre for the Study of Argumentation, 1991.

ROY, DONALD, "Banana Time: Job Satisfaction and Informal Interaction," *Human Organization,* 18 (1960), 158–168.

SCHEIN, EDGAR, "The Mechanisms of Change," in *Interpersonal Dynamics: Essays and Readings on Human Interaction,* Warren G. Bennis, Edgar H. Schein, Fred I. Steele, and David E. Berlew, eds. Homewood, Ill: Dorsey Press, 1964.

SCHEIN, EDGAR H., *Process Consultation: Its Role in Organization Development.* Reading, Mass.: Addison-Wesley, 1969.

SCHEIN, V. E., and LARRY E. GREINER, "Can Organization Developement Be Fined-Tuned to Bureaucracies?" *Organizational Dynamics,* 5 (1977), 48–61.

SCOTT, M. B., and S. M. LYMAN, "Accounts," *American Sociological Review,* 33 (1968), 46–62.

SMIRCICH, LINDA, "Is the Concept of Culture a Paridigm for Understanding Organizations and Ourselves?" in *Organizational Culture,* Peter J. Frost et al., eds. Beverly Hills, Calif.: Sage Publications, Inc., 1985.

SMITH, DAVID H., "The Master Symbol as a Key to Understanding Organizational Communication." Unpublished paper, Univ. of So. Florida, n.d.

STRINE, MARY S., and MICHAEL E. PACANOWSKY, "How to Read Interpretive Accounts of Organizational Life: Narrative Bases of Textual Authority," *The Southern Speech Communication Journal,* 50 (Spring 1985), 283–297.

SYKES, A. J., "Myths in Communication," *Journal of Communication,* 20 (1970), 17–31.

TAYLOR, JAMES C., "The Human Side of Work: The Socio-Technical Approach to Work System Design," *Personnel Review,* 4.3 (1975), 17–22.

TAYLOR, JAMES C., and DAVID G. BOWERS, *Survey of Organizations.* Ann Arbor, Mich.: Institute for Social Research, 1967.

TAYLOR, JAMES C., and DAVID F. FELTEN, *Performance by Design.* Englewood Cliffs, N.J.: Prentice Hall, 1993.

TOMPKINS, PHILLIP K., and GEORGE CHENEY, "Account Analysis of Organizations: Decision Making and Identification," in *Communication and Organizations: An Interpretive Approach,* Linda L. Putnam and Michael E. Pacanowsky, eds. Beverly Hills, Calif.: Sage Publications, Inc., 1983.

TRUJILLO, NICK, "Interpreting (the Work and Talk of) Baseball: Perspectives on Ballpark Culture," *Western Journal of Communication,* 56 (Fall 1992), 350–371.

WILKINS, ALAN, "Organizational Stories as an Expression of Management Philosophy: Implications for Social Control in Organizations." Unpublished doctoral dissertation, Stanford University, Stanford, Calif., 1978.

WUTHNOW, R., D. J.HUNTER, A. BERGESON, and E. KURZWELL, *Cultural Analysis.* Boston: Routledge & Kegan Paul, 1984.

16

Where Do You Use Organizational Communication Theory and Methods?

The study of organizational communication holds much promise for those who have a sense of perspective about what such a program offers. The "tool" aspect of organizational communication is so apparent that many times there is a rush to "put it to work." One can hardly dispute the importance of gainful employment and economics. Indeed, we devote a substantial amount of this chapter to the discussion of employment. However, it is important to stress that the study of organizational communication offers more than "how-to skills" that lead to employment.

Materials have been presented that generate alternative ways of thinking. We believe that one of the ways to learn how to think is to think in different ways. This is a step in developing creative and critical competencies. The development of these competencies is a primary function of education. These same competencies not only serve well in any organizational context but they are a significant part of individual development. We also ask that you consider "appreciation" as well as "use" when looking at communicating and organizing. There is the matter of the complexity and the challenge of creating and sustaining organizations. There is art as well as science in the teamwork required to sustain a productive and civilized organization. Those who can do it well are worthy of recognition.

We caution that courses and programs in organizational communication do *not* create instant managers or consultants. Pat Freston, Personnel Services Manager for Questar Corporation, states the issue very well with her reference to potential managers when she says: "Newly graduated students come to me and say, 'I want to be a manager.' I say what do you want to manage? They then say, 'I will manage anything.' But entitlement doesn't come with a degree! There must be an appreciation for a body of knowledge in a particular context." You can substitute the word "consultant" for manager in the preceding exchange to get a notion of what is required to be a consultant.

You should have something to consult about before rushing out to "hang up a shingle." A number of our former students are involved as consultants, and this is certainly an attainable and worthy goal. But they have reached their positions by advanced study and experience at a number of levels where they could develop their knowledge and leadership skills. The later part of this chapter deals with ethical issues that must be part of the responsibility and vision of both organization members and consultants. This has the greatest meaning when it is experienced.

WHERE COMMUNICATION MAJORS FIND EMPLOYMENT!

When people graduate from college they often look for employment to which they can devote a great deal of time throughout much of the rest of their lives. Many graduates prefer entrepreneurial work where they are basically self-employed, whereas others look to be employed by others in an organization. Both approaches are exciting and satisfying, and communication graduates may find either self-employment or employment in an organization a fulfilling accomplishment in their lives.

College degree programs, however, tend to prepare students from a wide variety of points of view, ranging from a very general liberal education to professional education. Curricula in communication are eclectic and tend to prepare students in the liberal tradition as well as in the more contemporary professional tradition. Thus, the preparation of communication graduates may not be as predictable as the preparation of either liberal arts students or students in professional schools, making it more difficult to advise students about employment opportunities.

Some of the difficulty arises from the way in which courses and curricula are created in departments. Peter Drucker (1968) identified one major issue when he explained that "the search for knowledge, as well as the teaching thereof, has . . . traditionally been dissociated from application. Both have been organized by subject, that is, according to what appeared to be the logic of knowledge itself. The faculties and departments of the university, its degrees, its specializations, indeed the entire organization of higher learning, have been subject focused"; however, "work . . . cannot be defined in terms of disciplines [or subject matter]. End results are interdisciplinary of necessity" (p. 352).

Ernest Boyer (1987) of the Carnegie Foundation in a seminal work about undergraduate education offers a solution that should be considered by communication departments:

> The challenge then is to enlarge lives by bringing meaning to the world of work. And the special task of the undergraduate college is to relate the values of liberal learning to vocation. Therefore, what we propose, as a centerpiece of the undergraduate experience, is the *enriched major*. By an *enriched major* we mean encouraging students not only to explore a field in depth, but also to help them put their field of special study in perspective. The major, as it is enriched, will respond to three essential questions: What is the history and tradition of the field to be examined? What are the social and economic implications to be understood? What are the ethical and moral issues to be confronted? The goals of general education, when properly defined, can be accomplished through the major. The liberal and useful arts can be brought together in the curriculum just as they inevitably must be brought together during life. Such linkage should be cultivated in all disciplines, and be exemplified in the lives of those who teach them (p. 112).

If communication curricula provide "enriched" programs of study in which knowledge is made useful, then students will be prepared to identify areas of application and, consequently, employment possibilities. The discussion that follows assumes that communication graduates have enriched curricula and programs of study and are prepared to move into the world of work.

As a general rule, the places where communication graduates find employment and apply theories and methods of organizational communication are categorized according to areas of professional use. Organizational communication graduates more often than not learn to apply knowledge in a select number of professional settings. For example, they apply their knowledge in *public contact* positions in organizations, such as sales, marketing, public relations, advertising, fund raising, and community affairs; on the other hand, they may apply their knowledge in *development* positions in organizations, such as counseling, career development, organization development, internal consulting, technical training, and management development, as well as *general management* (both line and staff) positions.

These major career areas have similarities and differences that allow communication students to specialize within or to move across categories. For example, all of the *public contact* professional areas require both interpersonal skills and media skills, but *development* professional areas also require similar skills, even though the manner in which they are applied may differ, and *general management* relies heavily on basic communication skills. Interpersonal skills are important in counseling, staff or line management, consulting, and management development; media skills are important in technical training and consulting, as well.

Employment opportunities exist in every major business and industrial group, including health care, manufacturing, retailing, banking, construction, communications, transportation, agriculture and forestry products, military, educational institutions, beverages, chemicals and pharmaceuticals, computer and data processing, energy and petroleum, hospitality and recreation, insurance, justice systems, utilities, government, and the consulting and training industry.

Development Career Opportunities

Development employment opportunities generally fall into six categories: organizational effectiveness, management development, training services, sales training, career development, and technical training (Pace, Smith & Mills, 1991).

Organizational Effectiveness

Major companies are recognizing the impelling need to create work environments that promote open communication and responses based on mutual respect where personal risk taking, innovation, and individual and team participation in goal setting, problem solving, and decision making are encouraged and recognized. Methods used to achieve this new environment and culture include idea systems, focus groups, and employee and management forums designed to enhance employee involvement in improvements in the workplace.

Organizational effectiveness or "systems refinement" is an approach to organization improvement that progressively develops individuals, work teams, and systems to their maximum level of effectiveness. The process embodies a variety of team structures such as quality circles, autonomous work groups, task forces, and integrated management teams. Team members are provided with training in work methods, problem solving, project management, leadership, group dynamics, and team building. Organizational effectiveness promotes a culture of excellence by emphasizing continual improvements, teamwork, and participative management in all areas of work life.

Staff are assigned responsibility for the design, employee training, and implementation of the organizational effectiveness or systems refinement process.

Management Development

There are more than five million managers in U.S. companies. Managers are the fifth most frequently trained occupational group in the work force, after technical and non-technical professionals, technicians, and management support personnel. Most management development is provided in order to qualify managers for their jobs and for upgrading their positions.

Individuals trained for development careers are employed to create, conduct, and administer programs for three levels of managers: supervisors, middle managers, and executives. Staff may be responsible for conducting development programs in leadership effectiveness, managing conflict, communication, power and influence, team building, innovation and change, management styles, group processes, creative thinking and problem solving, bargaining and negotiating, and setting and achieving goals.

Training Services

The training industry consists of companies that provide training tailored to the needs of specific employers. Large companies buy almost 40 percent of their formal training from outside providers, mid-sized employers buy an even larger share, and small employers go outside for nearly all of their formal training. Professionals are employed to perform a wide range of services in the training industry, including the design and production of materials, the presentation and facilitation of programs, and the sales and marketing of vendor products.

Sales Training

Dramatic changes have occurred in the philosophy and culture of major segments of the business community regarding sales and marketing. Financial institutions, for example, are using professionals to prepare employees for the transition from a product orientation to a service philosophy. Staff members design and present programs in customer service, platform skills, office operations, management skills, and direct marketing.

Many entry-level specialists are given responsibility for managing the sales training program, which often includes skills in marketing, sales, and customer service. Nearly every company that distributes products and services has a comprehensive sales training program that strengthens specific skills and prepares sales personnel for managerial responsibilities; thus, sales training and management development are often closely allied.

Career Development

With increasing concerns about downsizing, dislocating workers, and technological change, employees have begun to recognize that they have diminished job security and must take more responsibility for their own career progress and work vitality. To accept this new responsibility, employees will need new tools, more information, and access to support systems that have not been available in the past. Professionals train employees in the new methods, how to use information systems, and how to find and use support systems.

Technical and Skills Training

In companies where technological superiority is a goal, graduates are employed to design ways and to conduct programs for helping employees learn computer skills, operate computer-controlled equipment, and to coordinate the use of subject-matter experts in training programs, such as assisting buyers to learn automated inventory management.

Development is a career area that may be for you if you have the ability to interact with organization members at all levels, an interest in helping others develop, and the talent to conceptualize, design, and implement programs that integrate people, technology, and systems both vertically and horizontally within the organization; if you can teach people to analyze work systems, identify areas that need improvement, and assist them in acquiring the skills to refine their work systems; and if you can take a broad "systems view" of organization processes in learning and developing problem solving, decision making, leadership, and management skills so as to apply them to real work situations.

Public Contact Career Opportunities

One of the broadest career areas for which students in organizational communication receive explicit preparation is that of public contact. *Public contact* opportunities exist in all types of organizations. Public contact work may be divided into four areas: public affairs, community relations, media relations, and employee relations.

Public affairs involves addressing issues and legislation that have an impact on the way an organization conducts its business.

Community relations has to do with the management of local issues in communities where the offices, plants, and headquarters of organizations are located.

Media relations involves working with trade and industry media that cover the organization, including financial analysts who follow the status of the organization.

Employee relations has to do with the development of programs and publications that deal with employee issues.

Public contact professionals handle activities such as political campaigns, interest-group contacts, fund raising, and employee information programs. However, public contact specialists also focus on understanding the concerns of customers, employees, and other publics, helping keep organization officers informed so they can formulate sound policies.

Public contact professionals coordinate information programs that keep the general public, special-interest groups, stockholders, and employees aware of organization policies, activities, and accomplishments. They contact media (radio, television, newspapers, magazines, etc.) representatives to assist them in preparing materials for distribution through their channels.

Public contact professionals may set up speaking engagements and often help prepare speeches for organization representatives. They also represent the organization at community meetings, make videos, slides and other visual presentations to support presentations to school groups, conventions, and for fund-raising campaigns.

With public contact skills, you might also find success as a research interviewer, a sales representative, or a speech writer. Some graduates have taken positions as manager of a sports stadium or a shopping mall, as a congressional aide, and an employment agency counselor. Then, of course, a graduate might also manage a restaurant, work as a customer service representative, as a personnel interviewer, as a travel agent, a real estate agent, as a literary agent, or as a retail store manager.

Marketing is, in fact, the largest employer in the American nongovernmental/non-military work force (Boone & Kurtz, 1986, p. 574). Those who are interested in marketing careers find that marketing often encompasses public relations and advertising as well as sales, but also includes product planning, research, and purchasing. The U.S. Department of Labor's Bureau of Labor Statistics publishes the *Occupational Outlook Handbook*, which lists occupations. Marketing is divided into ten different occupational areas: buyers in retail and wholesale trades; insurance agents and brokers; manufacturers' sales workers; public relations workers; purchasing agents; real estate agents and brokers; reservation agents and ticket clerks; retail trade sales workers; securities sales workers; and wholesale trade sales workers. The majority of people in marketing tend to work in the area of personal sales, so the remainder of this discussion focuses on employment in personal sales work.

Personal sales involves making presentations on a person-to-person basis with potential purchasers. Salespeople are problem solvers who typically seek a mutually beneficial relationship over an extended period of time with a buyer. Personal selling does occur, however, in a variety of settings such as by telephone, over-the-counter, and in the field (Boone & Kurtz, 1986, pp. 436–455).

Personal selling tends to be the key element in an organization's marketing approach when customers are more concentrated in a single geographical area, when orders may be larger, when the products or services are more expensive, technically complex, and require special handling, when trade-ins or exchanges are involved, and when the number of customers is relatively small.

Telephone sales or telemarketing involves making personal telephone calls to a potential customer's home or business. On occasion, a WATS line with an 800 number allows customers to initiate the sales contact, which is convenient for both parties.

Over-the-counter sales are usually associated with retail organizations in which customers take the initiative to come to the organization's location, often in response to advertising or direct mail.

Sales done in the field involve making contact with customers at their homes or places of business who have a relatively long-standing relationship with the salesperson or the organization, or who represent initial and, often, original contacts and require innovative solicitation and order taking.

General Management Careers

The job of a manager is involved, at its core, with some functional area, such as marketing, public relations, development, retailing, manufacturing, sales, finance, or engineering. Managers, however, have responsibility for the work of others within the functional area, and they must direct their energies toward contributing to the success of the organization (Drucker, 1974, pp. 398–418). Managers do what is necessary to help their associates attain the objectives of the organization as a whole, but they must also have the best interests of their team in mind at all times.

The skills of a manager are first and foremost communication skills, both interpersonal and intraorganizational. Most of the issues of communication are summarized in the concept of organizational communication *climate* as discussed in an earlier chapter. Managerial communication should enhance trust and risk taking; it should demonstrate supportiveness and responsibility; involve open and accurate information; reveal an attentive, reliable, candid attitude; show considerate receptivity to information from team members; involve team members in decision making; and demonstrate a concern for high performance goals.

Students of organizational communication usually have the preparation that leads naturally to careers in management. You may be one of the organizational communication students who find a career in general management particularly appealing. A background of courses in management and organizational behavior should be very supportive of preparation in organizational communication when you want to pursue a career in general management.

ETHICAL ISSUES IN ORGANIZATIONS

Ethical issues arise in situations involving other people wherever they occur, but organizations often highlight ethical issues more than other settings. Violations of generally accepted ethical guidelines have become alarmingly apparent in organizations. To some, ethical behavior in organizations has hit an all-time low. Charles Saxon, cartoonist for *The New Yorker* magazine, published a series of business cartoons under the title, "Honesty Is One of the *Better* Policies" (1984). The cartoon from which the title derives shows six executives seated around a boardroom table in the process of making some decision. One of the top management team says, "Of course, honesty is one of the better policies" (p. 13). It may be that Saxon is suggesting that some discussion of ethics in business organizations is warranted, and it may be appropriate for us to explore some ethics issues in the context of making decisions about working in organizations. Whatever career area you choose to pursue will no doubt involve real-life ethical dilemmas and paradoxes.

What do we mean by ethics? One set of theorists (Solomon & Hanson, 1985) suggests that ethics has to do with both thinking and behaving. Ethical thinking consists of evaluating issues and decisions in terms of how they contribute to one's own possible gains while avoiding harmful consequences to others and to oneself. Ethical behavior concerns acting in harmony with the relevant decisions that conform to a set of guidelines that articulate possible gains and harmful consequences to others.

Ethical Issues

Ethical issues in organizations can be divided into two categories: (1) those involving organization practices in the workplace, and (2) those involving individual decisions (Ezorsky, 1987).

Organization Practices

1. *Respect, dignity, and civil liberties.* This issue has to do with the way in which organizations treat their members. From the perspective of a large number of organization members, the organization comes first and the member comes last, not even second. Personal experience, common practice, and legal decisions reveal and support the assumption that the organization member must act for the sole benefit of the organization in matters connected with the business of the organization. The organization member is obligated to avoid speaking or acting contrary to the organization's interests. Although there is a great deal of protection for groups of employees, individuals are often treated unjustly and without political strength and without organization support. Is it unethical for an organization to deny employees their full civil liberties?

2. *Personnel policies and practices.* This issue concerns the ethics of employing, compensating, promoting, disciplining, firing, and retiring organization members. The general obligation of the organization is to treat prospective organization members in a fair way at each of the stages in a person's career. Such practices as testing applicants, promoting exclusively from within, showing favoritism to relatives and close friends, having due process procedures, and appropriate salaries and wages represent some of the difficult decisions involving some fundamental ethical issues.

3. *Privacy and influence over private decisions.* The implicit and explicit contracts between employees and the organization that employs them allow the organization to have an interest in factors that significantly affect performance on the job. Ethical questions arise, however, when the organization takes a special interest in aspects of members' private lives that do not directly affect their performance in the organization. Some of these areas include off-duty conduct that might affect an organization's image, participation in civic affairs such as community activities and service organizations, contributions to charitable agencies, and involvement in political action groups. To what extent should an organization be able to influence the personal lives of its members?

4. *Monitoring behavior.* The issue involved here concerns the extent to which the organization has a right to pressure its members to reveal information about themselves through the use of hidden devices, administration of physiograph and personality tests, and drug testing. The legal argument hinges on what is widely known as *informed consent*. This means that organization members must have enough information about what is happening to be able to make an informed decision about its consequences as well as the procedures involved. Organization members should not be pressured to engage in information-revealing activities, but they should be fully informed and consent to participate in a completely voluntary manner. To what extent and under what conditions should the organization engage in practices that attempt to elicit confidential information from its members?

5. *Quality of work life.* This issue involves a wide range of activities, including problems of health and safety, maternity and child care, and manager–employee relationships. Hazards in the workplace that result in disabling injuries are widespread and often very serious. In addition to toxic and hazardous materials as sources of endangerment to health and safety, stress on the job may be a major contributor to inadequate quality in the work life of organization members. Add to the above the critical problems associated with maternity leaves and child-care policies. Because women continue to have the primary responsibility for child care, reasonable maternity leaves and affordable child-care services are becoming essential. Beyond the safety and child-care dimension of work, one's relationship with managers is a critical contributor to the quality of work life in the organization. Although there is probably no single correct way for managers to establish relationships with organization members over whom they have authority, the ethical position is that managers should create a climate that is respectful of organization members and conducive to optimum productivity. A leadership style that avoids infighting and political maneuvering that does an injustice to organization members' interest is likely to be the most ethical. What should the guidelines be for maintaining ethical managerial behavior? Finally, to what extent does using autonomous work groups and other forms of organization member involvement in workplace decisions represent and support an ethical way of managing?

Individual Decisions

While we may look at the ethics and ethical decisions of the organization, there are also a number of ethical issues that involve decisions of organization members. We shall briefly review a few of the most common problems.

1. *Conflicts of interest.* The issue involved here is whether organization members allow their judgment to be impaired or clouded by an interest they have in the outcome of a transaction. The most common forms of conflict of interest involve financial investments in other organizations that provide supplies, handle distribution of the organization's products and services, or purchase or consume the products and services of the organization; use of an organization member's formal position in the organization for personal gain; and bribery, kickbacks, gifts, and entertainment. When an organization member is engaged in any of these practices, questions of ethics almost always arise, although sometimes they involve only marginal conflicts of interest. What are the ethical guidelines that apply to conflicts of interest and related issues?

2. *Obligations to others.* The issue involved here concerns conflicts between members' obligations to the organization and their loyalty to others, often called third parties. In general, organization members are obligated to deal with others, such as customers, fairly, truthfully, and so as to avoid physical, psychological, financial, and other forms of injury. One of these obligations may dominate a particular situation more than the other obligations. This means, nevertheless, that organization members must monitor both their own decisions and the practices of the organization for actions that violate one or more of these basic ethical guidelines. For example, if an architect or engineer discovers or suspects some irregularities in design, he or she should be guided most strongly by noninjury ethics, since the design of a bridge, building, automobile, or even a sewer system can involve serious injuries to others. However, should an organization member carry out a manager's unfair instructions or report the manager to a higher authority? Should an organization member report the falsification of data about the number of quality circles operating in the organization or should the person simply ignore the untruthful report?

In a larger context, should an organization member who is directed to do something illegal, unfair, untruthful, or injurious to third parties inform the general public? When organization decisions and actions are injurious to the public, the person who informs the public is called a "whistle blower." On the other hand, organization members who publicize internal organization indiscretions are referred to as "gossip mongers" because they ignore their obligation of loyalty to the organization. Whistle blowing, however, is justified because it is motivated by the desire to avoid unnecessary harm or violations of human rights.

3. *Discrimination at work.* The legal basis of unlawful discrimination is that an employer should not be able to make work decisions involving employment, performance appraisal, compensation, work assignments, training, and firing using race, sex, age, national origin, or disability status as the reason—intentionally or unintentionally—for any particular decision. The law provides assistance to "protected" groups of organization members who fall into one or more of the clusters of people described above. That is, females are a protected group, as are members of religious groups and individuals of certain national origins such as Hispanics (Bouie, 1991).

Apart from the legal aspects of discrimination, it is widely accepted that the fundamental perspective of nondiscrimination goes hand-in-hand with effective management practices. From the perspective of this chapter, the question of greatest concern is: What are the ethical implications of nondiscrimination policy and practices?

4. *Sexual Harassment.* In some settings, sexual harassment is discussed as a form of discrimination, but the most common interpretation nowadays comes within the purview of civil rights. The definition of sexual harassment involves sexual advances, requests for sexual favors, and other verbal or physical conduct of a sexual nature in which submission to such advances, requests, or conduct is made a term or condition of an individual's employment.

Sexual harassment also includes remarks directed at members of one sex in general that express contempt or stereotyped assumptions about abilities and ambitions. Regardless of intent, such remarks have the effect of being derogatory or dehumanizing. Sexual harassment involves verbal comments (oral and written) that use sexual innuendo, that are suggestive, involve insults, humor and jokes about sexual traits, and sexual propositions and threats. It also involves nonverbal sounds that are suggestive or insulting, leering, whistling, and obscene gestures. Finally, it involves physical contact such as touching, pinching, brushing the body, coerced sexual intercourse, and direct assault.

Although our purpose here is to raise the issue of sexual harassment as an ethical issue, there are practical and serious consequences that should be explored in more detail. The affirmative action office of the university or other employing organization has specific information about the process and procedures for dealing with sexual harassment. Please take the time to become informed on your rights in this area. Our final question is about the ethics of sexual harassment. What ethical guidelines are violated by sexual harassment?

ETHICAL GUIDELINES

Five guidelines should be considered very important in assessing ethical behavior (Shaw & Barry, 1989, pp. 46–47). We shall briefly review each of the guidelines below. What might be the deeper meaning of each of these guidelines for people who work in organizations?

1. *Make a contribution to others where it is reasonable to do so and avoid consequences that are harmful to others.* This principle embodies the golden rule in that it asks each person to take into account the effects of individual behavior on other people regardless of the effect it might have on oneself or the organization. Although there is nothing in the golden rule that insists that you deny your own interests or to make unwarranted sacrifices for the public good, the principle asks all people to be aware of ways in which they can contribute to the well-being of others and avoid harmful consequences.

2. *Respect agreements and contracts that go beyond courtesy and protocol.* When you make an agreement with another person or another organization, consider fulfilling the contract a very high priority. Organization effectiveness, in the long run at least, depends on having respect for contracts and agreements, paying one's debts, and producing and marketing goods and services that have quality.

3. *Go beyond just obeying the law and avoid decisions and actions that are repulsive.* It seems obvious, as a matter of ethics as well as general prudence, that people should obey the law, but there are many decisions and actions that are disgusting, unfair, and repulsive, even if they are not clearly illegal. Some of these disgusting behaviors have been identified as abrasive and have been mentioned under headings such as sexual harassment. Innuendo, insults, obscenity, and intimidations seem to fit clearly within the scope of this principle. In general, taking advantage of others, crudities of behavior, and disrespect may not be illegal, but they are repulsive in ethical terms.

4. *Make decisions and take actions that are compatible with basic moral impera-tives.* A moral imperative is an ethical rule that applies generally, in a unqualified man-ner, to everyone in the society, in every walk of life in that society, without exception, and even to people who work in organizations. Moral imperatives in Western society include such directives as: Be kind, trustworthy, honest, truthful, respectful, and gentle. This principle encompasses the concept that the principles of ethics should apply equally to everyone. Failing to do so is in itself a violation of basic ethical principles.

5. *Preserve everyone's reputation and good name.* The term *ethics* comes from the Greek word *ethos*, which is equivalent to the concept of *character.* A person's character is captured in the expression "a person's good name." That is, one's reputation, good name, and character constitute one's ethos, and character represents the integrity, moral turpitude, and ethical position of a person and an organization. Although moral imperatives, and ethi-cal imperatives, may appear to vary from culture to culture, respect for one's character may be as general a principle as one can find in the folkways of most cultures. Individuals who preserve their own character while at the same time supporting the character of others will usually find themselves treading the fine line of ultimate ethical behavior.

SUMMARY

In this chapter we discussed where organizational communication majors find employ-ment. Public contact, development, and general management were identified as some of the career areas for students of organizational communication. Finally, the issue of ethics in organizations was discussed, including ethical problems that occur as a result of indi-vidual decisions and organization practices. Guidelines for evaluating the quality of ethi-cal decisions and actions were presented.

REFERENCES

BOONE, LOUIS E. and DAVID L. KURTZ, *Contemporary Marketing* (5th ed.). New York: The Dryden Press, 1986.

BOUIE, JACOB, JR., *Equal Employment Opportunity Manual for Managers and Supervisors.* Chicago: Commerce Clearing House, 1991.

BOYER, ERNEST L., *College: The Undergraduate Experience in America.* New York: Harper & Row, Pub., 1987.

"Communications Occupations," *Occupational Outlook Handbook.* Washington, D.C.: U.S. Department of Labor, Bureau of Labor Statistics, April 1990.

DRUCKER, PETER F., *The Age of Discontinuity,* New York: Harper & Row, Pub., 1968.

DRUCKER, PETER F. *Management: Tasks, Responsibilities, Practices.* New York: Harper & Row, Pub., 1974.

EZORSKY, GERTRUDE, ed., *Moral Rights in the Workplace.* Albany: State University of New York Press, 1987.

PACE, R. WAYNE, PHILLIP C. SMITH, and GORDON E. MILLS. *Human Resource Development: The Field.* Englewood Cliffs, N.J.: Prentice Hall, 1991.

SAXON, CHARLES D., *Honesty Is One of The Better Policies.* New York: The Viking Press, 1984.

SHAW, WILLIAM H., and VINCENT BARRY, *Moral Issues in Business* (4th ed.). Belmont, Calif.: Wadsworth, 1989.

SOLOMON, ROBERT C., and KRISTINE HANSON, *It's Good Business.* New York: Atheneum, 1985.

Appendix

ORGANIZATIONAL COMMUNICATION PROFILE

Brent D. Peterson and R. Wayne Pace

The *Organizational Communication Profile (OCP)* instrument is an approach for surveying organization member attitudes, perceptions, expectations, and satisfactions so as to provide information about communication and the climate of the organization from the point of view of organization members.

The *OCP* focuses on such organizational communication concerns as: communication climate, organizational satisfaction, media quality, information accessibility, information load, organization culture, information dispersion, and message fidelity.

Before beginning the questionnaire wait for special instructions from the facilitators. Thank you for your willingness to participate!

In the box below write the name of your organization. As you are timed for one minute, write all the words that come to your mind when you think of your organization. *Use only one word on each line.*

```


```

1. _____   3. _____

2. _____   4. _____

5. _____   11. _____

6. _____   12. _____

7. _____   13. _____

8. _____   14. _____

9. _____   15. _____

10. _____

Thank you! You have completed this portion of the instrument. **Do not turn the page until given further instructions.**

Please respond to all questions as honestly and frankly as you possibly can! Unless the wording of a particular item specifically indicates otherwise, respond in terms of your own impressions of this organization. Indicate your response to each item by circling a number. Please answer each item! Use the following instructions to interpret the meaning of the numerical symbols:

1 — Fill in this blank if the item is a false description of conditions in the organization.

2 — Fill in this blank if the item is more false than true as a description of conditions in the organization.

3 — Fill in this blank if the item is about half true and half false as a description of conditions in the organization.

4 — Fill in this blank if the item is more true than false as a description of conditions in the organization.

5 — Fill in this blank if in your judgment, the item is a true description of conditions in the organization.

Please, do not attempt to intensively analyze each question, and—of course—your responses should reflect your own judgments, not those of other people. There are no right or wrong answers.

You may now begin. Thank you and good luck!

		False True
1.	Your supervisor disciplines with tact and does not try to embarrass you publicly.	1 2 3 4 5
2.	Personnel at all levels in the organization demonstrate a commitment to high performance goals (high productivity, high quality, low cost).	1 2 3 4 5
3.	This organization provides adequate pension plans and other special benefits.	1 2 3 4 5
4.	Supervisors seem to have a great deal of confidence and trust in their subordinates.	1 2 3 4 5
5.	Your co-workers generally do quality work.	1 2 3 4 5
6.	Personnel at all levels in the organization are communicated to and consulted with concerning organizational policy relevant to their positions.	1 2 3 4 5
7.	Your organization's policy concerning vacations is fair.	1 2 3 4 5
8.	Your organization has no dead-end jobs—everyone has a chance to be promoted.	1 2 3 4 5
9.	Your supervisor congratulates you when you do good work.	1 2 3 4 5
10.	Subordinates seem to have a great deal of confidence and trust in their supervisors.	1 2 3 4 5
11.	Your co-workers are good people and enjoyable to be around.	1 2 3 4 5
12.	Information received from subordinates is perceived by supervisors as important enough to be acted upon until demonstrated otherwise.	1 2 3 4 5
13.	Your organization has a good system for evaluating your performance.	1 2 3 4 5
14.	Your supervisor lets you know where you stand.	1 2 3 4 5
15.	All personnel receive information that enhances their abilities to coordinate their work within the organization.	1 2 3 4 5
16.	Your organization pays you well for the work you do.	1 2 3 4 5

		False				True
17.	Your organization provides adequate coffee and rest breaks.	1	2	3	4	5
18.	A general atmosphere of candor and frankness seems to pervade relationships between personnel through all levels of the organization.	1	2	3	4	5
19.	Your working conditions are as good as your organization could possibly provide.	1	2	3	4	5
20.	Your organization provides you with every opportunity to gain a sense of accomplishment in your work.	1	2	3	4	5
21.	There are avenues of communication available for all personnel to consult with management levels above their own.	1	2	3	4	5
22.	Your organization provides you with plenty of freedom to work on your own and not be closely supervised.	1	2	3	4	5
23.	Your chance for promotion is excellent if you do your best work.	1	2	3	4	5
24.	All personnel are able to say "what's on their minds" regardless of whether they are talking to subordinates or supervisors.	1	2	3	4	5
25.	Your organization provides you with every opportunity to turn out quality work.	1	2	3	4	5
26.	Your organization promotes qualified individuals on a regular basis.	1	2	3	4	5
27.	Except for necessary security information, all personnel have relatively easy access to information that relates directly to their immediate jobs.	1	2	3	4	5
28.	Your co-workers get along well with one another.	1	2	3	4	5
29.	A high concern for the well-being of all personnel is as important to management as high performance goals.	1	2	3	4	5
30.	Your fellow workers are supportive of one another and do their best to help one another.	1	2	3	4	5
31.	Supervisors at all levels in the company listen continuously and with open minds to suggestions or reports of problems made by personnel at all subordinate levels in the organization.	1	2	3	4	5
32.	Your work is interesting and it provides you with a challenge.	1	2	3	4	5
33.	The communications sent out by the company help you identify with and feel a vital part of the company.	1	2	3	4	5
34.	Company publications are interesting and helpful.	1	2	3	4	5
35.	Written directives and reports from the company are clear and concise.	1	2	3	4	5

Instructions for Questions 36 through 51.

You receive information from various sources within the organization. For each source listed below, circle the number that best indicates the amount of information you are now receiving from that source.

		This is the amount of information I receive now				
	Source of information	Very Little	Little	Some	Great	Very Great
36.	Your immediate supervisor	1	2	3	4	5
37.	Co-workers/colleagues in your own unit	1	2	3	4	5
38.	The "grapevine"	1	2	3	4	5

		Very Little	Little	Some	Great	Very Great
39.	The manager of your immediate supervisor	1	2	3	4	5
40.	Top management (executive management team)	1	2	3	4	5
41.	Subordinates (if applicable)	1	2	3	4	5
42.	Written communications (newsletters, memos, etc.)	1	2	3	4	5
43.	Electronic communications (mail, video, telephone, etc.)	1	2	3	4	5

Now, circle the number that best indicates the amount of information you want to receive from that source.

This is the amount of information I want to receive

Source of information		Very Little	Little	Some	Great	Very Great
44.	Your immediate supervisor	1	2	3	4	5
45.	Co-workers/colleagues in your own unit	1	2	3	4	5
46.	The "grapevine"	1	2	3	4	5
47.	The manager of your immediate supervisor	1	2	3	4	5
48.	Top management (executive management team)	1	2	3	4	5
49.	Subordinates (if applicable)	1	2	3	4	5
50.	Written communications (newsletters, memos, etc.)	1	2	3	4	5
51.	Electronic communications (mail, video, telephone, etc.)	1	2	3	4	5

Prior to receiving this questionnaire, what did you know about the information in the box below?

The person who administers the OCP puts a message in the box and writes a 10 item list for the blank spaces.

52. Please check one: 1. _____ I knew nothing about it.

 2. _____ I knew something about it.

If your answer to item 52 was "I knew nothing about it," you have completed this portion of the questionnaire. Proceed to question number 60.

If your answer to item 52 was "I knew something about it," then read the following message and circle the number following item 53 closest to the approximate number of information items you know prior to reading the message.

MESSAGE

53.   1   2   3   4   5
        0–2   3–4   5–6   7–8   9–10

By what method did your receive the information in the message? Circle True (T) if you received the information by the method indicated. Circle False (F) if you did not.

54. T F Memo
55. T F Notice on bulletin board
56. T F Personal letter
57. T F Immediate supervisor
58. T F Talking over the telephone
59. T F Attending an organized group meeting or conference
60. Now if you would like, in the space provided below, state how you really feel about your organization. (Use 25 words or less.)

YOU ARE FINISHED! THANK YOU VERY MUCH!

Name Index

Abel, Kenneth Ross   89, 97
Aburdene, Patricia   47, 51, 61, 73, 88, 98
Adams, A.   146, 154
Adams, John D.   232, 255
Adelman, M.B.   232, 242, 257
Agarwala-Rogers, Rekha   121, 122, 124, 132, 154
Alberti, Robert E.   202, 208
Albrecht, Terrance L.   145, 151, 232, 242, 257
Alderfer, Clayton   82, 83, 93, 97
Allen, Myra Watkins   147, 151
Allsen, Philip   236, 258
Anatol, Karl W.E.   107, 115
Anderson, James A.   92, 98
Applbaum, Ronald E.   107, 115
Argyris, Chris   21, 25, 42, 48, 51
Athos, Anthony G.   252, 253, 256
Atkinson, J.W.   291, 321
Avila, Donald L.   282, 320
Axley, Stephen R.   149, 151
Aydin, Carolyn   146, 154

Bachrach, P.   173, 185
Baird, John E., Jr.   123, 151
Bakke, E. Wight   21, 25, 42, 48, 51
Bales, Robert F.   215, 231
Bandura, Albert   180, 185, 240, 241, 257, 290, 291, 292, 319
Bantz, Charles R.   69, 72, 324, 325, 327, 352, 353
Baratz, M.S.   173, 185
Barley, Stephen R.   66, 74, 254, 256, 323, 353

Barnard, Chester I.   38, 39, 40, 41, 48, 51, 157, 169
Barnett, Rosalind C.   232, 255
Barnlund, Dean C.   251, 255
Barrett, Dermot   120, 151
Barry, Vincent   365, 366
Bartlett, Alton C.   284, 288, 319
Barton, Grant E.   306, 307, 319
Baruch, Grace K.   232, 255
Bass, Bernard M.   189, 208
Bastien, David T.   70, 72
Baugh, Steven   107, 115
Bavelas, Alex   120, 151
Beckhard, Richard   226, 231, 345, 347, 353
Bednar, David A.   107, 115
Bell, Cecil H., Jr.   259, 320
Bellman, Geoffrey   278, 319
Benne, Kenneth   217, 231
Bennis, Warren G.   46, 48, 51, 215, 231
Benson, Herbert   235, 258
Berger, P.L.   65, 72, 175, 178, 185
Bergeson, A.   326, 355
Berlo, David   28, 36
Berne, Eric   201, 208
Bertalanffy, Ludwig von   43, 44, 51
Bettinghaus, E.P.   146, 152
Biddle, Bruce J.   293, 319
Biener, Lois   232, 255
Bikson, T.   162, 169
Birch, D.   292, 319
Bittner, E.   65, 72
Blair, Steven   224, 258

Blake, Robert R. 189, 190, 191, 192, 193, 195, 208, 251, 255
Blanchard, Kenneth H. 189, 193, 195, 208
Blank, A. 246, 256
Blau, Peter M. 27, 36
Block, P. 181, 183, 185
Blumenstock, David I. 100, 115
Bois, J. Samuel 103, 115, 282, 319
Bolton, Robert 202, 208
Boone, Louis E. 361, 366
Boren, Robert R. 138, 153
Bormann, Ernest G. 211, 231, 327, 353
Bormann, Nancy C. 211, 231
Borysenko, Joan 242, 256
Bosmajian, H.A. 176, 181, 185
Boster, Franklin J. 112, 115
Bouie, Jacob, Jr. 364, 366
Boulding, Kenneth E. 43, 51, 172, 174, 175, 179, 183, 185
Boundy, B. 146, 154
Bowditch, James L. 216, 231, 253, 256
Bowen, Donald D. 295, 320
Bowers, David G. 348, 355
Boyer, Ernest L. 357, 366
Bracey, Hyler J. 140, 154
Bramson, Robert M. 200, 208
Brief, Arthur P. 101, 116
Brown, Donald R. 327, 329, 330, 354
Brown, H. 2, 14
Brown, Mary Helen 327, 353
Bruhn, John G. 242, 257
Brunvand, Jan H. 327, 353
Bryman, Alan 326, 353
Buchanan, D.A. 165, 169
Buckholdt, D.R. 327, 353
Burgess, R.L. 120, 121, 151
Burke, W. Warner 226, 227, 231, 344, 345, 353, 354
Burnett, M. Dallas 229, 231, 251, 252, 276, 288, 321
Burns, Tom 13, 14, 50, 51
Burrell, G. 65, 72, 159, 169
Burrell, Nancy A. 328, 353
Buscaglia, Leo 246, 257
Buttny, Richard 327, 353
Buzzanell, Patrice M. 328, 355
Byham, W.C. 182, 185

Calas, Marta B. 61, 62
Calder, Bobby J. 206, 208
Carey, J.W. 175, 185
Carlton, G.G. 293, 321
Carnarius, Stan 302, 311, 319
Carroll, Stephen 104, 116
Case, D. 159, 166

Casse, Pierre 297, 320
Cervone, D. 291, 292, 319
Chamberlain, Jonathan M. 282, 320
Chanowitz, B. 246, 256
Charlesworth, Edward A. 232, 255
Chase, Dennis J. 232, 256
Cheney, George 177, 186, 327, 353, 355
Christie, B. 163, 169
Clark, David L. 35, 36, 53, 72
Clark, R.A. 291, 321
Clegg, S. 149, 151, 171, 172, 173, 174, 185
Clurman, Carol 88, 97
Coffey, Robert E. 252, 253, 256
Cohen, M.D. 328, 353
Coleman, J.S. 124, 151
Combs, Arthur 282, 307, 320
Conard, William A. 149, 150, 151
Conboy, William A. 130, 151
Conger, J.A. 180, 182, 185
Contractor, Noshir S. 129, 152
Coonradt, Charles A. 210, 231
Coons, Alvin E. 189, 209
Cooper, Cary Lynn 232, 256
Courtwright, John A. 145, 152
Craighead, W. Edward 282, 287, 320
Crawford, A.B. 166, 169
Csikszentmihalyi, Mihaly 233, 256
Culnan, M.J. 159, 161, 169
Cummings, L.L. 268, 272, 320
Cummins, Robert C. 201, 209
Cushman, Donald P. 146, 152

Daft, Richard L. 129, 152, 153, 155, 149, 163, 164, 169
Dahl, R.A. 172, 186
Dance, Frank E. 17, 25
Dandridge, Thomas 63, 72, 327, 353
Danowski, James A. 121, 152
D'Aprix, Roger 16, 25, 69, 72
Dass, Ram 248, 257
Davis, James H. 292, 320
Davis, Keith 124, 127, 131, 135, 136, 137, 152
Davis, Larry Nolan 316, 320
Davis, W.L. 137, 152
Deal, Terrance E. 61, 63, 66, 67, 72, 323, 353
Deetz, Stanley 68, 72, 185, 186, 328, 354
Dennis, Harry S. 107, 115
Depaoli, P.A. 161, 169
de Vries, Hein 240, 241, 257
Dickson, William J. 40, 52
Diese, James 199, 208, 291, 320
Dillard, James P. 112, 115
Doherty, V. 162, 170
Donnelly, James H. 103, 115
Dowling, John R. 267, 320

Downs, Cal W. 110, 112, 113, 115, 259, 280, 320, 331, 353
Drake Beam Morin 200
Drecksel, G. Lloyd 327, 353
Drolet, Robert P. 267, 320
Drucker, Peter 86, 97, 357, 361, 366
Dukstra, Margo 240, 257
Dushkin, David A. 199, 280
Dyer, William G. 226, 227, 231, 307, 320

Earle, Ralph B., Jr. 94, 98
Eisenberg, Eric M. 70, 129, 145, 146, 148, 152, 153
Ellerbroek, W.C. 237, 256
Ellis, Albert 232, 258, 282, 320
Ellis, B.H. 232, 257
Emery, F.E. 50, 51
Emmons, Michael L. 202, 208
Enterline, P.E. 234, 258
Evans, Michael R. 85, 98
Eveland, J.D. 162, 169
Ezorsky, Gertrude 362, 366

Fairhurst, Gail T. 145, 152
Falcione, Raymond L. 101, 115
Fantoli, A. 161, 169
Farace, Richard V. 121, 123, 152
Faules, Don F. 327, 328, 353
Fayol, Henri 135, 152
Felten, David F. 214, 231, 350, 352, 355
Ference, T.P. 19, 23, 25, 26
Fiedler, Fred E. 190, 196, 200, 208
Filley, Alan C. 250, 256
Fisher, B. Aubrey 43, 51, 215, 231
Foote, Nelson N. 91, 97
Form, William H. 40, 41, 51
Foucault, M. 177, 181, 182, 186
Francis, Carol 347, 350, 354
Frankl, Viktor 224, 243, 244, 257
Frantz, Roger S. 76, 77, 78, 97, 106, 115
Freadhoff, Keith 329, 355
French, J., Jr. 172, 186
French, Wendell L. 259, 320
Fromm, Erich 86, 97
Frost, Joyce Hocker 249, 250, 256
Frost, Peter J. 325, 354
Fulk, Janet 157, 159, 163, 164, 169

Gaertner, Karen 347, 350, 354
Galle, William P., Jr. 128, 153
Gardner, John 245, 257
Garfinkel, Harold 12, 14, 60, 72
Garson, Barbara 92, 97
Gaventa, J.P. 173, 186
Geertz, C. 53, 63, 64, 65, 69, 72

Geier, John G. 201, 208
Gerloff, Edwin A. 201, 209
Gibson, James L. 103, 115
Giddens, A. 173, 178, 186
Giffin, Kim 264, 321
Gilbert, Thomas F. 90, 91, 97
Globerson, T. 242, 257
Goethe, Johann Wolfgang von 245
Goldberg, Gale 296, 321
Goldhaber, Gerald M. 19, 20, 26, 123, 138, 152, 331, 354
Goodstein, Leonard D. 344, 345, 354
Gordon, Alice Koplan 289, 320
Gordon, George N. 292, 320
Gorman, Paul 248, 257
Gorman, Walter 290, 320
Gotcher, J. Michael 147, 151
Gradous, Deane 90, 98
Graff, P.W. 107, 116
Green, Hannah 224, 257
Greenwood, James W. 232, 256
Greenwood, James W., III 232, 256
Greiner, Larry E. 345, 355
Grove, Theodore G. 297, 320
Gubrium, Jay F. 327, 353
Guetzkow, Harold 118, 152
Guilbot, O. Benoit 41, 51
Guzley, Ruth M. 105, 106, 116
Guzzo, Richard A. 101, 116

Habermas, J. 68, 72, 173, 181, 186
Hackman, J. Richard 211, 231
Haiman, Franklyn S. 251, 255
Haldeman, Jeffery 347, 350, 354
Hale, Guy A. 263, 321
Hall, Bradford 145, 151
Hall, Douglas T. 295, 320
Hall, Francine 295, 320
Hall, Joy 251, 256
Hall, P.M. 181, 186
Hallowell, A.I. 65, 72
Hampton, David R. 216, 218, 231
Haney, William V. 119, 143, 152
Hanson, Kristine 362, 366
Haray, F. 124, 154
Harper, Roberta 282, 320
Harriman, Bruce 130, 131, 153
Harris, Reubin T. 345, 353
Harrison, Allen F. 200, 208
Harrison, Joyce M. 236, 258
Harrison, M.I. 165, 169
Harrison, Michael I. 293, 354
Harrison, Roger 320, 329, 330
Hart, David K. 210, 231
Hart, P. 164, 170

Harvey, Donald F.   329, 330, 354
Havelock, Mary C.   313, 320
Havelock, Ronald G.   313, 320
Hawes, Leonard C.   46, 51
Hazen, Michael D.   112, 115
Heaney, Catherine   232, 256
Hegstrom, Timothy G.   143, 153
Hellriegel, Don   86, 97
Herden, Richard P.   101, 115
Hersey, Paul   189, 193, 194, 195, 208
Herzberg, Frederick   82, 83, 93, 97
Hewitt, John P.   91, 97
Hill, Napoleon   291, 320
Hill, Richard L.   293, 294, 320, 321
Hill, William Fawcett   202, 208
Hiltz, S.R.   166, 167, 169
Hobbs, Charles R.   245, 258
Hoerr, John   210, 231
Hoffman, L.   140, 153
Hollihan, Thomas A.   329, 355
Holmes, D.   239, 256
Hoopes, Ned E.   138, 153
House, J.S.   242, 257
Houston, B.K.   239, 256
Hunt, Gary T.   140, 154
Hunter, D.J.   326, 355
Huse, Edgar F.   216, 231, 253, 256
Hyman, M.M.   234, 258

Immel, R.A.   165, 169
Irey, K.V.   232, 257
Ivancevich, John M.   103, 115, 232, 256

Jablin, Frederic M.   140, 142, 153
Jackofsky, Ellen F.   107, 116
Jackson, Jay M.   131, 139, 140, 153
Jacobsen, E.   235, 258
Jacobson, Eugene   124, 153, 155
Johnson, B.M.   167, 168, 169
Johnson, C.B.   162, 169
Jones, John E.   304, 306, 321
Joyce, William   63, 72, 327, 353
Jung, Carl   199, 206, 208

Kahn, Robert L.   19, 26, 45, 48, 51, 120, 127, 153
Kanter, Rosabeth Moss   89, 97, 161, 182, 186
Kanungo, R.N.   180, 182
Karasick, B.W.   112, 116
Kast, Freemont T.   350, 354
Katz, Daniel   19, 26, 45, 48, 51, 120, 127, 153
Katz, Elihu   124, 125, 153
Kazdin, Alan E.   282, 320
Kennedy, Allan A.   61, 63, 66, 67, 72, 323, 353
Ketchum, Lyman D.   211, 214, 231

Kiesler, S.   156, 158, 159, 161, 162, 166, 167, 168
Kilmann, Ralph H.   251, 256, 328, 354
King, Sara Sanderson   146, 152
King, Stephen W.   292, 320
Kirkpatrick, Donald L.   275, 320
Kobasa, S.C.   224, 234, 244, 245, 258
Koch, Susan   328, 354
Kolb, David A.   200, 208, 295, 320
Koontz, Harold   139, 153
Kopleman, Richard E.   101, 116
Kovach, Kenneth A.   78, 79, 98
Kreps, Gary L.   54, 72
Krivonos, Paul   140, 153, 331, 354
Kuhlman, Piet   240, 257
Kur, C. Edward   344, 354
Kurtz, David L.   361, 366
Kurzwell, E.   326, 355
Kushner, Harold S.   224, 246, 257

Lake, Dale G.   94, 98
Langer, Ellen J.   242, 246, 256, 257
Larson, Carl E.   17, 25
Lauffer, Armand   25, 26
Laurence, Paul R.   11, 13, 14, 50, 51, 259, 320
Lawler, Edward   84, 98
Lazarfeld, Paul F.   124, 125, 153
Lazarus, R.S.   224, 257
Leavitt, Harold J.   120, 153
LeBaron, Mel   210, 231
Lee, Irving   20, 26
Lee, Laura L.   20, 26
Leibenstein, H.   76, 98
Lengel, Robert H.   129, 152, 153, 155, 163, 164, 169
Lenhart, Levi   232, 256
Level, Dale A.   128, 153
Lewicki, Roy J.   295, 320
Likert, Rensis   42, 48, 51, 145, 153
Lincoln, Yvonna   53, 54, 72
Littauer, Florence   199, 208
Litvin, G.   112, 116
Locke, E.A.   132, 154
Long, James D.   284, 285, 321
Loo, Robert   87, 98
Lorsch, Joy W.   11, 12, 14, 50, 51, 259, 320
Louis, Meryl Reis   62, 64, 72, 325, 326, 354
Love, G.   164, 170
Lowell, E.L.   291, 321
Luckman, T.   65, 72, 175, 178
Lukes, S.   173, 178, 186
Lundberg, Craig C.   54, 72, 323, 325, 354
Luthans, Fred   19, 26, 42, 46, 47, 51
Lyles, J.S.   232, 257
Lyman, S.M.   327, 355

Lynch, Dudley   200, 208, 209
Lynton, Rolf P.   311, 321

Machaver, William   130, 132, 154
Macher, K.   181, 186
Mackenzie, Ralph   103, 116
Macleod, Jennifer S.   86, 87, 98
Maddi, S.R.   244, 258
Mager, Robert F.   306, 321
Mahoney, Michael J.   282, 320
Maier, Norman   140, 153
Main, J.   78, 98
Malone, T.W.   161, 170
Maltz, Maxwell   291, 321
Manz, Charles C.   205, 208
March, J.G.   328, 353
Markus, M.L.   159, 161, 169
Marshall, Judi   232, 256
Marston, William Moulton   201, 208
Martin, Ernest 280, 320
Martin, Joanne   13, 14, 67, 68, 72, 325,
    328, 354
Maslow, Abraham H.   81, 82, 83, 93, 98
Matteson, Michael T.   232, 256
Mayo, Elton   40, 41, 48, 51
McCallon, Earl   316, 320
McClelland, David   94, 98, 291, 321
McGregor, Douglas   188, 195, 208
McGuire, William J.   159, 292, 321
McIntyre, James M.   295, 320
McKenney, J.   162, 170
McMillian, Jill J.   329, 353
McPhee, Robert D.   12, 14, 114, 116, 160
Mehrabain, Albert   123, 153
Mellinger, Glen D.   140, 153
Merrihue, Willard V.   131, 153
Merrill, David W.   201, 209
Meyer, Alan D.   115, 116
Meyerson, Debra   70, 73
Miani, G.   161, 169
Michalak, Donald F.   266, 277, 295, 321
Middleman, Ruth R.   296, 321
Miller, Delbert C.   40, 41, 51
Miller, Katherine I.   145, 152, 232, 258
Miller, Sherod   202, 209
Mills, Gordon E.   94, 98, 205, 206, 209, 229,
    259, 331, 344, 354, 358, 366, 321
Mintzberg, Henry   10, 14, 103, 116, 164,
    172, 186
Mitroff, Ivan I.   60, 63, 72, 73, 327, 328,
    353, 354
Mok, Paul   200, 206, 209
Monge, Peter R.   23, 25, 121, 124, 145, 148,
    152, 153

Moore, Larry F.   325, 354
Moorehead, Alan   40, 51
Moosbruker, Jane   228, 231
Morgan, Gareth   2, 3, 8, 9, 14, 15, 17, 26, 60,
    65, 72, 73, 159, 161, 169
Mouton, Jane S.   189, 190, 191, 192, 193,
    195, 208, 251, 255
Mowday, Richard T.   106, 116
Mundy, A.K.   232, 257
Myers, Alan D.   66, 72
Myers, Isabel Briggs   199, 200, 208
Myrsiades, Linda S.   328, 354

Nadler, David A.   84, 98
Naisbitt, John   47, 51, 61, 73, 88, 98
Nathan, Ronald G.   232, 255
Newstrom, John W.   290, 321
Nilakanta, Sree   145, 153
Niniger, James Robert   86, 98
Noland, James R.   201, 209
Nunnally, Elam W.   202, 209

O'Connor, J. Regis   137, 152
Odiorne, George S.   288, 321
O'Donnell, Cyril   139, 153
O'Donnell-Trujillo, Nick   9, 11, 15, 26, 63, 64,
    67, 69, 70, 73, 74, 324, 325, 326, 354, 355
Ogilvy, J.   53, 147, 154
Oldham, Greg R.   211, 231
Oliveras, Louis   290, 321
Olsen, J.P.   328, 353
Oravecz, M.T.   201, 209
O'Reilly, Charles A.   121, 154
Osborn, Alex F.   224, 231

Pacanowsky, Michael E.   9, 11, 15, 26, 47,
    48, 51, 63, 64, 67, 68, 69, 73, 74, 92, 98,
    180, 186, 322, 324, 325, 326, 354, 355
Pace, R. Wayne   93, 94, 98, 107, 108, 116,
    138, 143, 153, 205, 206, 209, 231, 234,
    240, 251, 252, 257, 259, 276, 288, 296,
    321, 331, 332, 344, 350, 354, 358, 366
Palmer, R.S.   224, 258
Pareek, Udai   311, 321
Parkinson, C. Northcote   32, 33, 37
Parnes, Sidney J.   224, 231
Parsons, Talcott   60, 73, 182, 186
Pasmore, William A.   347, 350, 354
Patton, Bobby R.   264, 321
Pearce, W.B.   175, 186
Pelletier, Kenneth   241, 257
Pelz, Donald C.   140, 141, 154
Penman, Robyn   6, 15
Perrow, Charles   29, 37, 38, 41, 51

Peters, T.J.   16, 61, 73
Peterson, Brent D.   107, 108, 116, 125, 138, 153, 154, 229, 231, 251, 252, 276, 288, 321, 332, 354
Pettigrew, Loyd S.   207, 209
Pfeffer, Jeffrey   49, 52, 66, 73
Pfeiffer, J. William   304, 306, 321
Pincus, J. David   110, 114, 116
Planty, Earl   130, 132, 154
Plunkett, Lorne C.   263, 321
Pondy, Louis R.   60, 73
Pool, Ithiel de Sola   21, 26
Poole, Marshall Scott   100, 101, 105, 114, 116
Porter, Lyman W.   106, 116
Postman, L.J.   20, 26
Pritchard, R.D.   112, 116
Puccetti, M.C.   245, 258
Purkey, William W.   282, 320
Putnam, Linda L.   9, 15, 23, 26, 66, 73, 148, 154

Rapaport, Anatol   43, 52
Raven, B.   172, 186
Ray, Eileen B.   232, 242, 258
Read, W.   140, 153, 154
Reddin, William J.   189, 192, 193, 195, 209
Redding, W. Charles   19, 26, 100, 105, 107, 112, 116, 132, 149, 154
Reddy, M.   149, 154
Redfield, Charles E.   31, 37
Reid, Robert D.   85, 98
Reid, Roger   201, 209
Reynolds, Peter A.   252, 253, 256
Rhodes, Lucien   66, 73
Rice, Ronald E.   146, 154, 158, 159, 161, 162, 164, 166, 167, 168
Richards, William   121, 148, 154
Ricoeur, Paul   60, 73
Riker, William H.   172, 186
Riley, Patricia   66, 73, 329, 355
Rizzo, John R.   104, 116
Robbins, Stephen B.   104, 116
Roberts, Karlene   121, 154
Robey, D.   162, 170
Rochart, J.F.   161, 170
Rodin, J.   244, 257
Roethlisberger, Fritz, J.   40, 52
Rogers, Don   331, 354
Rogers, Everett M.   121, 122, 124, 132, 145, 152, 154
Rosch, Paul J.   234, 235, 256
Rosen, Michael   70, 73
Rosenbaum, Bernard L.   290, 321
Rosenzweig, James E.   350, 354

Ross, I.C.   124, 154
Roy, Donald   324, 355
Rubin, Irwin M.   295, 320
Russell, B.   172, 186
Russell, E.   121, 124, 146, 152, 154
Russell, Hamish M.   23, 25
Ryu, D.   163, 170

Sackman, Sonja A.   61, 62, 73, 100, 116
Salomon, G.   242, 257
Sanborn, George   19, 26
Sanford, Audrey C.   140, 154
Saxon, Charles D.   362, 366
Sayers, Susan   201, 209
Scamell, Richard W.   145, 153
Schattschneider, E.E.   173, 183, 186
Schein, Edgar H.   229, 231, 252, 253, 285, 321, 349, 355
Schein, V.E.   330, 345, 355
Scherbloom, J.   162, 170
Schilit, W.K.   132, 154
Schmidt, Warren H.   190, 196, 209
Schneider, B.   112, 116
Scholl, Maryan S.   66, 73
Schrank, Robert   92, 98, 114, 116
Schutz, A.   65, 73
Schutz, William   212, 213, 231
Schwab, Donald P.   268, 272, 320
Schwartz, Donald F.   124, 154
Schwartz, P.   53, 73, 147, 154
Scott, James C.   185, 186
Scott, M.B.   327, 355
Scott, William G.   37, 52, 210, 231
Scott, W. Richard   27, 36, 42, 46 Seashore, Stanley   124, 153
Seibert, Joy Hart   147, 151
Seligman, Martin E.P.   224, 240, 257
Senge, Peter M.   88, 183, 184, 186
Seyle, Hans   232, 256
Shani, Abraham   347, 350, 354
Sharma, Jitendra M.   130, 131, 155
Shaw, M.E.   120, 155
Shaw, William H.   365, 366
Sheats, P.   217, 231
Shepard, H.A.   215, 231
Sherril, Elizabeth   246, 257
Sherril, John   246, 257
Shook, Douglas E.   146, 154, 164, 170
Short, J.   163, 170
Siegel, J.   159, 170
Silverman, David   49, 50, 52, 60, 73
Simmons, Valerie M.   66, 74
Sims, Henry P., Jr.   205, 208
Skrtic, Thomas M.   70, 93

Slocum, John C. 86, 97, 107, 116
Smeyak, G. Paul 280, 320
Smircich, Linda 2, 3, 8, 9, 14, 15, 23, 26,
   58, 61, 62, 64, 65, 67, 70, 73, 323, 355
Smith, Alfred G. 143, 144, 155
Smith, David H. 327, 355
Smith, Dennis R. 18, 26
Smith, Kensvyn K. 66, 74
Smith, Martin E. 280, 317, 321
Smith, Peter B. 122, 155, 211, 231
Smith, Philip C. 344, 354, 358, 366
Smith, Ruth C. 70, 74
Sofer, Cyril 37, 41, 52
Solomon, Robert C. 362, 366
Sommer, Robert 121, 155
Spice, Martha B. 282, 321
Springer, Ilene 224, 236, 258, 321
Springer, Judy 295, 321
Sproull, L. 156, 158, 159, 161, 162, 166
Stalker, G.M. 13, 14, 50, 51
Staw, Barry M. 92, 98, 152
Steers, Richard M. 106, 116
Stein, Jess 137, 152
Steinfield, C.W. 157, 163, 169
Stephan, Eric 205, 206, 209
Stewart, John 23, 26
Stewart, John M. 47, 52
Stewart, John P. 121, 152
Stogdill, Ralph M. 11, 15, 189, 209
Stohl, Cynthia 132, 155
Strine, Mary S. 68, 74, 322, 355
Stringer, R. 112, 116
Strodtbeck, F.L. 215, 231
Stubbs, Irving 293, 321
Summer, Charles E. 216, 218, 231
Sussman, Lyle 101, 115
Sviokla, J. 162, 170
Swanson, Richard A. 90, 98
Sweetland, John 224, 256
Sykes, A.J. 327, 355
Syme, S.L. 234, 258

Tannenbaum, Robert 40, 52, 190, 196, 209
Taylor, Frederick W. 32, 35, 37, 38
Taylor, James A. 121, 152
Taylor, James C. 214, 231, 348, 350, 352, 355
Ten Boom, Corrie 246, 257
Thomas, Edwin J. 293, 319
Thomas, Kenneth 251, 256
Thomas, Milt 23, 26
Toffler, Alvin 46, 47, 48, 52
Tompkins, Phillip K. 177, 186, 327, 355
Torobin, J. 164, 170
Tosi, Henry L. 11, 15, 16, 104, 116
Trevino, Linda K. 129, 155, 163, 164, 167

Trist, E.L. 50, 51, 211, 214, 231
Tuckman, B.W. 215, 231
Turner, Barry A. 60, 74
Turoff, M. 167, 169

Uttal, Bro 68, 74

Vance, Barbara 236, 258
Van Maanen, John 66, 74, 254, 256
Van Ryn, Michelle 232, 256
Varney, Glenn H. 228, 231
Veroff, J. 292, 319
Vroom, Victor 83, 93, 98

Wackman, Daniel B. 202, 209
Wallace, R.K. 235, 256, 258
Wallis, C. 232, 256
Walonick, Dane 281, 321
Warshaw, Leon J. 232, 256
Waterman, R.H. 16, 61, 73
Watson, Tony J. 66, 74
Webber, Ross E. 216, 218, 231
Weber, Max 29, 31, 32, 35, 37, 160, 170
Weick, Karl E. 6, 7, 11, 12, 13, 15, 45, 52,
   54, 55, 56, 57, 58, 59, 60, 63, 65, 68, 74,
   149, 152, 181, 183, 186
Weiner, Hannah 288, 321
Weingartner, Charles 20, 26
Weiss, R.S. 124, 155
Wenburg, John 87, 98
Wendlinger, Robert M. 132, 155
Wheatley, Margaret 89, 98
Wigand, Rolf T. 112, 115
Wilkins, Alan L. 210, 231, 328, 355
Williams, E. 163, 169
Williams, Robert L. 284, 285, 321
Williamson, John N. 87, 98
Williamson, L. Keith 18, 26
Wilmont, William W. 249, 250, 256
Wilson, Clark 281, 321
Winans, James A. 292, 321
Wittgenstein, Ludwig 60, 74
Wofford, Jerry C. 201, 209
Wohlking, Wallace 288, 321
Wolf, Stewart 242, 257
Woodman, Richard W. 86, 97
Woodward, Joan 50, 52
Wuthnow, R.D. 326, 355

Yager, Edwin G. 135, 155, 266, 277, 295, 321
Yankelovich, Daniel 87, 98
Yates, Jeri E. 232, 256

Zemke, Ron 139, 155, 281, 321
Zenger, Jack 290, 321

Subject Index

Ability, 308
  accurate information, 308
  appreciation, 308
  deficiencies, 309
  favorable attitudes, 308
  psychomotor skills, 308
  understanding, 308
Achievement theory, 290
  aspirations, 291
  attention, 292
  group support, 292
  positive affirmations, 292
  psychological success, 291
  self-efficacy, 292
  standing ovation, 292
  success theory, 290
  visualization, 291
Ad-hocracy theory, 46–48, 161
  associates, 47
  Buck Rogers, 46
  temporary, 46
Analysis, individual, 259
  definition, 259–260
  proactive, 264
  process model, 261
  reactive, 264
Authority-Communication theory, 38–40
  communication techniques, 40
  zone of indifference, 39

Behavior modeling, 290
  good example, 290

  videotaped, 290
Behavioral theory, 284
  duration of behavior, 286
  frequency counting, 286
  goal, 285–286
  observable behaviors, 284
  punishing consequences, 287
  reinforcement, 284
  results of behavior, 286
  self–management, 285
  structuring contingencies, 285
  verbalize contingencies, 287
Brainstorming, 276
Bureaucracy, Weberian, 29
  characteristics of, 30–31

Card sort 278
Careers, 357–358
  interdisciplinary education, 357
  enriched major, 357
Classification of problems, 265–266
Clinical observations, 273
Communication, 17–18, 176
  display, 18–20
  information as message displays, 19
  interpret, 19
  meaning, 19
  message, 21
  as power, 176
  as power mechanism, 176
  transfer fallacy, 19–20
Communication audit, 330

Communication climate, 99–107, 114–115
  definition, 99–100
  importance, 100–101
Communication Climate Inventory, 107–108
Communication effects, 105
  effort, 106
Communication methods, 128
  availability, 128
  cost, 128
  import, 129
  least effective, 128
  most effective, 128
  relevance, 129
  response, 129
  skills, 129
Communication technology, 157–160
  efficiency, 165–167
  and organizational change, 158–159
  productivity, 165–167
  and social effects, 168
  structure, 160
Communication unit, 21
Comparison, 264
Complexity, 13–14
Concern, 261
  symptom, 261–262
Conflict, 249–253
  as struggle, 249–250
Consensus ranking, 278
Consequence, 247, 261–262
Contingency theory, 196–197
Continuum theory, 196
Control, 13
Conventional research, 69
Cross–channel communication, 133, 135–136
  methods of, 134–135
  purposes of, 134
Cultural artifacts, 62
Cultural content, 62
Cultural theory, 59–60
  accomplishment, 60, 63
  enacted sense making, 60
  language game, 60
  text, 60
Culture, 61
  cognitive perspective, 62
  corporate, 61
  definition, 63
  holistic perspective, 62
  organizational, 62
  variable perspective, 62

Deficiency theories, 80
  need, 80
  prepotent need, 81

Development careers, 358
  career development, 359
  management development, 359
  organization effectiveness, 358
  sales training, 359
  skills training, 360
  systems refinement, 358
  technical training, 360
  training services, 359
Direct indexes, 272
Directing practice, 300
  form a habit, 301
  four steps in practice, 301
  set the pattern, 301
Directions of information flow, 126
  downward communication, 127
Documentation, 262
  cause, 262, 263

Emergent social structures, 145
  conduit metaphor, 149
  deep, 149–150
  organizational boundaries, 146
  surface, 149–150
  technology, 146
Empowerment, 179–184
  and communication practices, 181
  efficacy expectations, 180
  ideal speech situation, 181
Environment, role of, 13
ERG theory, 82, 83, 93
Ethical issues, 362–365
  civil liberties, 362
  conflicts of interest, 364
  dignity, 362
  discrimination, 364
  guidelines, 365–366
  individual decisions, 364–365
  monitoring behavior, 363
  obligations, 364
  organization practices, 362–363
  personnel policies, 363
  privacy, 363
  quality of worklife, 363
  respect, 362
  sexual harassment, 365
Evaluation issues, 318
Expectancy theory, 83
  effort expectancy, 84
  outcome expectancy, 83
  valence, 83, 84
Expectations, 85–86
Experience, 294–295
  fractured puzzle, 297
  structured experience, 296

Experience *(cont.)*
   supervising experiences, 296
Experiential theory, 294
   advantages of, 295
   model, 296

Facilitating analysis, 299
   buzz groups, 300
   discussion formation, 300
   fishbowl, 300
   information processing, 299
   phillips 66, 300
   reporting formats, 300
   ring response, 300
Files analysis, 273
Force field analysis, 277
Forgiveness, 246
   model, 247
Formal organization, 29, 38
   characteristics, 29
Four-systems theory, 195
Fulfillment, 86–87
Functional methods of analysis, 329
Fusion theory, 42

Games, 289
   board, 289
   role-play, 289
General management, 361–362
General systems theory, 50
Grapevine communications, 136–137, 147
Grid theory, 190–191
Group, 212, 215–216
   competition and conflict, 218–220
   development, stages in, 215–216
   dynamics, 216–219
   formation, 212
   norms and status, 218
   roles, 217
Group consensus, 278
Group ranking, 278

Hardiness, 245
   challenge, 245
   commitment, 245
   control, 245
Hill interaction matrix, 202
Holograph metaphor, 54
Horizontal communication, 133
Human action, 10
   object/subject, 10
Human nature assumptions, 3–5, 9
Human relations theory:
   Hawthorne effect, 41
   Hawthorne studies, 40–41

Improving systems effectiveness, 344
   administrative, 344, 346
   agenda-setting, 349
   change agent, 344
   change process model, 345
   coaching, 350
   conditions for interventions, 347–348
   counseling, 350
   cultural, 344
   giving feedback, 350
   individual, 344
   intervention, definition, 348
   open system, 345
   process consultation, 349–350
   social, 344, 346
   structural, 344
   structural changes, 350
   survey feedback, 348–349
   technical, 344, 346
Individual change, 281
Information flow, 117–118
   dynamic, 117
   process, 117
Information technology, 156
   computer-mediated communication, 156
   COMSERVE, 165
   electronic mail, 161–163
   GRIPENET, 159
   media richness, 160, 163–164
Integration, 251–252
Intergroup conflict, 252
   ways to minimize, 253–254
Interpretation, 247
Interpretive methods, 322
   account analysis, 327
   artifacts, 323
   assumptions, 323
   cultural analysis, 324
   data interpretation, 326
   differentiation perspective, 325
   dreams, 328
   emergent perspective, 326
   interpretive core, 326
   interviews, 325
   legends, 327
   master symbols, 327
   messages, 325
   metaphor analysis, 328
   myths, 327
   participant observation, 325
   perspectives, 323
   physical, 325
   preconceptualized approach, 327
   researcher as instrument, 323
   sagas, 327

Interpretive methods *(cont.)*
  sense patterns, 324, 325
  story analysis, 327
  symbolic behavior, 323
  taken-for-granted behavior, 324
  talk, 325
  thick description, 329
  values, 323
  verbal justifications, 327
Interviews, 274
  exploratory, 274
  gap, 274
  group, 276
  individual, 275
  survey, 279
  telephone, 280

Leadership, 187–206, 207
  studies, 189, 190
Linking pin theory, 42

Management by objectives, 271
Management practices, 103
  managerial activities, 103
Maslow's hierarchy of needs, 81, 83, 93
Members, 103
  electro chemical activities, 103
  feeling activities, 103
  self-moving activities, 103
  thinking activities, 103
Metaphors, 8–9
Mindfulness, 242–243
  nonjudging, 243
  nonstriving, 243
  open perspective, 243
  patience, 244
  self-trust, 244
Motivation, 75–77, 79
  analysis of, 94
Motivator-hygiene theory, 82, 83, 84, 93
  maintenance/hygiene factors, 82
  motivators, 82

Needs analysis, 273
Network roles, 121–126
  bridge, 123
  clique member, 121–123
  cosmopolite, 125–126
  gatekeeper, 124–125
  isolate, 123
  liaison, 123–124
  opinion leader, 125
Nominal group process, 277

Objectives, 306
  criteria for, 309
  examples of, 310
  intermediate, 309
  terminal, 309
Objectivity definition, 2–7
  approaches, 4–5
One-best style, 205
  super leadership, 205
Ontological assumptions, 3–5
Operating style, 187
Operating Styles Profile, 203
  use of metaphors in, 204
Opportunity, 88–90
  aspirations, 89
  commitment, 90
  energy, 90
  problem solving, 90
  self-esteem, 89
Organization elements, 103–104
  perceptions of, 105
Organization guidelines, 104
Organization/Organizing, 7
  objective, 7
  subjective, 7
Organizational communication, 1
  functional definition, 21
  interpretive definition, 22
  systems, model of, 22
Organizational communication analytical
    process, 332
Organizational communication climate, 101
Organizational Communication Profile
    (OCP), 332, 367–371
  communication climate, 333, 337
  information accessibility, 333, 338
  information dispersion, 335, 339
  information load, 335, 339
  interpreting the OCP, 335
  media quality, 333, 338
  message fidelity, 335, 340
  model of variables, 333
  organization culture, 335, 341–343
  organizational satisfaction, 333, 336
  sources of information, 340
Organizational dysfunctioning, 330
  course of, 330–331
Organizational structure, 104
  centralization, 104
  complexity, 104
  decentralization, 104
  formalization, 104
Organizational symbolism, 63

Pareto diagram, 274
Perceptions theory, 85, 93
Performance, 90–91
    behavioral tasks, 90
    functional tasks, 90
    motives, 91
    vitality, 92–93
Performance analysis, 268
    absolute standards, 269
    alternative ranking, 269
    behaviorally anchored rating scales, 271
    comparative procedures, 268
    conventional rating scales, 270
    critical incident, 269, 326
    forced choice, 270
    forced distribution, 269
    halo effect, 270
    management by objectives, 271–272
    paired comparison, 269
    qualitative methods, 269
    quantitative methods, 270–272
    ranking, 268
    straight ranking, 268
    weighted check lists, 270
Personal conflict styles model, 250
Positional communication, 31
Positional theory, 292
    patterned forms, 293
    role, 293
    role analysts, 293
    role negotiation, 293
    setting priorities, 294
Power, 171–179, 182–185
    basis, 172, 176
    definition, 172
    and hierarchy, 174
    interface with organization, 173
    obedience, 174
    organizational dynamics and, 175
    relationships rules and, 177
    types, 175
Predictability, 13
Preference, 263
Presenting information, 299
Problem solving processes, 220–226
    decision-making, 225–226
    idea-generation, 223
    model, 221
Public contact careers, 360
    community relations, 360
    employee relations, 360
    marketing, 361
    media relations, 360
    over-the-counter sales, 361

personal sales, 361
public affairs, 360
telephone sales, 361

Questionnaire, 281

Rational theory, 281
    beliefs, 281
    hindering behavior, 284
    inner choices, 284
    personal meanings, 282
    rational-emotive, 282
    self-defeating behaviors, 282
    semantic therapy, 282
    thought selection, 282
Relationships, 138
    interpersonal, 138–139, 142
    positional, 139, 147
    quality circles and, 138
    serial, 143, 147
    superior-subordinate, 140–142
Relayor, 143
    controlling, 144–145
    linking, 143–144
    storing, 144
    stretching, 144
Resentment, 246
Role playing, 288
    enactment, 266
    objectives, 289
    spontaneous, 288
    structural, 288
    warm-up, 289

Satisfaction, 112–114
Scientific management, 32
    division of labor, 32–33
    functional, horizontal growth, 33
    scalar, vertical growth, 33
Serial message dissemination, 119
    circle pattern, 120–121
    wheel pattern, 120–121
Simplicity, 13–14
Simulation, 288
    simulator, 288
Simultaneous message dissemination, 118–119
Situational leadership, 193
    readiness, 193–194
S.O.B. theory, 207
Social organization, 27
    as related to communication, 28
Social reality, 2
Social systems theory, 45
Sociotechnical systems change, 350–352

Sociotechnical systems change *(cont.)*
    performance by design, 352
    scanning, 351
    social systems analysis, 351
    technical analysis, 351
    variance, 352
Stress, 232
    definition, 233
    event, interpretation of, 233–234
    model, 233, 239
    negative consequences, 234–235
    personal agenda, 233–234
    strategies of relief, 235–247
Structure, 33, 44
    line, 33–34
    span of control, 34–35
    staff, 34
    tall and flat, 34
Structure, in guiding behavior, 12
Styles, 197
    behavior style survey, 201
    behavioral matrix, 201
    humor, 199
    Myer-Briggs type indicator, 199
    other types, 200
    personality types, 199
    personnel profile system, 201
    social style profile, 201
Subjectivity, 2–7
    approaches, 3–4
Systems analysis, 322
Systems analysis model, 331
Systems theories, 42–45
    evolution, 44
    function, 44
    hierarchy, 44–45
    interdependence, 43
    nonsummativity, 44
    openness, 44
    structure, 44

Task analysis, 266–268
Team building, 226–230
    agenda-setting, 230
Team concept, 210–230
    project groups, 212
    self-managed teams, 212
    work teams, 211
Theory X, 188
Theory Y, 188, 189
Thick description, 69
3-D Theory, 192–193
Time, 313
    blocks, 313
    daily schedule, 313

    periods, 313
Topics, 303–306
    conducting meetings, 304
    leadership development, 306
    managing the unsatisfactory employee
        topics, 305
    supervisory, 303
Training, 311–317
    agenda fan, 312–314
    conducting, 316
    evaluation of, 317
    experiential, 312
    program, 311
    sequence, 311
    session, 311
Training design model, 302
Transactional analysis, 201

Upward communication, 130–133
    effective, 132–133

Weick's theory of organization, 54–59
    buzz words, 59
    connection, 59
    consensual validation, 56
    coupling, loosely and tightly, 57
    double interact, 56
    enactment, 56
    environment, 55
    equivocality, 56
    functionalists, 60
    grammar, 56
    interdependence, 57
    interlocked behavior, 55
    interpretive, 60, 63
    organizing, process of, 56
    punctuation, 59, 181
    retention, 56
    selection, 56
    subjectivism, toward, 53
    talk, 58
Work itself:
    content, 103
    context, 103
    requirements 103
Work Perceptions Profile, 94–97
World view, 10
    impact of, 11–12

X-efficiencies theory, 76–78
    directed effort, 77
    horizontal relationships, 78
    technical efficiency, 76
    worker effort discretion, 77